LTL

# INDIANA
# IN TRANSITION

## THE EMERGENCE OF AN
## INDUSTRIAL COMMONWEALTH

### 1880-1920

by Clifton J. Phillips

NDIANA HISTORICAL BUREAU & INDIANA HISTORICAL SOCIETY

Indianapolis 1968

# Indiana In Transition

## 1880-1920

THE HISTORY OF INDIANA

VOL. IV

*Published in observance of the sesquicentennial of Indiana's statehood in 1968 by the Indiana Historical Society and the Indiana Historical Bureau with the aid of a grant from Lilly Endowment, Inc.*

# INDIANA IN TRANSITION

## THE EMERGENCE OF AN INDUSTRIAL COMMONWEALTH

### 1880-1920

### by Clifton J. Phillips

INDIANA HISTORICAL BUREAU & INDIANA HISTORICAL SOCIETY
Indianapolis 1968

# PREFACE

The present work is Volume IV of a projected five-volume history of Indiana, of which Volume III, *Indiana in the Civil War Era, 1850-1880,* by Emma Lou Thornbrough, was published by the Indiana Historical Society and the Indiana Historical Bureau in 1965. The present volume covers the years from 1880 to 1920, which encompass most of the significant political, economic, and social changes involved in the transition of Indiana from a primarily rural-agricultural society to a predominantly urban-industrial commonwealth. While all historical periods may be considered transitional, it was chiefly within this forty-year span that there occurred in Indiana the changes that have characterized the urbanization and industrialization of society in America and elsewhere in the modern era. This process of urbanization and industrialization in Indiana, of course, did not begin precisely in 1880 or reach maturity in 1920, but it is the author's contention that modernizing elements which appeared at least as early as the 1850's and 1860's became major political, economic, and social forces in Indiana only in the last two decades of the nineteenth century. The First World War, moreover, played an important part in furthering industrialization, and its close found Indiana firmly established as an industrial state.

The transitional nature of this period is apparent also in the cultural sphere. During the years 1880 to 1920 Indiana experienced its "Golden Age" of literature as well as a modest flowering of the fine arts, especially painting, as seen in the work of the "Hoosier Group" of landscapists. Both literature and art reveal a strong regional flavor, to say nothing of a mild nostalgia for the rural-agricultural past, in the very years in which modernizing urban and industrial forces were integrating the state more closely into the national fabric. By the close of the period it could be said that Indiana no longer possessed a truly independent and distinctive regional culture. In intellectual and artistic life as in political, economic, and social development, the commonwealth had become largely absorbed into the nation by the beginning of the 1920's.

Most of this volume is taken up with a description of the actual events and developments of the period, though an attempt has been made to set them in a general interpretative framework, as suggested in the paragraphs above. The first chapters deal chiefly with political events, followed by chapters on economic, social, and cultural affairs in that order, with a final chapter on Indiana in the First World War. Both published and unpublished source materials have been the basis for much of the description and interpretation, but I also owe a great deal to the secondary accounts by historians and laymen on many topics. Both the footnotes and the bibliography give some indication of available resources and my debts in this regard.

The greater part of the research for this volume was done at the Indiana State Library. I should like to record my gratitude for the help of Hazel Hopper, Frances Macdonald, Louise Wood, and other members of the staff of the Indiana Division, Margaret Pierson and her staff in the Archives Division, and Caroline Dunn of the Indiana Historical Society Library. I am grateful to the staff of the DePauw University Library, the Indiana University libraries including the Lilly Library, the Indianapolis Public Library, and the Emeline Fairbanks Memorial Library in Terre Haute for assistance rendered. I have also received valuable advice from Hubert H. Hawkins, Director of the Indiana Historical Bureau, Donald F. Carmony and the late John D. Barnhart of Indiana University, and George B. Manhart and the late Andrew W. Crandall, both former colleagues of DePauw University. The maps of the individual railroad lines were made for the present volume by John T. McCord; the map showing the state highways as laid out in 1919 was made by George W. Phares.

I would like to thank Dorothy Riker, Gayle Thornbrough, and Shirley McCord for their work in editing the manuscript and seeing it through the press. Miss Riker especially has given an extra measure of time and energy to this project. Lastly, I am grateful to my wife, Rachel, for her unstinted efforts in typing the manuscript and related tasks.

DePauw University,     Clifton J. Phillips
August, 1968

# CONTENTS

# ILLUSTRATIONS

# MAPS

# INDIANA IN TRANSITION

# CHAPTER I

# THE POLITICS OF A PIVOTAL STATE,
## 1880-1896

THE PASSING OF THE CIVIL WAR and Reconstruction eras brought no truce to the political wars of Indiana, which a leading Hoosier politician dubbed the "Belgium of politics, the debatable land between great contending parties and opinions."[1] Like Illinois and Ohio in the Midwest, and New York, New Jersey, and Connecticut in the East, Indiana was a doubtful state, whose uncertain and shifting electorate could tip the scales toward either of the major political parties and determine the nation's choice of the President and control of the Congress of the United States. Both the Republican and Democratic parties recognized the peculiar political character of the two groups of states by choosing many of their presidential and vice-presidential nominees from them. Second only to New York in the number of men placed on the national party tickets between 1880 and 1896, Indiana had many favorite-son candidates for the highest office in the land. Yet it sent only one of its citizens to the White House—the Ohio-born Republican, Benjamin Harrison—and generally had to be content with vice-presidential hopefuls.[2]

Since the Civil War the two parties in Indiana had maintained an even balance, and neither achieved a dominant position before 1896. For this reason party strife was intense; Hoosier politics became, as a contemporary historian wrote, "a passion as strong as religion."[3] Because the margin of vic-

---

[1] Phrase attributed to Daniel W. Voorhees in David Turpie, *Sketches of My Own Times* (Indianapolis, 1903), pp. 302-303.

[2] John D. Barnhart and Donald F. Carmony, *Indiana: From Frontier to Industrial Commonwealth* (4 volumes, New York, 1954), II, 308-309.

[3] Jacob P. Dunn, *Indiana and Indianans . . .* (5 volumes, Chicago and New York, 1919), II, 729.

tory was small in most Indiana elections in these years, both major parties made strenuous efforts to secure the few additional votes needed to capture the state in the great quadrennial presidential contests. Not only did the Republican and Democratic national committees provide the services of important party leaders to help on the hustings, but they also often allocated extraordinary sums of money to the state campaign funds, a practice which led to charges of widespread vote purchase and fraud on both sides and gave Indiana an unenviable reputation for political corruption. In addition, since the responsibility for state leadership frequently shifted in so uncertain an electorate, each of the two major parties had to maintain a constant posture of readiness to campaign and take office, a condition which tended to professionalize political organization.

Why did Indiana maintain an even political balance between the parties—more so than the neighboring states of Illinois and Ohio?[4] One reason may lie in its comparatively stable social and economic position in the decades immediately following the Civil War. Indiana in 1880 was still an old-fashioned commonwealth. In the midst of a rapidly urbanizing and industrializing Middle West, the Hoosier state remained predominantly agricultural and rural, with few large cities and no metropolis. Its population also continued to be relatively homogeneous, little affected by the new currents of immigration in America until after the turn of the century. One scholar, noting that New York owed its doubtful political character to a "Democratic metropolis . . . balanced by a Republican rural population," pointed out that, on the contrary, "Indiana is doubtful because the voting constituency

4 Of the three doubtful states in the Midwest, Indiana shifted its party allegiance more frequently and usually had a smaller margin between parties at election time. Ohio, for example, gave its electoral vote to the Republican candidate in every presidential election between the Civil War and 1912, while Illinois wavered only once in that period, landing in the Democratic column in 1892. By the eighties, Illinois was "normally" Republican, according to its historian Theodore C. Pease, *The Story of Illinois* (Third edition, Chicago, 1965), p. 215.

of the two parties is distributed evenly between city and country in all sections of the State."[5]

Another important factor in the narrow division and harsh competitiveness of Hoosier politics was the impact of the Civil War, which left a bitter heritage of divided sympathies and distrust during and even after the Reconstruction era. Perhaps nowhere in the United States did the Grand Army of the Republic contribute more candidates to public office than in Indiana, where former generals ran for office in almost every election of the eighties on the Democratic ticket as well as that of the Grand Old Party. But according to a recent statistical study of Indiana election returns by two political scientists, the Civil War also bequeathed a legacy of traditional voting patterns persisting as late as 1900. Over this period they show that many counties in the state tended to retain fairly consistent partisan attachments apparently derived from Civil War traditions related to the previous proslavery or antislavery sentiments of their residents. Thus, counties in which a large part of the inhabitants had eastern or Quaker antecedents usually voted Republican, while those chiefly settled by Southerners or German immigrants were more often found in the Democratic column. Regardless of the issues raised in the campaigns, a large portion of the electorate rarely deviated from these long-established patterns of political behavior.[6]

Fervent partisanship and the habit of party regularity made Indiana a strong two-party state. Minor parties operated under severe handicaps and seldom elected candidates to office. Yet so narrow was the margin of success in many contests that they held a kind of balance of political power in the state. They often affected the outcome of a close election by significantly reducing the voting strength of one or both of

[5] Jesse Macy, *Party Organization and Machinery* (New York, 1904), p. 165.

[6] V. O. Key, Jr., and Frank Munger, "Social Determinism and Electoral Decision," in Eugene Burdick and Arthur J. Brodbeck (eds.), *American Voting Behavior* (Glencoe, Ill., 1959), pp. 282-285. Frank Munger has made a more detailed study of this in Two-Party Politics in the State of Indiana (Unpublished Ph.D. thesis in Government, Harvard University, 1955).

the major parties. Indeed, much of the strategy of Republican and Democratic politicians in this period was aimed at minimizing the appeal of minor parties among their respective traditional constituencies. Benjamin Harrison, for example, discussed this very problem with mathematical precision in a letter to a political associate in 1885: "I have very little hope of making Indiana a Republican state," he wrote, "with 4,000 Republican Prohibitionists and 8,000 Republican Greenbackers voting separate tickets."[7]

Another analysis of Hoosier politics after the Civil War traces partisan loyalties to sectional and socio-economic factors. The Democratic party, it is argued, was the radical party in Indiana because its main base of power was south of the National Road, in a region where poor soil and small farms contributed to rural discontent. It also drew part of its support from poorer counties in the north as well as from cities with large brewing and distilling interests and a relatively high proportion of the foreign born, many of them Roman Catholic in religion. On the other hand, Republicans were more numerous in the richer agricultural counties of the central plain and the rising manufacturing centers in the northern half of the state where the population was chiefly native born and Protestant. If the Democrats stood for "soft money and hard liquor," the GOP tended to favor temperance measures and fiscal conservatism. Likewise, the minor parties of agrarian and industrial protest gained greater backing in Democratic regions, while prohibitionists made inroads in Republican strongholds. Moreover, since the northern and central sections of the state were growing in population and wealth more rapidly than the southern, Indiana was becoming more conservative and, therefore, more Republican toward the end of the century.[8]

---

[7] Benjamin Harrison to Louis T. Michener, January 13, 1885, quoted in Harry J. Sievers, *Benjamin Harrison, Hoosier Statesman, From the Civil War to the White House, 1865-1888* (New York, 1959), p. 270.

[8] William G. Carleton, "Why Was the Democratic Party in Indiana a Radical Party, 1865-1890?" *Indiana Magazine of History,* XLII (1946), 216-228. Munger adds to this analysis the interesting suggestion that the Democratic and

In the last two decades of the nineteenth century, then, Indiana became a crucial, pivotal element in the American presidential sweepstakes. It was a "dark and bloody ground" where opposing partisan armies fought bitterly and long for political control of state and nation and the spoils of office. The struggle, though often harsh, was not always over important differences of policy. From 1880 to 1892 the protective tariff was the one outstanding issue dividing the Democracy from the GOP, but it was frequently obscured by local questions and personal rivalries. Furthermore, this was a transition period, when the new issues facing an emerging urban, industrial society had not yet fully replaced the older concerns of the Civil War and Reconstruction eras. The "bloody shirt" itself had only begun to disappear from political rhetoric after the death in 1877 of its chief Hoosier exponent, Senator Oliver Perry Morton, the war governor and powerful leader of the Republican political machine in Indiana. Indeed, the appointment and subsequent election of one of his most stubborn Democratic opponents, the choleric Daniel Wolsey Voorhees, to Morton's seat in the United States Senate insured the survival of the old animosities and points of view.[9]

The currency question also lingered on into the eighties. Senator Voorhees and former Democratic Governor Thomas A. Hendricks were both inflationists, though Voorhees' colleague in the Senate, Joseph Ewing McDonald, was a hard-money Democrat. But the successful resumption of specie payments by the national government in 1879 and the gradual return of commercial and agricultural prosperity tended to remove the currency issue from politics, though the Greenbackers continued for a few years to nominate candidates for office. By the mid-eighties the tide of agrarian unrest ex-

radical third-party vote tended to rise when wheat prices fell. Munger, Two-Party Politics in Indiana, pp. 44-46.

[9] For Morton's death and other events of the late seventies as symbolizing the end of an era in Indiana, see Emma Lou Thornbrough, *Indiana in the Civil War Era, 1850-1880* (*The History of Indiana*, Vol. III, Indianapolis, 1965), pp. 305-317.

pressed in the Granger and Greenback movements which had swept through the Midwest in the previous decade—yet never reaching as high a level in Indiana as in states farther west—had receded, leaving a residue of inflationary sentiment, particularly within the Democratic party, which absorbed much of the Greenback support when the GOP opted for financial orthodoxy.[10]

§ §

In 1880 the stage was set in Indiana for a political contest between what were thought to be nearly equal forces, for the state had given its electoral vote to Samuel J. Tilden and Thomas A. Hendricks four years earlier by the slim margin of about five thousand votes. Republicans planned a supreme effort to overcome the voting deficit of the previous election, while the Democracy counted on holding its precarious lead in Indiana in order to add its electoral vote of 15 to New York's 35 and the Solid South's 138 for a grand total of 188, or a majority of three votes in the electoral college. Another reason for Indiana's crucial importance in this campaign was that it was still an October state, holding general elections for state officers nearly a full month before the national balloting in November. Thus the outcome of the state elections in October would be closely watched for advance information concerning the direction of political currents which might influence voters in the rest of the country.

The October election date itself became an important issue in the campaign when the Indiana Supreme Court ruled on June 18 that a series of seven constitutional amendments, one of which would have moved the time of the state balloting to the Tuesday after the first Monday in November, had not been officially adopted. They had not received a majority of the total vote cast in the April township elections at which they had been submitted to popular referendum. Although more persons voted for the amendments than against

---

[10] William G. Carleton, "The Money Question in Indiana Politics, 1865-1890," *Indiana Magazine of History*, XLII (1946), 142-150.

them, those voting in favor did not constitute a majority of those casting votes in the election of local officials; therefore, according to the justices' interpretation of the state constitution, a "majority of the electors" had not approved the amendments.[11] Republicans assailed the Democratic-controlled court's decision. It was handed down on the eve of the Democratic national convention in Cincinnati, and the Indianapolis *Journal* went so far as to say that the principal object of the court was to keep Indiana an October state. "The Democratic managers believed this would inure to the interest of their party, and especially of Mr. Hendricks," said the *Journal,* "and hence the conspiracy. Under this decision they will go to Cincinnati and represent that Indiana is an October State, and that the nomination of Mr. Hendricks is necessary to carry it."[12]

In April, 1880, the National (Greenback) party held the first state nominating convention. Encouraged by their relatively strong showing in the 1878 election, when they won a seat in Congress and polled nearly forty thousand votes for the head of the ticket, Hoosier Greenbackers listened to a keynote address by Congressman Gilbert De La Matyr, a Methodist clergyman who had been elected from the seventh district as a fusion candidate with the Democrats, and named a Dearborn County man, Richard Gregg, for governor. Greenback presidential nominee James B. Weaver of Iowa made a personal appearance in the state during the campaign, and the local party organ, the Indianapolis *Sun,* kept enthusiasm at a peak with greatly exaggerated hopes for victory.[13]

---

11 The State *v.* Swift, 69 Ind. 505 (1880); Charles Kettleborough (ed.), *Constitution Making in Indiana . . .* (3 volumes, *Indiana Historical Collections,* Vols. I, II, XVII, Indianapolis, 1916, 1930), II, 166-176. For the earlier career of these amendments, see Thornbrough, *Indiana in the Civil War Era,* pp. 267-268.

12 Indianapolis *Journal,* June 19, 1880; Dunn, *Indiana and Indianans,* II, 711. This doubtful claim is repeated without additional evidence in Herbert J. Clancy, *The Presidential Election of 1880* (Chicago, 1958), p. 134.

13 Indianapolis *Sun,* May 6, August 17, September 29, 1880.

All the major party conventions, both state and national, were held in June. The Democrats chose Franklin Landers, a well-to-do dry-goods merchant and pork packer of Indianapolis, who had shown Greenback proclivities during a term in Congress and whose chief qualification for the nomination was his presumed ability to draw support away from the Greenbackers. The Indiana GOP awarded the gubernatorial nomination to Albert Gallatin Porter, a popular lawyer and former Democrat who rather reluctantly resigned from his position as first comptroller of the United States Treasury in order to head his party's state ticket. A "skilled debater and a captivating public speaker," Porter had an immense advantage over the less polished Landers in the series of joint meetings in which the two candidates participated around the state.[14]

The Indiana delegation to the Republican national nominating convention in Chicago was uninstructed, for the state leaders hoped to remain aloof from the tense struggle between Stalwarts and Half-Breeds which divided the party. But Benjamin Harrison, who headed the delegation and was gradually assuming the role of party leader formerly taken by Oliver P. Morton, held the largest bloc of Hoosier votes for James G. Blaine until the thirty-fifth ballot, when he helped to start the swing to Ohio's James A. Garfield, a compromise candidate and the ultimate victor. Although Harrison himself was a potential favorite-son candidate for the vice-presidential nomination, he and his delegation acquiesced in the naming of a New York Stalwart, Chester A. Arthur, as Garfield's running mate. Moreover, Harrison later accompanied Garfield to a "harmony meeting" in New York City which successfully united the warring factions of the GOP behind the convention's choice.[15]

On the Democratic side, the courtly Senator Joseph E. McDonald, who headed his party's delegation to the national con-

[14] Indianapolis *Journal,* June 18, 1880; Indianapolis *Sentinel,* June 10, 1880; Russel M. Seeds, *History of the Republican Party of Indiana* (Indianapolis, 1899), pp. 53-54, 325-326; John B. Stoll, *History of the Indiana Democracy, 1816-1916* (Indianapolis, 1917), pp. 289, 462.

[15] Sievers, *Benjamin Harrison, Hoosier Statesman,* pp. 170-175.

vention in Cincinnati near the end of June, abandoned his own presidential ambitions to support the candidacy of Thomas A. Hendricks, who had been Tilden's running mate on the "old ticket" of 1876. Senator Voorhees alluded broadly to the supposed advantage of having an Indiana man at the head of the ticket in his nominating address for the state's favorite son: "when the October sun goes down on the October election . . . you will have the enemy in full retreat." Although Hendricks received 49½ votes on the first ballot, the convention finally selected a Civil War general from Pennsylvania, Winfield Scott Hancock, for its presidential nominee. Indiana's claim to special consideration as a pivotal state was recognized by the award of the vice-presidential nomination to William Hayden English, a wealthy Indianapolis banker and former member of Congress, "whose qualifications were entirely geographic," as one historian has written. In an unusual maneuver, moreover, the Hoosier vice-presidential candidate, who has also been called a "banker with a 'barrel,'" was persuaded to retain the chairmanship of the state Democratic central committee and direct his party's Indiana campaign.[16]

16 Dunn, *Indiana and Indianans,* II, 713-714; Stoll, *History of the Indiana Democracy,* pp. 287-288; Democratic National Convention, *Proceedings,* 1880, cited in Clancy, *Presidential Election of 1880,* p. 134; Herbert Eaton, *Presidential Timber. A History of Nominating Conventions, 1868-1960* (New York, 1964), pp. 94-95; Eugene H. Roseboom, *History of Presidential Elections* (New York, 1957), p. 257. Ironically, English had written in January, 1880, that "the Vice Presidency especially would have no charms for me. . . . To be U. S. Senator or Secretary of the Treasury would be much more in accord with my wishes. . . ." William H. English to Lucius J. Gartrell, January 10, 1880, William H. English Papers, William Henry Smith Memorial Library of the Indiana Historical Society, Indianapolis. English, a native of Scott County, Indiana, served four terms in the lower house of Congress before moving to Indianapolis, where he founded the First National Bank in 1863, remaining as its president until 1877. He built English's Opera House on the Circle in Indianapolis during the campaign of 1880 and three years later returned to the presidency of the First National Bank when it encountered financial troubles. He died in Indianapolis in 1896, leaving an estate estimated at $3,000,000. *Dictionary of American Biography* (22 volumes, New York, 1928-1959), VI, 167-168; William G. Sullivan, *English's Opera House* (Indiana Historical Society *Publications,* XX, No. 3, Indianapolis, 1960), pp. 334-340, 358.

Both major parties made strenuous efforts to win Indiana in this last October election. From his farm in Mentor, Ohio, where he helped direct the Republican campaign, James A. Garfield frequently reminded his correspondents of the importance of Indiana in the national strategy. In August he wrote to his running mate, Chester A. Arthur: "If we carry Indiana in October the rest is comparatively easy. We shall make a fatal mistake if we do not throw all our available strength into that state." For a time Garfield even entertained the idea of approaching oilman John D. Rockefeller to obtain the aid of his sales agents in Indiana in the campaign, until warned that association with the founder of the Standard Oil Trust would lose him votes in Pennsylvania! In consideration of the importance of winning Indiana in October, especially after the victory of the Democratic-Greenback fusion ticket in Maine in mid-September, the GOP dispatched well-known national politicians to stump the Hoosier state, including such men as James G. Blaine, Roscoe Conkling, Levi P. Morton, Lyman Trumbull, and Carl Schurz. The Democrats likewise sent out-of-state speakers like the political turncoat Benjamin F. Butler, Cassius Clay of Kentucky, and Samuel J. Randall and William A. Wallace of Pennsylvania. State chairman English was willing to invite the former Greenbacker, Ignatius Donnelly of Minnesota, but refused to retain the services of George W. Julian, the Hoosier radical abolitionist who had helped lead the Liberal Republican bolt in 1872. The Democratic national committee, however, paid Julian $1,500 to make a series of campaign speeches in the state.[17]

---

[17] Garfield to Arthur, August 30, 1880, quoted in Theodore Clarke Smith, *The Life and Letters of James Abram Garfield* (2 volumes, New Haven, 1925), II, 1024, 1025-1026; Clancy, *Presidential Election of 1880,* p. 199; Paul T. Smith, "Indiana's Last October Campaign," *Indiana Magazine of History,* XIX (1923), 336; Albert V. House, "The Democratic State Central Committee of Indiana in 1880: A Case Study in Party Tactics and Finance," *Indiana Magazine of History,* LVIII (1962), 196; Martin Ridge, *Ignatius Donnelly. The Portrait of a Politician* (Chicago, 1962), pp. 194-195; Journal of George W. Julian, August 22, 1880, Julian Papers, Indiana State Library; Patrick W. Riddleberger, *George Washington Julian. Radical Republican* (*Indiana Historical Collections,* XLV, Indianapolis, 1966), pp. 299-300.

In the absence of clearly defined issues, the campaign often descended to the level of political mud-slinging. The reputedly enormous wealth of William H. English made him an obvious target of scandal. In late August a Republican journal in nearby Cincinnati with a wide circulation in Indiana published a two-page list of the Indianapolis banker's real estate holdings in Marion County allegedly acquired by foreclosure of mortgages. To counter such abuse English felt compelled to subsidize the editor of a cheap, sensational Indianapolis weekly called *The People* for the duration of the canvass. The two leading members of the Indianapolis daily press, the Republican *Journal* and the Democratic *Sentinel,* engaged in an acrimonious debate in the closing days of the October campaign over the use of "repeaters" and the importation of "plug-uglies" and "blood-tubs" to "bulldoze" legitimate voters. The *Sentinel* especially warned against the importing of southern Negroes into the state to vote Republican at election time, a charge heightened by the recent investigation into the so-called "Negro exodus" conducted by a special Congressional committee under the chairmanship of Democratic Senator Daniel W. Voorhees.[18]

In the latter stages of the canvass, however, the Republicans found that they had a potent issue in their party's advocacy of a protective tariff and launched a heavy attack on the Democratic platform's "tariff for revenue only" phrase. While it is difficult to gauge fully the effectiveness of this tactic, the tariff question was cited as a major factor in the

[18] Cincinnati *Commercial* cited in Indianapolis *People,* August 21, September 18, 1880; anonymous note in W. W. Woollen Account Books, English Papers; Indianapolis *Journal,* October 4, 5, 1880; Indianapolis *Sentinel,* October 6, 7, 1880. Although George Langsdale, the Republican editor of the Greencastle *Banner,* admittedly encouraged some southern Negroes to settle in Putnam County and other parts of the state in late 1879 and early 1880, there is no evidence of a GOP conspiracy to "colonize" Indiana for political purposes. Greencastle *Banner,* January 1, 8, 1880; *Senate Reports,* 46 Congress, 2 session, No. 693, Pt. II, 485-512; John G. Van Deusen, "Did Republicans 'Colonize' Indiana in 1879?" *Indiana Magazine of History,* XXX (1934), 335-346; Stanley P. Hirshson, *Farewell to the Bloody Shirt: Northern Republicans & the Southern Negro, 1877-1893* (Bloomington, Ind., 1962), pp. 72-77.

defection of two outstanding Hoosier industrialists, John Studebaker of the South Bend wagon-manufacturing family and the New Albany plate-glass manufacturer, Washington C. DePauw, each of whom announced relatively late in the campaign that he was leaving the Democratic party to vote the Republican ticket in 1880.[19]

The victory of Republican gubernatorial candidate Albert G. Porter and the rest of the Republican state ticket by a plurality of nearly seven thousand in October spurred on the Indiana Democratic campaign leaders to greater efforts, but to no avail, for Garfield defeated General Hancock by only a slightly smaller margin in November. The GOP also won majorities in both houses of the General Assembly as well as eight of the state's thirteen seats in the lower house of Congress. A significant factor in the outcome was the shrinkage of the Greenback vote to considerably less than half that polled two years before. Not only had Landers failed to draw Greenback supporters into the Democratic camp, but the working alliance between the two parties in the Seventh Congressional District broke up when the Democrats refused to endorse the Greenback incumbent Gilbert De La Matyr, who thereby lost his bid for a second term in the House of Representatives. Moreover, as one Indiana historian analyzed the election results, many Hoosiers who had formerly voted the Greenback ticket apparently returned to the Republican fold, while most of those remaining in the National party ranks in 1880 had originally been Democrats.[20]

The election of 1880 brought forth sensational charges of the bribery of voters and the expenditure of extraordinarily

[19] South Bend *Tribune*, November 1, 1880; Edwin Corle, *John Studebaker. An American Dream* (New York, 1948), pp. 176-179; New Albany *Ledger-Standard*, October 2, 1880. After the election an Indianapolis correspondent in an eastern political weekly argued that DePauw's shift to the GOP "probably changed more votes than any other influence." *The Nation*, XXXI (1880), 289-290.

[20] W. H. Barnum to English, October 27, 1880, English Papers; Secretary of State, *Annual Report*, 1880, pp. 101-107 and folder at end; John W. Holcombe and Hubert M. Skinner, *Life and Public Services of Thomas A. Hendricks* (Indianapolis, 1886), pp. 343-347; Dunn, *Indiana and Indianans*, II, 715.

large campaign funds in the state. Not long after the October election returns proclaimed a Republican victory, Kentucky's eminent Democratic editor, Henry "Marse" Watterson, published the accusation that Indiana had been "bought right out of hand" by a flood of five-, two-, and one-dollar notes freshly printed for that purpose by the GOP-controlled United States Treasury. At a dinner party at Delmonico's restaurant in New York early the next year honoring Stephen W. Dorsey, a former Carpetbag senator from Arkansas who was acting as secretary of the Republican national committee, Vice-President-elect Arthur lent substance to such charges in an indiscreet address which hinted at the liberal use of political slush funds. "Indiana was really, I suppose, a Democratic State," he was reported to have said. "It had been put on the books always as a State that might be carried by close and perfect organization and a great deal of—(laughter [and cries of 'soap']). I see the reporters are present, and therefore I will simply say that everybody showed a great deal of interest in the occasion and distributed tracts and political documents all through the State."[21]

A few years later Dorsey himself admitted that the GOP had spent $400,000 in Indiana in the 1880 campaign, but the wily former Carpetbagger gave the chief credit for organizing the state successfully to state chairman John C. New, publisher of the Indianapolis *Journal,* and Colonel William W. Dudley, a one-legged Civil War veteran and political lieutenant of the late Governor Morton.[22] In another later account by a reform-minded Republican attorney in Indianapolis, William Pinckney Fishback, both Dorsey and William H. Barnum, chairman of the Democratic national committee, came to the Hoosier capital in the fall of 1880, disbursing large sums of money in the Denison House parlors for their respective par-

---

[21] Louisville *Courier-Journal,* October 22, 1880, cited by Clancy, *Presidential Election of 1880,* pp. 203-204; *The Nation,* XXXII (January-June, 1881), 122, cited by Matthew Josephson, *The Politicos, 1865-1896* (New York, 1938), pp. 300-301.

[22] *Harper's Weekly,* XXVIII (1884), 748.

ty's cause while they were actually business partners and personal friends outside their political roles.[23]

On the Democratic side, state chairman and vice-presidential candidate William H. English was bitterly criticized by some members of his own party for conducting too thrifty a campaign and particularly for not spending enough of his personal wealth. Finally, in a newspaper interview in February, 1882, the long-suffering English came to his own defense with a detailed statement of the source and employment of Democratic campaign funds in 1880—omitting only the precise sums involved :[24]

More money was used by the Democrats in the Indiana campaign of 1880 than was ever used in any previous canvass. More was used by the National committee, more by the State committee, more by the Democratic candidate for Vice-President, more by the Democratic candidate for Governor, and more for the party generally. The expense of the whole canvass up to the time of its close, prior to the October election, was paid out of money raised within the State; the money used on the day of the election and a few days before, came from abroad, almost entirely through the National committee, and was disbursed

[23] William P. Fishback, open letter to Stanton J. Peelle, 1883, quoted in *The Nation*, XLVII (July-December, 1888), 365-366; William P. Fishback, *A Plea for Honest Elections* (Indianapolis, 1886), pp. 13-15, quoted in Dunn, *Indiana and Indianans*, II, 733.

[24] Cincinnati *Enquirer*, February 9, 1882, quoted in Fishback, *A Plea for Honest Elections*, pp. 9-10. The interview is also found in an incomplete form in the Indianapolis *News*, February 9, 1882. English had also defended his management of the campaign a few months before in a private letter to an eastern Republican friend in which he wrote: "I expended much more in the contest than is generally supposed, more I think than was probably ever expended by any candidate for the same office, but I thank God it was expended for legitimate purposes as I never countenanced the use of money for buying votes or corrupting the ballot box or doing any dishonorable act to secure my own election. . . . Besides you well know that my efforts were not properly sustained in certain quarters in our own party, and that I was from the beginning beset by as vile a set of political deadbeats as ever disgraced the human family. Under the circumstances we did remarkably well in Indiana. Where else did the party do better? Altho' shamefully abused and misunderstood I am not distressing myself about my own defeat and there has been no time since the election that I would have exchanged places with either Garfield or Arthur." English to George F. Parker, September 30, 1881, English Papers.

among the counties by the chairman of the National committee, as he had done in 1876, and at the same period before the election.

Moreover, English and the Democratic state committee treasurer, William Wesley Woollen, kept remarkably full financial records which are extant today and throw more light upon the above statement as well as provide a revealing glimpse into political campaign practices of the time. These records show that the state central committee raised approximately $40,000, some of which came from out of state in response to a special appeal. English himself was the largest single contributor, being put down officially for $15,000, though he spent other smaller sums in addition from time to time. Most interesting of all, the records include a confidential statement of the exact amounts paid out directly to state, district, and county committees by the Democratic national committee in October. The total figure thus disbursed came to $97,622.15.[25]

How much, if any, of the campaign funds of either party was employed in purchasing votes or in other corrupt practices, and how much went to pay for legitimate election costs cannot well be determined. Although the moral climate of Indiana politics was probably little or no worse than that of many other states, the state's pivotal position in national

[25] Records of the Democratic State Central Committee, English Papers. Albert V. House has made extensive use of these records in his article, "The Democratic State Central Committee of Indiana in 1880: A Case Study in Party Tactics and Finance," *Indiana Magazine of History*, LVIII, 179-210. But he apparently overlooked the document which specified the amounts of money paid out to the local committeemen by the Democratic national committee, for he wrote that he had found no evidence for such a transaction. *Ibid.*, p. 189. The amount collected by the state committee is found in W. W. Woollen's Account Book and the individual sums and the grand total allocated to the counties by the national committee in a Confidential Statement of Payments Made by the National Democratic Committee to Indiana County Committeemen, October, 1880, enclosed in the letter, Charles J. Canda to English, October 16, 1880, English Papers. The Wayne County committee returned $124 of the $900 awarded it. Letter from the committee to English, February 18, 1881, English Papers.

elections undoubtedly intensified the inclination of the campaign managers to utilize whatever means were available to achieve their objective. Then, too, the rapidly rising cost of the quadrennial presidential contests which had been observed since 1876 might also be attributed to the professionalization of politics which was going on apace in this period, especially within the generally better organized and better financed GOP. More than anything else, perhaps, what the surviving records of the Democratic state central committee reveal is that English conducted the canvass of 1880 in a casual, haphazard fashion, with no regard for the careful organization of party workers and little sense of the issues. One student of the 1880 election has argued cogently that the wealthy banker, who had been largely out of politics since 1861, was, like many other Democratic leaders of the time, still attuned to obsolete political traditions and thus unable to cope with new questions and techniques. "The fact that he ran an old-fashioned campaign," he wrote, "should not have surprised anyone. . . . He was, after all, a Bourbon holding the fort in a region being subjected to dynamic upheaval."[26] In short William H. English was a political amateur and an anachronism in an age when skillful professionals like John C. New and William W. Dudley had begun to organize the Indiana GOP down to the precinct level, an effort which would bear fruit again as well as set off a notorious controversy in the state eight years later.[27]

[26] "Cost of National Campaigns," *World's Work*, I (1900-1901), 77; House, "The Democratic State Central Committee of Indiana in 1880," *Indiana Magazine of History*, LVIII, 210.

[27] An interesting description of the organizing role of New and Dudley in the Republican campaign of 1880 is found in Seeds, *History of the Republican Party in Indiana*, pp. 365-368. New, who was born in Jennings County, Indiana, in 1831, was Governor Morton's quartermaster general during the Civil War and later an officer in William H. English's First National Bank in Indianapolis. In 1875-1876 he served as treasurer of the United States under President Ulysses S. Grant and in 1882 was appointed assistant secretary of the treasury by President Arthur. Chairman of the Indiana state committee of the GOP in both 1880 and 1884, he was appointed Consul General in London by President Benjamin Harrison in 1889. *Commemorative Biographical Record of Prominent*

In January, 1881, the Republican majority in the Fifty-second General Assembly proceeded to the selection of Benjamin Harrison, the Indianapolis attorney who had emerged as a major figure in the Hoosier ranks of the GOP since his unsuccessful candidacy for the governorship in 1876, as United States Senator, replacing the Democratic incumbent, Joseph E. McDonald.[28] Although Harrison had campaigned for the office and thought himself best able to serve his country in the Senate, he had a hard choice to make when Garfield asked him to take a post in his cabinet. Harrison finally decided to remain in the Senate, even though his refusal of Garfield's offer meant that Indiana would be denied the representation in the new cabinet which its key role in the election had earned, for the President-elect would consider no one else from the state. Thus the situation remained until after the assassination of President Garfield, when his successor, Chester A. Arthur, picked Harrison's fellow Hoosier and bitter party rival, Walter Quintin Gresham, for the position of Postmaster General.[29]

and *Representative Men of Indianapolis and Vicinity* (Chicago, 1908), pp. 18-20. The Vermont-born Dudley came to Richmond, Indiana, in 1860, lost a leg at Gettysburg, and served as Wayne County clerk from 1866 to 1874. He was United States Marshal for Indiana 1879-1881, and in 1881 was appointed Commissioner of Pensions by President Garfield. After 1884 he practiced law in Washington, D.C. and accepted the position of treasurer of the Republican national committee in 1887. Dunn, *Indiana and Indianans*, II, 739-740.

[28] This brought an end to McDonald's active political career. "An independent and vigorous character who never lost a certain raciness and tang," according to Meredith Nicholson, McDonald, unlike his senatorial colleague Voorhees, was a hard-money man and protective tariff advocate who rose high in his party's favor during a period when these views were unpopular in Democratic circles. He died in Indianapolis in 1891. Meredith Nicholson, *The Provincial American and Other Papers* (Boston, 1912), p. 16; *Dictionary of American Biography*, XII, 17-18.

[29] Sievers, *Benjamin Harrison, Hoosier Statesman*, pp. 184-195. The "cordial and magnetic" Gresham was a distinguished Civil War veteran who as a Federal judge in Indianapolis in 1877 helped organize a committee of public safety to halt the great railroad strike of that year. A potential candidate for both the Indiana governorship and senatorial seat in 1880, Gresham served President Arthur not only as Postmaster General but also as Secretary of the Treasury for a few months before accepting appointment to the Federal Circuit Court in

The legislature also resubmitted the seven constitutional amendments disallowed earlier to popular ratification at a special election in March, 1881. This time they received a majority of the votes cast, no other questions being on the ballot, and were declared adopted. Besides changing the date of the general elections to November, these amendments also limited the bonded indebtedness of municipalities to 2 per cent of the value of their taxable property, modified voting requirements, and struck out the clauses in the constitution banning Negro residence and suffrage. The removal of these clauses, though already rendered inoperable by judicial decisions and the Fifteenth Amendment, finally brought Indiana into conformity with the Federal constitution.[30]

This was a period of intense interest in amending the state constitution, which many Hoosiers felt was becoming obsolete in view of the great increase in population and wealth during the thirty years since its adoption in 1851. Outgoing Governor Isaac P. Gray, who had succeeded Governor James D. Williams upon the latter's death in November, 1880, recommended that the legislature call a constitutional convention to revise the state instrument. But neither newly elected Governor Porter nor the Republican-controlled legislature concurred.[31] In a special session in March, 1881, however, the General Assembly proposed four new amendments, the most important of which would have granted the suffrage to women and prohibited the manufacture and sale of intoxicating liquors in Indiana. The latter provision proved particularly unpopular and roused the Indiana Liquor League, a group of brewers and distillers who organized to try to defeat the Republican legislators who were held responsible for its passage. The Democrats, formally condemning all sumptuary

Chicago in November, 1884. Nicholson, *The Provincial American*, p. 14; Matilda Gresham, *Life of Walter Quintin Gresham, 1832-1895* (2 volumes, Chicago, 1919), I, 402-408; II, 488-504.

[30] Kettleborough, *Constitution Making in Indiana*, II, 202-207.

[31] *Ibid.*, II, 198-201; Indiana *House Journal*, 1881, pp. 37, 83-84. In 1889, after being elected in his own right to the governorship, Gray also opposed holding a constitutional convention. *Ibid.*, 1889, p. 47.

legislation in their state platform, swept to a substantial victory in the election of 1882. The state ticket won by a margin of nearly eleven thousand votes, and the Congressional delegation was changed to a nine-to-four Democratic advantage.[32]

The Democratic majority in the 1883 General Assembly rejected out-of-hand the pending amendments and also began what was to become a long tug-of-war between the legislative and executive branches of the government by taking from Republican Governor Albert G. Porter the power of appointing such officers as the state geologist and members of the boards of state institutions. In similar fashion the legislature created a controversial metropolitan police board, to which was transferred the management of the police system of the Republican-dominated city of Indianapolis.[33]

In 1884 Indiana had two favorite sons who aspired to first place on the Democratic national ticket. Perennial presidential hopeful Thomas A. Hendricks nominated his colleague, Joseph E. McDonald, in return for his deference to Hendricks' candidacy four years before, but later permitted his name to go before the Chicago convention, setting off a gallery demonstration engineered by Tammany Hall and other opponents of Governor Grover Cleveland of New York. But the tactic failed and the reform-minded Cleveland won the nomination easily, Hendricks having to be satisfied with the second place on the ticket, just as in 1876. Despite his disappointment, the former Indiana governor campaigned vigor-

[32] *Laws of Indiana, 1881* (special session), pp. 719-721; Kettleborough, *Constitution Making in Indiana*, II, 188-196; Secretary of State, *Annual Report, 1882*, pp. 139-145; Dunn, *Indiana and Indianans*, II, 715-716.

[33] Kettleborough, *Constitution Making in Indiana*, II, 207-236; *Laws of Indiana*, 1883, pp. 15-16, 89-94, 104. The legislature chose the state geologist from 1883 to 1889, when the Supreme Court found this unconstitutional and ruled that the office should be filled by popular election. The State ex rel. Worrell v. Peelle, 121 Ind. 495 (1889). The metropolitan police board was later extended to cities of 10,000 to 35,000 population, an act concurred in by both Republican and Democratic legislatures. *Laws of Indiana*, 1893, pp. 284-285; 1897, pp. 90-96.

ously and played a role in keeping the Tammany Hall dissi-
dents in New York from bolting the Cleveland candidacy.[34]

The Indiana delegation to the Republican nominating convention in the same city was split between supporters of Benjamin Harrison and his old rival, Postmaster General Walter
Q. Gresham. Because of this no Hoosier candidate was presented to the convention, and Indiana Republicans were generally content with the nomination of James G. Blaine of
Maine. Although Blaine made overtures to both Gresham and
Harrison for the vice-presidential candidacy, neither made any
response, and the honor went to John A. Logan of Illinois.[35]

The presidential campaign was characterized by a dearth
of attention to political issues and concentrated attacks on
the personal lives of the candidates. In an attempt to counter
the earlier Republican exposé of Cleveland's illicit relationship with Mrs. Maria Halpin, the bitterly partisan Indianapolis *Sentinel* on August 8 published the allegation that Blaine's
marriage had been celebrated a mere three months prior to
the birth of a child to his wife, but failed to point out that
this was a second marriage ceremony performed after the
principals involved had discovered that their first one a year
before lacked full legal standing.[36] Senator Harrison himself
was not above waving the "bloody shirt" once more in making campaign appeals to Civil War veterans. That wartime
prejudices were not dead in Indiana was indicated in this
election-day entry in the diary of Ira J. Chase, a Protestant
minister and leader of the Grand Army of the Republic who
later served as lieutenant governor and governor of the
state: "We are not really ready for a rebel government yet
& this is what will happen if a *libertine* like Cleveland and

[34] Eaton, *Presidential Timber*, pp. 109-112; Holcombe and Skinner, *Life and Public Services of Thomas A. Hendricks*, pp. 356-364. Hendricks' biographers denied that their subject had anything to do with the diversion in his favor at the convention, for "he was unwaveringly true to his trust," they claimed. *Ibid.*, p. 358.

[35] Sievers, *Benjamin Harrison, Hoosier Statesman*, pp. 247-251.

[36] Indianapolis *Sentinel*, August 8, 1884. Blaine asked Benjamin Harrison to file a criminal libel suit against the editor of the *Sentinel* but let it drop after the election. Sievers, *Benjamin Harrison, Hoosier Statesman*, pp. 254-259.

a base Copperhead like Hendricks are elected." The GOP also tried, less successfully than in 1880, to make the protective tariff a major issue in the campaign.[37]

A novel element—though not a decisive factor in the election in Indiana—was the activity of civil service reformers and independent Republicans, or Mugwumps, who rejected the candidacy of the tarnished Blaine. Most such agitation centered in Indianapolis, where, according to Meredith Nicholson, "the animosities left by the Civil War were still so bitter that to be a Democrat was a social disqualification, but to be a Mugwump was to be 'queer'—at best an object of amused or cynical curiosity." It was a newcomer to the city, Lucius Burris Swift, who organized an Independent Committee of One Hundred to canvass the state for Cleveland. Other Republicans active in the Cleveland campaign were the Indianapolis law partners, John T. Dye and William P. Fishback. William Dudley Foulke of Richmond, later a leading civil service reformer and associate of Theodore Roosevelt, announced that he could vote for neither Blaine nor Cleveland. The old Republican bolter, George W. Julian, was also called upon once more to take the stump for the Democrats, though by 1884, as a recent biographer has noted, he had "dropped his mantle of independence."[38]

The Greenbackers, who had nominated Benjamin F. Butler for president at their national convention in Indianapolis in May, were again represented on the state ticket. Another minor party made its initial appearance in Indiana in July, 1884, when Eli Ritter and other temperance men organ-

[37]Sievers, *Benjamin Harrison, Hoosier Statesman,* pp. 258-259; Diary of Ira J. Chase, November 4, 1884, Indiana State Library, Indianapolis. A Republican clergyman noted in the last months of the campaign that "the tariff question is being worked for all that is in it. It is the only thing but the bloody shirt and our history that can be made available." Thomas A. Goodwin to W. W. Thornton, October 1, 1884, Thornton Papers, Indiana State Library.

[38] Meredith Nicholson, *Old Familiar Faces* (Indianapolis, 1929), pp. 97-98, 128-129; William D. Foulke, *Lucius B. Swift. A Biography* (Indiana Historical Society *Publications,* IX, Indianapolis, 1930), p. 15; William D. Foulke, *Fighting the Spoilsmen* (New York, 1919), pp. 10-15; Riddleberger, *George Washington Julian,* p. 300.

ized a Prohibitionist convention in Indianapolis and placed their candidates on both the state and national ballot after unsuccessful attempts to gain a hearing for their cause from the Republicans. Both Butler and the National Prohibition party presidential candidate, John P. St. John, made personal appearances in the state during the campaign.[39]

The election outcome in November brought a complete reversal of the 1880 decision. The national Democratic ticket garnered a plurality of 6,500 in the state, even though Butler won 8,800 and St. John 3,000 votes. Indiana sent nine Democratic Congressmen to Washington to support Cleveland, whose electoral victory made him his party's first President since James Buchanan. Colonel Isaac P. Gray, a former Republican turned Democrat, was elected to the governorship over his Republican opponent, Congressman William H. Calkins. Moreover, with an overwhelming Democratic majority in both houses of the Indiana General Assembly, Daniel Wolsey Voorhees, the "Tall Sycamore of the Wabash," was easily returned to the United States Senate for a third term.[40]

Rather surprisingly, the Democratic-controlled legislature of 1885 enacted a civil-rights law to replace those provisions

[39] Logan Esarey, *A History of Indiana* (Third edition, 2 volumes, Fort Wayne, 1924), II, 957-959; Indianapolis *Sentinel,* July 25, October 3, 1884. Apparently Hoosier Prohibitionists had proposed a state ticket in 1880 but withdrew it before the election. Ernest H. Cherrington (ed.), *Standard Encyclopedia of the Alcohol Problem* (6 volumes, Westerville, Ohio, 1924-30), III, 1308.

[40] Secretary of State, *Biennial Report,* 1886, pp. 240-253. Senator Voorhees of Terre Haute, who represented Indiana in the House of Representatives for five years and in the Senate for twenty years, was a colorful personality better known for his rather florid oratory and intemperate polemic than for constructive legislation. His chief monument, however, was the Library of Congress Building, which he helped plan and championed as chairman of a select committee of the Senate for many years. Leonard S. Kenworthy, *The Tall Sycamore of the Wabash: Daniel Wolsey Voorhees* (Boston, 1936), pp. 119-120. For other assessments of his life and career, see Frank S. Bogardus, "Daniel W. Voorhees," *Indiana Magazine of History,* XXVII (1931), 91-103; Henry D. Jordan, "Daniel Wolsey Voorhees," *Mississippi Valley Historical Review,* VI (1919-20), 532-555.

of the Federal act which had been invalidated by the United States Supreme Court two years before. This statute, which declared that all persons within the state were entitled to equal access to places of public accommodation such as hotels, restaurants, and theaters, proved to have little effect upon the general pattern of racial segregation, however, as Professor Emma Lou Thornbrough has shown in her study of the Negro in Indiana.[41] Perhaps the chief accomplishment of the Fifty-fourth General Assembly was a controversial reapportionment of the state's legislative districts—the notorious "gerrymander of 1885," as the GOP immediately labeled it—which may well have helped the Democrats maintain their majority position in the legislature for a nearly unprecedented ten-year span.[42]

But the Indiana Democracy was soon deep in political trouble, chiefly on account of its adherence to a system of patronage which provoked the wrath of the civil service reformers. Lucius B. Swift joined with William D. Foulke, Indianapolis *News* editorial writer Louis Howland, and Oliver T. Morton, son of the war governor, to promote the organization of the Indiana Civil Service Reform Association. Foulke, a Republican member of the Senate, had attempted unsuccessfully to secure passage in the 1885 legislature of a civil service bill patterned on the Federal Pendleton Act. One of the

[41] *Laws of Indiana,* 1885, pp. 76-77; Emma Lou Thornbrough, *The Negro in Indiana. A Study of a Minority (Indiana Historical Collections,* XXXVII, Indianapolis, 1957), pp. 259-266.

[42] *Laws of Indiana,* 1885, pp. 62-64. For a contemporary view of this apportionment act by a Republican critic, see Charles H. McCarer, *The Gerrymander. A Statement Showing the Disfranchisement of Those Opposed to the Democratic Party* (Indianapolis, 1886). When legal action was taken to test the constitutionality of various apportionment acts, those passed in 1879, 1891, 1893, 1895, and 1903 were all declared invalid by the Indiana Supreme Court. The act of 1885 was the only one not tested and therefore the only one to remain effective in this period. Parker *et al. v.* The State, ex rel. Powell, 133 Ind. 178 (1892); Denney, Clerk, *et al. v.* The State, ex rel. Basler, 144 Ind. 503 (1895); Brooks, Clerk, *et al. v.* The State, ex rel. Singer, 162 Ind. 568 (1903); Dunn, *Indiana and Indianans,* II, 724-725. See also Robert D. Seltzer, Rotten Boroughism in Indiana (Unpublished Ph.D. thesis in Government, Indiana University, 1952), pp. 181-197.

association's first tasks was an investigation, led by Swift, of the Central Hospital for the Insane in Indianapolis. The investigators' disclosures of grave scandals and abuses in the administration of the hospital brought embarrassment upon the ruling party in the legislature, which controlled the appointment of the institution's managers.[43] Partly as a result of these revelations, the GOP won the state offices and seven of the thirteen Congressional races in the off-year election of 1886. The Republicans also won a majority in the lower house of the General Assembly, but the Democrats retained control of the Senate. Since the latter had a numerical advantage on joint ballot of both houses, they were able, with the aid of a Greenback-Labor representative, to elect the Democratic candidate, David Turpie, to succeed Benjamin Harrison in the United States Senate.[44]

The legislative session of 1887 was chaotic and unproductive, displaying the state governmental machine at its worst. The trouble started when Lieutenant Governor Mahlon D. Manson resigned to accept a Federal post in August, 1886. To replace him, all parties presented candidates at the fall general election, but when Republican Robert S. Robertson was duly elected, the Democratic-controlled Senate repudiated him and chose one of its own members, Alonzo Greene Smith, as presiding officer. From that point on, the two houses, operating under mutually antagonistic party leadership, refused to co-operate with each other. The outcome was a legislative deadlock: little business was transacted and few laws enacted.[45]

---

43 Foulke, *Lucius B. Swift,* pp. 30-31.

44 David Turpie was born in Ohio and educated at Kenyon College. He served briefly in the United States Senate in 1863 as a replacement for the ousted Jesse D. Bright and was elected to two full terms in that body, serving from 1887 to 1899. In the Senate he was known chiefly as an advocate of the popular election of Senators and the independence of Cuba. See his autobiography, *Sketches of My Own Times,* and *Biographical Directory of the American Congress, 1774-1961,* p. 1735.

45 The imbroglio hurt the political ambitions of Governor Isaac P. Gray, who had to withdraw his name from consideration for election to the United States Senate because there was no lieutenant governor of his own party to

The campaign of 1888 was a memorable one in Indiana. The GOP, more determined than ever to win the state after the catastrophe of 1884, proffered the presidential nomination to former Senator Benjamin Harrison after the withdrawal of the popular idol, James G. Blaine. Judge Walter Q. Gresham, however, once more the choice of an anti-Harrison faction in the Indiana Republican party and elsewhere, received strong support during the early balloting at the Chicago nominating convention.[46] The selection of Levi P. Morton of New York for second place gave the ticket the normal sectional balance contained in the Republican strategy of this period; namely, to choose presidential nominees from the Midwest and vice-presidential nominees from the East, just the reverse of the usual Democratic practice. Since Vice-President Thomas A. Hendricks had died in November, 1885, after less than a year in office, the Indiana Democracy hoped to replace him on the ticket with another Hoosier, Governor Isaac P. Gray, but the national convention preferred Allen G. Thurman of Ohio for Cleveland's running mate in 1888.

Indiana presidential politics were always colorful and boisterous, but the pageantry of this canvass was calculated to evoke memories of the log-cabin campaign of Benjamin Harrison's grandfather, "Old Tippecanoe," nearly a half century earlier. Elaborate torchlight processions and political barbecues entertained the electorate. In the capital city a group of business and professional men formed the Harrison Marching Club—later the exclusive Columbia Club of Indianapolis—and paraded in blue flannel coats and trousers and white derby

succeed him. Stoll, *History of the Indiana Democracy,* pp. 316-317; Dunn, *Indiana and Indianans,* II, 720-721.

[46] Among Indiana Republicans supporting Gresham for the presidential nomination were Charles W. Fairbanks, John W. Foster, and Albert J. Beveridge. Gresham, *Life of Walter Quintin Gresham,* II, 561-601. State Attorney General Louis T. Michener was Harrison's chief political manager at the Chicago convention, where he and William W. Dudley went up and down the aisles buttonholing delegates. Michener, The National Convention of 1888. Typescript draft in Louis T. Michener Papers, Library of Congress, Washington, D.C., microfilm copy in Indiana Division, Indiana State Library. See also Sievers, *Benjamin Harrison, Hoosier Statesman,* pp. 247-252, 319-356.

hats and canes.[47] For a few months the nation's attention was focused on Indianapolis, where representatives of the national press gathered to report the words and actions of the Republican candidate. There the austere, reserved Harrison, whom his enemies called cold and aloof, conducted a dignified "front-porch" campaign, receiving delegations from many parts of the country with careful speeches from his home, and later from a specially prepared platform in University Park. An old friend, Lew Wallace, author of the popular novel, *Ben-Hur,* made a welcome contribution to Harrison's election by writing a better-than-ordinary campaign biography of the warrior-statesman.[48]

Despite the presence of a Hoosier name at the head of the Republican ticket, the election was close and hotly contested in Indiana. President Cleveland's message to Congress in 1887 calling for a downward revision of tariff duties made the protective tariff the main substantive issue of the campaign, but lesser questions intruded in Indiana. The GOP, for example, appealed strenuously to state pride in sending an Indiana man to the White House, while the Democrats attempted to show that Harrison was aristocratic and unfriendly to labor.[49] The two major parties conducted a well-organized canvass, especially in attempting to locate and influence the so-called "floating vote," estimated at about thirty thousand persons who shifted political allegiances frequently, some of whose ballots were allegedly purchasable. Workers in both parties

[47] Seeds, *History of the Republican Party of Indiana,* p. 371.

[48] Lew Wallace, *Life of Gen. Ben Harrison* (Indianapolis, 1888); Sievers, *Benjamin Harrison, Hoosier Statesman,* pp. 357-373.

[49] R. C. Buley, "The Campaign of 1888 in Indiana," *Indiana Magazine of History,* X (June, 1914), 35-39, 46-47. The favorite calumny against Harrison, which apparently was first circulated in Indiana shortly after his nomination in July, 1888, was that he had broken the railroad strike of 1877 in Indianapolis by the use of bayonets and had used such expressions as "a dollar a day is enough for any workingman." There was no evidence of such antilabor sentiment on the part of Harrison, though he had antagonized some segments of organized labor by voting against the Chinese Exclusion Act in the United States Senate in 1882. Sievers, *Benjamin Harrison, Hoosier Statesman,* pp. 221-224, 395-397.

apparently took private polls at regular intervals in order to ascertain the comparative voting strength of the two tickets. Many charges of wholesale vote bribery were hurled on all sides, setting the stage for the celebrated "blocks of five" controversy which was precipitated at the very end of the election campaign.[50]

On the last day of October, 1888, the Indianapolis *Sentinel* exploded a political bomb in the Harrison camp by printing on its front page under the heading "The Plot to Buy Indiana" a document purporting to be a circular letter addressed to Indiana county chairmen by the treasurer of the Republican national committee, William W. Dudley, who had played a key role in the state during the 1880 campaign. The letter, which was dated October 24, contained such bald instructions to party workers as this: "Divide the floaters into blocks of five, and put a trusted man with necessary funds in charge of these five, and make him responsible that none get away and that all vote our ticket."[51] The publication of this document with these and other damaging phrases furnished the GOP's opponents with strong implications of corrupt Republican electioneering practices and caused an immediate uproar both in Indiana and in New York, where it was reprinted by Democratic newspapers. James N. Huston, Republican state chairman, immediately announced that "Colonel Dudley has nothing to do with the management of the Indiana campaign," and Dudley himself denounced the

[50] *Ibid.*, pp. 415-417; Gresham, *Life of Walter Quintin Gresham,* II, 603. Two Indiana University professors, R. H. Dabney and A. B. Woodford, described in letters to the editor of *The Nation* their observations of the methods of handling "floaters" employed by Republican party workers in Bloomington and Monroe County in 1888. Thirty thousand floaters is Dabney's figure. *The Nation,* XLVII (July-December, 1888), 412, 517-518.

[51] Indianapolis *Sentinel,* October 31, 1888. The letter is reproduced in facsimile in Dunn, *Indiana and Indianans,* II, 736. Louis T. Michener admitted later in a private memorandum that such a letter had been distributed to party workers in Indiana, but claimed that it had been "materially altered and enlarged so as to make it appear offensive to law and morals." "The Dudley Letter," a typed memorandum in the Michener Papers, cited by Sievers, *Benjamin Harrison, Hoosier Statesman,* p. 419.

letter as a forgery. However, there seems to be little doubt
of the authenticity of the letter, which had been purloined
by a railway mail clerk and forwarded to Indiana Democratic
state chairman Charles L. Jewett.[52] Most of the letter described the normal and legitimate methods of precinct work,
and nothing in it constituted justiciable evidence of advice to
bribe, as Hoosier Democrats discovered to their sorrow when
a Federal grand jury in Indianapolis refused to indict Dudley after the election.[53] Yet the Dudley letter pointed to long-
standing abuses in the pre-secret ballot conduct of elections.
While it probably did not materially affect the outcome of the
1888 election, it helped awaken Indiana and the nation to the
need for legislative reform of polling practices.[54]

This affair was at least partially offset by the conviction
earlier in the year of the Marion County Democratic boss,
Simeon Coy, and one of his associates of altering tally sheets
in a local election in 1886.[55] This and the civil service reformers' attacks upon Democratic misuse of political patronage
were put to effective use in the Republican campaign. The Indiana Mugwumps had become disillusioned by the Cleveland
administration's violation of Federal civil service regulations
in the Indianapolis post office and elsewhere in the state, and,
unlike Carl Schurz and their other eastern associates, supported Harrison in the campaign. Lucius B. Swift, who re-

---

[52] Indianapolis *News*, October 31, 1888; New York *Times*, October 31,
1888. Dudley instituted libel suits against three New York newspapers which
carried the story but dropped proceedings when retractions were printed. Harrison, however, never fully exonerated Dudley, and the breach between the
two men caused by the unfortunate letter remained unhealed. Sievers, *Benjamin Harrison, Hoosier Statesman*, pp. 420-421.

[53] Jacob P. Dunn, *Greater Indianapolis. The History, the Industries, the
Institutions, and the People of a City of Homes* (2 volumes, Chicago, 1910),
I, 298-306.

[54] Robert LaFollette, "The Adoption of the Australian Ballot in Indiana,"
*Indiana Magazine of History*, XXIV (1928), 112-114.

[55] Dunn, *Greater Indianapolis*, I, 292-298. Simeon Coy, who returned to his
old seat on the Indianapolis city council after serving a year in prison,
published his own account of the case, asserting his innocence and also discussing prison reform. *The Great Conspiracy. A Complete History of the Famous
Tally-Sheet Cases* (Indianapolis, 1889).

ceived assurances from Harrison that he would enforce the Pendleton Act in spirit and letter, made several speeches for him and in March, 1889, began publication in Indianapolis of a monthly journal, the *Civil Service Chronicle,* in order to keep watch over the administration's deeds.[56]

In an extremely close election, Benjamin Harrison won his home state by a 2,300 plurality while the combined vote for the Union Labor and Prohibition candidates was over 12,000. It was the capture of New York by a 14,000 plurality which proved decisive, for it gave Harrison the election by an electoral count of 233 to 168. But Indiana's favorite son was fated to be a minority President, for in the total popular ballot he fell behind Cleveland by more than 90,000 votes. Gubernatorial candidate Alvin P. Hovey, who headed the successful Republican state ticket in Indiana, slipped into office by an even smaller margin. Further evidence of the indecisiveness of the election was revealed when the Democrats won ten out of thirteen Congressional races and regained control of both houses of the state legislature.[57]

The Fifty-sixth General Assembly, which met in 1889, produced a very extensive record of reform legislation, some of it over Governor Hovey's veto but much of it bipartisan. It included laws aimed at the suppression of the so-called "White Caps," vigilante groups which flourished in certain southern Indiana counties, factory and charity organization laws, and election reform legislation. Publicity given to alleged corrupt practices at the polls for at least a decade and especially in the election just past lent urgency to the drive for reform of balloting methods. In his message to the General Assembly, outgoing Governor Gray, recommending immediate passage of a secret-ballot law, noted that "public faith in the purity of our elections has become shaken, and the feeling is wide spread that the decision at the ballot box no longer reflects the honest judgment of a majority of the

---

[56] Foulke, *Lucius B. Swift,* pp. 35-39.

[57] Secretary of State, *Biennial Report,* 1888, pp. 2-34; Walter Dean Burnham, *Presidential Ballots, 1836-1892* (Baltimore, 1955), pp. 140-141.

voters." Republican Governor Hovey agreed that "there is reason to believe that the ballot has been polluted."[58]

A Democratic journalist, Jacob P. Dunn, and an Indianapolis labor leader, Lafayette P. Custer, began the newspaper campaign for an Australian ballot system which culminated in the reform bill eventually passed by the legislature. The secret ballot adopted, one of the first in the nation, was the "party-column" type, listing nominees for office by party affiliation, with party emblem, name, and a circle for straight-ticket voting at the top of each column. The Indiana ballot, as this type was called to distinguish it from the Massachusetts ballot, which listed candidates by office rather than by party in order to discourage straight-ticket voting, became the model for a majority of the states of the Union. According to the new system, the state, rather than the political parties, as had been the practice before, furnished ballots uniform in size, color, and quality on election day to all qualified voters, who marked them in secret. Each of the two major parties was given equal representation on the election boards and all persons except election officials and voters were prohibited from approaching within fifty feet of the polling places. The legislature also passed an antibribery law, which penalized the purchaser rather than the seller of votes.[59] Although these enactments could not completely eliminate corruption of the ballot box, they undoubtedly led to greater purity at the polls and signaled the end of an era in Indiana politics.[60]

§ § §

The return of economic prosperity in the eighties proved to be short-lived, especially for Indiana's farmers, who found

[58] Indiana *Senate Journal*, 1889, pp. 45, 103.

[59] *Laws of Indiana*, 1889, pp. 157-186, 360-363; Dunn, *Indiana and Indianans*, II, 744-746; Eldon Evans, *A History of the Australian Ballot System in the United States* (Chicago, 1917), p. 40. The new election procedures were explained in Jacob P. Dunn, *A Manual of the Election Law of Indiana* (Indianapolis, 1889).

[60] Robert LaFollette, "The Adoption of the Australian Ballot in Indiana." *Indiana Magazine of History*, XXIV, 114-120.

that their own rising production together with the recovery of European agriculture soon began to depress farm prices in both the American and the world market. At the same time the new protective tariff legislation of the United States was raising the cost of manufactured goods bought by farmers. Caught in the pinch between rising costs and falling prices, many farmers began looking to governmental intervention of some kind to alleviate their depressed condition. An often accurate indicator of agricultural unrest is farm mortgage indebtedness. One contemporary study calculated the increase in mortgage debt in Indiana for the period 1882-1888 at $46,476,652, more than three quarters as much as the mortgage debt of $60,379,232 for the severe depression years 1873-1879.[61] During the late eighties and early nineties a new wave of agrarian organization and protest arose to express the political grievances of the agricultural classes who felt they were not getting a fair share of the economic progress of the country. An older association, the Patrons of Husbandry, or the Grange, remained an influential element in the social and economic life of Hoosier farmers, but gave ground before the rise of more politically oriented societies which appeared in Indiana and other states to the south and west at this time. Chief among these were the Farmers' Alliance and the Farmers' Mutual Benefit Association, both of which were well established in the state by 1890.[62]

The chief inspiration for agrarian political action at this time was derived from the St. Louis meetings of the Northern and Southern Alliances in December, 1889. Representatives of the F.M.B.A. and the Knights of Labor also were present as observers at consultations which many hoped would produce a unified farmer-labor movement. Although no such unity was achieved at St. Louis, the two Alliances drew up platforms remarkably similar in demanding the

61 Jacob P. Dunn, "The Mortgage Evil," *Political Science Quarterly,* V (1890), 66-69.
62 For the organization of the farmers' associations in this period, see below, Chapter IV.

abolition of national banks and the issue of legal tender treasury notes, governmental ownership and operation of railroads, the prohibition of alien land ownership, and other reforms. In addition, the Southern Alliance's platform called for the "free and unlimited coinage of silver" while the Northern Alliance demanded a graduated income tax and tariff reduction.[63] Hoosier farm leaders were quick to respond. At the call of James G. Kingsbury, editor of the *Indiana Farmer,* representatives of the Farmers' Alliance, the F.M.B.A., the Grange, and other farm organizations, were to convene in Indianapolis on June 19, 1890, to form a state league for united action.[64] Though failing in this purpose, the convention decided to advise its members to work actively within the old political parties, and adopted a series of resolutions denouncing trusts and high taxes and declaring for cheap currency, lower rates of interest, tax exemption for mortgaged farm property, and direct election of United States Senators. During the summer and early fall of 1890, farmers' organizations actually nominated their own tickets in a few localities.[65]

The major parties in Indiana were not entirely unmoved by this grass-roots rebellion. The Democratic state platform of 1890 announced that "we are rejoiced at the evidences of an awakening of the farmers of the country to the necessity for organized efforts to better their own condition and protect themselves against unjust legislation and oppressive administration." Claiming to represent the farmers' interest, the Democrats incorporated in their platform planks favoring the prohibition of alien land ownership, the popular

[63] The story of the Northern and Southern Alliances and the formation of their political programs at St. Louis in 1889 is found in John D. Hicks and John D. Barnhart, "The Farmers' Alliance," *North Carolina Historical Review,* VI (1929), 254-280. The platforms are found in Appendix A of John D. Hicks, *The Populist Revolt. A History of the Farmers' Alliance and the People's Party* (Minneapolis, 1931), pp. 428-430.

[64] *Indiana Farmer* (Indianapolis), May 31, 1890.

[65] Indianapolis *Journal,* June 20, 1890; Ernest D. Stewart, "The Populist Party in Indiana," *Indiana Magazine of History,* XIV (1918), 341-344; Esarey, *A History of Indiana,* II, 1047-1052.

election of Senators, and the "free and unrestricted coinage of silver."[66] "It was a year," the historian of the Republican party reported, "when the politicians were tumbling over each other to cater to the new farmers' organization, and each party was careful to head its ticket with a farmer."[67] The GOP chose Milton Trusler of Fayette County, the Master of the Indiana Grange, as its candidate for secretary of state while the Democrats nominated Claude Matthews, a Vermillion County farmer and stockman, for the same office. Despite this attention to their cause, the farmers' organizations made preparations for the creation of a third party. On September 23, 1890, about one hundred delegates of the Alliance, the F.M.B.A., the Patrons of Husbandry, and a few Greenbackers and Union Labor party members gathered in Indianapolis to nominate an independent ticket. Calling themselves the People's party, as similar groups around the country were doing at this time, and adopting the plow and hammer for an emblem, they chose a slate of candidates for state offices headed by Leroy Templeton, a wealthy cattleman of Benton County.[68]

Nevertheless, it was the Democratic party which reaped immediate political advantage from the agrarian discontent. Its state ticket was elected in 1890 by the surprisingly large plurality of 19,500, while the People's party received 17,300 votes, and the omnipresent Prohibitionists 12,000.[69] The Democrats also won eleven Congressional seats and maintained their dominance of the state legislature, which returned Daniel W. Voorhees once more to the United States Senate. The only major reform enactment of the General

[66] William E. Henry (comp.), *State Platforms of the Two Dominant Political Parties in Indiana, 1850-1900* (Indianapolis, 1902), p. 87.

[67] Seeds, *History of the Republican Party in Indiana*, p. 73.

[68] Stewart, "The Populist Party in Indiana," *Indiana Magazine of History*, XIV, 345-347. Leroy Templeton later withdrew to accept the nomination of Democrats and Independents for the Ninth District Congressional race. He was replaced as candidate for secretary of state by another farmer, Martin V. Kindle.

[69] Secretary of State, *Biennial Report, 1890*, pp. 220-251.

Assembly, however, was the creation of the State Board of Tax Commissioners, which was given more power than the former Board of Equalization in determining fair assessment of taxable property, especially that of railroads and other corporations.[70]

Undismayed by the election returns, the agrarian reformers continued their agitation. On November 20 eighty delegates of the Indiana Farmers' Alliance, claiming to represent fifteen thousand members, adopted resolutions to be submitted to the General Assembly on reform of state and local government, and repeated demands for free silver, nationalization of railroads, and abolition of national banks. A state conference of the F.M.B.A. at Peru, Indiana, took a similar stand in December.[71] Hoosiers also played a part in the formation of the national People's party at Cincinnati in May, 1891. Charles A. Power of Terre Haute was one of those who drew up and signed the call for the Cincinnati convention, and his fellow townsman, Morton C. Rankin, was chosen the treasurer of the new party's national committee. In July the Indiana branch of the party was organized, and arrangements made to transfer a Populist newspaper, the *American Nonconformist,* from Winfield, Kansas, to Indianapolis. The Indiana capital was the scene in November of the simultaneous meetings of the Supreme Council of the Southern Alliance and the executive committee of the People's party, which stirred up additional enthusiasm for the farmers' cause. Finally, in May, 1892, the Indiana Populists named a state ticket for the fall election headed by gubernatorial candidate Leroy Templeton and drew up the most radical platform yet seen in the state, including planks favoring free silver, government ownership of railroads and other utilities, the subtreasury scheme of the Southern Alliance whereby the national government would lend money at low interest on

---

[70] *Laws of Indiana,* 1891, pp. 249-256.

[71] Indianapolis *Journal,* November 21, 22, December 18, 1890.

farmers' surplus crops stored in local warehouses, the initiative and referendum, and woman suffrage.[72]

Indiana was well represented at the great national convention of the People's party in Omaha, Nebraska, in July, 1892, and Hoosier delegates were active in the abortive attempt to draft Judge Walter Q. Gresham as a presidential candidate. Gresham, who had broken with the GOP over the protective tariff, was flirting with Populism but finally declined to let his name go before the convention. After considering several other possible candidates, including the Terre Haute labor leader, Eugene V. Debs, the People's party tapped the former Greenback standard-bearer, General James B. Weaver of Iowa for the presidential nomination and chose an ex-Confederate general, James G. Field of Virginia, as his running mate.[73]

L 1475450

The major parties largely ignored the Populist challenge in 1892 and fought on the old battleground of the tariff question. There was no real opposition to the renomination of either Harrison or Cleveland by their respective parties, but the Democratic state platform declared for Governor Isaac P. Gray for president "in the event that the national convention deems the nomination of Mr. Cleveland inexpedient."[74] However, the Democratic nominating convention refused even to name the Hoosier governor for second place on the ticket, choosing instead Adlai E. Stevenson of Illinois. The Indiana Democracy nodded to the farm vote by granting the

---

[72] Stewart, "The Populist Party in Indiana," *Indiana Magazine of History,* XIV, 352-361. Stewart is apparently wrong when he states that the 154-man Indiana delegation at the Cincinnati convention was second in size to that of Kansas. Hicks gives Ohio over three hundred delegates and Kansas more than four hundred. Hicks, *Populist Revolt,* pp. 209-213. A bound volume of the *American Nonconformist* for 1894 is in the Indiana State Library. The journal's editors were Lucius A. Stockwell and Charles X. Mathews, and its publisher Leroy Templeton.

[73] Gresham, *Life of Walter Quintin Gresham,* II, 663; Hicks, *Populist Revolt,* pp. 233-234.

[74] Henry (comp.), *State Platforms,* p. 97. Gray was appointed Minister to Mexico by President Cleveland in 1893 and died while in that office in 1895. Dunn, *Indiana and Indianans,* II, 724.

gubernatorial nomination to Claude Matthews, the Vermillion County farmer who had been elected secretary of state two years earlier. The Republican candidate opposing him was Ira J. Chase, the former lieutenant governor who succeeded to the governorship upon the death of Alvin P. Hovey in 1891. The Democratic party also gained a new organizational leader of great political skill in Thomas Taggart, an Irish-born Indianapolis restauranteur who replaced the convicted Simeon Coy as Marion County boss in 1888. He attained wide public notice by carrying Harrison's home county for Cleveland in 1888 and was chosen chairman of the state central committee in 1892.[75]

Benjamin Harrison had proven much less adept as President of the United States and national party head than he had been as Republican leader and campaigner in his home state. Political patronage was badly handled, and his civil service record disappointed such independents as William D. Foulke and Lucius B. Swift, who refused to support him for a second term in the White House.[76] Harrison included in his cabinet not only James G. Blaine, who became a strong Secretary of State, but also his Indianapolis law partner, William Henry Harrison Miller, as Attorney General. He rewarded wealthy contributors to the GOP, naming John Wanamaker of Pennsylvania Postmaster General and Stephen B. Elkins

[75] Thomas Taggart came to Indianapolis in 1877 as manager of the Union Station restaurant. He became a popular figure in the city and ran successfully for auditor of Marion County on the Democratic ticket in 1886. He was elected mayor of Indianapolis for three terms and rose to leadership of the Democratic political machine in city, county, and state. Later he was the proprietor of the famous resort hotel in French Lick, Indiana, chairman of the Democratic national committee, 1904-1908, and briefly a member of the United States Senate in 1916. He died in Indianapolis in 1929. Charles Roll, *Indiana: One Hundred and Fifty Years of American Development* (5 volumes, New York and Chicago, 1931), IV, 383-384. The only biography of Taggart is Alva C. Sallee, T. T. The Master Mind That Wrought Brilliant and Bewildering Achievements in Political Legerdemain (typescript in Indiana Division, Indiana State Library, n. d.)

[76] Swift, "Civil-Service Reform. A Review of Two Administrations," *Forum,* XIV (1892-93), 206-215; Foulke, *Lucius B. Swift,* pp. 47-50; Foulke, *Fighting the Spoilsmen,* pp. 88-89.

of West Virginia Secretary of War.[77] Moreover, his administration found places in the government for a host of "deserving" party workers from Indiana. "So great in fact was the
exodus of Republicans from the State to fill Federal offices,"
wrote one observer, "that the campaign of 1890 fell largely
into the hands of a new generation of leaders." His wife's
long illness and eventual death prevented Harrison from campaigning actively in 1892. The usual torchlight processions
and noisy demonstrations were also largely absent in Indiana.[78]

Ex-President Grover Cleveland led the entire Democratic
ticket to victory in the state in November by a plurality of
nearly seven thousand, though the Populists increased their
vote to twenty-two thousand.[79] The Democrats also captured
eleven seats in Congress and obtained a safe majority in the
General Assembly, which returned David Turpie once more
to the United States Senate, where he and his colleague,
Senator Voorhees, represented the last of the "old guard"
among the Indiana Democracy. Indiana gained representation
in the cabinet in 1893 when the new President appointed the
politically vacillating Walter Q. Gresham, who had announced

[77] In the Louis T. Michener Papers is a letter from Stephen B. Elkins written
in 1890 and marked "personal and confidential" in which he complained that the
"transaction" between Indiana and the East concerning Harrison's nomination
had been forgotten. Elkins was not given his cabinet post until 1891. Elkins to
Michener, June 12, 1890, Michener Papers, Library of Congress, microfilm copy
in Indiana Division, Indiana State Library.

[78] Seeds, *History of the Republican Party in Indiana*, p. 69; George Harmon
Knoles, *The Presidential Campaign and Election of 1892* (Stanford University
Press, 1942), p. 222. For an excellent account of Harrison's role in the cam-
paign, see Donald Marquand Dozer, "Benjamin Harrison and the Presidential
Campaign of 1892," *American Historical Review*, LIV (1948-49), 49-77.

[79] Secretary of State, *Biennial Report*, 1892, pp. 292-306. At the end of his
presidential term in 1893, Harrison returned to his home in Indianapolis, where
he resumed the practice of law. He campaigned for the Republican party in
1894 and 1896 and was senior counsel for Venezuela in its boundary dispute
with England at the international arbitration hearing in Paris in 1899. Some of
his public addresses and a series of articles on the Federal government were
published in book form. He remarried in 1896 and became the father of a
daughter by his second wife. He died in Indianapolis in 1901. *Dictionary of
American Biography*, VIII, 331-333.

for Cleveland during the campaign, Secretary of State. He replaced another native Hoosier, John W. Foster, who after a long and distinguished diplomatic career headed the Department of State for eight months after the resignation of James G. Blaine, Harrison's original choice for that office.[80]

The coming of the Panic of 1893 struck a disastrous blow to the hopes and plans of the newly inaugurated Democratic administration. When Cleveland called Congress into special session in August to repeal the Sherman Silver Purchase Act as a means of relieving the country's strained financial condition, the whole Indiana Congressional delegation supported the President. In an unexpected reversal of his inflationary views, Daniel W. Voorhees even led the fight for repeal in the Senate as chairman of the finance committee.[81] But this measure helped little to soften the impact of the economic downturn. The ensuing depression had a severe effect upon Indiana, causing an extraordinary number of factory closings, railroad bankruptcies, and bank suspensions. In addition to falling farm prices and industrial unemployment, a coal miners' strike in the southwestern part of the state and the Pullman strike in Chicago in 1894 seriously injured the state's economy. When two separate detach-

[80] Martha Alice Tyner, "Walter Q. Gresham," *Indiana Magazine of History,* XXIX (1933), 337. Gresham, who died in office on May 28, 1895, opposed the treaty annexing Hawaii which John W. Foster, his friend and predecessor, had negotiated. Neither Gresham nor Foster was an outstanding Secretary of State in an era when the Department of State itself was at low ebb. After Foster's brief term as Secretary of State, he acted as adviser to the Chinese government in its peace negotiations with Japan in 1895 and was a delegate for China at the second Hague Peace Conference in 1907. He died in 1917. For an assessment of their careers, see William R. Castle, Jr., "John Watson Foster," and Montgomery Schuyler, "Walter Quintin Gresham," in Samuel F. Bemis (ed.), *The American Secretaries of State and Their Diplomacy* (Volumes 1—, New York, 1927—  ), VIII, 187-223, 227-269.

[81] *Congressional Record,* 53 Congress, 1 session, pp. 591, 1009, 2958. Matilda Gresham claimed that her husband was influential in bringing pressure on Senator Voorhees from his Indiana constituency in favor of repeal of the Sherman Silver Purchase Act. Voorhees' biographer argued that Cleveland's handling of patronage as well as the changing economic climate in Indiana affected the Senator's willingness to work for repeal. Gresham, *Life of Walter Quintin Gresham,* II, 701-705; Kenworthy, *Voorhees,* pp. 104-110.

ments of Jacob S. Coxey's "industrial army" crossed the state in 1894, a "Hoosier Brigade" was waiting to join them.[82] Hoping to benefit from the economic unrest, the Indiana People's party put up a full slate of candidates for state offices and wrote a strong platform. Besides a general endorsement of the Omaha national platform of 1892, it included the following demands for the state: abolition of the metropolitan police board, the calling of a state constitutional convention to write an instrument permitting such innovations as the initiative and recall, a child labor law, municipal ownership of public utilities, and a state income tax.[83]

The political consequences of the depression were catastrophic for the party in power in both state and nation. In the off-year election of November, 1894, the GOP was victorious by an unprecedented majority of nearly forty-five thousand, winning control of both houses of the legislature for the first time since 1872 and making a clean sweep of the thirteen Congressional races. The Republican landslide not only virtually buried the Democratic party but also left the Populists with just under thirty thousand votes cast for the head of their ticket, Dr. Charles A. Robinson, president of the Indiana Farmers' Mutual Benefit Association.[84] This represented approximately 5 per cent of the total vote, the highwater mark of the People's party as an independent entity in Indiana. Yet it was actually ten thousand less than the Greenback vote cast at the peak of its influence in 1878—a graphic display of the comparative strength of the two radical agrarian protest movements in the state. One important difference in the appeal of the Greenback and the People's party may have been the extreme simplicity of the former's

82 D. L. McMurry, *Coxey's Army* (Boston, 1929), pp. 144-147, 236-237. The state statistician reported that three national banks and nine state banks were suspended during the period January 1 to October 31, 1893; also that 248 businesses failed in 1893 as against only 167 in 1892. Indiana Department of Statistics, *Biennial Report*, 1893-1894, p. vi.

83 *American Nonconformist* (Indianapolis), May 24, 1894; Stewart, "The Populist Party in Indiana," *Indiana Magazine of History*, XIV, 365-367.

84 Secretary of State, *Biennial Report*, 1894, pp. 252-284.

reliance upon currency inflation as a panacea for the farmers' economic ills as contrasted with the broad spectrum of more complex reforms put forward by the Populists. This may also explain why political reformers after 1892 became increasingly obsessed with the "free and unlimited coinage of silver" as the road to popularity and success at the polls.

William H. Harvey's celebrated pamphlet, *Coin's Financial School* (1894), played a part in persuading Hoosier farmers and others that the demonetization of silver had been the chief cause of the country's economic difficulties, and that unrestricted coinage of silver at the ratio of sixteen to one in relation to gold was the best remedy. "Why anybody should have taken this clever allegory as a record of historical events is almost beyond comprehension but there were thousands who did," reported a contemporary historian of Indiana.[85] This same historian, then a Democratic newspaper editor, the indefatigable Jacob P. Dunn, entered the debate with a pamphlet arguing for international bimetallism in place of either free silver or the single gold standard.[86]

Political discussion of this issue came to a climax in the election year of 1896, when the two major parties took antithetical stands on the question in the presidential campaign. At its state convention in early May, the Indiana GOP declared unequivocally for "honest money" in a currency plank which anticipated the national platform enunciated a month later. To give added strength to the state ticket the party chose a well-known and widely respected Montgomery County farmer, James Atwell Mount, for its gubernatorial candidate. Although many Hoosier Republicans would have liked to have seen Benjamin Harrison renominated for the highest post in the land, the doughty ex-President refused to permit his name to be considered, and the state convention pledged

---

[85] Dunn, *Indiana and Indianans,* II, 755.

[86] Jacob P. Dunn, *The World's Silver Question* (Indianapolis, 1894). Another pamphleteer of the time was Charles H. Bliss of Auburn, Indiana, who was the author of *The Populist Compendium* (1894) and *The Free and Unlimited Coinage of Silver, from a Business View* (1895). He also edited a Populist magazine entitled *Bliss' Magazine* at Auburn in 1894 and 1895.

its support to Ohio's Governor William McKinley, who with
the aid of his chief political adviser, Marcus A. "Mark"
Hanna, had been actively seeking backing in Indiana for
several months.[87]

Presiding over the state convention was Charles Warren
Fairbanks, a wealthy Ohio-born railway attorney of Indianapolis who was emerging as a major leader of the Indiana
GOP after Harrison's retirement from active participation in
politics. Fairbanks was also McKinley's personal choice for
temporary chairman of the national nominating convention in
St. Louis, where he was duly elected to that position and
threw his weight into the movement to produce a platform
with a strong gold standard plank. As a comparison of the
monetary clauses in the Indiana and the national Republican platforms shows, the language was remarkably similar
except for a provision in the latter pledging the GOP to promote an international agreement concerning bimetallism.[88]

---

[87] A. Dale Beeler (ed.), "Letters to William R. Holloway, 1893-1897," *Indiana Magazine of History,* XXXVI (1940), 371-396.

[88] The state platform is found in Henry (comp.), *State Platforms,* pp. 107-
108. The national platform appears in Roseboom, *A History of Presidential
Elections,* p. 305. John W. Foster wrote to Fairbanks from Washington, D.C.,
urging him to give special attention to the financial plank of the platform,
because he felt McKinley, a former inflationist, would be weakest at this point.
Foster to Fairbanks, May 12, 1896, Fairbanks Papers, Lilly Library, Indiana
University, Bloomington, Indiana. Credit for the gold plank of the Republican
national platform has been claimed by several others, including Henry Cabot
Lodge, Henry C. Payne, Joseph Foraker, and Thomas C. Platt. Roseboom,
*History of Presidential Elections,* p. 305. For Fairbanks' part in the national
convention, see William Henry Smith, *The Life and Speeches of Hon. Charles
Warren Fairbanks* (Indianapolis, 1904), pp. 42-56.

| Indiana Republican Platform (May, 1896) | National Republican Platform (July, 1896) |
|---|---|
| We are unalterably opposed to every scheme that threatens to debase or depreciate our currency. | We are unalterably opposed to every measure calculated to debase our currency or impair the credit of our country. |
| We favor the use of silver as currency, but to the extent only and under such regulations that its parity with gold can be maintained; and in consequence are opposed to the free, unlimited and independent coinage of silver at a ratio of 16 to 1. | We are, therefore, opposed to the free coinage of silver, except by international agreement with the leading commercial nations of the world, which we pledge ourselves to promote, and until such agreement can be obtained the existing gold standard must be preserved. |

The money question seriously divided the Indiana Democracy in 1896. As the time for the state convention approached, free silver advocates and gold standard Democrats held separate public rallies at English's Opera House in Indianapolis in order to drum up support for their respective views. Although many party leaders, including former state chairman Thomas Taggart, opposed them, the silverites dominated the state convention which met in late June and nominated a former Greenbacker, Congressman Benjamin Franklin Shively of South Bend for governor. The state platform, moreover, demanded "the immediate restoration of bimetallism by the free and unrestricted coinage of both silver and gold, as primary money, at the ratio of 16 to 1" and committed the Indiana delegation to the favorite-son candidacy of Governor Claude Matthews for the presidency "first, last and all the time."[89]

[89] Claude G. Bowers, *The Life of John Worth Kern* (Indianapolis, 1918), pp. 119-122; Henry, *State Platforms,* pp. 105-107. Benjamin F. Shively, a native of St. Joseph County, Indiana, was elected to Congress as a Greenbacker for a short term in 1884 and later served five additional terms as a Democrat. He was twice elected to the United States Senate and died in Washington, D.C., in 1916. H.S.K. Bartholomew, "The Political Career of Benjamin F. Shively," *Indiana Magazine of History,* XXVIII (1932), 251-268.

The ultimate nomination of William Jennings Bryan of Nebraska to head the national Democratic ticket on a free silver platform alienated many conservative Hoosier Democrats, some of whom broke with the party completely. One of the most prominent bolters was William Dallas Bynum of Indianapolis, former minority party whip in the United States House of Representatives, who helped organize gold standard Democrats as a separate party in order to defeat Bryan. In September the National Democratic party held its nominating convention in Indianapolis, naming Senator John M. Palmer of Illinois for President and former Confederate General Simon Bolivar Buckner for Vice-President, and placing Bynum and another Hoosier, John A. Wilson, on the executive committee. But the Gold Democrats, as they were usually called, attracted few supporters in Indiana, the best known being George W. Julian, who came out of political retirement to make his last public speech in an appearance before the Sound Money League in Indianapolis in October, 1896.[90]

The People's party of Indiana met in Indianapolis in July shortly after its national convention had endorsed Democratic nominee William J. Bryan for the presidency but replaced the conservative Arthur Sewall of Maine by the Georgia Populist, Thomas E. Watson, for second place on the ticket. The chief problem facing Indiana Populists in 1896 was the division of their members over the question of "fusion," or amalgamation with the Democrats. When the struggle between fusionists and the "middle-of-the-roaders," as those opposed to amalgamation were dubbed, threatened to destroy the party, the state convention agreed upon a compromise solution. Although a full state ticket was put into the field under the Populist label, a committee was appointed to negotiate with

---

[90] Stanley L. Jones, *The Presidential Election of 1896* (Madison, Wis., 1964), pp. 267-272; Riddleberger, *George Washington Julian*, pp. 314-315. Julian died three years later, in 1899. *Ibid.*, p. 321. William D. Bynum was rewarded for his services in the anti-Bryan campaign by being appointed to a Federal commission in Washington by President McKinley. He retired from public life in 1907 and died in Indianapolis in 1927. *Biographical Directory of the American Congress, 1774-1961*, p. 642.

Democratic leaders concerning the possible combining of presidential electors. After a prolonged battle, partial fusion of the two parties was secured in many local election districts as well as on the presidential ballot, which finally contained the names of ten Democratic and five Populist electors.[91]

The campaign of 1896 in Indiana was marked by the "most intense bitterness of partisan feeling that had been known since war times," according to the contemporary journalist-historian, Jacob P. Dunn. Although the GOP attempted to give equal weight to the tariff question, the free silver issue overshadowed all else, producing a flood of oratory on both sides throughout the canvass. On the Democratic side the outstanding orator was William J. Bryan himself, who crossed Indiana five times and electrified large and enthusiastic crowds at most of his stopping places.[92] McKinley, on the contrary, remained at home in Canton, Ohio, while his astute political manager, Mark Hanna, conducted an "educational" campaign in every state by means of pamphlets and a host of stump speakers. Among the Hoosier contingent of campaigners was a group of younger Republicans—Albert Jeremiah Beveridge, Charles Warren Fairbanks, James Franklin Hanly, and James Eli Watson—all of whom were at the beginning of successful political careers in state and nation.[93]

While some Hoosier Democrats maintained silence during the canvass because of their hostility to Bryan and free silver, others entered the hustings out of loyalty to the party, like John Worth Kern, who campaigned vigorously for subsidiary issues to which he was sincerely attached, such as the income tax and the popular election of Senators. But the

[91] Stewart, "The Populist Party in Indiana," *Indiana Magazine of History,* XV (1919), 56-62.

[92] Dunn, *Indiana and Indianans,* II, 757-758; William J. Bryan, *The First Battle. A Story of the Campaign of 1896* (Chicago, 1898), pp. 304, 362-365, 445, 526-533, 568-569. A prominent Hoosier feminist and Prohibitionist, Helen M. Gougar of Lafayette, was an active campaigner for Bryan under the auspices of the National Silver Party. *Ibid.,* p. 252.

[93] Esarey, *History of Indiana,* II, 1055-1056; Claude G. Bowers, *Beveridge and the Progressive Era* (Cambridge, Mass., 1932), pp. 59-62.

GOP's monetary orthodoxy regained the support of the former Mugwumps William D. Foulke and Lucius B. Swift, both of whom stumped throughout the state for McKinley. In September, 1896, moreover, Swift announced that in the event of the defeat of Bryan he would cease publication of his *Civil Service Chronicle* in the conviction that the battle for reform had been won.[94]

In November William McKinley carried Indiana by a plurality of over eighteen thousand and an absolute majority of eleven thousand, despite the presence on the ballot of four minor parties. The Prohibitionist vote was split, 2,900 for the "narrow-gage" candidate and 2,200 for the "broad-gage" candidate, whose platform included free silver and other radical planks, while the National (Gold Standard) Democrats tallied only 2,000 votes, most of their strength, as predicted, going to McKinley. The Republican state ticket led by Governor-elect James A. Mount swept into office by an even larger margin, as the middle-of-the-road Populists polled 8,600 for their gubernatorial candidate, Thomas A. Wadsworth. The GOP also obtained a nine-to-four preponderance in the state's Congressional delegation. Although the Populists managed by virtue of fusion with the Democrats to place nine men in the General Assembly, the Republicans controlled a firm majority in both houses of that body and in January, 1897, elected Charles W. Fairbanks to the United States Senate seat being vacated by the aging Democratic warrior, Daniel W. Voorhees.[95]

---

[94] Bowers, *Life of John Worth Kern,* pp. 123-125; William D. Foulke, *A Hoosier Autobiography* (New York, 1922), p. 105; Foulke, *Lucius B. Swift,* pp. 58-60. After the election, however, Swift was disillusioned with McKinley as President and severely criticized him for laxness in administering the Federal merit system. Foulke, *Lucius B. Swift,* pp. 61-64.

[95] Secretary of State, *Biennial Report,* 1896, pp. 226-278; Roll, *Indiana,* II, 357-358. There is some confusion concerning the number of Populists who were elected to the General Assembly in 1896, for they were all listed officially as Democrats in the report of the secretary of state. Stewart gives the names of eight representatives and one senator, while Kettleborough reports twelve Populist legislators, nine in the house and three in the senate. Stewart, "The Populist Party in Indiana," *Indiana Magazine of History,* XV, 65, 65n; Kettleborough, *Constitution Making in Indiana,* II, 317.

The results of the election were disheartening to both Democrats and Populists, many of whom blamed their defeat on the alleged political intimidation of farmers and working-men by Republican party and business spokesmen. Histo-rians, however, tend to place more weight on such factors as the general improvement in economic conditions of the time, which "dulled the edge of discontent and aided the Republi-can cause," as John D. Barnhart and Donald F. Carmony have stated. Although the People's party continued to hold state conventions and present candidates for office for another dec-ade, its following in Indiana rapidly dwindled. A few Hoosier party leaders remained faithful to the end, one of whom, Samuel W. Williams of Vincennes, was rewarded by the nom-ination for Vice-President on the last Populist ticket in 1908. A major weakness of the Populists was their lack of success in establishing an alliance with the labor movement, which was growing in size and importance during these years. It was perhaps not altogether coincidental that the decline in Populist fortunes after 1896 was simultaneous with the rise of the Socialist party with its special appeal to the industrial working class.[96]

The failure of the radical agrarian movement in Indiana, moreover, ushered in an epoch of Republican political domi-nance which reflected in part, at least, the gradual transfor-mation of the state from a primarily agricultural to an in-creasingly industrialized society. The rising business and manufacturing classes, together with a large segment of the industrial workers, endorsed such Republican policies as sound money and the protective tariff and were able to veto the inflationary demands of a fading agrarian radicalism as soon as they came to approximate a majority of the elector-ate. The swing to the GOP in 1896 also seemed to reveal the weakening influence of the older sectionalism, as Indiana and its neighboring states were beginning to identify and ally

[96] Barnhart and Carmony, *Indiana*, II, 325; Hicks, *Populist Revolt*, p. 402; Stewart, "The Populist Party in Indiana," *Indiana Magazine of History*, XV, 73-74.

themselves with the industrial East rather than the perennially discontented agricultural West. Even the farmers of this region were becoming, both economically and politically, "less colonials of the East and more the advanced guard of expanding industrialism. No longer were they strictly a part of the agrarian Middle West," as Horace S. Merrill has written.[97]

In contrast to much of the agrarian South and West, moreover, Indiana had become less dependent upon one or two main crops, a failure or sudden drop in prices of which could cause severe farm distress. Increased diversification of agricultural production, including the combining of stock raising and dairying with the cultivation of cereal crops as well as the expansion of commercial vegetable growing, usually meant better and more dependable profits, which probably inclined farmers to political conservatism. Related factors were the rise of cities and a spreading railroad network which brought markets nearer and lessened the sense of isolation of rural residents. By the turn of the century improved transportation and communication facilities had also made large parts of Indiana the agricultural hinterland of numerous urban centers, including not only Indianapolis and other major cities within the state but also Chicago, Cincinnati, and Louisville just beyond its borders.[98]

The social and economic development of Indiana undoubtedly helped to mold its changing political character in these years. In the eighties and nineties both urbanization and industrialization were proceeding apace in many sections of the state, though without producing the concentrated manufacturing complexes and dense population masses of the older industrial centers in the East. The national election statistics

[97] Horace S. Merrill, *Bourbon Democracy of the Middle West, 1865-1896* (Baton Rouge, La., 1953), p. 140. For a good description of this transformation in the Old Northwest in general and Wisconsin in particular, see Frederick Jackson Turner, *The Frontier in American History* (New York, 1920), pp. 218-219.

[98] Robert R. LaFollette, "Interstate Migration and Indiana Culture," *Mississippi Valley Historical Review*, XVI (1929-30), 253-255.

in 1896 reveal, for example, that Bryan ran best in some of the more highly industrialized cities as well as in rural areas in the less industrialized states; in Indiana, however, he received 48 per cent of the vote in rural districts and only 44 per cent in urban.[99]

In the last two decades of the nineteenth century, moreover, the growth of population and wealth in Indiana tended to favor the GOP. The southern half of the state, long predominantly Democratic in its politics, grew much more slowly and experienced considerably less urban-industrial development than the remainder of the state. On the other hand, in many of the central and northern counties with strong Republican traditions a great expansion of manufacturing and commerce took place, causing a surge in population and the raising of villages and towns to the level of good-sized cities. Richer and generally more diversified agricultural counties also tended to be found in the Republican column at election time. By the same token the depopulation of poorer rural counties may have played some part in silencing the voices of agrarian unrest. One writer has suggested, in a variant of the "safety-valve" theory, that Indiana's loss of population to states farther west in the seventies and eighties might well explain why it showed less support for the People's party than the latter region. Noting that there were over 98,000 Hoosiers resident in Kansas in 1890, historian Charles Roll wrote, "If these emigrants had remained in Indiana, they would have undoubtedly helped to swell the tide of discontent at home."[100]

While Indiana was still primarily an agricultural state as late as 1896, its agrarian character was being modified by the challenge of new social and economic forces as represented by the rise of cities and the large-scale development

[99] William Diamond, "Urban and Rural Voting in 1896," *American Historical Review*, XLVI (1940-41), 289.

[100] Carleton, "Why Was the Democratic Party in Indiana a Radical Party, 1865-1890?" *Indiana Magazine of History*, XLII (1946), 228; Barnhart and Carmony, *Indiana*, II, 325-326; Roll, *Indiana*, II, 345.

of industry. Politically, the age of agrarian dominance was drawing to a close, and an era more consonant with an emerging urban-industrial society was at hand. The election of 1896 inaugurated a period of Republican party hegemony which would last for slightly more than a decade, destroying the relatively even balance of political forces which had made Indiana such a critical element in presidential elections. No longer so doubtful a state, it was perhaps never again to be quite so bitterly fought over as it had been in the eighties. Yet Indiana did not cease to play a significant part in national politics. Producing a host of prominent state and national politicians in both major parties and at least one minor party, the Hoosier state continued to be the "mother of Vice-Presidents." The political battles of the twentieth century in Indiana would differ in many ways from those of the eighties and nineties yet retain much of the passion and partisan rivalry which characterized the politics of a pivotal state.

# CHAPTER II

# THE POLITICS OF IMPERIALISM, 1896-1901

THE ELECTION OF 1896 was a watershed in the political history of Indiana and the nation. On the one hand, the overwhelming Republican victory was soon followed by a decided upturn in the business cycle in the United States which outmoded much of the rhetoric and strategy of the politics of agrarian depression of the eighties and nineties. Almost all sectors of the economy felt the impact of the new prosperity. While crop failures abroad in 1897 and the resulting rise in farm prices benefited American agriculture, tariff-protected industrial production at home began a long period of unprecedented expansion which made possible high profits for manufacturers and an increase in real income for workers. On the other hand, a satisfactory answer to the long-prevalent demands for currency inflation and to the free silver argument was finally found when the opening of Alaskan and South African gold mines along with the introduction of the cyanide process of refining vastly enlarged the world's supply of gold. In Indiana, as in most of the nation, Republicans basked in the warm sunlight of broad popular approval, their party's policies seemingly vindicated by the fulfillment of their glowing promises of economic revival.

The end of the century also brought a heightened sense of nationalism as the United States began to attain a self-confident economic maturity and to move boldly into the international arena of commercial rivalries and power politics. The Spanish-American War was not wholly responsible for this new national consciousness, though it helped to give it direction and momentum. While the Democracy continued largely to voice nineteenth-century attitudes of isolationism, the GOP was able to maintain its dominant political position after 1896 partly because it reflected, both in domestic and foreign policies, the expansive, optimistic mood of America at that time. In a letter of congratulation to Charles W. Fairbanks for his keynote address at the Republican nominating convention in the summer of 1896—"It is in line and humming with the spirit of Young Republicanism of the day"—a Hoosier newspaper editor revealed his enthusiasm for a strong program of political and economic nationalism. Linking together the three strands of Republican orthodoxy—fiscal conservatism, a high protective tariff, and expansionism—he made this resonant declaration of national goals for the coming era:[1]

We want a sound money, a tariff sufficient to pay the current expenses of the nation, interest on the public debt, and afford sufficient protection to our manufactures. Also a broad foreign policy, so that our flag *shall* wave on every sea and ocean, our trade extend in every direction by means of reciprocity treaties, the building of the Nicaragua Canal, and the building up of our merchant marine. The time has come when we must spell Nation with a big N and no foolishness.

The late nineties also witnessed the rise of a new type of political leader in Indiana, less regional in outlook and more attuned to the economic currents and prospects of an expanding capitalistic society than the previous generation of politicians. Gone were the Civil War volunteer generals and colonels who had figured so largely in earlier campaigns. Benjamin Harrison, Walter Q. Gresham, Isaac P. Gray, Alvin P. Hovey, Mahlon D. Manson, and other former officers had either died or retired from active politics by the turn of the century. Ironically, the last G.A.R. veterans to occupy the governor's chair in Indiana had served as enlisted men rather than commissioned officers in the great sectional conflict— James A. Mount, who was elected in 1896, and Winfield T. Durbin, the successful Republican candidate in 1900.[2]

As in earlier years, most Hoosier politicians were lawyers, but after 1896 they were more likely to be closely associated

[1] S. E. Haight, Columbus, to Charles W. Fairbanks, June 16, 1896, Fairbanks Papers, Lilly Library, Indiana University, Bloomington, Indiana.

[2] Dunn, *Indiana and Indianans,* II, 759, 765.

with business and industry as well as identified with broad national interests instead of a narrow sectionalism. The old-fashioned courtroom pleader, such as Joseph E. McDonald or Benjamin Harrison, would give way to a successful corporation lawyer, such as Charles W. Fairbanks, who specialized in reorganizing bankrupt railroads and was said to have taken only one criminal case in his whole career.[3] Similarly, David Turpie, who, like Senator Voorhees, had been primarily a sectional advocate during his long years of service in the Democratic party, would find himself replaced in the United States Senate by an ardent nationalist in the person of Albert J. Beveridge.[4]

Charles Warren Fairbanks, like the man he defeated for the United States Senate in the Republican legislative caucus in 1897, William Riley McKeen, a Terre Haute banker and president of the Vandalia Railroad, was an example of the new breed of wealthy lawyers and businessmen who entered politics at this time—the Hoosier counterpart of Ohio's Mark Hanna. Indeed, during the spring of 1896 the reformer William D. Foulke sourly noted this phenomenon in an open letter to the Indiana press. Without naming Fairbanks or McKeen but in clear reference to them, he declared that "the candidates who are now pushing their claims most loudly and eagerly are men without distinction or experience in public life, whose chief qualification is the possession of great wealth, which it is believed they are willing to use, paying for the coveted honor by enormous contributions to the cam-

---

[3] Smith, *Life and Speeches of Fairbanks,* pp. 22-23.

[4] Neither Beveridge nor Fairbanks had ever held public office before their election to the United States Senate, unlike most of their predecessors, who built their careers step-by-step from the county courthouse or State House to Washington. Indeed, Beveridge refused nomination for the highly lucrative position of state attorney general in 1893 because he had already set his sights on a higher goal. "I think I am not ready to begin to have 'ex' written after my name," he explained to a friend. "I think that there may be something higher ahead for me—but I shall not care even for that unless I can [do] my country good in the better & nobler sense." Albert J. Beveridge to John C. Shaffer, November 20, 1893, Shaffer Papers, Indiana State Library.

paign fund, as well as in other ways."[5] In a personal letter to Carl Schurz a few days later Foulke attacked Fairbanks by name, charging that he sought to be elected to the Senate "principally by his use of money." "He is an attorney who has been the representative of one or more railroad companies in the state and holds a respectable though by no means eminent position at the bar," he added, "but his election will in fact be due to money. No one would ever have thought of him for such a place as the United States Senate were it not for his liberal contributions and financial aid to the party."[6]

Actually Fairbanks had carefully planned a political career for several years. A native of Ohio and a graduate of Ohio Wesleyan University, he began the practice of law in Indianapolis in 1874. There he built a considerable fortune as a railway attorney, eventually becoming a major stockholder in the Cincinnati, Hamilton and Dayton Railroad Company and a silent partner in the Indianapolis *News* with his uncle, William Henry Smith, former manager of the Associated Press.[7]

[5] *Harper's Weekly,* XL (1896), 458.

[6] Foulke to Carl Schurz, May 14, 1896, Foulke Papers, Indiana State Library. Fairbanks, whose whole career was probably hampered by the rumors and allegations of his tremendous wealth, was tagged a "millionaire" by his opponents in the GOP as early as 1896. He complained to his uncle, William Henry Smith, that this epithet was being used even though no one really knew "whether I am worth $50,000 or $1,000,000." Fairbanks to Smith, February 21, 1896, William Henry Smith Papers, Indiana Historical Society.

[7] Smith and Fairbanks purchased the *News* in 1893, at least partly with a view to advance the latter's political career. It was to remain an independent paper, however, and the editor, Charles R. Williams, Smith's son-in-law, often carried independence so far that Fairbanks could say in 1895 that "now I am neither consulted nor are my suggestions invited." Fairbanks to Smith, February 16, 1895, Fairbanks Papers, Lilly Library, Indiana University. In rebuttal, Williams explained, "My idea is just this: the News as an independent paper can help you; as your personal organ it could have no influence. It has been my understanding always that it was not to be known that you have any interest in the paper. I have acted on that theory." Charles R. Williams to Fairbanks, February 18, 1895, *ibid.* But because of friction with William J. Richards, a minority stockholder, Fairbanks sold his interest in July, 1896. When the paper went into receivership in 1899, Fairbanks and Delavan Smith, son of William Henry Smith, who had died in the meantime, repurchased it, the former remaining a silent partner with Smith as editor and publisher.

After acquiring a competency, he entered politics and quickly became an important figure in the Republican party in Indiana. He worked for the presidential nomination of Judge Walter Q. Gresham in 1888 but later supported Benjamin Harrison. He presided over state conventions of the GOP and took an active part in campaigning, both by public speeches and financial contributions. For two decades after his election to the United States Senate in 1897, he was the state's most distinguished conservative Republican leader. A strict, nonsmoking, nondrinking Methodist layman, Fairbanks was a politician of great personal dignity and unquestioned honesty whose chief defects were his relatively narrow point of view and lack of imagination.[8]

§ §

When the new administration took office in 1897, the two main items on the agenda were upward revision of the tariff and the establishment of a sound currency. President William McKinley called a special session of Congress for the first of these but was rebuffed by Great Britain when he appointed a commission to explore the possibilities of international bimetallism. Although the Gold Standard Act was not passed until 1900, Republican business and political leaders of Indiana took the initiative in the movement to secure such an enactment at the earliest moment possible. On November 7, 1896, the day after the election of McKinley, an Indianapolis *News* editorial suggested that local businessmen call a conference of representatives of midwestern commerce and finance to formulate a conservative program of currency reform.[9] Later in the month, upon the request of several businessmen in the city, a member of the Indianapolis Board of Trade, Hugh H. Hanna, presented a memorial to its board of

William J. Richards to Smith, July 25, 1896, *ibid.*; Hilton U. Brown, *A Book of Memories* ... (Indianapolis, 1951), p. 191.

[8] The best biographical account of Fairbanks is found in Herbert J. Rissler, Charles Warren Fairbanks, Conservative Hoosier (Unpublished Ph.D. thesis in History, Indiana University, 1961).

[9] Indianapolis *News*, November 7, 1896.

governors proposing that it sponsor such a conference. Pointing out how important it was that the currency question be led "by safe, strong hands very early into the right path," he argued that Indiana was in a position to play a special mediating role in this matter. "The West will not take up this cause; the East should not do so, and the central West, by reason of its importance as a factor in the commerce of the country and its geographical relation to other sections in which financial views are more or less extreme, should act." Thus, he concluded, "For such a movement to emanate from Indiana would probably be more acceptable to all parts of the country than for it to emanate from any other state."[10]

The Indianapolis Board of Trade responded immediately by convoking a preliminary conference in that city on December 1, 1896. Representatives from twelve cities—Cincinnati, Chicago, Cleveland, Columbus, Grand Rapids, Indianapolis, Louisville, Milwaukee, Minneapolis, St. Paul, St. Louis, and Toledo—met in the Indiana capital and after brief consultations issued a call for a more ambitious gathering, a "Monetary Convention of business men" to be drawn from all cities in the nation containing at least eight thousand inhabitants. In January, 1897, approximately three hundred delegates, representing boards of trade and chambers of commerce in over one hundred cities in twenty-six states and the District of Columbia met in Indianapolis. They chose an executive committee headed by Hugh H. Hanna of Indianapolis and authorized it to lobby in the United States Congress for the establishment of a monetary commission to consider the entire currency question. Since Congress refused to act, the committee appointed its own monetary commission of eleven members, including one Hoosier, Judge Robert S. Taylor of Fort Wayne, and a professional economist, James Lawrence Laughlin of the University of Chicago.[11]

---

[10] *Report of the Monetary Commission of the Indianapolis Convention* . . . (The University of Chicago Press, 1898), p. 3.

[11] *Ibid.,* pp. 5-14.

In January, 1898, the Indianapolis monetary convention was convened once more in order to accept the commission's report, and Republican Representative Jesse Overstreet of the seventh district of Indiana introduced into Congress a bill embodying its recommendations. In addition to the establishment of the gold standard, this bill included a number of moderate reforms in the national banking system, some of which were later incorporated into the Federal Reserve Act of 1913. But Congress was not ready to consider so far-reaching a measure at that time. Most Republican Congressmen were more interested in adjusting the protective tariff, which was accomplished by passage of the Dingley bill in the special session of 1897. The Spanish-American War also intervened, drawing public attention away from the currency issue to more pressing problems of financing the United States military machine and the administration of new territories acquired as a result of the peace treaty. Only in March, 1900, did Congress pass a modified form of the Overstreet bill, the Gold Standard Act, which finally fulfilled the monetary plank of the Republican party's 1896 platform by making the gold dollar the standard unit of value, but postponed serious reform of the national banking system for more than a decade.[12]

§ § §

The new Republican leadership in Washington was also confronted with perplexing problems in external affairs left over

12 *Ibid.*, pp. 14-74; Milton Friedman and Anna Jacobson Schwartz, *A Monetary History of the United States, 1867-1960* (National Bureau of Economic Research, *Studies in Business Cycles, 12,* Princeton University Press, 1963), pp. 118-119; Henry Parker Willis, *The Federal Reserve System: Legislation, Organization and Operation* (New York, 1923), pp. 8-16. Willis, who had been one of the two assistants employed by the commission in preparing its report, claimed that the monetary commission, despite its origins in the Indianapolis convention of businessmen, was dominated and financed by national banking interests. *Ibid.*, p. 10. After the Panic of 1907 Congress established its own monetary commission in 1908, one of the steps in the evolution of the Federal Reserve System which culminated in the passage of the Glass bill in 1913. *Ibid.*, p. 43. For antithetical views of the Indianapolis monetary convention by two contemporary Indianans, see Russel M. Seeds, The Story of a Great Movement (Unpublished typescript dated Indianapolis, 1900) and Flavius J. Van Vorhis, *The Currency Trust Conspiracy* (Indianapolis, 1910), pp. 260-289.

from the Cleveland administration, especially the question of what attitude the government should take toward the annexation of Hawaii and the Cuban insurrection. Sensational newspaper accounts of the latter particularly were beginning to arouse the American people at this time. In Indiana outgoing Democratic Governor Claude Matthews recommended in his message to the legislature in January, 1897, that a resolution be passed asking the state's Congressmen to urge the national government to accord the rights of belligerents to the Cuban rebels.[13] Two resolutions to this effect were introduced in the General Assembly, as well as one extending sympathy to the Cuban patriots and requesting the President and Congress to take measures to halt the war and secure independence, but the GOP-controlled legislature rejected all three.[14]

President McKinley was inclined to temporize, but Democrats in the United States Senate initiated debate on a resolution to recognize the belligerency of the Cuban insurgents during the special session called by the President to enact a tariff in the spring of 1897. This provoked the maiden speech in that body of Charles Warren Fairbanks, who in accepting election at the hands of the Indiana legislature had clearly stated his opposition to "any policy which shall tend to involve us in unnecessary international entanglements and possibly war."[15] In an address in which he reiterated sharply his desire for peace, Fairbanks offered an amendment recommending that the United States open negotiations with Spain to end the war and gain Cuban independence. Furthermore, he argued, the debate over Cuba was delaying urgent domestic legislation. "A tariff law and a currency commission are the imperative needs of the hour," he insisted. "Whatever will interfere with early securing them, no matter how important it is, I shall steadfastly oppose."[16]

13 Indiana *Senate Journal,* 1897, pp. 55-56.

14 *Ibid.,* pp. 86-88.

15 Indiana *House Journal,* 1897, p. 236.

16 *Congressional Record,* 55 Congress, 1 session, pp. 1178-1179.

Although Fairbanks, a close political friend of McKinley, was thought to have reflected the President's thinking on the amendment, it was defeated, and the original resolution easily passed. The House, however, failed to act, and the agitation subsided for the moment. On the question of annexing Hawaii, McKinley had come to take a more positive position and in June, 1897, sent to Congress a new treaty of annexation drawn up by one of Fairbanks' early political associates in Indiana, John W. Foster, Secretary of State briefly under Harrison and negotiator of the first such treaty of 1893.[17] But this measure received small support in or out of Congress before the coming of the war with Spain and increased operations of the American navy in the Pacific. In September the Indianapolis *News,* which also took a conservative stand on Cuban intervention, urged caution upon the nation's leaders in the matter of annexing Hawaii.[18] Two Indiana Republican Congressmen, Henry U. Johnson of Richmond and Edgar D. Crumpacker of Valparaiso, strenuously opposed annexation on the floor of the House in February and June, 1898.[19]

In general the Indiana press showed slight interest in expansionism. Nor did it display many characteristics of the war-mongering sensationalism of the "yellow journalism" so prominent in much of the eastern press at this time, especially as represented by Joseph Pulitzer's New York *World* and William Randolph Hearst's New York *Journal.*[20] The sinking of the U.S.S. "Maine" in Havana harbor in mid-February broke the journalistic calm momentarily but did not evoke an immediate demand for war. Although the conservative format of the front page of the Indianapolis *News*

[17] John W. Foster, *Diplomatic Memoirs* (2 volumes, Boston, 1909), II, 169-175.

[18] Indianapolis *News,* September 23, 27, 1897.

[19] *Congressional Record,* 55 Congress, 2 session, pp. 2031-2034, 5920-5925.

[20] George W. Auxier found most midwestern newspapers taking a similarly moderate point of view as opposed to the jingoism of some of the eastern press. Auxier, "Middle Western Newspapers and the Spanish-American War, 1895-1898," *Mississippi Valley Historical Review,* XXVI (1939-40), 523-534.

was drastically altered by a two-column streamer announcing the disaster, the editorial page retained its cautious posture, as did the strongly partisan Republican *Journal,* which asked the American people to "maintain their present attitude of coolness and self-control."[21] Even the ardently Democratic Indianapolis *Sentinel* refused to follow the lead of the eastern antiadministration press and indicated editorial skepticism about the responsibility of Spain for the sinking.[22] In Indianapolis only the *American Tribune,* a G.A.R. weekly edited by the arch-Republican George J. Langsdale, former editor of the Greencastle *Banner* and promoter of Negro colonization schemes in Indiana, revealed a strong streak of jingoism. The editor castigated McKinley for his patience with Spain and was eager for military measures.[23]

Outside the capital Republican journals generally supported McKinley's cautious policy. "Are newspapers and statesmen who want this country to rush into war with Spain on a mere supposition," demanded the New Albany *Weekly Tribune,* "aware of the character they would thus fasten on the United States? Such a course would deprive this nation of all claim to modern civilization."[24] Democratic editors tended to be more aloof, one observing fatalistically on February 18: "If it be war and bloodshed, let it come."[25] Not long after the explosion in Havana harbor, however, the Terre Haute *Gazette* expressed a deep-dyed isolationism far from the jingoism of the yellow press: "Let us not forget in all this turmoil about Cuba, Spain and the Maine," proclaimed an editorial in this Democratic organ, "that the comfort and convenience, the health and wealth and happiness of the peo-

21 Indianapolis *News,* February 16, 17, 1898; Indianapolis *Journal,* February 18, 1898.

22 Indianapolis *Sentinel,* February 18, 1898.

23 *American Tribune* (Indianapolis), February 10, 17, 24, March 3, 1898. Remarking upon the lack of jingoism in the city's press, the militant editor observed that "the Indianapolis papers are more than one year behind the American Tribune on the Cuban question." *Ibid.,* March 24, 1898.

24 New Albany *Weekly Tribune,* February 25, 1898. See also the Vincennes *Commercial,* February 16, 17, 1898.

25 Vincennes *Weekly Western Sun,* February 18, 1898.

ple of Terre Haute is [*sic*] more dependent on the speedy and correct and permanent settlement of the Ohio street opening question than it is on the future of Cuba or of Spain. We live in Terre Haute and not in Cuba."[26] Populists were also quite uninterested in intervention in Cuba and feared the outbreak of hostilities as a threat to domestic reforms. In a letter to a Populist newspaper in early March, Charles X. Mathews, former editor of the *American Nonconformist* in Indianapolis, wrote with foreboding: "Goodby Bryan movement and populist party, if there is a war with Spain."[27]

On the other hand, the state's Republican leaders adopted a conservative attitude toward the Cuban crisis. Senator Fairbanks, an intimate of McKinley in these crucial days, firmly backed the President in his reluctance to force events to a military showdown with Spain. "The attempt to misrepresent the situation and to involve the country in war will not succeed," he wrote to the editor of the Indianapolis *Journal* in March. "I can say to you in personal confidence that there is not the remotest expectation of war; and that war will be averted under any and all circumstances—unless the national honor is involved."[28] Judge Robert S. Taylor of Fort Wayne, a Republican candidate for the United States Senate in 1898, agreed with Fairbanks that justifiable conditions for war did not yet exist. To fight Spain over the destruction of the "Maine" would be a "dreadful set-back to the progress of civilization."[29] In similar fashion Clem Studebaker of the well-known wagon manufacturing company in South Bend confided to Taylor: "I too have admiration for the course the President has pursued in not allowing himself to be hurried to a decision. . . . I believe that he and his ad-

[26] Terre Haute *Gazette,* February 23, 1898.

[27] Shoals *Referendum,* March 31, 1898.

[28] Fairbanks to Harry S. New, March 6, 1898, New Papers, Library of Congress, microfilm in Indiana State Library.

[29] Robert S. Taylor to Fairbanks, April 3, 1898, Taylor Papers, Indiana State Library. Taylor expressed similar views to a reporter on his home town newspaper, the Fort Wayne *Weekly Gazette,* April 7, 1898.

visers are striving to do what they can to avert war, and I hope and pray they will succeed."[30]

The Republican state chairman described clearly the wait-and-see attitude of the party leadership in Indiana in a letter of political advice to Judge Taylor:[31]

All of the Love Feasts have been declared off, and are liable to remain so until after the policy of the administration is fully settled with regard to the Cuban affair. It is not a good time now to undertake to hold Republican meetings or conventions during the pending crisis, and the best thing to do is to keep down excitement, and let everybody keep perfectly cool and stand by the President, and he will solve this problem along right lines. As soon as the policy is fully settled by the administration, then it will be all right to hold our political meetings and solidify the public sentiment in the hearty support of the administration policy.

Yet when President McKinley sent his war message to Congress on April 11, Fairbanks and other Hoosier Republicans supported him unequivocally. "The Spanish flag must be withdrawn and cease forever to contaminate the air of this hemisphere," Fairbanks declaimed in the Senate. "To the high and holy cause of humanity and the vindication of our national honor we dedicate the lives and fortune of the Republic."[32] Indiana's Democratic Senator David Turpie attempted to add recognition of Cuban independence to the war resolution, but the Turpie amendment, though passed by the Senate, was rejected by the House, and the milder Teller amendment accepted in its place.[33] While Congress debated these matters, public opinion hardened perceptibly. "Since Spain refuses to evacuate Cuba," argued the Vincennes *Commercial*, "the only thing for Uncle Sam to do is to drive her out."[34] The rival Democratic paper in Vincennes queried local ministers on the issue and found that most favored contin-

---

[30] Clem Studebaker to Taylor, April 8, 1898, Taylor Papers.

[31] Charles S. Hernly to Taylor, April 12, 1898, *ibid*. Hernly was apparently unaware that McKinley's war message had been sent to Congress the day before.

[32] *Congressional Record*, 55 Congress, 2 session, p. 3846.

[33] *Ibid.*, pp. 3954, 3988.

[34] Vincennes *Commercial*, April 15, 1898.

ued peace negotiations but many thought war justifiable if such negotiations broke down. One Methodist clergyman, John A. Ward, revealed a more belligerent mood in his reply: "If honorable diplomacy fails, and Spain is still defiant, *sweep her from the seas!*"[35] On the other hand, the pro-Spanish *Catholic Record* of Indianapolis continued to oppose American intervention in Cuba.[36] A Republican county chairman reported in early May that "these are glorious days for Uncle Sam. The people are boiling over with patriotism. . . ."[37]

Congress declared the existence of a state of war on April 25, 1898, and two days later, before a single shot had been fired, a shrill new note of American imperialism was sounded in Boston by a young and ambitious Hoosier orator, Albert Jeremiah Beveridge. Born in Ohio and raised in Illinois, Beveridge had graduated from Indiana Asbury–DePauw University with honors and a reputation for collegiate oratory in 1885. Moving to Indianapolis the next year he read law in the office of ex-Senator Joseph E. McDonald and married Kate Langsdale, daughter of the Greencastle *Republican* editor, George J. Langsdale, who soon moved to the capital city himself to oversee the building of the Soldiers' and Sailors' Monument in the Circle. The charming, impetuous Beveridge became a successful attorney and sought-after speaker in Republican political campaigns.[38] Having attained some national fame for his Chicago speech refuting Democratic Governor John P. Altgeld of Illinois in the 1896 campaign, Beveridge was asked to present an address in honor of Ulysses S. Grant's birthday before the Middlesex Club of Massachusetts in Boston on April 27, 1898. Grant, the speaker boldly proclaimed, "never forgot that we are a conquering race, and that we must obey our blood and occupy new markets, and, if necessary, new lands." Beveridge's far-reaching vision included control of the world's trade and acquisition of great

---

[35] Vincennes *Weekly Western Sun,* April 15, 1898.
[36] *Catholic Record* (Indianapolis), April 14, 1898.
[37] M. C. Skinner to Taylor, May 9, 1898, Taylor Papers.
[38] Bowers, *Beveridge and the Progressive Era,* pp. 1-65.

colonies. "And American law, American order, American civ-ilization, and the American flag will plant themselves on shores hitherto bloody and benighted, but by those agencies of God henceforth to be made beautiful and bright." Analyzing the strategy of the war just about to begin, he noted that "Cuba must fall into our hands, but that will be only when Spain is conquered." Furthermore, he predicted in startling anticipa-tion of Admiral George Dewey's triumph in Manila Bay that "in the Pacific is the true field of our earliest operations. . . . The Philippines are logically our first target."[39] With this powerful invocation of a new manifest destiny, Albert J. Beveridge, who had already secretly initiated a well-organ-ized plan to secure a seat in the United States Senate at the next session of the Indiana legislature, made his bid for lead-ership in the imperial age of America.[40]

In the meantime, citizens of Indiana responded enthusias-tically to the call to arms for the conflict with Spain. On April 25, Governor James A. Mount received instructions from the War Department in Washington to provide four regiments of infantry, comprising approximately one thousand men each, and two batteries of artillery. That same day the Gov-ernor and his adjutant general, James K. Gore, ordered the entire National Guard mobilized and called for volunteers to fill any existing vacancies.[41] The Indiana National Guard, for-merly the Indiana Legion, had been reorganized and re-

39 *Ibid.*, pp. 68-70. The entire speech was published in Beveridge's *The Meaning of the Times, and Other Speeches* (Indianapolis, 1908), pp. 37-46. Bev-eridge was not the first Indiana political leader to advocate expansionism. Representative J. Frank Hanly, who was to be Beveridge's chief opponent in the race for the United States Senate in 1898, was the author of a speech in Con-gress in 1896 in which he called for a "revival of nationalism" and asked his fellow countrymen to "embrace every opportunity for the extension of Ameri-can commerce and American influence and power." *Congressional Record*, 54 Congress, 1 session, p. 3241.

40 Bowers, *Beveridge*, p. 79; John Braeman, "The Rise of Albert J. Bev-eridge to the United States Senate," *Indiana Magazine of History*, LIII (1957), 359.

41 *Record of Indiana Volunteers in the Spanish-American War, 1898-1899* . . . (Indianapolis, 1900), pp. 7-10.

equipped by the authority of the General Assembly in 1895 and was relatively well prepared. At the beginning of 1898 it comprised forty-one companies of infantry and three artillery batteries, with a total of 2,822 officers and men enrolled.[42]

As soon as the orders were received by telegraph, militia companies began converging upon the capital from all over the state. So many volunteers poured into the hastily improvised military camp set up on the State Fairgrounds in Indianapolis that Indiana became the first state to meet its full quota of troops. The first unit to be mustered into United States service was the Third Regiment, which on May 10 became the One Hundred and Fifty-seventh Indiana Volunteer Infantry, for in numbering it was decided to begin where the Civil War regiments had left off. Three more regiments followed closely, restyled the One Hundred and Fifty-eighth, One Hundred and Fifty-ninth, and One Hundred and Sixtieth Indiana, as well as the Twenty-seventh and Twenty-eighth Artillery Batteries. All but the One Hundred and Fifty-ninth Infantry Regiment, which was stripped of its arms and other equipment to furnish the others and thus was the last to leave Camp Mount, as the Fairgrounds encampment was named, proceeded immediately to Chickamauga Park, Georgia. None of these units, however, saw any action in the war, and all men were discharged from service by November, 1898, except those of the One Hundred and Sixtieth Regiment, which, after having its orders to land in Puerto Rico during the fighting countermanded at the last moment, was eventually assigned to occupation duty in Cuba in January, 1899, and remained there three months before being returned to the mainland and mustered out.[43]

In late May, 1898, President McKinley issued a second call for troops, but no quota was announced for Indiana until June 18, when the state was asked to furnish an additional infan-

[42] *Laws of Indiana*, 1895, pp. 102-127; *A History of the National Guard of Indiana* (Indianapolis, 1901), p. 294.

[43] *History of the National Guard*, pp. 295-369; *Record of Indiana Volunteers*, pp. 11-12, 22-53, 61-62.

try regiment plus two separate companies of Negro soldiers. The inclusion of the latter provision stemmed from an earlier request of Governor Mount for permission to enroll in the United States armed forces two companies of Negroes which had been incorporated in the Indiana militia since the mid-eighties despite a constitutional ban. The War Department had originally rejected the units because they were officered by Negroes but finally agreed to accept them after the intercession of Senator Charles W. Fairbanks with President McKinley, according to the former's biographer. As a result Indiana was represented in the War with Spain by two companies of Negro infantry under the command of two experienced Negro militia officers, Captains Jacob M. Porter and John J. Buckner of Indianapolis. These unusual units remained in Camp Mount until the fighting was over in September, however, and after a few weeks' training in the South were dismissed at the end of October.[44]

The white troops newly called into service constituted the One Hundred and Sixty-first Infantry Regiment, composed of volunteer companies organized in anticipation of the President's second call under the command of a member of the Governor's staff, Lieutenant Colonel Winfield T. Durbin.

[44] *History of the National Guard,* pp. 369-370; Indianapolis *News,* June 2, 3, 7, 1898; Rissler, *Charles Warren Fairbanks,* pp. 96-97. The first Negro militia company was organized in Indianapolis in 1882 and the second in 1885, and both became integral elements of the regular regimental structure of the Indiana militia under their own Negro officers. *History of the National Guard,* pp. 194-195. Unsuccessful attempts by the General Assembly to amend the state constitution to remove the bar to Negro enrollment in the militia were made in 1885, 1887, 1889, 1891, and 1921. Kettleborough, *Constitution Making in Indiana,* II, 240-241, 253-254, 258, 280; III, 212-213, 317. Shortly before the outbreak of the war, General Lew Wallace volunteered to raise a body of Negro troops in Indiana and lead it into the field. Recalling his experience as American minister to Turkey, he wrote the Secretary of War that "the most magnificent regiment in the Turkish army consists of Negroes. I think that it could be duplicated here in our country." Lew Wallace to Russell A. Alger, April 11, 1898, Lew Wallace Papers, Indiana Historical Society Library. One Indiana historian has claimed that the War Department prevented Indiana volunteer troops from seeing action in the war on account of the imbroglio over the Negro companies. William Henry Smith, *The History of the State of Indiana* (2 volumes, Indianapolis, 1903), II, 469-470.

This regiment was mustered into service on July 15 but remained at Camp Mount in training until August 14 and finally served three months in Cuba after the war. An engineer company and a signal corps company were also raised in Indiana, the former of which served four months of occupation duty in Havana, Cuba, building railroads and hospitals and installing waterworks for military camps.[45]

The war was too short to exhaust the patriotic and martial spirit it had elicited in Indiana. It was a source of disappointment to many that none of the volunteer units raised in the state saw combat duty, though the Twenty-seventh Artillery Battery landed in Puerto Rico on August 4, 1898, and was actually on the firing line on the San Juan road when news of the peace protocol was received. The women of Indiana responded to the call to the colors by organizing the Indiana Soldiers' Aid Society in July, 1898, under the presidency of Mrs. Charles W. Fairbanks. This organization sent large quantities of food, clothing, and other articles to camps and hospitals for the comfort of the soldiers. When the Indiana regiments and batteries returned to Camp Mount for mustering out, women of Indianapolis met them at the station with coffee and sandwiches and served a dinner for each organization when it was discharged. Although there were no battle casualties among Indiana's volunteer troops, seventy-three soldiers died of disease, and hundreds were cared for in a special hospital established by the state at Camp Mount to receive the sick and injured upon their return to the city.[46]

The total number of volunteers furnished by the state to the armed forces in the Spanish-American War was 7,421. In addition about one thousand served in the regular army, according to the estimate of the Indianapolis *News*.[47] President McKinley also handed out commissions as staff offi-

45 *Record of Indiana Volunteers*, pp. 54-60, 63-65. See also William E. Biederwolf, *History of the One Hundred and Sixty-First Regiment Indiana Volunteer Infantry* (Logansport, Ind., 1899).

46 *Record of Indiana Volunteers*, pp. 15-21; Esarey, *A History of Indiana*, II, 1078-1082. Hostilities ceased under the peace protocol of August 12.

47 *Record of Indiana Volunteers*, p. 366; Indianapolis *News*, July 30, 1898.

cers to twenty-five politically influential Hoosiers, including the ex-President's son, Russell B. Harrison, the senior Indiana Senator's son, Warren Fairbanks, William E. English, Republican scion of the Democratic vice-presidential candidate in 1880, and Harry S. New, son of the publisher of the Indianapolis *Journal*. In the fighting which took place in suppression of the Philippine insurrection after the Treaty of Paris, Indiana supplied a considerable number of regular army personnel as well as a score of volunteer officers who transferred from their Indiana militia units for that purpose.[48]

Hoosiers on the home front were united in support of the war. Acknowledging that he had been reluctant at first to see his country take up arms, Quaker reformer William D. Foulke wrote to Senator Fairbanks, whom he had deprecated two years before, that "when war became inevitable, I felt with you that we must all stand together and strengthen the President's hand by every means in our power." Striking an old-fashioned Radical Republican pose unexpected in a Mugwump, he added: "There must be no copperheads in the present struggle, and I trust that all efforts to cripple the administration by interjecting political and financial issues into the measures brought forward to sustain the war, shall be sternly rebuked."[49] Even the anti-war *Catholic Record,* which had bitterly opposed American intervention in Cuba before the outbreak of hostilities, encouraged Roman Catholic youth to prove their loyalty to the nation by volunteering for military service. After peace was re-established, however, the editor posed this question: "The war is over, but on whose hands is the blood that was shed in it?" A month later he

---

[48] *History of the National Guard,* pp. 369-402. Other important figures volunteered for service but were unable to serve. Despite his advanced years Lew Wallace sought unsuccessfully to be commissioned as a major general. Indianapolis *News,* June 7, 1898; Irving McKee, *"Ben-Hur" Wallace. The Life of General Lew Wallace* (Berkeley, Calif., 1947), p. 257. Governor Mount declined Senator Charles W. Fairbanks' offer to serve on the plea that he was more needed in the United States Senate. Smith, *Life and Speeches of Fairbanks,* p. 131.

[49] Foulke to Fairbanks, May 16, 1898, Foulke Papers.

added flatly, "It was a misnomer to call our war with Spain a war for humanity."[50]

Indiana opinion was divided on the issue of American expansion which the war brought to the fore. Democratic and Populist newspapers generally opposed annexation of non-contiguous areas, whether Hawaii, Puerto Rico, or the Philippines.[51] Many Republican newspapers showed a lack of enthusiasm for the new theory of territorial expansion outside the continental limits of the United States, though most eventually accepted it as the official party position. In discussing the possible annexation of the Philippines, in May, 1898, a Republican editor in Fort Wayne pointed out that "there was no thought of conquest when we entered upon the present war, but events are rapidly shaping our policy and giving a new turn to our manifest destiny. Our immense Pacific coast line demands an Oriental base of supplies."[52] A New Albany *Weekly Tribune* editorial made a broad case for American empire based on keeping the flag flying no matter where it might be planted: "Wherever the flag of the United States goes up in this war there it should stay, whether it be Hawaii by voluntary consent, or the Philippines and Porto Rico by force. Cuba will come in in due time."[53] On the other hand, the Republican Congressman from Richmond, Indiana, Henry U. Johnson, made a last stand against the annexation of Hawaii in a long, impassioned speech in the House of Representatives in Washington on June 14, just before Congress voted to annex the Islands. Proposing the neutralization of Hawaii by international agreement instead of annexation, he asked, ". . . is there not grave danger that this holy crusade

---

50 *Catholic Record,* August 18, September 22, 1898.

51 Indianapolis *Sentinel,* April 11, 1898; Vincennes *Weekly Western Sun,* August 19, 1898; Shoals *Referendum,* July 14, 1898. The intransigent editor of the *Catholic Record* bluntly asked at the time of the debate over the Treaty of Paris, "American mothers, do you know what the acquisition of the Philippines means to you? It means the death of your sons." *Catholic Record,* December 15, 1898.

52 Fort Wayne *Weekly Gazette,* May 12, 1898.

53 New Albany *Weekly Tribune,* May 13, 1898.

for liberty and the independence of Cuba is liable after all to
end in a disgraceful scramble for spoils, a scramble as disgraceful as any that ever characterized the people of ancient
Rome?"[54] In the same month the Indianapolis *News,* an
independent paper with a Republican bias, confessed to a
change of opinion concerning the annexation of Hawaii, which
it had formerly opposed. Since Dewey's capture of Manila,
it might be necessary to take both Hawaii and the Philippines,
the editor argued.[55]

Both major parties endorsed the war effort in their state
platforms in the summer of 1898. The Democrats, who met in
convention in May, attempted to take part of the credit for
the intervention against Spain and demanded vigorous prosecution of the war and prompt recognition of Cuban independence.[56] Postponing their state convention until near the end
of the war in August, the Republicans put into their platform the grand declaration that "having achieved its man-
hood, the Republic, under God, is entering upon its greatest
period of power, happiness and responsibility." The party's
imperial program included strengthening of American trade,
reform of the consular system, encouragement of the mer-

[54] *Congressional Record,* 55 Congress, 2 session, p. 5994. Johnson, feeling
completely out of sympathy with his party's position on the annexation question, was not a candidate for re-election in 1898. As a lame-duck Congressman
in early 1899, moreover, he strongly opposed the annexation of the Philippines
despite the fact that most Republican newspapers in his district repudiated
him and his views, as a fellow Republican legislator from Indiana, Charles B.
Landis, took pains to point out, wiring each of the editors concerned and having their replies printed in the *Congressional Record.* Another Hoosier Congressman, Edgar D. Crumpacker, had also doubted the policy of expansion
earlier, he admitted, but changed his mind and favored taking the Philippines.
*Ibid.,* 55 Congress, 3 session, pp. 1021-1029, 1036, 2323. After leaving Congress
in 1899, Johnson switched to the Democratic party and moved to St. Louis,
where he practiced law for several years before returning to his home town of
Richmond. He died in 1939. *Biographical Directory of the American Congress,*
p. 1125.

[55] Indianapolis *News,* June 16, 1898.

[56] Henry (comp.), *State Platforms,* p. 108. The Indiana Populist platform
also demanded recognition of Cuban independence. Shoals *Referendum,* April
14, 1898.

chant marine, creation of a powerful navy, establishment of coaling stations, and construction of a Nicaraguan canal.[57] Charles W. Fairbanks had presided over the Republican convention, but Albert J. Beveridge, by then an avowed candidate for the United States Senate, opened the Indiana campaign in September at Tomlinson Hall in Indianapolis with a rousing address attacking the Democratic opponents of expansion into noncontiguous areas: "The ocean does not separate us from the lands of our duty and desire—the ocean joins us, a river never to be dredged, a canal never to be repaired," he exclaimed to the applause of an overflow crowd, ready to cheer at the end of a short but glorious war waged by a Republican administration. "Steam joins — electricity joins us—the very elements are in league with our destiny. Cuba not contiguous! Porto Rico not contiguous! The Philippines not contiguous! Our navy will make them contiguous!"[58]

Beveridge proclaimed his gospel of imperialism tirelessly throughout the state in the campaign of 1898. Fairbanks' activities in Indiana were curtailed by his appointment by President McKinley as chairman of the Anglo-American Joint High Commission, which convened in Quebec in August to attempt to solve the outstanding disputes between Canada and the United States, especially that concerning the Alaskan boundary.[59] The election of November 7, 1898, resulted in a

[57] Henry (comp.), *State Platforms*, pp. 112-114.

[58] Indianapolis *Journal*, September 17, 1898. This speech, under the title, "The March of the Flag," is found in Beveridge, *The Meaning of the Times*, pp. 47-57.

[59] John W. Foster, who was also a member of the commission, described its work in his *Diplomatic Memoirs*, II, 187-189. The commission failed to reach agreement on the Alaskan boundary dispute and recessed without adjusting any of the questions before it. Senator Fairbanks himself visited Alaska at the request of President McKinley to study the problem and returned even more convinced of the justice of the American claims, which were finally upheld by an Anglo-American tribunal appointed in 1902. Smith, *Life and Speeches of Fairbanks*, pp. 142-153. Fairbanks, Alaska, was named for the Senator in 1902. Merle Colby, *A Guide to Alaska, Last American Frontier* (Federal Writers' Project, *American Guide Series*, New York, 1941), p. 296.

near Republican landslide. In Indiana the GOP won nine out of thirteen seats in Congress and all the lesser state offices as well as a large majority in both houses of the legislature.

Beveridge immediately announced his candidacy for the United States Senate, initiating one of the liveliest contests ever seen in the state among five Republican candidates: J. Frank Hanly, Major George W. Steele, Francis B. Posey, Judge Robert S. Taylor, and the thirty-six-year-old Beveridge. It was a struggle over control of the party in Indiana, in which the old organization was split between followers of Harrison and Fairbanks and younger men such as Hanly and Beveridge who were trying to build their own machines. Interestingly enough, Beveridge had the backing of over a hundred business leaders from all over the state who met in December in Indianapolis under the chairmanship of David M. Parry, president of the Manufacturers' Association of Indiana, and vice-president of the National Manufacturers Association, to endorse his candidacy. At the Republican legislative caucus on January 10, Hanly had an initial advantage in the voting, but after twelve ballots Beveridge had gained enough votes from legislators originally supporting the three older men to win nomination.[60] This surprising event marked a turning point in Indiana Republican politics, for it signaled the end of the Harrison organization and the rise of a younger faction led by Beveridge in rivalry with the Fairbanks ma-

[60] Bowers, *Beveridge,* pp. 79-91; Charles F. Remy, "The Election of Beveridge to the Senate," *Indiana Magazine of History,* XXXVI (1940), 123-135; John A. Coffin, "The Senatorial Career of Albert J. Beveridge," *Indiana Magazine of History,* XXIV (1928), 147-162. The most detailed account, however, is Braeman, "The Rise of Albert J. Beveridge to the United States Senate," *Indiana Magazine of History,* LIII (1957), 355-382. In a letter to a friend years later Beveridge recalled that "I literally held the party and the legislature up by the nap of the neck in that Senatorial campaign, as you know." Beveridge to Shaffer, April 18, 1905, Shaffer Papers. During the campaign for the Senate Robert S. Taylor, one of Beveridge's opponents, observed that he found it difficult to obtain business support for his candidacy. "I am more than ever disgusted with the business men," he wrote in November, 1898. "I wish there were some way to roast them in hot, free silver without scorching everybody." Taylor to H. H. Hanna, November 3, 1898, Taylor Papers.

chine. On January 17, 1899, the General Assembly formally elected Beveridge to the United States Senate to succeed Democratic Senator David Turpie. In his acceptance speech he solemnly pronounced his faith in the coming American empire. After solving the money question, he told the legislators, we must turn to "our greater tasks, our larger duty and our manifest destiny. Ships, canals, railroads and commerce, civilization, Christianity and free institutions—these are the purposes and these will be the achievements of the holy American people for the thousand years of American supremacy of which the old song tells."[61]

Within two months the impetuous young Senator-elect had closed his law office in Indianapolis and set off with his wife on a tour of China, Japan, and the Philippine Islands to obtain firsthand information and prepare himself to become the spokesman of the new manifest destiny. Before his election to the Senate he confided to a friend that the coming of the war with Spain had made him wish to be in public office where he could "shape the events" of his time. "I would rather take part in organizing our colonial system," he wrote, "than to do anything else on this earth. I would rather map out and advocate the imperial policy of the Republic than to have been the leading statesman of the late war. It means more for humanity, more for our country, and a larger place in history."[62] Now it seemed his ambition and his ego were to be fulfilled. His trip to the Orient brought him abreast of the fast-moving tides of American imperialism. On February 4, 1899, the Philippine insurrection erupted, and two days later the United States Senate ratified the Treaty of Paris providing for American acquisition of the Islands. Beveridge arrived in Manila in May and toured the battlefields in Luzon and elsewhere. He met there a dashing professional soldier

[61] Indiana *House Journal*, 1899, p. 257. Beveridge concluded his short address to the legislature with these words: ". . . for the people, and the people only, are my masters—and the people and the people only are my love, and to the people I will be true." *Ibid.*, p. 258.

[62] Beveridge to Charles G. Dawes, May 10, 1898, quoted in Bowers, *Beveridge*, p. 71.

from Indiana, General Henry Ware Lawton, a veteran of the Civil War and the Indian wars in the West, who had commanded the first American troops to land in Cuba. General Lawton, whose recklessness in the face of danger impressed the military-minded Beveridge, was to fall in battle in the Philippines in December, becoming a famous war hero in his home state of Indiana, which erected a monument to his memory in Indianapolis in 1907.[63]

When Beveridge returned to the United States, he made plans to launch his career in the Senate with a speech based on his findings in the Philippines. His private reports on the Islands already had made a good impression on both New York Governor Theodore Roosevelt and President McKinley before he rose in the United States Senate in January, 1900, to present a long maiden speech on a subject of first importance, in defiance of the tradition according to which new Senators generally remained silent for a probationary period before making their presence felt in that august body. "The Philippines are ours forever . . . ," he announced to a crowded Senate and gallery. Then, taking up the theme of his earlier addresses on imperialism, he added, "and just beyond the Philippines are China's illimitable markets. We will not retreat from either. . . . We will not renounce our part in the mission of our race, trustee, under God, of the civilization of the world."[64] The enthusiastic response of the press to this bold speech, with its unabashed demand for permanent American occupation of the Philippines as partial fulfillment of the imperial destiny of the Anglo-Saxon people to organize the world and administer government among the lesser races, gave the youthful Indiana Senator a striking entrance upon the American political scene. From that moment he was to be not a state but a national figure.

[63] *Ibid.*, pp. 101-102; Dunn, *Indiana and Indianans,* II, 761. Lawton's home town of Fort Wayne also erected a statue of him in 1921. John W. Oliver, "Historical Notes," *Indiana Magazine of History,* XVII (1921), 370-371.

[64] *Congressional Record,* 56 Congress, 1 session, p. 704.

Beveridge, however, took his hazing in March, 1900, when he was presumptuous enough to attempt to make a second major appearance on the Senate floor closely following upon his first. This time the galleries were again packed, but most of the Senators themselves walked out of the chamber during Beveridge's address. He had chosen to speak against the Puerto Rico tariff bill, a measure favored by most members of the protection-minded GOP, including the senior Senator from Indiana, Charles W. Fairbanks, who was one of only six Republicans remaining on the Senate floor at the close of Beveridge's remarks.[65] But the young Senator compromised his view and voted for the bill in the end, an act which called forth the private comment of Hoosier Mugwump Lucius B. Swift in a letter to his wife that Beveridge was "after all as we always thought — nothing but sounding brass."[66]

In spite of the attention paid to him by the press in these weeks, the colorful, aggressive Beveridge was not yet in a position to overshadow his older Indiana colleague, Senator Fairbanks. Like Beveridge, the reserved and rather aloof Fairbanks was a Hamiltonian nationalist, but he was not an ardent imperialist, just as he had not been a war hawk prior to the outbreak of the Spanish-American War. Yet Fairbanks was in the inner circle of the Senate, a position which Beveridge never achieved despite his powerful oratory and personal force. The former was also on intimate terms with President McKinley, who may have thought of the senior Indiana Senator as his natural successor in the White House. Indeed, after the death of Vice-President Garret A. Hobart in 1899, a movement was initiated among conservative Republicans, allegedly including Mark Hanna, to secure the nom-

---

[65] Bowers, *Beveridge,* pp. 128-129. This was a troubled time for Beveridge, who hurried from the Senate chamber immediately after his speech to go to the bedside of his wife, who was dying from an infection she had received on their recent trip to the Orient. Her death came in June, 1900. Beveridge married his second wife, Catherine Eddy, in 1907. *Ibid.,* pp. 129-130, 262.

[66] Swift to Ella Swift, April 1, 1900, Swift Papers, Indiana State Library.

ination of Fairbanks as McKinley's running mate in 1900.[67] Instead, the GOP nominating convention picked a man nearly Fairbanks' opposite in personality and political philosophy, and in fact closer to the Beveridgean mold, Colonel Theodore Roosevelt of the Rough Riders, a war hero and the crusading governor of the pivotal state of New York.

In April, 1900, Fairbanks presided over the Republican state convention in Indianapolis, and the platform adopted reflected his moderating influence on the question of imperialism. It praised the "open door policy in China," articulated only a short time before by McKinley's Indiana-born Secretary of State, John Hay, but only mildly endorsed the imperial program proclaimed by Beveridge:[68]

The possession of the islands which came to our hands as a result of the war with Spain was a consequence of it not foreseen, but which could not be avoided with honor and safety. . . . The guiding principle of our conduct in dealing with the people of these islands should be to promote their highest welfare, and we pledge the largest possible freedom of control in their affairs, as their ability for self-government shall be developed. . . .

For the governorship, however, the GOP chose as their candidate the best example of a war hero available, Colonel Winfield T. Durbin of Anderson, who as commanding officer of the One Hundred and Sixty-first Indiana Volunteers had served in Cuba on occupation duty. The platform also stated the traditional Republican views on currency and the tariff.

The Democratic state platform attacked both the domestic and foreign policy of the McKinley administration and

---

67 Rissler, Charles Warren Fairbanks, pp. 111-119. One of McKinley's first biographers, who knew Fairbanks well, reported that the Indiana Senator refused to be drafted for the vice-presidential place on the ticket even though "there is good reason to believe that he was the President's first choice." Charles S. Olcott, The Life of William McKinley (2 volumes, Boston and New York, 1916), II, 268. Recent biographers, however, neither mention Fairbanks as McKinley's favorite nor picture him as a major contender for the nomination. Margaret Leech, In the Days of McKinley (New York, 1959), pp. 529-533; H. Wayne Morgan, William McKinley and His America (Syracuse, N. Y., 1963), pp. 489-493.

68 Henry (comp.), State Platforms, p. 119.

pledged its fidelity to the person and program of the Great Commoner, William J. Bryan. On the issue of imperialism it had little to say specifically except to criticize corruption in the administration of occupied territories and to condemn military rule "whether used to administer government in Cuba or to crush liberty in the Philippines."[69] In light of the general pessimism in Democratic quarters in regard to electoral success at a time when the party in power enjoyed the advantages of economic prosperity and recent military victory in a popular war, there was a dearth of candidates for state offices. The Democratic leaders were forced virtually to draft John W. Kern, a party regular who had supported Bryan in 1896 even while opposing his free silver doctrine, for the gubernatorial nomination.[70] At the national nominating convention the Indiana Democracy for the first time in several campaigns had no favorite son to propose for either first or second place on the ticket and ratified the selection of Illinois' Adlai Stevenson, who had been Vice-President in Cleveland's second term, as running mate for William J. Bryan, still the party's popular hero and the inevitable presidential candidate for another contest with McKinley.[71]

Although many Democrats would have preferred to take to the people their old familiar program of currency and tariff reform, Bryan himself, who had accepted ratification of the treaty annexing the Philippines as a way of bringing the colonial question to a debate, chose to make imperialism the "paramount issue" in the campaign. In August the Democracy's "Peerless Leader" opened both the Indiana and the national campaign by making his acceptance speech in Indianapolis. Its main theme was anti-imperialism. Uncompromisingly attacking the extension of the American domain in the Pacific, he linked colonial empire abroad to the loss of

[69] Henry (comp.), *State Platforms,* pp. 115-116.

[70] Bowers, *Life of John Worth Kern,* pp. 127-130.

[71] According to one newspaper account, however, some Indiana delegates at the Democratic convention in Kansas City in 1900 wanted to propose Benjamin F. Shively for the vice-presidential nomination, but Shively refused to be a candidate. Greencastle *Banner,* July 6, 1900.

domestic liberty: "Those who would have this nation enter upon a career of empire must consider not only the effect of imperialism on the Filipinos, but they must calculate its effect upon our own nation. We cannot repudiate the principle of self-government in the Philippines without weakening that principle here."[72] John W. Kern and other Democratic campaigners tried to bring this issue home to Indiana voters, but it proved difficult, as Kern's biographer argued, to make a successful appeal on "an abstract question of political morals," and to discuss "the wrongs of a people thousand of miles distant, of another race and color, of whom hundreds of Americans had never heard."[73]

There was little or no organized anti-imperialistic expression in Indiana outside the official Democratic campaign materials, and few individual Hoosiers voiced their apprehensions about the course of American empire. One who did was General Lew Wallace, an old Republican stalwart, who spoke out publicly against Philippine annexation in 1900.[74] And perhaps the most powerful literary protest against colonialism was found in some of the writings of the former New Albany schoolteacher, William Vaughn Moody, who published his moving "An Ode in Time of Hesitation" in the *Atlantic Monthly* during the election campaign. The Indiana-bred poet and playwright was also the author of the sardonic elegy, "On a Soldier Fallen in the Philippines," written upon hearing the news of the battlefield death of the Hoosier soldier-hero, General Lawton, of whom he sang:[75]

72 Indianapolis *Sentinel*, August 9, 1900. The entire speech was published in *Speeches of William Jennings Bryan* . . . (2 volumes, New York, 1909), II, 17-49.

73 Bowers, *Life of John Worth Kern*, p. 126.

74 McKee, *"Ben-Hur" Wallace*, p. 258. Another Hoosier voice from the past —George W. Julian—expressed himself in opposition to imperialism not long before his death. In a letter to William D. Foulke he described the annexation of the Philippines as a "disastrous mistake." Julian to Foulke, December 16, 1898, Foulke Papers.

75 *Atlantic Monthly*, LXXXV (1900), 593-598; LXXXVII (1901), 288. Both poems were reprinted in William Vaughn Moody, *Poems* (Boston and New York, 1902), pp. 12-21, 24-25. Another Hoosier writer disagreed. Maurice

> Let him never dream that his bullet's scream
> went wide of its island mark,
> Home to the heart of his darling land where she
> stumbled and sinned in the dark.

In mid-August the American Anti-Imperialist League held a "Liberty Congress" in Indianapolis which attracted only about two hundred persons, many of them from out of state, at the opening session. No well-known Indiana political figures were associated with the movement, though the Democratic *Sentinel* gave it favorable, front-page publicity.[76] Called a "Bryan sideshow" by the equally partisan pro-administration *Journal,* the Congress closed by endorsing the Democratic nominee for the presidency despite an attempt on the part of a handful of independents meeting simultaneously in Indianapolis to form a third party on a completely anti-imperialist platform.[77]

Former Mugwumps supported McKinley in 1900 on the issue of imperialism, though Lucius B. Swift had bitterly attacked the Republican surrender to the doctrine that the United States Constitution did not follow the flag in passing the Puerto Rican tariff bill earlier in the year. In August Swift's colleague, William Dudley Foulke, addressed a public meeting at English's Opera House in Indianapolis on the subject of the unfitness of the Filipinos for self-government in a speech later published and circulated by the GOP as a campaign document.[78]

---

Thompson of Crawfordsville in an essay in *The Independent* exclaimed, "If our civilization is not good enough for Cubans, Porto Ricans and Filipinos is it fit for us? Shame upon the thought that our rule in those islands would not be better than any other rule under heaven." Thompson, "Writing the Record," *Independent,* LII (January-June, 1900), 932.

[76] Indianapolis *Sentinel,* August 15, 16, 17, 1900. Many of the local people present were Silver Republicans, according to the Indianapolis *Journal,* the chief representative being Dr. Flavius J. Van Vorhis of Indianapolis. Indianapolis *Journal,* August 16, 1900.

[77] Indianapolis *Journal,* August 17, 1900.

[78] *Ibid.,* August 25, 1900; Foulke, *A Hoosier Autobiography,* p. 107; Foulke, *Lucius B. Swift,* p. 137. After the election Senator Fairbanks wrote Foulke thanking him for "the most excellent and efficient work you did during the

President McKinley himself, though he had toured the West and spoken in Indianapolis in the 1898 campaign, played a passive role in 1900, but his running mate, Theodore Roosevelt, stumped the country, meeting an especially enthusiastic response in Indiana.[79] The irrepressible Roosevelt apparently thought his speeches in several Hoosier cities were effective, to judge from a letter he wrote to Henry Cabot Lodge in October: "I think we shall carry Indiana. I have waded into brother Bryan pretty heavily and he is beginning to feel sore."[80] Indiana Senators Beveridge and Fairbanks also campaigned actively both inside and outside the state, championing the administration's domestic and overseas policies alike.

The Republican economic program and McKinley prosperity—the "full dinner pail"—were election issues as important as the colonial question in Indiana. Indeed, the newly established, firmly Republican Indianapolis *Press* insisted that the real issue in the campaign was not imperialism but the money standard.[81] Some Democratic businessmen who had been utterly opposed to Bryan's monetary views in 1896 made their final break with the party of free silver only in this election, as did Herman Hulman, Jr., of the wealthy Terre Haute mercantile family, who announced for McKinley in September, 1900.[82] The Prohibitionists, who had been split in 1896 over the free silver issue, united to conduct a vigorous canvass over the entire state.

Two constitutional amendments were on the ballot in November. The Sixtieth and Sixty-first General Assemblies had adopted amendments to the state constitution to permit the enlargement of the Indiana Supreme Court from five to as

campaign which has just closed." Fairbanks to Foulke, November 19, 1900, Foulke Papers.

[79] Indianapolis *Journal,* October 11, 12, 1900.

[80] Theodore Roosevelt to Henry Cabot Lodge, October 14, 1900, in Theodore Roosevelt and Henry Cabot Lodge, *Selections from the Correspondence . . . 1884-1918* (2 volumes, New York, 1925), I, 478.

[81] Indianapolis *Press,* October 9, 1900.

[82] Indianapolis *Journal,* September 4, 1900.

many as eleven members and to authorize the legislature to prescribe qualifications for the practice of law beyond the constitutional provision that lawyers be voters "of good moral character." Since 1881 both of these questions had been before the legislature several times, but not until 1900 were they finally submitted to the people of the state for ratification.[83]

The outcome of the general election, while it was probably not a "mandate for imperialism," indicated clearly that most Hoosiers felt little dissatisfaction with Republican party leadership of the state and nation at the outset of the new century, with its optimistic promise of an ever-expanding economy at home and political prestige overseas. McKinley increased his plurality over Bryan to 26,500, while Republican Winfield T. Durbin won the governorship by only a slightly smaller margin. The GOP also maintained its comfortable majority in both houses of the legislature and once again captured nine out of thirteen Congressional seats.[84]

The two constitutional amendments up for ratification did not attract a large number of voters. Although both received more affirmative than negative votes, neither obtained a majority of all the votes cast for candidates for state and national office. On November 30, Governor Mount issued a proclamation announcing the official count of votes cast for and against the amendments without stating whether they had been adopted or rejected. In order to initiate a test case to determine the legal status of the lawyers' amendment, the Marion Circuit Court immediately established a set of qualifications for admission to the bar and appointed a board of examiners. When an applicant applied to be admitted to practice law but declined to take the bar examination, the court rejected his application on the assumption that the amendment had been adopted. On appeal, the Indiana Supreme Court reversed this action, a majority of the justices holding

[83] Kettleborough, *Constitution Making in Indiana,* II, 195-197, 244-248, 254, 259, 321, 338.

[84] Secretary of State, *Biennial Report,* 1900, pp. 256-259, 280-283, 295-305.

that the amendment had failed of adoption because a majority of those voting in favor of the amendments did not constitute a majority of those voting in the election.[85]

As in 1896, there were four minor parties on the ballot in 1900, but together they could not poll enough votes to prevent the Republican state and national ticket from winning an absolute majority. The Populists' vote total plummeted to 1,500, but the Prohibitionists with 13,500 votes continued their general advance, which had been temporarily interrupted by the quarrel over free silver four years before. In addition, a new political organization—the Social Democratic party of America—made its appearance on the ballot in this election, its national ticket headed by a native Hoosier presidential candidate, Eugene Victor Debs of Terre Haute.

In Eugene V. Debs the state of Indiana produced a home-bred middle western political reformer who was to play a major role in popularizing socialism in America in the next two decades. In Terre Haute he had risen from local to national office in the Brotherhood of Locomotive Firemen before organizing the American Railway Union on an industry rather than a craft basis in 1893. After the failure of the Pullman strike initiated by this union in 1894, Debs, who had an opportunity to reconsider his views on unionism and political action while spending six months in jail for leading the strikers in violation of a Federal court injunction, moved gradually toward socialism. A former Democratic minor officeholder and member of the Indiana legislature who had become a Populist sympathizer in 1896, the indefatigable Debs helped found the Social Democracy of America in 1897 with the notion of planting a co-operative colony in some western state. When Victor Berger and others bolted the organization the next year in opposition to the colonization scheme, he joined with them in forming the Social Democratic party based on a full-fledged program of socialism.[86] In a letter to the edi-

[85] *In re* Denny, 156 Ind. 104 (1901). See above, pp. 6-7.

[86] The best narrative of Debs's early career is found in Ray Ginger, *The Bending Cross: A Biography of Eugene Victor Debs* (Rutgers University Press, 1949), pp. 1-203.

tor of a Populist newspaper in southern Indiana in October, 1898, Debs explained that as a socialist he could not devote his time to any lesser political issues. "The battle is narrowing down to capitalism and socialism," he wrote, "and there can be no compromise or half way ground."[87]

In 1898 Debs consistently opposed the Spanish-American War and the annexationist policy of the McKinley administration, but the new party largely ignored national issues and presented candidates only for local office in Indiana, polling, for example, seventy-eight votes in Terre Haute and Vigo County.[88] On March 6, 1900, the Social Democratic party held its first national convention in Indianapolis and named Debs as its presidential standard-bearer. Job Harriman, an Indiana-born resident of California, the candidate of the Kangaroo faction which had split off from the main body of the Socialist-Labor party shortly before, was given second place on the ticket. In the following months Debs made an extensive speaking tour throughout the country, returning to Terre Haute on the eve of the election in November to conclude his campaign among home-town friends and associates.[89] He received approximately 2,400 votes in Indiana, while the candidate of the older Socialist-Labor party, which had been on the ballot in the state since 1896, polled only 650 votes.

§ § § §

The day after the election the pro-McKinley Indianapolis *News,* cautious as always on the issue of imperialism, announced that it would be a great mistake for the Republican party to construe the results as an "unqualified endorsement" of the administration program. "The question, for instance, of our relation to our new dependencies has yet to be solved," an editorial stated. "Nothing in that subject has been determined except that the American people are opposed to surrendering to men in arms against the flag."[90] Another Hoo-

---

87 Shoals *Referendum,* October 20, 1898.
88 Indianapolis *News,* November 12, 1898.
89 Indianapolis *Sentinel,* November 6, 1900.
90 Indianapolis *News,* November 7, 1900.

sier voice also expressed a lack of enthusiasm for the new direction of American policy, when ex-President Benjamin Harrison, who had kept his peace during the campaign, gave a well-publicized address on "The Status of Annexed Territory and of Its Free Inhabitants" at the University of Michigan in December, 1900. Concluding a lecture which read like a constitutional lawyer's brief, Indiana's elder statesman made clear his convictions in this personal confession: "I am one who has retired from the service, but not from the love of his country, and who finds himself unable to rejoice in the acquisition of foreign lands because of the abandonment of the old American idea that government by absolute powers is an intolerable thing and under the constitution of the United States, an impossible thing."[91]

A confrontation between the old and the new views of the role of the United States in world affairs occurred at the ultra-Republican Columbia Club in Indianapolis on New Year's Eve, 1900, when Harrison rose to reply to Senator Beveridge's toast to the twentieth-century future of American empire. Just a few months before his death, the ex-President calmly and simply summed up his old-fashioned point of view in these words: "I have no argument to make against territorial expansion, but I do not, as some do, look to expansion as the safest and most attractive avenue of national development."[92] The undaunted Beveridge, still planning a career as spokesman for an expansive foreign policy, prepared to make a second trip to the East by way of Russia, through Siberia

[91] Indianapolis *Sentinel,* December 17, 1900. The Democratic *Sentinel* carried the whole speech, which did not appear in the Republican newspapers of the capital city. It received wide circulation, however, from its publication in the *North American Review,* CLXXII (1901), 1-22. This periodical also published two more papers by Benjamin Harrison entitled "Musings on Current Topics," which attacked the idea of Anglo-Saxon supremacy and the "irresponsible nonsense about our being a world power." "The nation," he wrote, "that goes out to slay and to possess in God's name must give some other attestation of its mission than the facts that it is the mightiest of the nations and has an adaptable language." *Ibid.,* CLXXII, 177-190, 352-366.

[92] Indianapolis *Journal,* January 1, 1901, quoted in Bowers, *Beveridge,* p. 144.

and Manchuria to China, Japan, and the Philippines. "This trip," he confided to a friend, "will make me easily the authority on the Orient in American public life."[93] But when the globe-trotting Senator returned in October, 1901, to a nation shocked by the assassination of William McKinley, he soon found the political atmosphere subtly altered by the personality and character of the new President, Theodore Roosevelt. In the transition from the era of McKinley to the era of Roosevelt, Beveridge the imperialist discovered another avenue of leadership as Indiana's chief representative of progressive Republicanism in the crusade for domestic reform.

Imperialism may well have helped prepare the way for progressivism by awakening Hoosiers and other Americans to a broadened consciousness of national power and responsibility. Although Indiana public opinion for the most part had not demanded overseas expansion and a larger world role for the United States, it embraced them when they came with a heightened sense of nationalism which was channeled into a drive for American political, social, and economic betterment in the first decade and a half of the twentieth century.

[93] Beveridge to Albert Shaw, May 2, 1901, quoted in *ibid.,* p. 145.

# CHAPTER III

# POLITICS IN THE PROGRESSIVE ERA, 1901-1919

THE SHOOTING OF PRESIDENT WILLIAM MCKINLEY by an admitted anarchist in Buffalo, New York, on September 6, 1901, profoundly shocked the whole nation. In Indiana the press broke out in sharp denunciation of anarchism, which had previously been considered chiefly a European phenomenon. "Let us sternly resolve," editorialized the Indianapolis *News*, "that the murderous doctrine of anarchy shall hereafter have no open chance to pollute the free air of America or to corrupt weak men."[1] But the conservative *News* also urged that Americans not let themselves be persuaded by this criminal act to demand limitations upon the freedom of speech, unlike its more partisan Republican rival, the Indianapolis *Journal*, which recommended that anarchists be sent to a barren island in the newly acquired Philippines.[2] Going even farther, the latter newspaper hinted darkly that the Democratic standard-bearer in the last two elections, William Jennings Bryan, was partially responsible for the tragedy because he had promulgated demagogic principles which tended to turn people to anarchism. "Whoever attempts to excite personal animosities by arraying class against class is sowing the seeds of anarchy," trumpeted the *Journal*.[3] The Democratic *Sentinel* took the assassination attempt more calmly, noting that there were no anarchists in Indianapolis.[4]

[1] Indianapolis *News*, September 9, 1901.

[2] *Ibid.*, September 10, 1901; Indianapolis *Journal*, September 9, 1901.

[3] Indianapolis *Journal*, September 12, 14, 1901.

[4] Indianapolis *Sentinel*, September 7, 1901. The *Sentinel* appended a historical note to the news story on the assassination attempt, describing an earlier endeavor to form an anarchist group in Indianapolis. According to the newspaper's account, a Chicago anarchist, Josef Hauptmann, arrived in the city during the depression winter of 1893 and organized a twenty-seven member society, which shortly afterwards disappeared.

McKinley's subsequent death profoundly affected his close personal friend and political associate, Indiana Senator Charles W. Fairbanks, who had hastened to the bedside of the stricken president. In an address shortly afterwards before a Civil War veterans' meeting in Indianapolis, Fairbanks described the assassination as a "horrid nightmare" and seized the opportunity to castigate the doctrine of anarchism. "The blow was not struck alone at him; it was a blow struck at the state," he proclaimed. "Anarchy! What a hated word! . . . There is no room in this Republic, great and splendid as it is, for anarchy! The red flag must go down in the face of the Stars and Stripes!"[5] There is no record of Fairbanks' thoughts concerning the accession of Theodore Roosevelt to the White House, though this event proved to be an important turning point in the former's political career; for the naturally conservative Indiana Senator would be out of step with the new and more progressive era which Roosevelt was soon to inaugurate.[6]

The Indianapolis *News,* in which Fairbanks held a substantial financial interest, chose to give sturdy editorial backing to Roosevelt, while taking cognizance of his reputation for impulsiveness. "To those who think that the new President is a mere reckless boy," the paper stated on the day of McKinley's death, "we would say that they have mistaken superficial traits for indications of character. . . . We believe that the country is entirely safe in his hands, and are confident that he will rise fully to his opportunity."[7] Most Republican journals in the state took the same line as the *News,* arguing that Roosevelt had no choice but to continue the conservative policies of his predecessor, a much-revered figure in Indiana. But the intransigent Indianapolis *Sentinel* made a rather negative assessment of the new chief executive: "There is, unfortunately, not much in the character and career of Theodore Roosevelt, who, by the operation of the

5 Smith, *Life and Speeches of Fairbanks,* pp. 156-157.
6 Rissler, Charles Warren Fairbanks, pp. 118-120.
7 Indianapolis *News,* September 14, 1901.

constitution and the deed of a murderous fanatic, has become president of the United States, to inspire confidence in his qualifications for the great duties and responsibilities which have been suddenly thrust upon him." The same editorial, however, went on to admit more charitably that the presidential office "may develop qualities in him which have hitherto remained latent."[8] A few days later the *Sentinel* argued further that Roosevelt was the conservative captive of big business who would do nothing to curb the "power of the trusts." "He was born and reared within the shadow of Wall St.," the newspaper claimed, "and has caught the capitalistic fever for consolidation."[9]

Theodore Roosevelt was not entirely unknown in Indiana. As early as 1884 he had been in close touch with Benjamin Harrison's political manager, Louis T. Michener, and worked for Harrison's nomination at the Republican national convention in 1888.[10] More importantly, Roosevelt, whom Harrison named to the United States Civil Service Commission in 1889, was a warm friend and faithful correspondent of Indiana reformers William D. Foulke and Lucius B. Swift. The young civil service commissioner visited Indianapolis in 1889 and Terre Haute in 1893 to investigate violations of Federal regulations at the request of Swift, the self-appointed watchdog of the Pendleton Act in Indiana.[11] In the former year an Indianapolis newspaper took rather unfriendly notice of the New Yorker's activities in the state: "Mr. Roosevelt is an enthusiastic young man and an ardent supporter of present

8 Indianapolis *Sentinel,* September 14, 1901.

9 *Ibid.,* September 20, 1901.

10 Roosevelt to Louis T. Michener, May 5, 1884, March 12, 1888, Michener Papers, Library of Congress.

11 Foulke, *Lucius B. Swift,* pp. 37-38; *Fighting the Spoilsmen,* pp. 52-53, 97-98. Roosevelt had actually recommended Swift for the post of civil service commissioner before receiving his own appointment to it. Roosevelt to Charles J. Bonaparte, May 14, 1889, in Elting E. Morison (ed.), *The Letters of Theodore Roosevelt* (8 volumes, Cambridge, Mass., 1951-1954), I, 161. In his autobiography Roosevelt singled out Swift and Foulke for special praise as civil service reformers. Roosevelt, *An Autobiography* (New York, 1913), p. 146.

methods, but, though he means well, he is hasty."[12] In 1901 one of the first executive acts of the new President was to appoint William D. Foulke to the United States Civil Service Commission.[13] Both Swift and Foulke remained intimate associates of Roosevelt for the rest of his life, frequently visiting him at his home in Oyster Bay, New York, and advising him on Indiana political matters.

Roosevelt's accession to the presidency also heightened the rivalry between Indiana's two Republican members of the United States Senate. The death of McKinley had reversed the respective positions of the two Senators in their relationship to the White House. Beveridge, who was much closer to Roosevelt, both temperamentally and politically, won an initial skirmish by succeeding in having his candidate for the Federal district court judgeship in Indianapolis chosen over his rival's nominee.[14] Yet, Fairbanks, who still controlled the Republican organization in Indiana, permitted Beveridge to chair the state convention in March, 1902, for the sake of party unity. Senator Beveridge also met President Roosevelt at Logansport on his brief tour of the state in September and escorted him to Indianapolis, where the latter made two speeches before going to St. Vincent's Hospital in that city for a minor operation on his leg.[15] Senator Mark Hanna made a two-day visit to southern Indiana in October at the request of Fairbanks, who was campaigning actively for a second term in the United States Senate.[16]

[12] Indianapolis *Journal,* December 2, 1889.

[13] Roosevelt, who had suggested Foulke's appointment to McKinley shortly before the latter's death, named the Indiana reformer to the post on October 19, 1901. Roosevelt to McKinley, March 26, 1901, and telegram to Foulke, October 19, 1901, in Morison (ed.), *Letters of Theodore Roosevelt,* III, 26-28, 178. William D. Foulke remained in Washington only two years, resigning from the Civil Service Commission in 1903 to return to his home in Richmond, Indiana, where he continued to play a significant role in liberal Republican politics. Foulke, *Fighting the Spoilsmen,* pp. 144-198.

[14] Bowers, *Beveridge,* pp. 175-176.

[15] Indianapolis *Journal,* September 24, 1902.

[16] Rissler, Charles Warren Fairbanks, p. 132.

The popularity of the new President in Indiana probably helped the GOP to maintain its dominance of the state government in the off-year election, the Republican candidate for secretary of state receiving a plurality of 35,000.[17] The incumbent party also retained nine out of thirteen Congressional seats. In the heavily Republican-controlled legislature, Charles W. Fairbanks, nominated by Booth Tarkington, was easily re-elected to the United States Senate in January, 1903. In his acceptance address in the General Assembly Senator Fairbanks struck an anti-expansionist note: "We are not to be led by the consciousness of increased national power and prestige to become an international meddler. We are not to put upon the high seas fleets to disturb the peace of the world."[18]

With Theodore Roosevelt of New York almost certain to be his party's presidential nominee in 1904, Indiana's chances of providing a vice-presidential candidate once more loomed large. In fact both Senators Fairbanks and Beveridge were mentioned for second place on the Republican ticket in newspaper speculation, though Beveridge was more interested in advancing his career in the Senate, where he was just finishing his first six-year term. The two Indiana Senators reached a happy compromise whereby Beveridge agreed to clear the way for his rival's vice-presidential nomination in return for Fairbanks' support of Beveridge's bid for re-election to the United States Senate.[19] In April, 1904, the Fairbanks-dominated Indiana GOP convention drew up a platform commending President Roosevelt for "faithful enforcement of the laws applicable to combinations of capital" and chose a state ticket headed by gubernatorial candidate J. Frank Hanly, whom Beveridge had defeated for the senatorial nomination

---

[17] Secretary of State, *Biennial Report,* 1902, pp. 448-482.

[18] Indiana *Senate Journal,* 1903, pp. 272-273.

[19] Bowers, *Beveridge,* pp. 204-205, 208-209; John Braeman, Albert J. Beveridge, From Imperialism to Progressivism (Ph.D. thesis in History, Johns Hopkins University, 1960), pp. 121-122.

in the legislative caucus of 1899.[20] Fairbanks was also chairman of the state delegation to the Republican national convention in Chicago, where he was nominated by acclamation as Roosevelt's running mate, thus balancing the ticket both geographically and ideologically.

On the Democratic side the withdrawal of the popular hero and two-time loser, William J. Bryan, made room for a lively contest for the presidential nomination between supporters of the conservative Judge Alton B. Parker of New York and the crusading multimillionaire journalist, William Randolph Hearst. Hearst, hoping to inherit the midwestern following of Bryan, made a strenuous effort to secure delegates in Indiana, pouring out a "flood of gold" in the state according to the hostile Indianapolis *Journal*.[21] But after a bitter struggle the Democratic machine led by the anti-Bryan hotelman and former Indianapolis mayor, Thomas Taggart, was able to push through the state convention in May an endorsement of Parker. The state's free silver Democrats were further angered the next month by the national convention's harsh attitude toward the Bryan forces as well as by Judge Parker's telegram accepting the presidential nomination in which he stated that he would only run on a gold standard platform. "No Indiana Democrat," wrote the partisan biographer-historian Claude Bowers, "will ever forget the stunning effect of that telegram when it was flashed upon the bulletins. It practically assured the state to the Republicans, for it was interpreted by the rank and file of Mr. Bryan's followers as a direct insult to their idol."[22]

Since most signs seemed to point to a Republican victory in November, there was a dearth of able Democratic candidates for nomination for state office. But John W. Kern, who had

---

20 Indianapolis *Journal*, April 27, 28, 1904.

21 *Ibid.*, May 13, 1904.

22 Bowers, *Life of John Worth Kern*, p. 141. Bowers, a young Terre Haute journalist at the time, was himself the unsuccessful Democratic candidate for Congress in the fifth district in 1904. Bowers, *My Life. The Memoirs of Claude Bowers* (New York, 1962), pp. 56-59. He also ran for the same office in 1906, with the same outcome. *Ibid.*, pp. 59-60.

been his party's unsuccessful gubernatorial nominee in 1900, was persuaded to head the state ticket once more at the urgent request of Judge Parker, a close personal friend.[23] Indiana's colorful political boss, Tom Taggart, received his reward for supporting Parker's presidential nomination by being chosen chairman of the Democratic national committee in July.[24]

On the other hand, the GOP considered the Indiana election outcome as far from certain. President Theodore Roosevelt himself communicated his concern over the supposed weakness of the Republican position in the state. "I believe Indiana is more doubtful than New York," he wrote GOP national chairman George B. Cortelyou in late October.[25] His Hoosier running mate, Charles W. Fairbanks, bore the brunt of the national campaign, visiting almost every northern state and making sixty-seven speeches in Indiana alone during the last week before the election. Albert J. Beveridge, who was campaigning for re-election to the United States Senate, felt pessimistic and isolated, as revealed in a letter to the Chicago newspaperman John C. Shaffer, who had recently become associated with the publication of the new Indianapolis *Star*. "I am fighting for my life & am fighting alone," he complained gloomily. "It seems to be my fate always to fight alone. No paper in Indiana has yet told the people *even that* I am a *candidate to succeed myself* except our county papers. . . . The Dems [*sic*] are doing nothing else—*absolutely nothing* else—except to try to carry the legislature. And I am left entirely alone to carry it for our ticket."[26] Although he was considerably cheered by the prospect of journalistic support for his political career which his old friend's connection with the *Star* promised, Beveridge would

[23] Bowers, *Life of John Worth Kern*, pp. 142-143.

[24] Indianapolis *Sentinel*, July 26, 1904.

[25] Roosevelt to George B. Cortelyou, October 29, 1904, in Morison (ed.), *Letters of Theodore Roosevelt*, IV, 1004-1005. See also Roosevelt to Harry S. New, October 14, 1904, and Roosevelt to Henry Cabot Lodge, October 31, 1904, in *ibid.*, IV, 982-983, 1007.

[26] Beveridge to Shaffer, n. d. [1904], Shaffer Papers.

have to wait several more years before Shaffer gained full control of the Indianapolis newspaper and could provide consistent backing for the progressive Senator.[27]

Once again the popular Bryan, despite the absence of his name from the ballot, stumped Indiana for the Democrats, but with even less success than in 1896 and 1900. The November election returns indicated a victory of landslide proportions for the Roosevelt-Fairbanks ticket, which won the state's electoral vote by the astonishing plurality of almost 94,000, about 10,000 greater than Republican gubernatorial candidate J. Frank Hanly's margin over Kern. Moreover, the Roosevelt landslide helped the GOP virtually to sweep the state. The party gained a large majority in both houses of the General Assembly and eleven out of the thirteen Congressional seats. The unprecedented Republican plurality was attained in spite of an exceptionally large number of minor party ballots. The Prohibitionists, who held their national nominating convention in Indianapolis in July, reached their peak voting strength in Indiana in this election, attracting approximately 23,000 votes for their state and national candidates. The Socialist party, which had been formed by the successful amalgamation of the Social Democrats and a large section of the faction-ridden Socialist Labor party at an Indianapolis convention in June, 1901, polled 12,000 votes in Indiana in 1904 for its presidential candidate, Eugene V. Debs of Terre Haute. In January, 1905, the new General Assembly, which was three-to-one Republican, not only sent Albert J. Beveridge back to the United States Senate for a second term but also chose a relatively undistinguished GOP Congressman, James A. Hemenway of Warrick County, to take the senatorial seat vacated by Charles W. Fairbanks upon his elevation to the vice-presidency.[28]

[27] For the story of the establishment of the Indianapolis *Star,* see below, Chapter XIII.

[28] Secretary of State, *Biennial Report,* 1904, pp. 332-335. Debs's total of 12,-000 votes was 500 per cent higher than that cast for him in 1900 and 60 per cent higher than that cast for the Socialist candidate for secretary of state in 1902. The Socialist party, which never polled as much as 5 per cent of the

In the election of 1904 the Indiana Democracy, which was experiencing an extraordinarily severe decline in popularity at the polls, reached its nadir, and the road to political recovery proved to be a long and arduous one. Yet what was happening in Indiana was only a single instance of the general malaise affecting the older of the two major parties in the whole northern half of the country in these years. The rising tide of economic prosperity together with the heightened sense of nationalism fired by the Spanish-American War endowed the incumbent GOP with a large advantage over its rival party, which could find no popular issues on which to launch a successful counterattack. Furthermore, the intense factionalism which had divided Democrats since the nomination of Bryan in 1896 resulted in persistent weakness in political organization both at the state and national level. A witty Hoosier lawyer who became one of the most accomplished Democratic politicians in the state, Thomas Riley Marshall, later gave this vivid, if facetious, description of the internal condition of the Indiana Democracy during this period.[29]

It was a somewhat difficult thing to find a man who was a Democrat—just a plain, unadorned, undiluted, unterrified Democrat. You could find Jacksonian Democrats, Jeffersonian Democrats, Parker Democrats and

total vote in the state, was strongest in certain urban-industrial and coal-mining counties of Indiana. In 1904 the largest number of ballots cast for a Socialist candidate for Congress in Indiana was recorded in the first district including the city of Evansville, which gave Alvin L. Heim nearly 2,000 votes. The fifth district, including Terre Haute, was next, with 1,200 votes for the Socialist Congressional candidate. *Ibid.*, 1904, pp. 333, 360, 361. A table recording the Socialist vote in Indiana by counties for the years 1896 to 1912 is found in Ora Ellen Cox, "The Socialist Party in Indiana since 1896," *Indiana Magazine of History*, XII (1916), 116-118. James Alexander Hemenway, who was born in Warrick County, in 1860, was a small-town lawyer who was elected to six terms in the House of Representatives as a Republican before taking his seat in the United States Senate in 1905. Failing to win re-election in 1911 because the GOP was in the minority in the state legislature, he returned to the practice of law in Indiana until his death in 1923. *Biographical Directory of the American Congress,* p. 1038.

29 Thomas R. Marshall, *Recollections of Thomas R. Marshall, Vice-President and Hoosier Philosopher. A Hoosier Salad* (Indianapolis, 1925), pp. 159-160.

Bryan Democrats; the party was a party of hyphenated Democrats. . . .
The harmony banquets were really incipient riots. It was only the
proprieties of civilized life that prevented the participants from coming
to blows, and those who attended usually went away far more set in
their views and far more disgusted with those who did not agree with
them, than when together they began to eat olives.

Moreover, the Indiana GOP enjoyed an immense superior-
ity over the Democratic party in the degree of national
prominence attained by their respective leaders at this time.
With the passing from the political scene of such men as
Senators Turpie and Voorhees, the Democrats had no one of
the stature and prestige of Senator Beveridge or Vice-President Fairbanks. Not long after the 1904 election the state
GOP organization received the recognition due its remarkable victory in that year by the appointment of Harry S. New
to the vice-chairmanship of the Republican national committee. New, who had been long associated with his father, John
C. New, in the management of the influential Indianapolis
*Journal,* became acting chairman in July, 1906, and full
chairman in January, 1907, upon the final retirement of George
B. Cortelyou from that position.[30] In addition, by 1906 Fairbanks himself had become an all-but-avowed candidate for the
Republican presidential nomination in 1908. In September,
1906, for example, the Indianapolis *Star,* then controlled by
Daniel G. Reid, a former Richmond banker who became a
wealthy industrial promoter and Wall Street financier, endorsed the Indianan's candidacy for that office in an editorial
statement which emphasized the Vice-President's reputation
for political conservatism: "The character and attainments
of Mr. Fairbanks are those peculiarly qualifying him for the
presidency at a time when the country is menaced by ram-
pant radicalism proclaiming as its purpose revolutionary
changes in the very nature of American Government."[31]

Although Fairbanks' dominance over the Indiana Republican organization had begun to wane somewhat during his

[30] Indianapolis *News,* July 5, 1906, January 7, 1907.
[31] Indianapolis *Star,* September 8, 1906.

absence in Washington, conservative forces controlled the state convention of 1906 which wrote a platform upholding the protective tariff and other traditional GOP policies. The Vice-President took an active part in the closing weeks of the campaign, delivering as many as fifty-six speeches in the state. Senator Beveridge, who had begun to assume the role of a champion of progressive legislation with his fight for the passage of a meat inspection bill in the last session of Congress, also campaigned hard in Indiana, advocating such political reforms as an inheritance tax, a national child labor law, the direct primary, and a downward revision of the tariff. The last issue especially divided Indiana Republicans and may have been a factor in the loss of four Congressional seats to the Democrats in November.[32] Nevertheless, the GOP was able to maintain its tenure of the state offices and a firm majority in the General Assembly, though the margin of victory in the state-wide races in 1906 was considerably reduced from two years before.[33]

The first overt signs of the beginning of a cleavage in Hoosier Republican ranks between conservatives and progressives were visible by 1906, a year which also marked the emergence of Senator Beveridge on the national political scene as a reformer in the Rooseveltian manner.[34] Yet the roots of twentieth century progressive reform in Indiana may be found in some of the state legislative enactments of the preceding decade. During these years the Indiana General Assembly, while dominated by supposedly conservative Re-

32 *Ibid.*, October 21, 31, November 4, 1906; Rissler, Charles Warren Fairbanks, pp. 177-180; Bowers, *Beveridge,* pp. 226-233. Beveridge also played a lesser role in the passage of the Pure Food and Drug Act, which had been largely drawn up by Dr. Harvey W. Wiley, former Purdue University professor and Indiana state chemist who went to Washington in 1883 to become chief chemist in the Department of Agriculture. Oscar E. Anderson, Jr., *The Health of a Nation. Harvey W. Wiley and the Fight for Pure Food* (Chicago, 1958), pp. 176-189.

33 Secretary of State, *Biennial Report,* 1906, pp. 315-326.

34 John Braeman, "Albert J. Beveridge and the First National Child Labor Bill," *Indiana Magazine of History,* LX (1964), 4-8. See also Daniel Levine, "The Social Philosophy of Albert J. Beveridge," *ibid.,* LVIII (1962), 111-116.

publican forces, created an important body of political reform measures, albeit of a relatively moderate nature. As early as 1897 and 1899, for example, the legislature passed mild laws aimed at the regulation of building and loan associations, insurance companies, and monopolies as well as somewhat more stringent factory and labor legislation.[35] Moreover, an outbreak of mob violence and vigilantism in the state during Governor Mount's administration stimulated the enactment in 1899 and 1901 of antilynch laws.[36] Also included among progressive measures in these years were the laws establishing a mortgage exemption on the taxation of private citizens' homes and prohibiting the adulteration of drugs and food, including candy.[37]

On the other hand, more radical innovations promulgated in a few midwestern states such as the initiative and referendum, though briefly considered in the General Assembly in the late nineties in the form of constitutional amendments, never gained acceptance in Indiana.[38] Hoosier concern for the purity of the ballot, however, was reflected in the passage of bills legalizing and regulating the use of voting machines in 1899 and 1901. In addition, serious charges of vote buying in the 1904 election reminiscent of the eighties inspired outgoing Governor Durbin to recommend and the legislature to pass a new law penalizing both the purchaser and the seller of votes, unlike the Democratic-sponsored act of 1889 which applied a penalty only to the former.[39] In 1901 a direct primary was authorized for the nomination of candi-

[35] *Laws of Indiana,* 1897, pp. 101-108, 130-136, 159-161, 284-287, 318-333; 1899, pp. 231-240, 310-341. For labor legislation, see below, Chapter VIII.

[36] *Laws of Indiana,* 1899, pp. 132-133, 500-502; 1901, pp. 311-312.

[37] *Ibid.,* 1899, pp. 189-191, 368, 422-423. For the pure food and drug movement in Indiana, see below, Chapter XII.

[38] Indiana *Senate Journal,* 1897, pp. 221-223, 336; 1899, pp. 482-484, 664-665; Kettleborough, *Constitution Making in Indiana,* II, 321-323, 335-337.

[39] *Laws of Indiana,* 1899, pp. 365-368; 1901, pp. 591-603; 1905, pp. 481-482. Although smaller communities were slow in shifting to the use of voting machines, they were quickly adopted in large urban districts. The first recorded use of a voting machine in the state was in a township election in the Indianapolis suburb of Irvington on May 1, 1899. Indianapolis *Journal,* May 2, 1899.

dates for local offices in Marion and Vanderburgh counties and six years later was made mandatory in all counties containing cities of over 30,000 population and optional in all others.[40]

Although Indiana did not produce a progressive state leader of the stature of Wisconsin's Robert M. La Follette or Missouri's Joseph W. Folk, it had in Republican Governor J. Frank Hanly a vigorous and relatively successful advocate of a variety of political and moral reform measures during his term of office from 1905 to 1909. The Illinois-born Hanly, an eloquent, largely self-educated lawyer and former Congressman, was a political maverick who often acted independently of his own party. As historian Jacob P. Dunn has written, "with the exception of Morton he had a more indomitable will than any other Governor of Indiana, and showed a more reckless courage in enforcing it."[41] An uncompromising foe of gambling and the liquor traffic as well as political corruption, Governor Hanly utilized his high office to conduct a veritable crusade against vice. In 1905 he halted all gambling operations in connection with horse racing at the state fair and the next year began an investigation of illegal gaming establishments located at the popular southern Indiana mineral springs resorts in French Lick and West Baden, Orange County, and at Dearborn Park near the city of Hammond. Perhaps his most spectacular move in this campaign was an attempt to link Democratic national chairman Tom Taggart of Indianapolis, owner of the lavish French Lick Springs Hotel, to the gambling casino located in the same community.[42]

[40] *Laws of Indiana*, 1901, pp. 495-505; 1907, pp. 627-652.

[41] Dunn, *Indiana and Indianans*, II, 766. Barnhart and Carmony have characterized Hanly as "a fearless man of strong convictions whose insistence upon principle sometimes hindered his reform efforts." Barnhart and Carmony, *Indiana*, II, 360.

[42] Indianapolis *News*, July 6, 1905, July 3, 1906, April 16, 1907; Leslie Ward Carson, The Life of J. Frank Hanly: Log Cabin Boy to Governor (Unpublished Master's thesis in History, University of Illinois, 1928), Chapter V. For Taggart's management of the French Lick Springs Hotel, see Richard W. Haupt, History of the French Lick Springs Hotel (Unpublished Master's thesis in History, Indiana University, 1953), pp. 94-150. The Hanly administration brought

Even earlier, the discovery that the state auditor had lost large sums at the gaming tables at the French Lick resort brought to light irregularities in the conduct of financial affairs by members of the Governor's administration. Hanly immediately took stringent action to maintain a high standard of morality among his political associates, shocking many of his fellow Republicans by removing from office the secretary of state, the attorney general, and the auditor and successfully prosecuting the last named for embezzlement of state funds.[43]

One of Hanly's major legislative accomplishments was the creation of the Indiana Railroad Commission, which the General Assembly authorized in 1905 after the Governor had made an impassioned appeal to the railroad interests to consent to the correction of abuses by such an agency in order to "stay, and perhaps to avert, the more radical sentiment of the country just now crystallizing in the demand for public ownership." Two years later Governor Hanly submitted a long list of recommendations to the legislature which included strong pleas for a state inheritance tax, an antilobby bill, regulation of private banking and the insurance business, and the abolition of capital punishment. In the longest governor's message on record up to that time, Hanly employed typically progressive rhetoric in attacking the lobbyists: "Human rights—the rights of the individual citizen, or the rights of the body of the people—are not safe where legislation can be procured or defeated or government administered through the corrupt and demoralizing influence of the paid

suit against Taggart to force forfeiture of his hotel charter on the grounds that he operated an illegal gambling establishment in connection with the hotel. Prosecution of the case was carried over into the administration of Democratic Governor Thomas R. Marshall and resulted in a court verdict in Taggart's favor. Charles M. Thomas, *Thomas Riley Marshall, Hoosier Statesman* (Oxford, Ohio, 1939), pp. 75-77.

43 Indiana *Senate Journal,* 1907, pp. 38-40; Dunn, *Indiana and Indianans,* II, 767; Carson, Life of J. Frank Hanly, Chapter IV. David E. Sherrick, the state auditor, was later released from prison by the Indiana Supreme Court on a legal technicality.

agents of organized wealth and greed."[44] The Hoosier reform temper, however, was particularly revealed in the extensive legislation passed during the Hanly administration in regard to control of the liquor traffic and even the manufacture and sale of cigarettes.[45]

Despite resentment of Hanly's highhanded tactics among members of his own party and the strenuous activities of a host of lobbyists for banking, insurance, and other interests, both the legislatures of 1905 and 1907 produced a number of significant reform measures, including bills to regulate trusts, railroads, and private banks and to outlaw "bucket-shops," where illegal transactions amounting to wagers on security prices and commodity futures were handled. In 1907 the General Assembly also reorganized the state's charitable and correctional institutions on a nonpartisan basis and passed laws prohibiting contributions to political parties by employees of such institutions and requiring public officials to deposit to public account all moneys coming to them by virtue of their offices. In one of its most far-reaching acts the legislature placed Indiana in the company of Wisconsin and other progressive states by the establishment of a legislative reference department in the State Library for the purpose of collecting information and carrying on research for the use of legislators and others.[46] Yet the strong-minded Governor failed to obtain a large part of his program and was forced to exercise his veto power to an extraordinary degree against various proposals passed in contravention of his recommen-

[44] Indiana *House Journal,* 1905, p. 120; Indiana *Senate Journal,* 1907, pp. 32-123, especially p. 83.

[45] *Laws of Indiana,* 1905, pp. 82-83, 720-723; 1907, pp. 27-33, 281, 658-659, 689-691. In 1909 the legislature amended the antitobacco bill to prohibit the sale of cigarettes to minors. *Ibid.,* 1909, pp. 71-72. For temperance agitation and legislation in this period, see below, Chapter XII.

[46] *Laws of Indiana,* 1905, pp. 182-185, 199-201; 1907, pp. 138-143, 236-237, 391-404, 488-497. In 1913 the Legislative Reference Department was separated from the State Library and its name changed to the Bureau of Legislative Information. Abolished in an economy move in 1917, it was re-established in 1919 as the Legislative Reference Bureau. *Ibid.,* 1913, pp. 694-696; 1917, p. 200; 1919, p. 82.

dations. At the 1907 session of the General Assembly alone he vetoed 13 senate bills and 32 house bills, 5 of which were passed over his veto, and killed 4 senate bills and 20 house bills by failure to sign them after the close of the session.[47] Among his most important vetoes was one against a weak, lobbyist-inspired bill for the regulation of the insurance business and another preventing the abolition of the metropolitan police boards which were appointed by the governor in certain Indiana cities. Hanly defended the latter veto in particular as guarding against the weakening of law enforcement by the surrender of police control to local political forces.[48]

For all his advocacy of a broader progressive program, Governor Hanly's predominant concern was for temperance reform. Having failed to obtain a county option law in the legislative session of 1907, the Governor persuaded the Republican state convention in the spring of 1908 to endorse such a measure in its platform. The concluding sentences in his address to the convention revealed both his characteristically florid style of oratory and his conviction that the crusade against the liquor traffic was equivalent to the historic Republican opposition to slavery:[49]

I hate it as Abraham Lincoln hated slavery. And as he sometimes saw in prophetic vision the end of slavery, and the coming of the time when the sun should shine and the rain should fall upon no slave in all the Republic, so I sometimes seem to see the end of this unholy traffic, the coming of the time when, if it does not wholly cease to be, it shall find no safe habitation anywhere beneath Old Glory's stainless stars.

Moreover, Hanly chose to cap his vigorous performance as governor by calling a special session of the General Assembly in September, 1908, in the midst of the fall election cam-

47 Indianapolis *Star*, March 13, 1907.

48 Indiana *House Journal*, 1907, pp. 2138-2140; Carson, Life of J. Frank Hanly, Chapter VII.

49 Indianapolis *Star*, April 2, 1908. This speech, entitled "The Liquor Traffic, Why I Hate It," was printed as a campaign document both by the Republican party in Indiana and the Anti-Saloon League. A long extract may be found in Dunn, *Indiana and Indianans*, II, 766-767.

paign, in order to enact a county option law which would permit rural "dry" voters to outlaw the saloon throughout a county regardless of the "wet" sentiments of many of the residents of the cities and larger towns. The Democrats, on the other hand, preferred a less drastic local option law based on the city, ward, or township as the voting unit. Despite the opposition of the brewery interests in the state, the lame-duck legislature proceeded to pass, though narrowly, the county option bill demanded by Hanly, thus setting the stage for a hard-fought election contest in which the control of the liquor traffic became the paramount issue.[50]

The Indiana Democracy held its state convention early, in March, 1908. Faced with an abundance of candidates for the gubernatorial nomination for the first time since 1896 and sensing the strong possibility of a Democratic victory in the state, the convention was bitterly divided between pro- and anti-Taggart forces. After a stormy session, however, a compromise candidate acceptable to all sides was found in the person of Thomas Riley Marshall, a little-known Columbia City attorney who had hitherto not run for public office. The equally divided Republicans finally chose Congressman James Eli Watson of Rushville, a member of the conservative Fairbanks wing of the party who was not notably enthusiastic about running on a strong temperance plank and had been opposed by Governor Hanly himself. Moreover, Watson was severely handicapped by the opposition of organized labor and the failure of the GOP to close ranks around him.[51] Marshall, on the other hand, conducted an attractive, low-

[50] *Laws of Indiana,* special session, 1908, pp. 4-9; Thomas, *Thomas Riley Marshall,* pp. 50-51; Carson, Life of J. Frank Hanly, Chapter IX.

[51] Thomas, *Thomas Riley Marshall,* pp. 43-50; Lawrence M. Bowman, Stepping Stone to the Vice Presidency: A Story of Thomas Riley Marshall's 1908 Gubernatorial Victory (Unpublished Master's thesis in History, University of Kansas, 1967), pp. 25-50. Samuel Gompers, president of the American Federation of Labor, personally entered the Indiana campaign to defeat Watson, whose Congressional record was considered particularly unfriendly to organized labor. Indianapolis *News,* September 17, October 1, 1908, cited in *ibid.,* pp. 152-154.

pressure campaign which gave new life to the Democratic party in Indiana and also launched a political career which was eventually to lead the witty small-town lawyer nearly to the White House. Although the brewing interests made available large amounts of money in an attempt to defeat the passage of the Republican-sponsored county option bill, Marshall allegedly rejected all such financial assistance for his own campaign, claiming to have spent only the incredibly small sum of $3,750, which he raised by a personal loan from his home-town bank.[52]

The election of 1908 also revealed the widening rift in the Indiana GOP. Early in the year Senator Beveridge, who had moved closer to insurgency against the conservative Congressional leadership of his party, confided to William D. Foulke of Richmond that "I have about made up my mind that the time is past when a man who is a bad man can put the placard 'Republican' on his coat and get the support of honest people who are faithfully attached to the Republican party because they think the success of the Republican party is the best way of advancing the interests of the nation." His letter concluded with the hope that he and other reformers might remold the party: "If we all pull together very earnestly from now on it strikes me that we may get the wagon out of the slue in Indiana, turn a hose on it, clean it up, paint it anew and make it an up-to-date clean vehicle that honest men can travel in with some self-respect."[53] Beveridge, how-

---

[52] Marshall, *Recollections*, pp. 169-170; Thomas, *Thomas Riley Marshall*, pp. 53-55; Indianapolis *News*, October 24, 27, 1908. An analysis of the campaign which attributed Marshall's success chiefly to his attractive personality and persuasive stump speeches is found in Keith S. Montgomery, "Thomas R. Marshall's Victory in the Election of 1908," *Indiana Magazine of History*, LIII (1957), 147-166.

[53] Beveridge to Foulke, February 10, 1908, Foulke Papers. Foulke, however, was not fully convinced of Beveridge's independence of the conservative GOP machine. In his reply to the Senator's letter quoted above, Foulke rather ungraciously scolded Beveridge for not taking a stronger stand against Watson and other standpatters: "But as for your own course, I am getting very weary of it, and when you talk of pulling together to get the wagon out of the 'slue' in Indiana, I do not feel like pulling very hard with a man that will

ever, was unable to prevent the nomination of Watson, a close associate of the arch-conservative Speaker of the House, Joseph G. Cannon, and was shunted aside as a possible keynote speaker at the GOP nominating convention in Chicago, even though President Roosevelt had recommended him for the post in a letter to Republican national chairman Harry S. New of Indiana.[54]

As head of the state delegation to the national convention in Chicago, moreover, Beveridge was forced to support Vice-President Fairbanks as Indiana's favorite-son candidate for the Republican presidential nomination. But the latter's presidential ambitions had received a severe setback during the previous summer, when *Collier's Weekly* had published a harsh muckraking attack upon him. Although David Graham Phillips, a native Hoosier and Senator Beveridge's college roommate, had given Fairbanks a brief unfavorable mention in the closing installment of his famous "Treason of the Senate" articles in *Cosmopolitan Magazine* in November, 1906, the Vice-President considered this to be very mild treatment compared with the full-scale exposé attempted by *Collier's*. In two articles entitled "The Real Mr. Fairbanks," the well-known political journalist Gilson Gardner revealed details of Fairbanks' silent partnership in the Indianapolis *News* as well as other alleged financial dealings.[55] Fairbanks' chances for the nomination, moreover, were significantly diminished by his loss to William Howard Taft in the Kentucky presidential primary election in April, 1908.[56] The genial Taft, who was Roosevelt's personal choice to succeed himself, won the presidential nomination easily over Fairbanks and a half-dozen

---

turn and pull in the wrong direction at the end." Foulke to Beveridge, February 13, 1908, *ibid.*

[54] Bowers, *Beveridge,* pp. 283-285.

[55] *Cosmopolitan Magazine*, XLII (1906-1907), 77-78; *Collier's Weekly,* June 1, 1907, pp. 13-16, and July 13, 1907, pp. 14-15. Fairbanks claimed that the *Collier's* articles were written not by Gardner but by a disaffected former private secretary, Jerry A. Matthews. Rissler, Charles Warren Fairbanks, p. 201.

[56] Indianapolis *Star,* April 13, 1908; Rissler, Charles Warren Fairbanks, pp. 207-208.

other aspirants. After Fairbanks and Beveridge both firmly rejected overtures from the Taft forces to accept second place on the ticket, that spot went to the elderly James S. Sherman of New York.[57]

On the other hand, the Democrats, who turned to their "Peerless Leader," William J. Bryan, for a third time to head the national ticket, chose an Indianan, John W. Kern, twice an unsuccessful candidate for governor, as their vice-presidential nominee. Kern, who had at first been reluctant to permit his name to go before the convention, accepted the nomination and campaigned strenuously in a losing cause despite the serious illness of his son, who was stricken with infantile paralysis in October.[58] Another Hoosier, Eugene V. Debs of Terre Haute, who received the Socialist party's presidential nomination for the third time in 1908, conducted a dramatic canvass of the whole country on board a three-car railroad train dubbed the "Red Special."[59]

Both Fairbanks and Beveridge went out on the campaign trail though the former largely confined his efforts to Indiana. Senator Beveridge undertook an extensive speaking tour of much of the nation but returned to his home state in the closing week of the campaign to try to help save what many of his fellow Republicans by that time considered a desperate situation for the party. Traveling on a special train and accompanied in his private coach by a group of congenial literary and journalistic friends, including the playwright-humorist George Ade and cartoonists John T. McCutcheon and Kin Hubbard, Beveridge rendered valiant service for the GOP throughout Indiana.[60] On the other hand, his friend Foulke and the stubbornly independent civil-service reformer, Lucius B. Swift, supported the election of Taft out of

---

[57] Bowers, *Beveridge,* pp. 286-287; Rissler, Charles Warren Fairbanks, pp. 212-216.

[58] Bowers, *Life of John Worth Kern,* pp. 156-187.

[59] For an account of that campaign, see H. Wayne Morgan, " 'Red Special': Eugene V. Debs and the Campaign of 1908," *Indiana Magazine of History,* LIV (1958), 211-236.

[60] Bowers, *Beveridge,* pp. 295-296.

friendship for Roosevelt but refused to participate in the state campaign managed by what the latter described as the "Fairbanks machine."[61]

Moreover, the Fairbanks-owned Indianapolis *News* displayed little enthusiasm for the Taft ticket. Following the lead of the New York *World,* the *News* published stories during the campaign linking the names of Charles P. Taft, the GOP presidential nominee's brother, and Douglas Robinson, President Roosevelt's brother-in-law, to an American "syndicate" alleged to have shared in the $40,000,000 paid by the United States Government for the Panama canal rights of a French company which had already begun construction of an isthmian canal. Although there was no evidence for these vague allegations, the Indianapolis newspaper kept the question before the voters, inquiring editorially on the eve of the election, "Where did the money go?"[62] Even more surprisingly, however, the independent-minded *News* gave the following accolade to the Socialist candidate for the presidency from Indiana, while clearly dissociating itself from his ideas, in an election-day editorial:[63]

As for Mr. Debs, we believe he is visionary, and that his plan of social reform in as far as he has promulgated it, is impracticable but he is sincere and his following includes a large number of honest, intelligent men, who believe there is something radically wrong in the organization of the present social system.

Although William Howard Taft defeated Bryan by a 10,-700 plurality in Indiana, the novice campaigner Thomas R.

[61] Foulke to William Howard Taft, September 10, 1908, Foulke Papers. In a letter to Taft in 1910 Swift explained that "I never joined in the humbug Fairbanks movement in Indiana, and I think I was the only man who gave the newspapers an interview openly opposing him. I did all I could in the campaign for your election and would have done more had not the Fairbanks machine shut me out." Swift to Taft, February 17, 1910, Swift Papers.

[62] Indianapolis *News,* September 26, October 20, November 2, 1908, William D. Foulke brought the *News* editorials to the attention of President Roosevelt, who later brought Federal libel suits against both Delavan Smith, Fairbanks' cousin and publisher of the *News,* and Joseph Pulitzer of the New York *World.* See below, Chapter XIII.

[63] Indianapolis *News,* November 3, 1908.

Marshall became the first Democratic governor in the state since 1893 by a startling 15,000-vote victory over the unfortunate Watson. In large part it was a personal triumph for the popular Marshall, who carried with him into the State House only the Democratic candidates for lieutenant governor and superintendent of public instruction while the GOP retained its hold on the lesser state offices. But the resurgent Democrats asserted their new voting power by sweeping eleven of the thirteen Congressional races.[64] Moreover, a sufficient number of Democrats were elected to the lower house of the state legislature to outvote the Republican-controlled senate in the joint session of the General Assembly, which was to choose a new United States Senator in January, 1909. After a spirited contest the choice went to former Congressman Benjamin F. Shively over John W. Kern, the defeated vice-presidential candidate.[65]

The conservative-progressive cleavage in the Indiana GOP widened perceptibly during the first two years of the new Republican national administration. In the bitter fight over the Payne-Aldrich tariff bill Beveridge broke publicly with President Taft and joined the ranks of the Senate insurgents who opposed its passage. By this action Beveridge not only angered Taft but alienated powerful leaders of the conservative wing of the party in Indiana, including James E. Watson and James A. Hemenway, who set to work to obtain an endorsement of President Taft and the Payne-Aldrich Act by the state convention which was to meet in the spring of 1910. Thus the impulsive Beveridge faced a major crisis in his political career, as he prepared to campaign for his re-election to the United States Senate by the new General Assembly to be chosen that fall. In a letter published in the Indianapolis *Star* in March, 1910, Lucius B. Swift claimed that "the trusts, the standpatters and all the interests represented by Cannonism and Aldrichism mean to crush Senator Beveridge in

---

[64] Secretary of State, *Biennial Report,* 1908, pp. 278-279, 300-319.

[65] Stoll, *History of the Indiana Democracy,* pp. 408-409; Bowers, *Life of John W. Kern,* pp. 188-195.

the coming campaign in Indiana." Like Samuel G. Blythe, a journalist friend of Beveridge who wrote an article for the *Saturday Evening Post* on the division of Republican opinion in the state which was strongly slanted in favor of the Senator, Swift was optimistic about the outcome, however, concluding that "we shall gain a victory that will be heard around the world."[66]

His conservative opponents could not prevent Beveridge from being selected as the temporary chairman of the state Republican convention, where he laid down a ringing challenge to the standpatters in his keynote address: "The coming battle is not so much between political parties as between the rights of the people and the powers of pillage."[67] His plan of action to portray himself as the progressive candidate crusading against reaction was weakened when the Democratic state convention under the astute leadership of Governor Marshall voted to pledge the senatorial nomination to John W. Kern, now clearly identified with the liberal Bryan faction of the party.[68] Marshall had conceived of this as a method of avoiding a repetition of the much-criticized secret legislative caucus of 1906, which had nominated Shively for the Senate rather than the popular and deserving Kern.

With the Indiana senatorial contest in the offing, the struggle between the two major parties to control the state legislature became a center of national attention in the fall of 1910. At the urging of Foulke and Swift, who visited Roosevelt at his home in Oyster Bay, New York, to request his assistance in the Indiana campaign, the former president invaded the state to praise Beveridge, though he hedged on the tariff issue, refusing to take a stand against the Payne-Aldrich Act. Other notable progressive leaders, including Sen-

---

[66] Indianapolis *Star*, March 5, 1910; *Saturday Evening Post*, April 2, 1910, pp. 3-4. The day before his letter appeared in the *Star*, Swift penned a blunt note to Roosevelt complaining about his successor in the White House. It read in its entirety: "My dear Roosevelt: Taft is a damn pig-headed blunderer. Affectionately yours, Lucius B. Swift." Swift Papers.

[67] Bowers, *Beveridge*, p. 385.

[68] Bowers, *Life of John Worth Kern*, pp. 202-203.

ators Joseph L. Bristow of Kansas, Albert B. Cummins of
Iowa, Moses E. Clapp of Minnesota, conservationist Gifford
Pinchot, and even the novelist, Winston Churchill, stumped
the state for Beveridge.[69] On the Democratic side, former
presidential candidates Bryan and Parker both came to Indiana to speak for Kern. Beveridge himself conducted a
strenuous campaign over the state, mostly by automobile for
the first time.[70] But treachery and division within his party
and a nationwide Democratic tidal wave swept him to defeat.
The returns of the off-year election of 1910 produced a re-
sounding victory for the Democrats, who gained a large majority in both houses of the legislature for the first time since
1893 and won all but one of the thirteen Congressional
races.[71] Both of Indiana's seats in the United States Senate
were held by Democrats when the General Assembly sent
John W. Kern to join Senator Benjamin F. Shively in Washington in January, 1911. The period of Republican dominance
in Indiana thus came to an abrupt close in the midst of the
progressive era.

The initiative passed to the Democratic party in forwarding a legislative reform program. Governor Marshall was an
independent-minded man of Jeffersonian principles whom a
contemporary historian called the ablest Democratic chief
executive in Indiana since Thomas A. Hendricks.[72] In his first
address to the General Assembly in 1909 he recommended
economy in government and warned against the passage of
superfluous laws. "Legislative enactments," he argued,
"should not precede, but should succeed, civic reform."[73]
He asked specifically for the creation of a board of accounts

[69] Bowers, *Beveridge,* pp. 390-399. Beveridge had become a friend and correspondent of Winston Churchill after reading and admiring his novels. The
letters between them at this time are found in Warren I. Titus (ed.), "The
Senator and the Author: Beveridge—Churchill Correspondence," *Indiana Magazine of History,* LV (1959), 169-178.

[70] Bowers, *Beveridge,* p. 401.

[71] Secretary of State, *Biennial Report,* 1910, pp. 222-241.

[72] Dunn, *Indiana and Indianans,* II, 769.

[73] Indiana *Senate Journal,* 1909, p. 93.

to audit the financial records of state and local officials, for
a new primary election law which would include the nomination of candidates for the United States Senate, and for
needed improvements in the state regulation of railroads, insurance companies, and other corporations. An advocate of
limited government, Governor Marshall warned the lawmak-
ers, however, that "there are certain phases of proposed legislation which can scarcely be distinguished from paternalism or socialism." "Theories are advanced, he claimed, "that
the State ought to raise and give to the people free fruit,
forest and ornamental trees and vines, that the State ought
to watch a man's work and if he is not doing it as some public official thinks it ought to be done, he should be supplied
with an assistant to show him how to make a success in life."
The Governor hoped that the legislators would resist such
demands in the realization that "under the guise of administering a free government, we are, in reality, rapidly turning
all the functions of government either into a business asset
or a guardianship over the incompetent, the ignorant and the
shiftless."[74]  Since the GOP, which controlled the upper
house of the 1909 General Assembly, was able to block most
Democratic-inspired legislation, little was accomplished in
that session except authorization of the state board of accounts, a popular measure which the legislature passed in
the face of fierce opposition from the county officers' lobby.[75] In 1910, as related above, Governor Marshall showed
his independence of the Democratic political machine by
successfully calling for the formal expression by the state
convention of its choice for United States Senator. This defeated the senatorial aspirations of party boss Tom Taggart,
who lost the nomination to the popular John W. Kern in the
balloting but might have won election by the same kind of

74 *Ibid.,* p. 102.
75 *Laws of Indiana,* 1909, pp. 136-150; Thomas, *Thomas Riley Marshall,*
pp. 69-70. For an account of the passage of this bill, see Louis E. Lambert,
"The Indiana State Board of Accounts," *Indiana Magazine of History,* LV
(1959), 115-147.

secret legislative caucus which had chosen Benjamin F. Shively over Kern in 1906.[76]

In 1911 Governor Marshall had large Democratic majorities in both houses of the General Assembly and proceeded to ask for a much more extensive legislative program. The legislature not only honored the Democratic pledge to make the township instead of the county the local option unit, but also passed a series of significant labor laws as well as a corrupt-practices act and a new registration law.[77] Failing to become law were such recommendations of the Governor as a state inheritance tax, automobile tax, state regulation of stock and bond issuance, and similar extension of the regulatory power of the state government. An old-fashioned Jeffersonian Democrat who had become a cautious advocate of progressive reform at the state level, Thomas Riley Marshall was described as a "liberal with the brakes on."[78] In his parting address to the General Assembly in 1913, he stated his conviction that reform was necessary to avoid socialism. "Representative government," he said, "does not mean that present-day conditions cannot be remedied. Upon the contrary, progressive legislation may be enacted with no disturbance to the checks and balances of our system of government. Unless progressive legislation is enacted, the people, some day, will open up the cul-de-sac even though the opening may lead representative government over a precipice into pure socialism or paternalism."[79]

The most striking event of Marshall's administration was his bold attempt to rewrite Indiana's sixty-year-old constitution, which many progressives felt stood in the way of needed

[76] Bowers, *Life of John Worth Kern*, pp. 188-202. The Democratic state convention in April, 1910, first voted approval of the Governor's plan by a close margin and then went on to select Kern over Taggart as its choice for Senator. Actually a mistake had been made in the tabulation of the first vote, which, if corrected, would have defeated the proposal. Since it was discovered only after the enthusiastic nomination of Kern, it was not brought to the attention of the delegates. Thomas, *Thomas Riley Marshall*, p. 67.

[77] *Laws of Indiana*, 1911, pp. 145-149, 288-305, 363-370, 371-384, 511-513.

[78] Thomas, *Thomas Riley Marshall*, p. 68.

[79] Indiana *Senate Journal*, 1913, p. 11.

reforms. Not only was the state constitution extremely difficult to amend under ordinary circumstances, but an Indiana
Supreme Court ruling that an 1897 amendment prescribing
qualifications for lawyers was still "pending" before the electorate prevented the submission of new amendments.[80]
Marshall decided to cut the Gordian knot by persuading the
legislature to submit a completely new constitution to the
people for ratification without calling a constitutional convention. With the help of his advisers, he drew up an instrument which greatly simplified the procedure of amendment
and embodied such other changes as restricting the right to
vote to literate male citizens of the United States who were
registered in the state and had paid a poll tax for two
years. The proposed constitution also would have permitted
the enlargement of the house of representatives and extension of the regular session of the legislature from sixty to one
hundred days, as well as specifically authorizing it to enact
legislation providing for the initiative, referendum, and recall, workmen's compensation, lawyers' qualifications, and
municipal home rule. Under it the Supreme Court would have
been increased from five to eleven members, and the governor's powers expanded by the item veto in appropriation
bills and by requiring a three-fifths majority vote in the General Assembly to override his veto.[81]

[80] As related in the previous chapter, this and another amendment had
been submitted in popular referendum in 1900 after having been approved by
the legislatures of 1897 and 1899. The Indiana Supreme Court ruled that both
had failed of ratification since they had not received a majority of all votes
cast in the general election, though they received a majority of the votes cast
on the amendments themselves. The lawyers' amendment was resubmitted to
the voters in 1906 and 1910 with the same result. In 1912 the Supreme Court
ruled that since the amendment had been neither approved nor rejected, it
had not been disposed of and was still pending. *In re Denny,* 156 Ind. 105
(1900); *In re Boswell,* 179 Ind. 292 (1912); Barnhart and Carmony, *Indiana,*
II, 365. The constitution provided that "while an amendment or amendments,
which shall have been agreed upon by one General Assembly, shall be awaiting
the action of a succeeding General Assembly, or of the electors, no additional
amendment or amendments shall be proposed."

[81] The proposed constitution may be found in Kettleborough, *Constitution Making in Indiana,* II, 388-424. Jacob P. Dunn, who was Marshall's chief

Thomas R. Marshall Scrapbooks,
Indiana State Library

OUR MODERN LAW GIVER

Thomas R. Marshall Scrapbooks,
Indiana State Library

**It Needs It**

Evansville *Courier,* January 7,
1911

*COAX ME.*

Indianapolis *Sentinel,* May 10,
1904

adviser in drawing up the constitution, defended it in a series of newspaper
articles and in a pamphlet, *The Proposed Constitution of Indiana* (Indianapolis,
1911). In a paper presented to the American Political Science Association in
1912, Dunn argued that the main point of the constitution was to purify elections, which he considered of much greater importance than such matters as
direct primary, initiative, and referendum. Dunn, "The Proposed Legislative
Constitution of Indiana," American Political Science Association, *Proceedings,*
1912, in *American Political Science Review,* VI (1912), Supplement, pp. 43-52.

The "Marshall Constitution" outraged not only the conservatives who opposed any constitutional changes but also the advocates of temperance and woman suffrage, who were indignant over the omission of their own particular reforms. Nevertheless, the new instrument was quickly approved by both houses of the General Assembly and submitted to the people for ratification. In July, 1912, however, the judge of the Marion County Circuit Court granted two Republican opponents of the constitution an injunction preventing the referendum from taking place on the grounds that the legislature had acted unconstitutionally in failing to follow the ordinary amendment procedure. When the Indiana Supreme Court upheld this ruling by a three-to-two majority, Governor Marshall, though he thought it a "flagrant interference on the part of the judicial with the rights, privileges and duties of the legislative and executive branches of government," obeyed the judgment and withdrew the controversial constitution.[82]

The doughty Indiana Governor, who had gained a measure of national fame from his extraordinary bid to establish a new state constitution, was a favorite-son candidate and a serious contender for the Democratic presidential nomination in 1912. In March the state Democratic convention endorsed Marshall for the presidency, and named his former political rival, Samuel Moffett Ralston of Lebanon, as its gubernatorial candidate. At the Baltimore convention in June, Tom Taggart, the Hoosier Democratic boss who had no special affection for Marshall, held the Indiana delegation's thirty votes intact for the Governor until the twenty-eighth ballot, when he shifted twenty-nine votes to Woodrow Wilson, thus helping to break the long deadlock between Wilson and Champ Clark. After Wilson's final nomination on the forty-sixth ballot, the convention rewarded the Indiana Governor with the

[82] Ellingham v. Dye, 178 Ind. 336 (1912); Marshall, *Recollections,* p. 210. Governor Marshall appealed to the United States Supreme Court on a writ of error, but it refused to hear the case. Thomas, *Thomas Riley Marshall,* pp. 89-90.

vice-presidential place on the ticket, largely because of the shrewd bargaining and political tactics of the man he had blocked from the senatorial nomination two years before, Tom Taggart.[83] Democratic Senator John W. Kern of Indiana also played a significant role in the convention, taking part in the fight for the temporary chairmanship between Bryan and Parker and finally presiding over the resolutions committee which drew up the platform.[84]

The election of 1912 brought the deep division in the Indiana GOP between conservatives and progressives to a crisis. Since both former Senators Fairbanks and Beveridge were in temporary political retirement, there was no outstanding Republican leader in the state to take charge of the party organization. On December 12, 1911, Republican state chairman Edwin M. Lee signaled the start of a severe intra-party contest when he made a blunt statement to the press in Washington, D.C.: "Mr. Taft cannot carry Indiana. If he is the Republican nominee our fight is lost before a gun is fired."[85] Although Lee claimed to have based this conclusion on a sampling of the opinions of party workers throughout the state, he was repudiated by the state committee, which chose a conservative, Fred A. Sims, for its new chairman in February, 1912. Anti-Taft sentiment, however, continued to grow in Indiana. Senator Robert M. La Follette carried his campaign for the presidential nomination into the

---

[83] The Wilson-Marshall combination was apparently agreed upon at a secret conclave of Wilson's managers with Taggart and other political bosses during the adjournment of the convention for the weekend after the twenty-sixth ballot. Wilson's own choice for the vice-presidency was Senator Oscar W. Underwood of Alabama, who refused to be considered for the office. Wilson was also reported to have objected to Marshall at first on the grounds that he was "a very small calibre man." Thomas, *Thomas Riley Marshall,* pp. 123-124; Arthur S. Link, *Wilson. The Road to the White House* (Princeton, N.J., 1947), pp. 458-463.

[84] Kern also received a scattering of votes for the presidential nomination on several ballots taken at the convention. Bowers, *Life of John Worth Kern,* pp. 252-281.

[85] Carl Painter, "The Progressive Party in Indiana," *Indiana Magazine of History,* XVI (1920), 180.

state, but most Hoosier progressives preferred Theodore Roosevelt, who entered the race in February. On March 1, 1912, Senator Beveridge announced his adherence to Roosevelt and opened his campaign for the latter's nomination in Indianapolis twelve days later.[86]

The progressives carried on a spirited struggle to gain control of the district conventions, but the Taft forces, led by such men as James E. Watson, Harry S. New, James A. Hemenway, Addison C. Harris, and Merrill Moores managed to capture eight out of thirteen Congressional districts and a clear majority of convention delegates. At the nominating convention in Chicago in June, after the credentials committee accorded the contested seats to the conservatives, the thirty-man Indiana delegation split, twenty for Taft, ten for Roosevelt. Taft's floor leader was the ultraconservative former Hoosier Congressman James E. Watson, who helped to push through the President's renomination in a packed convention. Seven out of the ten progressives in the Indiana delegation attended the "rump" convention which met in Orchestra Hall afterwards to make Roosevelt the presidential nominee, but neither Beveridge nor any other prominent Hoosier figure took any part in these proceedings.[87]

In Indiana the former GOP state chairman, Edwin M. Lee, took the lead in organizing a new party to work for Roosevelt's election. District and county chairmen were chosen and delegates elected to attend the national Progressive convention called for Chicago in August. Beveridge, who had hesitated to throw in his lot with the new party at first, eventually accepted the state convention's nomination for governor and went to Chicago to deliver a fighting keynote address to the national delegates assembled there to begin their march to Armageddon with Theodore Roosevelt.[88]

[86] *Ibid.*, pp. 184-185, 191-192; Bowers, *Beveridge*, p. 417.

[87] Bowers, *Beveridge*, pp. 419-421; Painter, "The Progressive Party in Indiana," *Indiana Magazine of History*, XVI, 182-184, 192-201.

[88] Bowers, *Beveridge*, pp. 423-431.

Indiana Progressives were much like their fellow Progressives in other parts of the country.[89] They were lawyers, newspaper editors, clergymen, physicians, and professors, as well as ordinary politicians who had broken with the GOP for various reasons. Former Mugwumps Foulke and Swift joined the movement in Indiana, as did the playwright and humorist, George Ade. An historian of the Indiana Progressive party described it as mostly made up of "young professional and business men, educators and literary men," though he admitted that there were others "who might have been classified as disgruntled office seekers, radical reformers and agitators."[90] Another Hoosier historian had the Progressives chiefly in mind when he wrote that "from an educational standpoint the campaign of 1912 in Indiana was one of the best ever known." "Teachers, preachers, reformers, literary men, agitators of all kinds," he added, "threw themselves into the great revival. Some had political sense, others only enthusiasm, but it made little difference."[91] The Indianapolis *Star* and its sister papers in Terre Haute and Muncie, owned by Beveridge's good friend, traction magnate John C. Shaffer of Chicago, were the leading journals to espouse the Progressive cause, though smaller newspapers in Lafayette, Richmond, Anderson, and elsewhere also supported the new party. Two years later the Progressive Press Association claimed as many as one hundred weeklies and dailies in the state.[92]

[89] For an analysis of the make-up of the Progressive party, see Alfred D. Chandler, "The Origins of Progressive Leadership," in Morison (ed.), *The Letters of Theodore Roosevelt*, VIII, 1462-1465, and George E. Mowry, *The California Progressives* (Berkeley, Calif., 1951), pp. 86-104. A more recent study has shown that Old Guard leaders were remarkably like Progressives, who differed chiefly from the former in being younger and having less political experience. Norman Wilensky, *Conservatives in the Progressive Era. The Taft Republicans of 1912* (University of Florida Monographs, *Social Sciences, No. 25*, Gainesville, 1965), pp. 32-38.

[90] Painter, "The Progressive Party in Indiana," *Indiana Magazine of History*, XVI, 218.

[91] Esarey, *A History of Indiana*, II, 1062.

[92] Painter, "The Progressive Party in Indiana," *Indiana Magazine of History*, XVI, 257.

The Indiana Republican state convention met in Indianapolis on August 6 and endorsed a platform little different from that of the Progressive party, including planks calling for child labor laws, workmen's compensation, woman suffrage, good roads, and the calling of a constitutional convention. Ex-Governor Winfield T. Durbin was chosen to head the state ticket, though Harvey W. Wiley, the Agriculture Department chemist and pure-food crusader, had been invited to enter the contest by the Indiana Republican Editorial Association. "But the disturbed condition of the Republican party," Wiley wrote later in his autobiography, "prompted me to decline the invitation to become a candidate. I did not want to enter a hopeless political struggle."[93] Former Senator Charles W. Fairbanks did not take an active part in the Republican canvass. When Woodrow Wilson visited Indianapolis in October during his campaign tour, Fairbanks joined with the Democrats in welcoming him to Indiana. He rode with Wilson to the Fairgrounds for his address on conservation of our natural resources and also attended the dinner given in Wilson's honor.[94]

The split in Republican ranks virtually insured victory for the Democrats, both at state and national levels. Woodrow Wilson carried Indiana by a plurality of 120,000 over Roosevelt, who in turn won 10,000 more votes than President Taft. But Beveridge, the Progressive party's nominee for governor, while losing to the Democratic candidate, Samuel M. Ralston, proved to be a better vote getter than his chief, receiving about 4,000 more votes than Roosevelt while coming in ahead of ex-Governor Durbin, the Republican candidate. The Progressive presidential ticket won in Elkhart, La Grange, Lake, Randolph, Wabash, and Wayne counties, but the GOP was victorious in Steuben and Warren counties. Progressive candidates received enough support in the Congressional

---

[93] Harvey W. Wiley, *An Autobiography* (Indianapolis, 1930), p. 299. Wiley eventually shifted his support to the Democratic party and campaigned for Wilson in Indiana and elsewhere in 1912. *Ibid.,* p. 301.

[94] Indianapolis *Star,* October 4, 1912.

races to enable the Democracy to capture all thirteen seats for the first time in history. In the General Assembly all the new senators were Democrats and ninety-five out of one hundred representatives, while the GOP elected four and the Progressives one of the members of the lower house—John W. Judkins of Wayne County, the strongest center of Progressivism in the state.[95] In the 1912 election the Republican party in Indiana was about evenly divided between insurgents and regulars, the latter actually polling more votes at the local level because the Progressives chose not to put up candidates in all counties.[96]

Both the Socialists and Prohibitionists made significant gains in the election, the former polling approximately 37,-000 votes for their fourth-time presidential nominee, Eugene V. Debs, and only slightly less for their gubernatorial candidate, Stephen M. Reynolds, long-time Terre Haute friend and colleague of Debs. This was the high tide of Socialist strength in Indiana, which ranked eighth among the states in total number of votes cast for the Socialist presidential candidate in 1912. The year before the Socialist party had elected for the first time several local officials in nine small communities mostly located in the coal-mining region of the state and in 1912 won seats on the city council in Marion and Elwood.[97]

Indiana Progressives, encouraged by the election results of 1912, attempted to strengthen their party by presenting candidates for local office. In the municipal elections in 1913, for example, the Progressive party won the mayoralty races in five cities—Elkhart, Marion, North Vernon, Richmond, and Seymour—and helped the Democrats defeat the GOP in In-

95 Secretary of State, *Biennial Report,* 1912, pp. 92-95, 152-159.

96 Painter, "The Progressive Party in Indiana," *Indiana Magazine of History,* XVI, pp. 230-233. The total vote in Indiana in 1912 fell about 67,000 short of that cast in 1908, which may indicate that many Republicans who disliked their convention's choice of presidential nominee stayed at home on election day.

97 Cox, "The Socialist Party in Indiana since 1896," *Indiana Magazine of History,* XII, pp. 118-119.

dianapolis and elsewhere.[98] When voices were heard in the land proposing a merger of the Progressives with the regular Republican organization, Beveridge vigorously championed the permanence of the new party, which, he predicted, would survive its first defeat and increase its political strength greatly in the coming years, a prophecy which proved tragically false.[99]

In fact the mid-term election of 1914 marked virtually the last stand of the Progressive party in Indiana. Beveridge, by then deeply engrossed in researching and writing his biography of Chief Justice John Marshall, was persuaded to accept the party's nomination in the state's first direct election of a United States Senator. The Democrats renominated the old Greenbacker, Benjamin F. Shively, who ran under the banner of President Wilson and won by a 45,000-vote plurality over Republican Hugh Th. Miller. Beveridge ran a poor third, revealing the severe decline of the Progressives since the election of two years before. The Democratic party also retained control of the state legislature, though by a slightly decreased margin, and elected eleven of the thirteen Congressional representatives.[100] Much of the success of the Indiana GOP in reducing Progressive inroads in this election resulted from the efforts of Will H. Hays, a young Sullivan attorney who had been chosen state chairman in February, 1914. Hays brought enthusiasm and organizational innovation to the task of rebuilding the shattered Republican party, and in the next two years was able to reunite the bulk of the Progressives with the Old Guard.[101]

Governor Samuel M. Ralston, who had been previously known more as a member of the Taggart political machine

[98] Painter, "The Progressive Party in Indiana," *Indiana Magazine of History,* XVI, pp. 242-243.

[99] Beveridge, "The Progressive-Republican Merger," *Saturday Evening Post,* June 28, 1913.

[100] Secretary of State, *Biennial Report,* 1914, pp. 140-173, 212-214.

[101] Will H. Hays, *Memoirs* (Garden City, N.Y., 1955), pp. 89-100; Garland C. Routt, Will Hays. A Study in Political Leadership and Management (Unpublished Master's thesis, University of Chicago, 1937), pp. 62-77.

than as a reformer, urged the General Assembly in 1913 to approve a series of progressive measures left over from earlier administrations, including a state inheritance tax, a public utilities commission, workmen's compensation, and a broad primary election law. He also favored the calling of a state constitutional convention, one of the planks in both the Republican and Progressive party platforms but not in that of his own party. In recognition of the growing popular clamor for control of corporations, he reminded the Democratic majorities in the legislature that

the acquisition of riches by the special interests, through the perversion of the functions of government, tends to divide the people into classes and weakens their confidence in the government. The supremacy of the people over combinations of all kinds is the demand of the day and the political party now entrusted with power that does not meet this demand will be repudiated by the people at their first opportunity.[102]

The Sixty-eighth General Assembly not only passed legislation establishing a public utilities commission in place of the existing railroad commission, an inheritance tax, and similar reform measures, but persisted in the endeavor to change the state constitution. It adopted a set of twenty-two amendments named after their sponsor, Democratic Senator Evan B. Stotsenburg of New Albany, which incorporated most of the features of the Marshall Constitution, and submitted a proposal calling for a constitutional convention to a popular referendum.[103]

The movement for constitutional reform was halted once more, however, when the electorate rejected the proposed convention at the 1914 general election, and the next legislature refused to reapprove the Stotsenburg amendments.[104] On the other hand, the Sixty-ninth General Assembly which convened in January, 1915, had a prolific progressive legislative session, culminating in the final passage of an antilobby

---

102 Indiana *House Journal,* 1913, pp. 75-76.

103 *Laws of Indiana,* 1913, pp. 79-80, 167-214, 812-819; Indiana *House Journal,* 1913, pp. 2143-2152.

104 Kettleborough, *Constitution Making in Indiana,* II, 540-602.

law and setting up a system of workmen's compensation, state-wide primaries, and permanent registration of voters, as well as other long-sought reform measures.[105] The Ralston administration was also credited with planning the celebration of the centennial of Indiana's statehood. This project began badly, with the General Assembly in 1913 rejecting various proposals for observance of the centennial. Finally, provision was made in the appropriation bill for submitting to the voters in the regular fall election in 1914 the question of appropriating $2,000,000 for a centennial memorial building to house the State Library and similar agencies. The proposal was rejected by a vote of 466,700 to 97,718, along with the call for a constitutional convention. The chief argument urged against the measure was economy.[106] In 1915, at Governor Ralston's request, the General Assembly voted to appropriate the smaller sum of $25,000 and to create a nine-man centennial commission to promote the celebration of the state's hundredth anniversary.[107]

In March of the centennial year of 1916, Indiana conducted its first state-wide direct primary elections. Charles W. Fairbanks received 176,000 votes in the GOP presidential preferential primary and was loyally supported by the members of the state delegation to the Republican national convention

[105] *Laws of Indiana,* 1915, pp. 5-11, 359-391, 392-417, 530-546. Passage of a "blue sky law" aimed at the fraudulent issue of stock by corporations has sometimes been included among the accomplishments of the Ralston administration. See Dunn, *Indiana and Indianans,* II, 779. Actually Governor Ralston vetoed such a bill in 1913 because he disapproved of its wording, and the next legislature postponed action on it indefinitely. Not until 1920 was a similar law passed, this time by a Republican-dominated special session of the General Assembly. *Laws of Indiana,* special session, 1920, pp. 83-96; Indiana *Senate Journal,* 1915, pp. 54-58.

[106] *Laws of Indiana,* 1913, pp. 526-257; Secretary of State, *Biennial Report,* 1914, pp. 168-169. Jacob P. Dunn blamed the defeat of the proposal on the liquor lobby, which feared temperance provisions might be incorporated into a new constitution and fought both the constitutional convention and the memorial building on the ostensible grounds of extravagant cost. Dunn, *Indiana and Indianans,* II, 781.

[107] *Laws of Indiana,* 1915, pp. 455-457. For an account of the work of the commission, see below, Chapter XIII.

in Chicago. State Chairman Hays, Indianapolis attorney Joseph B. Kealing, and George B. Lockwood, editor of the Muncie *Press,* were the chief managers of the Fairbanks-for-president boom.[108] The Indianan received 74½ votes on the first ballot at Chicago in June as one of the "Allies," including Theodore E. Burton of Ohio, Elihu Root of New York, and John W. Weeks of Massachusetts, who tried to stop the nomination of the favorite, Charles Evans Hughes. When Fairbanks, along with the other candidates, withdrew on the third ballot in favor of Hughes, whom the convention then selected as its standard-bearer, he reluctantly accepted the vice-presidential nomination.[109] This election campaign was to be exceptional in having two Hoosier candidates seeking the vice-presidency, for the Democratic national convention renominated Thomas R. Marshall as Wilson's running mate a few days later.[110]

In the primary contests for the gubernatorial and senatorial nominations the Republicans chose James P. Goodrich of Winchester for the former, and former GOP national chairman Harry S. New defeated ex-Congressman James E. Watson in a bitter, disputed race for the latter. Named to oppose them in the Democratic primary were John A. M. Adair and John W. Kern, respectively. The death of Kern's colleague in the Senate, Benjamin F. Shively, shortly after the primary added another contest to the election. To fill the office until November, Governor Ralston appointed Democratic boss Thomas Taggart, whom the Democrats quickly

---

108 Lockwood, who had recently started publishing an ambitious political journal called the *National Republican* in Muncie, was perhaps the most determined backer of Fairbanks' presidential nomination. In a letter to the putative candidate in early 1916 he boldly announced, "One year from today I hope to witness your inauguration as President of the United States." Lockwood to Fairbanks, March 4, 1916, Fairbanks Papers, Lilly Library.

109 Fairbanks, for whom the vice-presidency held no glamor, especially since the death in 1913 of his wife Cornelia, a brilliant Washington hostess and former president of the Daughters of the American Revolution, honestly did not want the nomination and tried unsuccessfully to withdraw his name. Indianapolis *News,* June 10, 12, 1916.

110 Thomas, *Thomas Riley Marshall,* pp. 232-235.

named as their second senatorial choice. The GOP in turn offered the nomination to Watson as consolation for his recent primary defeat.[111]

Despite its declining fortunes, the Progressive party of Indiana made a final attempt to remain in the field. Former Republican Governor J. Frank Hanly won the Progressive primary nomination for the gubernatorial contest but eventually declined to run, choosing instead to become the National Prohibition party's candidate for the presidency! The nomination of Hanly showed how desperate was the plight of the Progressive party, for he agreed to run only on the understanding that the initiative, referendum, and recall should not be included in the state platform. This concession, however, resulted in the withdrawal from the senatorial race of William D. Foulke, who refused to run on a ticket which omitted these planks. Finally the Progressives named Thomas A. Daily, of Indianapolis, for governor and James B. Wilson, of Bloomington, and Clifford J. Jackman, of Huntington, for the Senate.[112]

The Indiana GOP under the efficient leadership of State Chairman Will H. Hays made a strenuous effort to bring the Progressives back into the Republican fold, even naming a few of their number to party posts. The defection of Theodore Roosevelt himself helped to turn the tide, and ardent Rooseveltians including Beveridge, Swift, and Foulke, as well as John C. Shaffer and his *Star* league of newspapers, soon followed the lead of the "Rough Rider" in declaring for Hughes for President. The Hoosier playwright George Ade expressed

[111] According to Will Hays, Watson was hurt by the primary vote and intended to fight it out in the state convention, which settled the matter by giving him the short-term senatorial nomination opened up by Shively's sudden death. Hays himself was proposed for the nomination but refused to consider it. Hays, *Memoirs,* p. 101.

[112] Painter, "The Progressive Party in Indiana," *Indiana Magazine of History,* XVI, 264-265, 277. Wilson and Jackman withdrew in August and were replaced by John Napier Dyer and John F. Clifford. *Ibid.,* XVI, 279.

the Progressive predicament in typically humorous fashion in a press interview in October:[113]

I marched with the Progressive party until it became a dwindling minority of bleeding martyrs and I would have continued to march if there had been a probability of our arriving anywhere. I liked my traveling companions and the scenery, but a man cannot continue a journey which offers no terminus. When a man has just one round of ammunition to shoot he can't afford to stand off on a hillside and shoot into the air. . . . This is no time for grieving over what might have been. The thing for every Progressive to do is to look pleased and vote for Hughes.

In September a Hughes Alliance was formed at Indianapolis to obtain the support of former Progressives who preferred not to rejoin the Republican party. Some Progressive candidates for office resigned, and in a few counties the whole ticket withdrew in favor of the Republicans.[114]

All three leading party platforms promised domestic reforms as well as preparedness in the face of the conflict raging in Europe. In addition, the Republicans stressed their protective tariff views while the Democrats put their faith in the accomplishments of the Wilson administration. The election returns sounded the death knell of the Progressive party, which polled less than 5,000 votes for any of its candidates, far below the Prohibitionists' 16,300 and the Socialists' 23,500. Eugene V. Debs, who had refused to run for the presidency a fifth time, was the Socialist candidate for Congress from his home district. He campaigned vigorously throughout the fifth district in a Model-T Ford, speaking mostly against the war. Despite the general reduction in the Socialist total for the state, he trebled the party's vote in Terre Haute, running ahead of the Democratic incumbent, but lost to both the Democrat and the victorious Republican in the final tabulation for the whole district.[115] Indiana's electoral

113 Indianapolis *Star,* October 21, 1916, quoted in Painter, "The Progressive Party in Indiana," *Indiana Magazine of History,* XVI, p. 281.

114 Painter, "The Progressive Party in Indiana," *Indiana Magazine of History,* XVI, 279-280.

115 The campaign is colorfully described in Ginger, *The Bending Cross,* pp. 334-337.

college vote went to the loser in a presidential contest for the first time since 1876, Hughes garnering 7,000 more votes than Wilson in the state. The GOP won the state offices by an even smaller plurality and captured both seats in the United States Senate. In addition, Republican candidates scored victories in nine out of thirteen Congressional races.[116]

Claude G. Bowers, private secretary and biographer of Senator John W. Kern, called the 1916 campaign "a cross between a comedy and a tragedy," and blamed the Democratic defeat upon poor morale and insufficient organization.[117] But several other important factors influenced the outcome. First, the return of large numbers of former Progressives to the Grand Old Party helped swell the Republican vote. Secondly, the outbreak of war in Europe complicated matters. Although both sides stressed "peace with honor," there is evidence that a considerable body of German-American voters deserted the Democratic party because of Wilson's firm stand in the face of Imperial Germany's violations of United States' neutrality on the seas.[118] In addition, charges of corruption in the city hall machines of Terre Haute and Indianapolis hurt the Democratic candidates, especially senatorial nominee Tom Taggart, who had been indicted for election fraud in 1915 along with Indianapolis Mayor Joseph E. Bell, even though charges were subsequently dismissed.[119]

[116] Secretary of State, *Biennial Report,* 1916, pp. 174-208. Because of holdovers in the senate the party line-up was Democrats twenty-five, Republicans twenty-four, Progressives one. In the lower house, however, the GOP had a sixty-four to thirty-six majority. *Ibid.,* pp. 238-240.

[117] Bowers, *Life of John Worth Kern,* p. 377. Bowers also claimed that wealthy Democrats refused to contribute to the campaign fund because they were out of sympathy with the policies of Wilson. In addition, most of the people in the party were poor, he argued. "In Indianapolis there were not among merchants in the shopping district half a dozen Democrats, and among the manufacturers an even smaller number." *Ibid.,* pp. 378-379.

[118] Cedric C. Cummins, *Indiana Public Opinion and the World War, 1914-1917 (Indiana Historical Collections,* XXVIII, Indianapolis, 1945), pp. 224-234. For the German-American attitude toward the war, see below, Chapter XV.

[119] New York *Times,* March 21, 1916; Indianapolis *News,* February 27, 1915; Indianapolis *Star,* October 20, 1916; Roll, *Indiana,* IV, 383-384.

The GOP, once more in control of the State House and the legislature, initiated its own program of constitutional and legislative reforms. In opening the Seventieth General Assembly in January, 1917, both retiring Governor Ralston and incoming Governor James P. Goodrich recommended the calling of a constitutional convention in order to draft an instrument more in accord with the current social and economic needs of the state; meanwhile, the latter also urged the adoption of a number of constitutional amendments.[120] Eighteen amendments were proposed, of which two, concerning woman suffrage and the terms and salaries of state officers, were adopted. The legislature also enacted a law partially enfranchising women and another one provided for state-wide prohibition, and attempted to call a constitutional convention without submitting the question to a popular referendum.[121] The Indiana Supreme Court, however, invalidated both the act calling for a constitutional convention and the one concerning woman suffrage.[122]

The United States' intervention in the First World War in April, 1917, rallied most Hoosiers to the support of the war-time policies of the administration of President Woodrow Wilson, but it did nothing to strengthen his party's minority position in the state. Wilson's personal plea for the election of Democrats to Congress in 1918 fell on deaf ears in Indiana, where the GOP proceeded to capture the whole Congressional delegation as well as win the lesser state offices and large majorities in both houses of the legislature.[123] Moreover, former Republican State Chairman Will Hays contributed to the party's stunning nationwide victory in the mid-term elections by his organizational activities in the post of GOP na-

---

120 Indiana *Senate Journal,* 1917, pp. 30-32, 62-65.

121 *Laws of Indiana,* 1917, pp. 5-12, 15-34, 73-74, 443-473, 704-705.

122 Bennett *v.* Jackson, 186 Ind. 533 (1917); Board of Election Commissioners of the City of Indianapolis *v.* Knight, 187 Ind. 108 (1917); Kettleborough, *Constitution Making in Indiana,* III, 43-108.

123 Indiana *Year Book,* 1918, pp. 20-56. The Republican plurality for the head of the ticket was 50,000.

tional chairman to which he had been elevated in February, 1918.[124]

§ §

The progressive era in Indiana ended in a flurry of attempts, almost completely unsuccessful, to revise the obsolescent state constitution. In the Seventy-first General Assembly in 1919 Governor Goodrich recommended that the two pending amendments be replaced by a new set of changes covering a broad range of political reforms, including such measures as a state income tax, woman suffrage, restriction of the ballot to citizens of the state, the item veto in appropriation bills, simplification of the amending procedure, the short ballot, and authorizing the enlistment of Negroes in the state militia.[125] The legislators thereupon adopted a series of sixteen amendments to the constitution embodying most of the Governor's requests, of which the next legislature approved thirteen. Yet only one of these, an amendment making United States citizenship a prerequisite for voting in Indiana, was actually ratified by the electorate in a special election in September, 1921.[126]

How progressive was Indiana in the progressive era? Saddled with a mid-nineteenth-century constitution which withstood change because of the difficulty of its amending procedure as well as the cautious attitude of both the electorate and the courts, the commonwealth certainly did not rank among the most progressive states of the Union. Indiana, moreover, rejected such radical innovations as the initiative, referendum, and recall, the state income tax, the short ballot, municipal home rule, and woman suffrage. An extreme view of the state's conservative posture was found in an eastern writer's unfriendly commentary in 1916:[127]

124 For Hays's own story of the successful 1918 campaign, see Hays, *Memoirs,* pp. 153-177.

125 Indiana *Senate Journal,* 1919, pp. 14-15.

126 *Laws of Indiana,* 1919, pp. 954-957; 1921, pp. 880-890; Kettleborough, *Constitution Making in Indiana,* III, 111-230.

127 Frederick M. Davenport, "The Pre-Nomination Campaign: The Light Breaking over Stand-Pat Indiana," *Outlook,* CXIII (May-August, 1916), 177.

Back in the East among the thoughtful, and in other more or less enlightened sections of the United States, dear old stand-pat Indiana has politically long been held in disesteem. And that is putting it mildly. To tell it as it is, Indiana has the reputation politically of being sodden, mediocre, deeply satisfied with things as they are provided they are bad enough. Some of its leading party managers, when they have not seemed to be unpatriotic and cunning, have certainly given the impression of being flat, insipid, and platitudinous. Indiana is the original lair of the stand-patter in the United States.

But this harsh assessment, if taken more than half seriously, was less than fair. As has been shown above, Indiana's record of reform legislation during the first two decades of the twentieth century was a large and significant one, which included voter registration, direct primaries, fiscal accountability of public officials, regulation of railroads and other public utilities, and protective labor laws. Indeed, Indiana's political mood was compounded of nearly equal parts of conservatism and cautious liberalism, neither dominant for long and each force acting as a check upon the other. It was this kind of political moderation which Governor Samuel M. Ralston described when he wrote to Democratic party leader Tom Taggart, "I think I am not in error in believing that the citizenship of Indiana has, in truth and in fact, always been conservatively progressive."[128]

Both major political parties contributed to the record of progressive legislation and executive leadership in the state, much of it in the guise of conservatism. For the GOP, Governor J. Frank Hanly was undoubtedly the most vigorous proponent of reform, though his main concern was for the prohibition of alcoholic beverages, a cause to which he allocated most of his energies after retiring from the State House.[129] Governors Thomas R. Marshall and Samuel M.

---

[128] Ralston to Taggart, February 14, 1914, Ralston Papers, Lilly Library.

[129] Hanly was much in demand as a temperance speaker and was an active member, and later president, of the Flying Squadron of America, an organization devoted to the extension of prohibition in the various states of the Union. In 1915 he founded two prohibition newspapers in Indianapolis and the next year was named the presidential candidate of the National Prohibition party, as mentioned above. He died in an auto-train accident on August

Ralston were old-fashioned, regular Democrats, who might have been conservatives at any other point in history but in the progressive era advocated moderate political reform in tune with the times. When removed from Indiana to the center of Wilsonian progressivism in Washington, Vice-President Marshall approved tariff reduction and banking regulation but instinctively recoiled from the more radical antitrust, child labor, and similar legislation proposed by the President, though as a loyal Democrat he avoided embarrassing the administration.[130] Not surprisingly, in view of its long preoccupation with the art and technique of politics, Indiana was perhaps best known during the progressive period for its political managers, notably the Democrats' Tom Taggart and the GOP's Will Hays, who built powerful state organizations and often wielded significant national power as the engineers of party victories.

Both parties were also divided between conservatives and liberals, the Democrats chiefly on the basis of anti- and pro-Bryan sentiment derived originally from the currency arguments of the nineties. But the Republican differences grew so bitter that the Progressives seceded from the party for four years. This rupture destroyed the political career of Albert J. Beveridge, the outstanding Republican national leader from Indiana of the time, who turned from politics to historical research and writing after encountering defeat at the polls as a Progressive.[131] Republicans who represented the state on the national political scene were chiefly ultraconservatives like

1, 1920, while on a speaking tour in Ohio. *Biographical Directory of the American Congress,* p. 1003.

[130] Thomas, *Thomas Riley Marshall,* pp. 142-144.

[131] Beveridge began work on his biography of John Marshall in 1913 after his defeat in the gubernatorial election of the preceding year. Ten years later, after another defeat at the polls, this time as the regular Republican candidate for Senator, he began the biography of Abraham Lincoln which remained unfinished at the time of Beveridge's death in April, 1927. Bowers, *Beveridge,* pp. 545-589.

Charles W. Fairbanks and James E. Watson, both of whom were leaders of the Old Guard in the United States Senate.[132]

The Indiana Democracy sent to Washington two moderates who were granted parts to play in the Wilsonian "New Freedom"—Senator John W. Kern and Vice-President Thomas R. Marshall. The latter, who had sponsored a modest program of progressive legislation as governor of Indiana, brought little more as a two-term vice-president to the Wilson administration than a rich sense of humor, the quality for which he has become most famous. "I soon ascertained," he wrote later, "that I was of no importance to the administration beyond the duty of being loyal to it and ready, at any time, to act as a sort of pinch hitter; that is, when everybody else on the team had failed, I was to be given a chance."[133] Even this, however, did not eventuate, for Marshall made no attempt to assume any of the duties of the presidency at the critical moments when Woodrow Wilson was incapacitated by severe illness in 1919.[134]

On the other hand, Senator Kern, who was a middle-of-the-road politician, a close friend, for example, of both Bryan and the conservative Alton B. Parker, became a sturdy, if unspectacular, advocate of progressive reform and social justice after his election to the United States Senate in 1910; he fought for the expulsion of Senator William Lorimer of Illinois for corrupt election practices and instigated an investi-

---

132 Although their careers overlapped, the younger Watson was in some ways Fairbanks' successor as Indiana's conservative Republican spokesman in Washington. Watson had completed one term in the House of Representatives in 1897, when Fairbanks entered the Senate, and returned there in 1899 and remained until 1909, when he was defeated for governor of Indiana. Fairbanks left the Senate in 1905 to assume the vice-presidency. After his defeat for another vice-presidential term in 1916, he returned to his law practice in Indianapolis, where he died in 1918. Watson entered the Senate in 1916, completing the term of the deceased Senator Shively, and was re-elected twice, serving until 1933. Defeated in the Democratic sweep of 1932, he retired to the practice of law in Washington, D.C., where he lived until his death in 1948. *Biographical Directory of the American Congress,* pp. 873, 1783.

133 Marshall, *Recollections,* p. 233.

134 Thomas, *Thomas Riley Marshall,* pp. 203-228.

gation of labor conditions in the coal fields of West Virginia. Chosen majority leader by his Democratic senatorial colleagues in 1913 after only two years in that body, he helped guide through Congress some of the key measures of the Wilson administration, including the Underwood Tariff, a credits law, the child labor law, the Seaman's Act, and the Kern-McGillicudy Workman's Compensation Act.[135]

In the progressive era Indiana, like most states in the Midwest, awoke to the need for political reform as a means of meeting some of the pressing social and economic problems of a twentieth-century commonwealth. The result was a substantial, but not radical, program of ameliorative legislation at home as well as the playing of a minor role in national progressive politics. The period ended as it had begun, with the GOP in political control of the state, but, for a time at least, Indiana seemed to have returned to its former political balance. After 1906 neither major party dominated the state for long, though the pendulum often swung farther between Republicans and Democrats than before. Viewed in another way, however, the progressive Democratic hegemony between 1909 and 1915 may be seen as merely an interlude in the long-range Republican dominance of the rapidly urbanizing, industrializing state, beginning in 1896 and enduring for more than a decade after 1920.

[135] Bowers, *Life of John Worth Kern,* pp. 226-251, 282-358. Senator Kern did not long survive his retirement from the Senate after his defeat in 1916 and died in July, 1917, in Asheville, North Carolina, where he had gone for rest and medical treatment. *Ibid.,* p. 469.

# CHAPTER IV

## THE EMERGENCE OF A SCIENTIFIC AGRICULTURE

IN THE TRANSFORMATION of Indiana into an industrial commonwealth in the last decades of the nineteenth and the first decades of the twentieth century, agriculture itself was transformed. While declining in relation to manufacturing, the agricultural sector of the economy advanced steadily in both output and total investment. Farm property values in Indiana, which increased comparatively slowly in the deflationary eighties and nineties, rose rapidly in the fifteen to twenty-year period after 1899 which, because of its general prosperity and high level of commodity prices, has been called the "golden age" of American, and, particularly, midwestern, agriculture.[1]

### VALUE OF FARM PROPERTY, 1880-1920[2]

| Year | All farm property | Land and building | Implements and machinery | Livestock |
|---|---|---|---|---|
| 1880 | $ 726,781,857 | $ 635,236,111 | $ 20,476,988 | $ 71,068,758 |
| 1890 | 869,322,787 | 754,789,110 | 21,172,255 | 93,361,422 |
| 1900 | 978,616,471 | 841,735,340 | 27,330,370 | 109,550,761 |
| 1910 | 1,809,135,238 | 1,594,275,596 | 40,999,541 | 173,860,101 |
| 1920 | 3,042,311,247 | 2,653,643,973 | 127,403,086 | 261,264,188 |

[1] Barnhart and Carmony, *Indiana,* II, 402-403; Harold U. Faulkner, *The Decline of Laissez Faire 1897-1917* (*The Economic History of the United States,* VII, New York, 1951), 315-321; Allan G. Bogue, *From Prairie to Corn Belt: Farming on the Illinois and Iowa Prairies in the Nineteenth Century* (Chicago, 1963), p. 287.

[2] United States Bureau of the Census, *Fourteenth Census* (1920), V, *Agriculture,* p. 52. Agricultural statistics are available for most of this period from three main sources, the Federal Census, the United States Department of Agriculture, and the Indiana State Bureau of Statistics, though discrepancies often occur among them. The author has generally relied on the first, with occasional resort to both of the latter to supply figures not found in the decennial sum-

Federal Census Bureau calculations also showed that the gross value of the state's farm products, which was estimated at $115,000,000 in 1879 and actually dipped slightly in 1889, almost doubled by 1899 and reached $341,000,000 in 1909 and $782,000,000 in 1919.[3] The rise in the value of farm property and farm products, moreover, was achieved without a major expansion of the area of cultivation. During this forty-year period total farm acreage remained fairly stable, though the amount of improved land increased somewhat. Between 1900 and 1910 Indiana dropped completely out of that class of states which were continuing to add to farm acreage, while the census year of 1920 was the first to show a decrease in improved land.

## LAND IN FARMS, 1880-1920[4]

| | Land in farms | | | Improved land | | |
|---|---|---|---|---|---|---|
| Year | Acres | Per cent of increase | Acres | Per cent of increase | Per cent of land in farms | Per cent of farmland improved |
| 1880 | 20,420,983 | .... | 13,933,738 | .... | 88.9 | 68.2 |
| 1890 | 20,362,516 | —0.3 | 15,107,482 | 8.4 | 88.7 | 74.2 |
| 1900 | 21,619,623 | 6.2 | 16,680,358 | 10.4 | 94.1 | 77.2 |
| 1910 | 21,299,823 | —1.5 | 16,931,252 | 1.5 | 92.3 | 79.5 |
| 1920 | 21,063,332 | —1.1 | 16,680,212 | —1.5 | 91.5 | 79.2 |

Some of the gains in improved land, especially in the earlier part of this period, came from the clearing of wooded tracts, which had gone on continuously since pioneer days. But much more resulted from the extensive drainage undertakings in the state. Indeed, the Federal Census of 1910 indicated that the draining of swamps and lakes had added over 102,400 acres in the previous decade to Indiana's total land area.[5] The largest zone of wetland lay in a group of counties

maries. The 1920 value figures here and elsewhere in this chapter should be discounted by the extraordinary inflation of the First World War period.

[3] United States Bureau of the Census, *Eleventh Census* (1890), *Compendium,* Pt. 3, p. 615; *Fourteenth Census* (1920), V, *Agriculture,* p. 18.

[4] *Ibid., Fourteenth Census* (1920), VI, *Agriculture,* Pt. 1, p. 325.

[5] *Ibid., Thirteenth Census* (1910), *Abstract, with Supplement for Indiana,* p. 632.

in the northwest corner of the state across which the mean-
dering Kankakee River flowed into Illinois. As early as 1882
Professor John L. Campbell of Wabash College completed a
drainage survey of the Kankakee basin commissioned by Governor Albert G. Porter, but the legislature took no further action except to appropriate funds in 1889 and 1891 to cut
rock blocking the channel at Momence, Illinois, near the state
border. For the rest the work was left to private enterprise.
Steam dredge boats were first used in Lake County in 1884,
and large-scale ditching operations were attempted in the
Kankakee area by the nineties.[6] After the first effective
legislation of 1889 for that purpose, scores of drainage associations and drainage districts were formed to reclaim
swamps and wetland in many parts of the state. By December, 1919, Indiana had the largest percentage of farms under
drainage in the nation, with 8,227.6 miles of tile drains, 17,-
470.7 miles of open ditches, and 165.8 miles of accessory
levees.[7]

The total number of farms in Indiana increased gradually
from 1880 until the turn of the century and then fell off regularly each decade. Average farm size fluctuated slightly in
inverse proportion to the number of farms but remained
fairly stable at approximately one hundred acres. The value
of farms and farmland rose appreciably in the first two decades and steeply in the last two decades of this period.

---

[6] John L. Campbell, *Report upon the Improvement of the Kankakee River
and the Drainage of the Marsh Lands in Indiana* (Indianapolis, 1882); *Laws of
Indiana,* 1889, pp. 291-295; 1891, p. 198; Charles G. Elliott, *A Report upon
the Drainage of Agricultural Lands in the Kankakee River Valley, Indiana*
(United States Department of Agriculture, Office of Experiment Stations, *Circular No. 80,* 1909), pp. 5-8; Timothy H. Ball, *Northwestern Indiana from 1800
to 1900* . . . (Crown Point, Ind., 1900), pp. 439-442.

[7] United States Bureau of the Census, *Fourteenth Census* (1920), VII,
*Irrigation and Drainage,* pp. 352, 464-466.

## NUMBER, SIZE, AND VALUE OF FARMS[8]

| Year | Total number of farms | Average acreage per farm | Average value per farm | Average value per acre |
|------|------|------|------|------|
| 1880 | 194,013 | 105.3 | $ 3,746 | $ 35.59 |
| 1890 | 198,167 | 102.8 | 4,387 | 42.69 |
| 1900 | 221,897 | 97.4 | 4,410 | 45.27 |
| 1910 | 215,485 | 98.8 | 8,396 | 84.94 |
| 1920 | 205,126 | 102.7 | 14,381 | 144.44 |

The decennial census reports showed the number of persons over ten years of age engaged in agriculture in the state virtually unchanged from 1880 to 1910 at 339,000-340,000 before dropping to 294,000 in 1920. On the other hand, the proportion of those engaged in agriculture to the total labor force decreased precipitously from 52.2 per cent in 1880 to 38.1 per cent in 1900 and 26.3 per cent in 1920.[9] A substantial majority of Hoosier farmers continued to own and cultivate their own land, though a separate class of landlords was clearly emerging. Since farm operation by hired managers was rare in Indiana, renters predominated on the lands of absentee owners. The proportion of tenant-operated farms made a considerable gain in four decades: 1880, 23.7 per cent; 1890, 25.4 per cent; 1900, 28.6 per cent; 1910, 30.0 per cent; 1920, 32.0 per cent.[10] Even this was slightly below the national average and significantly lower than other Corn Belt states like Illinois and Iowa. Tenancy in Indiana followed the general pattern of farm tenure in the Middle West in

[8] *Ibid., Fourteenth Census* (1920), VI, *Agriculture,* Pt. 1, p. 325.

[9] United States Bureau of the Census, *Tenth Census* (1880), *Compendium,* p. 1356; *Twelfth Census* (1900), *Special Reports, Occupations,* pp. 268-270; *Fourteenth Census* (1920), IV, *Population, Occupations,* pp. 48, 56-57. The figures for 1910 and 1920 are slightly too large because forest and lumber workers were included in the agricultural labor force. The proportion of those gainfully employed in agriculture in Indiana in 1920 is very close to the national average, though significantly higher than in neighboring Ohio and Illinois. The corrected figures for 1920 are found in Leon E. Truesdell, *Farm Population of the United States* . . . (United States Bureau of the Census, *Census Monographs,* VI, 1926), p. 123.

[10] United States Bureau of the Census, *Fourteenth Census* (1920), VI, *Agriculture,* Pt. 1, p. 326.

being adapted primarily to high-priced rather than low-priced land, and to the raising of hay, grain, and hogs. Twenty-one counties in the state reported over 40 per cent tenant-operated farms in 1920 and four of these—Benton, Jasper, Newton, and White—ran over 50 per cent.[11] A United States Department of Agriculture study of three townships in central Indiana in the summer of 1911 suggests that farm tenants there were making a fair return on capital invested. The average tenant, with an investment of only $1,758, received $755 for a year's work. Moreover, the investigators concluded that, while most tenants hoped to become owners as soon as possible, a man with limited capital should rent rather than attempt to purchase a farm.[12]

§ §

By the end of the nineteenth century Indiana agriculture had largely left behind the more primitive ways of the pioneer farmer. In an address before the State Board of Agriculture in 1892, James A. Mount, a successful Montgomery County farmer who was later elected to the governorship, described the changes in farm standards of living in highly euphoric terms at a time of considerable agrarian protest:[13]

The day of log-rollings, of raising the heavy log buildings has passed away. The wooden mouldboard plow, the reap hook and the flaile, are agricultural implements of the past. The sound of the loom, the hum of the wheel are seldom heard in the rural home. Sweet notes of music from the piano and organ may be heard instead of loom and wheel. If the spinning wheel is now found, it is in the parlor, a gilded relic of the past. Elegant farm homes are being erected, substantial stock barns constructed; everywhere evidence of luxury and comfort can be seen. The progressive farmers are constructing good gravel and macadamized roads. Good roads and good conveyances do much to overcome distances,

---

11 Benjamin H. Hibbard, "Tenancy in the North Central States," *Quarterly Journal of Economics*, XXV (1910-11), 714-725; Emanuel A. Goldenweiser and Leon E. Truesdell, *Farm Tenancy in the United States* . . . 1920 (United States Bureau of the Census, *Census Monographs*, IV, 1924), pp. 32-38, 223.

12 E. H. Thomas and H. M. Dixon, *A Farm-Management Survey of Three Representative Areas in Indiana, Illinois, and Iowa* (United States Department of Agriculture, *Bulletin No. 41*, 1914), p. 11.

13 Indiana State Board of Agriculture, *Annual Report*, 1892-1893, p. 568.

thereby bringing the farmer nearer markets and into closer proximity to the world. Improved machinery enables the farmer to do his work better and in less time, thereby increasing facilities for mental culture and social improvement.

In a somewhat more systematic fashion Professor William C. Latta, long-time head of agricultural extension work at Purdue University and historian of Indiana agriculture, divided the transition from primitive to modern farming into six categories of change:

1. From self-sufficing to commercial agriculture
2. From soil mining to soil renewal
3. From manpower to horse and mechanical power farming
4. From grain growing to mixed husbandry
5. From farming as a means of subsistence to agriculture as a business
6. From the cultivator and stockman to the citizen farmer

Some of these shifts were underway in Indiana by the time of the Civil War, but progress was slow and uneven for many decades. In reference to one of the most important changes of all, Latta argued that "not until about 1890 could it truthfully be said that the era of soil renewal and self-sustaining agriculture was fairly inaugurated in Indiana."[14] In general, most authorities are agreed that an "agricultural revolution" of some significance took place in America during the period 1880-1920, though special emphasis has often been put on the twenty years just preceding the First World War.[15]

At the outset of this period near-frontier farming conditions prevailed in many sections of Indiana. In its first official publication in 1879 the Department of Statistics and Geology noted that half of the state's soil was untilled and invited

[14] William C. Latta, *Outline History of Indiana Agriculture* (Lafayette, Ind., 1938), pp. 103, 107.

[15] Carl C. Taylor, *The Farmers' Movement, 1620-1920* (New York, 1953), p. 88. Other terms used to describe the changes in farming in the United States beginning around the turn of the century are the "new agriculture," and "agriculture comes of age." Faulkner, *The Decline of Laissez Faire*, pp. 315-341; Murray R. Benedict, *Farm Policies of the United States, 1790-1950: A Study of Their Origins and Development* (New York, 1953), pp. 112-137.

immigrant farmers to enter such neglected branches of agriculture as "dairying and cheese making, hop growing, gathering of clover and other seeds, and sheep husbandry." The report further stated that unimproved land could be purchased for as little as $10.00 to $20.00 per acre and improved farms for $20.00 to $60.00 per acre. "With the latter," the report optimistically stated, "a practical farmer, who can pay one fourth of the purchase money down, may, with economy and management, make the deferred payments from the profits of the farm within five years." For the best chance of success, however, a farmer was advised to have available for investment a capital of from $1,500.00 to $3,000.00.[16]

The annual reports of the county and district fair associations to the State Board of Agriculture in the early eighties painted a revealing picture of the gradually changing face of Indiana farming. Farm animals were still permitted to run at large and commonly grazed along the highways, though farmers were beginning to fence livestock in rather than out. In some areas Osage hedge and barbed wire were taking the place of the old-fashioned rail or "worm" fence, which one correspondent predicted would soon go the way of the "old oaken bucket." Although roads were generally described as in a "desperate condition," a "wonderful improvement" in farm homes and other buildings was frequently reported. From Bartholomew County in 1884 came the report that "on nearly every road in the county may be seen fine large dwelling houses, in contrast with the little old log or frame houses standing near. Also, more convenient and capacious barns are taking the place of the old ones." The secretary of another association noted with great satisfaction that both "children and stock are better housed than they were in ye ancient days."[17]

Improved tillage and care of the soil were also reported in many places. "The most approved kinds of implements are

16 Indiana Department of Statistics and Geology, *Annual Report*, 1879, pp. 11-12. The same statement was repeated the following year. *Ibid.*, 1880, p. 14.

17 Indiana State Board of Agriculture, *Annual Report*, 1882, pp. 249-250, 255, 267-269, 272, 281; 1884, p. 250.

in active, constant demand," it was reported in Putnam County in 1882. The old-fashioned breaking plow, the double shovel plow, oftener called "double trouble" by the boys, on account of its jiggling propensities, and the "A" harrow, that was several times more efficacious than Hoosier liniment to draw blisters on horses' shoulders, now lie, forgiven and forgotten, among the weeds of the old barnyard, and the sulky plow, the walking cultivator, and the disc harrow have taken their place. Farmers were laying tile for underdrainage and co-operating in the construction of ditches to carry off surplus water from wetlands. While commercial fertilizers were still relatively little known, stable manure was much utilized, clover was being grown and plowed under, and some form of crop rotation was coming into use in many counties in a dawning recognition of the need for soil replenishment after decades of exploitive soil-mining practices.[18]

The full realization of the promise of scientific treatment of the soil had to wait for several more decades of experimentation and agricultural education, but Hoosier farmers began to enjoy the benefits of a significant increase in farm mechanization around 1880. In the eighties and nineties a multiplicity of new or improved farm machines were introduced into the state, including the riding gang plow, disk plow, manure spreader, twine binder, fertilizer drill, side-delivery hay rake, and the two-row corn cultivator. Two machines particularly important for Indiana agriculture, the corn binder and corn picker, were added in the first two decades of the twentieth century.[19] Men and animals continued

[18] Ibid., 1881, pp. 265-267, 277-278; 1882, pp. 275, 286; 1884, p. 257. The State Board of Agriculture estimated in 1893 that Hoosier farmers used only 8,000 tons of commercial fertilizer in 1883 as compared with 35,000 tons in 1892. Ibid., 1892-1893, p. 248.

[19] For the approximate date of the introduction of these machines with illustrations of some, see Latta, Outline History of Indiana Agriculture, pp. 87, 117, 119, 129, 133, 142, 144, 146, 148, 150. In a table prepared from county assessors' reports in 1880 mostly simpler farm machines were listed, such as 8,815 sulky plows as compared with 46,733 bar-shear plows, 128,834 common breaking plows, and 144,303 double shovel plows; only 3,013 self-binding reapers were reported in contrast to 14,678 drop or rake reapers. Indiana Department of Statistics and Geology, Annual Report, 1880, p. 8.

to furnish the main sources of power on the farm throughout this period, though windmills were often employed for the pumping of water and stationary steam engines were replacing horse power in the threshing of grain by the early eighties.[20] Not until near the close of this period did the gasoline motor serve to lighten the tasks of the farmer, and then it was used chiefly for his and his family's transportation rather than for actual farm work. In 1920, for example, the Federal Bureau of the Census reported that while 46.4 per cent of Indiana farms boasted automobiles, only 4.3 per cent were equipped with tractors and 1.7 per cent with trucks.[21]

Moreover, good roads, improved conveyances, and the telephone combined to ameliorate farm conditions, particularly the burden of rural isolation. With the increasing productivity and prosperity of the years between 1900 and 1920, many Hoosier farmers also began to enjoy some of the benefits of the rising American standard of living. In the latter year not only did 66.4 per cent of Indiana farms report telephones but 11.4 per cent had water piped into the house and 10.0 per cent were lighted by either gas or electricity.[22] The Indiana Legislative Reference Bureau in its estimates for the same year added that one fourth of all farm homes possessed washing machines and one thirteenth vacuum cleaners.[23]

§ § §

Scientific education and technology played a major role in the agricultural revolution of this period. First, however, the traditional prejudice against "book farming" which persisted throughout most of the nineteenth century had to be over-

[20] According to the same table cited above, there were 2,178 "horse-power threshers" and 2,519 "steam threshers" in the state in 1880. *Ibid.* Steam power was successfully used in cutting a crop of wheat in Hendricks County in 1883 according to one advocate of mechanization. Charles E. Merrifield, "The Importance of Mechanical Appliances to Successful Farming," Indiana State Board of Agriculture, *Annual Report,* 1883, pp. 226-228.

[21] United States Bureau of the Census, *Fourteenth Census* (1920), V, *Agriculture,* p. 514.

[22] *Ibid.*

[23] Indiana *Year Book,* 1920, pp. 916-918.

come in order that new ideas of soil cultivation and renewal, seed selection, pest protection, and marketing could be successfully communicated to farmers. Undoubtedly the general educational awakening of the seventies and eighties helped greatly in this. Compulsory attendance, school consolidation, and the eventual introduction of vocational—agricultural—education in the public schools all contributed to the raising of standards of information and understanding in the rural community. Rural free delivery, made feasible by better roads and introduced in Indiana as early as October, 1896, had a particularly important part in conveying news of the outside world to the farmer.[24]

A leading retailer of the knowledge of new farming techniques was the agricultural press, which proliferated in Indiana in this period. In 1909 the *Cyclopedia of American Agriculture* listed fifteen farm periodicals published in the state, nearly all of which were founded after 1880.[25] One of the oldest and most influential of these was the *Indiana Farmer,* a weekly established in Indiana in 1866 which probably enjoyed its largest success under the vigorous editorship of James G. Kingsbury in the eighties and nineties. Second in importance was the *Farmers' Guide,* which Ben F. Biliter of Huntington founded in 1888 "on a shoestring" but soon reached a national audience. In 1917 these two journals were merged under the latter title, creating the farm paper with the largest circulation in Indiana.[26] Other significant farm periodicals established in the state in this period were

[24] The first rural free delivery route in Indiana was established on October 15, 1896, with Hope, Bartholomew County, as its distribution center. By June, 1900, Indiana had 270 routes, more than any other single state. United States Department of Agriculture, *Yearbook,* 1900, pp. 514-515. See also Wayne E. Fuller, *RFD: The Changing Form of Rural America* (Bloomington, Ind., 1964).

[25] Liberty H. Bailey (ed.), *Cyclopedia of American Agriculture* (4 volumes, New York, 1907-9), IV, 81-87. See also a *List of the Agricultural Periodicals of the United States and Canada Published . . . July 1810 to July 1910,* compiled by Stephen C. Stuntz (United States Department of Agriculture, *Miscellaneous Publications 398,* 1941).

[26] Frank L. Mott, *A History of American Magazines* . . . (4 volumes, New York and Cambridge, Mass., 1930-57), I, 444; IV, 340-341.

the *Agricultural Epitomist* (1882) of Indianapolis and Spencer, later called *Farm Life*; Austin H. Brown's *Farm, Herd and Home* (1881), Solon L. Goode's *American Farmer, Live Stock and Poultry Raiser* (1897), and James A. Everitt's *Up-to-Date Farming* (1898) of Indianapolis; and *Progressive Country Life* (1902), published by F. L. and C. L. Sherrill in Rockville. In addition to these general agricultural papers, a number of journals devoted to particular lines of farming were published in Indiana.[27]

Among educational institutions, Purdue University had an outstanding share in the development of a modern, scientific agriculture in Indiana. As soon as the School of Agriculture was opened in 1879—five years after the establishment of the university with the aid of a Federal land grant—Professor Charles L. Ingersoll laid out an experimental farm on a small campus tract and by December, 1884, began issuing agricultural bulletins to Hoosier farmers. Upon Ingersoll's departure from the state in 1882, William C. Latta took up and expanded the experimental work.[28] Another early advo-

[27] Examples of more specialized, smaller-circulation farm journals published in Indiana during this period were the following: the *Western Horseman* (1878), *Swine Breeders' Journal* (1882), *Jersey Bulletin* (1883), and *Live Stock Journal* (1889) of Indianapolis; *Bee-Keepers' Guide* (1877) of Kendallville, and *Inland Poultry Journal* (1896) of Indianapolis and Greenfield.

[28] Indiana State Board of Agriculture, *Annual Report*, 1896-1897, p. 358; Latta, *Outline History of Indiana Agriculture*, pp. 319-320; Alfred C. True and V. A. Clark, *The Agricultural Experiment Stations in the United States* (United States Department of Agriculture, Office of Experiment Stations, *Bulletin No. 80*, 1900), p. 209. Charles Lee Ingersoll was a native of New York who graduated from Michigan Agricultural College (now Michigan State University) and taught there briefly before going to Purdue. After leaving Purdue in 1882 he became the president of Colorado Agricultural College and was director of the Colorado Experiment Station from 1888 to 1891. His successor at Purdue, William Carroll Latta, was born on a farm in La Porte County, Indiana, and received his bachelor's and master's degree from Michigan Agricultural College before joining the Purdue faculty in 1882. Latta's tenure at Purdue as professor of agriculture, farm superintendent, and leader of farmers' institutes covered a span of forty-one years. After his retirement from active service in 1923 he remained as a consultant in the department of agricultural extension in order to write a history of Indiana farming. He died in Lafayette in 1935. Alfred C. True, *A History of Agricultural Experimentation and Research in*

cate of scientific experimentation in agriculture in Indiana was Harvey W. Wiley, professor of chemistry at Purdue University who was given the additional responsibility of state chemist in 1881, when the General Assembly voted to require laboratory analysis of all commercial fertilizers sold in the state.[29] In 1887 the Hatch Act made Federal funds available for establishment of an agricultural experiment station at Purdue, but the state legislature regularly refused to appropriate money for its support until 1905, when an annual appropriation of $25,000 was authorized. Two years later, however, making amends for its earlier neglect of the institution, the legislature voted $100,000 for a new building and in 1909 increased the station's annual appropriation from $25,000 to $75,000.[30] With adequate, if belated, support of this kind, the Purdue Experiment Station, like its counterparts in other states of the Union, was able to conduct extensive agricultural research, publish regular bulletins and other pamphlets, co-operate closely with farmers' associations and the Federal government in various types of educational projects, and handle the inspection and control of fertilizers, feed, vaccines, and serums, and perform other tasks which the state legislature assigned it from time to time.[31]

Since Purdue University's School of Agriculture attracted few students in its earliest years, and most Hoosiers had little direct contact with the work being done there in scientific farming, any effective effort to educate farmers in new and improved techniques had to be carried out at the local level.

the United States, 1607-1925 (United States Department of Agriculture, Miscellaneous Publication No. 251, 1937), pp. 108-109; Latta, Outline History of Indiana Agriculture, pp. 5-7.

[29] Laws of Indiana, 1881, pp. 511-513. In January, 1880, Professor Wiley gave a long, impassioned address before the State Board of Agriculture arguing for the immediate establishment of a full-fledged experiment station in the state. Indiana State Board of Agriculture, Annual Report, 1879, pp. 208-239. In 1883 Wiley left Purdue to become chief chemist in the United States Department of Agriculture in Washington, D.C.

[30] Laws of Indiana, 1905, pp. 142-143; 1907, p. 664; 1909, pp. 403-404.

[31] Ibid., 1913, pp. 336, 922-923; 1917, pp. 309-313.

In 1882 the State Board of Agriculture decided to sponsor a series of farmers' institutes in imitation of a movement inaugurated earlier in the neighboring states of Michigan, Ohio, and Illinois. The first such institutes were held in Columbus and Crawfordsville in March, 1882, when local farmers were invited to hear addresses on various agricultural problems by Professors Ingersoll and Wiley of Purdue and prominent members of the State Board as well as Governor Porter and other officials.[32] The idea did not gain immediate acceptance, however, and the few meetings held during the next several years were mostly pronounced failures by their organizers on account of meager attendance. Finally in 1888 a number of successful institutes were held in scattered counties under the joint auspices of the State Board and local farmers' associations.[33] The next year the General Assembly provided an annual appropriation of $5,000 for the organization of farmers' institutes and placed the responsibility for them in the hands of the Purdue agricultural faculty.[34] Under the direction of William C. Latta, who had replaced Ingersoll as professor of agriculture at Purdue, the program was inaugurated with fifty institutes in the winter of 1889-1890. By 1894 at least one institute was held annually in each of the state's ninety-two counties.[35] A selection of the titles of the papers read at a "round-up" institute in 1890 may serve to indicate the nature and range of subject matter presented: "Some Facts about Sheep Husbandry," "Growing Pigs for the General Market," "How to Increase the Profits of Farming," "The Ideal Horse of the Farmer," "Injurious Insects and How to Destroy Them," "What Can Co-operative Efforts Do

---

[32] The proposal grew out of the discussion of Governor Porter's speech before the State Board of Agriculture in January, 1882, in which he argued for greater dissemination of scientific knowledge among farmers. Indiana State Board of Agriculture, *Annual Report*, 1881, pp. 81-92, 445-520.

[33] *Ibid.*, 1888, p. 182.

[34] *Laws of Indiana*, 1889, pp. 273-274. The annual appropriation was increased to $10,000 in 1901. *Ibid.*, 1901, pp. 92-93.

[35] Indiana State Board of Agriculture, *Annual Report*, 1903-1904, p. 658.

J. Frank Hanly
*by Wayman Adams*

Thomas R. Marshall
*by Wayman Adams*

Samuel M. Ralston
*by Wayman Adams*

James P. Goodrich
*by Wayman Adams*

Coal Mining in Greene County

Limestone Quarrying in Lawrence County

for the Farmer," "The Privileges and Possibilities of Farm Life," and "Industrial Education."[36]

Farm wives often took an active part in the institutes, reading papers and discussing questions relating to food preparation, housekeeping, and literary culture. In 1890 the Indiana Farmers' Reading Circle grew out of the institute work and supplemented it by encouraging systematic study of both agricultural and general literature.[37] A common topic of discussion among farmers everywhere in this period was the difficulty of keeping the younger generation on the farm in the face of the growing attraction of city life and work.[38] The boys' and girls' clubs which appeared in Indiana and other states shortly after the turn of the century were in part attempts to meet this challenge. In 1904 the first boys' club in the state was organized in Noblesville by John F. Haines, superintendent of schools in Hamilton County, who distributed seed to a group of young men in the spring and awarded prizes in the fall to those growing the best corn.[39] Township schools, farmers' organizations, and local merchants often co-operated in sponsoring similar corn-growing and other contests for young people in their communities. In 1907 an act of the General Assembly authorized the expenditure of public funds by county farmers' institute associations for such contests.[40] By 1908 there were five thousand members of boys' corn clubs in thirty-five counties, and in the succeeding years sewing, canning, and poultry clubs for girls were also formed. Moreover, Indiana followed the lead of Iowa in arranging with the United States Department of Agriculture a

[36] *Ibid.,* 1889-1890, pp. 245-335.

[37] *Ibid.,* 1892-1893, pp. 516-518.

[38] Titles of some of the papers read before farmers' institutes in 1893 included "Why Educate the Boy Who Expects to Farm," "How I Kept My Boys on the Farm," and "Can a Young Man Save Money on the Farm." *Ibid.,* pp. 518-527.

[39] Similar clubs had been organized elsewhere in the country, but Superintendent Haines claimed that he conceived of the idea independently. *Ibid.,* 1905-1906, pp. 286-289.

[40] *Laws of Indiana,* 1907, pp. 183-186.

joint Federal-state project for the promotion of rural young people's clubs in September, 1912, when Zora Mayo Smith, a high school agricultural teacher and principal, was appointed state club leader.[41]

In the meantime Purdue University introduced new approaches to agricultural extension work for adult farmers. The first Purdue "agricultural train" was instituted in 1905, making eighty-two station stops along the Lake Erie and Western Railroad with a staff of instructors who talked with farmers and demonstrated scientific methods. Two years later the first Purdue "short course" was given at Rushville for farmers who could not or would not take time off for similar educational programs on the University's home grounds in Lafayette.[42]

The next step in bringing agricultural education directly to the farm community was the development of the county agent network, wherein specially trained resident technicians were employed as full-time advisers to local farmers, a system which originated in the farm demonstration work of Professor Seaman Knapp in Texas and in similar programs in Broome County, New York.[43] Leonard B. Clore, a highly successful corn grower in Johnson County, became the first county agent in Indiana in October, 1912, when he was employed by the La Porte County Crop and Soil Improvement Association. A few months later, farmers and businessmen of Montgomery, Parke, and St. Joseph counties also organized county-agent programs in co-operation with Purdue University and the United States Department of Agriculture. These ventures proved so popular that the General Assembly incorporated in the Vocational Education Act of 1913 a provi-

41 *Indiana—A Pioneer State in Agricultural Extension and 4-H Club Work* (Purdue University, Department of Agricultural Extension, *Special Bulletin,* 1944), pp. 8-11.

42 Dave O. Thompson, *A History: Fifty Years of Cooperative Extension Service in Indiana* (Lafayette, Ind., 1962), pp. 39-47.

43 Alfred C. True, *A History of Agricultural Extension Work in the United States 1785-1923* (United States Department of Agriculture, *Miscellaneous Publication No. 15,* 1928), pp. 58-64, 73-74.

sion for the support of county-agent work from state and local tax funds and placed the whole program under the direction of Purdue University. Within a single year twenty-three additional counties and one township were employing agents in accordance with this legislation.[44]

The language of the law emphasized the educational nature and all-embracing duties of the county agent, who was instructed to

co-operate with farmers' institutes, farmers' clubs and other organizations, conduct practical demonstrations, boys' and girls' clubs and contest work and other movements for the advancement of agriculture and country life and to give advice to farmers on practical farm problems and aid the county superintendents of schools and the teachers in giving practical education in agriculture and domestic science.[45]

To carry out this broad mandate, the agents, who were usually recent agricultural college graduates, spent most of their time explaining new scientific methods of farming and demonstrating the advantages of such practices as smut control, seed-corn testing, liming and fertilizing fields, prevention of hog cholera and other diseases, and co-operative marketing. After 1914, when the Smith-Lever Act allocated Federal grants for the work, the county-agent system expanded rapidly and became a permanent part of the state's agricultural extension program, headed by Professor George I. Christie of the Purdue Experiment Station. Unlike most other states, however, Indiana kept its farm demonstration work, which was partially financed according to law by local taxation, closely integrated with the county public school sys-

[44] Indiana Department of Statistics, *Biennial Report,* 1913-1914, pp. 665-666; Thompson, *A History,* pp. 23-24. In 1914 Indiana had more counties in which agricultural agents had been employed up to that time than any other northern or western state. True, *A History of Agricultural Extension Work,* p. 100. Leonard B. Clore, the "corn king of Johnson County," was the originator of Johnson County White Dent, a recognized improved variety of seed in Indiana and adjoining states at this time. He was also one of the authors of the Vocational Education Act of 1913, which established state support of the county-agent system.

[45] *Laws of Indiana,* 1913, p. 44.

tem for many years.[46] The entry of the United States into the First World War stimulated the growth of agricultural extension, and in 1918 eighty-three out of the ninety-two Indiana counties were employing male agents, while twenty-two had woman home demonstration leaders.[47]

§ § § §

Despite growing diversification, Indiana maintained primarily a grain and livestock pattern of agriculture. In the four decades after 1880 cereals and hay held their place as the main field crops grown in the state. Significant changes, however, took place in the amount of farmland devoted to the various types of cereal and forage crops, as the table below indicates:

## ACREAGE OF IMPORTANT FIELD CROPS[48]

| Year | Corn | Wheat | Oats | Rye | Barley | Hay and Forage |
|------|------|-------|------|-----|--------|----------------|
| 1879 | 3,678,420 | 2,619,695 | 623,531 | 25,400 | 16,399 | 1,274,364 |
| 1889 | 3,586,190 | 2,570,017 | 1,102,479 | 62,890 | 10,280 | 2,330,504 |
| 1899 | 4,498,249 | 2,895,293 | 1,017,385 | 43,562 | 9,533 | 2,442,414 |
| 1909 | 4,901,054 | 2,082,835 | 1,667,818 | 83,440 | 10,188 | 2,301,069 |
| 1919 | 4,457,400 | 2,798,657 | 1,718,748 | 350,908 | 74,239 | 3,303,056 |

[46] West Virginia and Georgia were the only other states following the example of Indiana in relating the county agents so closely to the county boards of education. Gladys L. Baker, *The County Agent . . .* (University of Chicago, *Studies in Public Administration,* XI, 1939), p. 10.

[47] *Statistics of Cooperative Extension Work 1920-21* (United States Department of Agriculture, *Circular 140,* 1920), p. 15. In 1918 Indiana also boasted as many as 204 pig clubs and 59 poultry clubs with a total enrollment of both boys and girls of 3,281. O. H. Benson and Gertrude Warren, *Organization and Results of Boys' and Girls' Club Work (Northern and Western States) 1918* (United States Department of Agriculture, *Circular 66,* 1920), pp. 25-27. Home economics was introduced into Indiana by Mrs. Virginia Claypool Meredith, widow of a successful cattleman, who joined the staff of the farmers' institutes in 1889 as a speaker on subjects of interest to women. She continued in this work for twenty-five years except for six years spent at the University of Minnesota School of Agriculture as an instructor in homemaking. In 1913 she helped form the Indiana Home Economics Association, becoming its first president, and in 1921 she was appointed to the Board of Trustees of Purdue University. H. S. K. Bartholomew, "Virginia C. Meredith," *Indiana Magazine of History,* XXXV (1939), 49-57.

[48] United States Bureau of the Census, *Fourteenth Census* (1920), VI, *Agriculture,* Pt. 1, pp. 464-466.

Of the three chief grain crops—corn, wheat, and oats—wheat alone failed to expand its area of cultivation except during the First World War, when heightened demand both at home and abroad stimulated its output at the expense of corn.[49] This table of the estimated production of these crops at ten-year intervals shows clearly the long-range decline of wheat in relation to corn and oats:

PRODUCTION OF CORN, OATS, AND WHEAT,
1879-1919[50]
(in bushels)

| Year | Corn | Wheat | Oats |
|------|------|-------|------|
| 1879 | 115,482,300 | 47,284,853 | 15,599,518 |
| 1889 | 108,843,094 | 37,318,798 | 31,491,661 |
| 1899 | 178,967,070 | 34,986,280 | 34,565,070 |
| 1909 | 195,496,433 | 33,935,972 | 50,607,913 |
| 1919 | 158,603,938 | 45,207,862 | 52,529,723 |

One factor in this decline was the general westward shift of grain growing into the Great Plains at this time, as illustrated by the fact that in 1879 Indiana ranked second among all the states in wheat production but fell to eighth place in 1909 and 1919.[51] Moreover, in the kind of mixed husbandry that was coming to prevail on Hoosier farms, wheat, a cash crop which must be sold at highly fluctuating world market prices, tended to give way to grain and fodder crops which could be fed profitably to livestock. Yet Indiana continued to be an important wheat-growing state, the value of its annual production surpassing $33,900,000 in 1909 and almost reaching $100,000,000 in 1919,[52] second only to the value of the corn crop. Virtually all the wheat produced in Indiana was a

[49] Wheat tended to displace corn acreage to some extent throughout the Corn Belt during World War I. A. B. Genung, "Agriculture in the World War Period," United States Department of Agriculture, *Yearbook*, 1940, pp. 280-284.

[50] United States Bureau of the Census, *Fourteenth Census* (1920), V, *Agriculture*, pp. 739, 745, 752.

[51] *Ibid., Tenth Census* (1880), III, *Agriculture*, p. 440; *Fourteenth Census*, V, *Agriculture*, p. 741. North Dakota led in both acreage and production in 1909 and Kansas in 1919.

[52] *Ibid., Fourteenth Census* (1920), V, *Agriculture*, p. 744.

soft red winter variety, which was claimed to make a superior flour. It was grown in nearly every county of the state;
its yield, while fluctuating widely from year to year, gradually rising from an average of 13.1 bushels per acre for the
years from 1880 to 1889 to 15.4 bushels for the years from
1911 to 1920, was considerably higher than the yields in
Great Plains wheat states such as North Dakota and
Kansas.[53]

The increase in the planting of corn, oats, and hay was
concomitant with the steady development of livestock feeding and dairy farming. In 1919, 79.6 per cent of the corn, 76.5
per cent of the hay, and 69.9 per cent of the oats grown in
the state were consumed on the farm rather than shipped to
market. Corn was a favorite crop throughout Indiana, but it
was most heavily concentrated in a central band of counties
edging northward in the western section of the state, the
fertile Tipton Till Plain.[54]

Most corn in Indiana was husked from standing stalks, a
labor-saving and less expensive method than cutting and
shocking. Hogs were often grazed in cornfields, too, a practice called "hogging-off." But some corn was also cut for
fodder and ensilage, along with other green grains and hay.
The growth of livestock and dairy farming created a belated
demand for silage for winter feeding. In 1892 it was reported
that the state contained not over fifty silos, the longest recorded use of any one of which was seven years.[55] The construction of silos, at first rectangular in shape before shifting

53 United States Department of Agriculture, *Report of the Secretary,* 1890,
p. 335; *Yearbook,* 1920, p. 555; C. R. Ball *et al.,* "Wheat Production and Marketing," *Yearbook,* 1921, pp. 93-96, 123, 125; Frances Doan Streightoff and
Frank Hatch Streightoff, *Indiana. A Social and Economic Survey* (Indianapolis,
1916), pp. 42-43.

54 The principal corn-producing counties were Benton, Boone, Clinton,
Montgomery, Randolph, Shelby, and Tippecanoe. The Tipton Till Plain, according to Visher, had the best land in the state, with the highest average
value per acre, in 1920. Stephen S. Visher, *Economic Geography of Indiana*
(New York, 1923), pp. 118-125.

55 Charles S. Plumb, *The Silo and Silage in Indiana* (Purdue University
Agricultural Experiment Station, *Bulletin No. 40,* 1892), p. 76.

to what eventually became the almost universal cylindrical design, advanced most rapidly in the second decade of the twentieth century. The total number rose from less than ten thousand in 1913 to over twenty-five thousand in 1916, or a ratio of one silo to every 8.6 farms in the state.[56] In 1919 Indiana produced 1,616,509 tons of silage of all kinds, as well as 1,222,679 tons of dry-corn fodder. In addition, 124,607 acres of corn and hay were grazed or hogged off in the same year, according to the Federal Bureau of the Census, which reported this kind of statistic for the first time in 1920.[57]

As befits a crop so crucial to the state's economy, Hoosier farmers paid special attention to the improvement of corn culture. Purdue University and the Indiana Corn Growers' Association, founded in 1900 with an annual appropriation from the state legislature, co-operated in holding an annual corn school at Lafayette and in encouraging proper cultivation, use of fertilizers, and careful seed selection.[58] Corn yields increased more than any other crop during this period, progressing from an average of 28.9 bushels per acre for the decade 1880-1889 to 36.4 bushels per acre for 1911-1920.[59] Indiana corn won twenty-three gold medals at the Panama-Pacific Exposition in San Francisco in 1915 and took the grand prize at the National Corn Show fourteen times during the first sixteen years it was held.[60]

After corn and wheat, oats predominated among grain crops, chiefly because of its value for feeding livestock, espe-

[56] Indiana Department of Statistics, *Biennial Report, 1915-1916*, p. 602.

[57] United States Bureau of the Census, *Fourteenth Census* (1920), V, *Agriculture*, p. 791; VI, *Agriculture*, Pt. 1, p. 352.

[58] The systematic corn breeding which led to the development of hybrids in the 1920's had hardly begun in Indiana in this period, but as early as 1875 a Hoosier stockman, James Riley of Thorntown, was beginning to produce by careful, repeated seed selection the improved type of corn called Boone County White, one of the most popular varieties in the eastern part of the corn belt by 1900. See Indiana State Board of Agriculture, *Annual Report*, 1901-1902, p. 593; 1904-1905, p. 259.

[59] United States Department of Agriculture, *Report of the Secretary*, 1890, p. 335; *Yearbook*, 1920, p. 541. During this period the average yield varied widely, between 21.6 bushels per acre in 1887 to 40.5 in 1920.

[60] Streightoff and Streightoff, *Indiana*, p. 41.

cially horses. Oats were grown mostly north of the southern limit of the Wisconsin Drift and extensively after 1900 in the reclaimed wetlands of the Kankakee basin. Of the lesser cereals, barley was grown largely in the sandy soils of northern Indiana, and winter rye was chiefly concentrated in the morainal region of the northeast.[61] The two crops were roughly equal in output in 1879 but moved in opposite directions in the next decades, barley slowly declining to a relatively minor position and rye generally expanding, both temporarily reaching unusually high peaks in 1919 because of the stimulation of wartime demands. Buckwheat, however, remained more or less stable at a relatively low level of production.

## PRODUCTION OF BARLEY, RYE, AND BUCKWHEAT[62]
### (in bushels)

| Year | Barley | Rye | Buckwheat |
|------|--------|-----|-----------|
| 1879 | 382,835 | 303,105 | 89,707 |
| 1889 | 250,200 | 877,532 | 99,959 |
| 1899 | 260,550 | 564,300 | 102,340 |
| 1909 | 234,298 | 1,121,589 | 84,991 |
| 1919 | 1,427,772 | 4,432,091 | 73,260 |

Hay, grown extensively in every county, was the third most valuable Indiana field crop after corn and wheat. The two chief varieties—timothy and clover—were sown both separately and mixed. The latter was utilized for its special soil-building qualities in the crop-rotation system and also for its seed. By 1889 Indiana led the nation in the production of both clover hay and clover seed.[63] Several thousand acres were planted to millet and other tame grasses, but the acreage of wild prairie grass was fast diminishing, though Hoo-

---

61 Visher, *Economic Geography of Indiana*, pp. 134-137. Oats tended to be grown less in the extreme south of Indiana because temperature and rainfall conditions were unfavorable as compared with the cooler parts of the state to the north. Stephen S. Visher, *The Climate of Indiana* (Indiana University Publications, *Science Series No. 13*, Bloomington, 1944), pp. 400, 406-407.

62 United States Bureau of the Census, *Fourteenth Census* (1920), V, *Agriculture*, pp. 756, 760, 764.

63 *Ibid., Twelfth Census* (1900), VI, *Agriculture*, pp. 204, 269.

sier farmers harvested over 60,000 tons in 1909.[64] Among the new leguminous hay and fodder crops, alfalfa was established in the state by the nineties, being grown chiefly in the south near the Ohio River and in the northern tier of counties. The area of cultivation rose from 844 acres in 1899 to 17,898 acres in 1909 and 62,351 acres in 1919.[65] Cow peas and soybeans were introduced around the turn of the century but gained acceptance only very slowly. In 1919 the Indiana *Year Book* reported for the year 1918, 25,448 acres in cow peas, 8,415 acres in cow peas mixed with other crops, 6,866 acres in soybeans, and 7,176 acres in soybeans mixed with other crops.[66] The cultivation of the fiber crop, flax, which was grown only for its seed in Indiana, the third largest producer in the country in 1880, declined so abruptly that it virtually disappeared by 1900.[67]

The only field crop other than grain or hay to be grown on relatively large acreage in Indiana was potatoes, of which between six to nine million bushels were produced annually between 1879 and 1889, before production fell to about two and a half million bushels in 1919.[68] But they were raised largely for local use, and by 1900 Hoosiers were consuming more potatoes than they produced. The weather was a factor in the generally low yields and eventual shift of the main area of potato culture from southern Indiana to the cooler

[64] *Ibid., Thirteenth Census* (1910), V, *Agriculture*, p. 646.

[65] *Ibid., Twelfth Census* (1900), VI, *Agriculture*, p. 219; *Fourteenth Census* (1920), V, *Agriculture*, p. 800.

[66] Indiana *Year Book*, 1919, p. 922. There is a striking discrepancy between these figures and those found in the Federal Census report for 1919, which gives only 5,775 acres for cow peas and 684 acres for soybeans in that year. United States Bureau of the Census, *Fourteenth Census* (1920), V, *Agriculture*, pp. 777-778. Illustrating the lag that sometimes took place between scientific demonstration and practical application is the fact that the Purdue Experiment Station had proven the value of cow peas and soybeans and published the results as early as 1898. Indiana State Board of Agriculture, *Annual Report*, 1899-1900, pp. 800-804.

[67] United States Bureau of the Census, *Twelfth Census* (1900), VI, *Agriculture*, pp. 331, 420-21.

[68] *Ibid., Fourteenth Census* (1920), V, *Agriculture*, p. 813.

climate of the northernmost counties in the first decades of the twentieth century.[69]

As early as 1900 Indiana had become one of the leading market and truck-gardening centers in the Middle West. The first market produce mentioned in the State Department of Statistics' *Annual Reports* included melons, cabbages, and onions, with acreages in 1880 of 6,315, 1,648, and 847, respectively.[70] The last soon became a major vegetable crop in Indiana, expanding its area of cultivation fivefold by 1919, when total production was valued at over $1,000,000.[71] Onions, like cabbage and celery in a less extensive fashion, were grown largely in the muck-land farms of northern Indiana, requiring a great deal of hand labor and usually marketed dry on about the first day of March each year, before the Texas crop was put on sale.[72] The state also became famous in these years for its production of both watermelons and muskmelons, or cantaloupes, which were raised on four to five thousand acres each, scattered at various points around the state, but particularly in Posey, Gibson, Knox, and other counties in the lower Wabash Valley.[73]

The development of the canning industry in Indiana by the end of the nineteenth century created a large demand for the cultivation of tomatoes, green peas, sweet corn, and cucumbers for pickles. Tomatoes were the leading commercial vegetable crop from 1904, when official statistics were first gathered on it, to at least 1919, when 8,469 farms reported

[69] Visher, *Economic Geography of Indiana*, pp. 137-138.

[70] Indiana Department of Statistics and Geology, *Annual Report*, 1882, pp. 53, 95.

[71] United States Bureau of the Census, *Fourteenth Census* (1920), V, *Agriculture*, p. 827.

[72] H. R. Smalley, *Management of Muck-land Farms in Northern Indiana and Southern Michigan* (United States Department of Agriculture, *Farmers' Bulletin 761*, 1916), p. 11.

[73] Visher, *Climate of Indiana*, pp. 400-401. According to Latta, commercial melon growing began in Knox County in 1882, when the first carload of watermelons was shipped from Vincennes; ten years later the first carload of cantaloupes was also shipped from the same place. Latta, *Outline History of Indiana Agriculture*, p. 266.

production valued at nearly $2,000,000.[74] Sweet corn and peas followed tomatoes in importance as canning crops, all three grown in the central and south-central part of the state—chiefly the counties of Bartholomew, Clark, Delaware, Hamilton, Hendricks, Henry, Howard, Jackson, Johnson, Marion, Scott, and Tipton—while cucumbers for pickling were raised in a smaller number of counties to the north—Fulton, La Porte, Marshall, Starke, and Tippecanoe.[75]

Other vegetables grown on a smaller scale for home use and local markets included sweet potatoes, carrots, radishes, turnips, lettuce, parsnips, pumpkins, kale, and green peppers. Sunflower seeds composed another minor product, grown largely for poultry feed.[76] A small but significant commercial crop was peppermint, which was grown in the northern muck lands after 1890, when New York relinquished its monopoly of the plant to Michigan and Indiana. By 1919 Indiana had surpassed Michigan and was producing nearly 60 per cent of the nation's supply.[77]

Tobacco was a marginal part of Indiana agriculture but an important cash crop to many farmers in a group of southern counties between the Ohio and White rivers, across from the burley-growing district of Kentucky. In a special

[74] Indiana Department of Statistics, *Biennial Report,* 1905-1906, p. 723; United States Bureau of the Census, *Fourteenth Census* (1920), V, *Agriculture,* p. 830. The following table shows tomato acreage, 1904-1915:

| Year | Acres | Year | Acres | Year | Acres |
|------|-------|------|-------|------|-------|
| 1904 | 19,189 | 1908 | 25,801 | 1912 | 27,068 |
| 1905 | 15,013 | 1909 | 25,650 | 1913 | 27,209 |
| 1906 | 19,194 | 1910 | 12,743 | 1914 | 28,015 |
| 1907 | 21,705 | 1911 | 18,402 | 1915 | 21,413 |

Indiana Department of Statistics, *Biennial Report,* 1911-1912, p. 608; 1915-1916, p. 578.

[75] United States Bureau of the Census, *Twelfth Census* (1900), VI, *Agriculture,* pp. 314-315, 318.

[76] Indiana ranked fourth in the nation in production of sunflower seeds in 1909 with 6,330 bushels but fell to sixth place in 1919 with just 838 bushels. United States Bureau of the Census, *Fourteenth Census* (1920), V, *Agriculture,* p. 790.

[77] *Ibid., Twelfth Census* (1900), VI, *Agriculture,* p. 590; *Fourteenth Census* (1920), V, *Agriculture,* p. 708.

study for the Federal Census of 1880 it was stated that tobacco in Indiana was usually grown by "renters and tenant
farmers in small patches, the average crop for each farmer
being about 2,500 pounds." "It may be added," the report
continued, "that the best farmers pay but little attention to
tobacco culture, nor are the best lands employed for its production. It appears to be a favorite crop only with a class of
roaming farmers, who can always find a ready market for
it, though at prices which ordinarily will barely pay for the
cost of production."[78] With the exception of Warrick and
Spencer counties, which continued to be large producers, the
center of tobacco cultivation shifted in the nineties from the
southwest to the southeast, particularly to the white burley-
growing counties of Ohio, Switzerland, Dearborn, and Franklin. Fluctuating market conditions and prices brought wide
year-to-year variations in planting, ranging from six to thirty
thousand acres. The best crop year for Indiana growers was
apparently 1910, when they produced 26,400,000 pounds
worth $2,508,000, though the postwar harvest of 1919, ten
million pounds smaller, was estimated at more than double
that value.[79]

The production of maple syrup and sugar, once a fair-
sized industry in Indiana, declined after the seventies. But
Hoosier farmers made up for it in the production of sorghum
for syrup, planting between seven and twelve thousand acres
annually in cane during the period 1889 to 1919, and producing over 52,000 tons worth approximately one million dollars
in the latter year.[80] The story of sugar-beet culture was
quite different. Sorghum could be grown profitably because
its syrup was made in small mills right on the farm, but the
manufacture of beet sugar required complex machinery and

[78] Ibid., Tenth Census (1880), III, Agriculture, pp. 634, 635.

[79] Ibid., Thirteenth Census (1910), Abstract, with Supplement for Indiana,
pp. 662-669; United States Department of Commerce, Statistical Abstract of the
United States, 1920, p. 160.

[80] United States Bureau of the Census, Fourteenth Census (1920), V,
Agriculture, pp. 842-843.

factories, which were nonexistent in Indiana. In spite of persistent encouragement by the Purdue Experiment Station, farmers did not plant sugar beets on any scale until the First World War, which created a higher than usual demand for sugar. In 1919 the Federal Census reported 622 farms raising sugar beets on 4,119 acres, almost a 500 per cent increase over that for 1909.[81]

The rise of commercial fruit growing in Indiana may be dated from the eighties and nineties. In 1880 the State Department of Statistics and Geology reported that "apples, pears, peaches, grapes and the small fruits and berries are the home production of almost every farm, and so commonly abundant and cheap that none but an expert can afford to grow them for market sale."[82] By 1900 Indiana was ranked seventh among the states in the total value of fruit products, estimated at over four and a half million dollars.[83]

By far the greatest part of this production was orchard fruit—apples, peaches, cherries, pears, plums, and even, on a smaller scale, apricots. Orchards were found in every section of the state, though commercial growers tended to be more and more concentrated in some of the southern unglaciated counties, with their milder climate as well as hilly land less suitable for field crops. Just as the industry was becoming established, however, disaster struck in the form of plant diseases and pests. The San Jose scale, the most destructive enemy of orchards, appeared around 1894 and was reported in sixty counties by 1897, when the Indiana Horticultural Society sought state governmental action to protect fruit growers.[84] In the emergency Governor Mount appointed Professor James Troop of Purdue University state entomologist, a position confirmed by the General Assembly in 1899, when a law was enacted requiring annual inspection

[81] *Ibid.*, p. 845.

[82] Indiana Department of Statistics and Geology, *Annual Report*, 1880, p. 7.

[83] United States Bureau of the Census, *Twelfth Census* (1900), VI, *Agriculture*, Pt. 2, p. 599.

[84] Indiana Horticultural Society, *Transactions*, 1897, pp. 86-87, 161, 166, 167.

of nurseries to prevent spread of the San Jose scale and other pests.[85]

In 1907 the post of state entomologist was made a full-time job with an office in the State House. Two years later he was allocated up to $15,000 a year to fight destructive insects and plant diseases.[86] This was the beginning of a vigorous campaign to eliminate pests by destroying infected trees and spraying healthy ones with insecticides and fungicides. However, in spite of all the efforts of the state government, the horticultural society, and individual growers, fruit orchards suffered heavy reversals after 1900. The production of apples fell off by two thirds in the first decade of the twentieth century, and the output of peaches, pears, and cherries declined steeply in the second. The rise and fall of Indiana orchards between 1890 and 1920 is graphically displayed in the following table:

### TREES OF BEARING AGE, 1890-1920[87]

| Year | Apple | Peach | Cherry | Pear | Plum | Apricot |
|------|-------|-------|--------|------|------|---------|
| 1890 | 6,089,106 | 953,980 | 617,168 | 204,579 | 146,378 | 9,049 |
| 1900 | 8,624,593 | 2,925,526 | 896,641 | 868,184 | 723,815 | 9,586 |
| 1910 | 5,764,821 | 2,130,298 | 815,742 | 708,723 | 566,988 | 7,337 |
| 1920 | 3,427,816 | 860,024 | 475,333 | 337,515 | 214,202 | 106 |

Although Hoosiers no longer aspired to reach the front ranks of fruit growers, apples remained an important crop in Indiana, and serious attempts were made to improve their quality. In 1899 the Indiana Horticultural Society purchased a twenty-acre tract in Lawrence County, where an experimental orchard was established under the supervision of Joe A. Burton, a successful commercial apple grower. Experiments with seeds, fertilizers, and insecticides were car-

[85] Indiana *Senate Journal,* 1899, p. 32; *Laws of Indiana,* 1899, pp. 224-227.

[86] *Laws of Indiana,* 1907, pp. 291-295; 1909, pp. 189-194.

[87] United States Bureau of the Census, *Eleventh Census* (1890), *Agriculture,* p. 508; *Twelfth Census* (1900), VI, *Agriculture,* pp. 617-618; *Fourteenth Census,* V, *Agriculture,* pp. 862-868. Another index of the decline of apple growing in the state is the virtual disappearance of the production of cider and vinegar, which fell from 5,944,144 gallons in 1899 to 181,454 gallons in 1919. *Ibid.,* p. 870.

ried on there for several years before the orchard was turned over to the Purdue Agricultural Experiment Station in 1917.[88] In 1911 the society also began sponsoring an annual Apple Show in Indianapolis for the promotion of Indiana fruit.[89] Of the $2,999,519 the state's growers received for all orchard products in 1919, $2,221,498 was earned from the sale of apples.[90]

The cultivation of other fruit also declined during this period. Grape vineyards, which were located chiefly in counties bordering Lake Michigan as well as a few counties near the Ohio River, lost even the small commercial significance which they had enjoyed earlier. The number of vines of bearing age fell from approximately 2,500,000 in 1900 to 750,000 in 1920.[91] Production of small fruits and berries dropped from about 22,000,000 quarts to less than 7,000,000 quarts between 1899 and 1919. Strawberries alone, the leading crop, declined 50 per cent in this period. Strawberry growing, however, began to expand somewhat after 1910, when Clark County on the Ohio River became a commercial center for the crop.[92]

Another minor horticultural industry in the state was the raising of flowers and plants in greenhouses and nursery products. Indiana was for a time widely known for its roses and in 1890 ranked sixth among the states in their cultivation.[93] In 1919 total receipts for greenhouse products

88 Indiana Horticultural Society, *Transactions,* 1915, p. 403; 1917, p. 283.

89 *Ibid.,* 1911, pp. 155-158.

90 United States Bureau of the Census, *Fourteenth Census* (1920), V, *Agriculture,* pp. 862-863.

91 *Ibid., Twelfth Census* (1900), VI, *Agriculture,* Pt. 2 p. 618; *Fourteenth Census* (1920), VI, *Agriculture,* Pt. 1, p. 333.

92 Latta, *Outline History of Indiana Agriculture,* p. 261; Visher, *Economic Geography of Indiana,* p. 142; United States Bureau of the Census, *Fourteenth Census* (1920), V, *Agriculture,* pp. 852-853.

93 United States Bureau of the Census, *Eleventh Census* (1890), I, *Agriculture,* p. 572. New Castle, a main center of floriculture in the state, was known as the "Rose City" because so many greenhouses specializing in this kind of flower were located there. A popular variety created by Heller Brothers Company, a pioneer firm of florists, was named the New Castle Rose. See the catalogue issued by that company entitled *The Roses of New Castle* (New

amounted to $3,056,094 and nursery products $409,475.[94]
Indiana farms also had forest products valued at $5,603,322
in 1909 and $10,955,856 in 1919.[95]

§ § § § §

Livestock raising, an important branch of farming in Indiana since pioneer days, not only helped to maintain the
fertility of the soil, which grain growing annually depleted,
but also provided a readily marketable and profitable product. The value of livestock products and domestic animals
sold or slaughtered on the farm accounted for a significant
part of the gross value of all farm products, though somewhat less than the total value of all crops and forest, nursery,
and greenhouse products, as the following table indicates for
the two census years in which fully comparable figures are
available:

### VALUE OF FARM PRODUCTS, 1909 AND 1919[96]

| Year | Livestock products | Domestic animals sold or slaughtered | Crops | Forest and nursery and greenhouse products |
|---|---|---|---|---|
| 1909 | 44,319,539 | 92,896,132 | 196,869,691 | 7,227,600 |
| 1919 | 99,350,023 | 171,100,000 | 497,229,719 | 14,421,425 |

As in pioneer days, many Hoosier farmers continued to
slaughter domestic animals on the farm, both for home use
and for sale of meat and related products. But by 1910 the
great majority of animals were sold rather than slaughtered.
In that year the value of those sold was $81,437,250 as com-

Castle, Ind., 1922). The Society of Indiana Florists also inaugurated an annual
Chrysanthemum Show in Indianapolis in the fall of 1887. Indiana State Board
of Agriculture, *Annual Report,* 1887, p. 487.

[94] United States Bureau of the Census, *Fourteenth Census* (1920), V, *Agriculture,* pp. 885, 887.

[95] *Ibid.,* p. 882.

[96] *Ibid.,* pp. 18, 651, 695, 710, 883, 885, 887. These figures contain some
duplication, of course, since a large part of the total production of certain crops
was fed to livestock. This fact, however, emphasizes the importance of livestock to the Hoosier farmer, who realized the cash value of many of his field
crops only through the sale or slaughter of his domestic animals and the sale
of livestock products.

pared with that of those slaughtered, $11,458,882.[97] Though many animals from Indiana farms were marketed at Chicago or Cincinnati, the Indianapolis stockyards became a major livestock market in this period. The following table illustrates its growth:

RECEIVED AT INDIANAPOLIS STOCKYARDS, 1894-1920[98]

| Year | Cattle and calves | Hogs | Sheep |
|------|-------------------|------|-------|
| 1894 | 91,017 | 963,511 | 108,924 |
| 1896 | 135,253 | 1,255,405 | 120,890 |
| 1898 | 134,786 | 1,681,362 | 84,665 |
| 1900 | 139,722 | 1,323,018 | 67,005 |
| 1902 | 213,179 | 1,251,351 | 102,580 |
| 1904 | 274,710 | 1,668,771 | 89,945 |
| 1906 | 350,016 | 1,869,353 | 76,570 |
| 1908 | 407,149 | 2,484,226 | 111,848 |
| 1910 | 417,759 | 1,487,174 | 128,001 |
| 1912 | 390,238 | 1,824,260 | 154,414 |
| 1914 | 344,245 | 2,099,787 | 124,591 |
| 1916 | 405,069 | 2,576,611 | 98,142 |
| 1918 | 504,190 | 2,749,976 | 113,828 |
| 1920 | 597,097 | 2,896,894 | 135,841 |

The heavy production of corn inevitably made hog raising the outstanding livestock interest in Indiana, which ranked fourth after Iowa, Illinois, and Missouri as a hog-producing state in 1910 and third in 1919.[99] In 1910 73.5 per cent of all Indiana farms raised hogs, the leading counties concentrated near the center of the state—Rush, Boone, Grant, Hamilton, Henry, Madison, and Montgomery. At the same

[97] United States Bureau of the Census, *Thirteenth Census* (1910), *Abstract, with Supplement for Indiana,* p. 358.

[98] United States Department of Commerce, *Statistical Abstract of the United States,* 1920, p. 362. By 1920 Indianapolis received more hogs than any other market except Chicago, Kansas City, Omaha, or St. Louis. Other stockyards in Indiana receiving smaller amounts of livestock were located at Evansville, Lafayette, and La Porte.

[99] United States Bureau of the Census, *Thirteenth Census* (1910), *Abstract, with Supplement for Indiana,* p. 328; *Fourteenth Census* (1920), V, *Agriculture,* pp. 690-692. This ranking is based on the number of pigs born on farms in Indiana in 1910 and 1919; in both of these years Missouri surpassed Indiana in the total number of swine of all ages in the state.

time 90 per cent of all farms boasted cattle, 89 per cent reporting dairy cattle and 19.3 per cent "other cattle." By 1920 the proportion of farms reporting hogs had risen to 84 per cent and cattle to 91.5 per cent, with dairy cattle down to 78.3 per cent and beef cattle up to 28.4 per cent. On the other hand, sheep were found on only 17.7 per cent of all farms in 1910 and 14.7 per cent in 1920, and were concentrated mostly in five counties in the northern moraine and lake region—Allen, DeKalb, La Grange, Noble, and Steuben.[100]

Although Indiana did not rank among the leading states in the cattle industry, cattle raising for both beef and dairy purposes was a major farm business throughout this period. Commercial dairying, however, was just beginning in the eighties. In 1882 an eloquent advocate pleaded with his fellow Hoosier farmers to help lift "the dairy business out of a disconnected, desultory and merely pin-money incidental economy into an organized, intelligent pursuit. . . ." Nothing is wanting, he argued, "but the organized system, the awakening of enterprise, to turn grasses and corn fodder, so much of which now goes to waste, into milk and its manufactured products. It is better than gold mines."[101]

The introduction of the centrifugal cream separator from Sweden in the eighties and the invention of the Babcock butterfat test in 1890 stimulated the dairy industry. Approximately a hundred creameries, both co-operative and privately owned, had been constructed in the state by 1897, though more than half failed either through mismanagement or lack of milk, according to a survey made by Professor Charles S. Plumb of the Purdue Experiment Station.[102] Butter pro-

[100] United States Bureau of the Census, *Thirteenth Census* (1910), *Abstract, with Supplement for Indiana,* p. 636; *Fourteenth Census* (1920), V, *Agriculture,* pp. 556, 565, 577; Visher, *Economic Geography of Indiana,* pp. 145-148.

[101] Indiana State Board of Agriculture, *Annual Report,* 1881, p. 367.

[102] *Ibid.,* 1897-1898, pp. 424-429. When Professor Plumb arrived in Indiana in 1890 to take charge of the Purdue University Agricultural Experiment Station, he found the Indiana Dairymen's Association defunct and little sustained interest in commercial dairying. He called a meeting of interested farmers who organized a new Indiana Dairy Association in January, 1891, with Plumb as first president. His enthusiastic efforts on behalf of the state dairy in-

duction advanced rapidly at this time, but the United States Census reports show that until sometime after 1909 the greater part of it was made on the farm rather than in the creamery.

BUTTER MADE ON FARMS, AND IN FACTORIES,
1879-1919[103]
(in pounds)

| Year | All butter made | Butter made on the farm | Butter made in factories |
|------|-----------------|-------------------------|--------------------------|
| 1879 | 37,659,029      | 37,377,797              | 281,232                  |
| 1889 | 50,154,854      | 48,477,766              | 1,677,088                |
| 1899 | 54,595,879      | 51,042,396              | 3,553,483                |
| 1909 | 54,894,267      | 43,181,817              | 11,712,450               |
| 1919 | 60,531,133      | 18,344,239              | 42,186,894               |

Dairying did not become highly specialized but tended to fit into the pattern of medium-sized, mixed husbandry characteristic of most of Indiana agriculture. The chief product was whole milk, which found a ready market in the growing cities located within and without the borders of the state. Lake and Porter counties, with their close proximity to Chicago, led in production of milk together with counties with large urban populations like Allen, Elkhart, Madison, Marion, and St. Joseph. The milk sold by Hoosier farmers jumped from 6,723,840 gallons in 1879 to 36,562,105 in 1899 and 45,167,166 in 1919. Total receipts from sale of all dairy products in 1919 was $38,003,286.[104]

The United States Bureau of the Census did not distinguish clearly between the number of dairy and beef cattle until 1920. In that year it reported 599,695 beef animals in Indiana, about two fifths of the total number of cattle.[105]

dustry continued until 1902, when he left Purdue to become professor of animal husbandry at Ohio State University. C. B. Harris, "Dairying in Indiana," in Indiana State Board of Agriculture, *Annual Report,* 1892-1893, pp. 87-91.

[103] United States Bureau of the Census, *Fourteenth Census* (1920), V, *Agriculture,* pp. 660-661. Very little cheese was made in Indiana and nearly all of that in factories rather than on the farm. Total production declined from 1,521,275 pounds in 1879 to 378,328 pounds in 1919. *Ibid.,* p. 664.

[104] *Ibid.,* pp. 665, 668.

[105] *Ibid.,* p. 556.

The rising value of land for crop purposes after 1910 led some farmers to begin buying young western range cattle as feeders rather than raise their own calves. By 1919 thousands of head of such feeder cattle were being fattened for market on hay and grain in northern and central counties of the state, though never on as large a scale as Corn Belt states farther west, especially Illinois and Iowa.[106]

Sheep raising alone of the major livestock lines in Indiana did not advance during this period. The number of sheep on farms remained fairly stable until 1910, after which it declined severely. Lambs and sheep were raised for meat to some extent, but the most important product was wool, which fluctuated in weight between five and seven million pounds from 1879 to 1909 but fell to four million in 1919, when it was valued at $2,319,545.[107]

Horses and mules furnished most of the motive power used on farms, though as late as 1890 there were still over six thousand working oxen in the state, largely in southern counties.[108] Before the First World War, horse breeding, including standard-bred harness racers, was a substantial industry in the bluegrass pasture region of south-central Indiana. Almost every county fair had its "speed" events, and Hoosier racing fans were proud of the state's reputation for home-bred fast pacers and trotters, especially after the mare Nancy Hanks ran the mile in 2.04 at a track in Terre Haute in 1892.[109] Favorable climate and cheap fodder and forage made Indiana a good breeding ground for horses,

[106] For surveys of cattle feeding in Indiana and other Corn Belt states at this time, see W. H. Black, *Beef Production in the Corn Belt* (United States Department of Agriculture, *Farmers' Bulletin 1218,* 1921) and R. H. Wilcox and others, *Costs and Methods of Fattening Beef Cattle in the Corn Belt, 1919-1923* (United States Department of Agriculture, *Technical Bulletin No. 23,* 1927).

[107] United States Bureau of the Census, *Fourteenth Census* (1920), V, *Agriculture,* pp. 674, 676.

[108] *Ibid., Eleventh Census* (1890), I, *Agriculture,* p. 284. For some reason, perhaps inaccurate reporting, this figure represents a rather large increase over the previous census figure of 3,970 oxen. *Tenth Census* (1880), III, *Agriculture,* p. 175.

[109] Virginia C. Meredith, *A Monograph on the Live Stock of the State of Indiana* (Indianapolis, 1893), pp. 4-5.

many of which were exported, chiefly to the South. Mules, outnumbered by horses ten-to-one, were found mostly in the extreme southern portion of the state.[110]

NUMBER OF LIVESTOCK ON FARMS, 1880-1920[111]

| Year | Swine | Cattle | Sheep | Horses | Mules |
|------|-------|--------|-------|--------|-------|
| 1880 | 3,186,413 | 1,363,760 | 1,100,511 | 581,444 | 51,780 |
| 1890 | 3,320,817 | 1,511,908 | 1,081,133 | 720,035 | 58,688 |
| 1900 | 3,763,389 | 1,684,478 | 1,742,002 | 751,715 | 66,717 |
| 1910 | 3,613,906 | 1,363,016 | 1,336,967 | 813,644 | 82,168 |
| 1920 | 3,757,135 | 1,546,095 | 643,889 | 717,233 | 100,358 |

Livestock breeding played an increasingly important role in Indiana after the first large-scale importation of purebred animals in the seventies and eighties. The state possessed two of the outstanding Hereford cattle-breeding farms in America in Adams Earl and Charles B. Stuart's "Shadeland" on the Wea River near Lafayette and Moses Fowler and William S. VanNatta's Benton County showplace, the herds on both of which had been founded around 1880. Another important cattle breeder in this period was J. G. Robbins, who founded the Robbinwood Shorthorn herd in Decatur County in 1882.[112]

The rise of breeders' associations attracted increasing attention to the use of purebred stock in upgrading the native domestic animals. In 1907, by request of a number of these associations, the Indiana State Bureau of Statistics collected the first figures on registered purebreds, which it was shown constituted only a small fraction of all farm animals. Registered purebred hogs, at 65,124, were only a little more than 3 per cent of the total number of hogs; purebred cattle, at 20,604, and purebred sheep at 13,348, made up 2 per cent each; and horses, at 4,950, were less than 1 per cent.[113]

[110] Visher, *Economic Geography of Indiana*, pp. 145-146.

[111] Compiled from the United States Bureau of the Census, *Fourteenth Census* (1920), V, *Agriculture*, pp. 547-548, 572, 586, 598.

[112] Latta, *Outline History of Indiana Agriculture*, pp. 192-193; Alvin H. Sanders, *The Story of the Herefords* (Chicago, 1914), pp. 442-472. For the earlier career of Moses Fowler and Adams Earl as large landowners and cattlemen, see Thornbrough, *Indiana in the Civil War Era*, pp. 384-385.

[113] Figures taken and percentages calculated from table in the Indiana Department of Statistics, *Biennial Report*, 1907-1908, p. 433.

Most herds and flocks were gradually coming to be composed of "grade," or mixed-blood animals, while the old "scrub" stock was fast disappearing with the intrusion of the pure blood lines. By 1920, when the first Federal Census report on purebred livestock was issued, the number of purebred hogs in Indiana had risen to 159,696, third largest in the nation after Illinois and Iowa, and cattle to 50,624, but purebred horses had barely held their own at 5,265, and sheep declined to 9,282.[114]

### PUREBRED LIVESTOCK: LEADING BREEDS, 1907 AND 1920[115]

| Breed | 1907 | 1920 | Breed | 1907 | 1920 |
|---|---|---|---|---|---|
| **Hogs** | | | **Sheep** | | |
| Duroc-Jersey | 26,729 | 46,364 | Shropshire | 6,774 | 5,743 |
| Poland-China | 24,632 | 66,786 | Oxford | 1,743 | 628 |
| Spotted | | | Merino | 1,142 | 185 |
|   Poland China | — | 21,123 | Cotswold | 1,202 | — |
| Chester White | 7,834 | 12,493 | Hampshire | 658 | 720 |
| Berkshire | 4,811 | 2,104 | Tunis | 509 | — |
| Hampshire | 337 | 6,858 | Rambouillet | 470 | 333 |
| Essex | 240 | — | Southdown | 341 | 110 |
| Yorkshire | 168 | 27 | Cheviot | 315 | 88 |
| Tamworth | 76 | 77 | Dorset | 160 | 250 |
| All others | 297 | 3,864 | All others | 34 | 1,183 |
| **Beef Cattle** | | | **Dairy Cattle** | | |
| Shorthorn | 7,564 | 16,147 | Jersey | 3,192 | 9,921 |
| Hereford | 3,586 | 6,615 | Holstein-Friesian | 643 | 8,477 |
| Aberdeen-Angus | 3,085 | 4,807 | Guernsey | 113 | 1,215 |
| Polled Durham | 1,699 | 1,183 | Ayrshire | 33 | 509 |
| Galloway | 172 | 21 | Brown Swiss | 15 | 131 |
| All others | — | 736 | All others | 502 | 862 |
| **Draft Horses** | | | **Saddle and Harness Horses** | | |
| Percheron | 1,249 | 2,796 | Standard-bred | 2,234 | 322 |
| Belgian | 288 | 1,162 | German Coach | 168 | 24 |
| Clydesdale | 166 | 221 | Hackney | 77 | 6 |
| French Draft | 154 | 155 | American Saddler | 60 | 20 |
| Shire | 162 | 157 | All others (draft and saddle) | 67 | 402 |

[114] United States Bureau of the Census, *Fourteenth Census* (1920), V, *Agriculture,* pp. 636, 639, 644.

[115] Compiled from Indiana Department of Statistics, *Biennial Report,* 1907-1908, pp. 434-523; United States Bureau of the Census, *Fourteenth Census* (1920), V, *Agriculture,* pp. 637-638, 640-643, 645-646.

Livestock losses from disease, especially hog cholera, were relatively large in the eighties and nineties, but the state government was slow to take effective measures to protect herds and flocks from infection. In 1884 the State Board of Health requested without success that an official veterinarian be appointed under its supervision to organize methods of prevention and control of disease among domestic animals. Five years later, however, an outbreak of pleuropneumonia in cattle herds in some sections of the state prodded the General Assembly into authorizing establishment of the State Live Stock Sanitary Commission.[116] In 1899 Governor Mount estimated the loss of livestock in Indiana from various infectious and contagious diseases at between three and five million dollars and asked the legislature to replace the largely ineffectual Sanitary Commission with a state veterinarian with large powers of quarantine. This was finally acted upon in 1901, in the same year that the General Assembly voted to require the licensing of the practice of veterinary medicine.[117]

Additional legislation was passed during the next two decades giving this office such duties as supervising the manufacture and use of hog-cholera serum and administration of the tuberculin test to cattle.[118] With the co-operation of the Purdue Experiment Station and the Bureau of Animal Industry of the United States Department of Agriculture, the state veterinarian made a determined drive to eradicate tuberculosis in cattle. By 1919 the state claimed 275 accredited tuberculosis-free herds, and the incidence of this disease was reduced from 12 per cent to 2.2 per cent for dairy cattle and 3.5 per cent for beef cattle. In that year the General Assembly created a new State Live Stock Sanitary Control

116 *Laws of Indiana,* 1889, pp. 380-387; William A. Rawles, *Centralizing Tendencies in the Administration of Indiana* (Columbia University, *Studies in History, Economics and Public Administration,* XVII, No. 1, New York, 1903), pp. 241-242.

117 Indiana *Senate Journal,* 1899, p. 27; *Laws of Indiana,* 1901, pp. 98-102, 421-422.

118 *Laws of Indiana,* 1911, pp. 690-693; 1917, p. 682.

Board composed of two veterinarians and two livestock farmers to assume broad powers and responsibilities for all such matters.[119]

Large numbers of poultry were raised in Indiana, especially chickens. Of purebred stock the leading breeds were Plymouth Rock, Leghorn and Wyandotte, though Rhode Island Reds, Orpingtons, Brahmas, and Minorcas were also found.[120] Egg production tripled between 1879 and 1919, when Indiana ranked fifth among the states in production and sale of chicken eggs. In 1919 Hoosier farmers sold eggs valued at $23,254,964 and chickens worth $7,665,513.[121] However, while chicken production increased, the number of other fowls on Indiana farms, chiefly turkeys, geese, and ducks, declined rapidly.

### NUMBER OF FOWLS, 1890 TO 1920[122]

| Year | Chickens | Turkeys | Geese | Ducks |
| --- | --- | --- | --- | --- |
| 1890 | 12,307,903 | 505,111 | 434,778 | 348,001 |
| 1900 | 11,103,006 | 345,379 | 271,604 | 230,432 |
| 1910 | 13,216,204 | 202,977 | 139,081 | 121,306 |
| 1920 | 16,754,293 | 105,715 | 89,216 | 104,961 |

Beekeeping, though expanding in the eighties, when Hoosier apiarists began importing Italian queens and using artificial hives for winter protection of their swarms, diminished radically by 1919, when less than 10 per cent of all farms reported bees. In 1880 Indiana contained 146,000 colonies and produced over a million pounds of honey. The severe winter of 1880-1881 killed over half of the bees, but honey production rose in 1887 to 1,624,000 pounds.[123] In 1919, how-

[119] Indiana *Year Book,* 1919, pp. 581-586.

[120] Indiana Department of Statistics, *Biennial Report,* 1907-1908, pp. 524-539.

[121] United States Bureau of the Census, *Fourteenth Census* (1920), V, *Agriculture,* pp. 678-685.

[122] Compiled from *ibid.,* pp. 610-611.

[123] Indiana State Board of Agriculture, *Annual Report,* 1889-1890, p. 547.

ever, about 87,000 hives produced only 582,380 pounds of honey valued at $186,359.[124]

§ § § § § §

The bountiful crop of farmers' organizations in the state seems to contradict the traditional view of farmers' isolation and fierce independence and individualism.[125] The oldest such organizations persisting through this period were the county and district agricultural associations, which were organized under a law of 1851 for the purpose of sponsoring annual fairs and farm exhibits. By 1880 every county in the state was represented, either by the formation of an association controlling its own fairground or as part of a district containing the whole or parts of two or more counties. Delegates from these associations met annually to elect the sixteen members of the State Board of Agriculture, a quasi-public body created in 1835 and reorganized in 1851 which received a subsidy from the legislature to hold the annual state fair in Indianapolis and generally to foster the progress of Indiana farming. It contributed little directly to the latter objective, however, except to serve as a clearinghouse for information, which it accomplished chiefly by publishing each year until 1907 a thick volume of its own proceedings, along with reports of various state and county agricultural associations, farmers' institutes, and the Purdue Experiment Station. After 1907 the State Board of Agriculture largely confined its efforts to conducting the state fair, which was moved to a new site on the northern edge of Indianapolis in 1892.[126] Unlike most other farm states, Indiana failed to establish a centralized commission to deal with agricultural affairs as a whole, though special agencies were created

[124] United States Bureau of the Census, *Fourteenth Census* (1920), V, *Agriculture*, pp. 613, 687.

[125] Barnhart and Carmony, *Indiana*, II, 218-219.

[126] Latta, *Outline History of Indiana Agriculture*, pp. 271-280. The state fairs had previously been held in the area centering around Nineteenth and Alabama streets.

from time to time to handle specific responsibilities, such as the office of the state entomologist and the Live Stock Sanitary Board described above.[127]

The oldest of the privately organized associations was the Indiana Horticultural Society, which was founded in 1842 and continued its able advocacy of fruit and, to a lesser degree, vegetable and flower growing. Other groups of farmers interested in special branches of agriculture formed their own societies in the seventies and eighties. Included among them were the shorthorn breeders (1872), poultry breeders (1875), wool growers (1876), dairymen (1877), tilemakers (1877), beekeepers (1879), florists (1880), cane growers (1882), Jersey cattle breeders (1883), and horse breeders (1885). Some of these were shortlived, and others were later reorganized, such as the poultrymen and florists in 1887 and the dairymen in 1891. In the early years of the twentieth century there appeared a whole new group of societies, of which the Indiana Corn Growers Association (1900) was the largest and most influential. Others were the Indiana Live Stock Breeders' Association (1904), the Indiana Potato Growers' Association (1905), which was merged with the Indiana Horticultural Society in 1906, the Indiana Cattle Feeders' Association (1907), the Indiana State Dairy Association (1907), the Indiana Draft Horse Breeders' Association (1912), the Indiana State Poultry Association (1919), the Indiana Grain Dealers' Association (1916), the Indiana Vegetable Growers' Association (1920), and the Indiana Fruit Growers' Association (1921).[128]

[127] In 1919 the office of state entomologist became the Division of Entomology within the Department of Conservation. Many other responsibilities which might have come under a department of agriculture, if such existed, were assigned by the legislature to the Purdue Experiment Station.

[128] Barnhart and Carmony, *Indiana,* II, 219; Latta, *Outline History of Indiana Agriculture,* pp. 280-284, 288, 292-293. Latta also includes information concerning the organization in Indiana of the American Shropshire Registry Association (1884), Indiana Trotting and Pacer Horse Breeders' Association (1886), Chester White Record Association (1890), American Tunis Sheep Breeders' Association (1896), Indiana Duroc Swine Breeders' Association (1897), Indiana Holstein-Friesian Association (1900), Indiana Aberdeen-Angus

Fraternal organizations also flourished among Hoosier farmers, just as secret societies and lodges proliferated among their urban contemporaries. The longest-lived of these societies was the Order of Patrons of Husbandry, or the Grange, which dated from 1869 in Indiana. Although Granger membership declined steeply from its peak in the mid-seventies of over 60,000 men and women organized in some 2,-000 lodges to approximately 5,000 persons and 150 lodges in the early eighties, it remained a permanent part of rural life. Helping to raise the social and intellectual level of farmers with its ritual and educational activities, and assisting them in the co-operative purchase of such farm needs as twine binders and sewing machines, the Indiana State Grange slowly grew to 5,531 members in 1916.[129] The Grange worked for good roads and tax reform in the state and rural free delivery and postal savings banks at the national level. But most Grangers were far from advocating extreme political measures, as shown in this 1887 statement of State Master Milton Trusler warning his fellow farmers to be on their guard against urban radicalism :[130]

The element that is disturbing the peace and quiet of our country is not found in the rural home, but in our large cities. This bad element is seeking to rule the country. Here we find the hot bed of the Socialists, the Anarchists, and the followers of Henry George. The American

Cattle Breeders' Association (1901), Indiana Hereford Cattle Breeders' Association (1902), Guernsey Breeders' Association (1904), Berkshire Swine Breeders' Association (1906 or 1908), Indiana Draft Horse Breeders' Association (1912), Indiana Polled Hereford Breeders' Association (1918), Polled Shorthorn Breeders' Association (1920), Indiana Ayrshire Breeders' Association (1920), Indiana Yorkshire Breeders' Association (1922), Central States Soft Wheat Growers' Association (1924), Rambouillet Sheep Breeders' Association (1928), Indiana Hampshire Swine Breeders' Association (1929). *Ibid.,* pp. 285-295.

[129] Indiana State Grange, *Proceedings,* 1884, p. 15; 1916, p. 28; Solon J. Buck, *The Granger Movement: A Study of Agricultural Organization and Its Political, Economic and Social Manifestations (Harvard Historical Studies,* XIX, Cambridge, Mass., 1913), pp. 58-59. Indiana's state master for eleven consecutive terms, Aaron Jones of South Bend, also served as master of the National Grange from 1897 to 1905. Thomas C. Atkeson, *Semi-Centennial History of the Patrons of Husbandry* (New York, 1916), p. 337.

[130] Indiana State Grange, *Proceedings,* 1887, pp. 9-10.

farmer should be aroused to a sense of duty; we should be thoroughly organized and educated so as to meet these threatening dangers.

Two new fraternal societies appeared in Indiana in the eighties and nineties. First was the Patrons of Industry, a ritualistic association of "agriculturalists and laborers" founded in Michigan in 1887 which spread into several northern counties of Indiana by 1890 but apparently died out before the end of the century. Another Michigan society was the Ancient Order of Gleaners, which was organized in 1894 on the general pattern of the Grange, with local lodges known as "Arbors" and stressed co-operative enterprises, especially insurance. Comparatively strong in the northern third of the state, the Gleaners survived into the twentieth century chiefly as a mutual life insurance company.[131] In the eighties occurred a boom for co-operative insurance companies, over a score of which came into existence and were organized into the Farmers' Mutual Fire Insurance Union of Indiana in 1897.[132]

The agricultural depression of the late eighties and early nineties brought a new wave of farmers' organizations, more politically oriented than those described above. The Alliance movement, which originated farther west and south around 1880, swept into Indiana before the end of the decade and disappeared silently by 1900. Three different branches of the movement made their appearance in the state. Although Hoosier delegates were present at the first convention of the National (Northern) Farmers' Alliance in Chicago in 1880, this particular society was weakly represented in Indiana. It was chiefly found in the north, where a state organization was effected in June, 1890, at Fort Wayne.[133] On the other

---

[131] Sidney Glazer, "Patrons of Industry in Michigan," *Mississippi Valley Historical Review*, XXIV (1937-38), 185-194; Latta, *Outline History of Indiana Agriculture*, p. 296; Taylor, *The Farmers' Movement, 1620-1920*, pp. 221, 233-234; Edward Wiest, *Agricultural Organization in the United States* (Lexington, Ky., 1923), pp. 533-539.

[132] Indiana State Board of Agriculture, *Annual Report*, 1897-1898, pp. 236-241. The legal basis for farmers' mutual insurance companies in Indiana was a law enacted by the General Assembly in 1881. *Laws of Indiana*, 1881, p. 714.

[133] *Indiana Farmer* (Indianapolis), June 21, 1890, p. 13.

hand, the Southern Alliance, an amalgamation of earlier Texas, Louisiana, North Carolina, and Arkansas societies known after 1889 as the National Farmers' Alliance and Industrial Union, found strong support in some central and southern counties. A state branch was organized in Indianapolis in April under the presidency of Thomas Force of Shoals, Martin County, and claimed over 5,000 members in 120 local Alliances.[134] Its state constitution enjoined from membership anyone except

a white person, over sixteen years of age, who is a believer in the existence of a Supreme Being, and has resided in the state more than six months, and is, either, first a farmer, or farm laborer; second a mechanic, a country preacher, country saw mill man, a country school teacher or a country doctor; and third, an editor of a strictly agricultural paper.[135]

But the most successful of all such organizations was the Farmers' Mutual Benefit Association, a secret, ritualistic society much like the Southern Alliance which was founded in Southern Illinois in 1883. Its main growth came only after 1887, when it spread into other states, especially Indiana, which with Illinois comprised almost half of the total membership in 1890. In that year forty counties in the southern and central sections of the state were said to have 40,000 members.[136]

Although the Alliances and the F.M.B.A. placed a great deal of emphasis on fraternal and economic objectives, including co-operative enterprises of various kinds, they chiefly voiced the agrarian political discontent of the period. As

[134] *Ibid.,* May 3, 1890, p. 8.

[135] Indiana State Farmers' Alliance and Industrial Union, *Constitution* . . . (Anderson, Ind., n.d.), p. 11. Specifically excluded from membership were merchants, brokers, city preachers, city teachers, land agents, book agents, peddlers, livery stable keepers, railroad officers, and speculators! The word "white" was finally struck out of the constitution in November, 1890. *Indiana Farmer,* November 29, 1890, p. 8.

[136] *Ibid.,* April 26, 1890, p. 6; Latta, *Outline History of Indiana Agriculture,* p. 296; Roy V. Scott, *The Agrarian Movement in Illinois, 1880-1896 (Illinois Studies in the Social Sciences,* LII, Urbana, 1962), pp. 45-50. The Indiana State Library has a copy of minutes of the Hickory Grove branch of the F.M.B.A. in Washington County for the year 1900.

described in an earlier chapter, these societies took an active part in political campaigns of the early nineties and contributed to the rise of the Populists. With the collapse of this movement after 1896, the Alliances quickly dissolved. Farm prices, which reached their nadir in the mid-nineties, began to climb in a nearly unbroken upward curve until after the First World War, as indicated below:

### AVERAGE PRICES RECEIVED BY INDIANA PRODUCERS, 1890-1920[137]
(Cents per bushel)

| Year | Corn | Wheat | Oats |
|------|------|-------|------|
| 1890 | 36 | 83 | 29 |
| 1891 | 52 | 90 | 37 |
| 1892 | 40 | 75 | 31 |
| 1893 | 39 | 58 | 31 |
| 1894 | 40 | 49 | 31 |
| 1895 | 35 | 59 | 25 |
| 1896 | 22 | 64 | 18 |
| 1897 | 22 | 83 | 18 |
| 1898 | 29 | 79 | 24 |
| 1899 | 29 | 66 | 25 |
| 1900 | 35 | 69 | 24 |
| 1901 | 45 | 70 | 30 |
| 1902 | 55 | 73 | 36 |
| 1903 | 42 | 74 | 32 |
| 1904 | 45 | 98 | 34 |
| 1905 | 45 | 92 | 28 |
| 1906 | 43 | 76 | 30 |
| 1907 | 48 | 81 | 40 |
| 1908 | 62 | 92 | 47 |
| 1909 | 63 | 113 | 44 |
| 1910 | 54 | 100 | 38 |
| 1911 | 50 | 86 | 36 |
| 1912 | 65 | 98 | 41 |
| 1913 | 57 | 92 | 35 |
| 1914 | 66 | 93 | 40 |
| 1915 | 68 | 118 | 43 |
| 1916 | 73 | 127 | 42 |

[137] Howard J. Houk, *A Century of Indiana Farm Prices, 1841 to 1941* (Purdue University Agricultural Experiment Station, *Bulletin No. 476,* 1943), pp. 51, 58-59, 62. These price figures, gathered chiefly from newspapers before 1910, differ slightly from the Indiana prices (as of December 1 each year) in United States Department of Agriculture, *Yearbook,* 1894, p. 545, and subsequent annual issues.

AVERAGE PRICES RECEIVED—Cont.
(Cents per bushel)

| Year | Corn | Wheat | Oats |
|------|------|-------|------|
| 1917 | 140 | 209 | 61 |
| 1918 | 135 | 207 | 73 |
| 1919 | 150 | 216 | 66 |
| 1920 | 136 | 227 | 75 |

Political agitation aside, however, a perennial concern of farmers was to exert a greater control over the market for farm commodities in order to assure better and more stable profits. Some ventures in co-operative marketing were attempted by the Alliances and other farm associations, but little success was achieved in this kind of enterprise until about 1915.[138] A major endeavor to persuade farmers to regulate both their production and marketing originated with James A. Everitt, an Indianapolis farm seed and tool shop proprietor and agricultural newspaper editor who founded the American Society of Equity in 1902.[139]

According to its founder the chief purpose of this society was "to secure equitable and profitable prices for all products of the farm, garden, and orchard, including livestock and dairy products and poultry." Through the columns of his sprightly journal, *Up-to-Date Farming and Gardening,* which became the official organ of the movement, Everitt exhorted his readers, most of whom were members of Equity by a combined membership-subscription scheme, to control farm

---

[138] In 1915 there were reported to be 27 co-operative grain elevators and warehouses, 27 creameries, 19 fruit and produce marketing associations, and 11 miscellaneous co-operatives in Indiana, according to O. B. Jesness and W. H. Kerr, *Cooperative Purchasing and Marketing Organizations among Farmers in the United States* (United States Department of Agriculture, *Bulletin No. 547,* 1917), p. 13. Another source gives 45 co-operative elevators in 1915 and 149 in 1920, both figures still considerably below those for Illinois. Joseph B. Kenkel, *The Cooperative Elevator Movement: A Study in Grain Marketing at Country Points in the North Central States* (Catholic University of America, Washington, D.C., 1922), p. 31.

[139] The best accounts of this society are found in Robert H. Bahmer, "The American Society of Equity," *Agricultural History,* XIV (1940), 33-63; Taylor, *The Farmers' Movement,* pp. 367-390; and Theodore Saloutos and John D. Hicks, *Agricultural Discontent in the Middle West, 1900-1939* (Madison, Wis., 1951), pp. 111-148.

prices themselves by means of such techniques as crop reporting, limiting production, holding crops off the market, and storing surpluses on the farm. Everitt put his faith in the self-organizing ability of farmers, who so organized could compete on a parity with industry and labor as the "third power."[140] Although Equity began largely as an Indiana association, with Everitt as president and all other officers but one Hoosiers, it soon spread to other midwestern states. By 1905 the national secretary reported that out of a total of slightly more than 140,000 members about 10,000 were residents of Indiana, which placed third among the states after its neighbors, Kentucky and Illinois.[141]

Although the American Society of Equity never achieved its founder's goal of a million members, it gained sufficient support among midwestern farmers to be able to form pools and other holding actions which were partially successful in maintaining the prices of certain crops, especially wheat and tobacco, in some parts of the country. Its most spectacular success was in the formation of a tobacco pool in Kentucky. One Equity-inspired group, the Kentucky Burley Tobacco Society, went so far as to use vigilante methods to enforce its crop limits, producing the infamous night-riding episodes of 1905-1906. Attempts on the part of local tobacco-growers' unions of the American Society of Equity in southeastern Indiana to form a pool in 1907 brought threats of night-riders in Ohio and Switzerland counties which apparently emanated from the other side of the Ohio River but stimulated Governor Hanly to request and the General Assembly to pass a bill during the special session of 1908 making it a crime to destroy tobacco or tobacco beds and to prevent the sale of tobacco by intimidation.[142]

[140] *Up-to-Date Farming* (Indianapolis), May 1, 1905. See also *Plan of the American Society of Equity of North America* (Indianapolis, 1902) and James A. Everitt's *The Third Power: Farmers to the Front* (Indianapolis, 1903).

[141] *Up-to-Date Farming*, December 1, 1905.

[142] Vevay *Reveille*, January 30, May 7, June 11, 1908; *Laws of Indiana*, special session, 1908, p. 14.

John S. Crump Street Railway, Columbus

Winona Interurban Railway Car

Making Glass Jar at Ball Brothers, Muncie

Van Camp Advertisement, 1890

Swans Down Girl, Trade-Mark
of Igleheart Brothers

Equity was ultimately most successful among wheat growers, who created co-operative elevators and marketing associations to secure higher prices for their grain crop. It was chiefly representatives of this interest who forced Everitt, who had conducted the organization's business almost single-handedly, out of the presidency in 1907 and moved the national union headquarters to Chicago. As the movement's center of gravity shifted to the wheat belt north and west of Indiana, Hoosier membership and influence declined. Everitt himself reorganized his dwindling group of supporters under the name Farmers' Society of Equity which he continued to direct through the pages of his *Up-to-Date Farming* until 1916, but neither the organization nor the journal prospered during its final decade of existence.[143]

In the same year as the founding of the American Society of Equity, Newton Gresham established the Farmers' Educational and Cooperative Union in Texas. Similar in its objectives to Equity but organized as a secret society, the Farmers' Union entered Indiana in 1907, when John K. Weinmeister of Daviess County was named state organizer. Two years later he reported the organization of one hundred and fifty local unions, and by 1910 claimed a state membership of nearly five thousand, or the largest in the north. The Farmers' Union was mostly active in Indiana in the relatively poor southeastern counties, where it was credited with organizing a number of co-operative elevators and stores as well as shipping associations. In the state as a whole, however, it was little more successful than Equity in holding the loyalty of Hoosier farmers.[144]

Crop diversification and comparatively easy access to markets were undoubtedly a factor in the failure of this type of

[143] *Up-to-Date Farming,* November 1, 15, December 8, 1907; Bahmer, "The American Society of Equity," *Agricultural History,* XIV, 54-56.

[144] Charles S. Barrett, *The Mission, History, and Times of the Farmers' Union* (Nashville, Tenn., 1909), p. 329; Commodore B. Fisher, *The Farmers' Union* (Lexington, Ky., 1920), pp. 45-48. Although Fisher reported only 743 members in 1919 in Indiana, Latta gave the total as 2,500 in 1925. Latta, *Outline History of Indiana Agriculture,* p. 298.

farmers' organization in Indiana, while both Equity and the Farmers' Union flourished in those less-favored regions of the West and South which tended to be dependent upon a single crop. A United States Department of Agriculture study of one hundred farms in Clinton County, Indiana, from 1910 to 1918 presents this picture of the reasonably profitable character of an average diversified farm operation in the state:

AVERAGE ANNUAL PRODUCTION AND INCOME FOR ONE HUNDRED FARMS IN CLINTON COUNTY, 1910-1918[145]

| Crops and livestock products | | Amount Harvested | Amount Sold | Cash Income |
|---|---|---|---|---|
| Corn | (43 acres) | 1,935 bushels | 486 bushels | $ 408 |
| Wheat | (10 acres) | 180 bushels | 166 bushels | 221 |
| Oats | (25 acres) | 1,075 bushels | 811 bushels | 375 |
| Hay | (12 acres) | 16 tons | 4 tons | 44 |
| Clover seed | | 7 bushels | 5 bushels | 42 |
| Hogs | | | 1,000 pounds | 1,225 |
| Cattle | | | 6 head | 290 |
| Butterfat | | | 329 pounds | 112 |
| Horses | | | 1 head | 41 |
| Sheep | | | 1 head ⎱ | 9 |
| Wool | | | 7 pounds ⎰ | |
| Poultry | | | 62 head ⎱ | 125 |
| Eggs | | | 330 dozen ⎰ | |
| Other Products sold | | | | 89 |
| | | | Total | $2,981 |

The final thrust of the farmers' movement in this period brought to the fore a quite different sort of organization than any of the earlier ones. In 1911, in order to organize and support the work of county agricultural agents in Broome County, New York, the Binghamton Chamber of Commerce established the first "farm bureau," the name eventually given to many of the societies connected with the agricultural exten-

145 E. Z. Russell *et al.,* "Hog Production and Marketing," in United States Department of Agriculture, *Yearbook,* 1922, p. 204. The data in the above article was taken in part from a study by H. M. Dixon and H. W. Hawthorne, *Farm Profits* . . . (United States Department of Agriculture, *Bulletin 920,* 1920).

sion program throughout the United States.[146] In Indiana farmers and businessmen began forming similar organizations to aid county agents in demonstration and educational work in local communities as early as 1912. Often incorporating representatives of various pre-existing farm and business associations, these groups sprang up in many counties over the state as the county-agent system expanded.

The First World War, which created a driving demand for increased agricultural production, strengthened the agricultural-extension movement and encouraged the formation of larger numbers of "Better Farming Associations," as most of the newly organized groups styled themselves in Indiana. In March, 1919, not long after the end of the war, four hundred delegates from such societies met in Indianapolis to organize the Indiana Federation of Farmers' Associations under the presidency of John G. Brown of Monon.[147] For the most part these men represented the more successful, substantial farmers of the state, many of whom shared the fear of anarchism and communism which infected the atmosphere of postwar America and planned to make their organization a sane, conservative force for civil order, dedicated to farm interests in a businesslike, utterly nonrevolutionary fashion. "We are not out for class legislation," stated an editorial in the federation's newsletter in June, "but a square deal between the three general classes—producers, distributors and consumers. . . . The farmers represent the land owners, the home makers, the law-abiding element. Hence this great movement of organizing and federating the farmers will make for the stability and perpetuity of our civil and religious institutions."[148]

[146] Orville M. Kile, *The Farm Bureau Movement* . . . (New York, 1921), pp. 94-96.

[147] *Organized Farmer* (Indianapolis), June, 1919, pp. 3-5.

[148] *Ibid.,* June, 1919, p. 16. The same issue of this journal contained a note emphasizing the difference between this organization and the radical Nonpartisan League farther west: "The farmers of Indiana will not go to extremes. They have grievances like the North Dakota farmers. But they will not take the same road to correct these grievances." *Ibid.,* p. 5.

The federation not only helped its member associations pool their orders for the purchase of binder twine and commercial fertilizers at less than retail market prices, but also successfully intervened with the United States Department of Agriculture to avert a quarantine of Indiana wheat in the summer of 1919, when the Australian "take-all" disease erupted. By November it was able to claim seventy-five counties organized with forty thousand farmers enrolled and had become the first state organization to affiliate officially with the newly formed National Federation of Farm Bureaus. In December, 1920, the Indiana Farm Bureau, as it was eventually called, entered fully into the co-operative purchasing business with the establishment of its Federated Marketing Service.[149]

The Farm Bureau movement marked the end of an era of agrarian protest and agitation in Indiana. While utilizing some of the co-operative methods and political lobbying promoted earlier by the Grange, the Alliances, the Society of Equity, and other groups, this newest farmers' organization eschewed any taint of agrarian radicalism and developed a conservative coalition with both business and government in order to create a more efficient and profitable agriculture. In an age when scientific agricultural techniques and rapidly advancing mechanization was making farming a complex, heavily capitalized business, the Indiana Farm Bureau became a fitting agency for Hoosier farmers who were beginning to take a businessman's view of both economics and politics.

149 *Hoosier Farmer* (formerly the *Organized Farmer*), August, 1919, p. 16; November, 1919, pp. 3, 12-13; December, 1919, pp. 4-5; Paul Turner, *They Did It in Indiana: The Story of the Indiana Farm Bureau Co-operatives* (New York, 1947), pp. 16-18.

# CHAPTER V

# THE EXPLOITATION AND CONSERVATION OF NATURAL RESOURCES

AT THE OPENING of the last quarter of the nineteenth century, the commonwealth of Indiana seemed to possess an almost inexhaustible plenitude of natural wealth in its soil, forests, lakes, rivers, and streams, as well as beneath the surface of the earth. The chief problem lay not in finding ways of conserving but in appropriating and utilizing most profitably these resources. Primarily an agricultural state, Indiana needed capital and skilled labor to exploit fully its extensive coal measures, clay and limestone beds, and other mineral deposits. Although sporadic geological surveys of the state had been carried out before the Civil War by David Dale Owen, Richard Owen, and Ryland T. Brown, not until 1869 did the Indiana General Assembly establish the permanent office of state geologist, charged with the task of collecting and disseminating information concerning natural resources for the "promotion of agriculture, mining, the arts and manufactures."[1] The first man appointed to this post was Edward T. Cox of New Harmony, who had served as an assistant and field worker under the Owen brothers. During his ten-year occupancy of the office he published seven volumes of reports containing geological surveys of thirty of the state's counties and a number of brief essays on miscellaneous aspects of its natural history, the whole presented in a rather repetitious and unsystematic manner.[2]

[1] *Laws of Indiana,* regular session, 1869, pp. 22-24.

[2] Indiana Geological Survey, *Annual Reports,* 1870-1879. The *Reports* for the years 1876, 1877, and 1878 were not published until 1879. For the geological surveys prior to 1879, see Willis S. Blatchley, "A Century of Geology in Indiana," Indiana Academy of Science, *Proceedings,* 1916, pp. 89-143, and Thornbrough, *Indiana in the Civil War Era,* pp. 658-662.

In 1879, however, in order to comply with a long-standing demand for a state statistical service, the General Assembly passed a bill which at the request of the frugal Governor James D. Williams incorporated this task with the geological survey in a combined Department of Statistics and Geology. Furthermore, the economy-minded legislature appropriated only the extremely small sum of $3,700 for the agency's annual budget, including a miserly salary of $1,200 for the director. Cox, whose salary had been raised to $3,000 in 1873, refused to continue the work under these conditions, and the dual appointment of state geologist and chief of the new department went to a Vermillion County native, John Collett, one of Cox's assistants.[3]

The reduced budget and doubled responsibility greatly limited the effectiveness of the geological survey. Collett, whose first report was virtually all statistics and no geology, immediately requested a substantially increased appropriation in order to carry on his work properly. In 1881, the newly elected Republican governor, Albert G. Porter, recommended such action to the legislature, which responded by creating two separate agencies, a Department of Statistics and a Department of Geology and Natural History, each with a relatively generous budgetary allowance.[4] Collett, who was named to head the latter department, remained in that office until 1885, when Democratic Governor Isaac P. Gray replaced him with a man of his own political persuasion. During his term of office Collett continued the system of county surveys begun by Cox and published notes on Indiana's natural re-

3 *Laws of Indiana*, 1873, p. 145; 1879, pp. 193-195; Blatchley, "A Century of Geology in Indiana," Indiana Academy of Science, *Proceedings*, 1916, p. 145. After leaving the survey Cox opened a geological consulting office in New York and later became a geologist for a large mining company in Florida, where he died in 1907. Blatchley, "A Century of Geology in Indiana," *loc. cit.*, p. 143. John Collett was a graduate of Wabash College, which also conferred an honorary Ph.D. upon him in 1879. His death occurred in 1899.

4 *Laws of Indiana*, 1881, pp. 523-524. The state geologist's salary was raised to $1,800 (see 1882 *Report* for the Department), still far below that paid Cox from 1873 to 1879; the total budget for the Department of Geology and Natural History was a respectable $5,000.

sources in a frankly promotional manner. In 1884, in answer to the charge that the annual geological reports were merely advertisements for the state, he argued that "the results show that they have been good advertisements, and that it pays well to advertise in that way." Publicity of this kind was necessary, he added, in order to attract settlers and develop the state's economic potential: "Indiana must show her attractions—must thrust her invitations into the hands of outsiders to enlist them in her army of productive citizens. We have room for millions. Our mines and quarries are only opened. Our forests offer the best of timber to the workers in wood. . . . We not only have room for immigrants, but we need their help."[5]

Governor Gray's choice of a successor to Collett fell upon Maurice Thompson, a civil engineer and popular Crawfordsville author who wrote his geological reports with more literary flair than scientific precision. His resignation in December, 1888, and the election of a Republican governor together with a Democratic-controlled legislature set the stage for a political tug-of-war which further mired the office of geological survey in partisan politics. In January, 1889, the General Assembly passed over Governor Alvin P. Hovey's veto a bill which attempted to transfer from the chief executive to the legislature itself the power to appoint the state geologist and also established a Department of Geology and Natural Resources under the latter's direction, with subordinate officials in charge of coal mining, "mineral oils," and natural gas, which had been recently discovered in east-central Indiana.[6] Rejecting the legislature's action depriving him of his power of appointment as unconstitutional, Governor Hovey proceeded to name John Collett state geologist and director of the new department. When the Democratic incumbent, Sylvester S. Gorby, who had filled the vacancy

[5] Indiana Department of Geology and Natural History, *Annual Report*, 1884, pp. 9-10.

[6] *Laws of Indiana*, 1889, pp. 44-49; Blatchley, "A Century of Geology in Indiana," Indiana Academy of Science, *Proceedings*, 1916, pp. 154-159.

left by Thompson's resignation first by appointment from Governor Gray and later the General Assembly, refused to surrender the office, Collett took the matter to court. The question was finally resolved by the Indiana Supreme Court, which in a sweeping decision ruled against the legislature's seizure of the appointive power but also declared that since the office of director of the Department of Geology and Natural Resources was an administrative one, under the state constitution it must be filled by popular election![7]

The political controversy took its toll of the scientific study of natural resources in Indiana. Gorby, who was duly elected state geologist in 1890, issued only three reports during his four years in office, and those were generally mediocre. But the state was peculiarly fortunate in the electorate's choice of his successor, Willis Stanley Blatchley, a Connecticut-born science teacher from a Terre Haute high school, who was elected on the Republican ticket in 1894. Blatchley, a gifted and dedicated naturalist, was re-elected three times and during his sixteen years in office made a systematic study of Indiana's natural resources, collecting scientific knowledge and disseminating practical information concerning their commercial value and industrial uses. Abandoning the county-by-county survey conducted by his predecessors, he reported on each resource separately, issuing annually a series of monographs prepared by himself and members of his staff on clays and sandstone, coal measures, petroleum, Portland cement, limestone, the lime industry, mineral waters and hot springs, and even gravel beds useful for road building materials.[8]

In 1907 Blatchley endeavored to extend the activities of the Department of Geology and Natural Resources to the

[7] State ex rel. Collett v. Gorby, 122 Ind. 17 (1889); Blatchley, "A Century of Geology in Indiana," Indiana Academy of Science, *Proceedings,* 1916, pp. 159-161. Blatchley noted that Indiana, which continued to elect its state geologist until 1919, was unique in this respect.

[8] See Blatchley's statement of purpose in the introduction to his first report in Indiana Department of Geology and Natural Resources, *Annual Report,* 1895, p. 5.

field of agriculture by making county soil surveys, beginning
with counties in the unglaciated southern section of the state
and continuing the work initiated five years earlier by the
Bureau of Soils of the United States Department of Agriculture.[9] Edward T. Barrett, who was elected to succeed Blatchley in 1910, conducted the soil surveys as the major work of
the department, on the assumption, perhaps, that his predecessor had exhausted the study of other natural resources in
the state. Barrett's statement of purpose in his first report,
"to assist farmers in increasing the productivity of the soil"
and to help "make two blades of grass grow where one had
grown before, by suggesting better methods of drainage,
aeration, adaptation, rotation, and tillage," clearly reflected
the prevailing concern with commercial exploitation rather
than conservation. The next year the United States Bureau of
Soils began a co-operative program of soil surveys with the
Indiana Department of Geology and Natural Resources which
continued until 1916, when the Federal agency resumed primary responsibility for this activity.[10] Barrett, moreover,
was the last elected state geologist, for in 1919 the General
Assembly created a Department of Conservation headed by
an appointee of the governor and containing a subordinate
Division of Geology whose chief, the state geologist, was
chosen from the staff of Indiana University.[11]

§ §

Although coal had long been mined in Indiana, by the
eighties it was just beginning to take its place as a major

[9] *Ibid.,* 1907, pp. 9-11.

[10] *Ibid.,* 1911, pp. 7-9, 27; 1912, p. 7; 1916, pp. 8-9. The study of soils
was still in its infancy in this period and mostly centered around the analysis of
glaciation. The first attempt to locate accurately the southern limits of the
Wisconsin Drift in Indiana was done in 1882-1883 by Professors T. W. Cham-
berlain of the University of Chicago and G. Frederick Wright of Oberlin College, according to Blatchley, "A Century of Geology in Indiana," Indiana
Academy of Science, *Proceedings,* 1916, pp. 164-165. The modern scientific
analysis of soils dates only from the 1920's, when C. F. Marbut and others
introduced into America the work of the Russian school of soil science. *Soil
Survey Manual* (United States Department of Agriculture, *Handbook No. 18,*
1951), pp. 3-4.

[11] *Laws of Indiana,* 1919, pp. 375-392.

factor in the development of the state's economy. As the state geologist reported in 1881, "production has been limited to the demands of a new country with few factories, but the promise for the future from these treasure houses is grand."[12] Comprising a small segment of the Eastern Interior Coal Region which included much of Illinois and western Kentucky as well, the Indiana bituminous coal field covered an area of approximately seven thousand square miles in the western and southwestern part of the state, extending from Warren County south to the Ohio River and stretching across

Visher, *Economic Geography of Indiana*

The Indiana Coal Field

the counties of Vanderburgh, Warrick, Spencer, and Perry. Workable veins were found in nineteen counties and thin outcrops in three additional ones. The most highly developed and productive seams in the mid-nineties were located in Clay, Sullivan, Greene, Daviess, and Pike counties, closely followed by Vigo, Owen, Warrick, and Spencer.[13] Clay County, with its valuable veins of "block" coal, a hard, noncaking bituminous type which came from the mines in large rectangular blocks, led production in 1880 with 57.2 per cent of the state's total output but declined to 27.5 per cent in 1890 and 5.4 per cent in 1920, when the largest producers were Vigo County with 27.1 per cent and Sullivan with 16.0 per cent. Greene

12 Indiana Department of Geology and Natural History, *Annual Report*, 1881, p. 16.

13 Indiana Department of Geology and Natural Resources, *Annual Report*, 1895, p. 8. For a thorough study of coal mining in Indiana in this period, see the survey made by George W. Ashley in *ibid.*, 1898, pp. 1-1573. This material was updated in *ibid.*, 1905, pp. 1061-1147.

and Vermillion counties, which had barely begun mining coal in the eighties, were next in order in 1920 with 10.7 and 11.3 per cent, respectively.[14]

Indiana's coal measures extended down from a few feet to as much as three hundred feet below the surface. The chief method of mining was by shafts sunk into the ground to reach the seams where miners working in "rooms" cut out the coal, largely by pick and shovel, and delivered it to the surface by mule cars and hoisting equipment. In the beginning mining was virtually unregulated by the state and was conducted under extremely hazardous conditions. To remedy this, the General Assembly in 1879 enacted its first significant piece of mining legislation, providing for the appointment of an inspector who was instructed to visit each mine twice a year in order to enforce safety measures called for in the law, such as the requirement for suitable outlets for miners in case of accidents, proper ventilation, and the workable condition of ropes, machinery, and other equipment.[15] The first mine inspector, Herbert H. Richards, found few of the 177 producing mines in the state in safe operating condition, and recommended the passage of additional legislation, advice with which nearly every subsequent General Assembly complied for many years.[16]

Mechanization of mining processes was comparatively slow in Indiana, partly because of the small size of many mines

[14] See the table in George W. Starr, *Industrial Development of Indiana* (*Indiana Studies in Business, No. 14*, Bloomington, 1937), p. 88.

[15] *Laws of Indiana*, 1879, pp. 19-25. For an account of the origin of this legislation, see Thornbrough, *Indiana in the Civil War Era*, pp. 450-451. The 1879 law also prohibited the employment of boys under fourteen years of age in the mines. For discussion of this and other child labor legislation in Indiana, see below, Chapter VIII.

[16] Indiana State Mine Inspector, *Annual Report*, 1879-1880, pp. 30-38. Mining laws were passed in 1883, 1885, 1889, 1891, 1893, 1895, 1897, 1903, 1905, 1907, 1909, 1911, and 1913. List of Mining Laws Passed by Indiana Legislators 1850-1913 (Typescript compiled by Indiana Legislative Reference Bureau, [1922], Indiana State Library). See also Kathryn D. Schakel, Some Aspects of Coal Mining in Indiana (Unpublished Master's thesis in History, Butler University, 1934), pp. 40-41, 41-42, 51-52.

and partly because the operators found it difficult to over-come the prejudices of the miners in favor of the customary techniques. Although steam-power hoists were commonly used by 1880, the first coal-cutting machinery in the state was reportedly installed by the Curriesville Coal Company in Sullivan County in 1884 as the result of a miners' strike.[17] In the next decades many other operators followed this exam-ple, introducing air-compression punching machines and electric chain machines for the cutting and removal of coal. Yet by 1909 only 50.6 per cent of the coal produced in Indiana was mined by machinery, as compared with 80.4 per cent in Ohio and 61.5 per cent in Kentucky.[18] As late as 1919, more-over, according to the Indiana Department of Mines and Min-ing, pick-mined coal still amounted to nearly half the total production, and only Greene, Knox, and Sullivan counties produced substantially more coal by machine than by hand.[19]

In 1919 the mine inspector also reported the existence of strip mining in Indiana, though noting that stripping opera-tions did not come under his jurisdiction. In fact strip mines had appeared in the state as early as 1904 and by 1917 were producing about a million tons a year in fifteen counties. This method of recovering high-quality coal from deposits too shallow to be excavated by underground mining required the removal of a twelve to forty-foot overburden by steam shovels and draglines, badly scarring the landscape. Little attention was paid, however, to the problem of reclaiming the thousands of acres of gouged surface affected by the new method of mining until the 1930's, when conservationists began their efforts to encourage the planting of trees in such areas.[20]

[17] Indiana State Mine Inspector, *Annual Report,* 1884, pp. 11-13.

[18] United States Bureau of the Census, *Thirteenth Census* (1910), XI, *Mines and Quarries,* p. 213.

[19] Indiana *Year Book,* 1919, pp. 340-341.

[20] *Ibid.,* p. 328; Robert D. Loring, "The Growth of Strip Mining in In-diana," Indiana Academy of Science, *Proceedings,* LXI (1951), 184; Lee Guern-sey, "Reclamation of Strip-mined Lands in Vigo County," *ibid.,* LXVII (1957), pp. 215-224.

Total coal production in Indiana climbed more or less steadily from 1880, when the annual tonnage exceeded a million for the first time, to 1918, when over thirty million tons were mined, falling off somewhat in the immediate postwar years. A major expansion took place around the turn of the century, as the failing supply of natural gas began to create a rising demand for coal as an industrial fuel. The expanded production was made possible by the investment of additional capital and increased mechanization as well as by the opening of new mines. At the same time a major consolidation of coal-mining properties was effected in Indiana. In the years 1904 and 1905 alone, the state mine inspector reported that eighty-one mines had changed hands and that seventy-two of them had been brought together into six large companies.[21]

The mining industry in Indiana experienced its greatest prosperity in wartime, when the entry of the United States into the European conflict made coal a chief economic weapon on the home front. Yet Indiana coal never became an important factor in the national or international market, partly because of its somewhat inferior quality. Unfavorable freight rates and relatively high labor costs have also been cited as factors in restricting the industry's growth. Within the state, however, coal mining carried great economic weight, aiding its industrialization and employing thousands of workers in the seventeen or more coal-producing counties themselves.[22] The table below indicates the annual production and value of all coal mined in Indiana during this period:

[21] Indiana Department of Geology and Natural Resources, *Annual Report,* 1908, pp. 28-29.

[22] Starr, *Industrial Development of Indiana,* p. 86.

## COAL PRODUCTION AND VALUE, 1880-1920[23]

| Year | Short tons | Value |
|------|-----------|-------|
| 1880 | 1,454,327 | |
| 1881 | 1,771,536 | |
| 1882 | 1,976,470 | |
| 1883 | 2,560,000 | |
| 1884 | 2,260,000 | |
| 1885 | 2,375,000 | |
| 1886 | 3,000,000 | $ 3,450,000 |
| 1887 | 3,217,711 | 4,324,604 |
| 1888 | 3,140,979 | 4,397,370 |
| 1889 | 2,845,057 | 2,887,852 |
| 1890 | 3,305,737 | 3,259,233 |
| 1891 | 2,973,474 | 3,070,918 |
| 1892 | 3,345,174 | 3,620,582 |
| 1893 | 3,791,851 | 4,055,372 |
| 1894 | 3,423,921 | 3,295,034 |
| 1895 | 3,995,892 | 3,642,623 |
| 1896 | 3,905,779 | 3,261,737 |
| 1897 | 4,151,169 | 3,472,348 |
| 1898 | 4,920,743 | 3,994,918 |
| 1899 | 6,006,523 | 5,285,018 |
| 1900 | 6,484,086 | 6,687,137 |
| 1901 | 6,918,225 | 7,017,143 |
| 1902 | 9,446,424 | 10,400,000 |
| 1903 | 10,794,692 | 13,244,817 |
| 1904 | 10,842,189 | 12,004,300 |
| 1905 | 11,895,252 | 12,492,255 |
| 1906 | 12,092,560 | 13,116,261 |
| 1907 | 13,985,713 | 15,114,300 |
| 1908 | 12,314,890 | 13,084,297 |
| 1909 | 14,834,259 | 15,154,681 |
| 1910 | 18,389,815 | 20,813,659 |
| 1911 | 14,201,355 | 15,326,808 |
| 1912 | 15,285,718 | 17,480,546 |
| 1913 | 17,165,671 | 19,001,881 |
| 1914 | 16,641,132 | 18,290,928 |
| 1915 | 17,006,152 | 18,637,476 |
| 1916 | 20,093,528 | 25,506,246 |
| 1917 | 26,539,329 | 52,940,106 |
| 1918 | 30,678,634 | 70,384,601 |
| 1919 | 20,912,288 | 46,345,750 |
| 1920 | 29,350,585 | 92,867,000 |

Indiana bituminous, which was chiefly used as a steaming coal, was too "spongy" to make good coke, though small amounts were being manufactured from it as early as 1886. By 1899 the state geologist reported only a single coke manufacturer, David Ingle, who operated twenty-four "beehive" ovens in Ayrshire, Pike County.[24] The introduction of retort ovens in the early twentieth century, however, revolutionized the manufacture of coke, especially by creating commercially valuable by-products such as tar, ammonia, and coal gas. After 1908 this process was extensively used in the iron and steel complex at Gary, where the United States Steel Company manufactured coke for use in its own blast furnaces. Ironically, between that date and 1912 Indiana moved abruptly from thirteenth to first place among coke-producing states, though virtually all the coal used to make coke was imported from West Virginia and other distant points. In the latter year the total value of coke and its by-products manufactured in Indiana, including illuminating and fuel gas, tar, anhydrous ammonia, and ammoniated liquids, amounted to $18,119,645.[25]

The seemingly huge reserves of coal in Indiana precluded any overt interest in the conservation of this natural resource until the First World War, when severe shortages occurred. Finally, in 1919 the state geologist, claiming that Indiana mining methods were more wasteful than those used in many other bituminous-producing states, made extensive recommendations concerning the removal of upper veins before lower ones, substitution, where possible, of the "long wall" system for the more commonly employed room and pillar system, and cleaner strip-pit mining. Since private oper-

23 Compiled from the United States Geological Survey, *Mineral Resources of the United States,* 1882-1920. No accurate figures are available for the value of coal mined prior to 1885. The statistics given here are slightly different from those reported in the Indiana Department of Geology and Natural Resources, *Annual Reports,* 1895-1910, and the Indiana *Year Book,* 1917-1920.

24 Indiana Department of Geology and Natural Resources, *Annual Report,* 1899, p. 20.

25 United States Geological Survey, *Mineral Resources of the United States,* 1912, II, *Nonmetals,* pp. 1182-1183, 1188, 1193.

ators showed little inclination to make such changes, the next year the mine inspection office called for immediate state regulation in order to "halt this reckless, useless waste . . . before it is too late."[26]

Whether or not Indiana's coal measures were being significantly wasted for lack of attention to the principles of conservation, natural gas provided Hoosiers with a recent and striking example of careless exploitation and the eventual exhaustion of one of the state's most valuable natural resources. Although it failed in the first decade of the twentieth century, the Indiana natural gas field had an unparalelled impact upon the economic development of the state. Its discovery and rapid commercial exploitation from the late eighties onward gave a sudden, powerful impulse to the industrialization of a predominantly agricultural economy. Brief as the natural gas era was, it spanned the years of Indiana's industrial "take-off," when large infusions of outside capital took place and important new industries were established.

The earliest recorded flows of natural gas in Indiana dated back as far as 1865 at Francesville, Pulaski County, Eaton in Delaware County, and Terre Haute. But it was only after large strikes were made near Findlay, Ohio, in 1884-1885, that prospectors began drilling in earnest in Indiana. At this time State Geologist Maurice Thompson also began gathering materials for a report on the geology of the natural gas field, a part of which was published in the Indianapolis newspapers. Before the full report could be officially released, however, the news came of the first successful well bored near Portland, Jay County, in March, 1886. In September two more gas strikes were made at Kokomo and Eaton, in the latter place by redrilling an old well first opened in 1876. By 1888 wells were in flow at or near such towns and cities as Alexandria, Anderson, Elwood, Hartford City, Marion, Montpelier, and New Castle.[27]

26 Indiana *Year Book,* 1919, pp. 401-404; 1920, p. 725.
27 Indiana Department of Geology and Natural History, *Annual Report,* 1886, pp. 320-331; Esarey, *History of Indiana,* II, 910-912.

The gas boom continued for almost two decades, but the main period of active prospecting continued only until 1896. By that time the Indiana natural gas field had become the largest in the world. The main gas pool was located in Trenton limestone underlying the east-central portion of the state. Centering on the city of Muncie, the "Gas Belt," as it was quickly dubbed, extended across an area of about 3,750 square miles made up of parts of nineteen counties, chief of which were Blackford, Grant, Howard, Delaware, Hamilton, Madison, Hancock, Henry, Randolph, Rush, and Tipton. Just outside this central zone gas was also found in Adams, Decatur, Jay, Marion, Shelby, Wabash, Wayne, and Wells counties.[28]

Since at first the gas was thought to be practically inexhaustible, little or no attempt was made to control or conserve its flow. The freely escaping high-pressure gas fed great flaming torches, or flambeaux, which often burned day and night for months at the well sites. Special excursion trains brought thousands of visitors to enjoy the unusual sights, and a spirit of carnival reigned for a time over the region. Scores of companies were formed to distribute natural gas to consumers, who began to use the inexpensive fuel for cooking, lighting, and heating. Towns and villages in the Gas Belt utilized flambeaux for street lighting, and by the early nineties pipelines had been constructed to carry natural gas to cities outside the producing area, such as Indianapolis, Lebanon, Crawfordsville, Frankfort, Peru, Wabash, Huntington, Bluffton, Fort Wayne, Decatur, Union City, Richmond, Connersville, Shelbyville, and even Chicago and a few places in Ohio.[29]

[28] Indiana Department of Geology and Natural Resources, *Annual Report,* 1891, pp. 328-329; 1899, pp. 205-209. Other counties which produced smaller amounts of natural gas were Daviess, De Kalb, Fayette, Franklin, Harrison, Jefferson, Jennings, Knox, Lawrence, and Ripley.

[29] Indiana Department of Statistics, *Biennial Report,* 1885-1886, pp. xvii-xxi; Indiana Department of Geology and Natural Resources, *Annual Report,* 1899, pp. 209-210. Accounts of the early gas boom are found in Barnhart and Carmony, *Indiana,* II, 282-284; C. C. Lydick, Natural Gas in Indiana (Unpublished MS, 1946, Indiana State Library) ; Margaret Wynn, "Natural Gas in Indiana: An Exploited Resource," *Indiana Magazine of History,* IV (1908), 31-45.

The immediate effect of the gas boom in Indiana was to accelerate an already developing industrial economy. It did so partly by stimulating the economic growth of nearby industrial cities such as Indianapolis, Fort Wayne, and Richmond, but also by creating an entirely new area of industrialization in the Gas Belt itself, which had been hitherto chiefly an agricultural region. Promoters hastened to advertise abroad the area's newly realized advantages for industry, some communities even offering both free gas and free factory sites to prospective manufacturers. Almost overnight the Gas Belt became a scene of intensive industrial activity, as eastern capitalists built plants to manufacture glass, tinplate, strawboard, and other products, some of them transplanted from Ohio and Pennsylvania, where the natural gas supply had begun to falter. Real estate values rose, and the new prosperity of the region not only affected the merchants and other townsmen but even the farmers in the surrounding countryside. New towns sprang up as if by magic, and old established communities doubled or tripled their population within the space of a few years. The ranks of Indiana's industrial cities swelled to include Alexandria, Anderson, Elwood, Gas City, Hartford City, Kokomo, Marion, Muncie, New Castle, and Noblesville. As early as 1890 the Department of Statistics calculated that 162 factories capitalized at nearly $10,000,000 had been located in the Gas Belt since the first strike, creating more than ten thousand jobs. Three years later it was estimated that the number of factories built in Indiana as a direct result of the discovery and development of natural gas was "not less than 300."[30]

This rapid industrial development placed a heavy burden on the productive capacity of the several hundred active wells in the Gas Belt. From the very beginning of the boom, moreover, the production, transmission, and consumption of natural gas were marked by a great deal of inefficiency and waste. In 1891 the General Assembly finally enacted a law

---

[30] Indiana Department of Statistics, *Biennial Report*, 1889-1890, pp. 5-7; Indiana Department of Geology and Natural Resources, *Annual Report*, 1893, p. 198.

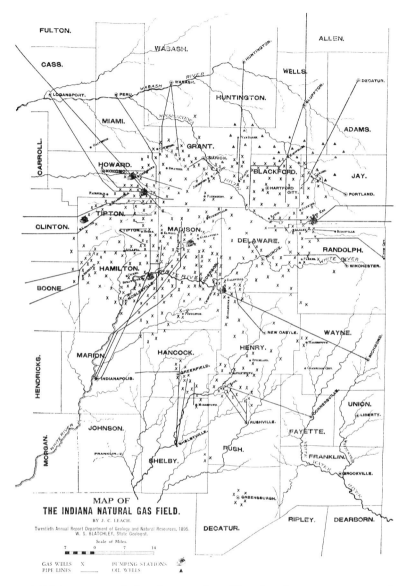

MAP OF
THE INDIANA NATURAL GAS FIELD.
BY J. C. LEACH.
Twentieth Annual Report Department of Geology and Natural Resources, 1895.
W. S. BLATCHLEY, State Geologist.
Scale of Miles.
7      0      7      14

GAS WELLS    X          PUMPING STATIONS
PIPE LINES   _____     OIL WELLS          ▲

prohibiting use of flambeaux for illuminating purposes and
providing for a state inspector of natural gas to enforce this
and other regulations. Public sentiment in the Gas Belt so
opposed this measure as to make it unenforceable until after
the Indiana Supreme Court declared its constitutionality in

1896.[31] Meters were almost unknown, and customers were encouraged to burn more fuel than necessary because they were charged by the month or year rather than for a measured amount of gas. Pipeline leaks and the failure to plug abandoned wells were other sources of waste. In 1893 the state inspector of natural gas estimated that 100,000,000 cubic feet per day had been wasted during the first few years of production and predicted the early exhaustion of the field. "The waste has been criminal," he wrote, "and the day of repentance is fast approaching, and can only be delayed by practicing the most rigid economy and unrelaxed efforts in the husbandry of this valuable resource of our State."[32]

By 1898 the state geologist, in a report planned four years before and in the process of preparation for almost two years, announced that the supply of natural gas for manufacturing purposes was virtually at an end. The problem remaining was "how best to retain within our State most, if not all, of the many factories which had been erected since 1888. . . . ." The only solution, he argued, was "to show the owners of those factories that within the bounds of Indiana was a supply of fuel sufficient to last for centuries, and of a quality equal almost to that of any other State." Three alternatives were proposed: the transport of coal from the Indiana coal fields to the Gas Belt factories; relocation of factories near the coal supplies; or relocation along the Ohio River, where coal could be brought in cheaply from West Virginia by water transport.[33] By the early years of the twentieth century, however, many newly built factories in the Gas Belt, especially the smaller glass-manufacturing establishments, were forced to close their doors or at least remove to other states with more favorable fuel resources. On the other hand, the impetus given Indiana's industrialization by the discovery of natural gas was not permanently checked. Some manufacturers followed the advice of the state geologist and switched to other fuels such as coal or manufac-

[31] *Laws of Indiana*, 1891, pp. 55-56; Townsend *v.* The State, 147 Ind. 624 (1896).

[32] Indiana Department of Geology and Natural Resources, *Annual Report,* 1893, p. 217.

[33] *Ibid.,* 1898, pp. xix, xxii-xxiii.

tured gas. By 1913, moreover, natural gas from the West Virginia field was being piped into the state in large volume and was available for industrial as well as domestic use.[34] Although greatly depleted, the Indiana natural gas field continued through the first few decades of the twentieth century to produce small amounts of fuel, which were utilized only for domestic purposes in a few communities. By 1920, however, Indiana had become chiefly a consumer rather than a producer of this once apparently plentiful resource. Recklessness and haste in exploiting large but not endless reserves of natural gas had wasted an irreplaceable source of energy and endangered, though fortunately it did not permanently damage, the economic development of the state. On the whole, despite some missed opportunities and the obvious lack of a true spirit of conservation, the story of natural gas in Indiana was one of limited but significant success in utilizing the state's natural wealth for industrial advancement. The table below shows the rise and fall of the gas industry:

VALUE OF NATURAL GAS PRODUCED IN INDIANA,
1886-1920[35]

| Year | Value | Year | Value | Year | Value |
|------|-------|------|-------|------|-------|
| 1886 | $ 300,000 | 1898 | $5,060,969 | 1910 | $1,473,403 |
| 1887 | 600,000 | 1899 | 6,680,370 | 1911 | 1,192,418 |
| 1888 | 1,320,000 | 1900 | 7,254,539 | 1912 | 1,014,295 |
| 1889 | 2,075,702 | 1901 | 6,954,566 | 1913 | 843,047 |
| 1890 | 2,302,500 | 1902 | 7,081,344 | 1914 | 755,407 |
| 1891 | 3,942,500 | 1903 | 6,098,364 | 1915 | 695,380 |
| 1892 | 4,716,000 | 1904 | 4,342,409 | 1916 | 503,373 |
| 1893 | 5,718,000 | 1905 | 3,094,134 | 1917 | 453,310 |
| 1894 | 5,437,000 | 1906 | 1,750,715 | 1918 | 899,671 |
| 1895 | 5,203,200 | 1907 | 1,572,605 | 1919 | 547,000 |
| 1896 | 5,043,635 | 1908 | 1,312,507 | 1920 | 758,000 |
| 1897 | 5,009,208 | 1909 | 1,616,903 | | |

[34] Ibid., 1915, p. 267; United States Geological Survey, Mineral Resources of the United States, 1913, II, Nonmetals, pp. 1434-1435; E. A. Stoneman, "The Natural Gas Industry of Indiana," Indiana Academy of Science, Proceedings, LX (1950) 261.

[35] Compiled from United States Geological Survey, Mineral Resources of the United States, 1886-1920. See also a table which gives additional information for some of these years up to 1917 in W. N. Logan, Petroleum and Natural Gas in Indiana. A Preliminary Survey (Indiana Department of Conservation, Publication No. 8, Fort Wayne, 1920), p. 20.

The widespread search for natural gas in the late eighties brought to light the petroleum resources of Indiana, as drillers boring for gas often struck oil. Small traces of oil had been discovered as early as 1865, but the first significant commercial production came only in 1889, with a strike near Montpelier, Blackford County, and another at the center of Terre Haute. The latter was brought in as a spectacular gusher shooting forty to fifty feet in the air. A second drilling in the same city resulted in the famous "Phoenix" well, which became the best-paying well in the state, pumping a thousand barrels of oil per month for more than a dozen years. A few more bores were sunk in the neighborhood, but the Terre Haute field, where the oil lay in a Corniferous limestone, turned out to be only a minor producer, most of its product being marketed locally.[36]

Visher, *Economic Geography of Indiana*

Indiana Oil Fields

The main field in Indiana was located close to the Gas Belt, where oil was found in the same Trenton limestone as natural gas. In June, 1890, the first major oil strike was made on a farm near Keystone, Wells County. By 1904 over twenty thousand bores had been sunk, most of them producing successfully, in a four-hundred-square mile area comprising six counties —Adams, Blackford, Grant, Huntington, Jay, and Wells— on the northeastern border of the old gas field. The Indiana Trenton rock field was a westward extension of the Ohio (Lima) field, producing a dark-colored, ill-smelling crude oil high in sulphur content, which sold for about fifty cents a

[36] Indiana Department of Geology and Natural Resources, *Annual Report,* 1906, pp. 539-544; 1907, pp. 473-474.

barrel less than the higher grade Pennsylvania product. Large companies were active in the field, but much of the drilling was done by small operators, "wildcatters," who leased land from farmers and bored for oil, taking a loss on dry holes and usually selling out to Standard Oil or a competing company if a producing well was sunk. Pipelines were built into the field to transport the oil to Ohio for refining and later to Whiting, Indiana, where the Standard Oil Company built the largest refinery in the world expressly to process the Indiana-Lima crude.[37]

Unlike the Pennsylvania oil, the product of the Indiana and Ohio wells contained so much sulphur that special refining methods were necessary in order to eliminate the offensive substance. Therefore, the directors of the Standard Oil Trust, which John D. Rockefeller and others had created in 1879, decided to build in the Middle West a new type of refinery using the copper-oxide process invented recently by Herman Prasch for the removal of sulphur compounds from crude petroleum. In 1889 the construction of the huge factory was begun near Chicago at Whiting, Indiana, in the desolate dune country along the southern shore of Lake Michigan. In the same year the Standard Oil Company of Indiana was incorporated, and the operation of the new installation, which was not completed until 1890, was placed under its jurisdiction. Pipelines and pumping stations, one of the largest located near English Lake, Starke County, were also built to supply the refinery with crude oil from the Ohio and Indiana fields.[38]

Later, however, with the gradual depletion of the Indiana-Lima oil field, the company was forced to turn to the West for the major part of its supply of crude, bringing it to Whiting by specially laid pipelines. When the growing popularity of the automobile in the early twentieth century created a heavy demand for gasoline, the research department at

[37] *Ibid.*, 1896, pp. 46-47, 55, 82-96; 1904, pp. 791-795.
[38] *Ibid.*, 1893, p. 191; Paul H. Giddens, *Standard Oil Company (Indiana) Oil Pioneer of the Middle West* (New York, 1955), pp. 2-18.

Whiting under the direction of chemist William M. Burton, later president of Standard Oil of Indiana, perfected the famous cracking process during the years 1909-1913.[39]

Meanwhile, a second oil boom occurred in the heart of the old Indiana gas field in 1897, when a few successful wells were sunk near Alexandria. Within a year seventy-five bores were drilled, forty of which produced oil and gas together. This initiated a harsh controversy between the oil companies and the state, for the producers usually permitted the unwanted gas to escape while pumping out the oil, contrary to a law of 1893 prohibiting such waste. Not until 1898, when the Indiana Supreme Court ruled against the Ohio Oil Company, was the issue resolved, though it meant virtually closing down most oil wells of the region.[40] Since oil and gas were often found together, a chief question in the conservation of these resources was how to prevent the loss of one while producing the other, a problem never satisfactorily answered. Both waste and excessive drilling, much of which produced dry wells, were costly to the gas and petroleum industry in the state. Indiana historian Logan Esarey seems to have been too pessimistic, however, in writing in 1918 that it was doubtful whether the income received from the combined product—a sum greater than $200,000,000, he estimated—would pay for all the labor expended in drilling for the two mineral resources.[41]

The Indiana oil field, like the gas field, was eventually near-depleted. During its heyday, which lasted roughly from 1893 to 1910, oil production surpassed two million barrels annually and reached a peak in 1904 with over 11 million barrels. Just before the Trenton rock field began to fade, a

---

[39] *Ibid.,* pp. 140-152; Moore, *The Calumet Region,* pp. 208-209.

[40] Indiana Department of Geology and Natural Resources, *Annual Report,* 1897, pp. 165-168; 1899, p. 219; *Laws of Indiana,* 1893, pp. 300-302; The State *v.* The Ohio Oil Company, 150 Ind. 21 (1897); The Ohio Oil Company *v.* The State, 150 Ind. 694-695 (1898). Other short-lived oil pools were discovered about the same time at Peru and Broad Ripple. Indiana Department of Geology and Natural Resources, *Annual Report,* 1901, pp. 321-325.

[41] Esarey, *History of Indiana,* II, 915.

new field was opened in the southwest, where a strike was made at Princeton, Gibson County, in 1903. This zone, in which oil was found in a Huron sandstone formation, eventually widened to include parts of Daviess, Martin, Pike, and Sullivan counties, the latter of which proved to be the largest producer of all by 1915, when it reported 547,500 barrels from 503 wells, by far the greater part of the Indiana total in that year.[42] The following table indicates the annual production and value of petroleum in the whole state:

PETROLEUM PRODUCTION IN INDIANA[43]

| Year | Barrels | Value |
|------|---------|-------|
| 1889 | 33,375 | $ 10,881 |
| 1890 | 63,496 | 32,462 |
| 1891 | 136,634 | 54,787 |
| 1892 | 698,068 | 260,620 |
| 1893 | 2,335,293 | 1,050,882 |
| 1894 | 3,688,666 | 1,774,260 |
| 1895 | 4,386,132 | 2,807,124 |
| 1896 | 4,680,732 | 2,954,411 |
| 1897 | 4,122,356 | 1,880,412 |
| 1898 | 3,730,907 | 2,214,322 |
| 1899 | 3,848,182 | 3,363,738 |
| 1900 | 4,874,392 | 4,693,983 |
| 1901 | 5,757,086 | 4,822,826 |
| 1902 | 7,480,896 | 6,526,622 |
| 1903 | 9,186,411 | 10,474,127 |
| 1904 | 11,339,124 | 12,235,674 |
| 1905 | 10,964,247 | 9,404,909 |
| 1906 | 7,673,477 | 6,770,066 |
| 1907 | 5,128,037 | 4,536,930 |
| 1908 | 3,283,629 | 3,203,883 |
| 1909 | 2,296,086 | 1,997,610 |
| 1910 | 2,159,725 | 1,568,475 |
| 1911 | 1,695,289 | 1,228,835 |

[42] *Ibid.*, p. 914; Indiana Department of Geology and Natural Resources, *Annual Report,* 1903, pp. 203-208; 1915, pp. 268-269.

[43] Compiled from United States Geological Survey, *Mineral Resources of the United States,* 1896-1921. A similar table, but with different figures for the value of production before 1896 and lacking statistics for 1918-1920, may be found in Logan, *Petroleum and Natural Gas in Indiana,* p. 18.

## PETROLEUM PRODUCTION IN INDIANA—Cont.

| Year | Barrels | Value |
|---|---|---|
| 1912 | 970,009 | $   885,975 |
| 1913 | 956,095 | 1,279,975 |
| 1914 | 1,335,456 | 1,548,042 |
| 1915 | 875,758 | 813,365 |
| 1916 | 769,036 | 1,297,265 |
| 1917 | 759,432 | 1,470,548 |
| 1918 | 877,558 | 2,028,129 |
| 1919 | 972,000 | 2,284,000 |
| 1920 | 945,000 | 3,407,000 |

Next in importance after coal, gas, and petroleum among Indiana's natural resources was building stone, chiefly limestone. Of the several varieties of limestone which underlay many parts of the state, oolitic, or Indiana, limestone proved by far the most valuable.[44] A handsome, light-colored stone —usually buff or gray—which was soft enough to be easily worked when first quarried, it hardened to an extremely durable material particularly suitable for large public buildings. Although limestone had been quarried in Indiana in a small way from the early nineteenth century, its development into a major industry began in the late seventies, when after ardent promotion by state geologists Cox and Collett it was selected for the construction of the Chicago City Hall and the new State House in Indianapolis. Further impetus to its career as a building stone was given when the well-known eastern architect, Richard M. Hunt, chose Indiana limestone for the sumptuous residences of William K. Vanderbilt in New York and Cornelius Vanderbilt in Newport, Rhode Island, in 1879-1880, as well as George M. Vanderbilt's country estate "Biltmore" at Asheville, North Carolina, in the nineties. A taste for monumental civic architecture created strong

[44] Also called Bedford stone from the name of the city at the center of the main district where it was quarried. The term oolitic was used to describe the egglike appearance of its soft, rounded, granular texture and was first applied to Indiana limestone by David Dale Owen in 1839. Indiana Department of Geology and Natural Resources, *Annual Report*, 1896, p. 298. This volume contains a good, detailed study of the Bedford oolitic limestone industry by T. C. Hopkins and C. E. Siebenthal. See pp. 291-427.

demand for the oolitic stone in the construction of Federal buildings, statehouses, and county courthouses, and for many churches and large private residences also. By 1913 its use was reported in 85 per cent of all courthouses and other public buildings in Indiana constructed during the preceding twenty years.[45]

The main oolitic district in Indiana lay in a 240-square mile area stretching from Gosport in Owen County south and southeast through Monroe County to Lawrenceport in Lawrence County. The most important quarries were located at Bedford, Bloomington, Ellettsville, Romona, and Stinesville. By 1896 there were twenty-eight active oolitic limestone quarries in the state, with a total value of over $2,000,-000 and employing 1,431 men. The majority of these were locally owned and operated, though Chicago, Louisville, Indianapolis, and Terre Haute capitalists began to secure control of some of the region's quarries in the early twentieth century, and railroads running through the three counties often had a financial interest in stone properties.[46]

The oolitic industry experienced a technological revolution in this period. Introduced into Indiana quarries around the year 1880 were such important instruments as the channeling machine, which made the original cutting, and the steam-operated derrick which lifted out the huge cut blocks of stone. Steam, and later compressed-air and electric drills were eventually employed to divide the blocks into the required sizes. At the stone mills improvements were also made by the nineties in the mechanical operation of gang saws and the overhead traveling cranes needed to remove the pieces of stone from place to place. Furthermore, a major shift oc-

[45] Joseph A. Batchelor, *An Economic History of the Indiana Oolitic Limestone Industry* (*Indiana Business Studies, No. 27,* Bloomington, 1944), pp. 23-33, 85-87. A long list of buildings constructed of Indiana limestone in various parts of the country up to that time is found in Indiana Department of Geology and Natural Resources, *Annual Report,* 1896, pp. 414-427.

[46] Indiana Department of Geology and Natural Resources, *Annual Report,* 1896, pp. 344-349; Batchelor, *Economic History of the Indiana Oolitic Limestone Industry,* pp. 47-54.

curred in the industry in the late eighties and early nineties
when semifinishing machinery and cut-stone shops were installed at many mills in the Indiana limestone district, partly
in order to take advantage of the freight savings in shipping
finished products over the bulkier uncut blocks. Stone could
also be finished more cheaply in the quarry districts, where
mechanization was far ahead of the big city cut-stone yards
whose skilled workers remained adamantly opposed to the
introduction of planing and jointing machinery.[47]

In the eighties the rapid expansion in the production of
oolitic quarries in the state quickly gave Indiana a premier
position in the national building stone industry. Although no
reliable separate statistics for the oolitic district were gathered until the United States Geological Survey began reporting the production of the Lawrence and Monroe county quarries in the mid-nineties, it has been estimated from other
sources that the amount of stone quarried annually rose from
519,420 cubic feet in 1880 to 3,814,000 in 1892.[48] Demand
for Indiana limestone reached a peak by the beginning of the
second decade of the twentieth century and gradually declined
for the rest of this period, with a dip in 1917 when America's
entry into the First World War shut down much building
activity. Probably the most important factor in the falling
demand for this building stone, however, was the shift in
architectural design away from heavy masonry to the steel
skeleton structure. The following table contains the annual
output and value of the quarries in the two Indiana counties
where the bulk of the state's production was concentrated.

[47] Batchelor, *op. cit.*, pp. 33-46. As Batchelor points out, the stone boom of
the early nineties resulted in a greater rise in the industry's capacity than in
actual volume of production, which was lowered by the Panic of 1893.
During the period 1892-1896 cubic footage produced increased 42 per cent,
channeling capacity increased 111 per cent, gang-saw capacity 181 per cent,
and planer and jointer capacity 56 per cent. *Ibid.,* p. 46. An illustrated
description of the mechanical equipment used in quarrying and milling oolitic
limestone is found in Indiana Department of Geology and Natural Resources,
*Annual Report,* 1896, pp. 326-336.

[48] See table in Batchelor, *Economic History of the Indiana Oolitic Limestone Industry,* p. 31.

INDIANA OOLITIC LIMESTONE QUARRIED IN
LAWRENCE AND MONROE COUNTIES, 1894-1920[49]

| Year | Cubic Feet | Value |
|------|-----------|-------|
| 1894 | 4,580,418 | $1,154,246 |
| 1895 | 5,368,307 | 1,523,260 |
| 1896 | 5,455,582 | 1,209,632 |
| 1897 | 5,382,889 | 1,344,158 |
| 1898 | 5,630,046 | 1,389,204 |
| 1899 | 7,128,121 | 1,400,854 |
| 1900 | 7,035,000 | 1,639,985 |
| 1901 | 7,400,820 | 1,787,474 |
| 1902 | 6,774,445 | 1,647,399 |
| 1903 | 6,521,445 | 1,576,139 |
| 1904 | 6,812,845 | 1,643,974 |
| 1905 | 8,465,188 | 2,393,975 |
| 1906 | 9,282,004 | 2,622,805 |
| 1907 | 7,489,027 | 2,321,892 |
| 1908 | 8,347,093 | 2,379,040 |
| 1909 | 9,411,871 | 2,479,520 |
| 1910 | 9,738,808 | 3,166,704 |
| 1911 | 9,528,442 | 3,000,728 |
| 1912 | 10,442,304 | 3,447,242 |
| 1913 | 9,010,672 | 3,087,747 |
| 1914 | 7,929,006 | 2,171,215 |
| 1915 | 8,685,213 | 2,933,427 |
| 1916 | 8,545,534 | 3,493,765 |
| 1917 | 6,774,674 | 3,261,107 |
| 1918 | 2,701,674 | 1,800,167 |
| 1919 | 4,788,639 | 3,946,332 |
| 1920 | 6,343,536 | 7,579,879 |

Less valuable stone quarried in Indiana in this period included Harrodsburg limestone, which formed a four- to five-mile-wide belt along the eastern outcrop of the oolitic and Mitchell limestone, found near and often overlying the oolitic beds. Both these harder varieties of stone were chiefly used as an ingredient in the macadam surfacing of roads and in

[49] Compiled from United States Geological Survey, *Mineral Resources of the United States,* 1894-1920. These statistics do not include limestone quarried for other purposes than building stone, such as that sold for rubble, riprap, curbstone, flagstone, or ground limestone.

the manufacture of lime and cement. By 1920 quarries were in operation in Abydel, Bedford, Bloomington, Corydon, Greencastle, Marengo, Milltown, Mitchell, Putnamville, Salem, and Spencer. Niagara limestone, though widely distributed throughout the state, was quarried mostly in the north-central section and used extensively for bridges and foundations for buildings, as well as for curbing, guttering, and flagging. Quarries were located in Anderson, Alexandria, Bluffton, Buena Vista, Delphi, Eaton, Greensburg, Harper, Holton, Huntington, Kokomo, Laurel, Longwood, Marion, Markle, Montpelier, Newpoint, Osgood, Peru, Sardinia, St.

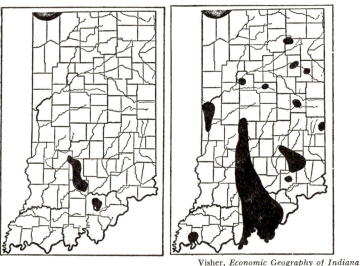

Visher, *Economic Geography of Indiana*
*Left,* Oolitic Limestone Area; *right,* Complete Limestone Area

Paul, and Westport. Limestone of various kinds was also used for miscellaneous purposes such as ballast for railroad tracks, flux in blast furnaces, and an ingredient in glass manufacturing. Mansfield sandstone, used for structural purposes, was found near the coal measures in western and southwestern Indiana from Warren County to the Ohio River and was quarried commercially at Attica, Bloomfield, Fountain, Mansfield, Portland Mills, Riverside, and St. Anthony. Another type of sandstone found in Lawrence, Martin, and Orange counties was used for abrasives. Whetstones from this district, especially the Hindostan oilstones, were in high demand abroad as well as in this country. By 1900 Indiana ranked second among the states in the production of whetstones and grindstones, though the total value of the output in that year was only $16,950.[50]

Most limestone found in Indiana was suitable for the manufacture of lime, which was produced by burning crushed rock in kilns and sold for agricultural, building, and chemical purposes. The principal lime-manufacturing center in the state was at Huntington, where the Western Lime Company, which was formed by an amalgamation of several firms in 1887, was the largest producer in the state. Successful kilns were also operated for many years at Delphi, Milltown, Putnamville, and Salem, but the amount of lime produced was hardly commensurate with the quantity and quality of raw material and fuel available in Indiana. Between 1904 and 1917 the state produced an average of 100,000 tons of lime valued at from $350,000 to $650,000 annually. In the latter year Indiana actually imported slightly more lime from outside the state than the amount of the home product that was consumed locally.[51]

A much more important product of limestone manufactured in Indiana was cement, which was also made from marl, an amorphous form of calcium carbonate found in the lake basins and former basins of extinct lakes in the northern part of the state. For a time the Devonian limestones of southeastern Indiana were extensively used in the manufac-

[50] William N. Logan et al., Handbook of Indiana Geology (Indiana Department of Conservation, Publication No. 21, Indianapolis, 1922), pp. 594-595, 601-603; Indiana Department of Geology and Natural Resources, Annual Report, 1896, pp. 15-17; United States Bureau of the Census, Special Reports, Mines and Quarries, 1902, p. 877. For whetstones, see Edith S. Stipp, "Unique Sharpening Stone Industry Founded in Pioneer Days," Society of Indiana Pioneers, Year Book, 1942, pp. 3-9.

[51] Indiana Department of Geology and Natural Resources, Annual Report, 1903, pp. 233-238; Logan et al., Handbook of Indiana Geology, pp. 770-771. In 1917 118,530 tons were produced in Indiana, of which only 43,086 tons were consumed within the state, while 46,772 tons were imported from outside.

ture of natural, or hydraulic, cement. In 1900 six plants in
Clark County produced over a million barrels, but by 1920
only a single firm was still in production.[52] The first Portland cement factory in Indiana and one of the first in the
United States was opened at South Bend in 1877 to use the
marl and clay of that area.[53] Although this closed in 1893,
others were built at Stroh, Syracuse, Mitchell, Buffington, and
Limedale in the next decade and a half. Most used limestone and shale, but the Buffington plant, located in the Calumet Region, also utilized slag from the nearby iron furnaces.
By 1920 Indiana ranked second in the nation after Pennsylvania in the manufacture of Portland Cement, shipping in
that year 10,191,126 barrels worth $18,649,115.[54]

The raw material for an unusual product, "rock wool,"
was discovered in the argillaceous limestone near Alexandria
in 1897, when C. C. Hall, a chemical engineer for a St. Louis
steel company operating a plant in that city came upon its
peculiar properties while searching for a suitable stone for
fluxing purposes in the steel mill. The wool, used chiefly for
insulating material, was produced by melting the limestone
in steel "cupolas" and blowing air through it to draw it out
into fibers or threads. Hall organized his first company in
Alexandria to manufacture rock wool in about 1899 but sold
out seven years later and formed the Banner Rock Products
Company in the same city. These two concerns were joined by
several other rock wool manufacturing companies after 1920,
but they remained for many years the largest producers in

[52] United States Bureau of the Census, *Special Reports, Mines and Quarries,* 1902, pp. 212-214; Logan *et al., Handbook of Indiana Geology,* p. 606.

[53] Indiana Department of Statistics and Geology, *Annual Report,* 1880, pp.
379-381. The South Bend cement plant was opened by a sewer pipe manufacturer from Syracuse, New York, just a few years after the installing of the first
American Portland cement kilns in Pennsylvania. United States Geological Survey, *Mineral Resources of the United States,* 1891, p. 535.

[54] Logan *et al., Handbook of Indiana Geology,* pp. 611-618; United States
Geological Survey, *Mineral Resources of the United States,* 1920, II, *Nonmetals,* p. 268.

Indiana, which in turn led all other states in production of this substance.[55]

An abundance of clays and shales found in almost every county but especially in the western and southwestern portions of the state, often in close proximity to the coal measures, formed the basis of the ceramic industry in Indiana. One of the earliest uses of this material was in the manufacture of drain tile, in which Indiana was already a leading state by the eighties.[56] Most of the clays were of the poorer quality used in making tile and common brick, but the presence of smaller amounts of fire clay and other better grades —their locations loudly proclaimed by the Department of Geology and Natural Resources—eventually stimulated the manufacturing of vitrified brick for street paving, terra cotta and pressed brick for architectural purposes, and similar ceramic products. By the second decade of the twentieth century a large number of kilns and factories had been built in cities such as Attica, Brazil, Evansville, Fort Wayne, Terre Haute, and Veedersburg to produce various types of bricks.[57]

Little pottery was made in Indiana, though a cruder kind of stoneware and later sanitaryware were produced. Despite a great deal of attention paid by the state geologists to "Indianaite," a white, porcelainlike clay similar to kaolin discovered in Lawrence County as early as 1874, only small quantities of it were mined in this period, partly for use in the manufacturing of aluminum sulphate and partly for potter's clay.[58] Indiana ranked seventh among the states by

[55] The story of the beginnings of the rock wool industry in Alexandria is found in W. D. Thornbury, "The Mineral Wool Industry of Indiana," Indiana Academy of Science, *Proceedings*, XLVII (1937), 162-175.

[56] Only Illinois produced a larger quantity of drain tile in the early eighties. United States Geological Survey, *Mineral Resources of the United States*, 1883-1884, pp. 700-701.

[57] Logan *et al., Handbook of Indiana Geology*, pp. 651-661. A long, detailed description of Indiana clays and clay-working industries is found in Indiana Department of Geology and Natural Resources, *Annual Report*, 1904, pp. 13-657.

[58] Indiana Geological Survey, *Annual Report*, 1876-1878, pp. 154-155; Logan *et al., Handbook of Indiana Geology*, pp. 714-756. Most of the clay used in the

1920 in the production of all clay products, which were valued at $11,634,097 in that year.[59]

Various kinds of sands found in the state provided raw materials for Hoosier industries. Building sand constituted the largest single item, but foundry sand and glass sand were also obtained locally, though in amounts considerably less than that consumed in Indiana. Much of the sand came from the dunes region in Lake, Porter, and La Porte counties, though some was supplied from other locations south to the Ohio River. The value of Indiana sands of all types sold in 1920 was $1,242,640.[60] A German method of making processed bricks from sand and lime was introduced into the United States at Michigan City in 1901, and Indiana became one of the leading states in their production.[61] Other minor mineral products of the state were diatomaceous earth from Dubois, Lawrence, Jackson, Sullivan, and Washington counties and mineral pigments for paints from Greene, Lawrence, Martin, Monroe, Orange, and Vigo counties.[62]

A natural resource more important economically to the state than any of these last was the supply of mineral waters which were obtained from more than eighty springs and artesian wells during this period. Several springs producing water containing various mineral salts alleged to possess medicinal properties had long been known and utilized in Indiana. But in the last two decades of the nineteenth century new sources were discovered when wells bored for gas or oil sometimes developed a flow of water showing the presence of moderate amounts of sodium, calcium, iron, sulphur, magnesium, and other chemical elements.

white-ware industry in Indiana was brought in from outside the state. Indiana Department of Geology and Natural Resources, *Annual Report,* 1904, pp. 602-604.

59 United States Geological Survey, *Mineral Resources of the United States,* 1920, II, *Nonmetals,* p. 326.

60 *Ibid.,* pp. 171-172.

61 United States Bureau of the Census, *Special Report, Manufactures, 1905,* III, 893.

62 Logan *et al., Handbook of Indiana Geology,* p. 1056.

The best known of the early springs were located in Orange County, at Frenck Lick and West Baden, where bathhouses and inns were flourishing before the Civil War. By the turn of the century these small communities had become famous health and recreation resorts, with luxurious hotels and gambling casinos catering to the fashionable and wealthy classes in the eastern half of the country.[63] In the nineties scores of additional springs and wells were being exploited commercially in Henry, Montgomery, Morgan, Warren, and other counties. Large sanatoriums were built at Spiceland, Attica, and Martinsville; the last-named city, with five of these health centers by 1900, nearly doubled its population in the decade after 1890.[64]

In 1901 state geologist Willis S. Blatchley, apparently in a professional endeavor to promote the development of the industry, compiled a survey of Indiana mineral waters, complete with chemical analyses of the products of the various springs and wells. Moreover, a medical paper by Dr. Robert Hessler of Logansport which was enclosed in the report endorsed, with only minor reservations, the consumption of such waters as an aid to health. State geologist Blatchley himself, however, stated as his personal opinion that "the change of surroundings . . . obtained by a few weeks spent at the sanatoriums and resorts, have quite as much to do with bringing about a cure of many patients as does the water itself."[65] Whether or not the mineral springs had any special health-giving effect upon the tens of thousands of visitors who flocked to the health spas, they provided a popular, quasi-medical added attraction for a resort industry which survived for many years.

Besides encouraging consumption of mineral waters at the health resorts, many proprietors bottled and distributed them to customers in and out of the state. One of the favorite bot-

[63] For an account of the development of one of these famous spas, see Haupt, History of French Lick Springs Hotel.

[64] Indiana Department of Geology and Natural Resources, *Annual Report,* 1901, p. 94.

[65] *Ibid.,* p. 15.

tled health drinks of this period was "Pluto Water," drawn from one of the springs at French Lick. By 1920 the total annual value of all such Indiana products was approximately $184,000.[66]

§ § §

The first major public plea for conservation of natural resources in Indiana was issued on behalf of the diminishing timber reserves in the state. In a lecture before the State Board of Agriculture in 1881, Professor Charles L. Ingersoll of Purdue University, arguing that most of the forests would soon be cut down to meet the need for cultivated land and manufactured wood products, posed the question, "Has the time arrived for us in Indiana to commence forestry—planting and preservation of trees for timber?" His own answer was affirmative, as his eloquent advice to Hoosier farmers indicated:[67]

In conclusion, let me urge you to plant trees. Plant! though you may never expect to pluck the fruits, gather the nuts, or garner the timber. Plant! for the influence on our climate. Plant! for shelter from the bleak winds. Plant! for shade for yourself, your children and your animals.

Few heeded the call.[68] Although most of the virgin forest had already disappeared, Indiana seemed to possess an impressive supply of native lumber, with the United States Department of Agriculture reporting almost 40 per cent of

---

[66] United States Geological Survey, *Mineral Resources of the United States,* 1920, II, *Nonmetals,* 163. The main economic value of the mineral springs lay in their ability to attract invalids and visitors in large numbers. The peak in their popularity as health resorts was reached during the two decades between 1890 and 1910, when at least thirty hotels or sanatoriums were in operation at Indiana springs. The automobile was probably a major factor in their decline after 1910. See W. D. Thornbury, "The Mineral Waters and Health Resorts of Indiana: A Study in Historical Geography," Indiana Academy of Science, *Proceedings,* L (1940), 154-164.

[67] Indiana State Board of Agriculture, *Annual Report,* 1880-1881, pp. 229, 237.

[68] The response of Dr. A. C. Stevenson of Greencastle, a well-known stock man and former president of the State Board of Agriculture, who saw no need for timber conservation, was probably representative of many Hoosier farmers

the state's land in timber.[69] Appearances were deceptive, however, for besides the continuing inroads into forested lands made by clearing for agricultural purposes, significant lumber losses were inflicted in a less immediately visible fashion by the selective cutting of valuable hardwoods for shipping to furniture, farm implement, and other fabricating plants in Indiana and other states. The residual stands of timber, much of it commercially worthless, became either wasteland or pasture, and was often burned off. Most of the state's forests were cut during the period from 1870 to 1900, when large acreages of wooded land were converted to fields for agricultural crops; this conversion was hastened by the advent of the steam-powered sawmill which made it possible to meet the high demand for wood products in the decades after the Civil War.[70]

Virtually all the commercial lumber production in Indiana was composed of hardwoods—oak, tulip or yellow poplar, maple, black walnut, beech, hickory, or red gum. Oak predominated, representing about 80 per cent of all lumber produced in the state, followed by poplar, a little over 10 per cent. Indiana's proportion of the total United States lumber cut declined radically from 18 per cent in 1869 to a mere 2 per cent in 1915.[71] Yet output remained fairly large until 1899, the peak year, and then fell rapidly, as the following table indicates:

at this time. "It was his opinion," the *Annual Report* of the Board noted, "that the best thing to do was to kill every tree. One or two crops of wheat or two years' pasture for stock will pay for all the timber you keep standing there for forty years." *Ibid.*, p. 238.

[69] United States Commissioner of Agriculture, *Annual Report,* 1875-1876, pp. 309-310.

[70] Stanley Coulter, "Forest Conditions in Indiana," Indiana Academy of Science, *Proceedings,* 1909, pp. 447-448; Daniel DenUyl, "Indiana's Old Growth Forests," *ibid.,* LXIII (1953), 74-75.

[71] DenUyl, "Indiana's Old Growth Forests," *loc. cit.,* LXIII (1953), 75-77.

HARDWOOD LUMBER PRODUCTION, 1879-1919[72]

| Year | Thousands of board feet | Rank in U.S. |
|------|------------------------|--------------|
| 1879 | 917,900 | 5 |
| 1889 | 893,359 | 8 |
| 1899 | 1,036,999 | 13 |
| 1904 | 563,853 | 23 |
| 1909 | 556,418 | .... |
| 1914 | 298,571 | .... |
| 1919 | 282,487 | .... |

By the nineties some Hoosier farmers had begun planting catalpa and black locust trees, chiefly in order to produce their own fence posts, but this never became a successful program of reforestation. The first official step taken toward practical conservation came in 1899, when the state legislature enacted a law establishing a nominal property tax rate of $1.00 an acre on certain farmlands set aside for tree planting. Although more than 1,500 persons attempted to take advantage of this provision, only twenty-four qualified within the first four years, and in 1905 the act was repealed.[73]

In 1901, however, the Indiana General Assembly created the State Board of Forestry, composed of five men appointed by the Governor, three representing different aspects of the lumbering enterprise, one a member of the faculty of Purdue University, and the last a trained expert in forest preservation and timber culture, who also acted as state forester. Two years later the legislature appropriated money to purchase land for a state forest reservation which might serve as a laboratory for forestry conservation. Accordingly the State Board of Forestry bought a 2,000-acre tract near Hen-

72 Compiled from R. V. Reynolds and A. H. Pierson, *Lumber Cut of the United States, 1870-1920* (United States Department of Agriculture, *Bulletin No. 1119,* 1923), pp. 30-33; Henry B. Steer, *Lumber Production in the United States, 1799-1946* (United States Department of Agriculture, *Miscellaneous Publication No. 669,* 1948), pp. 11-13.

73 *Laws of Indiana,* 1899, pp. 570-571; 1905, p. 65; Streightoff and Streightoff, *Indiana,* p. 24.

ryville in Clark County, where a small staff carried out experiments in tree planting and cultivation somewhat on the model of the Agricultural Experiment Station at Purdue University in Lafayette. Other legislation aimed at preservation of forests was enacted in 1905 making it unlawful to set fire to any woods belonging to another and authorizing the township road supervisors to employ helpers to extinguish such fires.[74]

Many private citizens agitated persistently for stronger measures of forestry conservation. Among these were John P. Brown, who published his own journal, *Arboriculture,* at Connersville, Indiana, in order to advocate general tree planting; Professor Stanley Coulter of Purdue University, a distinguished botanist and active member of the State Board of Forestry; and Professor Glenn Culbertson of Hanover College, who took to the public platform to stress the effect of deforestation on erosion and flooding and called for the planting of tens of thousands of acres of trees in southern Indiana at state expense.[75] In 1910 Vice-President Fairbanks helped organize and became the first president of the Indiana Forestry Association, which led the movement for the annual celebration of an officially designated Arbor Day, finally authorized by the General Assembly in 1913.[76]

Indiana had frequently suffered from serious floods along the banks of the Ohio and its interior rivers, especially

[74] *Laws of Indiana,* 1901, pp. 62-63; 1903, p. 132; 1905, pp. 64-65; Indiana State Board of Forestry, *Annual Report,* 1903, pp. 24-26. These projects were not popular in all political quarters. In 1909 Governor Marshall recommended in his address to the legislature that the state forest be sold, and that the state forester be employed to deliver lectures around the state as a more effective way of reaching the people with conservationist doctrines. Indiana *House Journal,* 1909, p. 97.

[75] Glenn Culbertson, "Deforestation and Its Effects among the Hills of Southern Indiana," Indiana Academy of Science, *Proceedings,* 1908, pp. 27-37.

[76] *Laws of Indiana,* 1913, pp. 422-423. For the story of the forestry conservation movement, see Daniel DenUyl, "History of Forest Conservation in Indiana," Indiana Academy of Science, *Proceedings,* LXVI (1956), 261-264. Manuscript records of the Indiana Forestry Association, 1910-1917, are in the Fairbanks Papers, Lilly Library.

the Wabash and the White. After the great flood of March, 1913, in which thirty-nine lives were lost and over $18,000,-000 worth of property destroyed, Governor Ralston appointed the Indiana Flood Commission in 1914 to make the first organized effort to study the cause of such disasters and to suggest ways of lessening their effect, but no action was taken as a result of its deliberations.[77] Likewise, little attention was paid in this period to the conservation of water resources in the state. Water power, long utilized by Indiana manufacturing enterprises, was still employed to operate a few small mills at several locations on the Wabash, Tippecanoe, White, Eel, Whitewater, and other rivers in the early decades of the twentieth century. But its most important use by 1920 had become the generation of electricity in cities in the northern half of the state, including Elkhart, Goshen, Logansport, Mishawaka, Monticello, Noblesville, Ontario, and South Bend.[78]

The lakes, rivers, and streams of Indiana provided the basis for a minor commercial fishery. Michigan City, the state's first port on Lake Michigan, had as many as fourteen firms engaged in lake fishing in the late seventies, but this business gradually contracted after 1880 and soon became a negligible industry.[79] In the eighties, however, Hoosiers attempted to create a new commercial fishery enterprise in carp culture. Introduced into America several decades before as a food fish, German carp were distributed to persons willing to provide small lakes or ponds for their culture by the United States Commissioner of Fisheries. By 1890 Indiana, with almost three thousand fish ponds, was a leading state in

[77] W. K. Hatt, "Flood Protection in Indiana," Indiana Academy of Science, Proceedings, 1914, pp. 149-156.

[78] Streightoff and Streightoff, Indiana, pp. 6-7; Visher, Economic Geography of Indiana, pp. 69-70; Logan et al., Handbook of Indiana Geology, pp. 286-287. Two detailed analyses of the water power of Indiana were published in Indiana Department of Geology and Natural Resources, Annual Report, 1910, pp. 11-77, and 1911, pp. 469-538.

[79] Indiana State Board of Agriculture, Annual Report, 1889-1890, pp. 571-572.

the production of carp.[80] But this venture soon proved unsatisfactory, for the rapidly multiplying German import
quickly spread through the state's lakes and streams,
muddying the waters, destroying vegetation, and driving out
the native fish. By 1900 the carp became known chiefly as a
menace to the waters of the state and their denizens, and its
culture altogether disappeared.[81]

One early carp culturist, William Shoup of Waldron, Shelby
County, shifted to the breeding and raising of goldfish on a
commercial scale around 1880. Eventually he and his partner,
Charles Heck, went back to the source of the original goldfish supply and imported breeders from China and Japan in
order to improve the American and European stock. So successful were they in raising and marketing their product that
by 1900 their goldfish farm in Waldron was claimed to be
the largest such establishment in the world, supplying more
than 100,000 fish annually.[82] A colorful, short-lived fishery in
Indiana was the freshwater mussel industry which began
around 1900 in the Wabash River. The mussel shells were
taken from the river in low water with a forked spade and in
high water by raking the river bottom with hooks suspended
from the rear of a boat. Some contained valuable pearls but
most were sold for making buttons. In 1908 the mussel fishery product in Indiana was worth $155,000, a modest sum,
perhaps, but far larger than the value of all food fish produced commercially in the state in the same year.[83] In 1913
the Indiana commissioner of fisheries and game reported that
mussel shells were being dug from the White and Kankakee

[80] United States Bureau of the Census, *Eleventh Census* (1890), *Compendium*, Pt. III, p. 890.

[81] Indiana Commissioner of Fisheries and Game, *Biennial Report*, [1915-1916], pp. 64-65.

[82] Indianapolis *News*, May 24, 1902. For the story of the Waldron goldfish farm, see E. I. Lewis, "Indiana Gold Fisheries," Indiana Commissioner of Fisheries and Game, *Biennial Report*, 1901-1902, pp. 249-259.

[83] United States Bureau of the Census, *Fisheries of the United States*, 1908, pp. 66, 121-122. For a firsthand account of the mussel fishery in the Wabash River in 1908, see A. O. Reser, "The Mussel Industry of Indiana," Indiana Commissioner of Fisheries and Game, *Biennial Report*, 1907-1908, pp. 421-425.

rivers, but that the industry was being destroyed by over-fishing.[84]

The taking of game fish by illegal methods, though on a relatively small commercial basis, was threatening to depopulate the state's lakes, rivers, and streams when the General Assembly in 1881 authorized the appointment of a commissioner of fisheries to take protective measures.[85] Little was accomplished for several years, however, for the commissioner had neither public opinion behind him nor police power to enforce the laws against the use of seines, gigs, and spears by poachers and farmers. Similarly the legislation protecting deer, quail, ducks, and other wild game animals from indiscriminate hunters was generally ignored.[86]

Finally, in 1889 the Indiana Fish and Game Association was organized by Commissioner of Fisheries William T. Dennis and a group of Indianapolis sportsmen including Colonel Eli Lilly and former Lieutenant Governor William P. Cumback, in order to gain greater public support for the enforcement of fish and game laws as well as the restocking of lakes and streams with fish.[87] In that same year the first fish ladders were constructed in dammed rivers and streams in order to permit the migration of fish in spawning time, though the law requiring them had been passed four years before. Various species of pike and bass were also planted with the aid of the United States Bureau of Fisheries.[88] In 1899 the legislature broadened the office of commissioner of fisheries to include protection of all wild game and also added jurisdiction over song and insectivorous birds.[89] In 1898 the

[84] *Ibid.,* 1913-1914, pp. 68-71.

[85] *Laws of Indiana,* 1881, pp. 516-517.

[86] The revised statutes of 1881 established closed seasons on deer, quail, pheasants, woodcocks, ducks, wild turkeys, and prairie hens, and prohibited the killing of most wild birds except the English sparrow; the shooting of wild pigeons while roosting—a notorious sport in some parts of Indiana at this time —was also prohibited. *Ibid.,* 1881, pp. 218-220.

[87] Indiana Commissioner of Fisheries, *Biennial Report,* 1891, pp. 38-88.

[88] *Laws of Indiana,* 1885, pp. 51-52; Indiana Commissioner of Fisheries, *Biennial Report,* 1891, pp. 8-9, 12.

[89] *Laws of Indiana,* 1899, pp. 44-46.

Indiana Audubon Society was organized, largely through the instrumentality of ornithologist Amos W. Butler of Brookville and the Indiana Academy of Science.[90]

The increasing sentiment in favor of the protection of wildlife undoubtedly came in large part from the growing numbers of amateur hunters and fishermen who left the teeming cities on weekends and at vacation time in search of sport in the still unspoiled countryside. In 1901 the General Assembly enacted a comprehensive game law establishing a regular closed season for most game animals, and in 1905 resident hunters were asked to purchase annual licenses for $1.00 while nonresidents paid $15.50.[91] Although legislation was passed limiting the number of certain game fish which could be caught legally, no fishing license was required until 1911 for out-of-state sportsmen and in 1913 for Indiana residents.[92] Proceeds from the sale of licenses went partly to pay for replenishing the state's supply of fish and game.

The attempt to establish European-bred pheasants and partridges in Indiana, in spite of the expenditure of $60,000 for that purpose, was a complete failure. On the other hand, the commissioner of fisheries and game was successful in inaugurating a program of restocking lakes and streams by means of state fish hatcheries at Indianapolis, Brookville, Lake Wawasee, and Tri-Lakes in Whitley County. By 1915 the commissioner's office was financially self-sustaining, all its expenses being paid out of license receipts, though scores

90 Indiana Academy of Science, *Proceedings,* 1909, p. 46, Indiana Audubon *Year Book,* 1944, pp. 6-7.

91 *Laws of Indiana,* 1901, pp. 442-447; 1905, pp. 727-733.

92 *Ibid.,* 1905, pp. 733-737; 1907, pp. 86-88; 1911, pp. 677-679; 1913, pp. 310-311. Other legislation aimed at protecting game fish included an antipollution law prohibiting the draining of oil, dye-stuff, or other refuse into rivers and streams, and an act making it unlawful to construct drainage ditches which might lower the waters of any lake in the vicinity. Sportsmen were unsuccessful, however, in their attempts to prevent the drainage of the game-filled swamps of the Kankakee Valley. *Ibid.,* 1901, pp. 77-81; 1905, pp. 447-448; C. H. Bechert, "History of Water Conservation in Indiana," Indiana Academy of Science, *Proceedings,* LXVI (1956), 286-290.

of game wardens and inspectors now guarded the fish and wild animal resources.[93]

In an increasingly industrial and urban society, Hoosiers turned more and more to the great outdoors for recreation. Indianans quickly discovered many good locations for summer resorts on the shores of lakes in the northern part of the state. One of the earliest of these to be developed was Lake Wawasee in Kosciusko County, where a group of sportsmen built a clubhouse in 1880. In the eighties and nineties several hotels were built, and businessmen such as Colonel Eli Lilly and A. H. Nordyke of Indianapolis erected the first private cottages.[94] Other water resorts which became popular in this period were Bass Lake in Starke, Lake James in Steuben, Lake Maxinkuckee in Marshall, and Tippecanoe and Winona lakes in Kosciusko County. The sand dunes along the shores of Lake Michigan also attracted outdoorsmen as well as naturalists. In 1904 the commissioner of fisheries and game estimated that tourist receipts in Indiana had risen in a relatively short time from practically zero to $3,000,000 annually.[95]

Interest in the conservation of the natural environment was heightened in the second decade of the twentieth century in Indiana as in the nation, under the stimulus of President Theodore Roosevelt. After attending the National Conservation Conference called by Roosevelt at the White House in 1908, Governor Hanly appointed an Indiana Conservation Commission, the members of which, however, resigned soon afterwards upon the accession of a new chief executive, Governor Marshall. Although Marshall duly named another commission, it apparently failed to function.[96] But private

[93] Indiana Commissioner of Fisheries and Game, *Biennial Report,* 1910-1911, p. 99; 1911-1912, pp. 40-45, 230-231; 1915-1916, pp. 6-7.

[94] *Ibid.,* 1903-1904, pp. 256-258; Eli Lilly, *Early Wawasee Days* (Indianapolis, 1960), pp. 29-42.

[95] Indiana Commissioner of Fisheries and Game, *Biennial Report,* 1903-1904, pp. 254-255.

[96] Robert A. Frederick, Colonel Richard Lieber, Conservationist and Park Builder: The Indiana Years (Unpublished Ph.D. thesis in History, Indiana University, 1960), pp. 91-93.

individuals and organizations, such as the Indiana Fish, Game and Forest League, an association of sportsmen formed in 1911 which began lobbying for abolishment of the office of commissioner of fisheries and game and its replacement by a centralized department of conservation, were active and influential in this movement. In 1912 the fourth National Conservation Congress stirred additional interest in the state by meeting in Indianapolis under the leadership, among others, of Richard Lieber, a civic-minded businessman and outdoorsman of that city who was chairman of the board of managers of the Congress.[97]

The arrival of the centennial of Indiana's statehood in 1916 reinforced the spirit of conservation in the state. As a means of celebrating this anniversary the Indiana Historical Commission decided to inaugurate a movement for state parks and appointed a committee under the chairmanship of Richard Lieber for this purpose. Mrs. Juliet V. Strauss of Rockville, a well-known woman's page newspaper writer, and others interested the committee in the acquisition of an unspoiled area of primeval forest and rocky glens at Turkey Run in Parke County which was to be sold at auction in the spring of 1916. The committee raised funds by popular subscription for its purchase, but a veneer manufacturing concern was the successful bidder and threatened to destroy the area's beauty by removing all the merchantable trees. In the meantime, an opportunity came to buy another similar tract on McCormick's Creek in Owen County, which thus became the first Indiana state park. With additional private donations and an appropriation from the legislature in 1917, the committee was able to acquire the Turkey Run property from the lumber company.[98] Thus began the system of In-

97 Indiana *Year Book,* 1919, pp. 473-474; Frederick, Colonel Richard Lieber, pp. 101-106.

98 Indiana *Year Book,* 1917, pp. 495-497. See also Charles G. Sauers, *McCormick's Creek Canyon State Park. A History and Description* (Indiana Department of Conservation, *Publication No. 38,* 1923), and E. Y. Guernsey, *Turkey Run State Park. A History and Description* (Third edition, Indiana Department of Conservation, *Publication No. 35,* 1930).

diana state parks, the chief purpose of which was, in the words of Richard Lieber, "to refresh and strengthen and renew tired people, and fit them for the common round of daily life."[99]

In December, 1916, Lieber, hoping for favorable action from the incoming Republican General Assembly and admin-

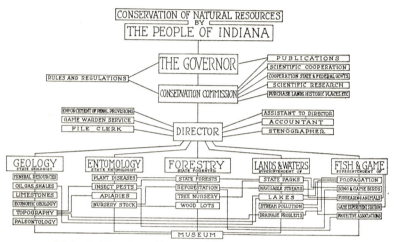

Lieber's Plan for a State Department of Conservation

istration, presented a comprehensive plan for a state department of conservation which would centralize the planning and work of the commissioner of fisheries and game, the State Board of Forestry, the Department of Geology and Natural Resources, and the state entomologist, and assume control and direction over the newly acquired state parks. Although the General Assembly rejected the proposal in 1917, the next Assembly passed an act creating the Indiana De-

[99] Indiana *Year Book,* 1917, p. 498. For Lieber's part in the origin of the state park system in Indiana, see Frederick, Colonel Richard Lieber, pp. 108-135; the movement to create a national park in the sand dune region of northern Indiana failed at this time, though Indiana's United States Senator Thomas Taggart submitted a resolution asking the Secretary of the Interior to investigate and report back to Congress the desirability of such a scheme. Hearings were conducted in Chicago in the fall of 1916, and the matter was reported favorably to Congress, but no action was ever taken. L. F. Bennett, "The Sand Dune Region as a National Park," Indiana Academy of Science, *Proceedings,* 1916, pp. 261-263; Moore, *The Calumet Region,* pp. 596-599.

partment of Conservation on almost exactly the lines originally drawn up by Lieber, with a conservation commission, a director, and five divisions—geology, entomology, forestry, lands and waters, and fish and game. The four-man commission immediately chose as first director of the department Richard Lieber, the man who brought progressive and imaginative leadership to the task of organizing for the first time a unified professional program of conservation of Indiana's natural resources.[100]

100 *Laws of Indiana,* 1919, pp. 375-392; Emma Lieber, *Richard Lieber* ([Indianapolis], 1947), pp. 80-90.

# CHAPTER VI

## THE EVOLUTION OF A MODERN TRANSPORTATION SYSTEM

By 1880 THE STEAM RAILROAD had triumphed over all other forms of transportation in Indiana. With five main trunk lines crossing the breadth of the state, three north-south systems, and about two score smaller roads, most of Indiana's cities and larger towns were served by rail, only six counties having no railroad connection whatever—Brown, Crawford, Ohio, Perry, Pike, and Switzerland, all of them relatively poor southern counties and all but two bordering the Ohio River.[1] Moreover, this rail network linked Indiana with Chicago, Cincinnati, Cleveland, Louisville, Pittsburgh, St. Louis, and other more distant American cities.

Railroad competition was a major factor in the decline of water transportation in the state. Not only had the canals closed by the seventies, but the steamboats were rapidly disappearing from the Ohio River. Although Evansville and, to a lesser extent, Madison remained centers of a local river trade in lumber, grain, tobacco, and coal, business at the once-flourishing Ohio River ports of Jeffersonville and New Albany fell off drastically in the eighties and never recovered.[2] By the turn of the century the steamboat was replaced on the Ohio by the small gasoline boat and, particularly, by the

---

[1] For railroad development in Indiana before 1880, see Thornbrough, *Indiana in the Civil War Era,* pp. 322-352.

[2] Only Evansville and Madison are included in the Federal census data on Ohio River ports in Indiana for 1906 and 1916. The following table represents the tonnage of freight handled at each in these years:

| Year | Evansville | Madison |
|------|-----------|---------|
| 1906 | 416,133 | 107,053 |
| 1916 | 251,549 | 135,382 |

United States Bureau of the Census, *Transportation by Water, 1916* (Washington, D.C., 1920), p. 176.

barge and towboat combination which became the prevailing system of freight haulage on the river. Five packet lines connected with Madison, New Albany, and Evansville, but Indiana ports figured little in the main barge traffic—mostly coal carried down river from the Pittsburgh area—which grew in volume up to the time of the First World War.[3]

In the eighties and nineties the United States Army Engineer Corps, which had supervised the work of deepening and widening the channel at the falls of the Ohio directly across from New Albany, attempted to improve the navigation of the Wabash and White rivers, which had become so badly obstructed by bars, reefs, and snags that they were navigable only at high stages of water. The original project proposed by the Army Engineers in the seventies would have opened the Wabash to year-round shipping all the way to Lafayette by a series of locks at twelve places and cleared the White River for a shorter distance, but neither goal proved feasible. The only permanent improvement made was a new dam and lock on the Wabash, which was installed at the Grand Rapids in 1893, since further Congressional appropriations were not forthcoming for work at other points. Engineering operations on White River were suspended in 1896 until the Wabash could be improved sufficiently to afford an outlet for its traffic; by 1907 through navigation at low water was impractical on either river.[4]

Before 1900 Indiana's single port on Lake Michigan was Michigan City. But its harbor was handling only a very modest freighting trade in such items as lumber and salt by this time. Not until the second decade of the twentieth century did

[3] Preliminary Report of the Inland Waterways Commission (Senate Documents), 60 Congress, 1 session, No. 325, pp. 110-111; Charles H. Ambler, A History of Transportation in the Ohio Valley (Glendale, Calif., 1932), pp. 285-291, 312-318; Louis C. Hunter, Steamboats on the Western Rivers. An Economic and Technological History (Cambridge, Mass., 1949), pp. 639-640.

[4] United States Army, Annual Report of the Chief of Engineers, 1907, pp. 570-580. By 1906 two Wabash River ports in Indiana handled only a minimum amount of shipping: Terre Haute, 4,980 tons, and Vincennes, 2,014 tons. United States Bureau of the Census, Transportation by Water, 1906, p. 184.

## INDIANA RAILROADS IN 1880

1. Anderson, Lebanon, St. Louis (Anderson to Noblesville), 19 m.
2. Baltimore, Ohio, and Chicago (formerly Baltimore, Pittsburgh, and Chicago), 146 m.
3. Bedford, Springfield, Owensburg, and Bloomfield, 41 m.
4. Chicago and Block Coal (Attica to Veedersburg), 15 m.
5. Chicago, Cincinnati, and Louisville (Peru to LaPorte), 71 m.
6. Chicago and Eastern Illinois (Bismark, Ill., to Coal Creek), 19 m.
7. Chicago and Grand Trunk, 56 m.
8. Cincinnati, Hamilton, and Indianapolis, 78 m.
9. Cincinnati, Lafayette, and Chicago (Lafayette to state line), 23 m.
10. Cincinnati, Richmond, and Fort Wayne (Fort Wayne to Richmond), 83 m.
11. Cincinnati, Rockport, and Southwestern (Rockport to Jasper), 38 m.
12. Cincinnati, Wabash, and Michigan (Anderson to Goshen), 111 m.
13. Cleveland, Columbus, Cincinnati, and Indianapolis (formerly Bellefontaine), 84 m.
14. Columbus, Chicago, and Indiana Central (Indianapolis to Richmond to Chicago), 416 m.
15. Eel River (Logansport to Butler), 93 m.
16. Evansville and Terre Haute, 108 m.
17. Evansville, Terre Haute, and Chicago (Terre Haute to Danville, Ill.), 43 m.
18. Fairland, Franklin, and Martinsville, 38 m.
19. Fort Wayne, Jackson, and Saginaw (Fort Wayne to Jackson, Mich.), 54 m.
20. Fort Wayne, Muncie, and Cincinnati (Fort Wayne to Connersville), 104 m.
21. Frankfort and Kokomo, 26 m.
22. Grand Rapids and Indiana (formerly Grand Rapids and Fort Wayne), 104 m.
23. Indiana Block Coal (Otter Creek to Brazil), 17 m.
24. Indiana, Bloomington, and Western, 78 m.
25. Indianapolis, Cincinnati, and Lafayette, 163 m.
26. Indianapolis, Decatur, and Springfield, Ill., 65 m.
27. Indianapolis, Delphi, and Chicago (Rensselaer to Delphi), 38 m.
28. Indianapolis, Peru, and Chicago (Indianapolis to Peru), 72 m.
29. Indianapolis and St. Louis (Indianapolis to Terre Haute), 71 m.
30. Indianapolis and Vincennes, 116 m.
31, 31a. Jeffersonville, Madison, and Indianapolis, 185 m.
    31b. Rushville extension, 18 m; Cambridge City extension, 20 m.
32. Lake Erie, Evansville, and Southwestern (Boonville to Ill. line), 17 m.
33. Lake Shore and Michigan Southern (including old Indiana Railroad), 167 m.
34. Lake Erie and Western (Muncie to Ill. state line), 158 m.
35. Louisville, New Albany, and Chicago (Monon), 288 m.
36. Louisville, New Albany, and St. Louis (New Albany to Milltown), 18 m.
37. Logansport, Crawfordsville, and Southwestern (Logansport to Terre Haute), 114 m.
38. Michigan Central, 43 m.
39. Michigan City and Indianapolis (Michigan City to LaPorte), 12 m.
40. Ohio and Mississippi (including spur from North Vernon to Jeffersonville), 266 m.
41. Pittsburgh, Fort Wayne, and Chicago, 153 m.
42. Terre Haute and Indianapolis, 79 m.
43. Terre Haute and Southeastern (Terre Haute to Clay City), 40 m.
44. Toledo, Delphos, and Burlington (Kokomo to Ohio state line), 37 m. completed.
45. Wabash, St. Louis, and Pacific (Lake Erie and Mississippi), 166 m.
46. Whitewater (Harrison, Ohio, to Hagerstown), 62 m.

RAILROADS
in INDIANA
in 1880

Indiana begin to get its share of Great Lakes traffic, when two new privately constructed harbors were created for the huge iron-and-steel complex at Gary and at East Chicago–Indiana Harbor.[5] These ports were used overwhelmingly in this period for incoming raw materials for the Calumet area industrial plants, though the Standard Oil Refinery at Whiting also shipped some petroleum products by way of Indiana Harbor. In 1916, the first year for which the United States Bureau of the Census gathered statistics for these ports, Gary and Indiana Harbor together handled shipments totaling 4,696,126 tons. The following table shows how this was distributed between the two ports and the types of commodities shipped and received.

### FREIGHT TONNAGE AT GREAT LAKES HARBORS IN INDIANA, 1916[6]

| Product | Gary | | Indiana Harbor | |
| --- | --- | --- | --- | --- |
| | Received | Shipped | Received | Shipped |
| Iron ore | 2,954,436 | —— | 927,073 | —— |
| Coal | —— | —— | 398,259 | —— |
| Sand, stone | —— | —— | 254,399 | —— |
| Petroleum | —— | —— | —— | 159,931 |
| Lumber | 1,508 | —— | —— | —— |
| Miscellaneous | 520 | —— | —— | —— |
| TOTAL | 2,956,464 | | 1,579,731 | 159,931 |

The railroad, however, continued to dominate the state's transportation system during virtually the full forty-year period after 1880. Although the initial thrust of railroad building was concluded by 1880, main track mileage contin-

---

5 Unlike other harbors built earlier on the Great Lakes, including that at Michigan City, these were constructed without substantial Federal assistance. Beginning in 1901, the East Chicago Company, which was organized to develop the Twin City—East Chicago–Indiana Harbor, built both the harbor and ship canal at Indiana Harbor before turning them over to the Federal government for maintenance. The United States Steel Company spent $2,450,000 on construction of the harbor at Gary. Moore, *The Calumet Region*, pp. 239-240, 276.

6 United States Bureau of the Census, *Transportation by Water, 1916*, pp. 146-149.

ued to expand steadily in the succeeding decades, rising from 4,373 in 1880 to 5,971 in 1890, 6,471 in 1900, 7,420 in 1910, and 7,426 in 1920.[7] A great deal of new capital was invested and several important new lines were constructed during these years, many counties and townships, as in the past, purchasing bonds or granting outright subsidies in order to secure railroad connections.[8] But the main growth resulted from the consolidation and extension of the great integrated systems which were acquiring a dominant position in the eastern half of the country. Moreover, in this expansion local capital played little part. Intense competition and recurring financial troubles resulting from the economic crises of 1873, 1884, 1893, and 1905 brought about widespread railroad bankruptcy and complicated reorganization schemes which culminated in most cases in the complete financial control of Indiana railroads by eastern investors and syndicates.

Indiana lay directly in the path of the expansion of American commerce and transportation. As the state's first official statistician put it in somewhat exaggerated phrases,[9]

the entire east-west commerce of the nation asks permit to cross Indiana, and willingly pays tribute with a trail of gold along each iron track. It is not only the highway of a people, but of nations. It is not unusual for cars laden with gold and silver bullion from the Pacific slope, trains filled with teas, spices and silks from China and Japan, to meet on Indiana soil other trains bearing the rich manufactures of Europe and our own country to Pacific continents and islands.

Chicago was the goal of most railroad trunk lines crossing the state. By 1880 five major roads reached that city through Indiana—the Michigan Central, the Lake Shore and Michigan Southern, the Pittsburgh, Fort Wayne and Chicago, the Columbus, Chicago and Indiana Central, and the Baltimore and Ohio. In that year the Canadian-based Chicago and Grand Trunk cut across the northwest corner of the state on its way

[7] United States Department of Commerce, *Statistical Abstract of the United States,* 1922, p. 309.

[8] See, for example, reports of the amount of such aid voted by counties and townships in Indiana Department of Statistics, *Biennial Report,* 1885-1886, p. 398; 1895-1896, p. 323.

[9] Indiana Department of Statistics and Geology, *Annual Report,* 1880, p. 13.

from Port Huron, Michigan, to Chicago by way of Valparaiso.[10] Between 1881 and 1883 the Chicago and Atlantic was
built from Marion, Ohio, to Hammond with the financial backing of the Erie Railroad Company. From Hammond it entered Chicago by way of a terminal railroad, the Chicago
and Western Indiana. In 1890 the Chicago and Atlantic was
reorganized as the Chicago and Erie and became an integral
part of the Erie system.[11] The last major trunk line to cross
Indiana en route to Chicago was the Chesapeake and Ohio,
which accomplished this by purchasing in 1910 the Chicago,
Cincinnati and Louisville, which had been constructed from
Cincinnati to Hammond between 1904 and 1907.[12]

The first of the large integrated rail networks to be fully
formed in Indiana was the Pennsylvania system. Having begun to acquire western lines as early as the fifties, the Pennsylvania Railroad Company strengthened its position in the
eighties and nineties by a series of reorganizations and new
acquisitions which were brought together in a tight corporate
structure in the first two decades of the twentieth century.
In 1883 its longest line in the state, the 431-mile Columbus,
Chicago and Indiana Central, was reorganized as the Chicago,
St. Louis and Pittsburgh. This in turn was merged in 1890
with the other principal roads of the Pennsylvania's South-

---

[10] Henry V. Poor (comp.), *Manual of the Railroads of the United States*
(volumes 1-  , New York, 1868-    ), 1885, p. 583. In 1900 the Chicago and
Grand Trunk was reorganized as the Grand Trunk Western Railway Company,
a subsidiary of the Grand Trunk Railway Company of Canada. *Ibid.,* 1901, p.
816.

[11] *Ibid.,* 1890, pp. 326-327; 1891, p. 110; Edward Hungerford, *Men of Erie.
A Story of Human Effort* (New York, 1946), pp. 166, 204-205. For the building of this road, see the pamphlet by Earle Steele, *The Chicago & Atlantic
Railway Company: Forty-third Anniversary, 1883-1926* (Huntington, Ind.,
1926).

[12] Poor's *Railroad Manual,* 1912, p. 453; Charles W. Turner, *Chessie's Road*
(Richmond, Va., 1956), pp. 158-159. Other railroads built across northwest
Indiana to reach Chicago in this period were the Louisville, New Albany and
Chicago, the Nickel Plate, and the Wabash, which are discussed below. The
Pere Marquette's Chicago Extension reached Porter in Lake County in 1903.
For the coming of all these Chicago-bound railroads to northwest Indiana, see
Moore, *The Calumet Region,* pp. 83-92.

western system, including the Jeffersonville, Madison and Indianapolis, the newly established Cincinnati and Richmond, and the Pittsburgh, Cincinnati and St. Louis—also known as the Panhandle Route, a trade name which devolved upon its successor company—to form the Pittsburgh, Cincinnati, Chicago and St. Louis Railway Company.[13] Three years later the Pennsylvania purchased a majority of the stock of the Terre Haute and Indianapolis Railroad, a locally owned enterprise which had remained financially independent up to that time under the leadership of its president, William Riley McKeen of Terre Haute. This line also controlled or operated a group of other railroads emanating from Terre Haute which the Pennsylvania soon began to incorporate in its system as well, acquiring the Terre Haute and Logansport in 1898 and the Logansport and Toledo—formerly the Eel River Railroad—in 1901. Then in 1904 an agreement was concluded consolidating these three roads with the Pennsylvania-built, but Terre Haute and Indianapolis-leased, St. Louis, Vandalia and Terre Haute and the Pennsylvania-controlled Indianapolis and Vincennes under the new corporate name of the Vandalia Company. This created a single vast system of rail communications between Indianapolis and St. Louis, with tributary branches south to Vincennes and north to South Bend and Butler, Indiana.[14]

Finally, in 1916 a grand consolidation merged the Vandalia Company with the Pittsburgh, Cincinnati, Chicago and St. Louis Railway Company and a few smaller roads to form the Pittsburgh, Cincinnati, Chicago and St. Louis Railroad Company, better known as the Panhandle, which for five years thereafter operated all Pennsylvania-controlled lines in Indi-

[13] Pennsylvania Railroad Company, *Annual Report of the Board of Directors*, 1890, p. 31; Howard W. Schotter, *The Growth and Development of the Pennsylvania Railroad Company* . . . (Philadelphia, 1927), pp. 206, 225; George H. Burgess and Miles C. Kennedy, *Centennial History of the Pennsylvania Railroad Company, 1846-1946* (Philadelphia, 1949), pp. 192, 380.

[14] Pennsylvania Railroad Company, *Annual Report*, 1904, pp. 15-16; Schotter, *Growth and Development of the Pennsylvania Railroad Company*, pp. 237, 253, 288-289.

The
PENNSYLVANIA RAILROAD
System in Indiana
(1920)

ana except the Pittsburgh, Fort Wayne and Chicago, which remained under the Pennsylvania Railroad Company, and the self-operated Grand Rapids and Indiana along with its subsidiary, the Cincinnati, Richmond and Fort Wayne.[15] In 1918 the huge Pennsylvania network in the state was rounded out by the construction of the short Indianapolis and Frankfort Railroad, which connected the Michigan and St. Louis divisions of the Pittsburgh, Cincinnati, Chicago and St. Louis Railroad Company and created a direct Pennsylvania-controlled route between Chicago and Indianapolis. Early in 1921 the Pennsylvania Railroad Company in the interest of greater efficiency took over the operation of the Pittsburgh, Cincinnati, Chicago and St. Louis, the Grand Rapids and Indiana, and the Indianapolis and Frankfort by 999-year leases.[16]

Even more extensive than the 1,550-mile Pennsylvania system was the New York Central, which operated approximately 1,900 miles of railroad lines in Indiana by 1920.[17] The latter organization's presence in the state dated from the late seventies, when the aging Commodore Cornelius Vanderbilt acquired a controlling interest in the Michigan Central, which reached Chicago by a route through Michigan City, Indiana, and the Lake Shore and Michigan Southern, which ran across a portion of the northern tier of Indiana counties and afforded the powerful eastern railroad company a direct link between New York and Chicago.[18] In 1882 the Commodore's son, William H. Vanderbilt, added a parallel line just south of the Lake Shore by buying out the newly constructed New York, Chicago and St. Louis. This road,

[15] Poor's *Railroad Manual,* 1915, pp. 247-248; Pennsylvania Railroad Company, *Annual Report,* 1916, p. 25; Burgess and Kennedy, *Centennial History of the Pennsylvania Railroad Company,* p. 555.

[16] Poor's *Railroad Manual,* 1919, p. 1239; 1921, p. 1551; Schotter, *Growth and Development of the Pennsylvania Railroad Company,* pp. 372, 381-382.

[17] The trackage of these two system within Indiana was computed from the mileages reported for the component parts of each in Indiana *Year Book,* 1920, p. 872.

[18] Alvin F. Harlow, *The Road of the Century. The Story of the New York Central* (New York, 1947), pp. 235-238, 281-300.

nicknamed the Nickel Plate, had been incorporated in Indiana in 1881 by an eastern financial syndicate, the most prominent members of which were George I. Seney of New York and Calvin S. Brice of Ohio. The only Hoosier involved was William Fleming, a Fort Wayne businessman who handled the purchase of a part of the old Wabash and Erie Canal for the route of the proposed railroad through his home town. The New York, Chicago and St. Louis was so feeble that it went into receivership in 1885 but was successfully reorganized in 1887.[19] Vanderbilt's acquisition of the Nickel Plate road not only eliminated the possibility of a dangerous rival to the highly profitable Lake Shore and Michigan Southern—probably the very strategy employed by the original promoters of the new line—but also forged a strong link in the New York Central system. The United States Interstate Commerce Commission later manifested its disapproval of a single operating company holding two parallel rail lines, however, and in 1916 the New York Central disposed of its interest in the Nickel Plate to the Cleveland capitalists, Oris P. and Mantis J. Van Sweringen.[20]

The next major line to become part of the New York Central holdings in Indiana was another Brice-Seney promotion, the Lake Erie and Western Railway Company. Beginning as a consolidation in 1879 and 1880 of several Ohio and Indiana roads, the most important of the latter being the Lafayette, Muncie and Bloomington (Ill.), it was reorganized in 1887 as the Lake Erie and Western Railroad Company and began to expand rapidly under the energetic presidency of Calvin S. Brice. Two routes leading to northern Indiana were added in 1887 by the purchase of the Indianapolis, Peru and Chicago (connecting Indianapolis to Michigan City), the Chicago,

[19] Poor's *Railroad Manual,* 1883, p. 591; 1887, p. 505; Taylor Hampton, *The Nickel Plate Road: The History of a Great Railroad* (Cleveland and New York, 1947), pp. 44-77, 177-178; John A. Rehor, *The Nickel Plate Story* (Milwaukee, Wis., 1965), pp. 13-45.

[20] Hampton, *The Nickel Plate Road,* p. 220; Rehor, *The Nickel Plate Story,* pp. 65-67.

The
NEW YORK CENTRAL
RAILROAD
System in Indiana
(1920)

Cincinnati and Louisville (Peru to La Porte), and the Michigan City and Indianapolis (Michigan City to La Porte). Three years later the Fort Wayne, Cincinnati and Louisville, often called the Muncie Road, was annexed by the Lake Erie and Western. This ambitious rail network profited from the development of the oil and gas discoveries in Indiana—it advertised itself as the "Natural Gas Route"—and connected several important commercial and industrial centers in the northern and central parts of the state, but it failed to obtain access to the eastern seaboard as planned by Brice, who died in 1898. A year later the directors of the Lake Erie and Western agreed to sell out to the New York Central-controlled Lake Shore and Michigan Southern. The Lake Erie and Western Railroad, dubbed the "Leave Early and Walk" after its initials and memorialized in a humorous verse by Indianapolis newspaperman William Herschell, remained a valuable section of the New York Central's midwestern system until its sale in 1922 to the Van Sweringen brothers of Cleveland, who added it to the Nickel Plate empire they were attempting to build.[21]

The New York Central's largest subsidiary in Indiana was the Big Four, or the Cleveland, Cincinnati, Chicago and St. Louis. This remarkably successful railroad was largely the creation of Melville E. Ingalls, a Massachusetts attorney sent out by eastern investors in the seventies to rescue the faltering Indianapolis, Cincinnati and Lafayette Railroad. After years of receivership, this road was reorganized in 1880 as the Cincinnati, Indianapolis, St. Louis and Chicago under Ingalls as president. Ingalls immediately began an ambitious program of expansion, leasing the Cincinnati, Lafayette and Chicago and helping to finance and then leasing two other small

---

[21] Poor's *Railroad Manual*, 1888, p. 472; *ibid.*, 1905, p. 669; Hampton, *The Nickel Plate Road*, pp. 259-295; Rehor, *The Nickel Plate Story*, pp. 82-109. In the period 1924-1929 the Van Sweringen brothers tried to put together a "Greater Nickel Plate" system which would have included lines running through Indiana belonging to the Chesapeake and Ohio, the Pere Marquette, and the Erie as well as the Lake Erie and Western and the Nickel Plate. Rehor, *op. cit.*, pp. 175-178.

roads initiated by local investors—the Columbus, Hope and Greensburg and the Vernon, Greensburg and Rushville in the early eighties. In 1889 he joined forces with the Vanderbilt interests controlling the Bee Line, or the Cleveland, Columbus, Cincinnati and St. Louis, which also operated the valuable Indianapolis and St. Louis Railway, to create the rail system generally known as the Big Four after the cities in its corporate title, the Cleveland, Cincinnati, Chicago and St. Louis Railroad Company.[22]

The next year the Big Four absorbed the Cincinnati, Wabash and Michigan Railway, the Whitewater Railroad, and a group of lines in Ohio and Illinois, and leased the Peoria and Eastern, formerly the Indianapolis, Bloomington and Western. The Cairo, Vincennes and Chicago, which became the Cairo division of the Big Four, had two extensions into Indiana, one from St. Francisville, Illinois, across the Wabash River to Vincennes, and a longer line across the southwestern corner of the state when the Evansville, Mt. Carmel and Northern Railway Company was organized under Big Four auspices in 1906. The Cleveland, Cincinnati, Chicago and St. Louis prospered exceedingly under the leadership of Ingalls, who gave up the presidency in 1900 to become chairman of the board until 1912, two years before his death. By the turn of the century it had become through financial control a part of the New York Central system, but it continued to be operated separately under the Big Four name for many years. With nine hundred and sixty miles of track in Indiana in 1920, the Big Four ran through forty-four counties in a broad band across the center of the state, connecting 237

22 Ared Maurice Murphy, "The Big Four Railroad in Indiana," *Indiana Magazine of History,* XXI (1925), 212-216, 234, 264-267; Poor's *Railroad Manual,* 1890, pp. 993-994. Harlow states that the name Big Four was first used to describe the Cincinnati, Indianapolis, St. Louis and Chicago before the Cleveland, Cincinnati, Chicago and St. Louis was organized. Harlow, *Road of the Century,* p. 388.

The
CHICAGO, TERRE HAUTE
& SOUTHEASTERN RAILWAY
and the
WABASH RAILWAY
Systems in Indiana
(1920)

Hoosier communities with such cities as Chicago, Cincinnati, Cleveland, Columbus, and St. Louis.[23]

Additional lines joining the New York Central family in the early twentieth century were the Indiana Harbor Belt Railroad, the Indiana, Illinois and Iowa, and the Danville and Indiana Harbor, the latter linking the Lake County industrial center with the Cairo division of the Big Four. These roads were consolidated in 1913 as the Chicago, Indiana and Southern and merged the next year with the Lake Shore and Michigan Southern and other lines directly into the New York Central corporate structure. The Big Four, like the Michigan Central, however, retained its identity within the system, the parent company being content with majority stock ownership. Not until 1930 did the New York Central finally sign ninety-nine-year leases with its two remaining subsidiaries.[24]

Another national railroad system, the Wabash, suffered a series of setbacks in this period. Running diagonally across the northern half of the state, the Wabash, St. Louis and Pacific Railroad Company was formed in 1879 by the consolidation of the Wabash Railway Company with the St. Louis, Kansas City and Northern. Bankrupt and in the hands of a receiver by 1884, it split into five separate companies but was reorganized in 1889 as the Wabash Railroad Company "after five years of constant and discouraging effort," as the official report candidly stated.[25] In the process it lost the Michigan City and Indianapolis line which was acquired by the Lake Erie and Western Railroad Company in 1887. The Wabash more than compensated for this loss in 1892, however, by building its profitable Chicago-Detroit Extension from Montpelier, Ohio, one hundred and fifty miles across Indiana

23 Murphy, "The Big Four Railroad in Indiana," *Indiana Magazine of History,* XXI, 251-252, 266-270; Harlow, *Road of the Century,* pp. 389-397; Indiana *Year Book,* 1920, p. 872.

24 Poor's *Railroad Manual,* 1905, p. 667; 1915, p. 97; Harlow, *The Road of the Century,* pp. 391, 418.

25 Poor's *Railroad Manual,* 1880, p. 720; 1887, pp. 544-545; Wabash Railroad Company, *Annual Report,* 1890, p. 4.

to Hammond. In 1901, after the Wabash was forced by the courts to relinquish its lease of the Eel River Railroad, which went to the Pennsylvania system, as mentioned above, a short cutoff was constructed from New Haven, near Fort Wayne on the main line, to a junction with the Detroit route at Butler, Indiana. Finally, in 1916 a second reorganization took place creating the Wabash Railway Company after a foreclosure sale in the preceding year and five years in the hands of a receiver.[26]

A number of railroads were operated primarily as freight lines in the coal and limestone regions of western and southwestern Indiana. The oldest of these was the Louisville, New Albany and Chicago, originally the New Albany and Salem, which ran almost due north across the state from New Albany to Michigan City. In 1881, in order to obtain direct access to Chicago, a consolidation was effected with the Chicago and Indianapolis Airline Railroad Company, which had been chartered a year before to construct a line between the two cities of its corporate name. The completion of this road gave the Louisville, New Albany and Chicago 165 miles of additional track and important terminals in Chicago and Indianapolis.[27] The Monon Route, as the line was familiarly called, owed much of its prosperity to the freighting of coal and limestone mined and quarried along the southern part of its route, but it also provided convenient passenger service for a chain of communities in western Indiana, including the college towns of Bloomington, Greencastle, Crawfordsville, Lafayette, and Rensselaer, as well as the capital city of Indianapolis. In 1887, moreover, the Monon took control of the

---

[26] Poor's *Railroad Manual,* 1888, p. 472; 1893, p. 656; Wabash Railroad Company, *Annual Report,* 1901, p. 5; Wabash Railway Company, *Annual Report,* 1916, p. 5.

[27] Poor's *Railroad Manual,* 1882, p. 634; Frank F. Hargrave, *A Pioneer Railroad. The Origin and Development of the Monon* (Indianapolis, 1932), pp. 194-195. Before this the Monon used the Michigan Central tracks from Michigan City to the Illinois state border, which the latter had originally constructed under the Monon charter by special agreement with the Hoosier road. Hargrave, *op. cit.,* pp. 105-109.

The
CHICAGO, INDIANAPOLIS
& LOUISVILLE (MONON)
RAILROAD
(1920)

proposed Orleans, West Baden and Frenck Lick Springs line and completed its construction, thus opening an important tourist route to the mineral springs resorts of Orange County.[28]

But the severe economic depression of the mid-nineties drove the Monon, like many other roads in the state, into bankruptcy and receivership, and in 1897 it was reorganized as the Chicago, Indianapolis and Louisville Railroad Company. Within the next decade the new organization expanded its operations into the coal fields of Clay, Greene, and Sullivan counties by obtaining control of over a hundred miles of track newly constructed in that area. In 1914 the Monon also absorbed the Chicago and Wabash Valley Railway, a thirty-four-mile road extending from McCoysburg to the town of Dinwiddie in Lake County. Yet the famed Hoosier railroad lost its financial independence in 1902, when the Louisville and Nashville and the Southern Railway jointly acquired a majority of its stock, though they permitted the Monon to retain its own name and separate operating management.[29]

A less well-known railroad line running into the coal-producing counties of western Indiana was the Chicago and Eastern Illinois. First organized as a coal road in Illinois, it gained entrance into Indiana by leasing the forty-three-mile Evansville, Terre Haute and Chicago in 1880. Ten years later it entered the coal mining district south of Terre Haute by a traffic agreement with the Evansville and Terre Haute, an older line which also controlled the Evansville and Indianapolis, a company formed from the Evansville, Washington and Worthington in 1880 to construct an extension to Indianapolis (which never reached that city). In 1894 the Chicago and Eastern Illinois finally purchased the Evansville, Terre Haute and Chicago along with two other smaller lines, the Chicago and Indiana Coal Railway and the Indiana Block Coal Rail-

28 Poor's *Railroad Manual,* 1888, pp. 485-486; John W. Barriger, *A Hoosier Centenarian. "The Monon."* (New York, 1947), p. 18.

29 Poor's *Railroad Manual,* 1897, p. 106; 1902, p. 334; 1915, p. 601; Barriger, *A Hoosier Centenarian,* p. 19.

road. In 1911 it completed its network in the western Indiana coal district by a consolidation which absorbed fully the Evansville and Terre Haute, including its subsidiary, the Evansville and Indianapolis, and the Evansville Belt Railway.[30]

In 1902 the Chicago and Eastern Illinois' attractive coal road properties were integrated into the "Frisco Line" through purchase of a controlling interest by the St. Louis and San Francisco Railroad Company. Within a dozen years, however, the parent organization's bankruptcy had forced both it and the Chicago and Eastern Illinois into receivership, the latter becoming a separate corporate entity once more in 1916. The Chicago and Eastern Illinois remained in the hands of a receiver until its reorganization in 1921. In the meantime, the Evansville and Indianapolis, which ran in a wide loop through several coal-producing counties on its route between Evansville and Terre Haute, was detached from the Chicago and Eastern Illinois in 1916 and reorganized as the Evansville, Indianapolis and Terre Haute in 1920-1921.[31]

Another coal road formed in this period which also ran through the oolitic limestone district was the Chicago, Terre Haute and Southeastern Railway. It originated as the Evansville and Richmond, a project of President David J. Mackey of the Evansville and Terre Haute to connect his road with Richmond, Indiana. By 1890 one hundred and one miles of track had been constructed between Elnora, Daviess County, on the Evansville and Terre Haute line, to Westport, Decatur County, which was as far east as the road ever went. In 1897 John R. Walsh, a Chicago banker with an interest in limestone quarries in the oolitic district through which the road ran, acquired the Evansville and Richmond at foreclos-

[30] Poor's *Railroad Manual,* 1885, pp. 626, 654; 1900, pp. 213-214, 280; 1911, pp. 1145-1146, 1148-1149.

[31] *Ibid.,* 1920, pp. 1607-1608, 2113; 1921, pp. 1882-1883. In 1920 the Big Four leased and in 1921 purchased the Evansville, Indianapolis and Terre Haute, which became the former's Evansville division. Cleveland, Cincinnati, Chicago and St. Louis Railroad Company, *Annual Report,* 1921, p. 7.

ure sale, renaming it the Southern Indiana Railway. The new leadership inaugurated an ambitious program of expansion, annexing the Bedford Belt Railroad and extending the Southern Indiana Railway westward to Linton and later to Terre Haute. A planned extension to Indianapolis was never carried through, but the road reached Chicago by 1907 by the construction of a line from Terre Haute to Hunrick, Illinois, and thence straight north along the Indiana-Illinois border. Meanwhile, Walsh was convicted of violating the national banking laws and sent to prison, and his railroad was forced into receivership. In the reorganization which was ordered by the courts in 1910, the banker's quarry and railroad properties were separated and the latter incorporated as the Chicago, Terre Haute and Southeastern Railway.[32] By 1920 this organization was operating a prosperous 247-mile coal and limestone road which curved through southwestern and southern Indiana to its eastern terminus at Westport in Decatur County. Moreover, in 1921 the Chicago, Terre Haute and Southeastern was absorbed into the Chicago, Milwaukee, St. Paul and Pacific system by a 999-year lease.[33]

The last major railroad built through the coal and limestone districts of Indiana was the Indianapolis Southern Railway, an enterprise projected in 1899 by a group of Indianapolis businessmen and promoted as the "Mineral Route" linking the capital city with the great natural wealth of the region directly southwest of it. Local capital proved insufficient for the task, however, and the Illinois Central financed its construction, which was completed in 1906. The line ran from Indianapolis south and west to Bloomington and then westward to connect up with the Illinois Central's road between Switz City, Indiana, and Effingham, Illinois, which had originally been built as a narrow-gauge railroad in the early eighties. Operated independently at first as the Indianapolis

32 Poor's *Railroad Manual*, 1893, pp. 255-256; 1898, pp. 120-121; 1908, p. 473; 1911, p. 1818; Batchelor, *An Economic History of the Indiana Oolitic Limestone Industry*, pp. 93-95, 149n.
33 Indiana *Year Book*, 1920, p. 872; Poor's *Railroad Manual*, 1921, p. 342.

The
ILLINOIS CENTRAL R.R.
and the
SOUTHERN RAILWAY
Systems in Indiana
(1910)

◯ The LOUISVILLE, NEW ALBANY & CORYDON Railroad.

Southern, in 1911 it was fully integrated into the Illinois Central Railroad as its Indiana division. The only other Illinois Central line in Indiana was acquired in 1900 from the Peoria, Decatur and Evansville Railway, extending less than forty miles between Evansville and the state line, with a short branch to New Harmony.[34]

The only major trunk line running completely across southern Indiana was the Baltimore and Ohio, which took possession of the long-established Ohio and Mississippi in 1893, under the name Baltimore and Ohio Southwestern Railroad. This road ran through a part of the limestone and coal districts of the state on its route between Lawrenceburg and Vincennes and operated two Indiana branches, a short line to Bedford, Lawrence County, and a longer one from North Vernon south to New Albany and Jeffersonville.[35] Two other railroads extended across the extreme southern portion of Indiana on their way to St. Louis. One was the Southern Railway, the main line of which ran between New Albany and the Illinois state line, with branches to French Lick, Evansville, Rockport, Cannelton, and Corydon. It was chiefly composed of the former Louisville, Evansville and St. Louis, a line projected in the mid-seventies which traversed the relatively sparsely settled knob country of Floyd, Harrison, and Crawford counties and encountered steep grades and financial crises before being consolidated with other lines in 1889 and finally selling out to the Southern Railway in 1900.[36]

34 Poor's *Railroad Manual,* 1908, p. 432; 1912, p. 855; W. T. Hicks, Indianapolis Southern Railroad (Unpublished paper read before the Monroe County Historical Society, Bloomington, Indiana, February 17, 1911; MS in Indiana University Library), pp. 3-25; Carlton J. Corliss, *Main Line of Mid-America: The Story of the Illinois Central* (New York, 1950), pp. 290-291, 333-334. A copy of the Indianapolis Southern Railway's *Prospectus* is in the Indiana State Library.

35 Poor's *Railroad Manual,* 1898, p. 329; Edward Hungerford, *The Story of the Baltimore and Ohio Railroad, 1827-1927* (2 volumes, New York, 1928), II, 227. See also Robert F. Smith, *From the Ohio to the Mississippi* (Cincinnati, Ohio, 1965).

36 Indianapolis *News,* April 18, 1903; Poor's *Railroad Manual,* 1890, p. 644; 1901, p. 374; Southern Railway Company, *Annual Report,* 1901, p. 14.

The
BALTIMORE & OHIO R.R.
and the
CHESAPEAKE & OHIO RY.
Systems in Indiana
(1920)

A much shorter route across a portion of the state was taken by the Louisville and Nashville Railroad, which acquired in 1880 the Southeast and St. Louis Railway, the Indiana section of which extended across parts of Vanderburgh and Posey counties between Evansville and Mount Vernon.[37]

Despite the general tendency toward amalgamation with large national organizations, a few independent railroads survived through the second decade of the twentieth century in Indiana. An example was the moderate-sized Clover Leaf Route, the trade name by which the Toledo, St. Louis and Kansas City and its successors was popularly known. This railroad originated as a group of small, narrow-gauge roads strung across central Ohio and Indiana in the seventies, including the Frankfort and State Line, the Toledo, Delphos and Indianapolis, and the Delphos, Bluffton and Frankfort. In 1879 these and a fourth line were consolidated to form the Toledo, Delphos and Burlington as part of an extraordinarily ambitious scheme to create a "Grand Narrow Gauge Trunk" reaching across the country. Three years later this became the Toledo, Cincinnati and St. Louis, the so-called "Little Giant Line," which went into the hands of a receiver in 1883 after a series of financial crises. In 1886, however, it was reorganized as the Toledo, St. Louis and Kansas City, which adopted the famous white three-leaf clover symbol and soon converted to standard gauge. Famous for its fast freights, the Clover Leaf went under during the Panic of 1893 but was reorganized in 1900 as the Toledo, St. Louis and Western. The latter company prospered for a decade and a half, though it finally entered the Van Sweringen empire in 1922 after eight years of receivership.[38]

A somewhat similar railroad which maintained its independence for most of this period was the Cincinnati, Hamilton and Dayton, an Ohio corporation of which Charles W. Fairbanks was a director in the early nineties. This road

---

[37] Poor's *Railroad Manual*, 1880, p. 787.

[38] *Ibid.*, 1886, pp. 937-938; 1900, p. 312; Hampton, *The Nickel Plate Road*, pp. 230-256; Rehor, *The Nickel Plate Story*, pp. 119-169.

operated an Indiana subsidiary, the Cincinnati, Hamilton and Indianapolis, which was merged in 1902 with the Indiana, Decatur and Western to form the Cincinnati, Indianapolis and Western Railway Company to give its parent company a through route across the state of Indiana and into the middle of Illinois.[39] In 1904-1905 an interesting attempt was made to create a "Great Central System" composed of the Cincinnati, Hamilton and Dayton, the Pere Marquette of Indiana, and the under-construction Chicago, Cincinnati and Louisville, but the project fell through after the Cincinnati, Hamilton and Dayton had actually begun the acquisition of the other two lines. Instead, in the drive for integrated national rail systems, the Chesapeake and Ohio acquired the Chicago, Cincinnati and Louisville in 1910, as related above, and the Baltimore and Ohio bought the properties of the Cincinnati, Hamilton and Dayton in 1917, though it had to wait ten years to obtain full control of its new subsidiary.[40]

Other railroad enterprises promoted in this period with less success were the Findlay, Fort Wayne and Western and the Cincinnati, Bluffton and Chicago. The former was organized in 1894 as a consolidation of two shorter roads in Ohio and Indiana and after going into receivership in 1901 was renamed the Cincinnati, Findlay and Fort Wayne, which was financially controlled by the Cincinnati, Hamilton and Dayton for a decade. After a few years of independent operation once more, it was abandoned in 1919. The Cincinnati, Bluffton and Chicago was founded in 1903 and eventually built about fifty miles of track between Huntington and Portland, Indiana, with branches to a gravel pit and a stone quarry. Reorganized in 1915 under the less ambitious name of the Huntington, Bluffton and Portland, it soon languished and died. By 1920 its track was dismantled.[41] A somewhat more

[39] Poor's *Railroad Manual*, 1893, p. 741; 1903, pp. 373-374.

[40] *Ibid.*, 1908, pp. 400-402; 1917, p. 1988; Hungerford, *The Story of the Baltimore and Ohio Railroad*, II, 259-263; Interstate Commerce Commission, *Statistics of Railways of the United States*, 1927, p. 214.

[41] Poor's *Railroad Manual*, 1897, p. 124; 1907, pp. 537-538, 543; 1915, p. 1305; 1917, p. 2025; 1919, p. 2081.

successful short road was the Central Indiana Railway, which ran across the center of the state between Muncie and Waveland, Montgomery County. Originating in 1876 as the Anderson, Lebanon and St. Louis with nineteen miles of track between Anderson and Noblesville, it gradually expanded both east and west under a series of reorganizations, first as the Cleveland, Indiana and St. Louis, later as the Midland Railway and the Chicago and Southeastern, and finally as the Central Indiana Railway in 1903, when the line came under joint control of the Big Four and Pennsylvania systems.[42]

The United States Steel Company controlled its own industrial railroad system in the Calumet district by acquisition in 1901 of the Elgin, Joliet and Eastern, which was organized as early as 1888 and later became known as the Chicago Outer Belt, with its eastern terminus at Porter and extensions to Whiting and Griffith, Indiana.[43] Two very short rail lines organized in the early twentieth century in Indiana were the grandiosely named New Jersey, Indiana and Illinois, which was chartered in 1902 and opened twelve miles of track between South Bend and Pine in 1905, and the Ferdinand Railway, which was founded in 1905 and began operating a seven-mile route from that small Dubois County community to Huntingburg in 1909. In receivership by 1910, the latter was reorganized in 1911 and has survived until the present time, though passenger service has been discontinued.[44]

By 1920 twenty-eight railroad companies operated lines in Indiana, though many of these were linked together as parts of great integrated systems. According to the Indiana *Year Book* for that date these companies owned a total of 7,812 miles of main and secondary track within the state.[45] This dense pattern of railroad trackage had its greatest con-

[42] *Ibid.*, 1891, p. 772; 1915, p. 278.

[43] *Ibid.*, 1911, pp. 787-788.

[44] *Ibid.*, 1911, pp. 793-794, 846-847; information from Huntingburg Public Library.

[45] Indiana *Year Book*, 1920, p. 872. These figures are presumably more accurate than the 34 operating companies and approximately 13,000 total miles of track given in Logan *et al., Handbook of Indiana Geology,* p. 41.

centration in the central and northern sections of the state where urbanization and industrialization were most advanced, but by 1920 only two counties—tiny Ohio and Switzerland— in the less developed south lacked rail connections with the outside world. Although such cities as Fort Wayne, Logansport, Lafayette, and Terre Haute were important railroad centers, Indianapolis with its geographically central position remained the hub for most of this transportation network, most of the major lines being represented in the city. Connecting all entering tracks was a belt railroad, one of the first in America. Constructed in 1877 for the Union Stockyards, the belt line was leased in 1882 to the Indianapolis Union Railway Company, an organization formed to represent the city's railroads and conduct switching and transfer operations for them, though most of the capital was furnished jointly by the Pennsylvania and New York Central systems. In 1888 the company erected a large new Romanesque-designed Union Railway Station, where all roads entering the city received and discharged their passengers. In 1910 it was estimated that about two hundred passenger trains arrived in Indianapolis each day, while the belt railroad itself handled more than a million freight cars each year.[46]

§ §

The first significant rival of the steam railroad in Indiana was the electric railway. The use of electric power for transportation began with the street railway, one of the earliest recorded attempts at electrification of which was made in South Bend in 1882. Three years later, on November 15, 1885, the Belgian-born Charles J. Van Depoele designed an electric carline in South Bend which operated for several months before reverting to horse power because of difficulties with dissipation of current. But it was the work of Frank J. Sprague in building a successful electric system in Richmond, Virginia, in 1887-1888 which opened the way to electrification of American street railways. The Lafayette Street

46 Dunn, *Greater Indianapolis,* I, 257-263.

Railway, which began operation in August, 1888, was the first fully electrified city transportation system in Indiana. Many other cities followed this example in the next few years. By 1895 Anderson, Columbus, Elwood, Evansville, Fort Wayne, Indianapolis, Kokomo, Logansport, Richmond, South Bend, and Terre Haute had functioning electric lines.[47]

The next step was to extend the tracks out into the countryside and to connect with neighboring communities. Apparently the first intercity electric road in the state was the Brazil Rapid Transit Street Railway, which began operation from Brazil to Knightstown and Harmony on July 16, 1893, though only about two weeks later another company opened traffic from Marion to Jonesboro and Gas City.[48] Two pioneer promoters in the Gas Belt who did much to stimulate the building of electric railways were Noah J. Clodfelter, a Marion banker, and Charles L. Henry, a lawyer and former Republican Congressman. The former, who conceived of building a line from Marion to Indianapolis by way of Anderson as early as 1894, organized four companies between that year and 1897, but the financial stringency of the time brought failure to each of them. Henry, who had purchased the Anderson mule line in 1891 and electrified it the next year, began making plans for an extensive interurban service throughout the Gas Belt. He failed, however, to obtain sufficient financing until September 3, 1897, when he organized the Union Traction Company with Philip Matter of Marion and others. On January 1, 1898, the company's first car ran from Anderson to Alexandria, an eleven-mile journey.[49]

---

[47] George K. Bradley, *The Northern Indiana Railways* (Electric Railway Historical Society, *Bulletin 6,* Chicago, 1953), p. 4; David W. Chambers, *The Lafayette Street Railway* (Electric Railway Historical Society, *Bulletin 32,* Chicago, 1958), pp. 5-6; Jerry Marlette, *Electric Railroads of Indiana* (Indianapolis, 1959), p. 5.

[48] Glen A. Blackburn, "Interurban Railroads of Indiana," *Indiana Magazine of History,* XX (1924), 221-222, 255-256.

[49] Fred B. Hiatt, "Development of Interurbans in Indiana," *Indiana Magazine of History,* V (1909), 122; George S. Cottman, *Centennial History and Handbook of Indiana* (Indianapolis, 1915), pp. 164-166; Streightoff and Streightoff, *Indiana,* pp. 77-78.

In 1899 the Union Traction Company was merged with the newly formed Muncie, Anderson and Indianapolis Street Railroad Company, largely controlled by George McCulloch, owner of the Muncie street railway and of franchises on the route to Indianapolis. The new Union Traction Company of Indiana reached Indianapolis in January, 1901, by which time it comprised 163 miles of track and connected the cities of Alexandria, Anderson, Elwood, Marion, and Muncie.[50] Although Henry soon left to undertake other ventures, the Union Traction Company of Indiana, reorganized, consolidated with other roads, and financially controlled by an eastern syndicate which also owned the Indianapolis street railways, became by 1912 one of the largest systems in the state under the leadership of Hugh J. McGowan, the syndicate's representative in Indiana.[51]

The first interurban to enter the capital city, however, was the Indianapolis, Greenwood and Franklin, which reached Indianapolis on January 1, 1900. This, one of the earliest interurban railroad organizations in the state, had been originally formed in 1894 but its line was not constructed until after Joseph I. and William G. Irwin of Columbus purchased the company in 1899. Reorganized as the Indianapolis, Columbus and Southern Traction Company in 1902, the Irwin road was later extended to Seymour, where it connected with an electric line to Louisville, thus providing through service from Indianapolis to that city. In 1912 both of these roads were leased by the Interstate Public Service Company, a

[50] Blackburn, "Interurban Railroads of Indiana," *Indiana Magazine of History*, XX, 225-226.

[51] *Ibid.*, pp. 240-242; George W. Hilton and John F. Due, *The Electric Interurban Railways in America* (Stanford, Calif., 1960), pp. 280-281. Charles L. Henry has been credited with coining the word "interurban" to describe the electric intercity railway, but it seems to have been used by others before him, though he certainly helped to popularize it. *Ibid.*, p. 26. When Henry left the Union Traction Company in 1902, he organized the Indianapolis and Cincinnati Traction Company, which built lines to Connersville and Greensburg but went bankrupt before reaching Cincinnati. The indefatigable Henry was still trying to extend the line to that city in the years just before his death, which occurred in 1927. *Ibid.*, pp. 26, 284-285.

holding company headed by electric utilities magnates Samuel and Martin J. Insull of Chicago.[52]

Another major interurban network centering in Indianapolis was operated by the Terre Haute, Indianapolis and Eastern Traction Company. Formed in 1907 as a consolidation of the Indianapolis and Richmond, Indianapolis and Danville, Dunreith and New Castle, and the Cambridge City and Milton lines, by Hugh J. McGowan and the same eastern capitalists who controlled the Union Traction Company, it expanded by leasing such companies as the Terre Haute Traction and Light, the Indianapolis and Northwestern Traction, the Indianapolis and Martinsville Rapid Transit, and the Indianapolis, Crawfordsville and Danville Electric Railway. This gave the Terre Haute, Indianapolis and Eastern a 402-mile system stretching from the eastern to the western border of the state and linking Indianapolis to such cities as Crawfordsville, Danville, Frankfort, Lafayette, Lebanon, and Martinsville, as well as extending from Terre Haute in three directions, to Clinton, Sullivan, and to Paris, Illinois.[53]

Among interurban systems centered in other cities but connected to Indianapolis lines was that operated by the Fort Wayne and Northern Traction Company. Incorporated in 1911 as a reorganization of the Fort Wayne and Wabash Valley Traction Company, its lines extended from Fort Wayne to Lafayette by way of Huntington, Wabash, Peru, and Logansport, and from Fort Wayne to Bluffton.[54] In the important manufacturing region of the northwestern corner of the state two valuable electric railroad properties were organized in the early twentieth century. One was the Gary and Interur-

---

[52] Blackburn, "Interurban Railroads of Indiana," *Indiana Magazine of History*, XX, 251-271; Richard H. Gemmecke, W. G. Irwin and Hugh Thomas Miller: A Study in Free Enterprise in Indiana (Unpublished Ph.D. thesis in History, Indiana University, 1955), pp. 82, 96-106.

[53] Blackburn, "Interurban Railroads of Indiana," *Indiana Magazine of History*, XX, 251-271; Hiatt, "Development of Interurbans in Indiana," *ibid.*, V, 125-126; Hilton and Due, *Electric Interurban Railways in America*, pp. 278-279.

[54] Hilton and Due, *Electric Interurban Railways in America*, p. 280.

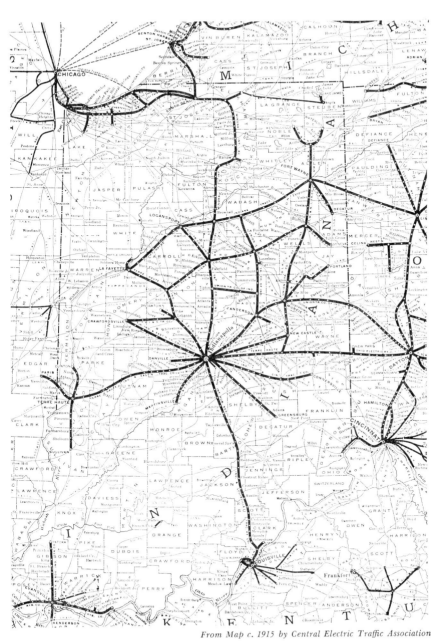

*From Map c. 1915 by Central Electric Traffic Association*

Electric Railway Lines in Indiana, 1915

ban Railway, which in 1913 took over several subsidiaries formerly belonging to the Chicago-New York Electric Airline, a company based on a grandiose project to connect those two cities which never materialized. The other was the Chicago, South Shore and South Bend, incorporated in 1901 as the Chicago and Indiana Air Line, promoted by the Samuel Insull and the J. B. Hanna syndicate of Cleveland. It developed such heavy traffic that it had to be double-tracked from Gary to Pullman, Illinois, and eventually became one of the most successful interurbans ever built, lasting down to the present time.[55]

Profiting from the densely populated South Bend-Elkhart area was the Northern Indiana Company, formed in 1905 out of several predecessor companies and operating city lines in South Bend, Elkhart, Goshen, La Porte, and Michigan City, as well as connecting these communities by interurbans. By 1910 this railway was linked to the Indianapolis systems by the Winona Interurban Railway, which was organized by the Winona Assembly in 1904 to build a line from Goshen to Warsaw, later extended south to Peru. These two companies also arranged schedules with steamers on Lake Michigan to meet cars at Michigan City and carry both passengers and freight across the lake to Chicago.[56] The only interurban lines not connected in some way with Indianapolis were three small systems in the Evansville area which were consolidated in 1919 as the Evansville and Ohio Valley Railway.[57]

By 1920 Indiana contained 2,600 miles of electric railway lines, of which 2,420 miles were main track. Indianapolis itself was the hub of the largest peripheral interurban network in the United States, linking it with almost every major city in the state and connecting at three points with railway sys-

---

[55] *Ibid.*, pp. 38-41, 337-338; Blackburn, "Interurban Railroads of Indiana," *Indiana Magazine of History*, XX, 415-416, 420-421.

[56] Blackburn, "Interurban Railroads in Indiana," *Indiana Magazine of History*, XX, 411-413; Hilton and Due, *Electric Interurban Railways of America*, pp. 276-277.

[57] Hilton and Due, *Electric Interurban Railways of America*, pp. 285-286.

tems in Ohio.[58] At the heart of this system was the huge interurban station on Market Street between the Circle and the State House. Built in 1904 by the Indianapolis Traction and Terminal Company under the presidency of Hugh J. McGowan, it consisted of a train shed covering nine tracks and an imposing nine-story office building housing the headquarters of the leading interurban companies. Operations in Indianapolis were further integrated in 1905 by the establishment of a joint ticket agency. Nearly four hundred cars a day entered the city, the majority of them making runs of forty or more miles, while some traveled as far as one hundred seventy miles in a day. On some of the longer lines deluxe services such as parlor, dining, and sleeping cars made their appearance.[59]

The Indiana electric railways industry was more highly concentrated and integrated than most, its major lines dominated after the turn of the century by the W. Kelsey Schoepf-Hugh J. McGowan syndicate backed by eastern banking interests. Yet by the second decade of the twentieth century the interurban had already begun to decline. Financial instability plagued the industry, caused by too rapid expansion and frequent over capitalization. Few new lines were constructed after about 1911, for opportunities for profit were insufficient to attract additional capital. Rivalry with the steam railroads, which had better facilities for handling freight and even began to win back some of the electric lines' passenger business except for distances under fifty

[58] Indianapolis replaced Detroit as the center of the largest peripheral network early in the twentieth century. *Ibid.*, p. 26. Hilton and Due give Indiana only 1,825 miles of track but place the state second after Ohio in the absolute size of the interurban network. *Ibid.*, p. 275. The figures of 2,600 and 2,420 miles are taken from Logan *et al., Handbook of Indiana Geology*, p. 42. For a map of the Indiana interurban system, see page 255.

[59] Marlette, *Electric Railroads of Indiana*, pp. 1, 9-10; Blackburn, "Interurban Railroads of Indiana," *Indiana Magazine of History*, XX, 425-426. In 1918 the Indianapolis station handled 128,145 cars carrying 7,519,634 passengers in or out of the city. Other large interurban terminals in Indiana were located at Muncie and Fort Wayne. Hilton and Due, *Electric Interurban Railways of America*, pp. 69-70.

miles, was a significant factor in the decline. But the coming of the automobile and the motor bus constituted the most dangerous threat to the interurbans, which struggled to survive through the twenties only to collapse in the next decade.[60]

§ § §

The urgent demand of farmers and others for railroad rate regulation in the seventies produced no significant legislative response from the General Assembly.[61] Moreover, the creation of the Interstate Commerce Commission in 1887 as a Federal regulatory agency seemed to relieve the government of Indiana of most of the responsibility for railroad affairs, so much of which extended beyond the jurisdiction of a single state. Nevertheless, by the eighties Hoosier legislators were becoming increasingly concerned about certain aspects of rail transportation within state boundaries, particularly the large number of injuries and deaths resulting from railroad operations. In 1885 Eugene V. Debs, a Democratic representative from Vigo County, fought unsuccessfully for a bill making railroad companies responsible for injuries to employees.[62] Not until 1893 was a similar measure enacted.[63] A few minor safety regulations were also written into law at this time, but enforcement was difficult in the absence of a state regulatory body.

A major complaint against railroad companies was their inclination and ability to evade fair assessment and property

---

[60] Blackburn, "Interurban Railroads of Indiana," *Indiana Magazine of History*, XX, 426-436; Logan *et al.*, *Handbook of Indiana Geology*, pp. 42-43; Marlette, *Electric Railroads of Indiana*, pp. 15-20. The ever-optimistic Charles L. Henry, however, said in a speech in 1916 that "the fad feature of automobile riding will gradually wear off, and the time will soon be here when a very large part of the people will cease to think of automobile rides, and the interurbans will carry their old time allotment of passengers." *Electric Railway Journal*, XLVII (1916), 403, quoted in Hilton and Due, *Electric Interurban Railways of America*, p. 235.

[61] See Thornbrough, *Indiana in the Civil War Era*, pp. 356-361.

[62] The bill passed in the lower house but did not come to a vote in the Senate. Indiana *House Journal*, 1885, pp. 136, 1293; Indiana *Senate Journal*, 1885, p. 881.

[63] *Laws of Indiana*, 1893, pp. 294-296.

taxation. In 1891, when Governor Alvin P. Hovey requested the legislature to establish a board of railroad commissioners having general supervision over common carriers' intrastate operations, the General Assembly instead replaced the State Board of Equalization by a somewhat stronger State Board of Tax Commissioners, with the power to assess railroad property fully and without favoritism.[64] This measure brought a sudden, dramatic rise in the valuation of railroads for tax purposes and apparently ended for the time being any demand for further regulation of transportation companies.[65]

Finally, upon the urgent recommendation of Governor Hanly, the legislature in 1905 authorized the establishment of the Indiana Railroad Commission, composed of three men appointed by the chief executive to be responsible for the regulation of railroad rates and both passenger and freight car service within the boundaries of Indiana.[66] The commission, moreover, was given the power to alter rates it considered unfair, while the railroads' only method of redress was to appeal to the courts. Two years later when Governor Hanly reiterated a request for wider regulatory authority, the General Assembly complied by prohibiting the distribution of free passes and granting the Railroad Commission jurisdiction over electric interurbans, express companies, and sleeping car companies as well as steam railroads.[67]

Meanwhile, public attention had been drawn to the need for improved safety measures by a tragic event in November, 1906, when a railroad wreck on the Baltimore and Ohio at Woodville, in Porter County, brought death to forty-eight persons and injuries to one hundred fifty. When more serious accidents took place on the Big Four at Fowler and at Sandford less than two months later, in which a total of twenty-

[64] Indiana *Senate Journal,* 1891, p. 27; *Laws of Indiana,* 1891, pp. 249-250, 256.

[65] Dunn, *Indiana and Indianans,* II, 750-753; William A. Rawles, *Centralizing Tendencies in the Administration of Indiana* (New York, 1903), pp. 272-277.

[66] *Laws of Indiana,* 1905, pp. 83-101.

[67] *Ibid.,* 1907, pp. 186-190.

four were killed and fifty-three injured, the General Assembly, which was in session at the time, passed bills requiring the installation of block signal systems for all steam railroads and the preparation of printed rules for operation of trains, calling an annual convention of superintendents and others with the Railroad Commission to discuss ways of increasing rail safety, and giving the latter agency more elaborate and specific authority.[68]

In 1910 five head-on collisions on interurban lines, the worst of which took place at Kingsland, in Wells County, on September 21, when one car telescoped another, killing forty-one passengers, created a strong demand for further safety legislation.[69] As a result the General Assembly in 1911 enacted a long series of laws affecting both railroads and interurbans requiring the installation of automatic bell ringers and storm windows in engineers' compartments, highway crossing signs, inspection of locomotive boilers, reporting of accidents by telegraph or telephone as soon as possible after the event, switching signal lights, and other safety devices.[70]

The Indiana Railroad Commission, though belated in making its appearance, was a relatively strong agency, with a good record of successful defense of its rate-setting and other regulatory activities in the courts. During its very first year of existence it was able to reduce rates for coal hauling, and after the passage of the Shippers' Bill in 1907 it regulated the distribution of freight cars within the state, a power especially useful at the time of the coal strike of that year

[68] *Ibid.*, 1907, pp. 353-354, 454-488, 584-586. The Railroad Commission had just begun to investigate the Baltimore and Ohio tragedy when the legislature asked for an additional report on the Big Four accidents of January, 1907. The report of the entire investigation is found in Indiana Railroad Commission, *Annual Report*, 1907, pp. 193-216.

[69] Indiana Railroad Commission, *Annual Report*, 1910, pp. 381-382. The Kingsland collision was the worst interurban disaster ever recorded in the United States. Hilton and Due, *Electric Interurban Railways of America*, pp. 88-89.

[70] *Laws of Indiana*, 1911, pp. 85-88, 127-130, 132, 133-134, 432-434, 466-467, 543-544, 643-644. Some laws regulating railroad safety had been passed in 1909. *Ibid.*, 1909, pp. 159-160, 232-233, 278, 323-324, 441.

and after the outbreak of the First World War.[71] The most controversial laws passed regarding railroad regulation were those establishing a two-cent-per-mile passenger fare and requiring a full train crew, which were later repealed.[72]

In 1913 the General Assembly, on the recommendation of Governor Ralston, replaced the Railroad Commission by another agency, the five-man Public Service Commission, which was given broad powers of supervision over the rates and service of all steam and electric railroads, street railways, telephone and telegraph companies, heat, light, power, and water companies, and elevators and warehouses, thus bringing for the first time all public utilities and transportation facilities under the full regulatory control of the state.[73] In both 1913 and 1915 the legislature also enacted several laws strengthening the authority of the Public Service Commission over railroad safety provisions as well as such matters as the right to buy and sell noncompeting railroad lines and the financial operations of public utility companies.[74]

§ § § §

The ramification of the steam and electric railroad network did not solve all the transportation problems of Indiana, especially for the farmer who still had to get his products to market or to the railroad over unpaved roads, often completely impassable many months of the year. Furthermore, until the nineties most of the improved highways were toll roads, constructed and operated for a profit by private companies chartered by the state or county government. In 1889 the General Assembly authorized counties to levy a special tax and to issue bonds for the purchase of such privately

71 *Ibid.,* 1907, pp. 434-443; Indiana Railroad Commission, *Annual Report,* 1906, pp. 7-8; Indiana *Year Book,* 1917, pp. 355-357.

72 The two-cent-a-mile law was passed in 1909 and repealed in 1919; the full crew law was passed in the same year and was applied to switching crews in 1911; both were repealed in 1921. *Laws of Indiana,* 1909, pp. 51-53, 68-69; 1911, pp. 124-125; 1919, pp. 470-471; 1921, p. 178.

73 Indiana *House Journal,* 1913, pp. 70-71; *Laws of Indiana,* 1913, pp. 167-214.

74 *Laws of Indiana,* 1913, pp. 74-76, 323-324, 462-465, 659-660; 1915, pp. 116-117, 319-320.

owned roads in townships where a majority of the voters registered their approval in a special election.[75] This proved to be a popular measure, particularly in the more densely settled northern and central sections of the state, where the toll roads were virtually eliminated within a few years after its passage. In 1905 the state geologist, who devoted almost the whole of his annual report to the subject of roads and road materials, reported that only 112 miles of private highways remained in the whole of Indiana, all of that in the counties along the Ohio River.[76]

The system of road supervision in Indiana was under jealously guarded local control. In 1877 and 1879 the first laws were passed permitting county commissioners to build and repair free turnpikes.[77] The construction of such roads was financed not by general taxation, however, but by assessments upon adjacent property owners, who had to petition for the improvement. Road repair and maintenance was done by the corvée, or forced-labor method, whereby all able-bodied men between the ages of twenty-one and fifty were required to work from two to four days each year on the public highways under the direction of elected road supervisors responsible to the township trustees.[78] This system long persisted despite its inefficiency and was actually reinforced by legislation of 1913 which authorized male taxpayers to work out their regular township road taxes. In that same year the General Assembly also provided for appointment of county highway superintendents by the county commissioners and the levying of a county road tax.[79]

[75] *Ibid.,* 1889, pp. 276-278.

[76] Indiana Department of Geology and Natural Resources, *Annual Report,* 1905, pp. 36-37.

[77] *Laws of Indiana,* 1877, pp. 82-89; 1879, pp. 226-228.

[78] *Ibid.,* 1883, pp. 62-74. Certain classes of persons, such as Civil War veterans, were exempted from the corvée, and anyone was permitted to substitute the payment of $1.25 for each day's labor.

[79] *Ibid.,* 1913, pp. 862-867, 877, 884. The highway superintendents were also charged with naming or numbering all public roads and preparing a road map of the county.

The conversion of common public roads into improved highways of gravel or stone went slowly until the nineties, when the popularity of the bicycle and the promise of free rural mail delivery awakened people to the need for good highways. Yet many, especially farmers, were fearful of higher taxes. In December, 1892, a Roads Congress held under the auspices of the Commercial Club of Indianapolis sought legislation to hasten the improvement of the state's highway system, but the State Board of Agriculture at its annual meeting the next month supported only mild reforms and instructed its legislative committee to "use all honorable means to prevent any further radical changes in our present road law, thus burdening the farmers with increased taxation."[80] In 1893, however, the General Assembly responded to the growing demand for better roads by passing a law authorizing the building of tax-supported highways upon the petition of fifty freeholders and the approval of a majority of the voters in any townships.[81] Road-making techniques remained rather primitive and inefficient, for most improved public highways were paved with gravel or crushed rock, at best a waterbound macadamized surface, needing repairs early and often.

The coming of the automobile did more than anything else to stimulate the good roads movement. Pioneer manufacturers and promoters of motor vehicles in Indiana were active in popularizing the new mode of travel and seeking the improved highways needed for its fullest enjoyment. As early as 1899 Elwood Haynes and his partner, Edgar Apperson, driving a phaeton manufactured in their own plant in Kokomo, made the first thousand-mile run on a journey to New York City.[82] The Indianapolis Automobile Trade Association

80 Indiana State Board of Agriculture, *Annual Report*, 1892, p. 149.

81 *Laws of Indiana*, 1893, pp. 196-200. In 1905 another public highway law permitted as few as twelve freeholders to petition to locate, change, or vacate a road. *Ibid.*, 1905, pp. 521-529.

82 Charity Dye, *Some Torch Bearers in Indiana* (Indianapolis, 1917), p. 158; Dunn, *Indiana and Indianans*, II, 949.

staged its first auto show in 1901, and the next year the Hoosier Motor Club was founded by capital city motorists "who banded together for mutual protection against irate owners of horse-drawn vehicles," according to a later secretary of the club.[83]

Racing events also played a part in popularizing the automobile. In June, 1909, two marathon road races were held over a 23-mile course in Crown Point, Lake County, the first won by Joe Matson in a Chalmers-Detroit and the second, for the Ira M. Cobe trophy, by Louis Chevrolet in a Buick. Attendance was disappointing, however, and the event was not repeated; thus the Cobe cup became one of the trophies awarded at the Indianapolis Motor Speedway,[84] which was built in the same year as the Crown Point race by Carl G. Fisher, an Indianapolis businessman and former bicycle racer, along with his partners, James A. Allison, Frank H. Wheeler, and Arthur C. Newby. The original macadam track was resurfaced with brick after a series of bad accidents marred the first "racing carnival" held in September, 1909. Two days of successful races were held in December on the new surface, and the third racing event in May, 1910, attracted a record attendance of thirty thousand persons. After two additional racing meets in July and September of that year, the annual 500-mile marathon was finally established as the single event of the year at the Motor Speedway on May 30, 1911, when the first such race was won by Ray Harroun in an Indianapolis-built Marmon "Wasp."[85]

Fisher, an indefatigable promotor of motoring, was also largely responsible for creating the first transcontinental

[83] *Hoosier Motorist,* March, 1918, p. 9.

[84] *Lake County Star* (Crown Point), June 18, 25, 1909; Rudolph E. Anderson, *The Story of the American Automobile: Highlights and Sidelights* (Washington, D.C., 1950), pp. 158-159. The national road races at Elgin, Illinois, which began in 1910 replaced the Crown Point race.

[85] Indianapolis *Star,* September 5, December 18, 19, 1909; May 27, 28, 29, 30, July 3, 4, 5, September 4, 5, 6, 1910; May 31, 1911; Anderson, *Story of the American Automobile,* pp. 160-163; Al Bloemker, *500 Miles to Go. The Story of the Indianapolis Speedway* (New York, 1961), pp. 38-97.

highway in the United States. In September, 1912, he laid
before a group of automobile manufacturers and dealers at a
meeting in Indianapolis his proposal for a hard-surfaced coast-
to-coast roadway which aroused national enthusiasm and support and spurred the construction of what became the Lincoln Highway.[86] In 1915 Fisher similarly helped to initiate
the movement for a national north-south highway by leading
a fifteen-car caravan from Indianapolis to Miami, Florida, on
the route that was later known as the Dixie Highway.[87]

The rapidly increasing number of motor cars in the state
brought demands for some form of regulation. In his final
address to the legislature in 1905, Governor Durbin drew
attention to the high level of accidents resulting from "the
careless and reckless driving of automobiles" and recommended legislation "regulating the speed and manner of handling of these machines upon the streets and highways of the
State."[88] In that year the General Assembly not only saw fit
to establish speed limits—eight miles an hour in the business and densely populated sections of cities, fifteen miles
an hour in other parts of cities and towns, and twenty miles
an hour in the rural countryside—but also required all owners of motor vehicles to register them with the secretary of
state and display the registration number on a circular metal
seal "conspicuously" on the car.[89] In the first year, 4,253 vehicles were registered in this fashion. But not until 1913 did
the state assess charges of from $2.00 to $20.00, according to
horsepower, for annual registration of motor vehicles and re-

[86] The Lincoln Highway: The Story of a Crusade that Made Transportation History (New York, 1935), pp. 9-20. Fisher was also one of the leaders of
the Hoosier Trail Blazers' Tour from Indianapolis to San Francisco in the
summer of 1913 which helped to publicize and popularize the idea of a transcontinental highway. Ibid., pp. 29-42; Jane Fisher, Fabulous Hoosier. A Story
of American Achievement (New York, 1947), pp. 82-88.

[87] Fisher, Fabulous Hoosier, p. 92.

[88] Indiana Senate Journal, 1905, p. 49.

[89] Laws of Indiana, 1905, pp. 202-205. The statute also required automobile
drivers to stop and signal before proceeding when meeting persons riding,
driving, or leading any draft animal on the road.

quire all chauffeurs to be licensed.[90] The table below indicates the rapid rise in the number of automobiles annually registered in Indiana after passage of that act.

REGISTRATION OF MOTOR VEHICLES IN INDIANA,
1914-1920[91]

| Year | Number | Year | Number |
|------|--------|------|--------|
| 1914 | 66,400 | 1918 | 227,160 |
| 1915 | 96,915 | 1919 | 227,255 |
| 1916 | 139,065 | 1920 | 333,067 |
| 1917 | 192,194 | | |

Yet Indiana was slow in establishing a unified system of improved highways throughout the state. The movement for such a system may be said to have begun with the formation of the Indiana Good Roads Association in December, 1910, under the presidency of Clarence A. Kenyon, an officer of the Western Paving and Supply Company and an enthusiastic advocate of better highways. On January 15, 1914, Kenyon addressed a special conference of "friends of good roads"—engineers, county commissioners, Purdue professors, and others—at the Indianapolis Chamber of Commerce, launching an ultimately successful fight for the organization of a state highway commission.[92] Later the same year Governor Ralston appointed a special commission to investigate highway conditions which presented a report strongly recommending establishment of a state road department.[93]

But the General Assembly did not act until after the passage by the United States Congress of a law in 1916 which appropriated $75,000,000 for distribution to the states for the

[90] Indiana *Year Book,* 1917, p. 42; *Laws of Indiana,* 1913, pp. 781-782. The same act raised speed limits to a maximum of ten miles per hour in business sections and fifteen miles per hour in residential sections, twenty miles per hour in cities and towns outside business and residential sections, and twenty-five miles per hour elsewhere. *Laws of Indiana,* 1913, pp. 788-789.

[91] United States Department of Commerce, *Statistical Abstract of the United States,* 1920, p. 312; 1922, p. 291.

[92] Dunn, *Indiana and Indianans,* II, 939.

[93] Indiana *House Journal,* 1915, pp. 40-41.

Plan of State Highways
as designated by
Indiana Highway
Commission, 1920

construction of rural post roads. In order to qualify for Federal assistance, the legislature in the closing hours of the 1917 session enacted a law establishing the Indiana State Highway Commission and creating a highway fund composed of receipts from the recently imposed inheritance tax and from special appropriations for road building and maintenance. The commission was authorized to receive and disburse Federal aid money as well as allocate state financial assistance to county road-building programs.[94] In accordance with the specific instructions set forth in the act, the commission designated five "main market highways," two passing through Indianapolis, one east-west along the "National Old Trail Road" and another north-south on the route of the so-called "Dixie Highway" promoted by Carl Fisher and others. One highway crossed the extreme northern part of the state along the route of the already well marked "Lincoln Highway," and two more were in the south, the first running from Lawrenceburg to Evansville, and the second branching off from the first at Mitchell and extending to Vincennes.[95]

The work of the Indiana Highway Commission was barely started when it was abruptly halted in May, 1918, by a court injunction which was granted upon the suit of a Hamilton County citizen contesting the validity of the state highway law.[96] On Governor Goodrich's recommendation, however, the General Assembly re-established the commission in 1919 with new instructions to lay out a system of state highways which would reach every county seat and every city with over 5,000 population and connect these communities with the improved trunk lines of adjoining states. At the same time the state highway fund was enlarged to include all motor vehicle registration fees as well as a new highway

94 Laws of Indiana, 1917, pp. 253-273.
95 Indiana Year Book, 1917, pp. 481-485.
96 Ibid., 1918, p. 521.

tax of ten cents upon each $100 of taxable property in Indiana.[97]

In accordance with the legislature's instructions, the reorganized Indiana Highway Commission drew up a plan for a 3,200-mile network of state highways, including the five main market roads originally proposed plus subsidiary routes reaching into every county. Wishing to satisfy as many citizens as possible and still give the state a system which would be the most economical from the standpoint of construction and maintenance, members of the State Highway Commission spent many days traveling over the state viewing various routes. Meetings were also held in order that individuals and communities might have the opportunity to present their views as to the best routes to select. The proposed routes were submitted to the Governor the latter part of February, 1920, and with a few changes were approved in April. The total mileage was estimated to comprise only about 5 per cent of the entire road system in the state. At the same time the commission recommended that the total be increased to 10 per cent, a figure which it was thought would include all the main highways. With its small annual appropriation from the legislature it was estimated that the commission would be able to construct about one hundred and twenty miles of hardsurface highways each year as well as to maintain the system as laid out.[98]

Although a few short stretches of highway were paved with concrete or asphalt, most roads continued to be maintained by grading, draining, and the application of gravel or crushed rock. The commission also instituted a system of state highway route numbers which at first were simply painted in black on white bands on telephone poles beside the roads.[99]

[97] *Laws of Indiana,* 1919, pp. 119-140.
[98] Indiana *Year Book,* 1920, pp. 1125-1126. See the map of the planned state highways on page 267.
[99] *Ibid.,* p. 1145.

It was a small beginning, but at long last a definite program of state responsibility for improved highways had been inaugurated in order to prepare Indiana to enter the dawning automobile age.[100]

[100] In this period Indiana also played a minor role in preparing the way for the air age yet to come. In 1896 the Frenchman Octave Chanute conducted experiments in gliding on the dunes in Lake County. Of the two Wright brothers who corresponded with Chanute and began their even more important experiments in powered flight at Kitty Hawk, North Carolina, in 1900, the oldest, Wilbur Wright, was born on a farm near Millville in Henry County. Moore, *The Calumet Region,* pp. 574-585; Marvin W. McFarland (ed.), *The Papers of Wilbur and Orville Wright* . . . (2 volumes, New York, 1953), I, vii-xi, 3n.

# CHAPTER VII

# THE INDUSTRIALIZATION OF AN AGRICULTURAL ECONOMY

MANUFACTURING GREW STEADILY but relatively slowly within Indiana's predominantly agricultural economy for several decades before 1880.[1] In the general westward march of American industrial development in the post-Civil War years, Indiana also lagged behind most other states of the Old Northwest, and especially Illinois and Ohio, which were far in the vanguard of the entire region. But by the eighties Indiana's growing network of rail transportation together with accumulating knowledge and increased exploitation of its natural resources provided a solid foundation for a rapid, if somewhat belated, expansion of the industrial sector of the economy. In particular, as related in Chapter V, the discovery and promotion of the natural gas field in the east-central section of the state furnished a powerful stimulus to industrialization, which the economic depression following the Panic of 1893 and the depletion of the gas field itself did not reverse. Contributing to the sustained growth of industry were improved transportation facilities which afforded easier access to markets as well as raw materials and the increasing productivity of the state's agriculture and extractive industries. In short, most, if not all, of the necessary preconditions for the "take-off" of an industrial economy were present in Indiana by the last two decades of the nineteenth century.[2]

[1] For the growth of manufacturing in the three decades prior to 1880, see Thornbrough, *Indiana in the Civil War Era,* pp. 411-424.

[2] According to the indexes used by George W. Starr, manufacturing in Indiana grew much more rapidly, especially in the decade after 1890, than in the country as a whole. Starr, *Industrial Development of Indiana,* pp. 12-13. The concept of "take-off" is borrowed from W. W. Rostow, who has used the term to denote the decisive point in the shift from a traditional, primarily

That the eighties and nineties were an era of burgeoning industrial growth in the state was indicated by a number of economic indexes. According to the published reports of the United States Bureau of the Census, between 1880 and 1900 the amount of capital invested in manufacturing of all types, including neighborhood and hand industry as well as factory production, rose from $65,742,962 to $234,481,528; the value of products manufactured, including custom work and repairing, from $148,006,411 to $378,120,140; the number of establishments from 11,198 to 18,015; the average number of wage earners from 69,508 to 155,956; and the amount of wages paid from $21,960,888 to $66,847,317. The proportion of wage earners to the total population of the state also increased from 3.5 per cent in 1880 to 6.2 per cent in 1900.[3]

At the close of the nineteenth century Indiana still drew the bulk of its wealth from the soil, primarily by way of agriculture, but to a lesser extent through mining and other extractive industries. These sectors of the economy, moreover, contributed an important share of the essential raw materials and fuels for the state's manufacturing enterprises. For this reason the gross value of product cannot be used to determine accurately the relative position of manufacturing in the state's economy. By subtracting the value of materials used

agricultural economy to a modern, industrial one. Rostow writes that the American economy in the North and West had taken off by the opening of the Civil War but that the South, for example, did not reach this stage for about eighty years, largely, he suggests, because of its "long, slow disengagement" from traditional society. W. W. Rostow, *The Stages of Economic Growth. A Non-Communist Manifesto* (Cambridge, England, 1961), pp. 4-40. Rostow does not treat the special case of Indiana's comparatively belated take-off, but among the factors in its relatively slow industrial development may have been the persistence of traditional, rural values in Hoosier life and society, as partially reflected, at least, in the literature and painting of this period. For a discussion of these values in these areas, see below, Chapters XIII and XIV.

3 United States Bureau of the Census, *Twelfth Census* (1900), VIII, *Manufactures,* p. 199. Comparisons among census reports for manufactures in these years are necessarily inexact, for changes were often made in the form of inquiry and method of compilation of statistics. For the most part census statistics after 1900 are much improved over previous decennial returns, though they are sometimes difficult to compare meaningfully with earlier reports.

it is possible to obtain a figure which Federal census reports after 1900 describe as the "value added by manufacture," which presumably better represents the real contribution of manufacturing to the state's wealth than the gross value of product. Yet, since it has not proven feasible to ascertain a "net value" of agricultural output, which might be considered statistically comparable to the value added by manufacture, it will be necessary to use the somewhat less satisfactory gross value of agricultural product for purposes of comparison, though with the recognition that the last is at least slightly overweighted in the equation.[4]

When, then, did manufacturing overtake the agricultural sector of the Indiana economy in the production of wealth? A comparison of the gross value of agricultural products with the value added by manufacture over these years reveals that the gap was finally virtually closed in the Federal census year 1920—actually, the production year of 1919—when out of a combined value of agricultural and industrial products totaling $1,500,000,000, agriculture accounted for $781,000,000 and the value added by manufacture, $724,000,-000, just $57,000,000 less than agriculture.[5] Considering the above-mentioned statistical advantage afforded the latter in this method of calculation, it is possible to assert that by 1920 the manufacturing sector had indeed caught up with, if not slightly surpassed, the hitherto dominant agricultural sector of the economy. In fact, manufacturing had been "catching up" with agriculture at least since the nineties. The first two decades of the twentieth century, moreover, were an era of unusually rapid industrial growth, especially the highly productive, as well as inflationary, years of the First World

[4] United States Bureau of the Census, *Twelfth Census* (1900), V, *Agriculture,* p. cxxvii; *Thirteenth Census* (1910), *Abstract, with Supplement for Indiana,* p. 676; Barnhart and Carmony, *Indiana,* II, 428. See also George D. King, The Industrialization of Indiana, 1860-1920 (Unpublished thesis in History, Indiana University, 1963).

[5] United States Bureau of the Census, *Fourteenth Census* (1920), V, *Agriculture,* p. 18; *ibid.,* IX, *Manufactures,* p. 375.

War. Ironically, because of the fact that certain other parts of the United States were industrializing even more rapidly in this period. Indiana's rank as a manufacturing state declined from eighth to ninth place in the decade from 1900 to 1910 and continued in that position during the next decade.[6] The following table indicates the respective increases in various indexes of manufacturing as reported in the quinquennial returns for this period.

### GROWTH OF INDIANA MANUFACTURES, 1899-1919[7]

| Year | Number of establishments | Capital | Value of product | Value added by manufacture |
|------|------|------|------|------|
| 1899 | 7,128 | $ 219,321,080 | $ 337,071,630 | $141,909,064 |
| 1904 | 7,044 | 312,071,234 | 393,954,405 | 173,447,398 |
| 1909 | 7,969 | 508,717,197 | 579,075,046 | 244,700,293 |
| 1914 | 8,022 | 668,863,232 | 730,795,021 | 306,937,864 |
| 1919 | 7,916 | 1,335,714,103 | 1,898,753,387 | 723,802,819 |

| Year | Number of persons engaged | Average number of wage earners | Salaries and wages | Wages |
|------|------|------|------|------|
| 1899 | — | 139,017 | $ 69,251,062 | $ 59,280,131 |
| 1904 | 176,227 | 154,174 | 87,086,888 | 72,058,099 |
| 1909 | 218,263 | 186,984 | 121,815,291 | 95,510,616 |
| 1914 | 233,270 | 197,503 | 155,854,826 | 119,258,329 |
| 1919 | 330,145 | 277,580 | 402,159,443 | 317,042,997 |

The emergence of Indiana as a leading industrial commonwealth in these years is closely related to at least four major factors: (1) large quantities of agricultural and forestry products which furnish the raw materials for manufactures; (2) deposits of mineral resources, especially abundant and cheap fuels such as coal, natural gas, and petroleum—though the last played a much less significant role in industrialization than the other two; (3) excellent transportation facili-

6 Barnhart and Carmony, *Indiana,* II, 430-431.
7 United States Bureau of the Census, *Fourteenth Census* (1920), IX, *Manufactures,* p. 374. Unlike earlier census reports, these statistics cover only production by the factory system, excluding neighborhood industries and hand trades, and are not fully comparable with returns before 1900.

ties with a dense network of railroads crisscrossing the state as well as waterways for freighting (the Lake Michigan ports beginning to function just as the traffic on the Ohio River and its navigable tributaries began to decline); (4) Indiana's fortunate geographic location at or near the center of the population of the United States and directly in the path of a large share of east-west commerce, with wide access to markets. Increasing urbanization was part of this pattern, Indianapolis and a dozen or more smaller cities in the state gaining population and economic weight during this period. Indiana also enjoyed the commercial advantages of proximity to the great urban marts of Chicago, Cincinnati, and Louisville outside the state boundaries.

Several changes took place in the nature of manufacturing enterprises during the period from 1880 to 1920. One involved the types of motive power used in factory production. Steam power grew slowly, remaining the leading prime mover until challenged by electricity about 1914; water power generally declined and the internal combustion engine became increasingly important, as the following table indicates:

HORSEPOWER OF TYPES OF PRIME MOVERS,
1880-1919[8]

| Year | Steam | Water | Electric | Internal Combustion |
|---|---|---|---|---|
| 1880 | 109,960 | 21,810 | — | — |
| 1890 | 174,060 | 16,305 | 323 | 176 |
| 1900 | 296,926 | 11,964 | 7,903 | 12,295 |
| 1905 | 336,932 | 9,685 | 33,582 | 21,171 |
| 1909 | 449,127 | 7,893 | 233,193 | 109,105 |
| 1914 | 430,504 | 9,905 | 450,357 | 66,691 |
| 1919 | 521,446 | 10,162 | 652,754 | 189,271 |

Another important shift was from the processing and fabrication of such local raw materials as lumber, wheat, and meat to the manufacture of durable goods, many of them

[8] Compiled from United States Bureau of the Census, *Census of Manufactures,* 1905, IV, 627, 630, 632, 636; *Fourteenth Census* (1920), IX, *Manufactures,* p. 390.

made from iron and steel.[9] Even native fuels such as coal
and natural gas tended to play a somewhat smaller part in
the state's manufacturing industries after 1900 than before.
Some manufactures flourished while utilizing little or none of
the state's natural resources. The blast furnaces of the Calumet Region, for example, transformed ores from the Mesabi
range in Minnesota by means of coke made from Pennsylvania and West Virginia coal, using limestone imported from
Michigan for fluxing.[10] In this case, Indiana's chief industrial advantage was its location, which, among other things,
made possible bulk transportation of raw materials by water.
Moreover, an industry like glass manufacturing, which used
practically no local raw materials, but was drawn to Indiana
by the promise of free or cheap fuel during the gas boom,
was able to remain in the state after the cessation of the
flow of natural gas by switching to coal or other sources of
heat.

A third shift was regional. As the earlier manufacturing
centers along the Ohio River declined in importance, the central and northern counties became more heavily industrialized. A northward movement of manufactures was already
well under way by the seventies but was greatly accelerated
in the succeeding decades. Of the seven leading industrial
counties which together produced approximately half of the
state's manufactures in 1879, only two—Vanderburgh and
Floyd—were located in the extreme south. With the abrupt decline of New Albany in the eighties, Floyd County dropped
out of the ranks of the principal industrial counties. Evansville alone among southern Indiana cities continued to keep
pace as a manufacturing center. In fact, its county, Vanderburgh, held fifth place in the value of manufactured products
in the state as late as 1919. Marion County, containing the capital city, Indianapolis, remained in first place until 1919, when

9 See Starr, *Industrial Development of Indiana*, pp. 19-20.
10 John B. Appleton, *The Iron and Steel Industry of the Calumet District.
A Study in Economic Geography* (University of Illinois *Studies in the Social
Sciences*, XIII, No. 2, Urbana, 1927), pp. 67-70, 78-80.

Lake County, a newly developed area, overtook it. Other leading industrial counties in this period were Vigo (Terre haute), St. Joseph (South Bend), Allen (Fort Wayne), and Madison (Anderson). The concentration of industry in certain regions was well shown in the 1920 census, when Marion and Lake counties together reported 48.8 per cent of the total products for the state and 33.6 per cent of the total number of wage earners.[11]

Indianapolis was the industrial as well as political capital of the state in 1909, with 21.8 per cent of the value of its manufactured products. Using the same measure of comparison South Bend was in second place in that year, having passed Evansville in 1904, largely because of the establishment of the automobile industry in the former place. By 1914, however, the comparatively young East Chicago in Lake County was ranked second, ahead of such older industrial cities as South Bend, Evansville, Fort Wayne, and Terre Haute. Five years later Indianapolis still held its supremacy, but second place would have to be awarded to Gary on the basis of the Lake County figures, for the Federal census reports omitted statistics of the new city to avoid disclosure of individual operations. Evansville fell to sixth and Terre Haute to eighth place or lower, depending on what position should be assigned to Whiting, another virtually single-industry city whose statistics were not revealed by the Bureau of the Census. Other important industrial cities in descending order of value of manufactured products in 1919 were Hammond, Anderson, Kokomo, Michigan City, Muncie, Mishawaka, Elkhart, Marion, Richmond, and La Porte.[12]

[11] United States Bureau of the Census, *Fourteenth Census* (1920), IX, *Manufactures,* p. 373. For a graphic presentation of this regional shift, see Starr, *Industrial Development of Indiana,* pp. 34-37, 39-40. The forty-two counties south of the National Road were credited with 37.3 per cent of the value of manufactured products in the state in 1880, but with only 16.5 per cent in 1920, according to a table in Starr, *op. cit.,* p. 51.

[12] United States Bureau of the Census, *Thirteenth Census* (1910), *Abstract, with Supplement for Indiana,* p. 685; *Fourteenth Census* (1920), IX, *Manufactures,* pp. 375, 387-388, 397-399.

Manufacturing in Indiana as in the rest of the nation was moving in the direction of large-scale factory production, which had far outdistanced neighborhood industries and hand trades in value of products by 1900, though the latter remained surprisingly numerous. If all manufacturing establishments with a product of less than $500 are included, the total number in 1899 was 23,657, of which 13,396, or 56.8 per cent, represented either small shops or hand trades. Yet the value of products of these last establishments amounted to only $30,515,265, or approximately 8 per cent of the total value of the state's manufactured goods in that year. On the other hand, in 1899 Indiana boasted 16 establishments out of 443 in the whole country employing over 1,000 persons.[13] Twenty years later manufacturing companies in the state doing over $1,000,000 worth of business accounted for only 3.8 per cent of the total number of establishments but 71.5 per cent of the gross value of products. In several industries the proportion of value of products manufactured by such concerns was much higher — agricultural implements, 87.0 per cent; automobiles, 97.0 per cent; and slaughtering and meat packing, 92.1 per cent.[14]

In the nineties occurred a series of industrial combinations affecting Indiana which stimulated a great deal of discussion of monopolies and "trusts." The Gas Belt alone spawned combinations in the glass, strawboard, and tinplate industries in this period.[15] Despite considerable unfavorable public opinion and some antitrust legislation by the General Assembly,

13 United States Bureau of the Census, *Twelfth Census* (1900), *Manufactures*, VII, 583; VIII, 200.

14 *Ibid., Fourteenth Census* (1920), IX, *Manufactures,* pp. 383-385.

15 For a contemporary discussion of Gas Belt "trusts," see the Indianapolis *Press,* December 22, 1899. Indiana sent a large delegation to the conference on trusts called by the Chicago Civic Federation in September, 1899. The speeches of several Hoosier delegates, including civil service reformer William D. Foulke, Grand Master Aaron Jones of the Patrons of Husbandry, wagon manufacturer Clem Studebaker, John B. Conner, chief of the Indiana Department of Statistics, and Professor James R. Weaver of DePauw University, were printed in *Chicago Conference on Trusts: Speeches, Debates, Resolutions, List of Delegates, Committees, etc.* (Chicago, 1900).

the process of integration of Hoosier manufacturing into the national economic sphere continued strongly into the twentieth century. By 1919 such huge corporations as the American Can Company, American Car and Foundry Company, American Hominy Company, American Seeding Machine Company, American Tin Plate Company, General Electric Company, General Motors Corporation, International Harvester Company, Pittsburgh Plate Glass Company, Standard Oil of Indiana, and United States Steel Corporation were each represented in the state by one or more factories. In addition, corporations were increasingly replacing individuals and partnership firms. The number of manufacturing enterprises owned by corporations rose from 27.2 per cent in 1904 to 37.4 per cent in 1919, while their average number of wage earners and value of products increased from 80.6 per cent each to 91.7 and 93.5 per cent, respectively. By 1919 the proportion of corporate ownership had reached 100 per cent in such industries as railroad car construction and repair, and cement, glass, and iron and steel manufacturing.[16]

§ §

Evidence of the continuing importance of agriculture in the production of raw materials for manufacturing in Indiana was the consistently high rank of the processing of meat, grain, and other foods among the state's industries throughout most of the period from 1880 to 1920. Yet the statistical significance of these particular industries was chiefly derived from the total value of products, which necessarily included a disproportionately large sum for the value of the materials used. Thus the processing of such agricultural products, significant as they were in total value, actually added less to the state's wealth than many manufacturing industries less dependent upon local raw materials, such as iron and steel and glassmaking. Nevertheless, meat packing, flour milling, and food processing made good economic sense in a

[16] United States Bureau of the Census, *Census of Manufactures*, 1905, I, 494; *Fourteenth Census* (1920), IX, *Manufactures*, pp. 374, 386-387.

state with both abundant agricultural resources and excellent transportation facilities. While this type of manufacturing was not sufficient in itself to place Indiana in the front ranks of industrial states, it clearly played a major role in the creation of an industrial base in a primarily agricultural region.

By 1899 slaughtering and meat packing constituted the leading industry in Indiana, computed according to value of products, which in that year amounted to $43,862,273, or 11.6 per cent of the total value of the state's manufactures. Although it fell to second place in 1914 and third place in 1919, its value of products remained relatively high. But the value added by manufacture amounted to only $12,339,000 in 1919. By this standard of measurement slaughtering and meat packing could not be counted among the state's ten leading industries.[17]

Before 1901 the principal slaughtering and meat-packing center in Indiana was Hammond, a Lake County city named for George H. Hammond, a meat wholesaler in Detroit and a pioneer shipper of dressed beef in refrigerator cars, who built a slaughterhouse in 1869 in what was then an uninhabited spot near the Indiana-Illinois boundary. In 1890, four years after the founder's death, the Hammond Packing Company was sold to an English syndicate, and its annual slaughtering capacity was enlarged to 300,000 cattle, 25,000 sheep, and 10,-000 hogs. Tragedy struck in October, 1901, when a disastrous fire almost completely destroyed the plant. J. Ogden Armour purchased the Hammond holdings in an attempt to create a giant meat trust, but, when this maneuver was rejected by the Federal courts, he closed the Indiana meat-packing plant permanently in May, 1903, and moved its operations to Chica-

17 *Ibid., Twelfth Census* (1900), VIII, *Manufactures,* pp. 201-202; *Fourteenth Census* (1920), IX, *Manufactures,* pp. 396-397. For tables of the twenty leading industries of the state ranked by value of products for the decades 1880-1920, see Barnhart and Carmony, *Indiana,* II, 241-243, 435-436. According to the system of ranking industries used by these authors, slaughtering and meat packing fell as far as fourth place in 1919.

go.[18] Not only was this a great blow to the economic well-being of the city of Hammond, but the loss meant a sharp drop in the state's meat production as shown vividly in the report of the census of manufactures in 1905, when the total value of slaughtering and meat-packing products fell by one third, to $29,352,593.[19]

Indianapolis succeeded Hammond as the center of slaughtering and meat packing in the state. The introduction of artificial refrigeration and the "summer pack" in the seventies through the experiments of George W. Stockman of the British-owned Kingan and Company helped to give the capital city a leading position in the industry.[20] In 1914 its value of products totaled $37,780,039 and in 1919 soared to $104,-805,746, according to which Indianapolis ranked fifth among meat-packing cities in the nation after Chicago, Kansas City, Omaha, and New York.[21] Other Hoosier cities with commercially significant facilities for slaughtering and meat packing were Fort Wayne, Evansville, Lafayette, and East Chicago. Indiana's main meat products were pork, both fresh and cured, beef, and sausage, plus lesser quantities of veal, mutton, and salted beef. Auxiliary products of the slaughtering and meat-packing industry included hides and pelts, lard, tallow, and oleomargarine, as well as glue, soap, and fertilizers, which were chiefly manufactured in separate establishments. The value of products of the entire industry rose to $51,022,000 in 1914 and $134,029,000 in 1919.[22]

[18] Moore, *The Calumet Region,* pp. 145-151, 173-174. Hammond's chief partner, Marcus M. Towle, was responsible for naming the city after the meat packer, who never took up residence in Indiana. *Ibid.,* pp. 153-156.

[19] United States Bureau of the Census, *Census of Manufactures,* 1905, III, 463.

[20] Dunn, *Greater Indianapolis,* I, 349-350.

[21] United States Bureau of the Census, *Fourteenth Census* (1920), X, *Manufactures,* p. 47.

[22] *Ibid.,* p. 59. Soap, for example, was usually produced in separate establishments, $5,678,183 worth in Indiana in 1919. *Ibid.,* p. 774. Yet the well-known soap product, "Old Dutch Cleanser," was manufactured by the Cudahy Packing Company in a plant built in East Chicago in 1909. *The Calumet Region Historical Guide . . .* (Gary, Ind., 1939), pp. 97-98.

In spite of the large livestock and slaughtering interests in the state, Indiana did not rank particularly high in the tanning of leather and its manufacture into finished products. The value of tanned and curried leather, which was $2,729,-000 in 1879, did not reach that large a sum again until 1914 and was only $4,730,000 in the inflationary year of 1919. Although the figures are not perfectly comparable because of the inclusion of small shops and hand trades in the earlier census returns, the manufacture of boots and shoes declined from a total value of products of $2,144,000 in 1879 to $1,-278,000 in 1914, before rising to $2,854,000 in 1919. Saddlery and harness manufacture remained fairly stable until 1914, but dropped significantly with the decreased use of horses by 1919, when the value of products was $2,520,000. Glove making, which was not even reported in the censuses of 1880 and 1890, was an extremely minor industry in Indiana, with products valued at just $588,000 in 1919. The only leather industry which expanded in the state in this period was the manufacture of trunks and valises, the value of such products rising from $84,000 in 1879 to $264,000 in 1914 and $1,348,000 in 1919.[23]

According to value of products, Indiana's leading industry in the eighties and nineties was the milling of grain, which slipped, however, to second place in 1899, fourth place in 1914, and finally, sixth place in 1919, when total output was valued at $75,111,000.[24] Since grain was grown commercially in most of the state, mills were relatively numerous and widely scattered. Their number, however, reached a peak in 1900 with 897 reported in the census returns of that year, and then declined to 563 in 1909 and 450 in 1919.[25] Indianap-

[23] United States Bureau of the Census, *Tenth Census* (1880), *Manufactures,* pp. 113-114; *Census of Manufactures,* 1914, II, 697, 705, 717, 723, 729; *Fourteenth Census* (1920), X, *Manufactures,* pp. 505, 518, 527, 536-537, 543, 549.

[24] *Ibid., Twelfth Census* (1900), VIII, *Manufactures,* p. 202; *Census of Manufactures,* 1914, I, 368; *Fourteenth Census* (1920), IX, *Manufactures,* p. 376.

[25] *Ibid., Twelfth Census* (1900), VIII, *Manufactures,* p. 202; *Fourteenth Census* (1920), X, *Manufactures,* p. 116.

olis was the leading flour-milling city in the state, closely followed by Evansville, though large mills were also found in cities like Fort Wayne, Lawrenceburg, and Terre Haute. The Igleheart Brothers Company in Evansville created a famous brand name, "Swans Down," which it introduced in 1876. In 1895 it began packaging Swans Down Cake Flour and three years later initiated a national advertising campaign which helped to make this product a family favorite throughout much of the United States.[26]

Wheat flour was the chief product of Indiana mills, though large quantities of corn meal and hominy were also manufactured, along with smaller amounts of rye and buckwheat flour and barley meal. More important commercially than the latter were livestock feeds—corn and oats ground together as well as bran and middlings, by-products in the manufacture of wheat flour. As the wheat belt moved northward and westward to Minnesota and Kansas, wheat-flour production declined in Indiana, as did most mill products except hominy and grits, of which the state remained the leading producer in the country through nearly the whole of this period. Indiana's "hominy king," Theodore Hudnut, founded a mill in Terre Haute just after the Civil War which became the foundation of a large corporation organized by him in that city and elsewhere in 1890. Most of his holdings outside Terre Haute went into the establishment of the consolidated American Hominy Company in 1902.[27]

[26] Igleheart Brothers Company and its famous brand name were acquired by General Foods Corporation in 1926. *General Foods Family Album* (n.p., 1948), pp. 8-9.

[27] C. C. Oakey, *Greater Terre Haute and Vigo County* . . . (2 volumes, Chicago and New York, 1908), I, 204-205.

## FLOUR AND GRISTMILL PRODUCTS IN INDIANA, 1899-1919[28]

| Year | Wheat Flour Pounds | Value | Corn Meal and Flour Pounds | Value |
|---|---|---|---|---|
| 1899 | 4,722,208 | $20,059,135 | 1,987,719 | $ 2,601,562 |
| 1904 | 5,181,906 | 25,282,880 | 909,622 | 2,076,266 |
| 1909 | 4,794,847 | 25,315,671 | 855,409 | 2,483,265 |
| 1914 | 4,526,879 | 21,183,688 | 984,239 | 3,030,308 |
| 1919 | 4,305,436 | 47,088,134 | 512,179 | 4,451,959 |

| Year | Hominy and Grits Pounds | Value | Bran, Middlings, and Feed Tons | Value |
|---|---|---|---|---|
| 1899 | 96,714,589 | $ 715,640 | 376,154 | $ 4,763,783 |
| 1904 | 182,106,165 | 2,147,012 | 374,314 | 6,703,490 |
| 1909 | 256,678,796 | 3,758,367 | 388,022 | 8,740,647 |
| 1914 | 292,131,101 | 4,620,892 | 337,627 | 8,412,421 |
| 1919 | 93,956,630 | 3,222,770 | 345,170 | 18,598,847 |

Another grain-using industry was the "wet" milling of corn in order to manufacture starch and related products. One of the earliest successful starch factories in the United States was built in Indianapolis in 1867 by a German immigrant, William F. Piel. In 1890 a consolidation of the Piel firm with several others in Indiana and elsewhere created the National Starch Manufacturing Company, which then controlled about 65 per cent of the American market, according to William F. Piel, Jr., vice-president and later president of the new corporation.[29] The state ranked second after New York in the production of starch in both 1889 and 1899, though the total value of products declined from $1,580,543 to $989,639

[28] United States Bureau of the Census, *Census of Manufactures,* 1905, III, 364-365; *Thirteenth Census* (1910), X, *Manufactures,* pp. 417-418; *Fourteenth Census* (1920), X, *Manufactures,* p. 112.

[29] Affidavit of William F. Piel, Jr., in *Trusts and Industrial Combinations* (*Report of the Industrial Commission,* XIII, *House Documents,* 57 Congress, 1 session, No. 182), pp. 671-673. Even larger consolidations were effected later, creating first the National Starch Company and then the Corn Products Refining Company, organized in 1900 and 1906, respectively. The Piels started another factory in Indianapolis in 1902, after disposing of their interest in the National Starch Company. Arthur S. Dewing, *Corporate Promotions and Reorganizations* (*Harvard Economic Studies,* X, Cambridge, Mass., 1914), pp. 52-71, 95, 103-108.

in this period, largely because of the closing of several plants brought about by the 1890 merger.[30]

Other products of starch mills were livestock feeds, glucose or corn syrup, and corn oil. Indiana became a major producer of the last two products in 1906, when the American Maize Products Company, which specialized in the manufacture of salad oil, built a large plant in East Chicago.[31] Largely for this reason, by 1909 Indiana ranked fourth among the states in the total value of starch and glucose products, which amounted to $5,750,000 in that year.[32]

Bread and other baked goods were also produced on an increasing scale in the state during this period. The industry was characterized by a comparatively large number of small and medium-sized bakeries, while Indianapolis led in value of products, followed by such other cities as Terre Haute, Fort Wayne, and Evansville. One of the most successful Hoosier entrepreneurs in this field was Alexander Taggart of Indianapolis, whose Parrot and Taggart Bakery in the capital city was merged into the United States Baking Company, later a part of the National Biscuit Company, a corporation formed in 1898 which also controlled bakeries in Fort Wayne and Terre Haute. In 1905, however, Taggart sold out his interest in the National Biscuit Company in order to organize the Taggart Baking Company in Indianapolis, which became the largest bakery in the state.[33] The steady growth of the industry, as shown in the table below, reveals the general shift from home to factory baking which occurred during this period.

30 United States Bureau of the Census, *Twelfth Census* (1900), IX, *Manufactures,* pp. 574-575.

31 *The Calumet Region Historical Guide,* pp. 96-97.

32 United States Bureau of the Census, *Thirteenth Census* (1910), X, *Manufactures,* pp. 430-434. Indiana remained in fourth position in 1919, though the Bureau of the Census did not publish the value of products for that year in order to avoid disclosing individual operations. *Fourteenth Census,* X, *Manufactures,* p. 121.

33 Dunn, *Indiana and Indianans,* IV, 1777-1778.

BREAD AND OTHER BAKERY PRODUCTS, 1879-1919[34]

| Year | Number of establishments | Average number of wage earners | Value of products |
|------|------|------|------|
| 1879 | 155 | 519 | $ 1,292,000 |
| 1889 | 264 | 1,025 | 2,282,000 |
| 1899 | 391 | 1,334 | 4,166,000 |
| 1909 | 754 | 2,505 | 10,209,000 |
| 1919 | 802 | 3,759 | 30,020,000 |

The most important food-processing industry to become firmly established in Indiana during this period was vegetable canning, which was closely related to the rapid growth of truck gardening in the central and northern sections of the state. Although pioneer canners like Gilbert C. Van Camp of Indianapolis and James T. Polk of Greenwood had begun commercial operations on a small scale in the sixties and seventies, the main advance came after 1890 with the discovery of natural gas and the subsequent rise of the domestic manufacture of tinplate. Indiana benefited particularly from the westward movement of the canning industry, which had been previously centered on the Atlantic Coast, and showed the most rapid increase among the ten leading states in the value of output in the first decade of the twentieth century.[35] The following table indicates the growth of the industry:

CANNING INDUSTRY IN INDIANA, 1879-1919[36]

| Year | Number of establishments | Average number of wage earners | Value of products |
|------|------|------|------|
| 1879 | 6 | 337 | $ 249,000 |
| 1889 | 11 | 2,020 | 885,000 |
| 1899 | 60 | 2,002 | 2,589,908 |
| 1909 | 134 | 3,406 | 8,758,000 |
| 1919 | 166 | 4,170 | 27,823,000 |

[34] United States Bureau of the Census, *Tenth Census* (1880), II, *Manufactures,* Pt. 2, p. 113; *Eleventh Census* (1890), XI, *Manufactures,* pp. 400-401; *Thirteenth Census* (1910), *Abstract, with Supplement for Indiana,* p. 695; *Fourteenth Census* (1920), IX, *Manufactures,* p. 396.

[35] *Ibid., Thirteenth Census* (1910), X, *Manufactures,* pp. 383, 384.

[36] *Ibid., Tenth Census* (1880), II, *Manufactures,* Pt. 2, p. 113; *Eleventh Census* (1890), XI, *Manufactures,* pp. 402-403; *Twelfth Census* (1900), VIII,

Canneries proliferated in this period. They were located in large cities such as Indianapolis as well as in dozens of small communities scattered throughout the vegetable-growing districts of the state, especially in Boone, Daviess, Delaware, Henry, Howard, Johnson, Madison, Scott, Tipton, Wabash, Washington, and Wayne counties. Among the chief products in Indiana were canned tomatoes, beans, peas, pumpkin, hominy, and sweet corn. Cucumber pickles and tomato catsup as well as a small quantity of fruit were also preserved. In the early nineties Frank Van Camp, son of Gilbert C. Van Camp, initiated the canning of a popular food combining pork and beans with tomato sauce, and the Van Camp Company remained for many years the leading manufacturer of that product, which was generally known to Americans as "Boston baked beans." Indiana was also the birthplace of another important innovation in the industry, the canning of hominy, which was apparently originated by Isaac V. Smith in Delphi in November, 1896. A leading canner in the southern part of the state was Joseph W. Morgan, who established the Morgan Packing Company in Austin, Scott County, and several other small nearby towns at the beginning of the twentieth century.[37]

By 1909 Indiana was ranked first among all the states of the nation in the canning of baked beans; second in pumpkin; and fourth in both peas and tomatoes. The canning industry was moving westward so rapidly by this time, moreover, that in 1919 Indiana had taken first place in the canning of pumpkin, hominy, and tomato pulp, while retaining its premier position in baked beans, and was in second place in tomato paste and kidney beans.[38]

*Manufactures*, pp. 210-211; *Thirteenth Census* (1910), X, *Manufactures*, p. 383; *Fourteenth Census* (1920), IX, *Manufactures*, p. 396.

37 Earl C. May, *The Canning Clan. A Pageant of Pioneering Americans* (New York, 1937), pp. 288-289; Lotys Benning, *The Vegetable Canning Industry* (Indianapolis, 1938), pp. 65-69.

38 United States Bureau of the Census, *Thirteenth Census* (1910), X, *Manufactures*, p. 395; *Fourteenth Census* (1920), X, *Manufactures*, pp. 76-78.

Other food products such as confectionery, ice cream, butter, cheese, and condensed or evaporated milk were manufactured on a fairly large scale in Indiana, their total value amounting to $8,563,000 in 1909 and $43,736,000 in 1919.[39] A major manufacturer of general dairy products was the Schlosser Brothers Company, a family concern which took its beginnings from a small creamery in Bremen, Marshall County, in 1884. Expanding operations to Indianapolis, Plymouth, South Chicago, and finally Frankfort, the company built a large modern plant in the last-named city in 1912. James T. Polk of the pioneer canning family of Greenwood entered the dairy business in 1888 and later founded the well-known Indianapolis firm which was incorporated in 1904 as the Polk Sanitary Milk Company. In 1893 another Hoosier canner, Frank Van Camp of Boston baked beans fame, formed the Indiana Condensed Milk Company with Frank L. Dittemore and built a plant to manufacture both sweetened and unsweetened canned milk in Sheridan, Indiana, and another later at Effingham, Illinois.[40]

An extremely important industry according to value of products and one heavily dependent upon locally grown raw materials, in this case corn and other grains, was the distilling of alcohol and neutral spirits. The excellent quality of the limestone water available near the Ohio River in Dearborn County had made Lawrenceburg and its vicinity a major distilling center since the early nineteenth century. The largest of several distilleries active there in this period was operated by the W. P. Squibb Company, which was incorporated in 1913 upon the death of the brothers, William P. and George W. Squibb, who had begun the manufacture of whiskey in

[39] *Ibid., Fourteenth Census* (1920), X, *Manufactures,* pp. 39, 99. In addition to these products, the Bureau of the Census reported "other food preparations not elsewhere specified" valued at $2,373,000 in 1914 and $9,318,000 in 1919. *Ibid.,* IX, *Manufactures,* p. 396.

[40] Dunn, *Indiana and Indianans,* II, 954-955; Elba L. Branigin, *History of Johnson County Indiana* (Indianapolis, 1913), pp. 592-594; May, *Canning Clan,* pp. 289-290. There were seven Schlosser brothers active in the firm. Roll, *Indiana,* III, 118-119.

the Lawrenceburg suburb of Greendale in 1868. Hammond and Terre Haute were centers of this industry, producing chiefly neutral spirits. Smaller distilleries in two Ohio River towns, New Amsterdam and Mauckport, Harrison County, manufactured brandies.[41]

By 1900 distilling ranked third among the state's industries according to value of products. In the same year the Federal census also reported Indiana in third place after Illinois and Kentucky in the production of distilled liquors of all kinds. In 1914, just a few years before national prohibition halted most production, the total value of distilled liquors in Indiana reached $31,483,823, of which $23,237,247 represented alcohol and neutral spirits, $8,208,944 whiskey, and $37,632 brandy.[42]

During the First World War the governments of the United States and Great Britain jointly purchased two large distilleries in Terre Haute and converted them to the production of acetone from corn by a new process invented by a famed European scientist, Dr. Chaim Weizmann. In 1919 a private concern, the Commercial Solvents Corporation, took over the plants and began manufacturing various chemical products.[43]

Unlike distilleries, which tended to be concentrated in a few places with adequate supplies of grain and good water, breweries, having a bulky product expensive to ship great distances, were found in many large Hoosier cities, including Indianapolis, Fort Wayne, Evansville, South Bend, and Terre Haute. Moreover, since most brewing companies served only local markets, they usually remained comparatively small,

[41] William H. Roose, *Indiana's Birthplace. A History of Harrison County Indiana* (1911), revised by Arville L. Funk (Chicago, 1966), p. 79; Archibald Shaw (ed.), *History of Dearborn County Indiana. Her People, Industries and Institutions* (Indianapolis, 1915), pp. 192, 831-832.

[42] United States Bureau of the Census, *Twelfth Census* (1900), VIII, *Manufactures,* p. 202; IX, *Manufactures,* p. 615; *Census of Manufactures,* 1914, I, 400-401.

[43] Fred C. Kelly, *One Thing Leads to Another: The Growth of an Industry* (New York, 1936), pp. 8-13.

independent businesses in an age of general consolidation. In 1889, however, the Indianapolis Brewing Company was formed from the merger of three long-established breweries in the capital city as the result of an attempt by a British syndicate, ultimately unsuccessful, to create a nationwide beer trust. One of the largest independent firms in this period and a major exporter of beer was the Berghoff Brewing Corporation in Fort Wayne, which was founded by Herman J. Berghoff and his two brothers in 1887. The value of all Indiana-brewed malt beverages was $11,936,237 in 1914.[44]

An industry based partly on a home-grown agricultural crop was the manufacture of tobacco products, chiefly cigars, though much of the leaf tobacco used was imported from outside the state. Cigar making was carried on mostly in small shops in the larger cities, but remained the center of the industry throughout this period. In 1919, for example, Evansville produced almost two thirds of the total value of all cigars and smoking tobacco manufactured in Indiana, amounting to $6,268,000 out of $10,345,000.[45]

Madison, a leading burley tobacco market in Indiana, was also the location of one of the largest businesses in the United States engaged in the processing and distribution of roots and herbs, or "crude drugs," used for medicinal purposes. A much more important Hoosier industry, however, was the manufacture of patent medicines and compounds and druggists' preparations, which grew rapidly in this period. The value of all such commodities made in Indiana rose from $2,403,000 in 1899 to $4,344,000 in 1909 and $13,738,000 in 1919.[46] The industry was centered in Indianapolis, where the

44 Max Hyman, *Hyman's Hand Book of Indianapolis* . . . (Indianapolis, 1897), pp. 284-289; Thomas C. Cochran, *The Pabst Brewing Company. The History of an American Business* (New York, 1948), p. 152; *Berghoff Brewing Corporation* (Fort Wayne, Ind., 1940), p. 3; United States Bureau of the Census, *Census of Manufactures,* 1914, II, 983.

45 United States Bureau of the Census, *Fourteenth Census* (1920), IX, *Manufactures,* p. 397.

46 Visher, *Economic Geography of Indiana,* p. 177; United States Bureau of the Census, *Thirteenth Census* (1910), IX, *Manufactures,* p. 322; *Fourteenth Census* (1920), X, *Manufactures,* p. 676.

leading firm was founded by Colonel Eli Lilly, a Civil War veteran and former druggist who opened a small pharmaceutical laboratory in the capital city in 1876. Incorporated in 1881 as Eli Lilly and Company, it soon became the chief purveyor of ethical, or prescription, drugs in the state and one of the three or four largest in the nation. After the founder's death in 1898, his son, Josiah K. Lilly, became president and served in that position for thirty-five years. Annual sales reached the million-dollar mark in 1905.[47]

Two additional Indianapolis pharmaceutical houses arose from the partnership of Harry C. Pitman and John C. Meyers who began manufacturing druggists' preparations in 1899. In 1909 Meyers left his partner to help found the Swan-Meyers firm in the same city, while Pitman joined with Harry C. Moore to form the Pitman-Moore concern. One of the leading manufacturers of patent medicines and compounds in Indiana was the Miles Laboratories in Elkhart, founded by Dr. Franklin Miles of that city in 1884. A highly successful enterprise somewhat related to those mentioned above was brought to Indiana in 1915, when the Mead, Johnson Company, a major producer of vitamins, dietary products, and baby foods, transferred its operations from New Jersey to Evansville.[48]

Few cosmetic products were manufactured in Indiana in this period. In 1910, however, a remarkable Negro woman from Louisiana established the Madam C. J. Walker Laboratory in Indianapolis for the manufacture of a secret hair-straightening formula which she had attempted earlier without much success to place on the market in St. Louis, Denver, and Pittsburgh. Eventually the Indianapolis cosmetics firm

[47] Glenn L. Jenkins et al., "Hoosier Pharmacy: An Historical Sketch," in Dorothy Ritter Russo (ed.), One Hundred Years of Indiana Medicine 1849-1949 (n. p., 1949), p. 144; Roscoe C. Clark, Threescore Years and Ten: A Narrative of the First Seventy Years of Eli Lilly and Company, 1876-1946 (n. p., 1946), pp. 17-47. A corporate history of Eli Lilly and Company is in preparation.

[48] Jenkins et al., "Hoosier Pharmacy," in Russo (ed.), One Hundred Years of Indiana Medicine, pp. 144-145.

became one of the outstanding Negro-owned and operated businesses in the United States.[49]

Indiana's forests provided the raw materials for another large segment of the industrial economy. But lumbering itself, which ranked third after meat and flour in value of products in the state up to the turn of the century, fell swiftly to eighth place in 1904. The number of lumber mills also decreased from 2,106 in 1879 to 995 in 1904, as the depletion of timber resources resulted in the abandonment of many small rural establishments and the transfer of others to the cities, where they were often operated in connection with large lumber yards and finishing mills. Yet southern counties continued to produce commercial hardwoods long after the industry's virtual disappearance in the north; and Evansville remained a main shipping center for lumber up to the First World War.[50]

A detailed analysis of the industry in the report of the Federal census of 1900 indicated that in addition to rough lumber, Indiana sawmills at that time produced large amounts of cooperage materials—hoops, staves, and headings—as well as stock for furniture, agricultural implements, and carriages and wagons, but relatively few laths and shingles.[51] Despite the general decline in the production of lumber in the state after the turn of the century, Indiana remained as late as 1919 an important producer of ash, beech, elm, hickory, ma-

---

[49] Indianapolis *News,* December 10, 1915. Mrs. Walker developed her hair treatment in St. Louis in 1900. After working with it in Denver and Pittsburgh, in 1910 she established her company in Indianapolis, where it remained after she retired and moved to New York in 1915. See the pamphlet, *The Madam C. J. Walker Year Book* (n. p., 1938), in the Indiana State Library.

[50] United States Bureau of the Census, *Census of Manufactures,* 1905, II, 259; Cottman, *Centennial History and Handbook of Indiana,* p. 429.

[51] The value of these products in 1899 was reported as follows: staves, $1,244,266; hoops, $617,710; headings, $526,221; carriage and wagon stock, $495,299; furniture stock, $340,608; agricultural implement stock, $277,396. In addition, the value reported for "all other sawed lumber" was $1,364,835, which presumably included stock for the manufacture of veneers. United States Bureau of the Census, *Twelfth Census* (1900), IX, *Manufactures,* p. 882-887.

ple, oak, sycamore, and walnut, much of which was used in making veneers. In the quantity of wood consumed in the manufacture of veneers the state ranked fifth nationally in 1909 but only tenth in 1919.[52]

The chief lumber-using secondary industries—those manufacturing carriages and wagons, furniture, and agricultural implements—maintained their position by importing hardwoods from other states as local supplies dwindled. In value of products Indiana's carriage and wagon industry, which was second only to that of Ohio by 1909,[53] was the largest of the three until the last years of the second decade of the twentieth century, when competition from the automobile was reflected in a severe decline in the production of horse-drawn vehicles. The leading carriage and wagon manufacturing centers in the state were Indianapolis and South Bend. The latter was the home of the Studebaker Brothers Wagon Works, which was one of the largest such factories in existence and exported its famous products all over the world by the eighties and nineties.[54]

Furniture manufacturing was next in importance as a woodworking industry. Factories were located in both large cities and small towns, mostly in the central and southern sections of the state, including Batesville, Bloomington, Connersville, Elwood, Evansville, Frankfort, Goshen, Jasper, Marion, Muncie, New Castle, Richmond, Tell City, and Wabash. Among Hoosier specialties were office desks, many of which were exported to Europe, Mexico, and South America, and kitchen cabinets, reputedly an Indiana invention. By 1919, Indiana's furniture industry ranked fourth in the nation in gross value of products.[55]

[52] *Ibid., Fourteenth Census* (1920), X, *Manufactures,* pp. 442-450, 457.

[53] *Ibid., Thirteenth Census* (1910), X, *Manufactures,* p. 832.

[54] Stephen Longstreet, *A Century on Wheels. The Story of Studebaker: A History, 1852-1952* (New York, 1952), pp. 44-56.

[55] Visher, *Economic Geography of Indiana,* pp. 177-178; United States Bureau of the Census, *Fourteenth Census* (1920), VIII, *Manufactures,* pp. 384-385.

*Gaar, Scott & Co. Catalogue, 1895*

Gaar-Scott Clover Huller

*Rumely Catalogue, 1887*

The Rumely Side-Geared Traction Engine

Its extensive agricultural enterprise made the state a natural center for the manufacture of farm implements and machinery. By 1905 South Bend and Richmond ranked sixth and eighth, respectively, among American cities in the production of these items.[56] Other important centers of the industry were Indianapolis, Evansville, La Porte, Kendallville, and Mishawaka. Plows were by far the leading product, though planters, drills, cultivators, and seed separators were also manufactured. Although International Harvester Corporation was represented in the state by a subsidiary in Richmond, most companies were locally controlled. James Oliver of South Bend, one of the largest agricultural implement manufacturers in the United States, actually prevented the creation of a plow trust at the turn of the century by rejecting overtures of Charles Deere of Moline, Illinois, and others who were interested in such a combination.[57]

MAJOR WOODWORKING INDUSTRIES IN INDIANA, 1879-1919[58]

| Year | Number of establishments | Average number of wage earners | Value of products |
|---|---|---|---|
| Carriages and Wagons | | | |
| 1879 | 239 | 4,711 | $ 6,328,000 |
| 1889 | 432 | 6,969 | 10,532,000 |
| 1899 | 323 | 8,714 | 15,811,000 |
| 1909 | 221 | 8,867 | 21,655,000 |
| 1919 | 100 | 2,216 | 12,785,000 |
| Furniture | | | |
| 1879 | 288 | 2,660 | 4,542,000 |
| 1889 | 131 | 6,096 | 7,663,000 |
| 1899 | 129 | 7,149 | 8,770,000 |
| 1909 | 201 | 11,284 | 18,456,000 |
| 1919 | 177 | 13,257 | 52,350,000 |

56 United States Bureau of the Census, *Census of Manufactures,* 1905, I, ccxxix.

57 Douglas L. Meikle, James Oliver and the Oliver Chilled Plow Works (Unpublished Ph.D. thesis in History, Indiana University, 1958), pp. 485-488.

58 United States Bureau of the Census, *Tenth Census* (1880), II, *Manufactures,* Pt. 2, p. 13; *Eleventh Census* (1890), XI, *Manufactures,* pp. 400-401;

MAJOR WOODWORKING INDUSTRIES IN INDIANA
1879-1919—Cont.

| Year | Number of establishments | Average number of wage earners | Value of products |
|---|---|---|---|
| | Agricultural Implements | | |
| 1879 | 96 | 2,471 | 4,460,000 |
| 1889 | 54 | 3,078 | 5,756,000 |
| 1899 | 45 | 3,419 | 6,415,000 |
| 1909 | 39 | 4,749 | 13,670,000 |
| 1919 | 29 | 5,533 | 31,824,000 |

Other Indiana products fabricated from lumber included children's carriages and sleds, coffins, burial cases, and undertakers' goods, turned and carved wood, and miscellaneous wooden goods, the total value of which was $13,191,000 in 1919.[59] Wood was also used in the manufacture of railroad cars, a major Indiana industry which is discussed below.

§ § §

Another group of industries took root in Indiana primarily because of the availability of cheap and abundant fuel. While Indiana-mined bituminous coal continued to play a significant role in manufacturing, the discovery of natural gas in the late eighties brought a sudden influx of new enterprises which had the effect of greatly accelerating the industrialization process. Most of these newcomers were engaged in the manufacture of glass, tinplate, and strawboard, all industries which valued cheap, clean fuel more than proximity to raw materials. Of these three, moreover, only glassmaking was substantially represented prior to the gas discoveries.

The chief glass manufacturing plant in Indiana before 1887 was the DePauw Glass Works in New Albany, which had been founded as early as 1869 by a former shipbuilder, John Baptiste Ford, who succeeded in making the first polished plate glass in America. In 1872 Ford lost control of the com-

Thirteenth Census (1910), Abstract, with Supplement for Indiana, pp. 695-696; Fourteenth Census (1920), IX, Manufactures, p. 396.

[59] Ibid., Fourteenth Census (1920), IX, Manufactures, pp. 396-397.

pany to his cousin and chief financial backer, Washington C. DePauw, a wealthy banker and merchant from Salem, Washington County, who lost more than half a million dollars before beginning to make a small profit by 1879, according to his written deposition to the United States Tariff Commission in 1882. His son and manager, Newland T. DePauw, personally testified before the same commission that the company was then earning an annual gross income in excess of a million dollars and manufactured about two thirds of all the plate glass made in the United States as well as window glass and jars. Despite the natural advantages of its location, which permitted easy access to glass sand dredged from the Ohio River and coal transported cheaply by water from the Pittsburgh region, the New Albany plant was dismantled a decade later and relocated at Alexandria in the natural gas region.[60]

Among the first and most successful glass manufacturers to become established in the Indiana Gas Belt were the Ball brothers—eventually all five, Edmund B., William C., Lucius L., Frank C., and George A. Ball, were involved in the enterprise—who moved their base of operations from Buffalo, New York, to Muncie in 1887. Accepting the Hoosier city's offer of free gas from its own well as well as a seven-acre industrial site and $5,000 in cash, the Ball brothers built a factory which began producing a patented fruit jar in 1888. By 1900 the United States Bureau of the Census reported that the Muncie firm had become the largest producer of

[60] *Report of the Tariff Commission* (*House Miscellaneous Documents,* 47 Congress, 2 session, No. 6), Pt. 1, p. 937, Pt. 2, pp. 1529-1531. For the beginning of the plate-glass industry in Indiana, see United States Bureau of the Census, *Tenth Census* (1880), II, Pt. 12, *Report on Glass Manufactures,* p. 99; and William E. Aiken, *The Roots Grow Deep* . . . (Cleveland, 1957), pp. 6-9. John B. Ford, after unsuccessfully attempting to make glass profitably in nearby Louisville and later Jeffersonville, Indiana, moved on to western Pennsylvania in the early eighties where he built the factories which became the foundation of the Pittsburgh Plate Glass Company. His son, Edward Ford, later established another glassmaking firm in Toledo, Ohio, which eventually became part of the Libbey-Owens Company. *Ibid.,* pp. 9-86.

glass fruit jars in the country.[61] Another early Muncie glass-making firm was the Hemingray Glass Company, which moved there from Covington, Kentucky, in 1887 and became a leading producer of insulators for telephone poles.[62]

Indeed, the lure of cheap, or even free, fuel together with other inducements sometimes offered by Gas Belt communities eager for industrial development attracted glass manufacturers from all over the eastern United States, but particularly from Ohio, where the gas supply had already begun to fail. By 1895 the following cities and towns, many of them formerly little more than rural villages, had acquired one or more glass factories: Alexandria, Anderson, Elwood, Frankton, Ingalls, Orestes, Pendleton, and Summitville in Madison County; Albany, Eaton, Muncie, and Yorktown in Delaware County; in Grant County, Fairmount, Gas City, Marion, Swayzee, and Upland; Hartford City in Blackford County; Arcadia and Cicero in Hamilton County; Greenfield in Hancock; Middletown in Henry; Kokomo in Howard; Dunkirk and Redkey in Jay; Peru in Miami; and Parker in Randolph County.[63]

The number of glass factories in the state climbed to a peak of 110 in 1899 before the reduction in the flow of natural gas checked the expansion of the industry. From eighth place in the nation in 1879, glass manufacturing in Indiana rose to become second only to Pennsylvania in 1899, with products valued at $14,758,000. It dropped back to third in

[61] The History of Ball Brothers Company 1878-1949, mimeographed document in letter of A. G. Emshwiller to Shirley Snyder, Muncie, October 31, 1949, Indiana Division, Indiana State Library; Frank C. Ball, *Memoirs* (Muncie, Ind., 1937), pp. 76-78; United States Bureau of the Census, *Twelfth Census* (1900), IX, *Manufactures*, p. 974.

[62] Frank D. Haimbaugh, *History of Delaware County Indiana* (2 volumes, Indianapolis, 1924), II, 592-594.

[63] Indiana Department of Statistics, *Biennial Report*, 1895-1896, p. 18. Within a dozen years glass factories were also found in these additional Gas Belt communities: Daleville and Gaston in Delaware County; Matthews and Sims in Grant County; Millgrove in Blackford; Shirley in Hancock; and Winchester in Randolph County. *American Glass Trade Directory* . . . (Commoner Publishing Company, Pittsburgh, 1908), pp. 8-22.

1909 and fourth in 1919, when the value of products was reported at $11,593,000 and $30,107,000, respectively.[64] At its
height in 1900, the Indiana glass industry produced 70.9 per
cent of the nation's fruit jars, 25.7 per cent of the prescription bottles, 50.2 per cent of the flasks and liquor bottles,
13.4 per cent of the milk bottles, 18.9 per cent of the patent
medicine bottles, 31.6 per cent of the bottles and jars for
the packing and preserving industries, 35.7 per cent of the
jelly glasses and pressed tumblers and goblets, 10.1 per cent
of the lamps, 45.1 per cent of the lamp chimneys, and 52.4
per cent of the lantern globes. Indiana was also a major
producer of building glass, especially window glass, but plate,
cathedral, and skylight glass were also manufactured.[65] The
state's production of building glass, however, declined much
more severely than bottles and jars and tableware after
1900, as revealed in the following table:

VALUE OF GLASS PRODUCTS IN INDIANA, 1879-1919[66]

| Year | Building Glass | Pressed and Blown Glass and Bottles and Jars |
|------|---------------|------------------------------------------------|
| 1879 | $  725,797    | $     64,984   |
| 1889 | 1,831,745     | 1,163,664      |
| 1899 | 5,711,948     | 9,045,935      |
| 1904 | 3,790,618     | 10,072,543     |
| 1909 | 1,616,092     | 9,756,506      |
| 1914 | 2,356,946     | 12,081,459     |
| 1919 | 5,485,490     | 23,782,059     |

During this period important changes took place in the
glass industry, including the introduction around the turn of
the century of the continuous tank furnace in the manufac-

[64] United States Bureau of the Census, *Thirteenth Census* (1910), *Abstract, with Supplement for Indiana*, p. 680; *Fourteenth Census* (1920), X,
*Manufactures*, p. 837.

[65] *Ibid., Twelfth Census* (1900), IX, *Manufactures*, pp. 974-981. Indiana was
second only to Pennsylvania in the production of both window and plate glass
in 1899, and with forty-six establishments and eighty-two furnaces devoted to
manufacturing window glass possessed an even larger capacity than that
state. *Ibid.*, pp. 961, 967.

[66] *Ibid.*, p. 954; *Fourteenth Census* (1920), X, *Manufactures*, p. 836.

ture of window glass and the annealing lehr in plate-glass production, one of the largest of the latter having been put into operation at Alexandria, Indiana, in the late nineties. At about the same time the invention of semiautomatic machinery revolutionized the bottle and jar industry, which also turned to the use of tank furnaces and annealing lehrs. In 1900, for example, the Ball plant in Muncie, where mechanization had been initiated by Frank C. Ball in 1892, had a daily capacity of 240,000 fruit jars, all machine-made.[67]

On the other hand, Indiana had its share of skilled designers and glassblowers, who produced a large quantity of fine glassware by hand. Especially famous for its production of chocolate and golden agate glass was the Indiana Tumbler and Goblet Company of Greentown, which was founded in 1894 and merged into the National Glass Company five years later. In 1903, however, the Greentown plant burned to the ground and was never rebuilt.[68]

As competition intensified among the growing number of glass-manufacturing concerns in Indiana and other states, a movement for industrial consolidation arose. In 1895, for example, the Pittsburgh Plate Glass Company, which had been formed out of enterprises begun in western Pennsylvania by the same John B. Ford who had inaugurated glassmaking in New Albany, Indiana, organized a merger which absorbed two plants in Kokomo and Elwood, leaving only one independent plate-glass company in the state—the former DePauw

[67] *Ibid., Twelfth Census* (1900), IX, *Manufactures,* pp. 962-963, 966-967, 974; Ball, *Memoirs,* pp. 85-86. The Ball Brothers Company developed a semiautomatic bottle machine based on the patents of Philip Arbogast of Pittsburgh. Later, in 1909, it obtained a license to use the fully automatic machine invented by M. J. Owens of the Toledo Glass Company. The Graham Glass Company of Evansville, Indiana, was on the verge of perfecting a similar machine when the Owens Bottle Company (which had been assigned the rights to the Owens machine) purchased the Evansville company in 1916 to eliminate a possible competitor. Warren C. Scoville, *Revolution in Glassmaking. Entrepreneurship and Technological Change in the American Industry, 1880-1920* (Cambridge, Mass., 1948), pp. 105, 162-165, 324.

[68] Ruth Herrick, *Greentown Glass. The Indiana Tumbler and Goblet Company and Allied Manufacturers* (n. p., 1959), pp. 5-6, 23-34.

Works which had been moved from New Albany to Alexandria—and, indeed, just three in the entire country.[69] Uncertain price conditions in the window-glass industry after the Panic of 1893 stimulated the creation of a selling pool in 1895 which controlled the production of 85 per cent of American factories, including several in Indiana. In 1899, moreover, this pool was refashioned into the American Window Glass Company, with direct ownership of individual plants, some of which were closed down in order to limit production and raise prices. In that same year the National Glass Company was also created, acquiring a large number of glass container and tableware manufacturing firms, five of them in Indiana, located at Albany, Dunkirk, Greentown, Marion, and Summitville.[70]

Consolidation did not cure the troubles of the glass industry, however, and glass manufacturing declined appreciably in Indiana by the first decade of the twentieth century. A chief reason for its decline was the failure of the natural gas supply. Yet there was no wholesale flight from the state, partly because the introduction of tank furnaces and increased mechanization made it more difficult to dismantle whole plants and move them to other localities, as had been done extensively earlier, when Indiana itself benefited greatly from the transfer of factories from eastern states. Some glass-manufacturing establishments in the Gas Belt, it is true, were removed to newly discovered natural gas fields in West Virginia and elsewhere, and others simply were forced

[69] Testimony of John Pitcairn, president of the Pittsburgh Plate Glass Company, in *Trusts and Industrial Combinations, Report of the Industrial Commission,* XIII, 225-242.

[70] Pearce Davis, *The Development of the American Glass Industry* (*Harvard Economic Studies,* LXXXVI, Cambridge, Mass., 1949), pp. 175-176; John Moody, *The Truth About the Trusts* . . . (New York, 1904), p. 264. In 1917 E. D. Libbey of the Libbey-Owens Glass Company attempted to effect a consolidation of bottle and jar firms which would have included the large Ball Brothers concern, but negotiations were dropped the next year after disagreements over the terms of merger among the interested parties. Scoville, *Revolution in Glassmaking,* pp. 304-305.

to close their doors, but many continued to carry on a profitable business by converting to alternative fuels, generally bituminous coal or manufactured gas at first and later natural gas piped in from outside the state. In addition several window-glass and bottle factories were established after the turn of the century in Indiana cities with nearby coal deposits, such as Loogootee, Evansville, Princeton, Terre Haute, and Vincennes. The huge Ball Brothers Company retained its manufacturing headquarters in Muncie but built branch plants in more favorable sites in other states and diversified its operations by adding mills for the production of paper and strawboard boxes as well as the zinc and rubber products auxiliary to the fruit-jar industry.[71]

A second major industry created in the natural gas region of the state in the nineties was the manufacture of tin- and terneplates, the former being iron sheets coated with tin and used chiefly for the commercial canning of fish, meat, fruits, and vegetables, while the latter were coated with an alloy of tin and lead and used primarily for roofing purposes. Before 1890, when the McKinley tariff raised the duty on tin- and terneplates from one to 2.2 cents per pound, American needs were being met largely by imports from Wales, the world's leading producer up to that time. Hoosier entrepreneurs were not slow in seizing the opportunity to enter the new tariff-protected field of manufacturing. In the spring of 1891 a factory was erected at Anderson, in the heart of the natural gas field, where on July 4 the first tinplates were produced and in October terneplates as well. But the Anderson plant contained only dipping facilities for coating the "black plates" manufactured in rolling mills elsewhere. Indiana's first tinplate factory equipped to carry on the entire process of manufacturing was constructed at Elwood in 1891 and began production by the summer of 1892. Within the next few years addi-

---

[71] United States Bureau of the Census, *Census of Manufacturers,* 1905, III, 854; *American Glass Trade Directory,* pp. 8-12, 32; *Indiana, A Guide to the Hoosier State* (American Guide Series, New York, 1941), pp. 227, 261, 275.

tional plants were located at Atlanta, Hamilton County; Gas City, Grant County; Middletown, Henry County; and Montpelier, Blackford County, while another one was planned at Summitville but abandoned before completion.[72]

The new tinplate industry managed to win most of the American domestic market from European producers, even though the Federal import duty was reduced to 1.2 cents a pound in 1895 and only partially restored—to 1.5 cents a pound—in 1897. But ruinous price competition among the numerous companies which had sprung up in the nineties brought the inevitable movement for consolidation. In 1898 a young Richmond bank cashier, Daniel G. Reid, and William B. Leeds, a railroadman from the same city, were associated with the Chicago industrial promoter, William H. Moore, in the organization of a "tinplate trust." Reid and Leeds, who had been among the first stockholders in the American Tin Plate Company which erected the Elwood plant, obtained a controlling interest in that firm by 1894 and assumed the presidency and vice-presidency, respectively, of the new consolidated company of the same name, which acquired all six plants in Indiana and enough of the remaining factories in Maryland, Pennsylvania, Ohio, and New York to control about 90 per cent of all tin- and terneplate production in the United States. As a result of the consolidation, both prices and profits rose in the tinplate industry.[73]

[72] United States Bureau of the Census, *Twelfth Census* (1900), X, *Manufactures*, pp. 99, 114-115; Ida M. Tarbell, *The Nationalizing of Business, 1878-1898 (History of American Life*, IX, New York, 1936), p. 198.

[73] Indianapolis *News*, May 4, 1901; Tarbell, *The Nationalizing of Business*, pp. 212-213; Moody, *Truth about the Trusts*, pp. 157-158. Howard A. Knox, "Development of the American Tin Plate Industry," *The Iron Age*, CLII, No. 22 (November 25, 1943), pp. 64-65. Daniel Gray Reid and William Batemore Leeds both became millionaires from their industrial promotions and left the state of Indiana for Chicago at the time of the consolidation of the American Tin Plate Company. Reid, who retained a deep interest in his home town of Richmond and made many large gifts to its churches and civic organizations, later lived in New York, where he engaged in successful financial speculation in Wall Street. He died there in 1925. Indianapolis *Star*, January 18, 1925.

By 1900 the United States Bureau of the Census placed Indiana in the second rank—after Pennsylvania—of tin- and terneplate-producing states, though actual figures were not reported in order to avoid disclosing individual operations, since the tinplate trust monopolized production in the state.[74] In 1901, moreover, Reid and his associates brought their American Tin Plate Company along with three additional consolidated organizations controlled by them, the American Steel Hoop Company and the National Steel Company, both created in 1899, and the American Sheet Steel Company, formed in 1900, into the billion-dollar United States Steel Corporation which was being organized by Elbert H. Gary, J. P. Morgan, and others. Eventually the smaller plants in the Indiana Gas Belt were closed or dismantled and production concentrated in the more efficient Elwood factory. In 1910, moreover, the United States Steel Corporation built an even larger and more modern sheet-steel and tinplate plant in the new industrial city of Gary, though the Elwood works remained in operation for another two decades. According to the 1920 Federal census returns Pennsylvania continued to hold the leading position in the industry, but Indiana with two large manufacturing establishments in Gary and Elwood maintained its importance as a major tinplate producer.[75]

The natural gas discoveries also attracted a number of paper and strawboard manufacturers to east-central Indiana. The availability of an adequate supply of straw, which was used as the main ingredient in the manufacture of heavy cardboard and corrugated boxes, was also important to the industry. By 1895 there were paper and strawboard mills in such Gas Belt cities as Albany, Anderson, Carthage, Gas City, Greenfield, Hartford City, Kokomo, Marion, Muncie, and

[74] United States Bureau of the Census, *Twelfth Census* (1900), X, *Manufactures,* p. 115.

[75] Arundel Cotter, *The Authentic History of the United States Steel Corporation* (New York, 1916), pp. 21-24; Moore, *The Calumet Region,* p. 327; United States Bureau of the Census, *Fourteenth Census* (1920), X, *Manufactures,* pp. 348-353.

Noblesville, as well as in older industrial centers like Elkhart, Indianapolis, Mishawaka, Richmond, South Bend, Vincennes, and Wabash.[76] By 1899 Indiana had become the leading producer of strawboard in the nation, making almost one half the nation's supply, valued at $2,041,881.[77] The state specialized in the manufacture of wrapping paper and cardboard containers rather than newsprint and fine paper. One of the leading firms making these products was the Fort Wayne Corrugated Paper Company, which was founded in that city in 1908 and acquired paper and strawboard factories in Eaton, Hartford City, and Vincennes during the next decade.[78] The total value of paper and strawboard products in Indiana reached $7,089,000 in 1909, $8,091,000 in 1914, and $18,482,000 in 1919.[79]

§ § § §

Although the part played by the gas boom was an indispensable stimulus in the process of industrialization, other factors were also significant in promoting manufacturing and helping to maintain momentum after the natural gas supplies dwindled. The large role of other commercially exploitable natural resources—particularly coal, oil, limestone, and clay—has been described in an earlier chapter. Moreover, Indiana's strategic location in relation to transportation facilities and markets tended to exert an increasing influence on its industrial development. This factor was especially important in the trend away from consumer industries dependent upon local raw materials to the large-scale production of durable goods which characterized Indiana's economic development in the early twentieth century.[80]

[76] Indiana Department of Statistics, *Biennial Report,* 1895-1896, p. 76.

[77] United States Bureau of the Census, *Twelfth Census* (1900), IX, *Manufactures,* pp. 1021-1022.

[78] Fort Wayne Corrugated Paper Company, *Forty Years of Container Making* (Chicago, 1949), p. 3.

[79] United States Bureau of the Census, *Fourteenth Census* (1920), IX, *Manufactures,* p. 397.

[80] Starr, *Industrial Development of Indiana,* pp. 19-20.

An example of the influence of strategic geographical position was the growth of the state's large share of the business of constructing and repairing railroad cars. While the availability of hardwoods was probably the original consideration in the location of this industry in Indiana, the state's central position in the nation's railroad network helped to retain it in an age of metal fabrication. The manufacture of passenger, baggage, and freight cars in the state was concentrated in the four cities of Indianapolis, Jeffersonville, Michigan City, and Terre Haute, the total products of which in 1899 equaled 10 per cent of the national output.[81] In that same year the Ohio Falls Car Manufacturing Company of Jeffersonville, the Terre Haute Car and Manufacturing Company, and the Indianapolis Car Company were consolidated with thirteen other firms to form the American Car and Foundry Company.[82] In total value of products Indiana moved from fifth place to third in the nation, after Illinois and Pennsylvania, between 1909 and 1914.[83]

Indiana's dense system of trunkline and other railroads also created a need for large, centrally located repair facilities. Of the larger roads, the Pennsylvania maintained car shops at Fort Wayne, Jeffersonville, Logansport, and Terre Haute; the New York Central at Wabash and Elkhart; and Big Four at Beech Grove, a suburb of Indianapolis virtually created by this industry. The Erie had its repair shops at Huntington; the Clover Leaf at Frankfort; the Monon at Lafayette; the Southern Railway at Princeton; the Chicago, Terre Haute and Southeastern at Bedford; and the Wabash, the Nickel Plate, and the Lake Shore and Michigan Southern at Fort Wayne. Small towns like Garrett in DeKalb County and Washington in Daviess County were chosen as locations for the shops of the Baltimore and Ohio and the Baltimore

---

81 United States Bureau of the Census, *Twelfth Census* (1900), X, *Manufactures*, pp. 268-269, 273.

82 Moody, *Truth about the Trusts*, p. 217.

83 United States Bureau of the Census, *Census of Manufactures,* 1914, II, 773.

and Ohio Southwest, respectively. A chief characteristic of this industry was the large number of persons employed, by which measure it deserves special recognition in the statistics of manufacturing.

## RAILROAD CAR CONSTRUCTION AND REPAIR
### 1889-1919[84]

| Year | Number of establishments | Average number of wage earners | Value of products |
|------|------|------|------|
| | Steam Railroad Car Construction | | |
| 1889 | 4 | 2,650 | $ 7,873,000 |
| 1899 | 4 | 3,337 | 9,007,000 |
| 1904 | 6 | 3,252 | 10,035,000 |
| 1909 | 7 | 4,084 | 9,498,000 |
| 1914 | 10 | 5,800 | 21,570,000 |
| 1919 | 9 | 6,650 | 86,021,000 |
| | Steam Railroad Repair Shops | | |
| 1889 | 48 | 6,613 | $ 7,289,000 |
| 1899 | 54 | 8,081 | 10,242,000 |
| 1904 | 44 | 11,348 | 14,515,000 |
| 1909 | 34 | 13,745 | 17,128,000 |
| 1914 | 49 | 15,410 | 20,586,000 |
| 1919 | 77 | 23,099 | 61,232,000 |

The development of the iron and steel industry in Indiana is an even more striking example of the shift from the processing of local raw materials to the manufacturing of durable goods based chiefly on location and transportation facilities. In the sixties and seventies several small blast furnaces utilizing Indiana and Missouri ores and Clay County block coal to produce pig iron were established in the Terre Haute–Brazil area, but these premature enterprises weakened in the eighties, largely because of a lack of high-grade raw materials

[84] United States Bureau of the Census, *Twelfth Census* (1900), X, *Manufactures*, pp. 269, 276; *Census of Manufactures*, 1905, I, 146-153; *Thirteenth Census* (1910), IX, *Manufactures*, p. 321; *Census of Manufactures*, 1914, II, 777, 784-785; *Fourteenth Census* (1920), X, *Manufactures*, pp. 913, 920-923. Although no electric or street-railway cars were built in Indiana, there were thirty-two repair shops for electric lines by 1914. *Census of Manufactures*, 1914, II, 790-791.

at hand. The last furnace went out of blast in 1895.[85] In the meantime, however, the production of steel products in rolling mills and similar establishments went on apace in Terre Haute, Brazil, and other Hoosier cities. In fact, Terre Haute's steel industry reached its height in the period from 1915 to 1920.[86]

Indiana iron and steel factories made sheet metal, bars, nails, wire, and other products, including black plates for tinning, as described earlier in this chapter. Because of its cheap fuel, the Gas Belt had a disproportionately large share of the steel industry in the nineties and later, especially the cities of Anderson, Elwood, Kokomo, and Muncie. Of the subsidiary firms which went to make up the United States Steel Corporation in 1901, the Shelby Steel Tube Company had two plants in Indiana, and the American Steel and Wire Company, the American Sheet Steel Company, and the American Bridge Company were represented by one apiece, to say nothing of the six Gas Belt plants belonging to another subsidiary, the American Tin Plate Company.[87] The effect of the gas boom on the steel industry is shown graphically by the rise in the amount of capital invested from $4,099,000 in 1889 to $14,994,000 in 1899 and $22,986,000 in 1904.[88]

Yet the great advance of the industry in Indiana came only in the early years of the twentieth century, when the nation's iron and steel tycoons decided to expand production in the Middle West and chose the Calumet Region for building new plants. This area in the northwestern corner of the state was almost an ideal location for such a purpose, with access to water transportation on the Great Lakes as well as excellent railroad connections and proximity to the Chicago metro-

[85] Esarey, *History of Indiana,* II, 896-900; Alden Cutshall, "Terre Haute Iron and Steel: A Declining Industry," *Indiana Magazine of History,* XXXVII (1941), 237-240.

[86] Cutshall, "Terre Haute Iron and Steel," *Indiana Magazine of History,* XXXVII, 241-242.

[87] Moody, *Truth about the Trusts,* pp. 143-145.

[88] United States Bureau of the Census, *Census of Manufactures,* 1905, IV, 5.

politan district. The strip of swampland and sand dunes lying east of Chicago along the southern shore of Lake Michigan which was a virtual wilderness before the erection of the Standard Oil Refinery at Whiting and the organization of the town of East Chicago in the late eighties, provided ample factory sites. In 1901 the Inland Steel Company accepted the offer of a fifty-acre lot from an East Chicago land company and commenced construction of open-hearth furnaces and rolling mills at nearby Indiana Harbor, where port and canal facilities were also being built. Inland grew rapidly into one of the largest independent steel concerns in the Middle West, transporting iron ore by way of the Great Lakes from company-controlled mines in the Mesabi range in Minnesota and manufacturing its own pig iron in two blast furnaces after 1912.[89]

In 1906 the United States Steel Corporation chose the same area for the location of a huge plant on nine thousand empty acres in Calumet Township in Lake County. On this desolate, barren site the gigantic corporation not only built the world's largest and most modern steel furnaces and mills but also laid out the model industrial city of Gary, named after Judge Elbert H. Gary, chairman of its board of directors. Actual steel production began in 1909, but the United States Steel Corporation continued to enlarge its operations in Gary, building plants in 1910 for two subsidiaries, the American Bridge Company and the American Sheet and Tin Plate Company, and increasing its capacity greatly with the coming of the First World War.[90] The Calumet Region's iron and steel industry was well integrated, making its own coke for use in blast furnaces, which in turn produced pig iron for the manufacture of steel in open-hearth furnaces and rolling mills. In iron alone Indiana advanced from sixth place in 1914 to fourth place in 1919, but in total value of iron and steel prod-

[89] Moore, *The Calumet Region,* pp. 219-236.
[90] *Ibid.,* pp. 257-276, 300-303, 327-331.

ucts the state ranked third after Pennsylvania and Ohio in 1919.[91]

IRON AND STEEL INDUSTRY IN INDIANA, 1899-1919[92]

| Year | Number of establishments | Average number of wage earners | Value of products |
|---|---|---|---|
| 1899 | 27 | 7,579 | $ 19,338,000 |
| 1904 | 21 | 7,215 | 16,920,000 |
| 1909 | 17 | 12,255 | 38,652,000 |
| 1914 | 19 | 11,106 | 58,883,000 |
| 1919 | 23 | 22,362 | 199,273,000 |

The fabrication of a large variety of products from iron and steel and other metals was carried on in the state during this period. By 1909, for example, there were 415 foundries and machine shops employing 15,809 wage earners and producing goods valued at $39,884,000.[93] Indiana, moreover, furnished a good part of the machinery used in some of its processing industries as well as machines for general and domestic purposes. In 1919 it was the leading state in the country in the manufacture of flour and gristmill machinery and lawn mowers, and the second state in the production of confectioners' machinery, vacuum cleaners, and windmills. Other similar products manufactured on a slightly smaller scale included dairy machinery, glassmaking machines, blowers and fans, and brick, pottery, and other clay-working machinery.[94]

The bicycle craze of the nineties introduced the short-lived manufacture of that two-wheeled vehicle in the state. In 1895 the Indiana Department of Statistics reported a to-

[91] United States Bureau of the Census, *Fourteenth Census* (1920), X, *Manufactures,* pp. 310, 315.

[92] *Ibid., Thirteenth Census* (1910), X, *Manufactures,* p. 260; *Fourteenth Census* (1920), X, *Manufactures,* p. 346. The value of pig iron produced in blast furnaces in Indiana was not included in the table above in order to avoid duplications, for it was all used to make steel at the mills where it was manufactured. The value of pig iron in 1919 was $51,591,467. *Ibid.,* p. 315.

[93] *Ibid., Thirteenth Census* (1910), *Abstract, with Supplement for Indiana,* p. 679.

[94] *Ibid., Fourteenth Census* (1920), X, *Manufactures,* pp. 369-371.

tal of 17 establishments engaged in making bicycles and bicycle parts in 8 cities, 9 shops being located in Indianapolis itself. The value of products was estimated at $3,085,377. Federal census returns showed that the industry reached its peak in 1899 with 19 establishments but declined suddenly, with only 2 manufacturing shops in 1904.[95]

Indiana, however, had a far larger share in the development of the American automobile industry. As early as 1891 an unsung and almost completely forgotten pioneer automobile maker, Charles H. Black, who was the proprietor of a small buggy factory in Indianapolis, constructed a self-propelled carriage equipped with a gasoline engine and a primitive kerosene-torch ignition system. Although this vehicle was successfully driven through the streets of the city, Black did not make another until 1899 and never undertook the manufacture of automobiles on a commercial scale.[96] David M. Parry, another buggy manufacturer in Indianapolis, was said to have designed an electric chair-car in 1892, but the enterprise proved abortive when the sudden death of a would-be purchaser canceled an order for one thousand of these conveyances.[97]

It was the Gas Belt of the nineties which provided the setting for the work of a better-known pioneer automobile builder, Elwood Haynes, an engineer educated at Worcester Polytechnic Institute and Johns Hopkins University. Haynes

95 Indiana Department of Statistics, *Biennial Report*, 1895-1896, p. 43; United States, Bureau of the Census, *Census of Manufactures*, 1905, II, 261.

96 Anderson, *Story of the American Automobile*, pp. 42-43; *Indiana. A Guide to the Hoosier State*, pp. 210-211; Wallace S. Huffman, "Indiana's Place in Automobile History," *Indiana History Bulletin*, XXXVIII (1961), 144n; XLIV (1967), 9-44. The evidence for Black's building such an automobile in 1891 depends chiefly upon his own recollection of the event, as given in a newspaper interview over twenty years later. Indianapolis *News*, December 27, 1913. See also an unpublished typescript prepared by Philip Flanagan for the Federal Writers' Project, Works Progress Administration, entitled First American Built Automobile, in the Indiana State Library. The Children's Museum in Indianapolis has on display a vehicle supposed to be the original model built in 1891, with some improvements added later.

97 Anderson, *Story of the American Automobile*, p. 50.

conceived of the possibility of a "horseless carriage" while supervising the laying of pipelines in the natural gas field in Jay and Howard counties in 1890-1891. Driving a horse and buggy many miles a day over his supervisor's route, the young engineer dreamed of building a mechanically powered vehicle which would do the job faster and more efficiently. Apparently unaware that both Charles Black in Indianapolis and Charles E. Duryea in Massachusetts were laboring on similar projects, Haynes settled in Kokomo and began to design such a machine. Not a practical mechanic himself, he hired two brothers, Elmer and Edgar Apperson, who operated a small machine shop in that city, to construct the vehicle according to his plans and install a single-cylinder, two-cycle gasoline engine purchased from a factory in Grand Rapids, Michigan. On July 4, 1894, the completed machine, which had a crude electrical ignition system and chain drive, was taken three miles outside the city limits of Kokomo and put through a successful eight-mile-an-hour trial run on a road called Pumpkinville Pike.[98]

In 1895 Haynes and the Appersons formed a partnership to manufacture automobiles based on this model. Incorporated three years later as the Haynes-Apperson Company, the partners eventually fell out and formed separate companies, continuing independently to make automobiles in Kokomo with great commercial success until the mid-twenties, when both firms went out of business. In the meantime, Haynes, whose primary training was in metallurgy, invented

[98] John B. Rae, *The American Automobile. A Brief History* (Chicago, 1965), pp. 9-10. Haynes recalled these events in a letter to Charity Dye printed in her *Some Torch Bearers in Indiana,* pp. 154-160. Haynes and Charles E. Duryea became involved in a long controversy, each claiming to have first conceived and built an automobile in America. Duryea's vehicle was actually completed and successfully operated in 1893, a year before Haynes's drive along Pumpkinville Pike. An early model built by each man was deposited in the Smithsonian Institution Museum in Washington, D.C. The quarrel seems to have begun in a publicity campaign planned to promote the Haynes automobile around 1913. Haynes published his claims for priority in an advertising pamphlet entitled *The Complete Motorist* (Kokomo, 1913), a copy of which is filed in the Indiana State Library.

Stellite and other metal alloys, and the company he formed to manufacture these products in Kokomo survived the closing of his automobile manufacturing concern.[99]

Other automobile manufacturers were soon established in various parts of the state, but Indianapolis became the main center of the new industry. A bicycle firm, the Waverley Company, made electric machines from 1896 to 1915. In 1903 Howard Marmon of Nordyke and Marmon, makers of flour mill machinery, built a gasoline-powered car for his own use and began manufacturing others like it for sale the next year. Many of the early auto makers were wagon and carriage manufacturers, such as David M. Parry and his former employee, Joseph J. Cole, both of whom were turning out motorcars in Indianapolis bearing their names by the first decade of the twentieth century. The Cole Motor Car Company reached its production peak in 1919, when six thousand automobiles came off the assembly lines. Until 1908 a Parry-controlled firm also built the Overland, a model originally created in Terre Haute by a subsidiary, the Standard Wheel Company. In that year John North Willys acquired the company and moved it to Toledo, where he manufactured the popularly priced Willys-Overland.[100]

In South Bend, the Studebaker Company, which had experimented briefly with the new type of vehicle in 1897-1898

[99] Wallace S. Huffman, "The Apperson Brothers and their Automobiles," *Indiana History Bulletin,* XLI (1964), 195-202; Dunn, *Indiana and Indianans,* II, 948-949; Joseph S. Powell, History of Elwood Haynes and Automobile Industry (Unpublished M.A. thesis in History, Indiana University, 1948). Elwood Haynes was an active campaigner for the National Prohibition party and several times ran for state office on its ticket, appearing in 1916 as a candidate for the United States Senate, but later returned to the Republican party. He died in Kokomo in 1925. See Roll, *Indiana,* III, 263-266.

[100] John B. Rae, *American Automobile Manufacturers: The First Forty Years* (New York, 1959), pp. 11, 37, 49-51, 62; *Nordyke & Marmon Company: An Institution. A History of the Development of a Leading Indianapolis Industry* (n. p., 1920), p. 43; Howard R. DeLancy, "The Cole Motor Company," *Business History Review,* XXX (1956), 260-273. See also DeLancy, The History of the Cole Motor Car Company (Unpublished D.B.A. thesis, in School of Business, Indiana University, 1954).

began building electric cars in 1902 and the next year added the production of gasoline-powered machines. Reorganized in 1911 as the Studebaker Corporation, it absorbed an automobile manufacturing firm in Detroit and entered the automotive field in a major way. In 1912 Studebaker discontinued its electric models and in 1920 finally abandoned its famous line of horse-drawn vehicles in order to concentrate upon automobiles. In 1916 the company sold 65,885 cars valued at $61,988,594, before devoting much of its productive capacity to war work.[101]

By 1920 automobiles were being manufactured in more than thirty cities in Indiana, including Anderson, Auburn, Decatur, Elkhart, Evansville, Knightstown, Marion, Mishawaka, New Albany, New Castle, Peru, and Richmond. In 1907 one of the largest factories in the state was erected at New Castle by the Maxwell-Briscoe Company.[102] An authoritative list of Indiana-built automobiles contains the names of 208 makes which were manufactured before 1920, many of them produced by comparatively small, short-lived companies.[103] Although by 1909 Indiana's automobile industry ranked fourth in the nation according to value of products, the state's annual production of cars was not large. Few electrics were built and few business vehicles. In 1919 Indiana turned out 49,740 touring cars, 6,325 closed cars, and 6,337 roadsters and other pleasure cars, all of these gasoline-propelled.[104]

101 Albert R. Erskine, *History of the Studebaker Corporation* (South Bend, 1924), pp. 25-26, 31-37, 45, 69, 79; Longstreet, *A Century on Wheels,* pp. 65-71; Kathleen A. Smallzreid and Dorothy J. Roberts, *More than You Promise: A Business at Work in Society* (New York, 1942), pp. 173-176, 188-191.

102 Indianapolis *News,* June 7, 1907.

103 Huffman, "Indiana's Place in Automobile History," *Indiana History Bulletin,* XXXVIII, 147-151; XLIV, 9-44. Many Indiana firms are also included in the list of automobile makers found in the appendix to Ralph C. Epstein, *The Automobile Industry. Its Economic and Commercial Development* (New York, 1928), pp. 377-382.

104 United States Bureau of the Census, *Fourteenth Census* (1920), IX, *Manufactures,* p. 392.

While Indiana, despite its early start, eventually failed to become a leading center of automobile manufacturing, the growth of the industry as a whole, including bodies and parts as well as complete machines, was extraordinarily rapid in the first two decades of the twentieth century, especially in the period 1914-1919, as shown in the following table:

PRODUCTION OF AUTOMOBILES, BODIES, AND PARTS, 1904-1919[105]

| Year | Number of establishments | Average number of wage earners | Value of products |
|---|---|---|---|
| 1904 | 11 | 816 | $ 1,639,000 |
| 1909 | 67 | 6,797 | 23,764,000 |
| 1914 | 86 | 7,219 | 29,389,000 |
| 1919 | 172 | 25,773 | 179,065,000 |

The manufacture of parts and accessories quickly became a significant feature of the Hoosier automotive industry. The Indianapolis carburetor firms, the Marvel Company and the Wheeler-Schebler Company, were based on the inventions and designs of two local violin makers, Burt N. Pierce and George W. Schebler. Around 1900 two brothers, Thomas W. and Harry Warner, developed an automobile differential and organized the Warner Gear Company in Muncie to manufacture it. Charles Davis, a native of Terre Haute, introduced the production of standardized transmissions for automobiles at the same company in 1920.[106]

In Anderson Frank L. and B. Perry Remy produced the first practical electric dynamo in 1895 and six years later formed the Remy Electric Company to manufacture magnetos, generators, and other electrical systems for automo-

[105] Ibid., Census of Manufactures, 1914, II, 743; Fourteenth Census (1920), X, Manufactures, p. 875. The Bureau of the Census also reported 358 automobile-repair shops in Indiana in 1919 with a total value of products of $3,353,-000. Ibid., pp. 880-881.

[106] William C. Oursler, From Ox Carts to Jets. Roy Ingersoll and the Borg-Warner Story: A Biography (Englewood Cliffs, N.J., 1959), pp. 147-154, 181-182. The Warner Gear Company and the combined Marvel and Schebler Carburetor companies became part of the Borg-Warner Corporation when it was formed in 1928.

biles. Sold to the Fletcher interests in Indianapolis in 1911, the company became part of the General Motors corporate structure between 1916 and 1918. In 1904 the automobile promoter Carl G. Fisher created the Prest-O-Lite Company for the manufacture of acetylene lamps for night driving. After joining with his partner, James A. Allison, and others in 1909 to build the Indianapolis Speedway, he moved the plant to the site of the new suburb which was growing up around the race track. In 1913 the Allison Engineering Company was established nearby to manufacture racing cars and experiment with automotive design and construction.[107]

A related industry that flourished in the early twentieth century was the manufacture of rubber tires. The first plant in the state was established in Kokomo in 1895 to produce bicycle tires, but in 1919 Indiana produced 308,670 automobile tire casings valued at $5,281,169 and 2,939,163 inner tubes valued at $7,975,250, ranking third nationally in the production of the latter.[108]

Indiana was also an important center for the manufacture of electrical apparatus. This industry was inaugurated in the state in 1881 when the Jenney Electric Company of Fort Wayne was organized to produce materials for an arc-lighting system invented by James A. and Charles D. Jenney. In 1899 this company and a second Jenney concern in Indianapolis were acquired by General Electric and later greatly enlarged and converted to the manufacture of tungsten incan-

---

[107] Arthur Pound, *The Turning Wheel: The Story of General Motors through Twenty-five Years, 1908-1933* (Garden City, N. Y., 1934), pp. 460-464; Fisher, *Fabulous Hoosier*, p. 59. After selling his interest in Prest-O-Lite in 1913, Fisher went to Florida, where he built and promoted the resort center of Miami Beach. After sinking a considerable part of his fortune in a less successful promotion scheme in Long Island, he died in Miami Beach in 1939. Fisher, *Fabulous Hoosier*, pp. 93-159, 260-261. The Allison Company was absorbed by General Motors in 1929, as was a second transmission firm organized by Thomas W. Warner in 1909 in Muncie. Pound, *The Turning Wheel*, pp. 460, 487.

[108] United States Bureau of the Census, *Fourteenth Census* (1920), X, *Manufactures*, p. 1002.

descent lamps and other electrical apparatus and supplies.[109] Indiana's electrical industry expanded rapidly in the early twentieth century, reaching a gross value of products of $7,-718,000 in 1909 and $41,594,000 in 1920.[110]

A relatively small industry in which Indiana played a major role in this period was the manufacture of musical instruments. Large numbers of pianos and a few organs were made in Richmond, Elkhart, New Castle, and other cities as early as the seventies. During the first two decades of the twentieth century, the state produced annually between 20,-000 and 25,000 pianos, valued at $3,513,127 in 1914 and $6,-870,350 in 1919.[111] Although the value of products was much smaller, Indiana was better known for its band instruments, and led all states in their production by 1900, with over half the total national output in that year.[112] The pioneer Hoosier manufacturer in this field was Charles Gerard Conn, a Civil War veteran and former Union Army musician who began making cornet mouthpieces in Elkhart in 1873. A few years later he turned to the manufacture of cornets and eventually other brass and wind instruments. When he sold his interests to the C. G. Conn Company in 1911, the Elkhart firm was the largest such factory in the country. Other instrument makers also built plants in Elkhart, making it the world capital of the band industry by 1920.[113] In 1919 Indiana not only led in the manufacture of all musical instruments except pianos and organs but also ranked third in phonographs, with products valued at $3,148,410 and $7,-977,495, respectively.[114]

[109] Bert J. Griswold, *The Pictorial History of Fort Wayne Indiana* (2 volumes, Chicago, 1917), I, 509-510; *Hyman's Hand Book of Indianapolis*, p. 374.

[110] United States Bureau of the Census, *Fourteenth Census* (1920), X, *Manufactures*, p. 953.

[111] *Ibid.*, p. 978.

[112] *Ibid.*, *Twelfth Census* (1900), X, *Manufactures*, p. 474.

[113] *Indiana. A Guide to the Hoosier State*, p. 289. See also the pamphlet entitled *Charles Gerard Conn* (n.p., n.d.), a copy of which is in the Indiana State Library.

[114] United States Bureau of the Census, *Fourteenth Census* (1920), X, *Manufactures*, pp. 986, 992.

Other significant manufacturing industries in the state were bookbinding, petroleum refining, printing and publishing, and shipbuilding. A listing of commercially important Hoosier products in this period, moreover, should include in addition to those mentioned above such items as ammunition and explosives, brick and tile, cement, chemicals, mattresses and spring beds, men's shirts, paints and varnishes, plumbers' supplies, pumps, refrigerators, rubber boots and shoes, saws, sewing machine cases, stoves and furnaces, and washing machines.[115] Indeed a chief characteristic of Indiana's industrialization during the four decades between 1880 and 1920 was the wide range and increasing diversification of its manufacturing interests.

§ § § § §

The extensive growth of industry and commerce in this period was reflected in a corresponding increase in banking activity in Indiana. By 1880 there were ninety-two national banks chartered under the National Banking Act of 1863 operating in the state, with total assets of $51,812,130. They were located in most of the large and many of the smaller cities. Indianapolis had six, Evansville, five, Lafayette and New Albany, four apiece, Fort Wayne and Richmond, three apiece, and Greensburg, Jeffersonville, Kokomo, Liberty, Madison, Muncie, New Castle, Peru, Rushville, South Bend, Terre Haute, Valparaiso, and Vincennes each had two, while there was a single national bank in each of the following cities: Anderson, Attica, Auburn, Aurora, Bloomington, Boonville, Cambridge City, Centerville, Columbus, Connersville, Crawfordsville, Crown Point, Danville, Elkhart, Frankfort, Franklin, Goshen, Greencastle, Huntington, Kendallville, Knightstown, La Grange, La Porte, Lawrenceburg, Lebanon, Logansport, Martinsville, Michigan City, Mount Vernon, Plymouth, Princeton, Rising Sun, Rockville, Seymour, Shelbyville, Sullivan, Thorntown, Vevay, Wabash, Warsaw, and

---

[115] See the detailed statement of specified industries, as well as a long list of "other industries" in *ibid.*, IX, *Manufactures*, pp. 400-407.

Washington.[116] The following table shows the growth of national banks in Indiana during the four decades after 1880:

NUMBER, CAPITAL, DEPOSITS, AND RESOURCES OF
NATIONAL BANKS IN INDIANA, 1880-1920[117]

| Year | No. of Banks | Capital | Deposits | Total assets |
|---|---|---|---|---|
| 1880 | 92 | $13,203,000 | $ 19,871,000 | $ 51,812,000 |
| 1890 | 100 | 12,652,000 | 30,906,000 | 57,016,000 |
| 1900 | 123 | 14,615,000 | 57,728,000 | 99,271,000 |
| 1910 | 262 | 28,055,000 | 131,113,000 | 229,876,000 |
| 1920 | 254 | 29,988,000 | 266,300,000 | 431,970,000 |

In addition to these banks of issue, there were 144 smaller state and private banks in Indiana in 1880 according to the report of the United States Comptroller of the Currency. The former were incorporated under the Discount and Deposit Act of 1873, which also established a banking department in the office of the state auditor, who appointed a bank inspector to examine their accounts periodically. Unincorporated banks owned by private individuals or partnerships remained free from regulation until 1907, when the General Assembly belatedly placed them under supervision of the state auditor.[118] Many private institutions of this kind became state or national banks in this period. Fletcher National Bank in Indianapolis, the oldest and largest of all private banking establishments in the state, received a charter as a national bank in 1898 and was consolidated with the American National Bank in 1910 to form the Fletcher American National Bank, the largest such institution in the state in 1920, with total resources of $43,970,232. Although in the latter year there were 172 private banks in Indiana, most of them were quite small, only three having assets of over a million

116 United States Comptroller of the Currency, *Annual Report*, 1880, pp. lxxxvii, 530-560. For the organization of national banks in Indiana prior to 1880, see Thornbrough, *Indiana in the Civil War Era*, pp. 433-434.

117 United States Comptroller of the Currency, *Annual Report*, 1920, II, 317.

118 *Ibid.*, 1880, lxxxvi-lxxxvii; *Laws of Indiana*, 1873, pp. 21-27; 1907, pp. 174-181.

dollars—Irwin's Bank in Columbus, A. T. Bowen's Bank of Delphi, and the Salem Bank, Goshen.[119]

Although the Indiana General Assembly had authorized the incorporation of mutual savings banks in 1869, the statute was so strict that few were organized. No more than ten were ever in existence at one time, and by the second decade of the twentieth century their number had leveled off at five. On the other hand, a somewhat different type of institution for the small saver, the building and loan association, was well represented in Indiana. By the eighties these associations, which had been organized under a series of laws going back as far as 1857, were extremely popular in the state. When the Department of Statistics undertook an extensive survey of them in 1888, it was discovered that 385 had been incorporated since 1880. They were not subject to state regulation until 1893, when the General Assembly enacted legislation severely restricting the activities of out-of-state associations and bringing both foreign and domestic types under the supervision of the auditor's office. Building and loan associations flourished greatly in Indiana, reaching a peak in 1896 with 505 institutions representing resources in excess of $38,000,000, a ratio of 45.2 per cent of all other bank assets in the state. Although their membership and resources tended to increase slightly over the next two and a half decades, their number and the ratio of their resources to those of other banking institutions in Indiana declined appreciably. Yet since these associations were organized primarily to enable workingmen and other low-income persons to obtain loans for the building of homes, their proliferation in the eighties and nineties undoubtedly contributed to the rapid growth of cities and towns in Indiana.[120]

119 Max R. Hyman, "A Bit of Banking History," *Indiana, Past and Present,* I, No. 1 (April, 1914), 17; United States Comptroller of the Currency, *Annual Report,* 1920, II, 520-521; Indiana *Year Book,* 1920, p. 172.

120 *Laws of Indiana,* 1869, special session, pp. 104-116; 1893, pp. 274-282; Indiana Department of Statistics, *Biennial Report,* 1888-1889, pp. lxxxviii-xci; *Report of the Study Commission for Indiana Financial Institutions* (Indianapolis, 1932), pp. 16-17, 20-26, 33-35.

In 1891 John P. Frenzel, president of the Merchants National Bank of Indianapolis, and others appealed to the state legislature to authorize the incorporation of trust companies. Although the General Assembly failed to act in that year, in 1893 it enacted a law permitting the organization of loan, trust, and safe deposit companies with broad powers to perform financial services for customers—so broad indeed that the institutions which came into existence under this legislation were often called "department store banks." The first to be organized was Frenzel's Indiana Trust Company, which was followed almost immediately by the Union Trust Company, also in Indianapolis, founded by John H. Holliday. The profitable trust companies grew rapidly in Indiana, reaching a total of 170 with resources of $248,720,825 in 1920, as compared with 463 state banks with resources of $237,138,736; 172 private banks with resources of $42,931,454; and 5 savings banks with resources of $18,016,432.[121]

The first attempt to organize the state's bankers took place in 1891, but the resulting society did not survive the Panic of 1893, which caused the failure of a number of Indiana banks and wrought some confusion in banking circles. Finally, in 1897 the Indiana Bankers Association was re-formed as a permanent organization.[122] A major modification of the traditional free banking system in the state was made in 1915, when the legislature established a bank charter board composed of the governor, the secretary of state, and the state auditor which was given the power to investigate the financial standing and character of persons seeking to organize a bank and to ascertain the public need for such an institution before granting a charter. This did not affect the vast majority of Indiana banks, which were organized prior to 1915, but

[121] *The City and the Bank 1865-1965. The Story of 100 Years in the Life of Indianapolis and the Merchants National Bank and Trust Company of Indianapolis* (Indianapolis, 1965), pp. 41-42; *Report of Study Commission*, p. 17; Indiana *Year Book*, 1920, p. 163. In 1915 the General Assembly finally authorized all banks in the state to perform the same services for customers as those performed by trust companies. *Laws of Indiana*, 1915, p. 310.

[122] *Hoosier Banker*, XXXI, No. 4 (April, 1947), 3, 8-10.

it tended to restrict the number of new ones chartered, though apparently not to the degree expected by the sponsors of the legislation. In 1919 the General Assembly passed the Southworth-Symons Act, which finally established a Department of Banking separate from the state auditor's office and under the direction of a bank commissioner appointed by the governor.[123]

[123] *Laws of Indiana,* 1915, pp. 550-551; 1919, pp. 112-115; *Report of Study Commission,* pp. 18-19.

# CHAPTER VIII

## THE ROLE OF LABOR

THE INDUSTRIALIZATION OF INDIANA greatly enlarged the class of wage earners within the total population, adding growing numbers of both skilled and unskilled workers to the labor force. Most of these found employment in manufacturing and ancillary industries such as trade, transportation, and mining, all of which expanded rapidly in the period from 1880 to 1920. Much of this growth was at the expense of agriculture, in which half or more of the state's work force was employed before 1880. The number of persons engaged in agricultural pursuits, while continuing to rise slowly each decade until about 1910, declined steadily in proportion to the total number of persons engaged in gainful occupations, as the following table indicates:

### NUMBER AND PERCENTAGE OF PERSONS ENGAGED IN GAINFUL OCCUPATIONS, 1890-1920[1]

| Year | Agriculture | | Manufacturing and mechanical industries | | Trade and Transportation | | Mining and Quarrying | |
|---|---|---|---|---|---|---|---|---|
| | Number | Per cent | Number | Per cent | Number | Per cent | Number | Per cent |
| 1890 | 322,339 | 44.5 | 144,485 | 20.0 | 92,344 | 12.7 | 8,026 | 1.1 |
| 1900 | 342,733 | 38.1 | 193,267 | 21.5 | 138,545 | 15.4 | 13,018 | 1.4 |
| 1910 | 344,454 | 33.2 | 310,402 | 29.9 | 223,957 | 20.6 | 24,300 | 2.3 |
| 1920 | 294,006 | 26.3 | 377,446 | 33.8 | 267,786 | 24.0 | 33,322 | 3.0 |

Although small contingents of craftsmen were imported from abroad to work in some of the new industries founded in the eighties and nineties—glassblowers from Belgium and

[1] Compiled from United States Bureau of the Census, *Twelfth Census* (1900), II, *Population*, Pt. II, cxxxv-cxxxvii; *Thirteenth Census* (1910), IV, *Population*, pp. 44-45; *Fourteenth Census* (1920), IV, *Population*, pp. 48, 50. The totals do not reach 100 per cent because figures for public, professional, domestic, and clerical occupations have been omitted.

England, tinplate technicians from Wales—and a flood of immigrants from southern and eastern Europe arrived to swell the ranks of common laborers in the oil refineries, steel mills, and other factories in the Calumet Region and elsewhere in the early twentieth century, the vast majority of industrial workers in this period were native-born Americans recruited from the rising towns and cities as well as from the declining farm population of Indiana and adjoining states. By 1920 only 7.5 per cent of all persons engaged in gainful occupations in the state were of foreign birth, compared with 25.8 per cent for Illinois and 16.9 per cent for Ohio. Of the remainder, 75.1 per cent were native white of native parentage, 13.6 per cent native white of foreign or mixed parentage, and 3.8 per cent Negro. East Chicago was the only city with a labor force more than half of which was foreign born, though Gary and Hammond followed closely behind. Outside of Lake County only South Bend counted as much as a quarter of its working population as foreign born. Indeed in two cities—Indianapolis and Evansville—Negro workers greatly outnumbered those of foreign birth.[2]

Working conditions in Indiana in this period paralleled those found in other industrializing regions. Long hours and low wages sum up much of the story of industrial labor in the state in the first two or three decades after 1880. Most factory employees worked at least a ten-hour day and a six-day week. As late as 1910 the United States Bureau of the Census reported that the prevailing work week in 7.7 per cent of Hoosier manufacturing industries was more than sixty hours, and that 2,505 persons were employed in establishments working over seventy-two hours per week. Industries with the longest hours of work included those manufacturing gas, cement, ice, paper and wood pulp, glucose and starch, flour, baked goods, and iron and steel. In fact steel-mill workers commonly put in a seven-day week. On the other hand 13.1 per cent of all manufacturing establishments in 1910 re-

[2] *Ibid., Fourteenth Census* (1920), IV, *Population,* pp. 363, 368-372.

ported that the prevailing hours of work totaled less than fifty-four per week. The glass, tobacco, and printing and publishing industries were the chief representatives of this group.[3]

In 1889 the Indiana General Assembly attempted to legislate an eight-hour day for all wage earners except those engaged in agricultural or domestic labor, but a provision permitting additional hours of work for extra compensation by mutual agreement of employers and employees made the act a dead letter.[4] Yet some progress was made in the direction of shorter hours, especially by the more highly skilled and the best-organized workingmen. The building trades—carpenters, bricklayers and masons, painters, and plasterers—won an eight-hour day and overtime pay in the larger cities around the turn of the century, Indianapolis leading the way in 1898. Certain skilled iron and steel workers as well as coal miners also enjoyed an eight-hour day and forty-eight hour week by this time. The length of the working day for blowers, gatherers, flatteners, cutters, and snappers was as short as six and two-thirds hours in some glass factories and generally no more than nine hours in others, though ordinary laborers in the glass industry often worked as long as twelve hours each day.[5]

A marked shortening of the hours of labor in Hoosier factories occurred in the second decade of the twentieth century, as it did in most of the country. In 1909 nearly half the total number of factory workers in the state were employed in establishments where the prevailing work week was sixty or more hours; by 1914 this figure was reduced to one third of the workers and in 1919 to just 16.1 per cent. At the other end of the scale, the proportion of workers in establishments where forty-eight hours constituted the maximum work week

3 *Ibid., Thirteenth Census* (1910), IX, *Manufactures*, p. 309.
4 *Laws of Indiana*, 1889, p. 143; Rawles, *Centralizing Tendencies in the Administration of Indiana*, pp. 319-320.
5 Indiana Department of Statistics, *Biennial Report*, 1899-1900, pp. 194-197; 1903-1904, pp. 717-722.

rose from 7.2 per cent in 1909 to 14.9 per cent in 1914 and 32.6 per cent in 1919.[6]

The first report on factory wages published by the Indiana Department of Statistics in 1881 revealed that the prevailing daily rate for common labor ranged from $1.00 to $1.50 for ten to twelve hours, while certain groups of skilled workmen earned up to $4.50 per day, with wide variations among different counties.[7] Wages were often paid only at long or irregular intervals. To prevent this practice the legislature in 1887 passed the first of a series of laws requiring employers to pay their workers every two weeks.[8] Among the most meagerly compensated wage earners in Indiana were the bituminous coal miners, who were normally paid according to the tonnage mined, and whose employment was often irregular, depending upon conditions in the highly competitive market in the Illinois-Indiana coal fields. Their gross wages were also reduced by the cost of blasting powder and other supplies which they had to purchase from the mine operators, who often ran "company stores" selling food, clothing, and similar commodities to their employees at a high profit, a practice which the General Assembly attempted to outlaw in 1889.[9] In a special investigation of the coal mining region in 1894, the director of the Indiana Department of Statistics estimated the average annual earnings of the operatives at $287 and published the following description of their drab living conditions:[10]

[6] United States Bureau of the Census, *Census of Manufactures,* 1914, I, 375-376; *Fourteenth Census* (1920), IX, *Manufactures,* p. 373. Indiana lagged slightly behind both Illinois and Ohio in the reduction of the hours of labor in manufacturing industries in this decade. *Ibid.,* pp. 309, 1139.

[7] Indiana Department of Statistics, *Annual Report,* 1881, pp. 140-161.

[8] *Laws of Indiana,* 1887, pp. 13-14. An 1899 law requiring weekly payments was declared unconstitutional by the Indiana Supreme Court in 1902. *Ibid.,* 1899, p. 193; Republic Iron and Steel *v.* the State, 160 Ind. 379 (1902). In 1911 the legislature again enacted a weekly payment law. *Laws of Indiana,* 1911, p. 110.

[9] *Laws of Indiana,* 1889, pp. 191-192.

[10] Indiana Department of Statistics, *Biennial Report,* 1893-1894, pp. 237-238.

The homes of the miners demonstrate that the wages are inadequate to supply the comforts of life. They are generally cabins, ill furnished and with nothing that is not absolutely necessary, the furniture consisting of wooden bottom chairs, the most ordinary bedsteads and bedding, and furnishings for the table of the least expensive kind. The floors are rarely carpeted, and the few exceptions show only the cheapest grades of hemp and rag carpets. . . . The fare, like the house furnishings, is of the plainest possible character.

Until the end of the century there was little or no improvement in the wages of most workers, who suffered in addition from periodic pay reductions and high levels of unemployment during the financial panics of the mid-eighties and mid-nineties. But by 1900 skilled journeymen in the glass, tin-plate, and the iron and steel industries were earning between $4.50 and $8.00 per day, union scale.[11] Wages in general rose gradually in the early years of the twentieth century and spectacularly after the outbreak of the First World War. According to a special Federal census report in 1929, the average yearly earnings of all factory workers in Indiana increased from $490 in 1899 to $501 in 1904, $576 in 1909, $636 in 1914, and an inflationary $1,412 in 1919, figures well above the national average though slightly below those for other industrialized states of the Middle West.[12]

Industrialization resulted in a significant increase in the number of women working outside the home. A study of working women in Indianapolis conducted by the office of the United States Commissioner of Labor in 1888, however, suggested that despite the low wages they received—described as "almost beggarly" in some cases—their social and economic state was superior to that of their counterparts in many parts of the country. This was attributed at least partly to the fact that nine-tenths of the female employees in the city, most of them native born, lived at home with their families rather than in rented rooms or boarding houses. In fact

11 *Ibid.*, 1899-1900, pp. 177-193.
12 Paul F. Brissenden, *Earnings of Factory Workers, 1899 to 1927* (United States Bureau of the Census, *Census Monographs*, X, 1929), p. 107.

the investigators reported further that they found working-class living conditions generally good in Indianapolis. Workers lived in small but neat and comfortable cottages in the "suburbs," paying only moderate rents and often owning their own homes. Moreover, the nearby farms supplied cheap and varied food. They saw little evidence of real poverty and noted especially that the streets in workingmen's sections seemed cleaner and more attractive than those in the crowded slums of great cities. As for the working girls themselves, the report stated, "though their manners are not fastidious, and carelessness or indifference as to looks prevails among them, their morals are good." Despite the existence of relatively poor working conditions in the factories, many of which were badly lighted and ventilated, "the shop regulations are kind and fair, the moral tone of the work-rooms respectable, and the employers as a class, just," the report solemnly concluded.[13]

An investigation by the Indiana Department of Statistics five years later produced a similar, if somewhat less optimistic, picture of working women in Indianapolis. The five hundred women studied, all but thirty-one of whom were born in the United States, were employed in bookbinderies, clothing factories, laundries, pork-packing houses, tobacco factories, chain and stamping works, and paper-box plants, and as salesgirls, secretaries, seamstresses, bookkeepers and cashiers, hairdressers, and telephone operators. Their average working hours were calculated at 9.4 per day and 56.3 per week. Those who were required to work for longer periods were often saleswomen in department and other retail stores which remained open for business thirteen hours or more on Saturdays. Complaints were also registered concerning noise and dirt in the workrooms, imperfect ventilation, lack of protection from inclement weather, poor sanitary conditions, and the necessity on some jobs of standing or sitting in one

[13] United States Commissioner of Labor, *Annual Report, 1889, Working Women in Large Cities,* p. 18.

position constantly. Average weekly earnings were only $5.66, a figure so patently inadequate that the author of the report suggested that many of the workers would have sunk deeply into debt had they not saved on expenses by living at home. The report was also concerned with the morality and reputation of female workers, but concluded happily that "improvement in the social status of the working woman is steadily taking place; she is no longer the unfortunate exception, but a self-reliant, free and independent person, demanding and receiving increasing respect both for herself and for her industrial abilities."[14]

The same official report contained the results of a study of the conditions of domestic labor in the eight largest cities of the state. The majority of girls and women in domestic service were also found to be native-born, though many were of foreign parentage. A somewhat larger share of these workers than of those found in factories in Indiana, however, were Negroes and recent immigrants, chiefly Irish and German. Sixty per cent, moreover, were country-bred, a fact which seemed to indicate that city girls preferred to work in factories rather than as domestics. Such servants, however, were usually able to reduce their living expenses by staying in the home in which they were employed, but they worked longer hours and drew smaller wages than women in industry, averaging only $2.64 per week.[15]

The number of working women in Indiana was rising rapidly by the turn of the century. In 1900 the United States Bureau of the Census reported a total of 116,716 women engaged in gainful occupations, of whom 9,893 were employed in agriculture, 12,981 in professional work, 50,478 in personal and domestic service, 13,464 in trade and transportation, and 29,900 in manufacturing and mechanical pursuits. By 1920, moreover, the total number had grown to 185,385, a

[14] Indiana Department of Statistics, *Biennial Report,* 1893-1894, pp. 3-59.

[15] *Ibid.,* pp. 173-227. For a good picture of the daily tasks of a hired girl in Corydon, Indiana, in 1889, see the letter of Katie Balcom in *Indiana History Bulletin,* XLIV (1967), 173.

60 per cent increase, with major gains recorded in manufacturing, professional, and clerical occupations.[16]

Despite the changing pattern of female employment, the Indiana legislature paid little attention to the special problems of women in industry. Not until 1913 did the General Assembly create a commission on working women to "investigate the hours and conditions of labor of women in this state" and "determine what limitation, if any, should be placed on the hours of labor of women in any or all employments, or what improvement should be made in the conditions under which women labor in any or all employments."[17] This commission, whose woman member, Mrs. Bertha J. Lockwood, virtually worked herself to death in attempting to carry out its responsibilities on a very small budget, held hearings in ten cities and sent questionnaires to employers in thirty different industries. At the request of the commission, the United States Department of Labor conducted a study of hours, wages, and conditions of employment in retail stores and garment factories, where almost half the female working force in Indiana was concentrated. It was found that long hours of work still prevailed in both types of establishment, though late Saturday night closings in department stores were being abandoned in Indianapolis and Lafayette. Average weekly wages were calculated at $6.92 in garment factories and $7.76 in mercantile houses, with some weeks of enforced idleness each year, especially for workers in the garment trade during the slack season. Working conditions were judged to be only fair. Although the state commission found no "pressing conditions that would seem to justify any radical legislation," it recommended the setting of additional

16 United States Bureau of the Census, *Twelfth Census* (1900), II, *Population*, Pt. II, 508-509; *Fourteenth Census* (1920), IV, *Population*, p. 54. The proportion of women in gainful occupations in Indiana remained consistently lower than that for most other midwestern states during this period. *Ibid.*, p. 18.

17 *Laws of Indiana*, 1913, pp. 707-708. The legislature appropriated only $2,000 for the commission, considerably limiting its scope of action.

safety and sanitation standards, rest periods for women workers, and limitation of their working week to fifty-four hours in mercantile establishments and fifty-eight in factories, with possible overtime in certain industries such as fruit and vegetable canning during the rush season. The General Assembly, however, failed to take any action concerning these mild recommendations.[18]

Child labor was also a prominent feature of the industrialization of Indiana, especially in the glass industry, where several young boys were traditionally employed as helpers for each set of skilled blowers and gatherers in a factory. By 1896, 2,056 boys as well as 443 women and girls were reported at work in glass factories in the state.[19] Girls, as well as older women, found employment in cotton and woolen mills, clothing factories, and laundries. Other industries utilizing child labor on a fairly large scale were coal mining, furniture manufacturing, and fruit and vegetable canning. One condition encouraging the employment of children of both sexes in factories and retail establishments as well as extensively on farms was the lack of any compulsory school attendance legislation in Indiana until near the end of the century.[20]

Although as early as 1867 the Indiana General Assembly enacted a law prohibiting the employment of persons under sixteen years of age in cotton or woolen mills for more than ten hours a day, little further progress was made in attempting to regulate working conditions of children for nearly two decades with the exception of the coal mining act of 1879 which set minimum safety standards and excluded boys un-

[18] Streightoff and Streightoff, *Indiana,* 90-91; *Hours, Earnings, and Conditions of Labor of Women in Indiana Mercantile Establishments and Garment Factories* (United States Bureau of Labor Statistics, *Bulletin No. 60,* 1914), pp. 8-91.

[19] John Spargo, *The Bitter Cry of the Children* (New York, 1906), pp. 154-161; Indiana Department of Statistics, *Biennial Report,* 1895-1896, p. 18.

[20] For the development of the movement for compulsory education, see Chapter X, 389-90n.

der fourteen from work in the mines.[21] In 1885 the legislature took the modest step of making it unlawful for any
individual or firm manufacturing iron, steel, nails, metals,
machinery, or tobacco to employ persons under twelve years
of age and limited the length of the working day for children of that age engaged in other legal occupations to eight
hours. Four years later an amendment was passed extending
the prohibition against the employment of persons under
twelve to certain other types of establishments and forbid-
ding persons under fifteen from being employed in places
where liquor was sold. Finally, in 1893 the minimum age was
raised from twelve to fourteen years. In both 1891 and 1893
the General Assembly also enacted laws aimed at the protection of the health of women and girls employed in manufacturing and mercantile establishments, with provisions such
as that requiring seats to be available for their use when not
actively engaged in their duties.[22]

Yet none of these legislative enactments seems to have
had much practical effect upon actual working conditions in
the state, for the simple reason that no special officials were
designated to administer them. Although local prosecuting
attorneys were assigned the duty of enforcing the acts of
1891 and 1893, they had, according to a contemporary observer of Indiana's administrative system, "neither the time
nor the inclination to make thorough inspections and investi-
gations in order to ascertain to what extent the laws were
violated."[23] In 1897, after a similar bill had failed in the Senate in the previous session, the General Assembly finally
passed a comprehensive labor law which prohibited the employment in any manufacturing establishment of children un-

---

[21] *Laws of Indiana*, 1867, p. 232; 1879, pp. 19-25. A provision prohibiting
persons under the age of eighteen from being employed in cotton or woolen
mills was included in the 1881 revised statutes. *Revised Statutes of Indiana*,
1881, sec. 2125.

[22] *Laws of Indiana*, 1885, p. 219; 1889, pp. 363-367; 1891, p. 331; 1893, pp.
147-148, 360.

[23] Rawles, *Centralizing Tendencies in the Administration of Indiana*, p.
316.

der the age of fourteen, as well as those persons fourteen or fifteen years of age who were unable to read and write English. In addition, no one under sixteen years and no woman under eighteen years was permitted to work more than ten hours a day or sixty hours a week. The minimum age of elevator operators was fixed at fifteen and, in some cases, at eighteen. Most importantly, the act provided for the appointment of a factory inspector whose responsibility it was to see that the above regulations were enforced and violators prosecuted. Appointed by the governor, this officer was authorized to inspect all manufacturing establishments in the state and, if he deemed it necessary, to require the installation of certain safety and sanitation facilities. Tenement-house shops were also forbidden, except upon the written permission of the inspector.[24] In 1899 an amendment broadened the minimum-age provisions to include children under fourteen employed in mercantile establishments, laundries, renovating works, bakeries, and printing shops, and also prohibited the employment of women and girls between the hours of 10:00 P.M. and 6:00 A.M. To strengthen enforcement of the act, moreover, a department of inspection staffed by a chief inspector and two deputies was established.[25]

The legislation of 1897 and 1899 helped to reduce the number of young children at work in Indiana factories, partly through the vigorous administration of the department of inspection but also because compulsory school attendance was required after 1897. Furthermore, the introduction of semi-automatic machinery in the glass industry around the turn of the century replaced many young boys along with other

[24] *Laws of Indiana*, 1897, pp. 101-108; Jay B. Kennedy, Protective Labor Legislation in Indiana (Unpublished Ph.D. thesis, Indiana University, 1961), pp. 123-124.

[25] *Laws of Indiana*, 1899, pp. 231-240. The department of inspection was also charged with enforcement of a law requiring fire escapes on certain buildings. *Ibid.*, pp. 473-476. In 1901 an act establishing health and sanitation requirements for food industries gave the department new duties. *Ibid.*, 1901, pp. 42-43.

unskilled workers. In 1906 the chief factory inspector reported that the state's glass plants at that time employed only 630 boys between the ages of fourteen and sixteen. He cited the case of one establishment which had reduced its employment of such boys from 260 in 1897 to just 35 in 1906. On the other hand, he pointed out that some retail stores were evading the ten-hour day provision by keeping their cash boys and girls as late as 10:00 P.M. by an extension of the lunch and dinner periods.[26] In general, Indiana lagged somewhat behind most other industrial commonwealths in successfully restricting the hours of labor and types of employment for both women and children. In 1910 the United States Department of Labor reported that Indiana had a higher proportion of child labor than any other northern states except Pennsylvania and Ohio.[27]

Out of the contemporary movement for a Federal child-labor law, in which Indiana's Senator Albert J. Beveridge was a prominent figure, came a heightened demand for further state legislation. In 1909 an Indiana Child Labor Committee was formed under the chairmanship of Professor Ulysses G. Weatherly of the Department of Sociology at Indiana University to lobby at the legislature for an improved child-labor law. After the General Assembly failed to act on it at that session, a watered-down version of the bill supported by the committee was passed in 1911 against the vehement opposition of many factory owners. This law extended the ban on the employment of children under fourteen years of age to all types of work except agriculture and domestic service

26 Indiana Department of Inspection, *Annual Report*, 1906, p. 6. It was estimated that as many as eight hundred boys were taken out of factories in the Gas Belt during the first year of operation of the law of 1897. Indiana Department of Statistics, *Biennial Report*, 1897-1898, p. 154.

27 *Glass Industry (Report on Condition of Women and Child Wage-Earners in the United States,* 61 Congress, 2 session, U.S. *Senate Documents No. 645,* III, 1911), p. 18. Indiana's child-labor legislation was inferior to that of the surrounding states, Kentucky, Ohio, Michigan, and Illinois, according to one writer. Edward N. Clopper, *Child Labor in Indiana* (National Child Labor Committee, *Pamphlet No. 91,* New York, n.d.), pp. 13-16.

but included a clause, at the behest of the canning industry, permitting persons between the ages of twelve and fourteen to be employed in canneries during the period from June to October only. It also prohibited the employment of children under the age of sixteen between the hours of 6:00 P.M. and 7:00 A.M. or in any tobacco factory or warehouse, hotel, theater, place of amusement, or other employment "where their health may be injured or morals depraved." Other restrictions applied to employment in breweries, distilleries, saloons, and in certain kinds of dangerous occupations. But the sponsors of the bill failed to secure an absolute ban on the employment of persons under sixteen years for more than eight hours a day or forty-eight hours a week, for as finally passed the law permitted a child to work up to nine hours a day and fifty-four hours a week with the authorization of his parent or legal guardian.[28]

Child labor declined precipitously in the second decade of the twentieth century. According to the Federal census statistics, the number of boys between the ages of ten and fifteen engaged in gainful occupations in Indiana dropped from 27,688 in 1910 to 12,248 in 1920, while the number of girls in this age bracket decreased from 6,005 to 4,483 in the same period.[29] In 1921 the General Assembly strengthened the law of 1911 by removing the exemption of the canning industry from the minimum age requirement during the summer months and requiring all persons between the ages of fourteen and sixteen to have completed the first eight grades of school before obtaining a work certificate. It also broadened the category of occupations forbidden to any child under six-

[28] Ulysses G. Weatherly, "Indiana's Child Labor Problem," *Indiana Bulletin of Charities and Correction,* December, 1910, pp. 335-338; *Laws of Indiana,* 1911, pp. 511-513.

[29] United States Bureau of the Census, *Fourteenth Census* (1920), IV, *Population,* p. 514. The number of boys engaged in gainful occupations in Indiana in 1920 was still proportionately higher than that for any other midwestern state.

teen deemed to be "dangerous to life or limb, or injurious to the health or morals of such minor."[30]

In the eighties and nineties the Indiana General Assembly enacted into law a whole series of safety measures aimed at protecting the health and welfare of coal miners, who were engaged in probably the most dangerous occupation in the state.[31] At the same time the high rate of general industrial accidents, many of them fatal, created a vigorous demand in some quarters for legislation giving injured workers and their families statutory relief from the increasingly out-moded common-law doctrines of assumed risk, contributory negligence, and fellow servant, which as interpreted by the courts often exempted employers from any responsibility for the injury or death of their employees during working hours. In 1893 the General Assembly took a first step in this direc-tion by passing an employer's liability act which was made applicable to "every railroad or other corporation."[32] Because of controversies over its meaning and constitutionality, a somewhat stronger law was enacted in 1911.[33] Finally, in 1913 the legislature authorized Governor Ralston to appoint a special commission to investigate the operation of work-men's compensation laws in other states and to make recom-mendations for Indiana. Two years later the commission made its report, urging a comprehensive program of compul-sory workmen's compensation, but industrial and insurance lobbies opposed it so effectively that the General Assembly

30 *Laws of Indiana*, 1921, pp. 345-346, 351-353.

31 The basic act concerning coal mining was passed in 1879. It was supple-mented by additional legislation over the next twenty years, and in 1905 and 1907 extensive compilations of mine regulations were made by the General Assembly. In 1915 an attempt to codify all coal mining laws failed, and two years later the chief mine inspector reported that increasing mechanization brought a need for new safety regulations. *Ibid.*, 1879, pp. 19-25; 1883, pp. 75-76; 1885, pp. 65-67; 1889, pp. 445-449; 1891, 7-62; 1897, pp. 127-128, 168-170, 226; 1905, pp. 65-81; 1907, pp. 347-353; 1915, pp. 597-598; Indiana *Year Book*, 1917, pp. 397-399.

32 *Laws of Indiana*, 1893, pp. 294-296.

33 *Ibid.*, 1911, pp. 145-149; Ben F. Small, *Workmen's Compensation Law of Indiana* (Indianapolis, 1950), pp. 6, 25.

in 1915 compromised by passing a bill which made coverage voluntary on the part of employers and permitted private insurance companies to write the policies. To administer the system, an Industrial Board appointed by the governor was established with full power to adjudicate conflicting claims and make awards to injured workers and beneficiaries.[34]

Another hard-fought contest was waged to require the inspection and regulation of steam boilers, the explosions of which often caused serious injuries and even death. Despite the submission of a spate of bills calling for boiler inspection in almost every session of the legislature since 1887, when Governor Gray included a strong plea for it in his biennial message to the joint session of the legislature, no action was taken until 1903, when steam boiler safety regulations were enacted and an inspector authorized to enforce them.[35] In an important statute of 1911, moreover, the General Assembly completely reorganized the state's machinery of industrial regulation by creating a new Bureau of Inspection with three subordinate departments responsible for the inspection of buildings, factories, and workshops, the inspection of mines and mining (which was transferred from the Department of Geology and Natural Resources), and the inspection of boilers, each headed by a deputy inspector with two assistants. Then in 1915, when the Industrial Board was created to administer the workmen's compensation system, the Bureau of Inspection was abolished and its duties and powers transferred to the former agency, co-ordinating all, or virtually all, of the state's industrial regulatory activities. Finally, in 1919 the General Assembly added to the Industrial Board a department for women and children headed by a woman director.[36]

In 1909 the state undertook another function on behalf of labor with the passage of a law authorizing the establishment of a free public employment bureau in the Indiana Depart-

<hr />

[34] *Laws of Indiana,* 1913, pp. 897-898; 1915, pp. 392-417; Kennedy, Protective Labor Legislation in Indiana, pp. 23-24.

[35] Indiana *Senate Journal,* 1887, p. 61; *Laws of Indiana,* 1903, pp. 535-536.

[36] *Laws of Indiana,* 1911, pp. 553-556; 1919, pp. 191-192.

ment of Statistics. Private employment agencies were also required to obtain a license from that department. Two years later the General Assembly extended the work of the bureau to include branch offices in Evansville, Fort Wayne, South Bend, and Terre Haute as well as Indianapolis. This agency provided a useful service to both employers and job seekers until 1917, when upon the entrance of the nation into the First World War its work was consolidated with that of the United States Employment Bureau.[37]

§ §

The industrialization of Indiana was accompanied by the emergence of a fairly militant organized labor movement. Among the earliest labor organizations represented in the state were the typographical union, the railroad brotherhoods, and a few of the building craft unions. By the late seventies the Knights of Labor, a broadly based secret society founded in 1869, was one of the most active forces among workingmen, both in some of the larger cities and in the coal mining districts. In 1880 the United States Bureau of the Census reported the existence of seventy-seven labor organizations in Indiana, of which twenty-three were local assemblies of the Knights.[38] At the peak of their influence in the mid-eighties, the Knights of Labor had six assemblies in the cities of Evansville, Indianapolis, South Bend, and Wabash made up entirely of women—housekeepers, seamstresses, cotton mill operatives, and others. Many women also belonged to mixed assemblies, and one Indianapolis woman, Mrs. Catherine Kirn, was a delegate to the 1889 and 1891 national conventions of the Knights.[39]

On Sunday, September 19, 1886, the Knights of Labor collaborated with independent trade unions in holding Indianap-

[37] *Ibid.,* 1909, pp. 375-377; 1911, 654-657; Indiana Department of Statistics, *Biennial Report,* 1909-1910, p. 17; Indiana *Year Book,* 1918, p. 301.

[38] United States Bureau of the Census, *Tenth Census* (1880), XX, *Report on Statistics of Wages* [Pt. 3], pp. 14-18.

[39] *History of Women in Trade Unions (Report on Condition of Women and Child Wage-Earners in the United States,* 61 Congress, 2 session, U.S. *Senate Documents, No. 645,* X, 1911), pp. 128-131.

olis' first Labor Day parade, in which an estimated four thousand persons took part, many of them from outside the city.[40] On December 20 of the same year a state assembly of the Knights of Labor was formed at a meeting in the capital city, and John T. Taylor of Chesterton, Porter County, was elected Master Workman. Early in the following year, the legislative committee of District No. 106, which included local assemblies in Indianapolis plus the area within a fifty-mile radius of the city claiming a membership of nearly seven thousand, met with state legislators from Marion County to propose a broad program of labor legislation which the Knights wished to see enacted during the current session of the General Assembly. Their demands included the abolition of prison contract labor, compulsory school attendance legislation, boiler inspection, a mechanics' lien law, and the establishment of a state labor bureau.[41]

Although a few local assemblies composed of workers in particular industries such as window glass making persisted in Indiana, the Knights of Labor as a whole experienced a sudden and irreversible decline in membership and influence in the late eighties. In its place the craft unions, many of them organized into a national federation by that time, flourished as the main type of labor organization. The first step toward the organization of such a federation was taken in Terre Haute, Indiana, on August 2, 1881, when a small group of

---

[40] Indianapolis *Sentinel,* September 20, 1886; Greencastle *Banner,* September 23, 1886. The first nationwide observance of Labor Day on the first Monday in September was attempted the year before, in 1885. The planners of the 1886 Indianapolis parade had postponed its celebration to a Sunday because participants could not get off work on the earlier Monday. Some Protestant ministers in the city, however, objected strongly to the parade as a violation of the Sabbath. Indianapolis *Sentinel,* September 27, 1886. Other Hoosier cities began to celebrate Labor Day within the next few years. On September 2, 1889, Fort Wayne had its first Labor Day parade. Griswold, *Pictorial History of Fort Wayne,* I, 519.

[41] Indianapolis *Sentinel,* December 21, 22, 1886; Knights of Labor, *Proceedings of the State Convention, 1880,* p. 8; *Organized Labor: Its Position and Some of the Laws It Will Ask For* (Legislative Committee of District No. 106, Knights of Labor, Indianapolis, 1887), pp. 5-7.

union delegates from Chicago, St. Louis, Cleveland, Dayton, Springfield, and Indianapolis met with leaders of the Terre Haute Amalgamated Labor Union to plan co-operative action. Since so few labor organizations were represented at the meeting, the delegates voted to call a larger convention to be held in Pittsburgh later in the year. Samuel L. Leffingwell of Typographical Union No. 1 of Indianapolis, one of the signers of that call, was chairman of the Committee on Planning and Principles at the Pittsburgh conference which on November 15, 1881, brought into existence the Federation of Organized Trades and Labor Unions of the United States and Canada, the predecessor of the American Federation of Labor which was formed five years later.[42]

Meanwhile Hoosier labor leaders initiated a movement for the organization of city and state trade assemblies or federations. Apparently the first city-wide body of this kind in Indiana was the Indianapolis Trades Assembly, which was formed in July, 1880, by representatives of three unions in that city, the printers, cigar makers, and iron molders, under the presidency of Samuel L. Leffingwell, who was also a prominent member of the Knights of Labor. By 1892 the Indianapolis Central Labor Union, as it was known after 1883, comprised eighty-three local labor organizations claiming approximately eleven thousand members.[43] On September 8,

---

[42] Terre Haute *Express,* August 3, 1881; Terre Haute *Saturday Evening Mail,* August 6, 1881; Philip Taft, *The A. F. of L. in the Time of Gompers* (New York, 1957), pp. 8-13. Labor historian Norman J. Ware mentions another Terre Haute labor union, the Knights of Industry, as sharing in the convention in that city in August, 1881. Ware, *The Labor Movement in the United States 1860-1895* (New York, 1929), pp. 245-248. The Indiana delegates present at the Terre Haute meeting were as follows: Samuel L. Leffingwell of the Indianapolis Trades Assembly; James Pierce, F. M. Light, and Simon Neale of Terre Haute Coopers' Union No. 16; Mark W. Moore of Terre Haute Typographical Union No. 76; J. R. Backus, E. P. Pagette, Moses Crapo, John Rupe, Jr., and N. A. Murphy of the Terre Haute Amalgamated Labor Union; and John Toit, James Herring, and Michael Howard of the Terre Haute Iron Molders' Union. Taft, *The A. F. of L. in the Time of Gompers,* p. 19.

[43] Indianapolis *Sentinel,* July 5, 1880; September 3, 1900; *Trade Unions of Indianapolis* [Indianapolis, 1896], p. 2.

1885, delegates from several trade unions plus two assemblies of the Knights of Labor met in Indianapolis to organize a state federation of trade and labor unions and elected Leffingwell its first president. At the second meeting, which was held in the same city on June 8, 1886, the president's opening address took note of the recent Haymarket riot in Chicago and stated his lack of sympathy with "those who perpetrate deeds of lawlessness, violence and disorder." Suggesting that the federation use its influence to elect legislators pledged to support labor reform measures, he announced:[44]

We must proclaim it as a fixed principle with us that our means of obtaining redress for the ills of which we complain are lawful and peaceful; that we recognize the fact that capital has rights which demand our respect, and that we intend to demand of capital a like respect to the rights of that labor which produces wealth and gives to capital all the powers it possesses.

Under the leadership of Leffingwell and his successors in office, especially Edgar A. Perkins, a fellow printer who served as president from 1895 to 1908 and from 1911 to 1913, the Indiana Federation of Labor, as it was later styled, was extremely active in helping form new local unions throughout the state and in lobbying for the passage of factory and labor legislation by the General Assembly. Measures for which it claimed at least partial credit included the child-labor acts of 1897 and subsequent years, the laws restricting prison contract labor, and the establishment of the State Bureau of Inspection in 1914.[45]

44 Indianapolis *Journal* and Indianapolis *Sentinel*, September 9, 1885, June 9, 1886; "State Federation History," in Indiana State Federation of Labor, *Year Book*, 1923, pp. 3-6. An earlier attempt to form a state federation of labor in Indiana in 1873 was apparently stillborn. See Thornbrough, *Indiana in the Civil War Era*, p. 444. Samuel L. Leffingwell, who was born in Ohio in 1830 and served in the United States Army in both the Mexican and the Civil wars, came to Indianapolis in about 1878, and took employment as a printer on the Indianapolis *Sentinel*. Besides his active participation in the organization of the Indianapolis Central Labor Union and the Indiana Federation of Labor, he published a labor journal entitled the *Organette*. He died in Indianapolis in 1903. Indianapolis *Sentinel*, January 16, 1903.

45 Ralph Walden Van Valer, "The Indiana State Federation of Labor," *Indiana Magazine of History*, XI (1915), 40-58. The Indianapolis Central Labor

In fact, the legislature showed itself peculiarly sensitive to the rights of organized labor at this time. As early as 1889, the General Assembly passed a bill which attempted to prevent "blacklisting," a device used by railroad companies in particular in this period to avoid employing union organizers, but an Indiana Supreme Court decision of 1904 considerably weakened the law's effect. In 1889 the legislature also enacted a law aimed at preventing the employment of Pinkerton detectives and similar persons as strikebreakers. This measure placed limits on the power of sheriffs and other law enforcement officers to appoint special deputies, marshals, or policemen to serve during labor disputes and made it unlawful to import any persons from out of state for that purpose. In 1891 the first Monday in September was officially proclaimed a state holiday as Labor Day, and legislation was enacted to legalize the use of union labels. The next session of the General Assembly in 1893 passed a number of bills supported by organized labor, including one making it unlawful to discharge or threaten to discharge an employee for union activities or to exact a pledge of an employee that he would not join a union as a condition of employment.[46] Thus Indiana was a pioneer in outlawing the so-called "yellow-dog contract," though there is little evidence to suggest that this provision was ever actively enforced.

Although the General Assembly authorized the gathering of state labor statistics in 1889, a quarrel between the legis-

Union did not affiliate with the American Federation of Labor until 1894; the Indiana Federation of Labor remained unaffiliated until 1903, when it finally received a charter from the national body. Hugh Gormley, "Indiana: A Union State," *American Federationist* (New York), LV, No. 6 (June, 1948), p. 12.

46 *Laws of Indiana,* 1889, pp. 301-302, 315-316; 1891, pp. 315-320, 394-395; 1893, p. 146; Wabash Railroad Company *v.* Young, 162 Ind. 102 (1904); Fred Witney, *Indiana Labor Relations Law (Indiana Business Report No. 30,* Bloomington, 1960), pp. 4-10. Witney is mistaken in dating the 1889 law as 1905, when it was merely included in a general recodification of statutes concerning public offenses. *Laws of Indiana,* 1905, p. 720. One of the state legislators most active in forwarding labor legislation in the 1893 session of the General Assembly was John W. Kern, later United States Senator from Indiana. Bowers, *Life of John W. Kern,* pp. 93-101.

lature and the chief executive over appointment of the officer in charge of the Department of Statistics delayed any such action for several years. Not until 1894 did William A. Peelle, Jr., a conscientious chief of bureau who was also notably sympathetic to the cause of labor, publish the first official report on trade union activities. Obtaining information from the secretaries of 217 labor organizations representing 66 trades in 22 cities, he reported a total union membership of 19,081, which he assumed, rightly or wrongly, to include 90 per cent of all organized labor in the state. He pointed out, however, that the abnormal industrial conditions following in the wake of the Panic of 1893 had adversely affected union organization. Meetings became irregular and infrequent, many unions collapsed completely, and "a lack of vitality was almost universally observable," he reported.[47]

The Department of Statistics made a further attempt to collect such information in the comparatively prosperous year of 1899, when 408 labor organizations submitted reports claiming 24,424 members. Moreover, the total membership was growing fairly rapidly, for this figure represented an increase of 3,468 over the previous year. Most were members of trade unions though 836 belonged to the Window Glass Workers' Local Assembly 300, apparently the only major element of the fading Knights of Labor remaining by that date.[48] A much more complete report in 1905 indicated that Indiana had become one of the leading states in the country in union membership. According to the calculations of the Department of Statistics in that year there were 72,504 members of 1,280 local unions, 1,278 of which were affiliated with 87 national and international organizations. This included 9,619 persons who belonged to the various unions and brotherhoods of steam and electric railroad workers. An independent organization composed chiefly of Negroes, the American

<hr>

47 Indiana Department of Statistics, *Biennial Report,* 1893-1894, pp. 116-117.
48 *Ibid.,* 1899-1900, pp. 175-176. This report included a long table listing each local union by city, with the name and address of its secretary. *Ibid.,* pp. 157-174.

Hod Carriers' Union, was one of the largest such associations in the United States. Indianapolis, with 7,301 union members, was a stronghold of organized labor and the headquarters of nine international unions, including the Carpenters and Joiners, the Teamsters, the Bricklayers, the Typographical Union, Journeymen Barbers, and the United Mine Workers. The Brotherhood of Painters, Decorators and Paperhangers of America had its international headquarters in Lafayette, Indiana. In addition, the department reported that the Women's Union Label League, which had been founded in Muncie in 1899, was extended throughout the nation with a membership in excess of two thousand, eight hundred of this number in Indiana.[49]

Two years later union membership was reported to have fallen to 66,902, perhaps reflecting the successful drive for the "open shop" on the part of many employers in Indiana which is discussed below. There were 1,043 local unions belonging to 77 national and international organizations, plus 19 local unions affiliated directly with the American Federation of Labor. By far the largest body of organized labor in

[49] *Ibid.*, 1905-1906, pp. 686-691. A number of official union organs were published in Indianapolis in this period, including the *Carpenter* (1905), *Locomotive Firemen and Enginemen's Magazine* (moved from Terre Haute in 1885), *United Mine Workers Journal* (1891), *Typographical Journal* (1893), the *Bricklayer and Mason* (1898), the *Teamster* (1903), and the *Journeyman Barber* (moved from Los Angeles in 1905). In addition the *Labor Signal* was established in 1881 as the organ of the Indianapolis Central Labor Union but was discontinued in 1896. Dunn, *Greater Indianapolis,* I, 395-396. In 1902 eight general labor papers were being published in Indiana: Indianapolis *Union* (official organ of the State Federation of Labor); Evansville *Union Label*; *Gas Belt Labor News* (Anderson); South Bend *Labor Journal*; Marion *Pharos*; Terre Haute *Toiler*; Vincennes *Labor News*; and Fort Wayne *Bulletin*. Indiana Federation of Labor, *Official Proceedings of . . . Annual Convention,* 1902, p. 23. In 1894 the American Federation of Labor transferred its headquarters from New York to Indianapolis as part of a western revolt against the organization's eastern leadership which also cost Samuel Gompers the presidency for one year. Re-elected in 1895, Gompers came to Indianapolis but was unhappy with the location of the federation's main office there and was able to have it moved to Washington, D.C., in 1896. Samuel Gompers, *Seventy Years of Life and Labor. An Autobiography* (2 volumes, New York, 1925), I, 355-361, 370-379.

the state was the United Mine Workers of America, with 18,-822 members in 200 locals, a net increase of 2,184 during the year.[50]

The first organizations among miners in the Indiana coal fields were local assemblies of the Knights of Labor, some of whom joined National District Assembly No. 135 formed in 1886. But a rival association founded in Indianapolis in September, 1885, the National Federation of Miners and Mine Laborers, later renamed the National Progressive Union, soon became the main organizational force among Hoosier miners. Finally, in January, 1890, in a meeting at Columbus, Ohio, the two organizations merged to form the United Mine Workers of America, Indiana's District 11 of the National Progressive Union becoming District 11 of the new association with headquarters at Terre Haute. A Clay County miner, English-born Philip Henry Penna, became an organizer for the United Mine Workers upon its formation in 1890 and served as its president in 1895-1896. Largely because of its geographical position near the center of the coal-mining region, Indianapolis became the site of the union's main offices in 1898.[51]

Although the United Mine Workers remained a relatively weak organization for several years, District 11 was able to negotiate its first state agreement on wage scales with the Indiana Bituminous Coal Association on April 21, 1892, when the latter agreed to pay seventy cents per ton for pick-mined

[50] Indiana Department of Statistics, *Biennial Report,* 1907-1908, pp. 615-625.

[51] Indianapolis *Sentinel,* September 10, 11, 12, 1885; Chris Evans, *History of United Mine Workers of America from . . . 1860 to 1890* (2 volumes, n. p., n. d.), I, 137; II, 4-29, 544. Philip H. Penna came to the United States in 1881 and later became a coal miner in Clay County, Indiana, where he was elected to the presidency of District 11, National Progressive Union, in 1889. After helping to bring District 11 into the United Mine Workers in 1890 and serving the latter organization as vice-president and president, Penna left the ranks of labor to assist in organizing the Indiana Bituminous Coal Association. Secretary of this association from 1902 to 1922, he was well known as a leading authority on coal mining and collective bargaining in Indiana. He died in Terre Haute in 1939. United Mine Workers of America, District Number 11, *50 Years of Progress and Achievement, Golden History 1890-1940* (n. p., 1940); Indianapolis *Star,* January 6, 1939.

coal and a smaller scale for that mined by machines, and offered no objection to the "checkoff" for the collection of union dues. In both 1894 and 1897 Hoosier coal miners suffered heavily when they obeyed the call of the UMW for a nationwide strike, but they also shared in the gains of the Joint Interstate Conference at Chicago in January, 1898, which won a wage increase and the eight-hour day for the four-state competitive field — Illinois, Indiana, Ohio, and western Pennsylvania. Subsequent interstate agreements made annually until 1904 and every two years after that were supplemented and reinforced by state agreements hammered out by representatives of District 11 with the Indiana Bituminous Coal Association, all of which helped to keep a certain measure of industrial peace in the coal mining district.[52]

Organized labor in some other industries, however, entered a severe test of strength with determined antiunion forces in the first two decades of the twentieth century. Employers' protective associations and citizens' alliances were formed shortly after 1900 in such Indiana cities as Columbus, Marion, and Shelbyville in order to fight the so-called "closed shop" by which employers contracted to hire only union members.[53] The open-shop movement in Indiana gained momentum after 1902, when Indianapolis carriage and automobile maker David M. Parry, the newly elected president of the National Association of Manufacturers, initiated a nationwide crusade

[52] The first interstate agreement was negotiated with operators in Ohio, Illinois, Indiana, Pennsylvania, and West Virginia by the National Progressive Union in 1886, but this was short-lived, the Indiana operators withdrawing in 1888. Frank Julian Warne, *The Coal-Mine Workers: A Study in Labor Organization* (New York, 1905), pp. 201-205. The provisions of the first state agreement in Indiana in 1892 are found in United Mine Workers of America, District Number 11, *50 Years of Progress and Achievement*. Besides District 11, the UMW was represented in Indiana by a smaller body of miners in the Brazil block coal field in Clay County, which negotiated separately with its own mine operators. Louis Bloch, *Labor Agreements in Coal Mines . . .* (New York, 1931), pp. 67, 84-85.

[53] Indiana Labor Commission, *Biennial Report*, 1903-1904, p. 18; John R. Commons *et al.*, *History of Labour in the United States* (4 volumes, New York, 1918-1935), IV, 131.

against unionization. A bitter foe of organized labor, Parry persuaded the NAM, which had formerly been concerned chiefly with the promotion of trade and commerce, to launch a campaign for the open shop, organizing for that purpose the Citizens' Industrial Association in 1903. Parry, who also became president of the latter organization, was the chief speaker at its first convention in Indianapolis in February, 1904, when resolutions condemning union labels, the eight-hour day, and an anti-injunction bill pending in Congress were enthusiastically adopted.[54]

The most active open-shop organization in Indiana and one of the most successful in the whole country was the Employers' Association of Indianapolis, founded in 1904 as a leading supporter of the Citizens' Industrial Association. It offered advice and aid to companies involved in strikes or lockouts and urged them to destroy the closed shop, hitherto generally practiced in many industries in the heavily unionized capital city. Absorbing the Commercial Vehicle Protective Association, which was formed to combat a teamsters' strike in 1913, the Employers' Association was reorganized as the Associated Employers of Indianapolis, Inc., comprising about five hundred individuals and firms, and under the aggressive leadership of its secretary, Andrew J. Allen, attempted to reverse the course of unionization in the city. It took credit for the defeat of labor-supported candidates in the local elections of 1914 and for the passage by the Indianapolis city council of an antiboycott ordinance in June, 1916, and an antipicketing ordinance in September, 1919. Moreover, it was so successful in destroying the power of organized labor almost everywhere except in the building trades that by 1920 it could boast that 85 per cent of the man-

[54] Indianapolis *News,* February 22, 23, 1904. Parry, who wrote an antisocialistic novel entitled *The Scarlet Empire,* which was published by the Indianapolis firm of Bobbs-Merrill in 1905, kept up his crusade against unionism until his death in Indianapolis in 1915. Milton Rubincam, "David M. Parry," *Indiana Magazine of History,* XXXIV (1938), 170-174; John Bartlow Martin, *Indiana: An Interpretation* (New York, 1947), pp. 123-128.

ufacturing and business enterprises of Indianapolis were conducted on open-shop principles.[55]

While organized labor remained influential in certain older industrial cities such as Terre Haute, employers in other communities strongly resisted unionization. The furniture manufacturers of Tell City in Perry County, for example, kept labor unions completely out of that small southern Indiana town despite a lengthy strike and lockout which shut down ten factories for a time in the summer of 1907. Other than Indianapolis itself, however, the most important center of antiunion sentiment in the state was highly industrialized Lake County. In 1898 Walter B. Conkey moved his huge printing and bookbinding plant from Chicago to Hammond primarily to avoid employing union printers and successfully fought off all attempts to organize his approximately one thousand employees for ten years in that Lake County city. The Standard Oil Company of Indiana, with a paternalistic policy of providing such benefits as free medical treatment and retirement pensions for its workers, was even more effective in preventing unionization of its great refinery in Whiting.[56]

But the United States Steel Corporation furnished the outstanding example of the influence of an official antiunion labor policy in Indiana. This policy became effective in the state with the building of the company's mills in Gary between 1906 and 1908, and in the latter year the proclamation of the open shop in the plants of its subsidiary, the American Sheet and Tin Plate Company, in Elwood and other cities brought on a long and bitter strike by the Amalgamated Association of Iron and Steel Workers which failed dismally and

[55] Andrew J. Allen, *Business Men in Politics: Political Defeat of Union Labor in Indianapolis* (Indianapolis, 1914); *Labor Conditions and the Open Shop in Indianapolis* (Indianapolis, 1920), pp. 3-7; Clarence E. Bonnett, *Employers' Associations in the United States: A Study of Typical Associations* (New York, 1922), pp. 499-544. See also Indiana Labor Commission, *Biennial Report,* 1905-1906, pp. 77-78, 98-116.

[56] Indiana Labor Commission, *Biennial Report,* 1901-1902, pp. 53-59; 1907-1908, pp. 41-49; Francis M. Trissal, *Public Men of Indiana* (2 volumes, Hammond, Ind., 1923) II, 63-64.

signaled the final decline of that once-powerful union. Moreover, the United States Steel Corporation maintained its policy of resisting union activities among its employees in Gary and elsewhere for the next two and a half decades.[57]

A significant factor in organized labor's loss of influence in Indiana in the early twentieth century was the unfavorable publicity of the dynamite cases involving the Bridge and Structural Iron Workers' Union, which had its international headquarters in Indianapolis. In April, 1911, John J. McNamara, secretary-treasurer of the Iron Workers, was arrested at an executive board meeting of the union in Indianapolis and secretly extradited to California to stand trial with his brother, James B. McNamara, for complicity in the dynamiting of the Los Angeles Times Building. The doubtful legality of the union officer's extradition brought loud protests from the Indianapolis Central Labor Union, the Indiana Federation of Labor, and other quarters, but the subsequent conviction and sentencing to prison of both brothers after they consented to plead guilty on the advice of their defense counsel, the celebrated Chicago attorney Clarence Darrow, badly damaged the cause of organized labor. Moreover, the investigation of the McNamara brothers led to the indictment of fifty-one additional persons on charges of transporting dynamite, most of them members of the Iron Workers' Union. The trial, which took place in the Federal circuit court in Indianapolis presided over by Judge Albert B. Anderson, lasted from October to December, 1912, and aroused tremendous excitement. Despite the efforts of Indiana's pro-labor Democratic Senator, John W. Kern, who acted as an attorney for the defense, the jury found thirty-eight of the forty men brought to trial guilty, including Frank M. Ryan, the Iron Workers' president. Their conviction, which was ultimately

[57] Indiana Labor Commission, *Biennial Report*, 1909-1910, pp. 84-85; Moore, *The Calumet Region*, pp. 492-494, 500-504; *Working Conditions and the Relations of Employers and Employees (Report on Conditions of Employment in the Iron and Steel Industry in the United States*, U. S. *Senate Documents*, 62 Congress, 1 session, *No. 110*, III, 1913), pp. 116-135.

upheld by the United States Supreme Court, was a harsh blow to organized labor and provided further ammunition for the antilabor campaign of manufacturers' associations and other advocates of the open shop.[58]

§ § §

The industrialization of Indiana was not accomplished without a high incidence of often harsh conflict between workers and management over wages, hours, working conditions, and other questions. From the violent railroad riots in the summer of 1877 to the great steel strike of 1919, the state experienced a wide variety of industrial disturbances. According to statistics compiled by the office of the United States Commissioner of Labor, in the twenty-five year period from 1881 to 1905 Indiana was the scene of 1,126 strikes affecting 3,533 establishments and 160,847 employees, as well as 53 lockouts in 233 establishments involving 4,373 employees. Only six states—New York, Pennsylvania, Illinois, Massachusetts, New Jersey, and Ohio—reported a greater frequency of strikes than Indiana, where the largest number of them occurred in the coal mining, glass, metal working, and tobacco industries. The following table shows the incidence of strikes year by year during this period:

STRIKES IN INDIANA, 1881-1905[59]

| Year | Number of strikes | Number of striking employees | Year | Number of strikes | Number of striking employees |
|------|------|------|------|------|------|
| 1881 | 11 | 1,056 | 1886 | 31 | 3,968 |
| 1882 | 10 | 713 | 1887 | 25 | 7,291 |
| 1883 | 15 | 3,208 | 1888 | 16 | 940 |
| 1884 | 11 | 4,211 | 1889 | 16 | 4,682 |
| 1885 | 21 | 1,949 | 1890 | 26 | 2,441 |

[58] Indianapolis *Star,* April 24, 25, May 3, 1911; Indianapolis *News,* December 25, 28, 1912; July 25, 1914; Indiana Federation of Labor, *Official Proceedings of . . . Annual Convention,* 1911, pp. 82-85; Louis Adamic, *Dynamite. The Story of Class Violence in America* (New York, 1931), pp. 200-253.

[59] United States Commissioner of Labor, *Annual Report, 1901, Strikes and Lockouts,* pp. 60-63; *ibid.,* 1906, pp. 184-195, 550-553, 652-655.

STRIKES IN INDIANA, 1881-1905—Cont.

| Year | Number of strikes | Number of striking employees | Year | Number of strikes | Number of striking employees |
|------|------|------|------|------|------|
| 1891 | 40 | 11,235 | 1899 | 36 | 5,397 |
| 1892 | 26 | 2,239 | 1900 | 65 | 6,765 |
| 1893 | 36 | 6,202 | 1901 | 123 | 18,322 |
| 1894 | 30 | 11,226 | 1902 | 133 | 11,185 |
| 1895 | 44 | 5,352 | 1903 | 172 | 22,678 |
| 1896 | 14 | 4,160 | 1904 | 91 | 13,398 |
| 1897 | 38 | 3,249 | 1905 | 55 | 4,455 |
| 1898 | 41 | 4,525 | | | |

From 1906 through 1913 no similar statistics were gathered, and those compiled by the United States Bureau of Labor Statistics after 1914 are less detailed. There is no information available concerning the number of employees involved, but the incidence of strikes seems to have declined from the peak years of 1901-1904. The number of strikes reported were 45 in 1914, 30 in 1915, 75 in 1916, 73 in 1917, 76 in 1918, 106 in 1919, and 99 in 1920.[60]

One of the most volatile labor situations in the whole state existed in the western Indiana coal fields, especially before the organization of the United Mine Workers. In 1881 over five hundred coal miners struck for three months in an unsuccessful attempt to prevent a reduction in wages. Another protracted strike involving a much larger number of men took place in the spring of 1884, when Parke, Sullivan, and Vigo County miners joined 3,500 strikers in the Brazil block coal region who had walked out to protest a 25 per cent reduction in the price of mining demanded by the operators. After a few weeks the miners returned to work at the reduced rates. Equally unsuccessful was the seven-month strike of the Clay County block coal miners in 1889 and the

60 Florence Peterson, *Strikes in the United States, 1880-1936* (United States Bureau of Labor Statistics, *Bulletin No. 651*, 1937), p. 37.

November, 1891, walkout of nearly every miner in the state.[61]

The first major outbreak of violence in the mining district occurred during the general strike called by the UMW in 1894, when striking miners of Clay, Daviess, and Sullivan counties attempted to prevent the operators from marketing coal on hand by stopping trains and detaching or derailing cars. In June, Governor Matthews dispatched nine companies of state militia to Cannelburg, Daviess County, but the mobs reported there had dispersed before the soldiers' arrival; six companies, plus others withdrawn from Daviess County, were sent to Sullivan County, where they remained twenty days before order was fully restored.[62] During the second general strike of 1897 little disorder occurred, though seventy-five Negro miners alleged to be "armed to the teeth" were brought in from Kentucky to work in Washington, Daviess County. Governor Mount appointed a two-man commission to visit the entire mining district and investigate the condition of the out-of-work miners. When the commission reported that the mine workers had not been paid "decent, living wages," and that they and their families were near destitution, the Governor took the unprecedented step of appealing to the people of the state for help and established a central relief committee to receive and distribute food and clothing to the needy strikers.[63]

[61] Indiana Mine Inspector, *Annual Report,* 1880-1881, p. 69; 1884, pp. 10, 15-16; Indiana Department of Statistics, *Annual Report,* 1884, pp. 224-225; Indiana Department of Geology and Natural Resources, *Annual Report,* 1891, pp. 275-276. In 1884 the Knights of Labor purchased a coal mine at Cannelburg, Indiana, as part of their scheme of producers' co-operatives, but sold it several years later after suffering large losses. Jacob H. Hollander and George E. Barnett (eds.), *Studies in American Trade Unionism* (New York, 1907), pp. 367-368.

[62] Indiana Department of Statistics, *Biennial Report,* 1893-1894, pp. 236-237; Indiana *House Journal,* 1895, pp. 26-27.

[63] Indiana Labor Commission, *Biennial Report,* 1897-1898, p. 18; Indiana Department of Statistics, *Biennial Report,* 1897-1898, pp. 19-25; Indiana *Senate Journal,* 1899, p. 25.

A few scattered eight-hour-day demonstrations and strikes took place in Indiana in early May, 1886, at the call of the Federation of Organized Trades and Labor. Walkouts in furniture factories, bakeries, metal shops, and elsewhere, as well as strikes among some of the building trades were only partially and temporarily successful. The Knights of Labor, whose national leaders were unenthusiastic about the eight-hour-day movement, celebrated the occasion by a mass meeting of workingmen in Indianapolis on May 1.[64] The Haymarket bombing in Chicago at this time, however, caused popular sentiment to turn against organized labor in general and anarchists, to whom the deed was attributed, in particular. When the Reverend Oscar C. McCulloch of Plymouth Congregational Church in Indianapolis publicly advocated a new trial for the convicted anarchists in November, 1886, he brought down upon his head a flood of abuse.[65]

Indiana also had a part in the Pullman strike in the summer of 1894, when Terre Haute's fiery labor leader, Eugene V. Debs, called upon the members of the American Railway Union, of which he was the founder and president, to cease handling Pullman cars on all lines. Work stoppages, most of them brief, occurred on the Big Four, the Vandalia, and other roads, and violence erupted in the shops of the Chicago and Eastern Illinois Railroad in Brazil.[66] But the chief dis-

64 Indianapolis *News,* May 3, 4, 5, 8, 1886. For an editorial vehemently opposing the eight-hour day, see the Indianapolis *Sentinel,* May 5, 1886.

65 Greencastle *Times,* May 6, 1886; *Indiana Christian Advocate* (Indianapolis), September 22, November 17, 1887; Indianapolis *News,* November 29, 30, 1886. In 1887 District No. 106 of the Knights of Labor of Indiana felt it necessary to state that "we are not anarchists," while at the same time expressing some sympathy for the accused Chicago anarchists. *Organized Labor,* p. 3.

66 Terre Haute *Express,* July 4, 6, 16, 1894. In Crawfordsville General Lew Wallace was reported to be organizing two companies of local militia to counteract possible disorders. *Ibid.,* July 10, 1894. Three years after the failure of the Pullman strike one small-town Hoosier editor voiced this harshly unfavorable assessment of Eugene V. Debs as a labor leader: "Debs may be sincere but he is wrong. His cleverness, affability and show of sympathy with laborers makes him all the more subtly dangerous. Debs needs an education which he may get only too late and at the end of a rope, if he does not cease his inflammatory and anarchistic utterances. The greatest favor he can bestow upon the

turbances took place in Lake County communities adjacent to
Chicago, where the struggle centered. Many citizens of Hammond, East Chicago, and Whiting sympathized with the strikers, and some participated in demonstrations. Thomas E.
Knotts urged strikers to defy a Federal injunction which
enjoined all persons from interfering with the mails and the
flow of interstate transportation. He was arrested and charged
with attempting to intimidate the engineer and fireman of a
locomotive. Knotts was said to be an agent of Debs, but unlike Debs, who was later sentenced to six months in prison
for contempt of court under the same injunction, Knotts was
never brought to trial. Soldiers of the United States Army
accompanying a work train fired upon rioters in Hammond
on July 8, wounding three persons and killing a bystander.
As a result both Hammond and Whiting were placed under
martial law. But after several companies of Indiana militia
equipped with a Gatling gun arrived a few days later to replace the Federal troops, no more lives were lost, and order
was restored.[67]

At its height in the nineties the glass industry was beset
by labor disputes, sixty-two strikes having been recorded by
1900.[68] Some disturbances took place in plate-glass factories,
which employed chiefly unskilled labor, but the window-glass
plants were the main focus of trouble. For more than two
years at the end of the century a furious struggle was waged
among the various branches of the highly organized window-
glass workers—blowers, gatherers, fasteners, and cutters—
most of whom belonged to Local Assembly 300, Knights of
Labor, though rival unions affiliated with the American Fed-

working men of this country would be retirement." Greencastle *Banner-Times,*
September 15, 1897.

67 Moore, *The Calumet Region,* pp. 494-496. In order to finance the dispatch of state militia to Lake County shortly after troops had been sent to restore order in the coal miners' strike in Daviess and Sullivan counties, Governor
Matthews had to borrow $41,917.49 from three Indianapolis banks on his own
personal note. Indiana *House Journal,* 1895, pp. 28-29.

68 United States Commissioner of Labor, *Annual Report, 1901, Strikes and
Lockouts,* p. 200.

eration of Labor were gaining strength. In the glass-bottle industry both major labor organizations, the American Flint Glass Workers' Union and the Glass Bottle Blowers' Association, fought the many nonunion factories which sprang up in the Indiana Gas Belt in this period. Jurisdictional disputes also broke out between the two unions, and in 1900 the A.F.G.W.U. attempted to compete successfully by establishing its own prescription bottle and flask plant at Summitville, a venture which lasted only three years and failed to prevent the majority of the flask workers from going over to the rival association.[69] Moreover, the introduction of labor-saving machinery at the turn of the century was the cause of a number of strikes and lockouts which eventuated in a sharp reduction in the unskilled working force in many Gas Belt glass factories.[70]

In 1897 the Indiana General Assembly passed a labor arbitration bill which established a two-man labor commission, appointed by the governor, to offer mediation and voluntary arbitration services to participants in labor disputes. Upon receiving information of any strike, lockout, boycott, or other labor disturbance, the commissioners, one of whom represented labor and the other the employing interest, were to proceed to the place of the dispute and tender their services as mediators. If they were unable to reconcile the parties, they were directed to endeavor to induce them to submit their differences to arbitration. In such a case the two commissioners together with the judge of the circuit court of the county in which the dispute took place constituted the board of arbitration. If arbitration was refused, the labor commissioners were empowered to investigate the dispute thoroughly and make their report to the governor.[71] At first the commission

69 Indiana Labor Commission, *Biennial Report*, 1899-1900, pp. 6-9; Ellsworth Steele, "The Flint Glass Workers' Union in the Indiana Gas Belt and the Ohio Valley in the 1890's," *Indiana Magazine of History*, L (1954), 237-250.

70 Indiana Department of Statistics, *Biennial Report*, 1899-1900, p. 210.

71 *Laws of Indiana*, 1897, pp. 130-136. The law was amended in 1899 broadening the powers of the labor commission to include investigation of disputes in which less than fifty persons were involved. *Ibid.*, 1899, pp. 202-209.

seemed to be extraordinarily successful in mediating labor difficulties, reporting in 1898 that despite the activities of "superserviceable labor agitators, whose zealous and often honest efforts are exerted in trying to promote legitimate ends by unwise counsels," it had ended thirty-two strikes or lockouts out of the thirty-nine investigated during the first eighteen months after the law's passage.[72] As late as 1906 the commission claimed that "the number of settlements by arbitration and conciliation during the past two years will exceed the number of strikes by a ratio of 20 to 1."[73]

Yet the bitter struggle over the open shop hindered efforts for mediation and conciliation, and both employers and organized labor became reluctant to accept the services of the commission. In the fourteen years of the law's operation, formal arbitration was elected by the parties in dispute in only four instances out of the 228 cases investigated. Moreover, in eighty-six cases the commissions failed to terminate a strike or lockout by the process of mediation.[74]

The most noteworthy failures of the labor commission to halt labor disturbances in the state occurred in a series of interurban and street railway strikes in which the companies involved refused to recognize or treat with the union and used strikebreakers to maintain service on their lines. The first took place in 1903 in South Bend, where strike sympathizers assaulted nonunion motormen and conductors and attempted to wreck the Indiana Railway Company's powerhouse. Two similar strikes brought great disorders to Evansville in 1907 and 1909, resulting in several deaths and injuries. In the latter dispute the presence of Governor Marshall, who came to the city to discuss matters with the strikers and others, failed to have any more effect than the efforts of the labor commissioners themselves. An even more serious situation arose in Muncie in 1908, when a strike against

---

[72] Indiana Labor Commission, *Biennial Report,* 1897-1898, pp. 8-15; Witney, *Indiana Labor Relations Law,* pp. 43-44.

[73] Indiana Labor Commission, *Biennial Report,* 1905-1906, p. 5.

[74] Witney, *Indiana Labor Relations Law,* p. 44.

the Indiana Union Traction Company initiated a demonstration and riot on January 3 which the local police proved unable to handle. The next day, upon the urgent request of the distraught mayor, Governor Hanly proclaimed a state of martial law in Muncie and the surrounding territory within a radius of four miles of the courthouse and dispatched thirteen companies of militia to restore order. But when the Delaware County sheriff deputized five hundred local businessmen and others and ordered them to patrol the city's streets, the disturbance ended without the active assistance of the troops who were gradually withdrawn after five days, though martial law remained in effect for two weeks. On March 2 the strikers surrendered, and business was resumed on the traction lines, thus ending what the labor commission called "the most costly strike in the history of the State."[75]

In 1911 the legislature abolished the labor commission and transferred its duties and powers to the deputy inspectors of buildings and mines under the newly established Bureau of Inspection.[76] Yet during the short four-year existence of that agency there was only one significant attempt to settle a labor dispute by mediation. This was in connection with the Indianapolis street railway strike of 1913, when eight hundred streetcar operators stopped work from October 31 to November 7 in an endeavor to gain union recognition as well as higher wages and improved working conditions. During the strike mob action destroyed a great deal of property and caused the deaths of three persons and injuries to many more. Governor Ralston called out the entire Indiana National Guard, 1,800 men, to re-establish order and intervened personally to halt the strike after the railway company rejected mediation offers by both the state Bureau of Inspection and the United States Department of Labor. Upon the Governor's suggestion, the newly created Public Service Commission acted as a board of arbitration, which finally

75 Indiana Labor Commission, *Biennial Report,* 1903-1904, pp. 34-39; 1907-1908, pp. 15-26, 66-84; 1909-1910, pp. 62-74.

76 *Laws of Indiana,* 1911, pp. 553-556.

made an award acceptable to both the company and its employees.[77]

The Indianapolis streetcar strike and another walkout by teamsters in the same city a few weeks later, both of which were accompanied by some violence, created a demand for a system of compulsory arbitration. After Governor Ralston made a strong plea for new and more effective legislation of this kind in his biennial message, the General Assembly enacted into law in 1915 a mediation bill similar to that of 1897. But not only did it omit any provision for compulsory arbitration, it also failed to establish a permanent, full-time agency to handle the mediation and conciliation of labor disputes. This proved to be a fatal defect in the administration of the act, for, though the governor was empowered to appoint a three-man board to mediate in specific disputes involving fifty or more employees, the law was rarely invoked.[78]

The reason for this inaction was certainly not the absence of industrial strife, since Indiana was plagued by a succession of severe labor disturbances in the next few years. In April, 1919, five companies of militia were sent to Linton in Greene County to halt rioting and demonstrations resulting from a strike of the operators of the Home Telephone Company in that coal-mining community. In August of the same year the inability of county and city officials to control lawlessness and riots in conjunction with a strike at the Standard Steel Car Company in Hammond required the dispatch of eleven companies of state troops, who remained in the city for a week.[79] The worst disorders of all broke out hardly more

[77] Indianapolis *Star,* November 7, 1913; United States Department of Labor, *Annual Report,* 1913, pp. 18-19; *Survey* (New York), XXXI (October, 1913-March, 1914), 193-194, 665; Carl H. Mote, *Industrial Arbitration . . .* (Indianapolis, 1916), pp. 202-204; Witney, *Indiana Labor Relations Law,* pp. 46-47.

[78] *Laws of Indiana,* 1915, pp. 507-512; Witney, *Indiana Labor Relations Law,* pp. 47-49.

[79] Indiana *Year Book,* 1919, pp. 739-740; Moore, *The Calumet Region,* pp. 524-527. An earlier strike at the Standard Steel Car Company in Hammond in January, 1910, was apparently the result of the organization there of a local

than a month later in Gary and East Chicago, where the great steel strike which began on September 22, culminated in violent clashes between strikers and strikebreakers. When the Lake County sheriff requested assistance "to protect life and property and the dignity of the state of Indiana," Governor Goodrich complied by sending twelve companies of militia to the beleaguered cities and later reinforced these units with four additional companies. In Gary, however, the National Guard could not cope with the situation, and after an unruly mob of strikers and strike sympathizers, many of them war veterans, defied the militia on October 7, Mayor William F. Hodges asked for Federal troops. Over a thousand soldiers of the United States Army were quartered in Gary until the end of the year.[80]

The presence of state and Federal troops not only brought law and order to Lake County but also helped to break the strike, which ended at the Gary mills of the United States Steel Corporation on January 8, 1920, without a single concession to the strikers. Another major factor in the strike's failure was the use of strikebreakers, many of them Mexicans and Negroes imported into the Calumet Region for that purpose. A great many of the strikers were foreigners while the native-born workers tended to be indifferent or even hostile to union efforts to organize the steel plants. Lack of harmony between the American Federation of Labor's Samuel Gompers and the radical strike leader, William Z. Foster,

union of the radical Industrial Workers of the World. Harry Slough, the Indiana labor commissioner who was sent to Hammond to attempt to mediate the struggle, was unsympathetic to the I. W. W. and unsuccessful in his endeavors at reconciliation. After a few weeks of picketing and some violence, the strikers went back to work with the promise of an adjustment of their grievances and increased wages but no recognition of the union. I. W. W. leaders, however, claimed a victory. Indiana Labor Commission, *Biennial Report,* 1909-1910, pp. 60-62; *Lake County Times* (Hammond), January 18, 28, 31, February 2, 1910; Philip S. Foner, *History of the Labor Movement in the United States* (4 volumes, New York, 1947-65), IV, 295-299.

80 Indiana *Year Book,* 1920, pp. 226-230; Moore, *The Calumet Region,* pp. 511-523.

also contributed to the collapse of the walkout. Moreover, the latter claimed later that the failure of the strikes in Gary and East Chicago weakened the whole movement to organize the steel industry in the rest of the nation.[81]

[81] Moore, *The Calumet Region,* pp. 523-524; William Z. Foster, *The Great Steel Strike, and Its Lessons* (New York, 1920), pp. 170-172.

# CHAPTER IX

# POPULATION AND URBANIZATION

IN 1916 INDIANA CELEBRATED the one hundredth anniversary of its admission to the Union as the nineteenth state. It was an occasion for the display of state pride and patriotism, with many a backward glance and nostalgic reminiscence. Under the guidance of the Indiana Centennial Commission, Indianapolis, Bloomington, and other communities organized parades and pageants colorfully portraying the scenes of the state's early history. Yet proud as they were of the pioneer past, Hoosiers in the second decade of the twentieth century were well aware of the rapid transformation of their state from a predominantly rural, agrarian order into an increasingly urban, industrial society. Even the rude, rustic popular image of the state's inhabitants was changing, as native-son critic Meredith Nicholson pointed out in a new edition of his study of Indiana literature, *The Hoosiers*, republished in 1915 in anticipation of the centennial. Indiana, he announced, "has contributed men and women of character and genius to every department of human activity, and in cultural fields their attainments often have won the crown of fame. Increasing respect, bordering upon affection, attends the name Hoosier (once employed in reproach!) wherever it may be spoken."[1]

Yet Nicholson and many of his contemporaries tended to conceive of Indiana as a "typical American State," which was considered to represent the mean rather than any particularly distinguishing feature of national character. Describing the state as a "barometer of American temper" in an

[1] Meredith Nicholson, *The Hoosiers* (Revised edition, New York, 1915), p. 290.

address in 1916 before the Ohio Valley Historical Association meeting in Indianapolis as part of the centennial celebration, the well-known historian Frederick L. Paxson argued that

Indiana approximates an average of America and closely resembles the composite that the various corners of our country might present could they be brought together and intermingled. It is an average that makes a State with fewer of the very rich, with fewer of the very poor, with fewer of the foreign born, with a larger proportion of the home born than most of our other States; that makes a community born within itself, enlarging its own traditions and carrying on its own ideals; and because of the trend of its history it is singularly American in its point of view.[2]

A few years later another observer, pointing out that at the turn of the century the imaginary center of United States population was located near Columbus, Indiana, commented that "a fair case might be made out to the effect that the typical American of 1900 had possibly more points of identity with the typical inhabitant of an Indiana community than with most other persons in other backgrounds."[3]

What does it mean to say that Indiana was a typical American state? These last, frequently cited, statements to that effect seem merely to argue that Indiana retained something of the older, nineteenth-century quality of American life and society at a time when much of the country was rapidly changing under the impact of industrialization and urbanization; or, stated somewhat differently, that Indiana itself, while moving in the same general direction as the more industrialized and urbanized states of the Union, was changing slowly enough to remain near the median point of the entire United States. An analysis of the composition and distribution of its population in the twenty years before and

2 Harlow Lindley (ed.), *The Indiana Centennial 1916* (Indiana Historical Commission, Indianapolis, 1919), pp. 330, 333.

3 Mark Sullivan, *Our Times, The United States, 1900-1925* (6 volumes, New York, 1926), I, 3. For similar reasons social scientists Robert and Helen Lynd selected Muncie, Indiana, as a representative American community for the subject of their *Middletown: A Study in Contemporary American Culture* (New York, 1929).

after the century's turning may throw some light on this proposition.

Indiana as a whole enjoyed a steady rise in population during this forty-year span, adding nearly a million residents by 1920, approximately a 50 per cent gain over the population in 1880. But its growth was considerably below that of most other midwestern states, and it declined from sixth to ninth place among all the states in the nation in size of population between 1880 and 1920. The urban-rural ratio remained very close to the national average, while manifesting a much slower pace of urbanization than neighboring Illinois or Ohio. According to the decennial reports of the United States Bureau of the Census, rural population continued to rise slowly until 1900, after which it began an abrupt downward slide. Over this whole period the urban sector—defined in the Federal census as comprising all those living in communities of 2,500 or more persons—rose both absolutely and relatively until it slightly exceeded half the total population of the state in 1920. The following table indicates the growth by decades:

### URBAN AND RURAL POPULATION IN INDIANA, 1880-1920[4]

| Year | Total population | Urban population | | Rural population | |
|------|------------------|--------|----------|--------|----------|
|      |                  | Number | Per cent | Number | Per cent |
| 1880 | 1,978,301 | 386,211 | 19.5 | 1,592,090 | 80.5 |
| 1890 | 2,192,404 | 590,039 | 26.9 | 1,602,365 | 73.1 |
| 1900 | 2,516,462 | 862,689 | 34.3 | 1,653,773 | 65.7 |
| 1910 | 2,700,876 | 1,143,835 | 42.4 | 1,557,041 | 57.6 |
| 1920 | 2,930,390 | 1,482,855 | 50.6 | 1,447,535 | 49.4 |

Moreover, population growth in Indiana was distributed unevenly, some counties experiencing rapid expansion while others actually reported a gradually shrinking number of residents during most of this period. In general the shift was northward and cityward at the expense of the largely rural counties south of the National Road. Although only three

[4] Compiled from the United States Bureau of the Census, *Thirteenth Census* (1910), I, *Population,* pp. 56-57; *Fourteenth Census* (1920), I, *Population,* pp. 46-47.

counties lost population absolutely in the seventies, twenty-five suffered such a loss in the eighties, fourteen in the nineties, and as many as fifty-six in the decade 1900-1910 and sixty-four between 1910 and 1920. Those most affected by this depopulation were Boone, Brown, Carroll, Crawford, Dearborn, Franklin, Jefferson, Ohio, Putnam, and Switzerland. In the south only Knox, Monroe, and Vanderburgh made appreciable gains, while Floyd remained stable. In the central district Delaware, Fayette, Grant, Henry, Howard, Madison, Marion, Tippecanoe, Vermillion, Vigo, and Wayne counties generally expanded, though the Gas Belt counties of Delaware, Grant, and Madison had their growth slowed or even halted for a time around 1900. In the north Allen, Elkhart, La Porte, and St. Joseph counties registered gains, but none so spectacularly as heavily industrialized Lake County, which quadrupled its population between 1900 and 1920.[5]

A key factor in this pattern of population distribution was urbanization, which in turn was closely related to access to natural resources and transportation facilities. The older Ohio River cities stagnated in this period with the notable exception of Evansville, which, close to workable coal deposits and with good transportation both by water and rail, remained the second city in Indiana until 1920, when it fell behind Fort Wayne, a major railroad and manufacturing center in the northeastern section of the state. Terre Haute, an important hub of coal mining and railroad development in the earlier part of this period, slipped from fourth to fifth rank in the same year, overtaken by fast-growing South Bend in the industrial north. But the community which experienced the most phenomenal growth of all was Gary, Chicago's new "satellite" city built by United States Steel on the southern shore of Lake Michigan in Lake County, Indiana, in 1906; by 1920 it had reached a population of 55,000. Of the six Hoosier cities which ranged between 25,000 and 50,000 inhabitants in 1920, all but Richmond were the product of comparatively

5 *Ibid., Fourteenth Census* (1920), I, *Population,* pp. 102-103.

recent industrialization: Anderson, Kokomo, and Muncie in the Gas Belt, and Hammond and East Chicago in Lake County. Nineteen cities in 1920 boasted a population of from 10,-000 to 25,000 residents, only three of which—Jeffersonville, New Albany, and Vincennes—were located in the south. Their number included the older, established commercial and industrial centers of Elkhart, Lafayette, Logansport, and Michigan City, as well as rising cities in or near the Gas Belt such as Elwood, Marion, and New Castle. Among the last to attain the class of 10,000 population were Clinton in the coal-mining district and the oil-refinery city of Whiting in Lake County.

The only city to reach 100,000 population in this period was Indianapolis, which passed that mark in 1890, slightly more than doubled in size during the next two decades, and approached a third of a million residents by 1920. The capital city's importance was enhanced by its central geographic location in the state and especially by its position at the intersection of a great network of steam railroads and, later, electric interurban lines. Yet, despite its rapid rate of growth in this period, Indianapolis did not become a great metropolis on the order of Chicago, Cleveland, or Detroit in neighboring states. Although it gained a few residential suburbs, most of them after the mid-seventies, and annexed some of them in the nineties and later, it failed to develop a populous "metropolitan district" in its environs. According to Federal census statistics, the suburban area within a radius of ten miles of Indianapolis grew only 19.5 per cent in population between 1910 and 1920, while the number of residents of the city proper increased 34.5 per cent.[6] With its broad, tree-lined

6 *Ibid.,* p. 64. The first of Indianapolis' suburban towns was Broad Ripple, which was laid out north of the city in 1837 in anticipation of the building of the Central Canal which connected it with the capital; it was annexed in 1923. In the early 1900's it became well known as a recreation and amusement center. *A History of Broad Ripple,* prepared and published by the Junior Historical Society and the Riparian newspaper of Broad Ripple High School (Indianapolis, 1968). Another suburban town was Irvington, which was laid out four miles east of the city in 1870 by Jacob B. Julian and Sylvester Johnson. Named for Washington Irving and carefully planned as a residential suburb

streets and diagonal avenues radiating from Monument Circle, Indianapolis was often described as a "city of homes." It had the air not so much of a large industrial urban center as of a "provincial capital," which had become "a city rather against its will," in the words of a distinguished resident.[7] The following table shows the changes in population of the thirty-one cities with 10,000 or more residents in 1920:

## POPULATION OF MAJOR INDIANA CITIES, 1880-1920[8]

| Cities | 1880 | 1890 | 1900 | 1910 | 1920 |
|---|---|---|---|---|---|
| Indianapolis | 75,056 | 105,436 | 169,164 | 233,650 | 314,194 |
| Fort Wayne | 26,880 | 35,393 | 45,115 | 63,933 | 86,549 |
| Evansville | 29,280 | 50,756 | 59,007 | 69,647 | 85,264 |
| South Bend | 13,280 | 21,819 | 35,999 | 53,684 | 70,983 |
| Terre Haute | 26,042 | 30,217 | 36,673 | 58,127 | 66,083 |
| Gary | — | — | — | 16,802 | 55,378 |
| Muncie | 5,219 | 11,345 | 20,942 | 24,005 | 36,524 |
| Hammond | — | 5,428 | 12,376 | 20,925 | 36,004 |
| East Chicago | — | 1,255 | 3,411 | 19,098 | 35,967 |
| Kokomo | 4,042 | 8,261 | 10,609 | 17,010 | 30,067 |
| Anderson | 4,126 | 10,741 | 20,178 | 22,476 | 29,767 |

it was not annexed to the city until 1902. Brightwood was platted in 1872 as an industrial suburb and was the location after 1877 of the repair shops of the Cleveland, Columbus, Cincinnati and Indianapolis Railroad. It was annexed to Indianapolis in March, 1897, along with such other industrial towns as West Indianapolis, where the stockyards were built in 1877, and Haughville, a manufacturing community with a large Negro and immigrant population. Woodruff Place, created in 1872 as a residential park, successfully resisted annexation until 1962 though it was soon entirely surrounded by the city. Two other separate suburban towns organized in this period were Beech Grove, which grew up around the huge Big Four (New York Central) Railroad shops located there in 1906 and University Heights, where Indiana Central College was built in 1905-1906. Taking on something of the character of a suburb was Fort Benjamin Harrison, a United States Army Post located northeast of Indianapolis in 1903. Dunn, *Greater Indianapolis,* I, 434-444.

[7] Nicholson, *The Provincial American and Other Papers,* p. 67. While noting that "the great wave of growth and prosperity" had made a new city of the Indiana capital, Nicholson argued that "the distinguishing quality of Indianapolis, however, continues . . . to be its simple domesticity. The people are home-loving and home-keeping." *Ibid.,* pp. 69-70. For a picture of life in Indianapolis just before and after the turn of the century, see Charlotte Cathcart, *Indianapolis from Our Old Corner* (Indiana Historical Society, 1965).

[8] Compiled from the United States Bureau of the Census, *Tenth Census* (1880), *Population,* pp. 147-155; *Twelfth Census* (1900), I, *Population,* Pt. 1, pp. 446-448; *Fourteenth Census* (1920), I, *Population,* pp. 320-321.

POPULATION OF MAJOR INDIANA CITIES—Cont.

| Cities | 1880 | 1890 | 1900 | 1910 | 1920 |
|---|---|---|---|---|---|
| Richmond | 12,742 | 16,608 | 18,226 | 22,324 | 26,765 |
| Elkhart | 6,953 | 11,360 | 15,184 | 19,282 | 24,277 |
| Marion | 3,182 | 8,769 | 17,377 | 19,359 | 23,747 |
| New Albany | 16,423 | 21,059 | 20,628 | 20,629 | 22,992 |
| Lafayette | 14,860 | 16,243 | 18,116 | 20,081 | 22,486 |
| Logansport | 11,198 | 13,328 | 16,204 | 19,050 | 21,626 |
| Michigan City | 7,366 | 10,776 | 14,850 | 19,027 | 19,457 |
| Vincennes | 7,680 | 8,853 | 10,249 | 14,895 | 17,160 |
| Mishawaka | 2,640 | 3,371 | 5,560 | 11,886 | 15,195 |
| La Porte | 6,195 | 7,126 | 7,113 | 10,525 | 15,158 |
| New Castle | 2,299 | 2,697 | 3,406 | 9,446 | 14,458 |
| Huntington | 3,863 | 7,328 | 9,491 | 10,272 | 14,000 |
| Peru | 5,280 | 7,028 | 8,463 | 10,910 | 12,410 |
| Bloomington | 2,756 | 4,018 | 6,460 | 8,838 | 11,595 |
| Frankfort | 2,803 | 5,919 | 7,100 | 8,634 | 11,585 |
| Clinton | 965 | 1,365 | 2,918 | 6,229 | 10,962 |
| Elwood | 751 | 2,284 | 12,950 | 11,028 | 10,790 |
| Whiting | —— | 1,408 | 3,983 | 6,587 | 10,145 |
| Crawfordsville | 5,251 | 6,089 | 6,649 | 9,371 | 10,139 |
| Jeffersonville | 9,357 | 10,666 | 10,774 | 10,412 | 10,098 |

Much of the increase in urban population in these years was drawn from the rural areas of the state and especially from the less-developed southern counties. But a large-scale migration from other states also helped to swell the number of residents in Indiana cities. By 1900 nearly five hundred thousand Hoosier residents had been born outside Indiana, including about 20 per cent of the native white Americans and over half the Negroes. The neighboring states of Ohio and Kentucky led in furnishing settlers, followed by Illinois, Pennsylvania, New York, and Michigan. Yet this influx was at least partially offset by the outward flow of population to other states. In the eighties and nineties thousands of native Hoosiers joined the western trek which created a "greater Indiana" in the plains of Iowa, Kansas, Missouri, and Nebraska. But in the twentieth century this emigration began to shift to the industrialized urban areas of Illinois, Ohio, Michigan, and even the far frontier of California, which thus competed with Indiana's own cities in attracting new residents.[9]

9 James V. Chittick, The Greater Indiana: A Study of the Movement of Hoosiers to Other States (M. A. thesis in History, Indiana University, 1940), pp. 21-22, 41-46.

Another element in the population of the state was made up of European immigrants. Although Indiana absorbed many thousands of Germans, Irish, and other northern Europeans in the nineteenth century, it remained remarkably homogeneous, with a proportion of foreign-born residents which was extremely small in comparison with most other industrial states. Moreover, Indiana was very little affected by the "deleterious influence," as one Hoosier historian described it, of the immigrants from southern and eastern Europe who entered the United States in such large numbers from the 1890's, to the 1920's. Expressing a popular contemporary view of the so-called "new immigrants," he boasted that the state had almost completely missed "the pollution of the stream of political and social intelligence by their thirty per cent of illiteracy and their inexperience in democratic government, their different culture and beliefs, their garliced meat and potato and bandanna handkerchief standard of living." On the other hand, he noted that Indiana also lacked "the invigoration that comes from the injection of new blood, the flow and cross-fertilization of ideas; the relief from the drabness of inbreeding by the bright colors and tone qualities of Latin and Slavic cultures."[10] The table below shows the generally declining proportion of first-generation immigrants in this period:

FOREIGN BORN IN INDIANA, 1880-1920[11]

| Year | Number | Per cent |
|------|--------|----------|
| 1880 | 144,178 | 7.3 |
| 1890 | 146,205 | 6.7 |
| 1900 | 142,121 | 5.6 |
| 1910 | 159,663 | 5.9 |
| 1920 | 151,328 | 5.2 |

[10] Robert R. LaFollette, "Foreigners and Their Influence on Indiana," *Indiana Magazine of History,* XXV (1929), 26-27.

[11] United States Bureau of the Census, *Twelfth Census* (1900), I, *Population,* Pt. 1, p. xcix; *Fourteenth Census* (1920), II, *Population,* p. 36.

In 1920 Indiana was found to have the highest proportion —92.1 per cent—of native-born white population in the entire nation. Yet the foreign-born element in the state possessed a significance disproportionate to its numbers because of its heavy concentration in certain cities, especially that portion deriving from eastern and southern Europe. For, though the total numbers were relatively small, an important shift occurred in the distribution of European immigration in the early twentieth century. Although Germans remained the dominant foreign-born and foreign-descended stock in Indiana, other segments of the older immigration from northern Europe declined. By 1910, for example, Poles and Hungarians outnumbered Irish and English immigrants in the state. At the same time, the number of persons born in Belgium, Canada, France, the Netherlands, Sweden, Switzerland, and Wales fell drastically while those coming from Austria, Greece, Italy, Rumania, and Russia increased. By 1920 nationals of the recently established states of Czechoslovakia and Yugoslavia were also represented. The bulk of the newcomers from eastern and southern Europe was composed of unskilled workers and their families, most of whom settled in the heavy-industry complex in the Calumet Region and in a few other manufacturing cities in the central and northern sections of the state. At approximately the height of this immigration in 1910, a majority of the residents of East Chicago and Whiting, nearly half of the citizens of Gary, and a quarter of the population of both Hammond and South Bend had been born abroad. The cities of Clinton, La Porte, Michigan City, and Mishawaka also contained a considerable body of foreign-born residents. On the other hand, such important industrial centers as Anderson, Evansville, Fort Wayne, Kokomo, Muncie, Richmond, and Terre Haute received only comparatively minor increments of immigrants in this period. Even Indianapolis, which attracted residents of almost every nationality, failed to maintain a significantly high proportion of foreign-born population, which fell from 10.1 per cent of the total in 1900 to 8.5 per cent in 1910 and just 5.4 per cent of 1920.[12]

Of equal or greater importance in many parts of the state was the influx of southern Negroes which began at the close of the Civil War and was greatly accelerated in the first two decades of the twentieth century. Although the proportion of Negro residents in Indiana remained small, rising from 2.0 per cent of the total population in 1880 to only 2.8 per cent in 1920, their impact upon society was heightened by their tendency to settle in racial ghettos in certain cities. The extreme degree of urbanization of Indiana's colored citizens is revealed below:

NEGRO POPULATION IN INDIANA, 1890-1920[13]

| Year | Total population | Urban population | | Rural population | |
|---|---|---|---|---|---|
| | | Number | Per cent | Number | Per cent |
| 1890 | 45,215 | 28,839 | 63.8 | 16,376 | 36.2 |
| 1900 | 57,505 | 42,274 | 73.5 | 15,231 | 26.5 |
| 1910 | 60,320 | 48,425 | 80.3 | 11,895 | 19.7 |
| 1920 | 80,810 | 71,813 | 88.9 | 8,997 | 11.1 |

Most Negroes entered Indiana from Kentucky, often settling at first in cities along the Ohio River. Many followed the railroad lines northward to become residents of such cities as Indianapolis, Muncie, Richmond, and Terre Haute. Within the state Negro population was redistributed in this period. Between 1900 and 1920 the Negro element of Jeffersonville fell from 16.9 to 14.0 per cent of the city's total population, and that of Evansville from 12.7 to 7.5 per cent. In Gary, on the other hand, the Negro ratio rose from 2.3 to 9.6 per cent in the single decade after 1910, chiefly because of the heavy demand for unskilled laborers during the First World War

---

[12] Ibid., Thirteenth Census (1910), II, Population, p. 570; Fourteenth Census (1920), II, Population, pp. 33, 53, 63-64, 713. For the distribution of the various nationalities represented in Indiana cities in 1920, see Fourteenth Census, III, Population, p. 304.

[13] United States Bureau of the Census, Negro Population 1790-1915 (Washington, D.C., 1918), p. 92; Negroes in the United States 1920-32 (Washington, D.C., 1935), p. 53.

and the recruiting of large numbers of strikebreakers during the steel strike of 1919. In the case of Indianapolis, which received the main brunt of this northward migration, the sharp decline in the proportion of foreign-born residents after 1900 was more than offset by the large-scale increase in Negro inhabitants. By 1920 the Negro element had reached nearly 35,000 and constituted 11 per cent of the total population of Indianapolis, one of the highest such ratios to be found among major cities in the northern United States.[14]

§ §

Many sections of Indiana, however, were little affected by the new currents of industrialization and urbanization. One particular legacy from the state's frontier past which persisted in some rural areas until late in this period was vigilantism. Apparently the first official attempt to deal with this phenomenon occurred in 1874, when Governor Thomas Hendricks designated a special fund to be drawn upon by the state attorney general for an investigation of vigilante activities in Crawford and Washington counties.[15] In the next decade the same general region gave birth to the "White Caps," a curious kind of regulator movement which flourished for many years in Indiana. Although their origins and mode of organization remained cloaked in mystery, the White Caps were thought to be members of a secret order somewhat akin to the Ku Klux Klan and dedicated to the enforcement of a private standard of morality upon the community, if necessary, by the rifle and lash. Like the Klansmen, they usually appeared by night as a band of hooded, masked men who first warned their chosen victims to reform their behavior or to leave the area; if this warning was ignored, it was followed by midnight visitations and frequently by very severe beatings. Since the night riders were sworn to secrecy and their

[14] United States Bureau of the Census, *Fourteenth Census* (1920), II, *Population*, pp. 53, 63-64, 77. Many rural areas were virtually free of Negro residents. In 1920 two counties, Adams and Scott, reported no Negroes and nineteen contained less than ten each. *Ibid.*, pp. 1337-1338.

[15] Indiana Attorney General, *Biennial Report*, 1873-1874, p. 20.

fellow citizens were too frightened or otherwise unwilling to testify against them, they were rarely brought to justice. A series of such incidents in the mid-eighties received a great deal of unfavorable attention in the New York *Times,* which also criticized the Indiana state government harshly in its editorial columns for failure to halt the regulators.[16]

Finally, in 1888 Governor Gray authorized Attorney General Louis T. Michener to make a thorough investigation of an outbreak of White-Cap activities in Crawford and Perry counties. Michener reported the existence of several bands of the secret order federated in "one grand organization" covering parts of three or four adjoining counties in southern Indiana. Although these vigilantes had been active for more than two years in Crawford County, they had aroused no effective opposition to their deeds. In fact, juries had failed to convict any of those who had been indicted as alleged participants in the raids. Describing the lawless actions of the White Caps, he wrote that

they have driven citizens out of the county and out of the State; they have cruelly whipped their victims in the villages of the county without molestation; they have dragged large numbers of persons from their beds, and whipped them until the blood flowed to the ground; they have repeatedly flogged helpless women until the life was nearly extinct, and have procured the publication of their law-defying motives in the newspapers of the county.[17]

The only significant result of Michener's investigation was the passage by the Indiana General Assembly in 1889 of an act making it a crime punishable by two to ten years impris-

---

[16] New York *Times,* October 12, 21, 1887, May 20, 25, August 1, September 8, 1888; *Appletons' Annual Cyclopaedia and Register of Important Events, 1888* (New York, 1889), p. 441. White Caps were also reported in existence in Ohio. *Ibid.,* pp. 670-671. The same name was used by vigilante bands in Tennessee in the nineties. See E. W. Crozier, *The White-Caps: A History of the Organization in Sevier County* (Knoxville, Tenn., 1899).

[17] Indiana Attorney General, *Biennial Report,* 1888, pp. 211-215. For another account of White Caps in southern Indiana, see Hazen H. Pleasant, *A History of Crawford County, Indiana* (Greenfield, Ind., 1926), pp. 338-342.

onment for three or more persons to combine for unlawful purposes wearing white caps or masks.[18]

Despite this legislation there was little diminution of vigilante incidents attributed to the White Caps. In the summer of 1891 a particularly atrocious case was reported from near Leavenworth, Crawford County, where a band of two hundred masked men abducted an elderly man and his eighteen-year-old daughter from their home and administered thrashings to both for some supposed infraction of the southern hill country's moral code. This outrage and the failure to indict any of the members of the band inspired a series of editorials in the Indianapolis *News* reproaching Indiana for providing "most congenial soil" for White Caps: "a great wealthy, long-settled State like this, seamed with railroads and dotted with school-houses, and yet that cannot bring one villain to punishment for a species of crime that has flourished for years."[19] In 1895 Governor Claude Matthews, who had sought stronger legislation unsuccessfully in 1893, announced that the secret order's depredations had been halted in the last few months by vigorous prosecution. Yet newspapers continued to carry accounts of the activities of bands of self-styled White Caps for another two decades. Eventually public opinion began to turn against the masked night riders, however, and several alleged White Caps were convicted and imprisoned in Bartholomew and Monroe counties in the period from 1908 to 1912.[20]

Despite the similarity of their method of operations to that of the Ku Klux Klan, the White Caps in Indiana largely confined their efforts to the intimidation and punishment of white persons who were suspected of violating their peculiar code of morality. The clandestine bands operated chiefly in those rural southern counties which contained few or no Negro residents and seemed to have been motivated by no racial

[18] *Laws of Indiana,* 1889, p. 50.

[19] Indianapolis *News,* June 29, July 1, 3, 1891.

[20] Indiana *Senate Journal,* 1893, p. 59; 1895, p. 42; Columbus *Republican,* January 9, 1908; Indianapolis *News,* February 8, 1912.

bias, though their presence may have acted as a deterrent to the settlement of colored people in districts infested by them. At any rate, there were few authentic incidents involving attacks upon Negroes.[21] Neither was religion apparently a factor in singling out victims. Perhaps because of the frontier tradition Hoosiers were extraordinarily tolerant of vigilante activities on behalf of social and moral conformity as well as in enforcement of property rights. A good example of an organization devoted to the latter was the horse thief detective company, which dated from before the Civil War. In 1892 James A. Mount, later governor of Indiana, was president of the state association, which in 1907 was authorized to receive assistance from local peace officers in its work of detecting and apprehending horse thieves and other criminals.[22]

In addition to the types of private law enforcement described above, mob violence frequently erupted in Indiana during these years. Both Negroes and whites suffered at the hands of lynch mobs which attempted to take the law into their own hands in order to deal out the punishment fitting to persons accused of murder or other violent crimes. The climax to a succession of such incidents involving colored men in the post-Civil War period occurred in 1878, when a band of masked men lynched five Negroes in Mount Vernon, Posey County, in the southwestern "pocket" of the state. In the summer of 1885, however, a Negro in Marion charged with raping a white woman was saved from a similar fate by the courageous action of the sheriff and several guards, who fired on the would-be lynchers, killing one and wounding others. On the other hand, early the next year a colored farm

21 An incident in which twelve masked men whipped two Negroes and two whites near the Indiana University campus in Bloomington in 1903 so aroused the ire of Governor Durbin that he wrote to the sheriff of Monroe County, threatening to remove the university if such affairs were not halted. There is some doubt whether this was actually the work of White Caps. Indianapolis *News,* April 27, 29, 1903.

22 National Horse Thief Detective Association, *Journal,* 1910, pp. 20-22; *Laws of Indiana,* 1907, pp. 230-232; Indianapolis *News,* September 23, 1897.

laborer in Greene County accused of both murder and rape was taken from jail in Vincennes, where law enforcement officials had removed him for safety, and hanged in the court-house square. No legal action was ever taken against members of the lynch mob, and public opinion in many sections of the state tended to condone such deeds, especially when the victim was a Negro accused of a crime of violence against a white person.[23]

Yet the number of whites lynched in Indiana was much larger than the number of Negroes. The victims were often notorious bandits, such as the famous Reno band of train robbers who were lynched at New Albany in 1868 and the Archer gang who were similarly treated at Shoals in 1886. Murder was also a popular pretext for mob action, as in the lynching in Vincennes in 1884 of a young man named Oliver Camfield, "the diabolical scoundrel who shot and killed his sweetheart, Mollie Gerber, Tuesday night, at Brown's boardinghouse," as the local newspaper reported the affair. Two white men were lynched in 1889 at Corydon and one each at Spencer and Shelbyville in 1891 without arousing any great public outcry.[24]

But the case of five white men accused of a series of petty robberies and burglaries who were taken from jail in Versailles, Ripley County, and hanged in the town square by a mob of angry citizens on September 15, 1897, inspired a sharp feeling of revulsion throughout the state. Moreover, the punishment seemed inappropriate to the relatively minor crimes with which the victims were charged. "There has hardly been a lynching in a Southern State in ten years," stated one newspaper editorial, "for which there was not a better excuse than can be pleaded in behalf of that which will blacken forever the history of Ripley County and the fair name of

---

[23] Emma Lou Thornbrough, *The Negro in Indiana. A Study of a Minority* (*Indiana Historical Collections*, Vol. XXXVII, Indianapolis, 1957), pp. 276-280.

[24] Vincennes *Commercial*, June 24, 1884, reprinted in Indianapolis *Journal*, June 25, 1884; Indianapolis *News*, July 20, August 24, 1891, September 23, 1897.

Indiana."[25] The state attorney general sent his deputy to the scene immediately to help bring the perpetrators to justice, but the only person indicted was triumphantly acquitted by a jury made up of his fellow townsmen, who thoroughly condoned the deed.[26] This episode, however, together with the lynching on Christmas Eve, 1898, of a Scott County man who had shot his wife, inspired Governor Mount to urge action upon the General Assembly. In the following session in 1899 the legislature enacted two antilynching laws. One permitted county commissioners to offer a reward for the apprehension of lynchers, while the other provided stiff penalties for those convicted of being members of a lynch mob, including life imprisonment or even death, and also made the county sheriff responsible for forming a posse to protect a threatened prisoner and for requesting military assistance from the governor, if necessary. In addition, any sheriff who surrendered his prisoner to a lynch mob could be removed from office by the governor.[27]

Yet no action of any kind was initiated under the terms of this legislation in December of the following year, when three Negroes jailed on murder charges were lynched in southern Indiana, two of them in Rockport and the other in Boonville. Although the sheriff apparently had time to organize a posse to protect his prisoners, he failed to do so. In 1901, moreover, another Negro was taken from jail in Terre Haute by a mob and hanged from the Wabash River bridge after the local authorities rejected the Governor's offer to call up the state militia. The next year, however, Governor Winfield T. Durbin enforced the law for the first time by declaring vacant the

25 Indianapolis News, September 16, 1897.

26 Indiana Attorney General, Biennial Report, 1897-1898, pp. 43-48. The local Methodist minister preached a sermon after the trial in which he pointed to the hand of God in the acquittal. Versailles Republican, March 16, 1898.

27 Indiana Attorney General, Biennial Report, 1899-1900, p. 18; Indiana Senate Journal, 1899, pp. 16-17; Laws of Indiana, 1899, pp. 132-133, 500-502.

office of the sheriff of Sullivan County after he had surrendered a Negro prisoner to a lynch mob.[28]

The Governor's firm stand may have helped to bring a halt to such incidents, for this proved to be the last lynching of a Negro in Indiana for nearly thirty years. Yet racial tensions remained high in some parts of the state. The most serious affair was an explosive near-race riot which was set off in the city of Evansville on July 4, 1903, by an attempted lynching of a Negro arrested after the fatal shooting of a white policeman. Although the prisoner was successfully removed from the danger zone, an excited mob formed and began to storm the local jail, while some of its members provoked clashes with Negroes belonging to the large colored community in Evansville. Governor Durbin mobilized a local company of militia, which took up positions in front of the besieged jail, where it soon came under attack by the angry crowd. In an exchange of shots eleven lives were lost and at least thirty-five persons wounded, including five guardsmen. Military reinforcements were rushed to the city, but the disorders quickly came to an end. Although Governor Durbin was praised by many for his quick action in resistance to mob spirit, the tragedy left its mark on relations between the races in Evansville and precipitated an extensive Negro exodus from the Ohio River port city.[29]

A minor racial disturbance occurred four years later, on April 25, 1907, when a mob of men and boys gathered in Greensburg, Decatur County, after the arrest there of a Negro itinerant laborer charged with assaulting a white widow of the community. Apparently no violence took place, since the sheriff hurried the accused person out of town in time to avoid any possible threat to his life from the inflamed populace. When journalist Ray Stannard Baker visited Greensburg the next year in the course of his study of race rela-

[28] Indiana Attorney General, *Biennial Report,* 1899-1900, pp. 18-19; 1903-1904, pp. 5-6; Thornbrough, *Negro in Indiana,* pp. 281-283.

[29] Thornbrough, *Negro in Indiana,* pp. 284-287.

tions in America, he was informed by local residents that several Negroes were beaten and a few families were forced to flee the city as a result of the incident, but that racial harmony had finally been re-established.[30]

§ § §

Although professional police and fire protection had been organized in most Hoosier cities for many years, municipal sanitation and sewage disposal systems remained fairly primitive as late as 1880, when the United States Bureau of the Census made a special report on the social statistics of American municipalities. While Indianapolis, Evansville, Fort Wayne, and Terre Haute had begun constructing sewers by that date, only about 10 per cent of their homes contained water closets. A city as large as Richmond had no sewer whatever, and New Albany but a single one, so that most of the latter community's drainage ran through the street gutters into the Ohio River. Many urban dwellers in Indiana still relied on private wells for a supply of fresh water, which was often contaminated by seepage from cesspools and privy-vaults, from which night soil was collected in some places for removal to the nearby farms for use as fertilizer. In the eighties and nineties a rising demand for improvement in sanitation in the rapidly growing larger cities brought about a wide extension of sewer systems, which often contributed greatly, however, to the pollution of water resources in the state by emptying huge amounts of untreated wastes into rivers and streams. As early as 1872 Evansville constructed a municipally owned waterworks, an example which was fol-

[30] Ray Stannard Baker, *Following the Color Line. An Account of Negro Citizenship in the American Democracy* (New York, 1908), pp. 126-128. Contemporary newspaper accounts of the incident suggest that Baker's informants may have slightly exaggerated the extent of the Greensburg "race riot." Greensburg *Weekly Review*, May 2, 1907; Columbus *Evening Republican*, April 27, 1907. Isolated racial incidents continued to occur, as in the burning of a Negro farmer's home and the dynamiting of the residence of Negro employees of a road contractor in Poseyville, Gibson County, in 1908. Rockport *Democrat*, September 4, 1908.

lowed by many other cities during the next decades. But Indianapolis, having rejected a similar proposal in 1874, continued to obtain its water supply from a private company, the Indianapolis Water Company, which created one of the first modern pure-water systems in the state by building a filtration plant in 1902. By the early years of the twentieth century the capital city also boasted an extensive system of sewers, regular garbage collection service, and even street cleaning.[31]

In the eighties electricity gradually replaced gas for city street lighting, except in a few communities in the Gas Belt which utilized their free-flowing supply of natural gas as long as it lasted. Wabash claimed to have been the first city in Indiana to demonstrate public electric lighting, when an arc lamp was placed on the flagstaff on the dome of the county courthouse on the night of March 31, 1880. In 1881 the Indianapolis common council granted a franchise to a private firm to install electric arc lights on five towers in the center of the city. Later both arc and incandescent lamps were included in the municipal lighting system of the Indianapolis Light and Power Company, which was formed by the consolidation of several smaller predecessor firms in 1902. The first publicly owned electric lighting plant in the state was built in Huntington in 1885, and seventeen more were reported by 1898. In general, however, municipal ownership of public utilities did not flourish in Indiana. By 1920 three quarters of the electric light plants and nearly half of the waterworks then functioning in the state were privately owned and operated. A novel and ultimately successful experiment in quasi-public ownership of another kind of public utility was initiated

31 United States Bureau of the Census, *Tenth Census* (1880), *Report on the Social Statistics of Cities,* Pt. 2, pp. 437-475; Dunn, *Greater Indianapolis,* I, 334-335; Frederick D. Kershner, Jr., A Social and Cultural History of Indianapolis, 1860-1914 (Ph.D. thesis in History, University of Wisconsin, 1950), pp. 261-263, 333. Indianapolis was one of only five major cities in the United States without publicly owned waterworks in 1910, the others being New Haven, Conn., Scranton, Pa., Paterson, N.J., and St. Joseph, Mo. Delos F. Wilcox, *Municipal Franchises* . . . (2 volumes, New York, 1910-1911), I, 398.

in Indianapolis in 1906, when the Citizens' Gas Company was granted a franchise with the proviso that the entire operation would become the property of the city at the end of twenty-five years, during which time the shareholders would have received repayment in full of the capital invested, plus 10 per cent annual interest.[32]

In 1879 Indiana's first telephone exchange was established in Indianapolis under the Bell patents by a company organized by E. T. and James Gilliland, local manufacturers of telephonic equipment. The next year a rival Gray system was set up, but it proved short-lived. In 1883 the Gilliland exchange was purchased by the Central Union Telephone Company, a Bell-controlled organization based in Chicago which operated in Illinois and Ohio as well as Indiana. An attempt by the General Assembly in 1885 to set maximum telephone rates met so much resistance that the act was repealed four years later. Although a group of Indianapolis businessmen organized a successful competing exchange in 1898, in order to give outside independent lines an entrance to the city, the Central Union Company prospered and in 1903 moved its headquarters from Chicago to the Indiana capital, where a substantial building was erected to house its main offices.[33]

After the expiration of the Bell patents in 1893 a host of smaller, independent telephone companies sprang into existence throughout the state. By 1902 the United States Bureau of the Census reported 261 commercial and 105 mutual, or co-operative, companies in Indiana, the latter chiefly found in less populous communities. The Bell system, confined to a few of the larger cities in the central region of the state, plus an area in the northwestern corner near Chicago, controlled

---

[32] *Indiana History Bulletin,* XIV (1937), 164; Dunn, *Greater Indianapolis,* I, 327-330; Wilcox, *Municipal Franchises,* I, 640-642; Edward W. Bemis, "The Latest Electric Light Reports," in Bemis (ed.), *Municipal Monopolies* . . . (New York, 1899), pp. 190-191, 204; Indiana *Year Book,* 1920, pp. 574-576, 588-590.

[33] Dunn, *Greater Indianapolis,* I, 340-341; *Laws of Indiana,* 1885, pp. 227-228; 1889, p. 49. See also a pamphlet entitled *Telephone Pioneers of America, Hoosier State Chapter No. 16* (Indianapolis, 1931).

only 25.0 per cent of the total number of telephones in Indiana in 1907 and 38.5 per cent in 1917. Not until 1920 was the Indiana Bell Telephone Company formed by the purchase and consolidation of the Indiana properties of the Central Union, the rival Indianapolis Telephone Company, and four independent exchanges in other cities in the state. While this merger eliminated direct competition in Indiana, a very large number of independent companies continued to serve the state, even in such major cities as Fort Wayne, South Bend, and Terre Haute.[34]

The growing complexity of urban life in the industrial era created a demand for better, more efficient administration of municipal government. Even the largest Hoosier cities retained through the eighties the old-fashioned councilmanic system, according to which the mayor also acted as police judge, and most other municipal affairs were handled by committees of the common council. The first reform measure originated in the Indiana General Assembly, which in 1883 enacted a law creating bipartisan boards of metropolitan police for the cities of Indianapolis and Evansville, designed in part, at least, to improve efficiency and eliminate corruption. Although this bill, which was passed by the Democratic majority in the legislature over the veto of a Republican governor, met considerable opposition at first on the grounds that it violated the principle of local self-government, the Indiana Supreme Court upheld its constitutionality. Moreover, a similar system was later extended to other cities in the state. Legislation enacted in 1889 which would have brought municipal fire departments under such a board and also established a board of public works and affairs, however, was invalidated by the court.[35]

34 United States Bureau of the Census, *Special Reports, Telephones and Telegraphs,* 1902, pp. 9-10; *Census of Electrical Industries* (1915), *Telephones,* p. 31; Indiana *Year Book,* 1920, pp. 832-833.

35 *Laws of Indiana,* 1883, pp. 89-94; 1889, pp. 222-225, 247-254; 1891, pp. 90-92; 1893, pp. 284-285; 1897, pp. 90-96; 1901, pp. 24-25; The State *ex rel.* Holt *et al. v.* Denny, Mayor, *et al.,* 118 Ind. 449 (1888); The State *ex rel.*

Another movement for municipal reform arose from the agitation for paved streets. The Barrett Law of 1889 helped matters somewhat by providing a legal method for property owners to pay for such improvements in installments over a ten-year period. In early 1890 the Commercial Club, which had just been organized in Indianapolis, chiefly through the efforts of William Fortune, a newspaper writer, and the prominent citizen, Colonel Eli Lilly, who became its first president, sponsored a paving exposition in the city in order to arouse interest in the latest and best techniques of street paving. At about the same time the Commercial Club began discussing with the Indianapolis Board of Trade a possible revision of the municipal government, with special emphasis upon the need for a board of public works. A joint committee of the two organizations set to work enthusiastically and soon drew up a completely new city charter for Indianapolis, which the General Assembly enacted into law with only a few changes in its next session in 1891. The chief feature of the charter was its division of the city government into three separate branches corresponding in general to the executive, legislative, and judicial functions of the national and state government. Under the new system the elected mayor was granted large executive authority, especially in his power to appoint members of the various administrative boards or departments without the approval of the common council. So popular was this innovation in municipal government that the General Assembly granted similar charters to Evansville and Fort Wayne in 1893, Terre Haute in 1899, and South Bend in 1901. Muncie, however, rejected such a scheme in 1903. Finally, in 1905 a uniform system closely patterned after the original plan drawn up for Indianapolis was adopted for all the state's cities, which were divided for this purpose into five classes according to size of population. All cities were to be governed by an elected mayor and council, with six execu-

Law et al. v. Blend et al., 121 Ind. 514 (1889) ; Rawles, Centralizing Tendencies in the Administration of Indiana, pp. 308-311.

tive departments including boards of public safety, public health, and public works. Larger municipalities were also to elect a city clerk and city judge. An unusual provision was incorporated into the statute which called for the election of city officers in odd-numbered years in order to avoid the outside political influences associated with the state and national campaigns.[36]

With the rapid growth of urban population in Indiana there arose a demand for city parks and other recreational facilities. In 1895 the General Assembly passed a law establishing a board of park commissioners as a part of the structure of municipal government in Indianapolis. Although the Indiana Supreme Court ruled this act unconstitutional, it was reenacted by the legislature in 1899 with only minor changes. Meanwhile, Mayor Thomas Taggart of Indianapolis had initiated the acquisition in 1897 of a large acreage along the White River which later became known as Riverside Park as well as three smaller pieces of land for public parks in other sections of the city.[37] The establishment of park boards in other large cities in the state did not come until the years 1909-1915, which the historian of Fort Wayne has called a period of "civic awakening." In addition to parks, the state legislature also authorized cities to construct playgrounds, public baths, and swimming pools for the use of their residents.[38]

---

[36] *Laws of Indiana,* 1889, pp. 237-246; 1893, pp. 65-133; 1899, pp. 270-341; 1901, pp. 198-278; 1903, pp. 432-501; 1905, pp. 219-410; H. O. Stechan, "The New Municipal Code of Indiana," *Forum,* XXXVII (1905), 286-296; Dunn, *Greater Indianapolis,* I, 312-321; Kershner, Social and Cultural History of Indianapolis, pp. 140-150.

[37] *Laws of Indiana,* 1895, pp. 63-74; 1899, pp. 386-397; Dunn, *Greater Indianapolis,* I, 422-423. Indianapolis already possessed Garfield Park, which had been purchased from a horse-racing association in 1874, but it was located far from the center of the city and was not connected by a streetcar line until 1895. *Ibid.,* I, 423.

[38] *Laws of Indiana,* 1909, pp. 210-232; 1911, pp. 566-589; 1913, pp. 232-233, 281-282, 382-383; 1915, pp. 49-73; Griswold, *Pictorial History of Fort Wayne,* I, 546-548.

The new system of municipal government failed to solve all the problems of Indiana's burgeoning cities. Despite the attempt to dissociate local from state and national elections, intense political partisanship marked the conduct of many officials in some of the larger cities. Party machines flourished, and cries of corruption were frequently heard. In 1914 an election-fraud and vote-bribery scandal of huge proportions erupted in Terre Haute which affected a major part of the Democratic city and county administrations. Not only were a large number of officials convicted and sentenced to long prison terms, but the mayor and the Vigo County circuit judge were both impeached. The next year a grand jury indicted the mayor and police chief of Indianapolis, along with several other persons, on similar charges, but the chief figures were ultimately acquitted.[39] Moreover, the strong mayor-council form of government created by the new municipal code successfully withstood the movement for more radical reform measures such as the commission or city-manager plans adopted elsewhere in this period. Not until 1921 did the General Assembly enact legislation permitting cities to choose one of these plans by a popular referendum, and only Michigan City experimented for a short time with the city manager system. In 1929 the Indiana Supreme Court invalidated the enabling act just as a majority of the voters in Indianapolis had approved a similar scheme for that city.[40]

Reform of local government outside of the cities also challenged the efforts of legislators in Indiana. Although the concentration of both legislative and executive powers in the hands of the township trustees and the county commissioners had long been criticized on the ground that it led to extravagance and corruption, the great political influence of these officers within the state defeated most attempts to effect

[39] Indianapolis *News,* April 7, 20, May 5, June 24, July 3, 1915; *Literary Digest,* L (1915), 87-88, 943-944; above, p. 125.

[40] *Laws of Indiana,* 1921, pp. 594-623; Roll, *Indiana,* II, 416-417.

changes. Finally, in 1899, after a succession of scandals concerning the administration of local government units, the
General Assembly voted to provide for the election of both
a seven-member county council and a three-member township
advisory board with the duties of fixing the annual tax rates
and exercising a general supervision over the work of the
county commissioners and township trustees, respectively.[41]
In addition to this check on county and township government,
the legislature in 1909 established the state board of accounts
to review the financial records of officials at all levels.[42]

[41] *Laws of Indiana,* 1899, pp. 150-158, 343-365.
[42] *Ibid.,* 1909, pp. 136-150.

# CHAPTER X

## THE EXPANSION OF EDUCATION

DURING THE SEVENTIES AND EIGHTIES, a period marked by what one Hoosier historian has called a "great awakening in education," a free, tax-supported system of common schools was securely established in Indiana. The last legal obstacle was successfully overcome in 1885 when the State Supreme Court upheld the constitutionality of the statute of 1867 which had re-enacted the local tuition-tax provisions of earlier laws previously invalidated. It was a highly decentralized system, with control of the schools largely in the hands of township trustees and appointive boards of education in the incorporated towns and cities. Before 1911 only Indianapolis had an elected board of school commissioners; in that year the General Assembly authorized the election in Terre Haute of a similar five-man board. Since 1873 county boards of education, presided over by county superintendents, exercised a general supervision over the rural schools while town and city school boards had their own superintendents. State control of education, minimal at first, slowly expanded as new statutory powers and responsibilities were granted to the State Board of Education, which was composed of the governor, the presidents of the two state universities and the state normal school, the school superintendents of the three largest cities in the state, and the state superintendent of public instruction, an elected official, who acted as its chief executive officer. In 1899 the board was enlarged to include three additional members actively engaged in education, one of whom must be a county superintendent, and in 1913 the governor was excluded and three representatives of vocational educational interests added.[1]

In the eighties the great majority of public educational institutions in Indiana were ungraded district schools holding classes in one-room rural schoolhouses, usually for no more than six months of the year. The movement for a system of graded schools and greater uniformity in instruction came largely from the Association of County Superintendents meeting in its annual conventions. As early as 1874 a committee of county superintendents drew up a proposed course of study for the district schools, but it was another ten years before the association officially adopted a standard course of five grades covering eight years of study, which was introduced into more than half of the counties of the state within the next few years. At the same time steps were taken to provide a regular procedure of graduation for those pupils who had successfully completed the course of study. In 1883 the county superintendents' convention created a committee under the chairmanship of the state superintendent of public instruction to prepare lists of examination questions, and graduation exercises began to be held in many counties with diplomas granted to pupils who had mastered the "eight common branches" of learning.[2]

With the co-operation of the Indiana State Teachers' Association, another committee prepared a new and more elabo-

[1] William O. Lynch, "The Great Awakening: A Chapter in the Educational History of Indiana," *Indiana Magazine of History,* XLI (1945), 125-130; Robinson, Treasurer, v. Schenck, 102 Ind. 307 (1885); Richard G. Boone, *A History of Education in Indiana* (New York, 1892, reprinted by Indiana Historical Bureau, Indianapolis, 1941), pp. 232-237, 246-251, 264-268, 271-276; *School Laws of Indiana,* 1917, pp. 38, 50-51, 161-164, 184-188. County superintendents, formerly appointed by the township trustees for two years, were given a four-year term in 1899. The constitution provided for an elected state superintendent of public instruction and set his term at two years. This gave a political character to the office which tended to weaken the state supervisory system. See the critique in Indiana Education Survey Commission, *Public Education in Indiana* (New York, 1923), pp. 163-165.

[2] Indiana State Superintendent of Public Instruction, *Biennial Report,* 1883-1884, pp. 102-107; Boone, *History of Education in Indiana,* pp. 281-291.

rate program which was approved by the county superintendents' convention in 1890 and formed the basis for the course of study incorporated into the first state manual issued in 1892 as a part of the biennial report of the state superintendent of public instruction. After 1895 the course was divided into eight grades, each corresponding to a school year. In the succeeding years the recommended course of study, which originally encompassed only spelling, reading, writing, arithmetic, grammar, geography, physiology, and American history, was gradually expanded to include such subjects as music, hygiene, art, agriculture, manual training, and domestic science. By law all work in the elementary schools was to be done in English. Courses in the German language had been authorized by the General Assembly as early as 1869 in any public school in which twenty-five parents requested them and were regularly offered in some Indianapolis schools up through the First World War.[3]

One remaining obstacle to uniformity of instruction lay in the selection of textbooks, which after 1873 had been entrusted to the county boards of education. Dissatisfaction with this system was expressed not only on the grounds of the lack of uniform standards of instruction but also because of the excessive prices charged and the high-pressure tactics often used by book publishers who dealt with individual boards of education. In the late eighties the Indianapolis *Sentinel* in particular campaigned for a uniform schoolbook law in order to combat the so-called "Book Trust," a group of Chicago and Cincinnati firms which it was alleged monopolized textbook sales in the state. In 1889, despite the opposition of the publishing interests and the superintendent of public instruction himself, the Indiana General Assembly authorized the State Board of Education to constitute itself a board of schoolbook commissioners to select textbooks for

3 Indiana State Superintendent of Public Instruction, *Biennial Report*, 1893-1894, pp. 8-11; 1895-1896, pp. 35 ff; Frances H. Ellis, "German Instruction in the Public Schools of Indianapolis, 1869-1919," *Indiana Magazine of History*, L (1954), 251-276, 357-380.

the eight elementary grades and enter into contracts for their publication and sale at stated prices. The books chosen were then purchased directly from the publishers and distributed to the county superintendents for sale to all pupils in their districts, a system which both made for cheaper textbooks and brought an increased measure of uniformity to the course of study in the common schools.[4]

The next major step in strengthening the common school system was the enactment in 1897 of a compulsory attendance law for which the state superintendents of public instruction and the State Teachers' Association had long been lobbying. This statute made it mandatory for parents and guardians to send all children under their control who were between the ages of eight and fourteen to either public or private schools for twelve consecutive weeks or more per year. Truant, or attendance, officers were to be appointed to enforce the act. Subsequent amendments enlarged the scope of this measure by reducing the lower age limit to seven, requiring attendance for longer terms, and providing for the furnishing of free clothing and books for indigent children whose poverty might otherwise prevent them from attending school.[5] The immediate result was a marked rise in public school attendance, though the increasing incidence of employment of children in glass factories and other industrial establishments at this time would seem to prove that the law was not fully effective. In 1913, the upper age limit for compulsory schooling was raised to sixteen, except for gainfully employed children fourteen years and over who had passed the fifth grade of the common school.[6]

4 Indianapolis *Sentinel,* January 5, 1889, February 25, 1898 (anniversary issue), p. 11; New York *Times,* August 1, November 4, 1889. In 1894 it was estimated that school books were reduced in cost from 50 to 60 per cent under the new law. Indiana State Superintendent of Public Instruction, *Biennial Report,* 1893-1894, p. 62.

5 *Laws of Indiana,* 1897, pp. 248-250; *School Laws of Indiana,* 1907, pp. 327-332.

6 *Laws of Indiana,* 1913, pp. 616-618. In 1921 the General Assembly made completion of the eighth grade mandatory for those children between the ages

The table below, excluding children enrolled in private and parochial schools, indicates that school enrollment actually did not quite keep pace with the expanding population of the state in a period of intensive industrialization.

INDIANA PUBLIC SCHOOL ENROLLMENT,
1880-1920[7]

| School year | Enrollment in all public schools | Per cent of total population | Per cent of school population |
|---|---|---|---|
| 1879-1880 | 511,283 | 25.9 | 82.4 |
| 1889-1890 | 512,955 | 23.4 | 79.2 |
| 1899-1900 | 564,807 | 22.4 | 81.1 |
| 1909-1910 | 531,459 | 19.7 | 78.4 |
| 1919-1920 | 566,288 | 19.3 | 79.4 |

One result of the expansion of the common school system in the eighties and nineties was the proliferation of small, one-teacher district schools with inadequate facilities for a modern educational program. Although legislation had been passed in the seventies providing for the establishment of joint graded schools within townships and even by two or more adjacent townships or counties, little progress was made in school consolidation before the end of the century. In 1898, for example, the state superintendent of public instruction reported that there were still two thousand schools in Indiana with an average daily attendance of fewer than twenty pupils each.[8] The difficulties of transporting children to joint schools from remote districts proved an effec-

of fourteen and sixteen who wished to leave school to go to work. *Ibid.,* 1921, pp. 337-355.

[7] Florence DuBois and H. R. Bonner, *Statistics of State School Systems, 1919-20* (United States Bureau of Education, 1922, *Bulletin No. 29*), pp. 12-13. The percentages in the last column of the table are based on the school population five to eighteen years of age as reported by the Bureau of the Census. While the compulsory school attendance law of 1897 brought a large, immediate rise in enrollment, it did not hold up, as the table indicates. Indiana State Superintendent of Public Instruction, *Biennial Report,* 1897-1898, p. 411.

[8] Boone, *History of Education in Indiana,* pp. 291-294; Indiana State Superintendent of Public Instruction, *Biennial Report,* 1897-1898, pp. 33-36.

tive bar to rapid consolidation. In 1899 the General Assembly attempted to solve this problem by passing legislation permitting local school corporations to furnish free transportation for pupils in their districts. Two years later another law was enacted authorizing the abandonment of sparsely attended schools. Finally, in 1907 the legislature made it mandatory that township trustees discontinue all district schools with an average daily attendance of less than twelve persons and provide free transportation to other schools for all pupils affected.[9]

The pace of school consolidation was greatly accelerated during the following decade, and the team-drawn, and later the gasoline-engine, hack carrying farm children to school over often barely passable country roads became a familiar sight in many rural regions of the state. Indiana's accomplishments attracted national attention through its rural consolidated school display at the Panama-Pacific Exposition in San Francisco in 1915. The next year the state superintendent of public instruction reported 706 consolidated schools in 76 counties, with a daily transportation of 37,456 pupils. But large numbers of small district schools survived, especially in those southern counties where topographical conditions and sparse settlement made consolidation difficult to achieve. The Indiana Educational Commission, created by the legislature in 1921 to survey the state's public school system and recommend possible improvements, concluded that the task of consolidation was far from finished. Its report pointed out that in 1920 there still remained 4,800 one-room schools in the state, though 3,990 had been abandoned since 1890. Furthermore, it noted that no county was fully consolidated; less than 40 per cent of the counties had eliminated as many as half their one-teacher schools, and three counties had done nothing at all.[10]

9 *Laws of Indiana,* 1899, p. 551; 1901, p. 437; 1907, pp. 444-445.

10 Indiana State Superintendent of Public Instruction, *Biennial Report,* 1915-1916, p. 658; Indiana Education Survey Commission, *Public Education in Indiana,* pp. 214-215.

School consolidation made possible an extension of the advantages of secondary education to a broader segment of the school-age population, especially in rural areas. Yet the high schools were comparatively late in adapting their curriculum to the needs of a widening constituency and attaining full acceptance as an integral part of the system of public education in Indiana. Critics contended that they catered to a small minority of students preparing for admission to colleges and universities. As late as 1887 an editorial in a major Indianapolis newspaper could speak disparagingly of the "petted few" who graduated each year with "high school diplomas tied up in blue ribbon."[11]

In their earliest development Hoosier high schools related their curriculum primarily to the entrance requirements of the colleges and universities to which their students sought admission. In 1873 the trustees of Indiana University voted to admit to its freshman class without examination the graduates of all those high schools which received the approval of the Indiana State Board of Education. After a six-month investigation, the board issued commissions to twenty-one high schools in Aurora, Bloomington, Elkhart, Evansville, Franklin, Goshen, Greencastle, Greensburg, Kokomo, Logansport, Mount Vernon, Muncie, New Albany, Plymouth, Princeton, Rushville, Seymour, Shelbyville, South Bend, Terre Haute, and Vincennes as having met the academic standards of the university. Similar arrangements were made later with Purdue University and the State Normal School, and most private colleges also eventually agreed to accept students on the same basis. The number of "commissioned" high schools grew steadily each year, reaching a total of one hundred by 1888, when the practice was initiated of granting a commis-

---

[11] Indianapolis *Journal,* April 21, 1887. In 1885, however, John W. Holcombe, superintendent of public instruction, stated in an address at the dedication of the new Indianapolis High School building: "The high school argument has been made, the fight has been fought in this State, and the high school is accepted as an essential part of our common school system." *Indiana School Journal,* XXX (1885), 309.

sion only after receiving a favorable report in writing by a member of the State Board of Education who had visited the school in person.[12]

In 1892 the first suggested course of study set forth in the report of the state superintendent of public instruction included two three-year "minimum" programs and one full four-year program, all of which contained varying proportions of mathematics, English, Latin or German, history, and natural science. By 1902 the revised course of study of commissioned high schools specifically recommended four years of English, three years of a foreign language, three years of mathematics, three years of history, two years of natural science, and two years of electives. The last might include another language, bookkeeping, commercial arithmetic, physical geography, or geology.[13] Latin was a staple subject in most Hoosier high schools, but German was commonly taught also in the larger cities until it was banned by the legislature in 1919. Before that date few schools offered either French or Spanish. There was no statutory curriculum until 1907, when the General Assembly belatedly passed legislation officially recognizing secondary education as part of the common school system and enumerating the following subjects which commissioned high schools were required to teach:[14]

MATHEMATICS: Commercial arithmetic, algebra, geometry
HISTORY: United States, ancient, medieval or modern
GEOGRAPHY: Commercial or physical
ENGLISH: Composition, rhetoric
LITERATURE: English, American
LANGUAGE (FOREIGN): Latin or German
SCIENCE: Biology, physics or chemistry

12 Indiana State Superintendent of Public Instruction, *Biennial Report,* 1873-1874, p. 108; 1887-1888, pp. 83-85; Boone, *History of Education in Indiana,* pp. 305-307.

13 Indiana State Superintendent of Public Instruction, *Biennial Report,* 1891-1892, pp. 41-43; 1901-1902, pp. 657-658.

14 *Laws of Indiana,* 1907, pp. 323-324. In 1908 the State Board of Education ruled that agriculture, zoology, chemistry, or "soil-analysis" might be substituted for Latin. Indiana State Superintendent of Public Instruction, *Biennial Report,* 1907-1908, p. 125.

CIVIL GOVERNMENT: General, state
DRAWING
MUSIC

In 1912, following the recommendation of the National Education Association, the State Board of Education described the requirements for graduation from a commissioned high school as sixteen units of work—fifteen units in schools having a nine-month term—with a unit defined as a year's study of five periods per week for not less than thirty-two weeks. This total was to include three units in English, two in a foreign language, two in mathematics, one in natural science, one in history, two in additional work in one or two of the above subjects, and five units of electives. It was permitted, moreover, to substitute a second unit of science and history for either two units of mathematics or a foreign language. Further uniformity was achieved in 1913, when the General Assembly authorized the State Board of Education to select official textbooks for use in all high schools under its jurisdiction.[15]

In addition to the commissioned high schools, the State Board of Education established two lesser classifications, certified and accredited high schools, which were expected to follow the same course of study as the former but either did not fulfill the requirements for length of term (certified) or had less than a full four-year course (accredited). Most of these latter types of schools were found in rural townships and small communities, where one or more high school years were often simply added on top of the elementary grades. Yet the general tendency was for certified schools, at least, to be gradually upgraded, and many of them reached commission status each year. The following table indicates the extraordinarily rapid growth of Hoosier public

[15] Indiana State Superintendent of Public Instruction, *Biennial Report,* 1911-1912, pp. 283-285; *Laws of Indiana,* 1913, pp. 115-116. The development of the high school curriculum is discussed at some length in Oscar Findley, *Development of the High School in Indiana* (n. p., 1925), 77-151.

high schools, especially commissioned schools, in the years after the turn of the century:

### NUMBER OF AND ENROLLMENT IN PUBLIC HIGH SCHOOLS IN INDIANA, 1900-1920[16]

| School year | Number of high schools | | Number of students | |
|---|---|---|---|---|
| | Commissioned | Total | Commissioned | Total |
| 1899-1900 | 156 | 717 | 19,450 | 35,246 |
| 1901-1902 | 185 | 704 | 23,093 | 36,307 |
| 1903-1904 | 205 | 763 | 24,807 | 38,242 |
| 1905-1906 | 230 | 702 | 31,687 | 44,781 |
| 1907-1908 | 267 | 749 | 35,306 | 47,592 |
| 1909-1910 | 355 | 730 | 43,236 | 50,820 |
| 1911-1912 | 365 | 801 | 44,225 | 55,331 |
| 1913-1914 | 434 | 803 | 50,414 | 59,795 |
| 1915-1916 | 527 | 809 | 62,625 | 69,719 |
| 1917-1918 | 583 | 763 | 67,176 | 72,989 |
| 1919-1920 | 620 | 751 | 74,947 | 78,849 |

In 1917 Indiana ranked fourth among the states in the number of high school pupils per thousand of the total population. Its ratio of 23.1 was far above that for the country as a whole (15.6) and was exceeded only by California (27.0), Kansas (26.5), and Iowa (24.9). But this was accomplished by the establishment of an unusually large number of very small, and presumably less effective, schools, for in 1920 nearly three fourths of the state's four-year high schools enrolled less than one hundred pupils. Moreover, Indiana had almost the worst record among the states for short academic terms in four-year high schools. In the school year 1917-1918 only 26 per cent of all four-year high schools in the state had terms of more than 160 days, as compared with 89 per cent for the country as a whole.[17]

16 Compiled from statistics in Indiana State Superintendent of Public Instruction, *Biennial Report,* 1900-1916, and Indiana *Year Book,* 1920.

17 Indiana Education Survey Commission, *Public Education in Indiana,* pp. 98-100. The commission recommended further consolidation and reorganization along the lines of the junior-senior high school system. Actually, a few cities had begun to experiment with junior high schools as early as 1914, but little progress was made before 1920. *Ibid.,* pp. 215-224; Indiana *Year Book,*

With a larger proportion of the population attending high school and most of the student body no longer desiring to prepare for admission to college or university, a gradual change took place in the philosophy of secondary education in Indiana. Fassett A. Cotton, superintendent of public instruction from 1903 to 1909, stated the argument for a broader approach in this fashion:[18]

The high school must be thought of in relation to the community and not in relation to the college. The community and not the higher institution must determine its mission. Its course of study, its mode of procedure, its text-books, must all be determined from below instead of from above. . . . It is the finishing school for a very large majority of the people who go beyond the common school branches; in other words, it is the people's college, and as such its aim is to meet the needs of the community—to prepare the children, in large measure, for their life work.

In order to make the high schools of the state truly "people's colleges," Superintendent Cotton and others called for greater attention to practical and industrial training in the spirit of the "progressive education" proclaimed at that time by Professor John Dewey of the University of Chicago and later Columbia University in New York. Some form of manual training had been introduced in Indiana schools in the eighties, but the first "vocational" secondary school was not founded until 1895. This was the Indianapolis Manual Training School, which took its inspiration from a private *Gewerbeschule* organized earlier by members of the city's German-American community and combined industrial courses with the regular secondary school curriculum. Opened with 526 students in 1895, it quickly attained great popularity and was the model for industrial high schools in other parts of the

1920, p. 619; Indiana State Superintendent of Public Instruction, *Biennial Report,* 1915-1916, pp. 588-600.

[18] Indiana State Superintendent of Public Instruction, *Biennial Report,* 1905-1906, p. 724. Cotton also opposed such college-type activities in the high schools as organized athletics and social fraternities, the latter of which were banned in public schools by the legislature in 1907. *Ibid.,* pp. 726-730; *Laws of Indiana,* 1907, p. 616.

state, a similar institution being established in Fort Wayne in 1904. The most innovative program of progressive, practical education in Indiana, however, was the work-study-play plan inaugurated in 1900 in Bluffton by a young school superintendent named William A. Wirt. The heart of this scheme was a "platoon" system of rotating classes, whereby all students alternated each half day between practical and academic education, with additional time given to organized recreation. In 1907 Wirt was called to the school superintendency of the newly organized industrial city of Gary, where he had an unexcelled opportunity to create an entire school system from its very foundation on his own principles. An important part of his program was the inclusion of all classes from kindergarten to high school, plus adult classes, in a single large center, with special facilities for art, music, manual training, and recreation. The first school building in Gary had been constructed along traditional lines and had to be remodeled to serve Wirt's purposes, but in 1909 the Emerson School, which was designed by architect William B. Ittner exactly to the innovating superintendent's specifications, was opened, followed by the even better-known Froebel School in 1912 and others built in subsequent decades and named for Horace Mann, Theodore Roosevelt, and Lew Wallace. These institutions became world-famous as educators began to make frequent pilgrimages to Gary to investigate Wirt's remarkable success in organizing a practical and efficient school program seemingly so well adapted to the new industrial age.[19]

[19] Indiana State Superintendent of Public Instruction, *Biennial Report,* 1899-1900, pp. 709-710; 1905-1906, pp. 357, 377-428. John Dewey and Randolph S. Bourne were chiefly responsible for calling public attention to the work of William A. Wirt in the Gary schools. By 1914 Wirt had achieved a national reputation and was invited to reorganize the New York City schools in a similar fashion, but the project proved abortive. John and Evelyn Dewey, *Schools of Tomorrow* (New York, 1915), pp. 175-204, 251-268; Randolph S. Bourne, *The Gary Schools* (Boston, 1916), pp. 9-10, 64-66, 87-92, 182-198; Moore, *Calumet Region,* pp. 471-474, 483n; Lawrence Cremin, *The Transformation of the School. Progressivism in American Education, 1876-1957* (New York, 1961), p. 160.

In 1913, upon the recommendation of a vocational education commission appointed by Governor Ralston, the General Assembly enacted a law requiring the teaching of agricultural, domestic, and industrial courses in both elementary and secondary schools of the state. This act also provided for the establishment of full-time vocational schools and part-time and evening classes and authorized a special local tax levy as well as state aid for the support of vocational educational programs approved by the State Board of Education. Agricultural education, which was confined to town and township schools, was reinforced by the system of county agents, who were commissioned to work closely with the school authorities in legislation enacted in the same year. In 1916, moreover, an official survey was made in Indianapolis, Evansville, Richmond, Madison, and in Jefferson County to determine specific needs and recommend suitable programs of vocational education in those communities. Finally, the Smith-Hughes Act of 1917 strengthened the entire state system by providing Federal subsidies for the salaries of vocational education teachers and supervisors.[20]

Such subjects as art and physical education were also admitted into the curriculum in many schools in Indiana in these years. But not until after the First World War heightened the interest of the American public in the health and vigor of the nation's youth did the General Assembly in 1919 finally authorize the State Board of Education to prescribe a regular program of physical training for students in both elementary and high schools of all cities and incorporated towns of five thousand or more population.[21]

The expansion of the public school system downward to the kindergarten level began only after private charitable organizations had introduced such programs into Indianapolis and

[20] Charles H. Winslow, *Report of the Indianapolis Survey for Vocational Education* (2 volumes, Indiana State Board of Education, *Educational Bulletin No. 21, Survey Series No. 6*, 1917), I, ix-xiii; *Laws of Indiana*, 1913, pp. 37-46; *School Laws of Indiana*, 1917, pp. 196-205.

[21] *Laws of Indiana*, 1919, pp. 682-686.

other cities in the late seventies and early eighties. The best-known organization of this kind was the Indianapolis Free Kindergarten Society, which was formed in 1882 by a group of civic-minded women in order to furnish preschool training for underprivileged children of the capital city. Under the leadership of Mrs. Eliza A. Blaker, whom the society brought from Philadelphia to organize and supervise its work, twenty-three free kindergartens were established in the city by 1900.[22] In 1889 the state legislature empowered cities and incorporated towns to establish kindergartens for the instruction of children between the ages of four and six in connection with the common schools but disallowed the use of any state financial aid for them. This limited encouragement resulted in the organization of as many as fifty-eight public kindergartens by 1900. In 1901 cities of over six thousand population were permitted to levy a tax of one cent on each $100 of taxable property to support free kindergartens, whether publicly controlled or conducted by private associations approved by the local school board. Ten years later the General Assembly gave its further approval to the kindergarten movement by authorizing the tax levy to be doubled to two cents on each $100 of property.[23]

Hoosiers increasingly taxed themselves in order to finance an expanding public educational system in this period. Indiana possessed a relatively large permanent common school fund derived from such sources as the congressional township fund, the swampland fund, and various miscellaneous contingent funds, the interest from which was distributed to the counties for school purposes. By action of the General Assembly in 1889, the management of the school fund was entrusted to the county auditors, who were authorized to make real estate mortgage loans. But the main revenue for the support of the common schools came from state and local

22 Emma Lou Thornbrough, *Eliza A. Blaker, Her Life and Work* (Indiana Historical Society, Indianapolis, 1956), pp. 16-18.

23 *Laws of Indiana*, 1889, p. 355; 1901, p. 123; 1911, p. 112; Indiana State Superintendent of Public Instruction, *Biennial Report*, 1899-1900, p. 744.

taxation, the latter coming to bear by far the larger proportion of the burden.

By 1917 local school corporations were given the power to levy a maximum of 75 cents on each $100 of taxable property as well as $1.00 on each taxable poll, and under certain conditions a supplementary levy of 50 cents and 25 cents, respectively, was authorized. The state tax levy for schools stood at 13 cents and 6 mills on each $100 of taxable property plus a 50-cent poll tax for most of this period. Until 1905, moreover, all state school funds were distributed to the counties strictly according to the enumeration of pupils. In that year the General Assembly passed a so-called deficiency act, which enabled the state superintendent of public instruction to apportion 5.2 per cent of the state tax on the basis of need rather than school census, in order to aid those school corporations which could not maintain the minimum six-month school term even after assessing the maximum local property tax. In 1919 the proportion of state revenue so distributed was raised to 8.2 per cent and in 1921 to 30.0 per cent, in growing recognition of the advantages of equalizing financial support and educational opportunity throughout the commonwealth.[24]

Adding to the financial burden was the fact that the public school system of Indiana was in large part racially segregated in this period. According to a statute of 1877, however, Negro children were permitted to attend schools with white pupils if no separate facilities were provided for them or wherever the Negro students had advanced beyond the highest grade available in their own schools. While Negro children attended classes with whites in many areas, especially in the northern half of the state, most communities with a relatively large number of colored residents continued to operate segregated elementary schools. Not only were the Negro schools usually inferior in their facilities and the

24 *School Laws of Indiana,* 1907, pp. 147, 172-174; 1917, pp. 190-192; 1923, pp. 204-206; Boone, *History of Education in Indiana,* pp. 324-335.

Haynes-Apperson Factory, Kokomo, 1899

Composing Room of the Jasper *Courier,* 1912

Froebel School, Gary, Built 1912

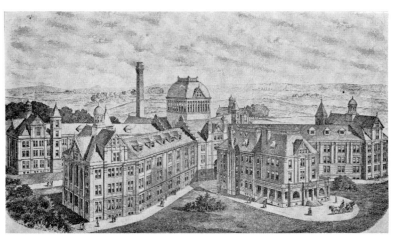

Plan of Southern Hospital for the Insane, Evansville
Opened in 1890

quality of education provided, but they generally reported a low rate of enrollment of children. In 1897 Gabriel Jones, a Negro member of the lower house of the General Assembly from Marion County, submitted a bill to equalize educational opportunities for white and colored pupils by completely eliminating separate schools for the two races, but it failed to be enacted into law, partly because of opposition from within the Negro community itself.[25]

In 1876 the first Negro graduated from an Indiana high school—in Indianapolis—and during the next few decades an increasing number of colored pupils attended white high school classes on the basis of the 1877 statute. In the south, however, many cities began to organize separate Negro high schools in the eighties, mostly by simply adding on "high school departments" to existing colored elementary institutions. When this was done in New Albany in 1880, a part of the Negro community objected strenuously and at least one colored student attempted to enroll in the white high school in the fall, but without success. By 1908 there were eight Negro high schools, none of them in separate buildings, and all located in the southern half of the state, in Corydon, Evansville, Jeffersonville, Madison, Mount Vernon, New Albany, and Princeton. Their general educational quality was indicated by the fact that only three of them—in Evansville, Madison, and New Albany—had been accorded commissioned status by the State Board of Education. By the early twentieth century virtually all the teachers in colored schools were Negroes. In 1916 there were 76 men and 168 women of that race employed as instructors—apparently none of whom taught in white or mixed schools. In the eyes of the Negro community in Indiana the chief advantage of the system of segregated schools lay in the opportunity it provided

<hr>

[25] *Laws of Indiana,* 1877, p. 124; John W. Lyda, *The Negro in the History of Indiana* (Terre Haute, Ind., 1953), pp. 86-87; Thornbrough, *The Negro in Indiana,* pp. 329-340.

for the professional employment of at least a small number of its educated members.[26]

§ §

Before 1880 Indiana possessed hardly any substantial public collections of books despite the work of private associations such as the Workingmen's Institute of New Harmony and legislation authorizing the organization of township and county libraries. The outstanding exceptions were the fifty-five-year-old Indiana State Library in the State House, the Indianapolis Public Library, which was opened in 1873 with a collection of nearly fourteen thousand volumes, and the smaller Muncie Public Library, founded in 1875 under a statute of 1873. A subscription library begun in Evansville in 1855 was turned over to the municipality in 1874 and formed the basis for the Willard Library built in that city in 1883 through the gift of Willard Carpenter. In both 1881 and 1883 the General Assembly passed legislation permitting cities and incorporated towns to levy taxes to establish and maintain public libraries, but few responded. The lack of good library facilities was partially remedied by the formation of a Chautauqua-style teachers' reading circle in 1883 and a young people's reading circle in 1887, each of which fostered inexpensive distribution and circulation of books throughout the state.

In 1891 the Indiana Library Association was organized to promote the establishment of local libraries and press for more liberal legislation. Women's literary societies were frequently active in urging the same cause, and the Indiana Union of Literary Clubs played a leading role in securing passage of the act of 1899 which extended permission to levy taxes for library purposes to townships and established the Public Library Commission. This commission, which worked in conjunction with the Indiana State Library until 1901, ar-

---

[26] Indiana State Superintendent of Public Instruction, *Biennial Report,* 1907-1908, pp. 515-516; Indiana *Year Book,* 1917, p. 197; Thornbrough, *The Negro in Indiana,* pp. 341-343.

ranged for the circulation of traveling libraries, gave advice to local communities on creating their own book collections, and even helped train librarians in summer programs.[27]

Gifts of private citizens formed the basis for such municipal libraries as the Willard Library in Evansville (1883) and the Emeline Fairbanks Memorial Library in Terre Haute (1903). The major impetus to the establishment of new public libraries, however, came from the gifts of the Pittsburgh steelmaker and philanthropist, Andrew Carnegie, whose large contributions for public libraries included several million dollars to Indiana cities and towns toward the erection of one hundred and fifty buildings between 1899 and 1920. Most communities receiving such aid, even the smaller towns, were able to fulfill their pledges to raise sufficient funds by local taxation to maintain the Carnegie libraries. As a result of this great library-building campaign, Indiana had only five cities or towns of over 3,000 population without public libraries in 1920, and only three predominantly rural counties—Crawford, Dubois, and Pike—lacked such institutions. In its report of that year the Indiana Public Library Commission noted that the number of public libraries in the state had risen from 57 in 1899, when the commission was first organized, to 213 in 1920, and that a total of 569 librarians and assistants had received summer training under its auspices during the past twenty years.[28]

§ § §

The preparation and recruitment of competent teachers posed a perennial problem for the whole public school sys-

[27] *Laws of Indiana,* 1881, pp. 588-589; 1883, pp. 200-202; Jacob P. Dunn, *The Libraries of Indiana* (Indianapolis, 1893), p. 26; William E. Henry, *Municipal and Institutional Libraries of Indiana* (Indianapolis, 1904), pp. 59, 73-76. In 1895 the Indiana State Library was placed under the jurisdiction of the State Board of Education, which was given the authority to choose the state librarian. *Laws of Indiana,* 1895, pp. 234-237.

[28] Henry, *Municipal and Institutional Libraries of Indiana,* pp. 42, 146; Indiana *Year Book,* 1920, pp. 396-409; Indiana Public Library Commission, *Biennial Report,* 1920, pp. 2-11.

tem. Low pay and poor working conditions, especially in the rural schools, discouraged many persons from either entering or remaining long in such a career. In the eighties male teachers still predominated in the schoolroom, but the tide soon turned in favor of the schoolmistress, largely because the meager salaries discouraged men, who were more likely to be heads of families. Some arguments were heard, moreover, that women were superior to men as teachers of young children. In 1880, when Indiana had 7,802 men and 5,776 women employed as instructors in the public schools, one county superintendent predicted that

as soon as that lingering prejudice which is still found in many localities, in favor of male and against female teachers, can be removed, women will immediately demonstrate, by the excellence of their work, that they do possess a superior fitness for the greater part of the work to be done in the country schools. Then will the patrons of these schools consent for a man to teach their children only when the services of a woman cannot be secured.[29]

At any rate, women soon began to dominate the teaching profession, particularly in the elementary grades. By 1900 they slightly outnumbered male teachers in all public schools in the state and sixteen years later had gained more than a two-to-one advantage over them.[30]

At first the state required no specific educational standards for teachers, many of whom in the district schools had not had the benefit of even a single year of high school training. Teaching licenses were granted by the county superintendents to candidates who passed certain written tests covering the subjects to be taught. After 1899 the State Board of Education was responsible for the preparation of all examination questions, but prospective teachers could choose between having their papers graded by either the state or the county superintendent, the license conferred by the latter having validity only within his jurisdiction. Despite this restriction,

[29] Indiana State Superintendent of Public Instruction, *Biennial Report,* 1879-1880, Pt. II, 124, 209.

[30] *Ibid.,* 1899-1900, p. 425; 1915-1916, p. 864.

as late as 1920 most elementary teachers were content to hold the county license, presumably because it was easier to obtain. After 1915, however, the county superintendent could issue licenses only for the first eight grades. The State Board also granted upon examination professional licenses valid for eight years as well as life licenses.[31]

In 1907 the General Assembly gave a major impetus to the professionalization of teaching by naming the State Board of Education a teachers' training board to "arrange for a regular system of normal school instruction throughout the state." The board was authorized to approve courses of study and to accredit normal schools and the education departments of colleges and universities. Teaching licenses valid in township and graded elementary schools were granted without examination to those who had completed a two-year professional course at the State Normal School or any other accredited institution. Another law enacted the same year also required that all previously unlicensed candidates presenting themselves for examination must be graduates of a commissioned or certified high school or the equivalent, with at least twelve weeks of professional training. In 1919 an amendment was passed which extended the system of licensing teachers on credentials rather than on examinations and specifically demanded that one fifth of the total number of credits needed for either elementary or secondary licenses should be in "professional subjects, including observation and practice teaching." Finally, in 1923, upon the recommendation of the Indiana Education Survey Commission, the legislature eliminated licensing by examination and gave the State Board of Education the responsibility of issuing all new teaching licenses on the basis of training and experience.[32]

31 *Laws of Indiana,* 1899, pp. 488-491; 1915, pp. 627-734; Indiana Education Survey Commission, *Public Education in Indiana,* pp. 51-53.

32 *Laws of Indiana,* 1907, pp. 147, 451-453; 1919, pp. 753-758; *School Laws of Indiana,* 1923, pp. 35-42; Indiana Education Survey Commission, *Public Education in Indiana,* pp. 54-60.

The main form of in-service training for teachers in this period were the county and township institutes, the former extending for a period of five consecutive days each year and the latter for at least one Saturday of each month that the township schools were in session. By a legislative enactment of 1889, teachers were paid for attending the township but not the county institutes. Furthermore, after 1917 Saturday institutes might also be held in cities and towns at the discretion of the local school boards. The annual meetings of the Indiana State Teachers' Association as well as regional associations also provided a forum for discussion of educational matters. Connected with the former was the Indiana Teachers' Reading Circle, organized in 1883 in order to improve both the professional and literary knowledge of its membership, which rose to more than sixteen thousand by the school year 1907-1908, before declining rapidly with the advent of the higher educational qualifications required for the teaching license. The *Indiana School Journal,* which began in 1856 as the organ of the State Teachers' Association, continued to be the leading professional magazine in the state until 1900, when it was merged with a Terre Haute periodical founded in 1895, the *Inland Educator,* under the name of the *Educator-Journal.* Another popular educational paper was *The Teachers' Journal,* a monthly which began publication in Marion, Indiana, in July, 1901.[33]

In an attempt to improve the standards of remuneration for teachers, the General Assembly in 1907 established a graduated minimum wage scale based on experience, scholarship, and professional training. All teachers, both elementary and high school, were grouped together in three classes, A, B, and C, with experience the main determining factor in classification. The minimum guaranteed annual salary for the beginner was set at $450 for nine months' work and for the most highly rated and experienced teacher, $630. Al-

[33] Boone, *History of Education in Indiana,* pp. 393-406; Fassett A. Cotton, *Education in Indiana (1793 to 1934)* (Bluffton, Ind., 1934), pp. 294-316, 368-370.

though the aggregate wages paid to teachers in Indiana immediately rose nearly $1,000,000 in the single year, 1908-1909, the average annual salary remained relatively low, $510.53 in 1909, and $593.70 in 1914. Moreover, teachers in rural schools were paid considerably less than those in towns and cities, women received less than men, and elementary school less than high school instructors. Wartime inflation affected school financing as it did other areas of the economy, and the minimum wage was raised in 1921 to $800 for beginning teachers and $1,170 for the most experienced teacher with the highest grade of license.[34]

The first teachers' retirement program in the state was established in 1907, when the General Assembly approved the Indianapolis school corporation's plan to build a pension fund by a special tax levy as well as by an assessment upon wages. Six years later a similar contributory pension scheme was authorized in all cities of over twenty thousand population, with a separate program for Terre Haute. Not until 1915, however, did the legislature create a state retirement fund to be drawn upon for the payment of annuities to all public school teachers who had completed a stated period of service. School corporations with their own pension plans were permitted, but not required, to come under the operation of the state retirement system.[35]

§ § § §

The rapid expansion of the public school system in Indiana, especially at the secondary level, signaled the end of an era for many of the private academies which had trained earlier generations of Hoosier leaders. By the eighties most of the Protestant church-affiliated academies — Baptist, Methodist,

[34] *School Laws of Indiana,* 1907, pp. 261-262; 1923, pp. 79-80; Indiana State Superintendent of Public Instruction, *Biennial Report,* 1913-1914, p. 351. The Indiana Education Commission of 1921 found salary scales still too low, especially at the higher levels of training and experience, and concluded that the minimum wage legislation had chiefly benefited beginning teachers. Indiana Education Survey Commission, *Public Education in Indiana,* pp. 58-59.

[35] *School Laws of Indiana,* 1917, pp. 350-376.

Moravian, Presbyterian, and Quaker—had either vanished completely or been taken over by local school corporations as tax-supported institutions. The Society of Friends, which maintained the largest number of academies, managed to keep many of them open into the second decade of the twentieth century partly by accepting pupils whose tuition was paid by communities lacking a public high school according to the provisions of a 1909 statute. A decision of the state attorney general in 1917 that this law did not apply to private and parochial schools, however, was a harsh blow. The last two academies of the Western Yearly Meeting, Bloomingdale Friends' Academy and the Central Academy of Plainfield, ceased to be operated by Friends in 1916 and 1919, respectively. In the Indiana Yearly Meeting only Fairmount Academy and Spiceland Academy remained in existence by 1920.[36]

On the other hand, despite seemingly adverse conditions for institutions of this kind, a few new schools were founded by religious organizations, such as the coeducational academy founded by the Chicago synod of the Evangelical Lutheran Church at Colburn, Tippecanoe County, in 1902 and later moved to Mulberry, Clinton County, under the name of the Weidner Institute. In 1902 the Seventh Day Adventists also started a small school at Boggstown, Shelby County, which in 1919 became the core of a larger institution, Indiana Academy, located on a farm in Cicero, Hamilton County. In 1905-1906 the Interdenominational Winona Assembly opened separate boys' and girls' boarding schools at Winona Lake as

[36] John Hardin Thomas, "The Academies of Indiana," *Indiana Magazine of History,* XI (1915), 8-30; Ethel H. McDaniel, *The Contribution of the Society of Friends to Education in Indiana* (Indiana Historical Society *Publications,* XIII, No. 2, Indianapolis, 1939), pp. 210-220; *Laws of Indiana,* 1909, pp. 331-332; Indiana Attorney General, *Opinions,* 1916-1920, pp. 247-249. In 1921 the Indiana General Assembly outlawed payment of any public funds to private academies. *Laws of Indiana,* 1921, pp. 743-745. Spiceland Academy ceased operation as a Friends' school in 1922, and Fairmount Academy closed its doors in 1923.

a part of the educational complex being created by that evangelistic organization.[37]

Furthermore, Roman Catholic academies continued to flourish, especially boarding schools for girls such as those long conducted by the Sisters of Providence at St. Mary-of-the-Woods near Terre Haute, the Sisters of St. Francis at their Oldenburg convent in Franklin County, the Sisters of St. Benedict at the Convent of the Immaculate Conception in Ferdinand, Dubois County, and the Sisters of the Congregation of the Holy Cross at St. Mary's in Notre Dame. These and other religious orders also operated girls' schools in Indianapolis, Vincennes, Lafayette, Logansport, Fort Wayne, La Porte, and Tipton, where the Sisters of St. Joseph organized the last of this group, St. Joseph's Academy, in 1903. Catholic boys' schools were fewer in number, those organized after 1870 including St. Michael's Academy in Plymouth, St. Joseph's Institute in Indianapolis, and Immaculate Conception in Avilla, Noble County.[38]

Another type of private educational institution was represented by a small number of college-preparatory and finishing schools launched by individuals in this period. The first venture of this kind was the Indianapolis Classical School, which Theodore Lovett Sewall, a recent graduate of Harvard, founded in 1876 primarily to prepare young men for admission to eastern colleges. In 1882 he and his educator-wife, May Wright Sewall, opened an adjunct known as the Classical School for Girls, which proved so successful that he later

[37] Weidner Institute, *Catalogue*, 1920-1921; Indiana Academy, *Announcement*, 1924-1925, p. 3; Thomas Kane, *Winona Booklet. Winona Assembly and Schools* (Indianapolis, 1906), pp. 25-26. Weidner Institute was closed in 1927 and the buildings later used for a home for the aged. C. R. Defenderfer, *Lutheranism at the Crossroads of America: A Story of the Indiana Synod of the U. L. C. A.* [1948], p. 60.

[38] Elizabeth Denehie, "Catholic Education in Indiana: Past and Present," *Indiana Magazine of History*, XII (1916), 337-350; Thomas, "The Academies of Indiana," *Indiana Magazine of History*, XI, 31-34; Marvin W. Pershing, *History of Tipton County Indiana. Her People, Industries and Institutions* (Indianapolis, 1914), p. 205.

sold the boys' school in order to concentrate upon the institution for young women, which he served as co-principal with his wife. Mrs. Sewall introduced feminine dress reforms and physical training along with the rigorous course of study which stressed both ancient and modern languages as well as mathematics. After her husband's death in 1895, she conducted the Girls' Classical School, which had become by then a celebrated Indianapolis institution, for another dozen years before leaving it to devote her energies to other causes.[39]

In 1902 Fredonia Allen, a member of Mrs. Sewall's teaching staff, established Tudor Hall School for Girls in Indianapolis, a somewhat similar institution which Miss Allen directed for a quarter of a century and which has long survived its model. In 1907 Julia Ethel Landers, daughter of the Democratic gubernatorial candidate in 1880 and a former student and assistant of Mrs. Sewall, became the principal of Knickerbacker Hall School, which was operated under the auspices of the Indianapolis Diocese of the Protestant Episcopal Church. After classes were discontinued in that institution in 1912, she conducted the nonsectarian Miss Landers'

39 Indianapolis Classical School, *Catalogue*, 1878-1879, p. 8, and miscellaneous catalogues, programs, and newspaper clippings in May Wright Sewall Scrapbooks in Indiana State Library; Charlotte Cathcart, *Indianapolis from Our Old Corner* (Indiana Historical Society, Indianapolis, 1965), pp. 20-23. Anna F. Weaver, who conducted a girls' academy in Logansport from 1903 to 1905 and was co-principal of the Girls' Classical School with Mrs. Sewall from 1905 to 1907, continued the latter institution until 1910 before becoming an instructor at Butler College. Butler College, *Annual Catalogue*, 1911-1912, p. 10. May Wright Sewall was born in Wisconsin and was educated at Northwestern University. In 1872 with her first husband, Edwin Thompson, she came to Indianapolis to teach in the public high school. After Thompson's death she married Theodore L. Sewall and collaborated closely with him in administering and teaching in the two private schools operated by them. She not only became an almost legendary educator in the capital city but also was an active leader in the woman's suffrage and woman's club movements in both state and nation. An ardent spiritualist in her later years, Mrs. Sewall wrote an interesting account of her psychic communications with her second husband in *Neither Dead Nor Sleeping*, a book published in 1920 with an introduction by Booth Tarkington. Her death occurred in Indianapolis in 1920. *Dictionary of American Biography*, XVI, 610.

School for Girls in the same city for a few years. Indianapolis, however, lacked a male counterpart of these establishments from 1889 (the date of the closing of Sewall's Boys' Classical School) to 1914, when a newcomer to the city, Yale-graduate Wendell Stanton Brooks, opened the Brooks School for Boys, a highly regarded college preparatory institution. Literary Hoosiers such as Booth Tarkington and Meredith Nicholson served on its advisory board and the sons of Indiana Senators Albert J. Beveridge and John W. Kern were among its students. However, it survived only six years.[40]

Coates College, a girls' school inaugurated in Terre Haute in 1885 through the benefactions of a Greencastle woman, Jane P. Coates, was carried on under Presbyterian auspices for about a decade. A more enduring establishment in that city was the King Classical School, a nonsectarian day school organized by Bertha Pratt King and Mary Sinclair Crawford in 1906 which admitted both boys and girls to its lower grades while accepting only the latter in the high-school department. Miss King, a Smith College graduate from New York, remained at the head of the popular school for nearly forty years. Another highly successful institution was the exclusive Elmhurst School for Girls, which Isabel Cressler and Caroline Sumner established in 1909 on a palatial estate near Connersville in Fayette County, where it remained until its removal to Rye, New Hampshire, in 1926.[41]

Two boys' military schools in Indiana trace their beginnings to the last two decades of the nineteenth century. The first

[40] Kate Milner Rabb and William Herschell (eds.), *An Account of Indianapolis and Marion County* (Vols. III and IV of Logan Esarey, *History of Indiana* . . ., Dayton, Ohio, 1924), IV, 606-609; Indianapolis *Star,* February 4, 1912, p. 10; Blanche Foster Boruff (comp.), *Women of Indiana* (Indianapolis, 1941), p. 189; Dunn, *Indiana and Indianans,* IV, 1803-1804; Brooks School for Boys, *Catalogue,* 1918-1919.

[41] William F. Cronin (ed.), *An Account of Vigo County from Its Origins* (Vol. III of Logan Esarey, *History of Indiana* . . ., Dayton, Ohio, 1922), pp. 87-88; sketch of Bertha Pratt King Ehrmann in Indiana Biographical Series, XXX, 95, Indiana State Library; Frederic Irving Barrows (ed.), *History of Fayette County Indiana* . . . (Indianapolis, 1917), pp. 384-385; Indianapolis *News,* June 8, 1926, p. 16.

of these had its origin in a bequest of several thousand dollars for the education of candidates for the Protestant Episcopal ministry left by John Badlam Howe, an attorney of Lima, La Grange County, who died in 1883. The next year his widow founded Howe Grammar School in the town of Lima with the assistance of Bishop David Buel Knickerbacker and the Reverend Charles N. Spaulding, the latter becoming the headmaster. When Spaulding resigned in 1895, Howe School came under the leadership of the Reverend John H. McKenzie, a young Episcopalian who reorganized the institution on a modified military basis and served as its rector until 1920. In the meantime, a St. Louis stove manufacturer, Henry Harrison Culver, founded Culver Military Academy on the shores of Lake Maxinkuckee in Marshall County in 1894. Losing its first building by fire, it was consolidated in 1895 with a similar academy in Mexico, Missouri, which had also been burned out, and under the superintendency of the latter institution's founder, Colonel A. F. Fleet, and with the financial aid of the Culver family, began to grow rapidly. By 1903 it had become, next to the United States Military Academy at West Point, the largest military school in the nation.[42]

One of the most unusual educational experiments ever undertaken in Indiana was the Interlaken School for Boys which Dr. Edward A. Rumely established at La Porte in 1907. Transferred to a large farm on Silver Lake near the La Porte County village of Rolling Prairie in 1911, the Interlaken School incorporated agricultural and industrial work fully into the academic program on the pattern of certain experimental schools which Dr. Rumely, a graduate in medicine, had observed in Europe. Its motto, "to teach boys to live," and its system of combined work and study smacked of the progressive educational philosophy of John Dewey, who visited and warmly praised the school before its demise

---

42 John W. Hanan (comp.), *LaGrange County Centennial History 1828-1928* (LaGrange, 1928), p. 35; Cottman, *Centennial History and Handbook of Indiana,* pp. 293, 297; Thomas, "The Academies of Indiana," *Indiana Magazine of History,* X (1914), 349-350; Smith, *History of Indiana,* I, 275-276.

during the First World War, when the Federal government took over the property for use as a training center.[43]

The largest sector of private elementary education consisted of the parochial school systems operated mainly by the Roman Catholic, Evangelical, and Lutheran churches. Accurate figures for such institutions, however, are difficult to obtain. In 1879 the state director of statistics reported the existence of forty-six Catholic and twenty-one Lutheran schools, together with a single Protestant Episcopal school. A county-by-county survey included in the report of the state superintendent of public instruction for 1887-1888 revealed the following enrollments in parish schools: Catholic, 16,200; Lutheran, 4,592; Evangelical, 328. Ten years later the bureau of statistics reported 29,171 pupils in Catholic, 7,919 in Lutheran, and 1,110 in Evangelical schools, together with a few score more scattered among smaller denominations. A Federal report on state school systems, however, gave only 35,857 as the total number enrolled in all private and parochial schools in Indiana in 1919-1920.[44]

Although Lutherans continued to maintain a relatively large parochial school system, the Roman Catholic church made the chief educational gains in this period. Out of 120 schools in the Indianapolis Diocese in 1924, 44 had been organized since 1880; in the younger Fort Wayne Diocese 68 out of 104 schools dated from 1880. Moreover, Sisters from the various teaching orders gradually replaced lay teachers in most parishes, while the Brothers of the Sacred Heart conducted one school in Indianapolis. Indeed, Sisters were employed as teachers in twenty-three public schools in southern Indiana communities with a predominantly Catholic pop-

[43] Indiana. A Guide to the Hoosier State, p. 444; Dewey, Schools of Tomorrow, pp. 87-90. Dr. Rumely discussed his educational philosophy in a pamphlet, The Interlaken School (La Porte, 1915).

[44] Indiana Department of Statistics and Geology, Annual Report, 1879, pp. 402-409; Indiana State Superintendent of Public Instruction, Biennial Report, 1887-1888, Pt. II, pp. 481-500; Indiana Department of Statistics, Biennial Report, 1907-1908, p. 130; DuBois and Bonner, Statistics of State School Systems, 1919-20, p. 10.

ulation. Fort Wayne, moreover, boasted one of the first central, or diocesan, Catholic high schools in the country, established in that city in 1909. In Indianapolis Sacred Heart Parish inaugurated regular high school classes in September, 1915, shifted to a two-year commercial course three years later, and finally in 1921 permanently established its four-year high school. Meanwhile, the Brothers of the Holy Cross opened Cathedral High School for boys in Indianapolis in September, 1918.[45]

§ § § § §

At the head of the public educational system of the state was Indiana University, located at Bloomington, which entered a period of vigorous growth in the eighties. After a fire in July, 1883, destroyed most of the library, scientific apparatus, and the university records, the trustees decided upon a move to a more spacious site on a twenty-acre wooded tract located on the eastern edge of the town, where the erection of two new structures was begun in the spring of 1884. Here David Starr Jordan, the professor of natural history who was chosen president in 1885, and his successors laid the foundations for a bigger and better university. Although Jordan left to become the first president of newly established Leland Stanford Junior University in California in 1891, during his six years of presidential leadership he strengthened the Indiana institution by calling to the faculty many men who became distinguished scholars and by helping to gain popular and legislative support for the state-supported university. A prominent ichthyologist himself, Jordan particularly promoted the development of scientific research at Indiana University, which in 1895 established a biological sta-

---

[45] Sister M. Salesia Godecker, *History of Catholic Education in Indiana: A Survey of the Schools, 1702-1925* (St. Meinrad, Ind., 1926), pp. 45, 66-69, 71-77; Edward F. Spiers, *The Central Catholic High School: A Survey of their History and Status in the United States* (Washington, D.C., 1951), p. 29; *Indiana Catholic and Record* (Indianapolis), special supplement, August 30, 1935, pp. 46, 81. Catholic parishes in a few other Indiana cities began offering high school training in these same years. *Ibid.*, pp. 81-88.

tion at Lake Wawasee and later one at Winona Lake. He also led a revolt against the traditional fixed curriculum, successfully persuading the faculty to adopt a system of elective courses and specialized "major subjects."[46]

Enrollment gradually rose from under 400 in 1890, when the preparatory department was finally abolished, to 3,200 by 1919. Much of the university's expansion in educational facilities took place during the thirty-five year presidency of educational psychologist William Lowe Bryan, who was elevated to that position in 1902. In 1910 standards for the School of Law, which had been re-established in 1889 after a lapse of a decade, were raised by requiring entering students to have completed two years of college. In 1912 an Extension Division was formed to supervise the growing off-campus courses which had begun as early as 1891, when Professor Jeremiah W. Jenks was invited by the Indianapolis Association of Collegiate Alumnae to deliver a series of lectures on economics. The Graduate School was formally organized in 1904, though the first earned masters' degrees were granted as early as 1882. But Indiana University did not greatly expand its graduate work until after the First World War. In 1915 seventy-eight graduate degrees—only six of them doctorates—constituted the largest total awarded in any single year in this period. The School of Medicine was opened in 1903, but there was no School of Dentistry until 1925, while

[46] James A. Woodburn and Burton D. Myers, *History of Indiana University* (2 volumes, Bloomington, Ind., 1940, 1952), I, 332-333, 360-400, 432-433. David Starr Jordan was born in New York state and graduated from Cornell University. After teaching briefly at Indianapolis High School and Butler University in the late seventies, he went to Indiana University as professor of natural history in 1879 and was chosen president five years later. Some of the faculty he had recruited for Indiana followed him to Stanford University, where he served as president for twenty-two years; he also became a widely known spokesman for anti-imperialism and pacifism. In his autobiography, *Days of a Man*, published nine years before his death in 1931, Jordan related his experiences in the reform and rebuilding of Indiana University. David Starr Jordan, *The Days of a Man: Being Memories of a Naturalist, Teacher, and Minor Prophet of Democracy* (2 volumes, New York, 1922), I 288-300; Edward McNall Burns, *David Starr Jordan: Prophet of Freedom* (Stanford, Calif., 1953), pp. 1-33.

the School of Commerce came into existence in 1920 and the School of Music in 1921.[47]

In the eighties and nineties Purdue University, the Federal land-grant college which had opened in Lafayette, Indiana, in 1874, began to have its goals of practical education more clearly defined and more generally accepted. From the beginning, however, more students tended to enter the school of mechanics than the school of agriculture, each of which had been separately organized in 1879. By 1882 a full course in mechanical engineering was available, and schools of civil engineering and electrical engineering were opened in 1887 and 1888, respectively. The university also built an engineering laboratory, which acquired the famous steam locomotive, "Schenectady No. I," in 1891. With the assistance of pharmacist John N. Hurty of Indianapolis who agreed to lecture twice a week at Purdue, a school of pharmacy was begun in 1884. Under the presidency of Winthrop E. Stone, in the early years of the twentieth century, Purdue University further enlarged its facilities, adding departments of education, home economics, applied mechanics, and chemical engineering. By 1919 student enrollment, which had barely exceeded 100 in 1880 and reached only 849 in 1900, was recorded at 2,605.[48]

At first Indiana was parsimonious in its support of state institutions of higher education. Before 1895 the General Assembly made separate biennial appropriations for Indiana University, Purdue University, and the State Normal School at Terre Haute. Purdue, however, failed to obtain any money from the state in either 1883 or 1887, when the legislature refused to appropriate funds for it. On the other hand, in

---

[47] Trustees of Indiana University, *Biennial Report,* 1899-1900, p. 5; Woodburn and Myers, *History of Indiana University,* II, 57-59, 238, 265-266, 451, 462-465, 636-656, 660-665; Indiana *Year Book,* 1919, p. 1177.

[48] Purdue University, *Annual Report,* 1901, p. 11; William Murray Hepburn and Louis Martin Sears, *Purdue University: Fifty Years of Progress* (Indianapolis, 1925), pp. 68-70, 82-83, 84, 85-86, 91-93, 120-123; H. B. Knoll, *The Story of Purdue Engineering* (West Lafayette, Ind., 1963), p. 33; Indiana *Year Book,* 1919, p. 1177.

1883 the legislature established a small permanent endowment for Indiana University by voting a tax of 1/2 cent on each $100 of taxable property for that purpose. Finally, in 1895 the General Assembly levied a tax of 1/6 of a mill on the dollar to be apportioned among all three of the state's institutions of higher education, 1/15 going to Indiana University and 1/20 each to Purdue and the State Normal School. The constant pleading of the three presidents and their trustees over the next several years produced increasingly generous tax legislation as well as frequent appropriations for buildings and equipment.[49]

The chief competitors of the state universities in professional education were the independent proprietary schools. As late as 1920 large numbers of lawyers were still being trained by two private Indianapolis institutions, the Indiana Law School, which was founded in 1894 by William P. Fishback, Charles W. Fairbanks, and other local attorneys, and the Benjamin Harrison Law School, the successor to the Indianapolis College of Law, which was opened in 1898. In the training of musicians Indianapolis also led, with the Metropolitan School of Music, organized in 1895, and the Indiana College of Music and Fine Arts, which was established in 1907 as the College of Musical Art. The name was changed in 1918. Two additional schools were the Fort Wayne Conservatory of Music, founded in 1871, and the South Bend Conservatory of Music which was inaugurated in 1906. After Purdue, the most important engineering college in Indiana was Rose Polytechnic Institute, a private institution opened in Terre Haute in 1883 through the beneficence of the wealthy railroad man, Chauncey Rose. Its student body slowly expanded, outgrowing the original campus to such a degree that

---

[49] *Laws of Indiana,* 1883, pp. 82-84; 1895, pp. 171-172; Hepburn and Sears, *Purdue University,* pp. 73, 79-80; Woodburn and Myers, *History of Indiana University,* I, 428-429. In 1913 the legislature raised the tax levy to seven cents on each $100 of taxable property, with two fifths of the proceeds going to each of the state universities and one fifth to the State Normal School. *Laws of Indiana,* 1913, pp. 506-507.

in 1917 the college was moved to a completely new site on the eastern edge of Terre Haute.[50]

The first school of dentistry in the state was founded in 1879, when the Indiana State Dental Association took the initiative in organizing the Indiana Dental College in Indianapolis. A shorter-lived institution, the Central College of Dentistry, was conducted in the same city from 1897 to 1905. Finally, in 1925 the Indiana Dental College was purchased by the state and incorporated into Indiana University as its School of Dentistry. The Indianapolis College of Pharmacy was opened in 1904 as a department of Winona Technical Institute and long survived that ambitious but ill-fated trade school. Two institutions for the training of veterinarians existed in the state, Indiana Veterinary College, established in Indianapolis in 1892 by Louis A. Greiner, and Terre Haute Veterinary College, incorporated in 1909.[51]

Medical education was conducted largely on a proprietary basis until the consolidation of the most significant institutions with the Indiana University School of Medicine in 1908. At the turn of the century the principal schools were the Central College of Physicians and Surgeons (1879) and the Medical College of Indiana (1869), both located in Indianapolis, and the Fort Wayne College of Medicine (1879), all three of which were combined in 1905 under the name of the Indiana Medical College as the School of Medicine of Purdue University. In the meantime Indiana University, which had established a preprofessional School of Medicine in Bloomington under Dr. Burton D. Myers in 1903, began negotiations for clinical facilities in Indianapolis. In 1906 the affiliated State College of Physicians and Surgeons was opened

[50] Cottman, *Centennial History and Handbook of Indiana,* pp. 352-353, 436-438; Benjamin Harrison Law School, *Catalogue,* 1920-1921; Homer L. Patterson (comp.), *Patterson's American Educational Directory,* XI (1914), pp. 103-104, 109; Indianapolis *Star,* January 27, 1918, p. 12.

[51] Jack D. Carr, History of the Indiana Dental College, 1879-1925 (Unpublished Master's thesis in Education, Butler University, 1957), pp. 19-20, 68-69, 80; Woodburn and Myers, *History of Indiana University,* II, 265-269; Cottman, *Centennial History and Handbook of Indiana,* pp. 353-354, 438.

in the capital city to conduct the last two years of the full four-year course of the Indiana University School of Medicine. The next year both Purdue and Indiana Universities applied to the state legislature to legalize their respective medical training programs, but in the heated struggle between the officers and supporters of the two competing institutions neither received the nod of the General Assembly at that session. Finally, in 1908 a successful compromise was effected whereby Purdue agreed to withdraw from medical education, and Indiana Medical College was united with the Indiana University School of Medicine. The main facilities of the school were to remain in Indianapolis, though up to two years of preclinical work were still offered on the Bloomington campus. After 1910 the university also required two years of college work for entrance to the School of Medicine. Within the next decade medical education in the state was established more securely with the erection of a modern teaching hospital in 1914 through the gifts of Dr. and Mrs. Robert W. Long of Indianapolis and a new classroom and laboratory building adjacent to it in 1919.[52]

There was little or no professional teacher training available in Indiana until the opening of the State Normal School in Terre Haute in 1870. The next two decades, however, witnessed the birth of nearly a score of private normal schools. Many of them were hardly more than academies, though a very few eventually became standard four-year colleges. In 1892 a historian of Indiana education listed fifteen such institutions in existence at that time:

[52] Burton Dorr Myers, *The History of Medical Education in Indiana* (Bloomington, Ind., 1956), pp. 137-150, 158, 167-169. In 1924 the James Whitcomb Riley Memorial Hospital for Children was added to the Indiana University Medical Center. *Ibid.*, pp. 176-177.

## PRIVATE NORMAL SCHOOLS[53]

| Year of establishment | Location | Name of Institution |
|---|---|---|
| 1873 | Valparaiso | Northern Indiana Normal |
| 1876 | Ladoga | Central Indiana Normal School |
| 1876 | Danville | Central Normal College and Commercial Institute |
| 1880 | Mitchell | Southern Indiana Normal College |
| 1883 | Hope | Hope Normal School |
| 1884 | New Providence | Borden Institute |
| 1885 | Covington | Indiana Normal College |
| 1885 | Angola | Tri-State Normal College |
| 1888 | Princeton | Southern Indiana Normal College |
| 1889 | Marion | Marion Normal College |
| 1889 | Columbus | Normal School and Business Institute |
| 1890 | Ridgeville | Ridgeville College and Indiana Normal School |
| 1890 | Rushville | Academic and Music Institute |
| 1890 | Evansville | Indiana Normal University |
| 1891 | Muncie | Normal and Classical Institute |

By the mid-eighties other institutions also occupied the teacher-training field. In 1886 Indiana University, which had experimented from time to time with normal courses since 1852, organized a regular department of pedagogics under the headship of Richard G. Boone, who had been city superintendent of schools in Frankfort. Some private liberal arts colleges also offered degrees in education during this period,

[53] Adapted from table in Boone, *History of Education in Indiana*, p. 437. Other institutions of the same type not included in this list were Richmond Normal School, which lasted from 1883 to 1887, and Rochester Normal School, founded in 1895. *Ibid.*, pp. 392-393; Cotton, *Education in Indiana* (*1793 to 1934*), pp. 364-365, 365-366.

such as DePauw University, which operated a school of pedagogy from 1885 to 1890.[54]

Most normal courses of study at the turn of the century
covered simply the common school branches, with some
attention paid to professional training, including educational
psychology and the history and philosophy of education.
Academic standards were generally low, for many students
had only an elementary school background before enrolling,
and academic terms were short, often only a few months.
In 1907, however, the passage of a teacher training law
which made the State Board of Education an accrediting
agency for normal schools brought a sudden change. Many
of the weaker institutions were forced to close their doors,
while others upgraded their programs in order to meet the
new standards, including the demand for a high school diploma as a prerequisite for admission. Even the State Normal
School at Terre Haute, which had previously offered a variety
of courses of study extending from one to four years in
length, remodeled its program radically. The first regular
college course was initiated in 1907 and the first bachelors'
degrees were granted the next year. Although both Indiana
and Purdue universities, as well as several private colleges,
enrolled many students in their education departments, the
State Normal School continued to produce a large proportion
of Indiana's public school teachers.[55]

During the First World War another publicly supported
normal school took form in Muncie in order to provide equal
educational opportunities for students in the eastern half of
the state. This was made possible partly through the philan-
thropy of the glass-manufacturing Ball brothers, who purchased and turned over to the state of Indiana the property
of the former Muncie Normal Institute, a private school and

[54] Boone, *History of Education in Indiana,* pp. 382-386, 391-392. The Indianapolis Normal School was operated as a part of the public school system
of that city after 1869 in order to train teachers for the city schools.

[55] *Laws of Indiana,* 1907, pp. 451-453; William O. Lynch, *A History of
Indiana State Teachers College* (Terre Haute, Ind., 1946), pp. 220-221, 255, 256.

successor to the Marion Normal College which moved to Muncie in 1911. The new institution opened its doors in June, 1918, as the Eastern Division of the Indiana State Normal School but was separated from the latter under an independent administration as Ball State Teachers College eleven years later.[56]

Teachers College of Indianapolis, a private normal school founded in 1884 by Eliza A. Blaker under the auspices of the Free Kindergarten Society of that city, offered a more specialized type of education. "Mrs. Blaker's College," as it was often called, became widely known throughout the nation for its training of highly skilled kindergarten and primary-grade teachers. A somewhat similar institution was the South Bend Training School organized by Alma O. Ware in 1909 to train kindergarten teachers for that city. The German Turner tradition, long represented in Indianapolis by a number of local societies, was largely responsible for the reorganization and permanent removal in 1907 of the Normal College of the North American Gymnastic Union from Milwaukee to the Hoosier capital, where it had previously been conducted between 1889 and 1891. While many of the male graduates of this institution were employed as instructors by the gymnastic association, most of the men and virtually all of the women who completed this course entered the public schools to supervise the growing physical education programs.[57]

Some private normal schools expanded their offerings and developed successfully into broader institutions of higher education. Although it did not change its name, Central Normal College in Danville, which became the property of a group of

[56] Lynch, *op. cit.*, pp. 357-365; Indiana State Superintendent of Public Instruction, *Biennial Report*, 1915-1916, pp. 131-136; Ball State Teachers College *Bulletin*, XXXVI, No. 2 (1960), p. 10.

[57] Indiana State Superintendent of Public Instruction, *Biennial Report*, 1915-1916, pp. 175-177, 183-189. After Mrs. Blaker's death in 1926, Teachers College was continued as an independent institution until 1930, when it became part of Butler University. Thornbrough, *Eliza A. Blaker*, pp. 66-67.

local stockholders in 1900, included liberal arts, law, and music departments along with its accredited teacher training course in the early decades of the twentieth century. Tri-State College in Angola, which opened as a normal school in 1884, added new departments of law, pharmacy, and engineering between 1900 and 1902. Most spectacular of all, however, was the transformation of Northern Indiana Normal School, which became Valparaiso College in 1900 and Valparaiso University in 1907. Sometimes dubbed the "poor man's Harvard" because of its low student costs, this institution grew rapidly, its student enrollment becoming the largest in the state, with a peak of approximately five thousand in the academic year 1914-1915. Besides operating a school of law after 1907, the privately owned university maintained affiliations with a medical and a dental school in Chicago, and later added schools of agriculture, Bible study, and engineering. After the death of its founder-president, Henry Baker Brown, in 1917, Valparaiso entered a period of decline in both enrollment and financial resources and was finally sold in 1925 to the Lutheran University Association, an Indiana corporation composed of members of the Evangelical Lutheran Synodical Conference.[58]

Winona Assembly, which had been conducting summer Bible institutes and other religious meetings at Winona Lake in Koskiusko County since 1894, fathered a group of year-round educational enterprises in the first two decades of the twentieth century. The first of these was a combined agricultural and technical school which was established on the Assembly grounds in 1902 but divided the next year into the Winona Agricultural College at Winona Lake and the Wi-

58 Indiana State Superintendent of Public Instruction, *Biennial Report,* 1915-1916, pp. 164-165, 199; Cotton, *Education in Indiana (1793 to 1934),* pp. 127-129, 140; Central Normal College, *Catalogue,* 1909; Cottman, *Centennial History and Handbook of Indiana,* pp. 290-291; Alice Ann Parrott, *History of Tri-State College, 1884-1956* (Angola, Ind., 1959), pp. 37, 78-82; John Streitelmeier, *Valparaiso's First Century: A Centennial History of Valparaiso University* (Valparaiso, Ind., 1959), pp. 48-49; Moore, *The Calumet Region,* pp. 457-471.

nona Technical Institute in Indianapolis. The latter opened in 1904 as a multidepartmental trade school with wide support from Indianapolis business leaders, a group of whom raised the money to purchase the buildings and grounds of the former Federal Arsenal for its site. Despite this auspicious beginning, the institute became bankrupt in 1910 and gave way three years later to the establishment of Technical (later Arsenal Technical) High School by the Indianapolis school commissioners. In the meantime the same religious association organized Winona Normal School at Winona Lake in 1908 and transformed it the next year into Winona College, a coeducational institution with liberal arts, education, business, and music departments. Winona College survived the Assembly's reorganization in 1918 but faded out in the early twenties even after eliminating all its functions except summer sessions at the popular Winona Lake resort.[59]

The period from 1880 to 1920 was one of substantial growth for most of Indiana's denominational colleges, despite occasional setbacks. In Greencastle Indiana Asbury recovered from financial uncertainty by accepting a large endowment gift from the New Albany glassmaker, Washington C. DePauw, and gratefully changed its name to DePauw University in 1884. Although ambitious plans to establish schools of theology, art, medicine, music, pedagogy, mechanical industries, and horticulture did not come to full fruition, the Methodist-affiliated institution was enabled to erect new buildings and generally strengthen and enlarge its educational program. In the period from 1885 to 1919 DePauw produced more than 2,500 liberal arts graduates, three times as many as during the whole forty-seven year existence of Indiana As-

---

[59] Cottman, *Centennial History and Handbook of Indiana*, pp. 390-391; Indianapolis Public Schools, *Annual Report*, 1916, pp. 61-64; Vincent H. Gaddis and John A. Huffman, *The Story of Winona Lake. A Memory and a Vision* (Revised edition, Winona Lake, 1960).

bury.[60] In 1890 the struggling Fort Wayne College was sold to the theologically conservative National Association of Local Preachers of the Methodist Episcopal Church. Reorganized as Taylor University, it was moved to a new campus in Upland, Grant County, in 1893. Another small Methodist institution, Moores Hill College in rural Dearborn County, encountered such severe financial reverses that it was forced to seek relocation in an urban environment in 1917. Finding fresh sources of support in Evansville, it was reopened under a new charter as Evansville College in September, 1919.[61]

The largest Roman Catholic institution of higher learning in the state was the University of Notre Dame, comprising colleges of science, engineering, architecture, and law, in addition to the college of arts and letters. In 1916 its teaching staff of around eighty was almost equally divided between laymen and members of the Congregation of the Holy Cross. In 1889, the Benedictine Fathers of St. Meinrad's Monastery inaugurated a secular commercial college which was moved the next year to nearby Jasper, Dubois County. The preparatory college at St. Meinrad was later made exclusively a senior seminary. A third Catholic men's college was opened in 1891, when the Society of the Precious Blood established St. Joseph's College at Rensselaer, Indiana, on a tract of land donated by the bishop of Fort Wayne. Two of the older Catholic girls' academies expanded their educational programs to the college level in this period. At Notre Dame, St. Mary's Academy granted its first bachelor's degree in 1898 and St. Mary-of-the-Woods in Terre Haute in the following year,

60 George B. Manhart, *DePauw Through the Years* (2 volumes, Greencastle, 1962), I, 170-183, 292. Schools of theology, law, pedagogy, art, and music were established almost immediately but the school of law closed in 1894, the school of theology in 1898, the school of pedagogy in 1890, and the schools of mechanical industries and of horticulture as well as the college of medicine never materialized at all. *Ibid.,* I, 190-204.

61 Cotton, *Education in Indiana (1793 to 1934)*, pp. 111-113; John W. Winkley, *Moores Hill College: An Intimate History* (Evansville, 1954), pp. 65-69.

though these institutions were not formally opened as colleges until 1903 and 1909, respectively.[62]

Other than those controlled by the Roman Catholic Church, nearly all denominational colleges in Indiana had become coeducational by the eighties. The last to open its doors officially to women in these years was Hanover College, a Presbyterian institution which had enrolled a few girls as special students in previous years, but did not admit them on a regular basis until 1880. One of the main arguments for admitting women to formerly all-male colleges was that the resulting enlargement of the student body might be expected to increase their total resources. For this and other reasons the faculty and students, alumni and other supporters of Presbyterian-founded Wabash College in Crawfordsville warmly debated the introduction of coeducation in the nineties, but the trustees handed down what became the seemingly final decision against the admission of women in 1899.[63]

Butler University, the former North Western Christian University which had been moved from Indianapolis proper to the newly built suburb of Irvington in 1875 and two years later renamed in honor of founder-benefactor Ovid Butler, survived a series of financial and theological crises in the last two decades of the nineteenth century. Dissension arose particularly over the question of sectarian control of the Bible department, which came under severe attack by many of the state's clergy for the allegedly heretical teachings of its head, Professor Hugh C. Garvin, who was forced to resign in 1896.

[62] Indiana State Superintendent of Public Instruction, *Biennial Report,* 1915-1916, pp. 96-97, 108; Cotton, *Education in Indiana (1793 to 1934),* pp. 141-143; Albert Kleber, *History of St. Meinrad Archabbey, 1854-1954* (St. Meinrad, Ind., 1954), pp. 375-386; Marion McCandless, *Family Portraits: History of the Holy Cross Alumnae Association of Saint Mary's College, Notre Dame, Indiana, 1879-1949* (Notre Dame, Ind., 1952), p. 39.

[63] William A. Millis, *The History of Hanover College from 1827 to 1927* (Hanover, Ind., 1927), p. 184; Daniel W. Fisher, *A Human Life: An Autobiography with Excursuses* (New York, 1909), p. 224; James I. Osborne and Theodore G. Gronert, *Wabash College, The First Hundred Years, 1832-1932* (Crawfordsville, Ind., 1932), pp. 207-211.

After recovering from this controversy, Butler became associated with a collection of private law, medical and dental schools in the city as the liberal arts college of the proposed University of Indianapolis. Although the Reverend Burris A. Jenkins, pastor of the Third Christian Church of Indianapolis, was chosen the university's first president in 1899, the merger was never more than an informal alliance which failed to strengthen any of the institutions and was dissolved by 1910. In the meantime Butler Bible College was established in 1898 in order to provide training for the Disciples of Christ ministry. Within a few years, however, this, the first three-year graduate seminary in the denomination, was discontinued, and not until 1913 did Butler resume granting the degree of bachelor of divinity. In 1910 the Christian Woman's Board of Missions established a College of Missions on the Irvington campus, though it had no organic connection with Butler. Another kind of institution sponsored by Indiana Disciples was the Bloomington Bible Chair, which was founded in 1910 as a means of providing religious education for students of that denomination enrolled at Indiana University. In 1917 it was reorganized as the Indiana School of Religion.[64]

Earlham College remained a vital center of Quaker learning in Richmond, Indiana, though it was buffeted by the winds of religious change within the Society of Friends. The most serious controversy concerned the critical interpretation of the Bible and led to the resignation of the professor of Biblical literature and others in the second decade of the twentieth century. Baptist-affiliated Franklin College, which had reached its nadir in the immediate post-Civil War period, experienced a virtual rebirth under the leadership of William Taylor Stott, who served as president for over a quarter of a

[64] Indianapolis *Sentinel,* February 22, 1899; Butler College, *Annual Catalogue,* 1897-1898, p. 5; Henry K. Shaw, *Hoosier Disciples: A Comprehensive History of the Christian Churches (Disciples of Christ) in Indiana* (n. p., 1966), pp. 225, 226, 228, 259-271, 298-301, 309-312, 338. In 1928, Butler made a second move, this time to Fairview Park in Indianapolis. Shaw, *op. cit.,* p. 352.

century from 1872 to 1905. During these years the institution achieved increasing support from Hoosier Baptists as the prejudices against higher education in this denomination were gradually dispelled. In 1891, however, a small dissenting group, the General Baptists, opened their own college in Oakland City, Gibson County, on a site furnished by a prominent resident of that community, Colonel William W. Cockrum. While maintaining its sectarian character, Oakland City College made a significant contribution to a region of the state almost devoid of institutions of higher education by its programs of agricultural and industrial, as well as normal, training. On the other hand, Union Christian College, which had been established by the "New Light" Christians in Merom, Sullivan County, in 1860, struggled unsuccessfully to build a firm foundation in rural western Indiana, finally closing its doors in 1924 and uniting with Defiance Christian College in Ohio.[65]

Several small Protestant denominations became actively engaged in higher education in this period. When the main buildings of Hartsville College, a former academy in Bartholomew County under the control of the church of the United Brethren in Christ (Old Constitution), burned to the ground in 1897, its trustees voted to relocate in Huntington, Indiana. Under the new name, Huntington Central College, it extended its course of study to four years under the administration of Thomas H. Gragg, who was president from 1905 to 1911. Manchester College, founded in 1889 as a successor to Roanoke Classical Seminary, was under the jurisdiction of the United Brethren in Christ (New Constitution) until 1895, when it was purchased by representatives of the

---

[65] Opal Thornburg, *Earlham: The Story of the College, 1847-1962* (Richmond, Ind., 1963), pp. 167-272; John F. Cady, *The Centennial History of Franklin College* (Franklin, Ind., 1934), pp. 110-127; Indiana State Superintendent of Public Instruction, *Biennial Report*, 1915-1916, pp. 179-181; Cotton, *Education in Indiana (1793 to 1934)* pp. 131-133; James W. Conlin, A History of Union Christian College, 1859-1924 (Unpublished Master's thesis in Education, Indiana University, 1931), p. 1.

Dunkers, or German Baptist Brethren, later known as the Church of the Brethren. Turned over to the five state districts of this denomination in 1902, Manchester College grew slowly but steadily under the leadership of Professor Otho Winger, who was elevated to the presidency in 1911. In the meantime, the reform wing of the United Brethren in Christ built Indiana Central College in 1905 on a tract of land donated by Indianapolis businessman William L. Elder in a tract on the southern outskirts of that city, where the suburb of University Heights eventually grew up around the college. In 1903 the Mennonites of northern Indiana established Goshen College, which derived from Elkhart Institute, an academy founded in a neighboring Elkhart County city in 1894. Extending only through the second year of college at first, it became a full four-year institution in 1898.[66]

While many denominational colleges gave serious attention to Bible study and religious instruction, there were few attempts in the state to carry on full-scale pastoral training. Concordia College, which the Missouri Synod of the Evangelical Lutheran Church organized in Fort Wayne in 1861, enrolled only preministerial students up through junior college who were expected to complete their seminary education in St. Louis. Roman Catholics had a similar institution at Floyd Knobs in Floyd County, where the Order of Friars Minor Conventual built a monastery in 1896 and opened Mt. St. Francis Proseminary for the preliminary training of young men for religious vocations. Fairmount Bible School was organized in 1907 by the Wesleyan Methodists, who had been holding a summer theological institute in Fairmount, Grant County, since the early eighties. In 1917 the General Ministerial Assembly of the Church of God opened a Bible

[66] Huntington College *Bulletin,* XXXII, No. 1 (1934), p. 5; Ira H. Frantz (ed.), *Manchester College. The First Seventy-Five Years* (Elgin, Ill., 1964), pp. 33-35, 42-47, 153-155; Russell E. Vance, Jr., *Fifty Years of Christian Education: A Short History of Indiana Central College, 1905-1955* (n. p., 1955), pp. 3-7; John Sylvanus Umble, *Goshen College, 1894-1954: A Venture in Christian Higher Education* (Scottdale, Pa., 1955), pp. 1-25.

Training School at Anderson, seat of the denomination's national headquarters. This institution, which was created to produce lay as well as clerical leaders, later became Anderson College and Theological Seminary.[67]

In the eighties and nineties college life on Indiana campuses was still largely dominated by the literary societies, which had sprung up in earlier decades as student debating groups supplementing the rather narrow classical and mathematical curriculum. Intense student enthusiasm was evoked by the annual speech contests sponsored by the Interstate Oratorical Association, which had been organized in the mid-seventies among midwestern colleges. One of the best-known Hoosier winners in the interstate final competitions was Indiana Asbury's Albert J. Beveridge, whose later platform success launched his meteoric political career. Yet by the turn of the century both oratorical contests and the literary societies had declined, partly, perhaps, because of the greater breadth of the college curriculum as well as the rise of organized athletics. Departmental clubs made their appearance and the Greek-letter fraternal societies became an increasingly significant, and sometimes dominant, factor in many Indiana colleges and universities.[68]

The major change which took place in the character of higher education in this period was the introduction of the elective system as advocated by such nationally prominent edu-

[67] Cotton, *Education in Indiana* (*1793 to 1934*), pp. 143-147; Anderson Bible School and Seminary, *Catalog,* 1926-1927, p. 6; *Concordia Centennial Edition,* 1939, pp. 16-17; Rolland L. Whitson (ed.), *Centennial History of Grant County Indiana 1812-1912* (2 volumes, Chicago, 1914), I, 218; Mt. St. Francis Pro-Seminary, *Silver Jubilee, 1936* (Louisville, Ky., 1936), pp. 53-60.

[68] Woodburn and Myers, *History of Indiana University,* I, 314-317; Manhart, *DePauw through the Years,* I, 128-133, 249-256, 270-274. Although fraternities had existed on Indiana college campuses since before the Civil War, the first Greek-letter sorority in the state and one of the first in the nation was Kappa Alpha Theta, founded at Indiana Asbury University in 1870. Manhart, *op. cit.,* I, 136. A few Hoosier colleges, Earlham being one, had neither fraternities nor sororities, and Valparaiso University did not lift its ban on such societies until 1919, though several had maintained an illegal existence previously. Streitelmeier, *Valparaiso's First Century,* pp. 63-64.

cators as Presidents Charles W. Eliot of Harvard and David Starr Jordan of Indiana University. By the eighties a drift away from the classical-mathematical curriculum was evident in some quarters, though a general shift to departmental specialization and elective courses did not occur until around 1900. Wabash College, with its strong classical tradition, was among the last to abandon the older system and accepted the inevitable change only after an extensive faculty debate in the first decade of the twentieth century. The passing of the fixed curriculum not only opened the way to a larger emphasis upon the natural sciences and modern languages but also helped to modify the old-fashioned lecture-recitation method of teaching, as college professors trained in Germany or in the emerging graduate schools in America introduced laboratories and seminars and encouraged their students to engage in research. President John P. D. John of DePauw University, one of the most enthusiastic advocates of the elective system, described the "spirit of the new education" in 1891 as "not so much to expand the circumference of human knowledge as to determine more fully and accurately what there is within the existing circumference."[69]

The only state-wide organization of colleges and universities was the Indiana College Association, which had been formed in 1877 to bring together representatives of both publicly and privately supported institutions for discussion of common problems. Although the association held annual meetings for over two decades, few concrete efforts toward co-operation were undertaken.[70] In fact, a certain amount of mutual suspicion and hostility continued to mark the relations between the state and denominational colleges up

[69] Cady, *Centennial History of Franklin College,* pp. 143-146; Manhart, *DePauw through the Years,* I, 205-209, 230-242; Osborne and Gronert, *Wabash College,* pp. 230-236; John P. D. John, *The College in the New Education: Presidential Address before the Indiana College Association, December 28, 1891* (Indianapolis, 1892), p. 4.

[70] Indiana College Association, *Addresses and Proceedings,* 1878, p. 2; 1883, pp. 26-28; 1889, p. 53.

through the early years of the twentieth century. In 1897 passage of a bill increasing the powers of the State Board of Education, which included the presidents of the two state universities and the State Normal School, incited the private college educators to form a committee to seek representation on this important policy-making body. As a result, in 1899 the General Assembly voted to authorize three additional members, two of whom were soon appointed from among the ranks of the denominational college presidents—William T. Stott of Franklin and Joseph J. Mills of Earlham. Even this did not put an end to the fears of the denominational and other privately supported institutions. In his first message to the legislature in 1909, Governor Marshall, an alumnus and trustee of Wabash, opposed "lavish aid" to the state universities on the grounds that it threatened the existence of the private colleges. In a conference between the Governor and the heads of the state and private colleges, however, President Francis J. McConnell of DePauw and Thomas Howe of Butler strongly supported the position of the public universities and argued that no basic conflict existed between the two types of institutions in the state, a conclusion which apparently satisfied Governor Marshall and others who feared for the future of the private establishments.[71]

By 1919 a broad spectrum of institutions of higher education had been created in Indiana, with a great deal of variation in size, library facilities, and sponsorship, as indicated in the following table of selected colleges and universities:

[71] Indianapolis *News*, February 2, 23, 1897, October 14, 15, 1909; *Laws of Indiana*, 1899, pp. 426-427; Thomas, *Thomas Riley Marshall*, pp. 103-105; Woodburn and Myers, *History of Indiana University*, II, 105-120. Some advocates of the denominational colleges attacked the state universities on religious grounds, as did the Rev. Thomas A. Goodwin, a Methodist clergyman and alumnus of Indiana Asbury, who published such pamphlets in this cause as *Facts and Figures Showing that State Universities Are Needlessly Expensive, Radically Non-American and Unavoidably Non-Religious* (Indianapolis, n.d.).

Meredith Nicholson, James Whitcomb Riley, Hewitt H. Howland

Indiana State House, Completed in 1888

Union Station, Indianapolis, Completed in 1888

## INDIANA COLLEGES AND UNIVERSITIES[72]

| Institution | Control or Sponsorship | Number of Faculty | Number of Students | Volumes in library |
|---|---|---|---|---|
| Butler University | Christian | 28 | 786 | 15,000 |
| Central Normal College | Nonsectarian | 25 | 846 | 2,600 |
| Concordia College | Lutheran | 11 | 237 | 12,000 |
| DePauw University | Methodist | 50 | 1,062 | 48,000 |
| Earlham College | Friends | 36 | 400 | 26,000 |
| Evansville College | Methodist | 18 | ........ | 10,000 |
| Franklin College | Baptist | 19 | ........ | 22,000 |
| Goshen College | Mennonite | 22 | 351 | 5,806 |
| Hanover College | Presbyterian | 16 | 281 | 30,000 |
| Huntington College | United Brethren | 16 | 190 | 4,600 |
| Indiana Central College | United Brethren | 14 | 174 | 4,100 |
| Indiana State Normal | State | 65 | 3,238 | 80,000 |
| Eastern Division | State | 26 | 1,325 | 3,000 |
| Indiana University | State | 140 | 3,210 | 131,442 |
| Manchester College | Brethren | 20 | 480 | 5,500 |
| Marion Normal Institute | Nonsectarian | .... | ........ | ........ |
| Oakland City College | General Baptist | 16 | 528 | 5,500 |
| Purdue University | State | 183 | 2,605 | 51,795 |
| Rose Polytechnic Inst. | Nonsectarian | 22 | 230 | 16,000 |
| St. Joseph's College | Roman Catholic | 24 | 311 | 11,000 |
| St. Mary's College | Roman Catholic | 56 | 279 | 12,516 |
| St. Mary-of-the-Woods | Roman Catholic | 17 | 115 | 17,937 |
| Taylor University | Methodist | 25 | 245 | 7,150 |
| Teachers College of Indpls. | Nonsectarian | 35 | 1,089 | 7,776 |
| Tri-State College | Nonsectarian | 20 | 450 | 4,000 |
| Union Christian College | Christian | 15 | 95 | 4,350 |
| University of Notre Dame | Roman Catholic | 81 | 2,031 | 103,000 |
| Valparaiso University | Nonsectarian | 104 | 2,200 | 25,000 |
| Vincennes University | Nonsectarian | 18 | 325 | 12,600 |
| Wabash College | Presbyterian | 21 | 325 | 56,000 |

The last two decades of the nineteenth century were marked by a rapid growth in the popularity of organized

[72] Indiana *Year Book*, 1919, p. 1177.

sports and athletic contests. The first to be introduced was baseball, which was widely played both in and out of schools and colleges by the seventies. Perennially popular among students and other amateurs, as a professional game it had an unremarkable career in Indiana. In 1887 Indianapolis retail merchant John T. Brush purchased the National League's St. Louis club and brought it to the Hoosier city, but the team's poor performance over several seasons caused the loss of the franchise in 1890. Ten years later the statutory prohibition of Sunday baseball was the chief reason given for dropping the Indianapolis club from the newly organized American League, formerly the Western League. Even the repeal of the ban on Sunday games in 1909 did not bring back major league baseball to Indianapolis, though it and other Indiana cities were well represented in lesser leagues.[73]

Intercollegiate athletics in Indiana began in a serious way with both baseball and association football, a sport more like English soccer than the American game which later replaced it. According to the Greencastle *Banner,* Indiana Asbury and Butler played a dual baseball and football match on May 15, 1880, though a contemporary Butler College team captain has stated that the same institutions played the first intercollegiate football contest in Indianapolis in 1884, the game going to Butler by a score of four touchdowns to none. In that year Wabash College claimed the state championship by defeating Butler in the fall by the same score. Hoosier teams began to play American football with enthusiasm within the next few years after graduates of eastern colleges introduced the new and more violent game to Indiana. In 1886 the Indianapolis Athletic Club formed a league to sponsor football games among Butler, Wabash, Indiana, Franklin, and Hanover, and by 1890 the Indiana State Athletic Associa-

---

[73] Indianapolis *Sentinel,* February 25, 1898, p. 46; Thomas, *Thomas Riley Marshall,* pp. 70-71; Allison Danzig and Joe Reichler, *The History of Baseball: Its Great Players, Teams and Managers* (Englewood Cliffs, N.J., 1959), pp. 52-53, 61-62. Brush later had a much greater success in baseball as the owner of the New York Giants. Danzig and Reichler, *op. cit.,* pp. 63-64.

tion, which included all these except Franklin and added Purdue and DePauw, was created to organize intercollegiate contests in all sports. Wabash, Butler, and Purdue were early champions in football and Indiana and DePauw in baseball, but the association broke up in the nineties, partly because the small private colleges were becoming outmanned by the large state universities. In 1895 President James H. Smart of Purdue called a meeting of representatives of the University of Chicago, Northwestern, Minnesota, Illinois, Wisconsin, and Purdue universities to draw up plans for the formation of the Western Conference, which eventually became the foremost midwestern athletic association. Indiana University joined the conference in 1899. Notre Dame, which played its first intercollegiate football match in 1887 with the University of Michigan, belonged to the Western Conference only briefly at the turn of the century but later became the strongest independent athletic power in the state, especially during the era of Knute Rockne, who was appointed football coach in 1918.[74]

Field and track events were held frequently at Indiana colleges and universities in the eighties, and by the middle of the next decade tennis had been introduced on some college campuses. Golf arrived somewhat later in Indiana, its introduction being attributed to Alvin S. Lockard of Indianapolis, who brought the game back from India after a world tour in 1897. Basketball was apparently first played in the state at Crawfordsville, where a Y.M.C.A. secretary, N. C. McCay, taught the newly invented game in 1892. Wabash College organized a team which played neighboring

[74] Greencastle *Banner,* May 20, 1880, cited in Manhart, *DePauw through the Years,* I, 143-144; Andrew J. Stott, *Indiana Foot-Ball: College, Athletic Club and High School* (Indianapolis, 1896), pp. 29-30; Osborne and Gronert, *Wabash College,* pp. 257-265; Woodburn and Myers, *History of Indiana University,* II, 396-397; Howard Roberts, *The Big Nine: The Story of Football in the Western Conference* (New York, 1948), pp. 14-17; Arthur J. Hope, *Notre Dame: One Hundred Years* (Notre Dame, 1943), pp. 241, 299-301.

Purdue as early as 1897, and soon basketball became one of the most popular intercollegiate sports in Indiana.[75]

In the nineties many Indiana high schools also began engaging in regular interscholastic athletic contests, especially basketball and football. Most matches were arranged between individual schools, though Indianapolis and a few neighboring cities held four track and field meets under the auspices of the Indiana Interscholastic Athletic Association between 1899 and 1902. In 1903 the Indiana High School Athletic Association was organized in order to regulate competition and record the official scores. From an initial membership of 40 schools in 1904, the association quickly expanded to embrace 450 high schools by 1916. Although football was the most popular sport for many years, it was discontinued in Indianapolis high schools from 1906 to 1915 after a student fracas during a championship match in the city, and attempts were made in the legislature to ban it throughout the state as a dangerously violent game. By the second decade of the twentieth century Wabash College sponsored an annual high school track and field meet. On March 10, 1911, Indiana University inaugurated the interscholastic state basketball tournament with twelve high schools participating. A similar tournament was held at Bloomington each year under the same auspices until 1919, when Purdue University acted as sponsor at Lafayette. In 1921, after Indiana University had regained the contest for only a single year, Indianapolis became the host city for this highly popular annual event.[76]

[75] Kershner, Social and Cultural History of Indianapolis, p. 237; Grady Franklin, "Hoosier Hoop Hysteria Started Here," Indianapolis Star Magazine, March 14, 1965, pp. 50-51; Osborne and Gronert, Wabash College, pp. 267-268.

[76] Indiana High School Athletic Association, Board of Control, Handbook and Annual Report, 1904, pp. 11-12; Indiana State Superintendent of Public Instruction, Biennial Report, 1915-1916, pp. 581-583; Stott, Indiana Football, pp. 181-194; Kershner, Social and Cultural History of Indianapolis, pp. 242-243. See also the pamphlet by Nick Ricos, A History of Basketball at Shortridge, containing a supplement by Thomas Koch, "A History of Football at Shortridge" [Indianapolis, 1944].

# CHAPTER XI

# ORGANIZED RELIGION

In the period 1880 to 1920 Indiana displayed a great multiplicity of sectarian religious divisions but remained overwhelmingly Protestant. According to Federal census calculations, in 1906 the Methodist Episcopal Church was numerically the largest single ecclesiastical organization in the state, though it fell slightly behind the more rapidly growing Roman Catholic Church by 1916. Yet in the latter year Catholics comprised just 23.1 per cent of all religiously affiliated Hoosiers, a proportion appreciably less than that found in the neighboring industrial states of Michigan (48.4 per cent), Illinois (46.4 per cent), and Ohio (36.8 per cent). In third place stood the Disciples of Christ, followed at a little distance by the Baptists (Northern Convention), and the United Brethren in Christ, the Presbyterians, the Lutherans (Synodical Conference), and the Society of Friends (Orthodox), plus a host of smaller Protestant bodies.[1]

Despite the seeming stability, significant changes took place in the structure and practices of much of organized religion in Indiana. Perhaps chief of these was the precipitous decline, particularly noted after the turn of the century, of the rural church, hitherto a main bulwark of Protestantism in mid-America. A careful survey made in 1911 in Boone, Daviess, and Marshall counties—chosen as representative rural areas in the central, southern, and northern sections of Indiana, respectively—showed that almost half of the existing congregations were failing. While 50 per cent of the village churches had resident pastors, only 1.7 per cent of the churches in the open country were so served. In gen-

[1] United States Bureau of the Census, *Religious Bodies,* 1916, I, 109.

eral, the picture emerging from the survey was one of sectarian strife and jealousy, with more separate congregations in each county than the declining population could support, and heavy reliance upon an old-fashioned, fundamentalist gospel which gave scant attention to social and community problems and utilized frequent "religious revivals" as the main methods of attracting new members and revitalizing the old congregation.[2]

Indeed, revivalism flourished in both urban and rural Indiana, though it tended to lose much of its emotional spontaneity in later years. In the spring of 1881 the young evangelist Thomas Harrison aroused many of the people of Indianapolis and reportedly harvested more than 1,200 conversions in a series of revival meetings at Roberts Park Methodist Episcopal Church which spread to several other congregations in the city. On the other hand, when he returned on a similar errand twenty years later he evoked a somewhat less enthusiastic response at the scene of his former triumphs, according to newspaper reports of the meetings. In a period marked by the prevalence of professional revivalism after the pattern of Dwight L. Moody and his many imitators, Indiana produced such prominent evangelists as the Presbyterian J. Wilbur Chapman, who was born in Richmond and was actively associated with interdenominational Protestant enterprises at Winona Lake for several years, and Charles Reign Scoville of the Disciples of Christ, a DeKalb County native and graduate of Tri-State College who became one of the most successful full-time revivalists in the United States.[3]

<hr />

[2] Presbyterian Church in the United States of America, Board of Home Missions, *A Rural Survey in Indiana* (n.p., n.d.), pp. 9-10, 19, 23, 63-64.

[3] J. C. Belman, *The Great Revival at Roberts Park M. E. Church and Other Churches* (Indianapolis, 1881), p. 298; Kershner, Social and Cultural History of Indianapolis, pp. 214-216; Indiana Biographical Series, III, 50, Indiana State Library; Charles R. Cravens, *History of Central Christian Church* . . . ([Anderson], 1925), pp. 401-403. Cravens reported that Scoville was responsible for 1,281 admissions to the church during a fifty-two-day revival in Anderson in early 1906.

By the eighties the old-time camp meeting which had remained from pioneer days was fast disappearing, as more commodious churches were built and Sunday schools and similar institutions developed rapidly, especially in the larger towns and cities. In its place, however, sprang up the summer assemblies, where individual denominations or larger groups sponsored annual evangelistic and other meetings under canvas or in specially constructed auditoriums, following the model of Methodist Bishop John H. Vincent's enormously successful Chautauqua Lake, New York, program begun in 1874. Often former camp meeting sites were utilized for this purpose, as at Battle Ground in Tippecanoe County, where the Methodists held conferences in the mid-seventies. In the eighties the Disciples of Christ founded Bethany Assembly in Morgan County, and the Baptists built Pine Lake Assembly near the city of La Porte. Eventually many of these establishments incorporated a wide variety of educational and recreational as well as purely religious activities. This was especially true of those created as semicommercial enterprises, such as Island Park Assembly on Sylvan Lake near Rome City, Noble County, which was opened in 1891 and soon became known as the "Chautauqua of the West."[4]

Best known of all organizations of this kind in Indiana was Winona Assembly, founded in 1895 by the Reverend Solomon C. Dickey as an outgrowth of his work in Presbyterian home missions. Planned with the advice of the famed evangelist Dwight L. Moody and Bishop John H. Vincent and backed by a board of businessmen which included John M. Studebaker of South Bend, Winona Assembly was built on the shores of Eagle, later Winona, Lake in Koskiusko County.

[4] Indiana Commissioner of Fisheries and Game, *Biennial Report*, 1903-1904, pp. 265, 267-272, 288-290, 308-312; 1913-1914, pp. 156-157; Jack J. Detzler, *The History of the Northwest Indiana Conference of the Methodist Church 1852-1951* (Nashville, Tenn., 1953), pp. 61-64; Shaw, *Hoosier Disciples,* pp. 239-240. German Methodists in southern Indiana did not give up their annual camp meeting at Santa Claus, Spencer County, until 1913. Herbert Heller, *Indiana Conference of the Methodist Church 1836-1956* [Greencastle, Ind., 1956], pp. 210-211.

While Dickey remained the active head of the whole assembly program, J. Wilbur Chapman was brought in to preside over the Winona Bible Conference, which held annual summer sessions and soon became one of the leading centers of interdenominational evangelism in the Middle West. Hotels and cottages were built to house the thousands of summer visitors to this "playground of the Christian world," as the Winona Lake resort was sometimes called, and luminaries of the "sawdust trail" such as revivalist William S. "Billy" Sunday and his musical assistant, the gospel-song composer and publisher, Homer Rodeheaver, became residents of the community. In 1915, however, Winona Assembly was forced into bankruptcy by the financial failure of one of its subsidiary enterprises, an interurban railway line which connected the lake resort with nearby cities. Reorganized and reopened three years later, Winona regained its place as a major American institution of revivalistic fundamentalism with the establishment there of the Reverend G. Campbell Morgan's School of Theology in 1920 and the building of the Billy Sunday Tabernacle in 1921.[5]

At the other end of the theological spectrum were a few representatives of Protestant liberalism who responded to the challenge of an increasingly industrial-urban society by preaching a "social gospel" aimed at the amelioration of oppression and injustice rather than the religious salvation of individual sinners. Among the pioneers of the social interpretation of Christianity in Indiana were such Protestant leaders as Gilbert de la Matyr, a Methodist clergyman in Indianapolis in the seventies who was elected to Congress as a Greenbacker from the district in which the city was located in 1878; Charles R. Henderson, a native of Fountain County who was the pastor of the First Baptist Church in Terre Haute from 1873 to 1882 and later became a noted professor of sociology at the University of Chicago; Myron

<hr />

[5] Solomon C. Dickey, "Winona Assembly and Summer School," *Chautauquan,* XXXI (1900), 635-638; Gaddis and Huffman, *The Story of Winona Lake,* pp. 9-12, 25-28, 56-65, 72.

W. Reed, a popular Presbyterian minister in Indianapolis until his removal in 1884 to Denver, where he founded the interdenominational Broadway Temple in 1895 and was active in Populist political circles; and Worth Marion Tippy, who served Methodist churches in Lafayette, Oxford, and Terre Haute in the nineties before going to Indianapolis and later Cleveland, where he became one of the founders of the Methodist Federation for Social Service in 1907.[6]

The most effective and influential exponent of the Protestant social gospel in Indiana in this period was the Reverend Oscar C. McCulloch, a Congregationalist minister who was called to the pastorate of the small, run-down Plymouth Church located on the Circle in Indianapolis in 1877. Constructing a larger, modern building on another site with reading, recreational, and lecture rooms in 1884, he reorganized the congregation as an "institutional church," with an open membership policy, no creed, and a special concern for the social problems of the city. McCulloch was also an independent thinker and social reformer who boldly supported the demands of organized labor and other unpopular causes in his pulpit utterances. In the fall of 1886 he stood virtually alone among Hoosier public figures in speaking out against the conviction of the Chicago anarchists for their alleged part in the Haymarket riot. He was also a pioneer advocate of organized charity and influenced the drawing up of legislation concerning the state's charitable and correctional institutions and the treatment of dependent children. His early death in 1891, however, cut off his work of socializing the message and activities of the church before it was well enough established to make a permanent impact on Protestant

---

[6] Dunn, *Indiana and Indianans,* III, 1245-1246, 1260; George Irving Reed (ed.), *Encyclopedia of Biography of Indiana* (2 volumes, Chicago, 1899), II, 333-335; *Who's Who in the Midwest* (1956 edition), pp. 844-845; Creighton Lacy, *Frank Mason North: His Social and Ecumenical Mission* (Nashville, Tenn., 1967), pp. 129-130; *Zion's Herald* (Boston), July 6, 1949, p. 629. Reed's liberal humanitarianism can be sampled in a small book of his Denver sermons entitled *Temple Talks* (Indianapolis, 1898).

life in the capital city. His successor, Frederick E. Dewhurst, initiated a neighborhood settlement house and continued the operations of Plymouth Institute, an adult education annex to Plymouth Church where John Dewey gave a series of six lectures in 1893, but the removal of the church to another location to make room for the construction of the Federal building in 1903 virtually ended its institutional program and character.[7]

The social gospel was inspired in large part by the growing realization of the cleavage between organized religion and the workingman. In December, 1890, Indianapolis newspaperman Morris Ross raised this issue in a controversial speech before the Central Labor Union of that city, in which he vehemently criticized the churches for their hostility to labor. In the storm of excitement which ensued, the Reverend John Hilliard Ranger of Christ Episcopal Church published an open letter to Ross heartily endorsing his criticism of ecclesiastical organizations, which the Indianapolis Central Labor Union published in a tract along with the original address by Ross. There is little evidence, however, to indicate that many Hoosier clergymen paid much attention to the industrial problems of the age. Among the scores of published sermons emanating from Protestant pulpits in these years, few contained any reference to the social gospel. One striking exception was a book of short sermons entitled *Samson and Shylock or, a Preacher's Plea for the Workingmen* by a Fort Wayne clergyman who praised the Knights of Labor and proclaimed that "Christianity is communism according to a divine plan." In 1902 the Reverend Worth M.

---

[7] Oscar C. McCulloch, *The Open Door. Sermons and Prayers* (Indianapolis, 1892), p. xxi; George Willis Cooke, "The Institutional Church," *New England Magazine*, XIV (1896), 648-651; Indianapolis *Journal*, October 26, 1885; Indianapolis *News*, November 29, 30, 1886; Plymouth Church *Year Book*, 1893, p. 26; Genevieve C. Weeks, "Oscar C. McCulloch Transforms Plymouth Church, Indianapolis, into an 'Institutional' Church," *Indiana Magazine of History*, LXIV (1968), 87-108; Ruth McCulloch, "Plymouth Church-II," *Indiana Magazine of History*, VII (1911), 89-99. For an account of McCulloch's work in organized charities see below, Chapter XII.

Tippy of Broadway Methodist Church in Indianapolis stirred up a controversy among his fellow Methodist ministers by an address on the duties of the church toward the wage earner. His leading critic was the Reverend Thomas A. Goodwin, a veteran Methodist clergyman and former newspaper editor, who published a polemical attack upon the views of the Indianapolis pastor.[8]

The state and regional denominational conventions were often able to voice somewhat more radical statements of the social application of the Christian gospel than individual ministers dared express in their home pulpits. The historian of the Northwest Conference of the Methodist Episcopal Church has noted that in the nineties and later this group had begun to affirm its sympathies with organized labor in a cautious way while reserving its strongest pleas for personal rather than social morality. In 1905 the General Association of Congregational Churches and Ministers of Indiana upheld the action of the denomination's foreign mission board in rejecting the "tainted money" gift of Standard Oil millionaire John D. Rockefeller. Its resolution hailed "with satisfaction the rising of a public conscience against all methods of money-making, which impair the inalienable right of every man to the reward of his honest labor, and against every form of civic and industrial dishonesty, wherever found." A year later the Baptists invited the well-known social gospel theologian Walter Rauschenbusch to address their state convention, which shortly afterwards appointed a special committee

8 Indianapolis *Sentinel,* December 9, 1890; Indianapolis *News,* February 20, 1891; Morris Ross, *Labor, Society and the Churches* (Indianapolis, 1891); Eli Lilly, *History of the Little Church on the Circle. Christ Church Parish Indianapolis 1837-1955* (Indianapolis, 1957), p. 248; John Merritte Driver, *Samson and Shylock or, a Preacher's Plea for the Workingmen* (Chicago, 1891), pp. 41-42, 211; Indianapolis *News,* June 9, 1902. Goodwin's attack upon Tippy was printed in a pamphlet entitled *Methodist Episcopal Churches and Organized Labor* [Indianapolis, 1902]. Goodwin had earlier shown his deep hostility to organized labor and especially to the Chicago anarchists convicted of murder in the Haymarket riot in 1886 as the editor of a short-lived Methodist journal. *Indiana Christian Advocate* (Indianapolis), September 22, November 17, 1887.

on social service. In one of the strongest statements of "Christian socialism" on record in Indiana, this committee declared to the Baptist state convention in 1914 that "the present world system of capitalistic competition is wrong; it must be superseded by a world system of industrial co-operation, permeated by the spirit of Jesus."[9]

Increased interest in the social interpretation of Christianity also greatly strengthened the ecumenical movement among Protestants, culminating in 1908 in the organization of the Federal Council of Churches of Christ in America. An affiliated state interdenominational council was formed in Indiana the next year, though it functioned for only a brief period. More effective in promoting denominational co-operation were local associations such as the Indianapolis Federation of Churches, which was founded in 1912 as an outgrowth of the Men and Religion Forward Movement, a socially oriented revivalistic campaign which swept through many large cities of the United States in that year.[10] One Indianapolis minister expressed the ecumenical character of the social gospel in the broadest possible fashion in an address before the State Conference of Charities and Correction in 1917:[11]

We are now beginning to search for the roots of responsibility and I thank God that day is at hand when Jew and Gentile, Catholic and Protestant, high and low, meet not upon the plane of theological argument, but upon the splendid territory of that neglected hemisphere, social service, and together we are learning that when we argue religiously we argue apart, but when we love in social service, we love together.

---

[9] Detzler, *Northwest Indiana Conference,* pp. 125-126; General Association of Congregational Churches and Ministers of Indiana, *Minutes of the Annual Meeting,* 1905, pp. 10-11; John F. Cady, *The Origin and Development of the Missionary Baptist Church in Indiana* (Franklin College, 1942), pp. 288-290; Indianapolis *News,* May 11, 1905, p. 5.

[10] Cady, *Baptist Church in Indiana,* pp. 280-281; Indianapolis *Star,* June 8, 1912.

[11] Frank L. Loveland, "Social Service and Religion," *Indiana Bulletin of Charities and Correction,* No. 113 (June, 1918), 172.

§ §

Despite this slowly rising tide of Christian social concern and ecumenicity, organized religion in Indiana remained strongly marked by sectarian sentiment. Methodists, who accounted for the largest sector of Protestantism, were themselves divided into a half dozen or more separate ecclesiastical jurisdictions, of which the dominant body was the Methodist Episcopal Church (North), with 261,228 Indiana members in 1916. Divided into three annual conferences after 1896, when the Southeast Indiana and the Indiana Conferences were merged, the Methodist Episcopal Church in this period gradually completed its shift from a frontier inspirational sect to an ecclesiastical establishment as fully at home in the larger towns and cities as in the rural countryside. Itinerancy gave way to the settled pastorate, and the old familiar Methodist institution of the class meeting was replaced by Sunday schools, women's missionary societies, and the Epworth League. But the church continued to emphasize a strict code of personal morality and regularly issued condemnations of dancing, card playing, the desecration of the Sabbath, tobacco, and especially intoxicating liquors. Perhaps no religious organization took a more fanatical stand for temperance than did the Methodist Church. In 1907, when President Roosevelt was served alcoholic cocktails at a party in the Indianapolis home of the prominent Methodist layman, Vice-President Charles W. Fairbanks, the ensuing publicity helped to prevent the latter from being elected as a Hoosier delegate to the denomination's general conference in Baltimore the next year.[12]

Largest of the independent Methodist bodies in Indiana was the Methodist Protestant Church with 10,367 members in 1916. Originating in a schism from the parent organization

---

[12] United States Bureau of the Census, *Religious Bodies,* 1916, II, 458; Horace N. Herrick and William W. Sweet, *A History of the North Indiana Conference of the Methodist Episcopal Church from Its Organization in 1844 to the Present* (Indianapolis, 1917), pp. 140-141; Detzler, *Northwest Indiana Conference,* pp. 95-97, 128-130; Rissler, Charles Warren Fairbanks, pp. 187-191.

because they demanded greater lay leadership, Methodist Protestants were represented in the state by a single conference created in 1878 by the reunion of two branches which had separated over the slavery question before the Civil War. In 1916 the 4,511-member Indiana Conference of the Wesleyan Methodist Connection of America was the largest state conference of that vehemently antiepiscopal sect, while the somewhat similar Free Methodists claimed 1,128 members in Indiana. Although a few Negroes were enrolled in some of the above churches, the great majority of Negro Methodists were found in the African Methodist Episcopal Church, with 4,961 members in 1916, and the African Methodist Episcopal Zion Church, with 2,465 members. A small number of German Methodist congregations survived into this period, as well as a few affiliated with the Methodist Episcopal Church (South) located near the southern border of the state.[13]

As the churches in the mainstream of the Wesleyan tradition came to place less emphasis on the perfectionist doctrine of "entire sanctification," various holiness and pentecostal sects appeared which drew their membership partly from Methodist ranks. The largest organization of this kind in Indiana was known after 1907 as the Pentecostal Church of the Nazarene, with 1,141 members reported in 1916. In 1898 the Reverend Thomas N. Nelson made Indianapolis the headquarters of the Pentecost Bands of the World, a missionary-minded society organized a decade earlier out of the Free Methodist Church. Other small sects of the perfectionist type centered in Indiana included the following: the Church of God as Organized by Christ, which was founded in 1886 by a Mennonite circuit preacher and maintained its publishing

[13] United States Bureau of the Census, *Religious Bodies*, 1916, II, 465, 471, 488, 497, 504; John C. Coons, *A Brief History of the Methodist Protestant Church in Indiana* (n. p., 1939), pp. 56-58; Heller, *Indiana Conference*, pp. 192-193, 203-204. In 1916 the Methodist Episcopal Church (North) included Negro congregations in its jurisdiction totaling 2,096 members, while the Colored Methodist Episcopal Church, a Southern Methodist affiliate, claimed 258 members. United States Bureau of the Census, *Religious Bodies*, 1916, I, 562.

office in Wakarusa; the Missionary Church Association, which was organized in Berne in 1898 and operated a Bible training school in Fort Wayne; and the Christian Congregation, established in Kokomo in 1899. It is not clear why this kind of religious phenomenon seemed to flourish so vigorously in Indiana, but in 1908 the Indianapolis *News* reported a startling influx of such sects and cults in the capital city. Most of these made their chief appeal to the poorer classes among the white population, though Negro newcomers to the city were also beginning to be affected by the second decade of the twentieth century. In 1915, for example, a Negro evangelist in Indianapolis founded the Apostolic Church of Jesus Christ, which rejected the doctrine of the Trinity and baptized its members in the name of Jesus only.[14]

By far the most important of the holiness sects in Indiana was the Church of God, a loosely organized fellowship formed originally by seceders from the General Eldership of the Church of God, a revivalistic society which had its beginnings under John Winebrenner in the early nineteenth century. The chief founder of the new sect, which stressed the individual's ability to attain full Christian perfection, was an Ohio Winebrennerian named Daniel S. Warner, who moved to Indiana in 1878 and began editing a religious journal, the *Gospel Trumpet,* at first in Rome City, Noble County, and later in Indianapolis. In 1881 the first church in the

[14] United States Bureau of the Census, *Religious Bodies,* 1916, II, 277, 278, 283-284, 286-287, 539; Elmer T. Clark, *The Small Sects in America* (Revised edition, New York, 1949), pp. 77-78, 104; Indianapolis *News,* April 18, 1903, December 26, 1908. The Reverend J. M. Wines described how holiness and pentecostal convictions led him from the Methodist Church to the pastorate of the First Church of the Nazarene in Indianapolis in 1909 in his autobiography, *Hoosier Happenings* (Kansas City, Mo., 1926), pp. 69-71. Similar small evangelistic and holiness groups in Indiana by 1916 were the Apostolic Christian Church, the Holiness Church, the International Apostolic Holiness Church, the New Apostolic Church, and the Churches of the Living God, the last a Negro organization. United States Bureau of the Census, *Religious Bodies,* 1916, I, 168-170. After two or three unsuccessful attempts, the Salvation Army was established in Indianapolis in 1892 and the Volunteers of America in 1902. Dunn, *Greater Indianapolis,* I, 623.

"reformation," as Warner termed his movement, was "called out" in the small community of Beaver Dam in Kosciusko County. Utilizing religious tracts and itinerant lay preachers, the reformed Church of God spread rapidly in rural villages and small towns of the Middle West. Upon Warner's death in 1893 Enoch E. Byrum of Randolph County succeeded to the editorship of the *Gospel Trumpet,* which was published at various places in Ohio, Michigan, and West Virginia before finding a permanent home in 1906 in Anderson, Indiana, which thus became the official headquarters for the Church of God movement. The rise of an increasingly urban membership in the early years of the twentieth century created a need for a regular pastoral ministry and a more complex ecclesiastical organization. Finally, in 1917 a Bible training school was established in Anderson and a general ministerial assembly formed. The latter eventually assumed control of the company which published the church organ, the *Gospel Trumpet,* though the journal's editor remained the acknowledged theological spokesman for the denomination.[15]

Second only to the Methodists in total number of communicants among Protestants were the Christians, or Disciples of Christ, a group which had developed on the American frontier as a "New Testament church" in opposition to denominational divisions. Despite their name and original intentions, Christians in Indiana and elsewhere gradually took on the characteristics of an ordinary ecclesiastical organization. Indianapolis was the headquarters of the Christian Woman's Board of Missions from its foundation in 1874, and Hoosiers

[15] Clark, *Small Sects in America,* pp. 80-81; Charles Ewing Brown, *When the Trumpet Sounded. A History of the Church of God Reformation Movement* (Anderson, Ind., 1951), pp. 81-82, 114, 128-133, 359, 365-369; Frederick G. Smith, *Brief Sketch of the Origin, Growth and Distinctive Doctrine of the Church of God Reformation Movement* (Anderson, Ind., 1926). There are no Federal census statistics for the Church of God until 1926, when 3,801 members were reported; meanwhile, the General Eldership of the Church of God (Winebrennerian) had seen its Indiana membership rise slightly from 2,064 in 1916 to 2,590 in 1926. United States Bureau of the Census, *Religious Bodies,* 1916, II, 215; 1926, I, 172.

dominated the leadership of this national body for many years. A monthly journal, *Missionary Tidings,* was also published in Indianapolis from 1883 to 1919, when it was replaced by the *World Call.* Denominational unity was seriously threatened in the eighties and nineties by a controversy concerning the Biblical authority for missionary societies, church colleges, and the use of instrumental music in worship services. Many congregations were split over these issues, and a large number of conservative brethren, mostly in south-central Indiana, separated themselves from the majority of the fellowship, who accepted organs in the churches. A leading journal for the former was the *Octographic Review,* which its publisher, the Reverend Daniel Sommer, moved to Indianapolis from Illinois in 1894. The main body of the denomination was served by the *Indiana Christian,* which was published in the capital city from 1887 to 1889 and 1892 to 1902 and was revived as the *Indiana Worker* in 1914. The cleavage between the two groups was more or less complete by 1900 and was formalized in the 1906 Federal census of religious bodies, which divided the Christian churches into two separate classifications: the Disciples of Christ, embracing the progressive faction, and the Churches of Christ, which was the name given to the anti-organ congregations. The former emerged as the dominant element in Indiana, with 137,727 communicants reported for 1916 as compared with 16,512 for the conservatives. Moreover, the Disciples were particularly well represented in the growing towns and cities and could claim at least one congregation in every county, while the Churches of Christ were chiefly to be found in smaller communities in the southern half of the state.[16] A separate, though distantly related, body of churches, known collective-

16 Shaw, *Hoosier Disciples,* pp. 211-220, 272-274, 488-489; Alfred T. DeGroot, *The Grounds of Divisions among the Disciples of Christ* (Chicago, 1940), pp. 136-163; United States Bureau of the Census, *Religious Bodies,* 1906, I, 308-310; 1916, I, 258-259. DeGroot, who held an Indiana pastorate for a few years, made a case study of the denominational split within one county in his *The Churches of Christ in Owen County, Indiana* (Spencer, Ind., n. d.).

ly as the Christian Connection or as the American Christian Convention, also preserved a distinct identity, with 20,253 members in 1916.[17]

Hoosier Baptists, most of whom continued to manifest a high degree of traditional congregational independence, had even less organizational unity than the Christians. The largest and most closely knit group was the state convention representing thirty-one associations of "missionary" Baptists, so-called because they supported foreign missions and other forms of denominational co-operation. Their state organ was the *Indiana Baptist,* which was founded in Indianapolis in 1881 and was reorganized in 1896 as the *Baptist Outlook* and in 1902 as the *Baptist Observer.* It was published at Greensburg from 1902 to 1911, and at Seymour from 1911 to 1918, when it was moved back to Indianapolis. Affiliated with the Northern Baptist Convention in 1907, these churches had 75,374 names on their membership rolls by 1916. By the close of the nineteenth century, however, most Negro members had withdrawn from the predominantly white congregations and were separately organized in churches associated with the National Baptist Convention. With 10,412 communicants in 1916, this denomination was the most numerous Negro religious body in Indiana.[18]

The next largest fellowship comprised the General, or Arminian, Baptists, who attained a membership of 7,497 by 1916 but were largely confined to a few southwestern counties of the state. In 1886 the *General Baptist Messenger* was established at Owensville, Gibson County, which became the national publishing headquarters for the denomination. In the first decade of the twentieth century a small schism arose when eight Indiana congregations and one in Kentucky

[17] United States Bureau of the Census, *Religious Bodies,* 1916, II, 198-199. Another similar group of congregations unaffiliated with any of the above but calling themselves Churches of Christ in Christian Union reported 1,366 members in 1916. *Ibid.,* II, 201-203.

[18] Cady, *Baptist Church in Indiana,* pp. 251-252, 261; United States Bureau of the Census, *Religious Bodies,* 1916, I, 562; II, 51, 55.

repudiated the doctrine of original sin and withdrew to form an independent association. On the other hand, General Baptists usually maintained friendly relations with the main body of Baptists in Indiana, though a proposed plan of union was abandoned after a short trial in the years 1914-1915. The somewhat similar Free Baptists, who reported only 1,931 members in 1906, were completely merged with the Indiana state convention of the Northern Baptists in 1913, seven years after fraternal delegates were first exchanged between the two bodies.[19]

Among those rejecting missionary and other denominational societies as unscriptural were the Old School or Primitive Baptists, who were uncompromisingly Calvinistic in doctrine and congregational in polity. A semimonthly journal founded in their interest in 1886 by Elder R. W. Thompson was published for many years in the Hancock County town of Greenfield. While remaining widely scattered in small communities in the southern half of the state, the Primitive Baptists lost considerable ground in this period, their total membership declining from 8,132 in 1906 to 5,432 in 1916. In addition, four congregations of the even more intensely Calvinistic Two-Seed-in-the-Spirit Predestinarian Baptists were reported in Indiana in 1916. In the same year the Separate Baptists, who formed a state association as late as 1898, and the more independent Regular Baptists, both of whom tended to eschew Calvinism and to observe the scriptural rite of foot washing, claimed 1,698 and 1,214 members, respectively.[20] Related distantly to the Baptists were the millenialist sects, which preached the imminent Second Coming of Christ. Of these the Seventh-Day Adventists predominated in Indiana,

19 United States Bureau of the Census, *Religious Bodies*, 1906, I, 186; 1916, II, 122-123; Theophilus A. H. Laslie, *Laslie's History of the General Baptists* (Revised edition, Poplar Bluff, Mo., 1938), pp. 318, 347-348; Cady, *Baptist Church in Indiana*, pp. 76-79, 282, 284-286.

20 *Primitive Monitor*, I (1886), 24-26; United States Bureau of the Census, *Religious Bodies*, 1906, I, 186; 1916, II, 126-129, 136-139, 150-152; Cady, *Baptist Church in Indiana*, pp. 55-57, 80.

with 1,800 adherents in 1916, while the smaller Advent Christian Church and the Churches of God in Christ reported only a few hundred members each.[21]

Present in a few counties of northern Indiana was a fairly large contingent of German Baptist Brethren. Members of a pietistic sect popularly known as Dunkers or Dunkards, the Brethren tended to separate themselves from the world and were for a long time recognizable by their distinctive garb, the women in "very plain dresses, full skirts, three-cornered capes, and large stiff bonnets with short, pleated tails," and the men wearing "long whiskers, hats with broad brims, plain coats and pants, and no neckties."[22] Almost exclusively rural in the eighties, they were beginning to be found in towns and cities by the second decade of the twentieth century and were losing much of their isolation. In 1881-1882 they were split into three separate organizations over questions of polity, discipline, and mode of life. The middle-of-the-road group was styled Conservative Dunkers, who in 1908 assumed the corporate name of the Church of the Brethren, with 12,558 members by 1916. Second in size by the same date with 5,879 members were the Progressive Brethren, who stressed greater congregational independence and preferred later to be called the Brethren Church. The Old Order Baptist Brethren, who attempted to preserve faithfully the traditions of strict nonconformity to the world, never totaled more than a few hundred members in Indiana. Unrelated but similar radical separatists were the Plymouth Brethren and River Brethren, who were also present in the state in very small numbers.[23]

Another Hoosier community of religious sectaries were the Mennonites and Amish, descended from German, Swiss, and Dutch pioneers who had moved westward from Pennsyl-

[21] United States Bureau of the Census, *Religious Bodies,* 1916, II, 17, 25, 33.
[22] Edith Iredale, *A Promise Fulfilled* (Elgin, Ill., 1962), p. 13.
[23] Otho Winger, *History of the Church of the Brethren in Indiana* (Elgin, Ill., 1917), pp. 190, 216-220; United States Bureau of the Census, *Religious Bodies,* 1916, II, 157, 160-161, 164, 167-180.

vania in the early decades of the nineteenth century and settled chiefly in Elkhart and La Grange counties. Most remained on farms in northern Indiana, though a few families
made a short-lived attempt to establish a colony in Brown
County in the period 1896-1910. Somewhat like the Dunkers,
they tended to subdivide into sects according to the degree
of separation from the world practiced by each. In 1916,
however, the Indiana-Michigan conferences of the two major
groups, the Mennonites and the Amish Mennonites, were
united to form the Mennonite Church, with 2,903 members in
Indiana. The next largest division, with 1,942 members, was
composed of Old Order Amish Mennonites, who clung faithfully to the plain style of costume, with hooks and eyes in place
of buttons, and used the German language for worship services, which were generally held in private homes rather
than churches. Minor schismatic groups which maintained a
separate corporate existence in Indiana in these years were
the Conservative Amish Mennonite Church, the Reformed
Mennonite Church, the Defenseless Mennonites, the Mennonite Brethren in Christ, and the Old Order Mennonites or
Wislerites, who seceded in 1870 under the leadership of Jacob
Wisler, first Mennonite bishop in Indiana.[24]

Although small in numbers, Indiana Mennonites published
a large quantity of religious literature in both English and
German. In 1867 a leading Mennonite editor, John F. Funk,
moved from Chicago to Elkhart, bringing with him his three-
year old *Herald of Truth* and the German-language *Herold
der Wahrheit,* which he published in that city until 1908,
when the former was merged with the *Gospel Herald* in Scottdale, Pennsylvania. Funk also founded the Mennonite Publishing Company in 1875 and for fifty years issued religious
books from his Elkhart headquarters. Berne, a Swiss-de-
scended community in Adams County, was another important

24 John C. Wenger, *The Mennonites in Indiana and Michigan* (*Studies
in Anabaptist and Mennonite History,* No. 10, Scottdale, Pa., 1961), pp. 37-38,
385-392, 398; United States Bureau of the Census, *Religious Bodies,* 1916, II, 418-
421, 424-437.

publishing center for the denomination, with two journals issued there, the *Christlicher Bundesbote* (1882) and the *Mennonite* (1885), the latter becoming the official organ of the Mennonite General Conference, which also published other literature through the Mennonite Book Concern in Berne.[25]

By far the largest Protestant denomination in Indiana deriving from an originally German-speaking population was the Church of the United Brethren in Christ, an organization very similar in both doctrine and polity to the Methodist Episcopal Church. In the eighties the church was deeply divided by a controversy over a new constitution, which modified the traditional ban on membership in secret societies among other things. The majority of the congregations in the four Indiana conferences accepted the innovations, but a conservative faction seceded and appealed to the state courts to obtain the rights to ecclesiastical property. The "Old Constitution" United Brethren kept control of the denominational college at Hartsville, which was subsequently moved to Huntington, Indiana, where a publishing house was also established. The seceders gradually lost ground in the state, however, and by 1916 were outnumbered 59,955 to 3,655 by the main body of the United Brethren in Christ. Not to be confused with either branch of the United Brethren in Christ was the older Unitas Fratrum, or Moravian Church, which had only three congregations in Indiana in 1916.[26]

Another church of German origin which suffered a cleavage in this period was the Evangelical Association, also a Methodist-type organization. Long-standing differences over episcopal discipline came to the surface at an annual conference

---

[25] Wenger, *The Mennonites in Indiana and Michigan,* pp. 25-26; Harold S. Bender, *Two Centuries of American Mennonite Literature. . . . (Studies in Anabaptist and Mennonite History,* No. 1, Goshen, 1929), pp. 30-31, 97, 99; *Indiana. A Guide to the Hoosier State,* p. 417.

[26] Adam Byron Condo, *History of the Indiana Conference of the Church of the United Brethren in Christ* (n. p., 1926), pp. 80-81; Augustus Cleland Wilmore, *History of the White River Conference of the Church of the United Brethren in Christ . . .* (Dayton, O., 1925), pp. 204-209; United States Bureau of the Census, *Religious Bodies,* 1916, II, 526, 694-699, 701-703.

in Indianapolis in 1891, resulting three years later in the secession of the United Evangelical Church. All but two Indiana congregations, however, remained with the Evangelical Association, which reported 8,787 members in 1906.[27]

Indiana's extensive German and German-descended population also supported a wide variety of Lutheran churches. The majority of them belonged to the theologically conservative Missouri Synod in the Evangelical Lutheran Synodical Conference. This group conducted Concordia College, a training institution for preseminarians in Fort Wayne, as well as eighty-five parochial schools throughout the state by 1920. Also represented was the Joint Synod of Ohio and Other States, which broke with the Synodical Association in 1881 when the latter began to emphasize the doctrine of predestination. Congregations affiliated with the more liberal General Synod and the General Council of the Evangelical Lutheran Church tended to make greater use of the English language in their religious services than the predominantly German-speaking Missouri and Ohio synods. According to the Federal census of religious bodies in 1916, Indiana Lutheran membership was distributed as follows: Synodical Conference, 38,309; General Synod, 10,505; Joint Synod of Ohio and Other States, 9,570; General Council, 6,209. In addition two congregations reporting 1,342 members adhered to the independent Immanuel Synod, which, however, disbanded the next year. In 1920 the formation of the United Lutheran Church brought all the congregations belonging to the General Synod and the General Council into a single state organization, the Indiana Synod.[28]

27 United States Bureau of the Census, *Eleventh Census* (1890), III, *Report on Statistics of Churches,* p. 371; *Religious Bodies,* 1906, II, 269-272; 1916, II, 269. In addition, two congregations of the liberal Evangelical Protestant Church of North America, which was formed by the union of a number of independent German-American churches in the Middle West, existed in Indiana in 1916. *Ibid.,* 1916, II, 271-272.

28 Missouri Synod, Evangelical Lutheran Church, *Central District School Bulletin,* I, No. 2 (September, 1920), 6; United States Bureau of the Census, *Religious Bodies,* 1916, II, 351-354, 359-371, 381-384, 399-400; Indiana Synod of

Another important group of German-speaking congregations, claiming 25,403 communicants in 1916, were identified with the German Evangelical Synod, which took its origin from the union of Lutheran and Reformed elements in the State Church of Prussia. In contrast, the German Reformed Church, which was presbyterian in polity and Calvinist in theology, could claim only 10,642 adherents in Indiana in that year.[29]

The Indiana Synod of the Presbyterian Church in the United States of America, which was formed by the consolidation of the state's northern and southern synods in 1881, a decade after the reunion of the Old School and New School factions, comprised eight presbyteries and 59,209 members in 1916. Unlike some of the more popular sects, the chief strength of the Presbyterians lay in the larger towns and cities from the beginning, with little following in the rural countryside. The synod's first official organ was the *Indiana Presbyterian*, a monthly which began publication in Indianapolis in 1914. In 1907 the Cumberland Presbyterian Church, which was represented only in certain southern counties, agreed to merge with the larger body, but a minority of congregations rejected the union and decided to continue as an independent ecclesiastical organization, reporting a total of 1,146 members in Indiana in 1916. Another related denominational entity was the Scottish Covenanter-derived United Presbyterian Church, which claimed 2,844 Hoosier members in that same year.[30]

Among major religious groups in Indiana, only the Quakers declined absolutely in total numbers in this period, membership in the Orthodox Society of Friends falling from 29,-

---

the United Lutheran Church in America, *Proceedings of the First Convention,* 1920, pp. 7-13; Defenderfer, *Lutheranism at the Crossroads of America,* pp. 58-59.

[29] United States Bureau of the Census, *Religious Bodies,* 1916, II, 306-308, 629-632.

[30] *Ibid.,* 1916, II, 560-562, 573, 585; Synod of Indiana of the Presbyterian Church, *Minutes,* 1906, pp. 38, 46.

255 in 1906 to 26,658 in 1916. In addition, a small contingent of the more liberal Hicksite Friends existed side by side with the Orthodox Indiana Yearly Meeting in the eastern half of the state, while in 1877 a number of Conservative, or Wilburite, Friends separated from the Western Yearly Meeting centered at Plainfield, Hendricks County. By the eighties evangelistic revivalism was a powerful force among many Quakers in Indiana, resulting in the rapid introduction of such innovations as congregational singing and a settled pastorate in place of the traditional silent worship and lay ministry. While quietism did not altogether die out, the Society of Friends tended to lose its distinctive characteristics and to move closer to the mainstream of evangelical Protestantism in this period, though failing to maintain its former level of membership.[31]

Nevertheless, Indiana remained one of the chief centers of Quaker life, and Indiana friends played an important part in the national movement for a unified faith and polity. It was two active Quaker leaders in Richmond, Timothy Nicholson and Allen Jay, who in 1886 initiated the call for a general conference of Friends to explore the possibilities for greater unity. The following year delegates from all over the world gathered at Richmond, where after some discussion they drew up a Declaration of Faith which was eventually adopted by most Orthodox Friends' Yearly Meetings in the United States. Subsequently a series of three quinquennial conferences held in Indianapolis between 1892 and 1902 resulted in the formulation of a uniform discipline and constitution to which eleven Orthodox Quaker organizations subscribed, thus constituting the Five Years Meeting of Friends in America as an advisory and co-ordinating agency for the denomination. The first conference of the new body was con-

---

[31] United States Bureau of the Census, *Religious Bodies,* 1906, I, 109; II, 303-305; Willard Heiss, *A Brief History of Western Yearly Meeting of Conservative Friends and the Separation of 1877* (Indianapolis, 1963), pp. 3-6; Elbert Russell, *Elbert Russell, Quaker. An Autobiography* (Jackson, Tenn., 1956), pp. 89-104, 116-120.

vened in Richmond, the birthplace of the movement, which was then appropriately chosen by the delegates for the national headquarters. In 1913 the *American Friend,* a long-established Quaker journal, was also moved from Philadelphia to Richmond to become the official organ of the Five Years Meeting.[32]

The Protestant Episcopal Church enrolled relatively few communicants in Indiana, though its membership rose from 5,185 to 8,848, or over 40 per cent in the period 1890-1916, according to statistics reported to the United States Bureau of the Census. Moreover, Hoosier Episcopalians, among whom were included many persons of wealth and high social position, chiefly residing in the larger cities of the state, exercised an influence disproportionate to their numbers. Bishop David Buell Knickerbacker inaugurated the monthly *Church Worker* in Indianapolis in 1883 and was active in the founding of Howe Grammar School in Lima, La Grange County, and in other educational projects. In 1898 the General Convention of the Protestant Episcopal Church authorized the division of the Diocese of Indiana, with a second episcopal seat to be established in the northern half of the state at Michigan City. The next year Bishop John Hazen White, who had succeeded Bishop Knickerbacker in Indianapolis upon the latter's death in 1894, was transferred to the new diocese, while the Reverend Joseph Marshall Francis, pastor of an Evansville parish, was elected to replace Bishop White at the capital where the new All Saints Cathedral was dedicated in 1911.[33]

Even less numerous than Episcopalians were Congregationalists, who failed to put down deep roots in the state,

32 Allen Jay, *Autobiography* (Philadelphia, 1910), pp. 356-363; Walter C. Woodward, *Timothy Nicholson, Master Quaker* (Richmond, Ind., 1927), pp. 189-198; *American Friend,* N. S., I (1913), 3-4.

33 United States Bureau of the Census, *Eleventh Census* (1890), III, *Report on Statistics of Churches,* p. 707; *Religious Bodies,* 1916, II, 616; Sarah S. Pratt, *Episcopal Bishops in Indiana. A Churchwoman's Retrospect* (Indianapolis, 1934), pp. 32-37, 50; Lilly, *Christ Church,* p. 263.

despite the active extension work of the Home Missionary Society of Indiana. Created originally in 1880 as an auxiliary of the New England-based American Home Missionary Society, this organization was merged with the General Association of Congregational Churches and Ministers of Indiana in 1911 to form the Congregational Conference of Indiana. Congregationalist membership grew from 3,881 in 1890 to 5,768 in 1916 but was largely concentrated in a few cities. Special efforts were made to found new congregations in the Gas Belt and in southern Indiana, but with little permanent success. Even the ten churches in Indianapolis—eight of them organized in the nineties—were reduced to five by 1919, the largest, First Congregational Church, having been formed from a consolidation of three others, North Congregational Church, Plymouth Church, and Mayflower Church. Moreover, attempts to maintain a small church academy, taken over from the Free Baptists, and to start a state journal were doomed to failure.[34]

The Universalist churches, which were once scattered widely across rural Indiana, suffered a severe decline in number and membership in the early twentieth century. The total of 44 congregations and 2,506 members reported to the United States Bureau of the Census in 1906 shrank to 24 congregations and 1,656 members ten years later. Far less numerous in Indiana, the urban-oriented Unitarians were represented in 1916 by only two societies, the largest having been re-established in Indianapolis as All Souls Unitarian Church in 1903 after a lapse of more than thirty years.[35]

In 1888 the Indiana Association of Spiritualists held its first convention in Anderson, though Spiritualism had been practiced in the state since before the Civil War. Four years later a campground was secured at Chesterfield, where an-

---

[34] United States Bureau of the Census, *Religious Bodies,* 1916, II, 242; Herbert L. Whitehead, *History of Indiana Congregationalism* (n.p., 1919), pp. 5-9, 12-13.

[35] United States Bureau of the Census, *Religious Bodies,* 1906, II, 657; 1916, II, 692, 712; Dunn, *Greater Indianapolis,* I, 622.

nual summer assemblies rivaling those at the more famous Spiritualist center in Lily Dale, New York, were held. In 1904 another state body was organized as an auxiliary to the National Spiritualist Association, which claimed 1,161 adherents in Indiana in 1916. In that same year three small Indiana societies were reported as affiliates of the Theosophical Society, an Oriental cult stressing the essential unity of all world religions. Other religious movements represented in the state by only a few hundred adherents were the Mormons, almost equally divided between the orthodox Church of Jesus Christ of Latter Day Saints and the "reorganized" church of the same name, and the Swedenborgians, or the Church of the New Jerusalem.[36] More influential than any of these minor sects were the followers of Christian Science, which was introduced into Indiana in 1889, when a study group was formed in Indianapolis to inquire into its principles. One of the members of this class, Annie B. Dorland, who went to Boston to receive training under the founder of the movement, Mary Baker Eddy, became the first Christian Science practitioner in the state. In 1897 the First Church of Christ, Scientist, was established in Indianapolis, followed by a second congregation six years later. In 1906 the United States Bureau of the Census reported a total of 1,931 Christian Scientists in Indiana.[37]

Materialism and unbelief also made themselves heard occasionally amid the dominant voices of Protestant Christianity in Indiana. From the late seventies on the famous atheistic orator, Colonel Robert G. Ingersoll, was a frequent visitor to the state while on his popular speaking tours. One of the most effective statements of his religious position was

36 Anna Stockinger, "The History of Spiritualism in Indiana," *Indiana Magazine of History*, XX (1924), 282-283; United States Bureau of the Census, *Religious Bodies*, 1916, II, 225, 335, 343, 680, 686, 688.

37 Indianapolis *News*, December 25, 1909; Dunn, *Greater Indianapolis*, I, 623-624; United States Bureau of the Census, *Religious Bodies*, 1906, II, 200. No statistics were reported for Christian Science membership in 1916. *Ibid.*, 1916, I, 14.

contained in an often-published reply to a group of Indianapolis clergymen who posed a series of questions to him on the occasion of one of his visits to the city.[38] Indiana produced its own little-known but no less colorful rationalist of this period in the person of Dr. Jasper Roland Monroe, a Seymour physician and editor who moved his small-town newspaper to Indianapolis in 1882 and published it there as a lively skeptical weekly under the title *The Iron-Clad Age,* until his death in 1891. Also founder and first president of an association rather grandly called the North American Confederation of Atheists, Dr. Monroe was described in an oration at his funeral by the veteran rationalist, Benjamin F. Underwood, as "an infidel, pure and undefiled." In 1909 another physician, Dr. Thomas J. Bowles of Muncie, and others founded the Indiana Rationalists' Association, which at its fifth annual conference in Indianapolis in 1913 ambitiously transformed itself into a national organization, but little more was ever heard from it.[39]

The German rationalist tradition was also carried to Indiana along with the more orthodox religious opinions of persons of that nationality. In 1883 the Socialer Turnverein of Indianapolis organized a Freethinkers' Sunday School, which enrolled as many as 120 children by 1904. One of the most earnest advocates of free thought was Clemens Vonnegut, a leading figure in the German-American community in that city, who was the author of a pamphlet published in 1900 entitled *A Proposed Guide for Instruction in Morals from the Standpoint of a Freethinker.* German-born J. A. Lemcke of Evansville straightforwardly expressed his own personal

[38] Ingersoll's reply was published in a short-lived Hoosier rationalist journal edited by W. H. Lamaster called *The Iconoclast* in 1882 and later reprinted in Indianapolis as a pamphlet entitled *An Open Letter to Indiana Clergymen by Col. Robert G. Ingersoll* (Indianapolis, 1893). Indiana historian John Clark Ridpath read one of Ingersoll's poems as part of the simple funeral rites following Ingersoll's death in 1898. Orvin Larson, *American Infidel: Robert G. Ingersoll, A Biography* (New York, 1962), p. 272.

[39] Obituary of Dr. Jasper Roland Monroe in Indiana Biographical Series, VII, 55-60, Indiana State Library; Indianapolis *Star,* November 9, 1913.

skepticism about the tenets of revealed religion in his
sprightly 1905 autobiography:[40]

The capsule containing the story of the creation, the fall of man, the
atonement, transubstantiation, the immaculate conception, and all the
innumerable miracles, so eagerly swallowed by the faithful, will not go
down with me; I prefer the conclusions evolved from the study of
nature's secrets by scientific methods, to the dicta of religious sooth-sayers
and dogmatic expounders of the unknown and the unknowable.

Jews constituted a slowly growing religious minority in
Indiana. Most were of German origin and resided in Indianapolis, Evansville, and other large cities where there were
congregations belonging generally to the Reform branch of
Judaism. But in the eighties Jews from Eastern Europe
began to arrive in the state in large enough numbers to
establish more conservative religious societies conforming
to the stricter rules of Orthodox Judaism. The first congregation of this type was Shara Tefila, which was organized in Indianapolis in 1882 by Polish Jews, followed three
years later by Ohev Zedek, a synagogue composed of Hungarian Jews. In 1890 the Eleventh Census reported 1,299
Orthodox Jews compared with 2,318 adherents of Reform.
A few Sephardic Jews of Spanish-Portuguese origin arrived
much later, establishing a synagogue in Indianapolis in 1913.
In the early years of the twentieth century a heavy influx of
Jewish immigrants from Eastern European countries brought
into existence a half-dozen Orthodox congregations in the
industrial communities of Hammond, Gary, and East Chicago–
Indiana Harbor. It is difficult to estimate the total number of
Jews in Indiana because the Federal Census of Religious
Bodies reported only the number of heads of households offi-

40 George Theodore Probst, The Germans in Indianapolis, 1850-1914 (Unpublished Master's thesis in History, Indiana University, 1951), pp. 111, 126;
J. A. Lemcke, Reminiscences of an Indianian. From the Sassafras Log Behind
the Barn in Posey County to Broader Fields (Indianapolis, 1905), p. 83. Vonnegut, an Indianapolis merchant and long-time member of the city school board,
also translated into German Robert G. Ingersoll's famous reply to the Indianapolis clergy as Offener Brief an die Indianapoliser Geistlichkeit (Milwaukee,
n. d.).

cially listed as members of specific congregations. Thus the figure of 5,461 for 1916 is probably too small by half or even more in calculating the true size of the Jewish community, a religious minority which apparently enjoyed a large measure of toleration and respect in Indiana in this period.[41]

§ § §

In spite of a background of anti-Catholic sentiment among Indiana Protestants, the Roman Catholic Church encountered remarkably little overt hostility as it expanded steadily in these decades, becoming the largest religious organization in the state by 1916, with 272,283 communicants. The American Protective Association, a secret society founded in Iowa in 1887 for the purpose of preventing the election of Catholics to public office, made its appearance in a few Indiana cities by 1892, but never gained a large following. The only violent incident that took place was a two-hour riot in Lafayette on January 26, 1893, provoked by an attack upon a former priest who was speaking in a public hall under A. P. A. auspices. Although some Protestant journals—notably the *Indiana Baptist*—occasionally joined in denouncing alleged Catholic political influence in the state, the secular press, both Republican and Democratic, repudiated the injection of religious intolerance in Hoosier politics. In an ill-considered attempt to influence the election of school commissioners in Indianapolis in June, 1893, the A. P. A.-backed candidates were soundly defeated.[42]

German and Irish elements predominated in the Catholic population, but Southern and Eastern European immigration in the first two decades of the twentieth century brought about the formation of many Italian- and Slavic-speaking par-

[41] Myra Auerbach, A Study of the Jewish Settlement in Indianapolis (Unpublished Master's thesis, Indiana University, 1937), pp. 10-13; United States Bureau of the Census, *Eleventh Census* (1890), III, *Report on Statistics of Churches,* pp. 414-416; *Religious Bodies,* 1916, II, 331; *The Calumet Region Historical Guide,* pp. 37, 185-186, 211.

[42] United States Bureau of the Census, *Religious Bodies,* 1916, II, 655; *Catholic Record* (Indianapolis), February 2, 9, April 20, 27, May 4, 1893; Indianapolis *Journal,* April 26, 1893; Indianapolis *Sentinel,* June 10, 12, 1893.

ishes. The first congregation composed entirely of Catholics of Italian origin was established in Indianapolis in 1908, and by 1920 there were Croat, Hungarian, Polish, Rumanian, and Slovak parishes in the cities of East Chicago, Gary, Hammond, and Whiting. Moreover, a schismatic body, the Polish National Catholic Church of America claimed 1,904 members in Indiana in 1916. In the same year two more distantly related communions, the Greek Orthodox Church and the Serbian Orthodox Church, reported 2,530 and 2,232 Hoosier communicants, respectively, a large proportion of whom were members of congregations organized after 1900 in the Calumet Region.[43]

Although the original Gallic character of Indiana Catholicism had almost disappeared, the older of the two Roman Catholic dioceses which comprised roughly the southern half of the state remained centered at the old French city of Vincennes on the southwest border of the state as late as 1878. In that year the newly appointed bishop, the Right Reverend Francis Silas Chatard, moved his episcopal seat to Indianapolis. Not until twenty years later, however, was the name finally changed from the Diocese of Vincennes to the Diocese of Indianapolis by a brief of Pope Leo XIII. During his long tenure Bishop Chatard was an energetic organizer who promoted the rapid establishment of parochial schools and the building of the new diocesan Cathedral of SS. Peter and Paul, which was completed in 1907. Although a Hoosier-born priest of Irish descent, the Reverend Denis O'Donoghue, was named auxiliary bishop in 1900 and served until his appointment as bishop of Louisville in 1910, the choice of coadjutor for the ailing Bishop Chatard in that year fell upon the Reverend Joseph Chartrand, whose elevation to the See of Indianapolis upon the former's death in 1918 continued an unbroken chain of French or French-descended prelates since the foundation of the diocese.

43 Dunn, *Greater Indianapolis*, I, 620; *Calumet Region Historical Guide*, pp. 35-38; United States Bureau of the Census, *Religious Bodies*, 1916, II, 257, 263, 548.

Indianapolis was also an active center of the Ancient Order of Hibernians, a secret society dedicated to Irish independence which had been brought to the state by Pennsylvania coal miners just after the Civil War and flourished despite the vehement opposition of the conservative Chatard. In 1899 the first local council of the Knights of Columbus, a fraternal order organized in New Haven, Connecticut, in 1882, was established in Indianapolis.[44]

On the other hand, the Diocese of Fort Wayne, whose jurisdiction covered the northern half of the state, was headed exclusively in this period by clerics of German birth or descent. In fact, the first native American prelate in Indiana was the Right Reverend Joseph Dwenger, who served as bishop of Fort Wayne from 1872 to 1893. He was followed by Bishop Joseph Rademacher, who was transferred from the See of Nashville in 1894 and died six years later. In 1900 the Reverend Herman Joseph Alerding, German-born pastor of an Indianapolis parish, was chosen to succeed him. At the episcopal seat of Fort Wayne was located Colony No. 1 of the American Sons of Columbus, a secret society for Catholic men founded in that city by P. S. O'Rourke in 1892. It was a priest of this diocese and a native of Fort Wayne, the Reverend John Francis Noll, who established the weekly *Our Sunday Visitor* in Huntington in 1912. Originally conceived as an antidote for the socialist and antireligious arguments put forward by such popular rationalist magazines as *The Appeal to Reason*, this journal soon became one of the most influential Catholic periodicals in the United States and brought national fame to its editor-founder. Its phenomenal success undoubtedly helped to elevate Father Noll to the Fort Wayne episcopacy upon the death of Bishop Alerding in 1925.[45]

[44] Charles Blanchard (comp.), *History of the Catholic Church in Indiana* (2 volumes, Logansport, Ind., 1898), I, 94, 105; Humbert P. Pagani, *200 Years of Catholicism in Indiana* (Indianapolis, 1934), pp. 30-33; Dunn, *Greater Indianapolis,* I, 385-386, 615.

[45] Blanchard (comp.), *History of the Catholic Church in Indiana,* I, 171, 175, 642; Richard Ginder, *With Ink and Crozier: A Biography of John Francis*

Many Catholic religious orders were active in Indiana during this period, conducting schools, colleges, and universities, and operating hospitals, orphan asylums, and homes for the aged, as did many Protestant organizations. But no single denomination of Protestant Christians carried on a more extensive program of education and social service than the various arms of the Roman Catholic Church. Male orders included the Benedictines, Franciscans, Fathers and Brothers of the Holy Cross and of the Precious Blood, and Brothers of the Sacred Heart. Women's orders included the Benedictine, Dominican, and Franciscan Sisters, Little Sisters of the Poor, Poor Clares, Poor Handmaids of Christ, Sisters of Charity, of Mary, of Notre Dame, of St. Agnes, of St. Joseph, of the Good Shepherd, of the Holy Cross, of the Holy Family of Nazareth, of the Precious Blood, and the Ursuline Sisters.[46]

The major Catholic educational institution in the state, Notre Dame University, played an increasingly important role in the religious and intellectual affairs of the church at large. In the summer of 1894 the first American Eucharistic Congress was convened on its campus. Moreover, Notre Dame furnished one of the leading figures in the "Americanist" controversy which raged toward the end of the nineteenth century over the adaptation of the Roman Catholic Church to contemporary life and thought. He was the Reverend John Augustine Zahm, C.S.C., the brilliant Ohio-born professor of chemistry and physics and vice-president of the university, who boldly defended a theistic interpretation of biological

Noll, *Fifth Bishop of Fort Wayne and Founder of Our Sunday Visitor* (Huntington, Ind., 1952), pp. 106-116, 189-191; *Our Sunday Visitor,* May 1, 1932. The only other major Catholic paper in the state was the *Indiana Catholic and Record,* a consolidation in 1916 of the *Indiana Catholic,* founded in 1910 by J. P. O'Mahony, and the Indianapolis edition of the *Catholic Columbian-Record,* which had earlier absorbed the *Catholic Record,* an Indianapolis weekly edited by Alexander Chomel and established as the *New Record* in 1882. Dunn, *Greater Indianapolis,* I, 406-408.

46 Godecker, *History of Catholic Education in Indiana,* pp. 54-55, 66-67; *Catholic Encyclopedia* (15 volumes plus index, New York, 1907-14), VI, 150-151; VII, 744-745. For an account of Catholic hospitals in Indiana, see below, Chapter XII.

evolution and advocated the reconciliation of Catholic dogma and modern science. A friend and associate of liberal Bishops John Ireland and John J. Keane, Father Zahm took an active part with them in the Americanist movement through his lectures and writings. But ecclesiastical conservatives attacked the Notre Dame professor for his controversial views, and in 1898 the Sacred Congregation of the Index in Rome placed his book *Evolution and Dogma* (1896) on the restricted list. Although the Pope was persuaded to suppress the edict by friends of Zahm, who had recently been named American Provincial Superior of the Holy Cross Community, the author made his submission to the Vatican by withdrawing the book from sale.[47]

[47] Blanchard (comp.), *History of the Catholic Church in Indiana,* I, 558; Ralph E. Weber, *Notre Dame's John Zahm. American Catholic Apologist and Educator* (Notre Dame, Ind., 1961), pp. 32-93, 121-124; Robert D. Cross, *The Emergence of Liberal Catholicism in America* (Cambridge, Mass., 1958), pp. 149-151; Thomas T. McAvoy, *The Great Crisis in American Catholic History, 1895-1900* (Chicago, 1957), pp. 262-264.

CHURCH MEMBERSHIP OF MAJOR DENOMINATIONS IN INDIANA, 1890-1916[48]

| Denomination | 1890 | | 1906 | | 1916 | |
|---|---|---|---|---|---|---|
| | Number | Per cent of total | Number | Per cent of total | Number | Per cent of total |
| Roman Catholic | 140,118 | 19.6 | 205,705 | 21.2 | 272,288 | 23.1 |
| Methodist Episcopal | 162,989 | 22.8 | 210,593 | 21.7 | 261,228 | 22.2 |
| Disciples of Christ | 78,942 | 11.0 | 108,188 | 11.2 | 137,727 | 11.7 |
| Northern Baptist | 54,080 | 7.6 | 60,203 | 6.2 | 75,374 | 6.4 |
| United Brethren in Christ | 35,824 | 5.0 | 48,059 | 5.0 | 59,955 | 5.1 |
| Presbyterian | 35,464 | 5.0 | 49,041 | 5.1 | 59,209 | 5.0 |
| Lutheran (Missouri Synod) | 24,666 | 3.5 | 34,105 | 3.5 | 38,309 | 3.3 |
| Friends (Orthodox) | 25,915 | 3.6 | 29,255 | 3.0 | 26,658 | 2.3 |
| German Evangelical Synod | 15,274 | 2.1 | 21,624 | 2.2 | 25,403 | 2.2 |
| Christian Connection | 19,832 | 2.8 | 21,397 | 2.2 | 20,253 | 1.7 |
| Churches of Christ | ......... | .... | 10,259 | 1.1 | 16,512 | 1.4 |
| Church of the Brethren | 10,224 | 1.4 | 9,949 | 1.0 | 12,558 | 1.1 |
| Evangelical Association | 6,738 | 0.9 | 8,787 | 0.9 | 10,876 | 0.9 |
| German Reformed | 6,269 | 0.9 | 8,289 | 0.9 | 10,642 | 0.9 |

[48] United States Bureau of the Census, *Religious Bodies*, 1916, I, 109.

# CHAPTER XII

## PUBLIC HEALTH, WELFARE, AND SOCIAL REFORMS

BEFORE 1880 THERE WAS LITTLE CONCERN in Indiana for centralized control or direction of public health and welfare. Among the first voices heard urging state action of this kind were those of physicians, some of whom, like Dr. Thaddeus M. Stevens of Indianapolis, had become ardent advocates of preventive medicine as a result of the gradual acceptance of the germ theory of disease. In 1875 the Indiana State Medical Society named a special committee under the chairmanship of Dr. Stevens to draw up and present to the legislature recommendations for the creation of an agency for the collection of accurate reports of contagious diseases and similar matters, but the General Assembly rejected such proposals in three successive sessions in 1875, 1877, and 1879, partly because of the fear that state regulation of medicine was somehow entailed. In the meantime, in 1878 the resourceful Dr. Stevens reorganized his committee of physicians as an informal state health commission with the addition of three lay representatives. Although this privately supported body attempted to gather health statistics with the help of members of local medical societies and published annual reports which included special articles on sanitation and disease, it soon discovered that it could not function effectively without the official stamp of governmental authority. Finally, in 1881 a former physician, State Senator Flavius J. Van Vorhis, sponsored a successful bill in the General Assembly which established the Indiana State Board of Health, with the assigned duties of collecting vital statistics, making sanitary inspections, and investigating the causes of disease. The temperance-minded legislators also requested the board

members to report "what, in their best judgment, is the effect of the use of intoxicating liquors as a beverage upon the
industry, prosperity, happiness, health and lives of the citizens of the State." In addition the act provided for the creation of co-operating local boards of health in counties, townships, and cities where such did not already exist.[1]

Governor Albert G. Porter appointed four prominent physicians to the State Board of Health, including Dr. Thaddeus
M. Stevens, who was appropriately chosen as its secretary and
thus became Indiana's first state health officer. Yet neither he
nor his immediate successors, who were often named for their
political rather than their medical qualifications, were able
to obtain sufficient backing for a full-fledged program of public health and preventive medicine, though a beginning was
made in collecting vital statistics and disseminating information concerning the cause and control of epidemics of diphtheria, typhoid fever, and other contagious diseases which
frequently appeared in various parts of the state. In the
eighties many Hoosier physicians remained unconvinced of
the existence of disease-causing microorganisms, as revealed
in the statements published in the *Annual Report* of the board.
Finally this official endorsement of the germ theory appeared
in the *Report* for 1889: "Each disease has its own particular
germ or seed that will produce the disease which it represents,
when taken into a susceptible body." Moreover, the Indiana
State Board of Health took an interest in the question of pure
foods, sponsoring some of the early researches of Purdue
chemist Harvey W. Wiley in adulterated sugars and syrups.[2]

---

[1] Thurman B. Rice, "History of the Indiana State Board of Health," in
Dorothy R. Russo (ed.), *One Hundred Years of Indiana Medicine, 1849-1949*
(n.p., 1949), pp. 41-42; John N. Hurty, "Review of Public Health Work in
Indiana," Indiana Academy of Science, *Proceedings,* 1916, pp. 225-227; *Laws of
Indiana,* 1881, pp. 37-42. The annual reports of the state health commission
organized by Dr. Stevens were published in the Indiana Department of Statistics and Geology, *Annual Report,* 1879, pp. 456-496, and 1880, pp. 319-368.

[2] Rice, "History of the Indiana State Board of Health," in Russo (ed.),
*One Hundred Years of Indiana Medicine,* pp. 42-43; Indiana State Board of

In 1896 the board chose as its secretary Dr. John N. Hurty of Indianapolis, a pharmacist and chemist who had earned a medical degree though he was not a practicing physician. An indefatigable crusader for public health, Dr. Hurty served continuously as state health officer until 1922 and was associated with many of the most significant advances in preventive medicine in Indiana during that time. Under his leadership the State Board of Health began publishing first a quarterly, and in 1899 a monthly, bulletin and greatly improved the system of collecting and reporting vital statistics, based chiefly on the new death-registration act of 1899, and the birth-registration act of 1907. In 1899, during the national controversy over the preserved-meat scandals of the Spanish-American War, the legislature passed a bill drawn up by Hurty prohibiting the manufacture or sale within the state of any adulterated drug or article of food. Although this was said to be the first fully comprehensive pure food and drug act in the country and was used as a model by some other states, it proved difficult to enforce, especially prior to 1905 when Dr. Hurty obtained an appropriation from the legislature for a chemical and bacteriological laboratory. In 1906 Harvey W. Wiley, who had left Purdue University to become chief of the Bureau of Chemistry in the United States Department of Agriculture, won his fight for the Federal Pure Food and Drug Act, and the next year the General Assembly rewrote the Indiana law to ensure uniform enforcement. Hurty was also instrumental in the passage of such public health legislation as the quarantine act of 1903, the rabies control and sanitary schoolhouse laws of 1911, and the vital statistics

Health, *Annual Report*, 1885, pp. 156-157; 1889, p. 190; Harvey W. Wiley, "The Early History of Chemistry in Indiana," Indiana Academy of Science, *Proceedings*, 1916, p. 183. Dr. Thaddeus Stevens, who was a nephew of the famous Pennsylvania Congressman of the same name, was dismissed from the secretaryship of the State Board of Health in 1883 and opened a medical laboratory in Indianapolis. He was in poor health, however, and died in 1885 in obscurity, despite his pioneer work in public health. Thurman B. Rice, *The Hoosier Health Officer. A Biography of John N. Hurty* (Indianapolis, 1946), pp. 57-62.

act of 1913. An aggressive and sometimes controversial pioneer in the field of preventive medicine, he conducted tireless campaigns against typhoid fever, smallpox, tuberculosis, and venereal diseases throughout the state during his many years in office.[3]

Meanwhile, the prejudices against state regulation of private medical practice gradually disappeared. Although the Indiana State Medical Society recommended legislation regulating entry into the profession as early as 1879, the General Assembly did not act favorably until 1885, when it was made unlawful for any person to practice medicine, surgery, or obstetrics in the state without obtaining a license from the clerk of the circuit court of the county in which he resided. This document was granted simply upon presentation of a diploma from a "reputable" medical school or upon proof of the candidate's residence and practice of medicine or surgery in the state for a certain period of time—ten years in the case of those without special educational qualifications or three years for those having attended one full course of medical lectures. In 1891 the legislature added the provision that a physician licensed in one county could practice in any county of the state. The chief weakness of the county licensing system under these laws was the lack of professional standards for medical education, the reputability of any particular institution being left to the judgment of lay officials in the ninety-two counties. But the mutual jealousies of the various "schools" of medicine represented at that time in the medical profession made it particularly difficult to ob-

3 Rice, *The Hoosier Health Officer*, pp. 25-32, 69-72, 105-108, 121-124, 141-144, 169-180, 201-204, 213-216, 353; *Laws of Indiana*, 1899, pp. 17-20, 189-191; 1903, pp. 161-166; 1905, pp. 42-43; 1907, pp. 153-160, 246-248; 1911, pp. 118-123, 161-163; 1913, pp. 668-672. In 1922 Dr. Hurty resigned from his post in order to run for the state legislature in the hope of reorganizing the State Board of Health and authorizing full-time local public health officers. Although he was successful in winning election to the lower house, his reorganization bill was not passed. In disappointment he retired from politics and died not long afterwards, in 1925. Rice, *The Hoosier Health Officer*, pp. 369-376, 381-383.

tain agreement upon a uniform method of accreditation. When the law which established the State Board of Medical Registration and Examination was eventually passed in 1897, it required that a representative of each of the four schools having the largest number of practitioners in Indiana—homeopathic, eclectic, physio-medical, and allopathic or regular—was to be included among the five board members appointed by the governor. The board was given the power to set minimum standards for institutions of medical education and to issue certificates to their graduates without further question and to all others upon examination, as well as to physicians already licensed under the preceding law. County clerks were then authorized to grant licenses to practice medicine to holders of these certificates. Four years later, however, the law was amended to provide that after January 1, 1905, no certificate was to be issued until the candidate showed evidence both of graduation from a recognized institution and of having passed a "satisfactory examination as to his qualifications to practice medicine, surgery and obstetrics." By an act of 1905 osteopathy, the practice of which had been licensed since 1901, was added to the schools of medicine represented on the State Board of Medical Registration.[4]

In somewhat different fashion, the practice of dentistry had been legally regulated since 1879 by a five-man board of examiners named by the privately organized Indiana State Dental Association. In 1887 the General Assembly invested the board with a more public character by including one mem-

---

[4] Charles N. Combs, "History of the Indiana State Medical Association," in Russo (ed.), *One Hundred Years of Indiana Medicine*, p. 11; Albert Stump, "Regulation of the Practice of Medicine in Indiana since 1897" in *ibid.*, pp. 53-54; *Laws of Indiana*, 1885, pp. 197-199; 1891, pp. 396-397; 1897, pp. 255-260; 1901, pp. 475-482; 1905, p. 194. In 1927 the General Assembly added a chiropractor to the board. When the board was reorganized in 1945, both the osteopath and chiropractor remained, while the other five members were chosen from among the ranks of reputable physicians with no recognition of the four schools of medicine existing in 1897 but obsolete a half-century later. Stump, "Regulation of the Practice of Medicine in Indiana since 1897," in Russo (ed.), *One Hundred Years of Indiana Medicine*, p. 55.

ber appointed by the governor and one by the State Board of Health in addition to three nominated by the dental association. Finally, in 1899 and 1903 the State Board of Dental Examiners was given the same authority over the practice of dentistry as the State Board of Medical Registration and Examination exercised over medical practice, and all applicants for dental licenses were required to submit to an examination by the former agency.[5]

Despite the active lobbying of the Indiana Pharmaceutical Association, which was organized in 1882, the state did not undertake the regulation of pharmacy until 1899, when the legislature created a State Board of Pharmacy and provided for the registration of all practicing pharmacists. In 1907 the board was given the power of examining the qualifications of applicants seeking to be registered. In the same year a State Board of Examination and Registration in Optometry was also established for the licensing of optometrists. Similar regulatory agencies which came into existence by legislative action in the first decade of the twentieth century included the State Board of Embalmers in 1901 for the licensing of members of that profession, the State Anatomical Board in 1903, charged with the protection and distribution of cadavers for medical research and teaching, and the State Board of Veterinary Medicine in 1905 to license veterinarians.[6]

The oldest continuous medical publication in the state was the *Transactions* of the Indiana State Medical Society (Association since 1903), which were issued annually from 1849 through 1907. The following year it was replaced by the

[5] *Laws of Indiana,* 1879, pp. 122-123; 1887, pp. 58-60; 1899, pp. 479-485; 1903, pp. 355-356. In 1913 qualification for membership on the Board of Dental Examiners was changed to include five years' practice of dentistry, and all dentists were required to obtain annual license renewal certificates. *Ibid.,* 1913, pp. 340-348.

[6] Glenn L. Jenkins, "Hoosier Pharmacy: An Historical Sketch," in Russo (ed.), *One Hundred Years of Indiana Medicine,* pp. 147-149; *Laws of Indiana,* 1899, pp. 159-163; 1901, pp. 562-564; 1903, pp. 84-85; 1905, pp. 165-170; 1907, pp. 311-316, 317-321.

*Journal* of the same association, which was published in Fort Wayne by Dr. Albert E. Bulson until his death in 1932. Dr. Bulson had previously been editor of the *Fort Wayne Medical Journal-Magazine,* which had been formed in 1897 by consolidation of the *Fort Wayne Journal of the Medical Sciences* (1881) and the *Fort Wayne Medical Magazine* (1893).

In 1882 Drs. Frank Ferguson and Alembert W. Brayton founded the *Indiana Medical Journal,* which had the endorsement of the Indiana Medical College and the Central College of Physicians and Surgeons of Indianapolis. Another Indianapolis journal was the *Central States Medical Monitor,* edited by Dr. Samuel E. Earp, which came into existence in 1905 as the result of the merger of the *Medical and Surgical Monitor* of Indianapolis (1898) and the *Central States Medical Magazine* at Anderson (1903). In 1909 the *Indiana Medical Journal* and the *Central States Medical Monitor* were combined to form the *Indianapolis Medical Journal* under the joint editorial supervision of Drs. Brayton and Earp.

Other schools of medicine in Indiana were represented by the short-lived *Indiana Medical Journal* edited by Dr. Daniel Lesh for the Indiana Eclectic Medical College in Indianapolis, followed by the *Eclectic Medical Journal* (1883), the *Indiana Eclectic Medical Journal* (1884), and the *Medical Free Press* (1889-1897). Another publication, the *Physio-Medical Journal,* was published in Indianapolis from 1875 through 1895, and the *Indianapolis Polyclinic* (1898) was followed by the *Physio-Medical Record* (1902-1907). The Indiana State Dental Association published its *Transactions* annually after 1858, and the *Indiana Dental Journal* was issued from 1898 to 1900. A German-language medical journal, the *Gesundheits-Bote,* was edited in Indianapolis by Von W. Denke-Walter in the years 1886 to 1899.[7]

7 Selected from a bibliography of medical journals in Indiana compiled by Allan Hendricks in Russo (ed.), *One Hundred Years of Indiana Medicine,* pp. 180-184.

Professional nursing and hospital care for the sick and injured had their beginnings in Indiana in the two decades
following the Civil War. In this period Roman Catholic religious orders for women were especially active in establishing
hospitals in an attempt to extend to the general public, and
the poor in particular, some of the services formerly rendered
to sick and wounded soldiers. Apparently the first such institution was St. Mary's Hospital in Evansville, established
between 1870 and 1872 by the Daughters of Charity of St.
Vincent de Paul, who came to that city during a cholera
epidemic and purchased the former United States Marine Hospital built there in 1856. In 1893 St. Mary's Hospital was
moved to a new and larger building in Evansville. In 1876
the Sisters of St. Francis Seraph of the Perpetual Adoration,
a German order, founded St. Elizabeth Hospital in Lafayette, where they also established their mother house, and in
1881 the Sisters of Charity responded to an invitation of
Bishop Francis Silas Chatard by founding St. Vincent's Hospital in Indianapolis. Other hospitals established by Catholic
religious orders were St. Joseph Hospital in South Bend
(1882), St. Anthony Hospital in Terre Haute (1882), St.
John's Hickey Memorial Hospital in Anderson (1894), and
St. Margaret's Hospital in Hammond (1898). Additional privately sponsored institutions, supported in part at least by
religious organizations, were the Protestant Deaconess Hospital, Evansville, and Union Hospital, Terre Haute, both
opened in 1892, Memorial Hospital, South Bend (1893), and
Protestant Deaconess Hospital, Indianapolis (1895). Individual Protestant denominations were also represented, notably by the Methodist Hospital opened in Indianapolis in 1908
after a building fund for that purpose had been started with
a $4,000 surplus remaining at the close of an Epworth
League conference held in the capital city in 1899.[8]

[8] Dotaline E. Allen, *History of Nursing in Indiana* (Indianapolis, 1950),
pp. 13-17; James E. Morlock, *The Evansville Story. A Cultural Interpretation*
(Evansville, 1956), pp. 90, 130; Dunn, *Greater Indianapolis*, I, 552-553; Heller,
*Indiana Conference,* pp. 271-275.

The oldest publicly supported general hospital in Indiana was Indianapolis City Hospital, which was converted from military to civilian use in 1866. Under the superintendency of Dr. William Niles Wishard during the years 1879 to 1887 major advances were made in hospital practice, including the state's first school of nursing, which was organized in 1883 under the auspices of the Indianapolis Flower Mission, a private charitable society composed of women who visited the sick poor of the city. In 1884 a surgeon attached to the hospital, Dr. John Chambers, first used carbolic acid as an antisepsis in the treatment of an amputation wound, and about the same time Dr. Wishard himself introduced antiseptic methods in the obstetric department, which resulted in the virtual disappearance there of puerperal peritonitis.[9]

Private institutions, however, long bore the main burden of hospital care in Indiana. Not until 1903 and 1905 did the General Assembly enact the necessary legislation to authorize boards of county commissioners to construct hospital buildings with local tax funds, provided that an association was formed to furnish and equip the hospital. The first county facility built under this authority was Good Samaritan Hospital in Vincennes, which was opened in 1908.[10]

The professionalization of nursing developed rapidly with the growth of nurses' training programs, which were instituted in at least eight private hospitals in addition to Indianapolis City Hospital before 1900. By 1908 thirty-eight out of the more than seventy hospitals in the state were conducting their own schools of nursing. The lack of uniform standards in such programs led the Indiana State Nurses Association, which was organized in 1903, to lobby for legislation to regulate admission to the profession. In 1905 the

9 Allen, *History of Nursing in Indiana*, pp. 45-51; Dunn, *Greater Indianapolis*, I, 550.

10 *Laws of Indiana*, 1903, pp. 167-171; 1905, pp. 37-38; Amos W. Butler, *A Century of Progress: A Study of the Development of Public Charities and Correction 1790-1915* (n.p., 1916), pp. 32, 39; Vincennes *Sun-Commercial*, May 7, 8, 1953.

General Assembly created a Board of Examination and Registration of Nurses to which Governor Hanly appointed four practicing nurses and a woman physician. By a careful system of inspection and accrediting, the board helped to raise standards of training and establish uniform requirements for the registration of nurses in Indiana.[11]

As early as 1890 the Indianapolis Flower Mission set up a registry for private-duty nurses and was also active in the movement to employ visiting nurses among the city's poor. By the second decade of the twentieth century some city schools along with the Metropolitan Life Insurance Company, the State Tuberculosis Association, and the American Red Cross were utilizing the services of visiting nurses, who organized their own professional association in Indianapolis in 1913. In 1920 a Division of Public Health Nursing was formally organized in the State Board of Health.[12]

The most rapidly expanding area of state responsibility in public health during these years lay in the housing and treatment of the mentally disturbed. In 1883 Dr. Joseph Goodwin Rogers, superintendent of the thirty-five-year-old and greatly overcrowded Hospital for the Insane in Indianapolis, brought to a successful culmination a campaign to obtain legislative authorization for the erection of three additional hospitals in other sections of the state. Under the guidance of Dr. Rogers, who was appointed medical engineer by the commission named to plan and construct the facilities, each of the three institutions was built according to a different scheme based on what were then advanced theories of mental health care: the Northern Hospital at Logansport on the block or pavilion plan; the Eastern Hospital at Richmond on the cottage plan; and the Southern Hospital at Evansville on the radiate plan. The first of these was opened for patients in 1888 and the

11 Allen, *History of Nursing in Indiana,* pp. 27-41, 45-56; *Laws of Indiana,* 1905, pp. 55-58; Indiana *Year Book,* 1920, pp. 558-561.

12 Allen, *History of Nursing in Indiana,* pp. 35-41; Charlotte Akins, History of Visiting Nurse Association of Indianapolis, 1913-1959 (Unpublished Master's thesis in Education, Butler University, 1960), pp. 8-20.

last two in 1890. Yet by the first years of the twentieth century the four hospitals could no longer meet the needs for which they were intended, and in 1900 the Marion County Asylum for the Incurable Insane was founded at Julietta, and a fifth state hospital was established ten years later in Madison. Moreover, in 1911 a Hospital for Insane Criminals was located on grounds adjoining the state prison in Michigan City. By 1915 the State Board of Charities reported 6,293 known insane persons, of whom 5,305 were in state hospitals, 516 in county poor asylums or county jails, and 472 outside public institutions.[13]

One of the largest benevolent institutions in the state was the School for Feeble-Minded Youth. Established in 1879 as the Asylum for Feeble-Minded Children and located at the Soldiers' and Sailors' Orphans' Home in Knightstown, it was made an independent agency in 1887 and occupied temporary quarters in the newly built Eastern Hospital for the Insane in Richmond until 1890, when it was moved to its own buildings in Fort Wayne. Besides mentally retarded boys and girls between the ages of six and sixteen who were sent to the institution on voluntary application of their parents or guardians, by a law of 1901 court-committed women under forty-five years of age were also received when space was available. By the close of 1915, 1,312 inmates were enrolled, but large numbers of similarly afflicted persons resided in county asylums and in private homes. Another class of defectives found scattered throughout the public institutions of the state received special attention in 1905, when the General Assembly authorized the establishment of the Indiana Village for Epi-

13 *Laws of Indiana,* 1883, pp. 164-168; Dunn, *Indiana and Indianans,* II, 1018-1020; Max A. Bahr, "A Hundred Years of Psychiatry in Indiana," in Russo (ed.), *One Hundred Years of Indiana Medicine,* p. 120; Butler, *Century of Progress,* pp. 52-55; Evelyn C. Adams, "The Growing Concept of Social Responsibility Illustrated by a Study of the State's Care of the Insane in Indiana," *Indiana Magazine of History,* XXXII (1936), 8-9.

leptics, which was opened near New Castle two years later, though with accommodations for men only.[14]

By the second decade of the twentieth century public concern for mental illness was mounting in Indiana. In 1915 the annual report of the Board of State Charities described conditions in this fashion:

The state faces no more serious problem than that involved in the care of mental defectives. No other class of public wards is increasing so rapidly, none other is so burdensome, socially and economically. The state has established seven great institutions for their care and treatment. It spends one and one-third million dollars annually for their maintenance. With all this it is not even keeping pace with the problem. Faster than the state can receive them in its institutions, the number of defectives increases, largely, as we are coming to know, through bad heredity, syphilis, and drug habits, including alcoholism. The task before the state is one not only of institutional care but of prevention.

The board strongly recommended, therefore, that a special committee be appointed to investigate thoroughly and suggest solutions to the whole problem of mental defectives in Indiana. Governor Samuel M. Ralston appointed an eight-man committee headed by the Reverend Francis H. Gavisk, an Indianapolis Catholic priest and a member of the Board of State Charities. Father Gavisk's committee, which was twice reconstituted and granted legislative appropriations, in 1917 and 1921, conducted social surveys of eleven counties and two cities, which revealed the existence of thousands of mental defectives who were not receiving institutional care. Chiefly, it recommended the expansion of state facilities of all kinds, including provisions for voluntary treatment of the mentally disturbed, traveling clinics, mental as well as physical examination of school children, and establishment of a psychiatric department at the Robert W. Long Hospital in Indianapolis. Although the General Assembly authorized voluntary treatment and traveling clinics, lack of funds pre-

14 *Laws of Indiana,* 1879, pp. 76-79; 1887, pp. 46-55; 1901, pp. 156-158; 1905, pp. 484-489; Butler, *Century of Progress,* pp. 28-29, 77-82; George S. Bliss, "Indiana's Feeble-Minded," Indiana Academy of Science, *Proceedings,* 1916, pp. 186-188.

vented either from being carried out effectively. The major physical expansion occurred with the establishment of the Farm Colony for the Feeble-Minded for male adults at Butlerville in 1920 and the construction of separate cottages for women and girls at the Indiana Village for Epileptics in 1924.[15]

In addition to institutions for the mentally ill and retarded, the only hospitals operated by the state were the Hospital for Treatment of Tuberculosis in Rockville, completed in 1911, and the Robert W. Long Hospital, which was opened in Indianapolis in 1914 in connection with the Indiana University School of Medicine.

§ §

The clergy played an important part in promoting social welfare programs in Indiana. One of the most prominent reformers was the Reverend Oscar C. McCulloch, pastor of Plymouth (Congregational) Church in Indianapolis, where, shortly after his arrival in the late seventies, he became an assiduous worker for the relief of urban poverty and a pioneer midwestern advocate of the work of organized, or associated, charities which the Reverend S. H. Gurteen had initiated shortly before in Buffalo, New York. In 1878 McCulloch attended the annual meeting of the forty-three year-old Indianapolis Benevolent Society and persuaded the seven members present, who were discouraged and ready to disband, to reorganize its work upon a more systematic basis. Under his energetic leadership an ambitious expansion of the society's operations was inaugurated, including the opening of an employment bureau, registration and investigation of the poor,

[15] Indiana Board of State Charities, *Annual Report,* 1915, p. 11; Indiana Committee on Mental Defectives, *Third Report: Mental Defectives in Indiana* (Indianapolis, 1922), pp. 4-17, 28-46; *Laws of Indiana,* 1919, pp. 91-93, 734-735; *Indiana Bulletin of Charities and Correction,* June, 1920, pp. 146-147; *ibid.,* September, 1924, p. 157. One of the field workers for the Gavisk committee, Miss Hazel Irene Hansford, published a detailed analysis of Monroe County under the auspices of Indiana University, *A Social Study of Mental Defectives in County H, Indiana, in 1918* (*Indiana University Studies,* X, No. 59, Bloomington, Ind., 1923).

and the establishment of a work yard and a lodging place for transients called the Friendly Inn. In December, 1879, McCulloch succeeded in bringing together a number of existing agencies in the capital city to create the Indianapolis Charity Organization Society, with headquarters in Plymouth Church. The social-gospel minister was also largely responsible for the establishment in the eighties of the Children's Aid Society, the Flower Mission Training School for Nurses, and the Dime Savings and Loan Association (for those who could deposit only a few cents a week), as well as being actively involved in the organization of a community fundraising project for local charities and summer camps for poor children.[16]

The influence of McCulloch's work in charity organization helped to spread the movement outside Indianapolis itself. In 1882 another Congregational minister, the Reverend Charles R. Henderson, became the founder and first president of the Terre Haute Society for Organizing Charity, and by 1899 similar organizations were organized in Anderson, Fort Wayne, Hartford City, Muncie, New Albany, Peru, Richmond, Vincennes, and Warsaw. In 1912 the Indiana State Federation of Organized Charities was founded with twenty cities represented.[17]

Like many social workers of the time, Oscar C. McCulloch was influenced by the theory that heredity was a major cause of pauperism, though this did not prevent him from advocating the amelioration of the environmental conditions of the poor. The startling study of hereditary poverty and degeneracy in the Juke family published by Richard L. Dugdale in 1877 led McCulloch to make a similar investigation of a group

16 Dunn, *Greater Indianapolis*, I, 606; Genevieve C. Weeks, "Oscar C. McCulloch: Leader in Organized Charity," *The Social Service Review*, XXXIX (1965), 209-217.

17 W. C. Ball, "The Work of the Terre Haute Society for Organizing Charity," *Indiana Bulletin of Charities and Correction*, December, 1909, p. 423; "Benevolent and Correctional Institutions and Organizations in Indiana," *ibid.*, December, 1899, pp. 23-47; "The State Federation of Charities," *ibid.*, June, 1912, p. 91.

of Indianapolis slum-dwelling families known as "Ishmaelites." In a report dealing with them which he read at a meeting of the National Conference of Charities and Correction in 1888, he recommended the discontinuance of public outdoor relief and "indiscriminate" private benevolence as encouraging pauperism but suggested that special efforts should be made on behalf of the children of the poor, who he hoped might somehow be able to escape the vicious circle of poverty, disease, and crime. McCulloch's social welfare work brought him national recognition, and he was not only a frequent speaker and discussant at the National Conference of Charities and Correction, but also served as chairman of its committee on organized charities in cities and held office successively as secretary and vice-president, and finally as president in 1891, when the annual meeting was held in Indianapolis.[18]

In Indiana McCulloch's major contribution to public welfare was his work for the Board of State Charities, which the General Assembly created in 1889 after a long campaign waged by the Congregationalist minister and others. Appointed to the first board, he helped to shape its initial policies, along with such fellow charter members as the Quaker bookseller, Timothy Nicholson, and a Catholic laywoman, Margaret Fitzgibbon Peele. This agency, which was designed primarily as an investigative body with power simply to examine the condition of the state's charitable and correctional institutions, managed gradually to reform and modernize the whole system of public welfare, largely through the reports and recommendations of a series of very competent executive secretaries chosen by the members of the board. Those who held that position before 1920 were Alexander Johnson, Ernest P. Bicknell, and Amos W. Butler, all of whom were eventually elected to the presidency of the National Conference of Charities and Correction. In 1890

18 Oscar C. McCulloch, "The Tribe of Ishmael: A Study in Social Degradation," in National Conference of Charities and Correction, *Proceedings,* 1888, pp. 154-156; Weeks, "Oscar C. McCulloch," *The Social Service Review,* XXXIX (1965), 218-221.

the board convened in Indianapolis the first state conference on charities and correction, which after a lapse of two
years was held annually in different cities and helped to publicize and promote the work of social welfare throughout Indiana. Its proceedings were published in the quarterly *Indiana
Bulletin of Charities and Correction,* which also served as an
important medium of information on public welfare.[19]

The board's supervisory responsibility extended to the
state prisons and hospitals, the Indiana School for the Blind
and the Indiana State School for the Deaf in Indianapolis, the
Soldiers' Home at Lafayette, and the Soldiers' and Sailors'
Orphans' Home at Knightstown, as well as generally to all
county poor asylums, hospitals, and orphans' homes. But it
was given no direct administrative powers over any state
institution, each of which was operated independently. Not
until 1907 did the General Assembly remedy some of the
worst features of this system, particularly the appointment
of officials through political patronage, by placing all such institutions under the administration of nonpartisan boards of
control.[20]

Indiana also provided for dependent children under a county system which was only partially made subject to state
supervision in this period. In 1881 the legislature authorized
the county commissioners to establish orphanages after an
investigation the previous year revealed that seven hundred
children under sixteen were living in county poor asylums. In
1889, the General Assembly passed a bill drafted by Oscar
C. McCulloch establishing boards of children's guardians in
townships of 75,000 or more population, in order to afford
protection to children who were not necessarily dependent

19 *Laws of Indiana,* 1889, pp. 51-52; Butler, *Century of Progress,* pp. 13-16,
152; Alexander Johnson, *Adventures in Social Work* (Fort Wayne, Ind.,
1923), pp. 87-169.

20 *Laws of Indiana,* 1907, pp. 138-143. The State Soldiers' Home, which
was established in Lafayette in 1896 for disabled or destitute military veterans
and their wives or widows, was partially supported by the Federal government which contributed $100 a year for each soldier residing there. Butler,
*Century of Progress,* pp. 30-31.

but were without proper parental care or guardianship. Such boards were extended to all counties in 1901. The legislature of 1897 assigned the Board of State Charities full supervisory responsibility over all orphanages wholly or partly supported by tax funds and prohibited the retention of any children between the ages of three and sixteen in county poor asylums for more than ten days. At the same time a state agent was appointed to make regular visitations and to place children in private foster homes in so far as possible rather than maintain them for extended periods of time in orphanages. In 1903 the legislature gave the board responsibility for the inspection of both public and private institutions caring for dependent or neglected children, and in 1909 required annual licensing of such institutions, including maternity hospitals. By 1915 the Board of State Charities had eight field workers supervising the care of 4,887 children, 3,136 of whom were in foster homes subject to periodical visitation and only 1,751 in private or county orphanages. Moreover, the organization of the Indiana Children's Bureau in 1911 and its continued activity under the leadership of Professor Ulysses G. Weatherly of Indiana University demonstrated a growing and vital public interest in child welfare in the state.[21]

Outdoor, or noninstitutional, poor relief was first brought under a measure of centralized control in 1895, when the township trustees, acting as overseers of the poor, were required to file reports with the county commissioners and the Board of State Charities. Two years later the General Assembly authorized trustees to levy taxes in order to reimburse the counties for poor relief funds expended. Finally, in 1899 and 1901 the legislature further reformed the local administration of poor relief by establishing boards of county charities and correction and laying down regulations con-

[21] Laws of Indiana, 1881, pp. 10-11; 1889, pp. 261-263; 1897, pp. 44-48; 1901, pp. 369-373; 1903, p. 537; 1909, pp. 369-375; William B. Streeter, "Child-saving Work under the Law of 1897," Indiana Bulletin of Charities and Correction, June, 1898, pp. 21-28; Butler, Century of Progress, pp. 4, 87-88.

cerning such matters as the investigation of applicants' need and ability to work. By 1908 the secretary of the Board of State Charities claimed a significant reduction in the expenditure of funds for poor relief as a result of these changes.[22]

The discovery of urban poverty in this period also led to the founding of social settlements patterned after Jane Addams' Hull House in Chicago. The first and longest-lived of these in Indiana is Flanner Guild, now Flanner House, which came into existence as an outgrowth of neighborhood work among Negro residents on the west side of Indianapolis initiated by the Charity Organization Society in 1889. In 1898 a local mortician, Frank W. Flanner, donated a building for its use and contributed liberally to its support until his death in 1912. The next year the Christian Woman's Board of Missions began a decade-long period of sponsorship of the institution. Other neighborhood centers of this kind in Indianapolis were the Harley Gibbs Settlement, founded in 1900, and the College Settlement, or Christamore House, which two graduates of Butler University, Anna C. Stover and Edith D. Surbey, established in a predominantly white residential section in 1905. As early as 1896 Judge David N. Taylor also organized a social settlement in Terre Haute, and similar centers arose in a few other communities. The new industrial city of Gary with its burgeoning foreign-born and Negro population had the largest number of such institutions, chiefly under ecclesiastical auspices. Two Presbyterian ministers founded Neighborhood House in 1909, the Reverend John B. de Ville, a Catholic parish priest, opened the Judge Gary—Bishop Alerding Settlement House in 1912, and the Methodist Episcopal Church supported Stewart House and

---

[22] *Laws of Indiana,* 1895, pp. 241-242; 1897, p. 230; 1899, pp. 50-52, 118; 1901, pp. 323-332; Alice Shaffer and others, *The Indiana Poor Law. Its Development and Administration with Special Reference to the Provision of State Care for the Sick Poor* (Chicago, 1936), pp. 48-55; Amos W. Butler, "A Decade of Official Poor-Relief in Indiana," *American Journal of Sociology,* XI (1905-1906), 765-767.

Friendship House, the first located in a Negro residential district and the second serving an originally all-white neighborhood in the steel city.[23]

Another attack upon poverty was launched in the early years of the twentieth century by Albion Fellows Bacon, an Evansville housewife and volunteer social worker. Horrified at what she had witnessed of the home life of poverty-stricken families in the slum tenements of her home city, Mrs. Bacon began virtually a one-woman crusade for housing reform as a chief method of ameliorating living conditions among the urban poor. In 1909 she went to Indianapolis as a self-appointed "Ambassador of the Poor" to lobby successfully for Indiana's first housing law, which prescribed minimum building and maintenance regulations for the state's two largest cities, Indianapolis and Evansville. But a campaign waged two years later with the assistance of the State Association of Architects to obtain an improved law, which would have covered all incorporated cities in the state, failed of passage by a single vote. Undaunted, Mrs. Bacon undertook a strenuous program of traveling and lecturing throughout the state, securing firm backing from the State Federation of Women's Clubs and organizing her supporters in the Indiana Housing Association. In 1913 she returned to the State House to win the General Assembly's final approval of a comprehensive housing law applying to all incorporated cities in Indiana.[24]

23 Indianapolis Charity Organization Society, *Annual Report,* 1908-1909, pp. 36-37; Shaw, *Hoosier Disciples,* pp. 326-327; C. B. Coleman, "The College Settlement in Indianapolis," *Indiana Bulletin of Charities and Correction,* December, 1909, pp. 432-435; Robert A. Woods and Albert J. Kennedy (eds.), *Handbook of Settlements* (New York, 1911), pp. 82-83; *Calumet Region Historical Guide,* pp. 193-197.

24 Albion Fellows Bacon, "The Awakening of a State—Indiana," *The Survey,* XXV(1910-11), 467-473; *Laws of Indiana,* 1909, pp. 108-120; 1913, pp. 377-408. Mrs. Bacon has described her work for housing reform in her moving autobiography, *Beauty for Ashes* (New York, 1914), originally published serially in *The Survey.*

§ § §

In the post-Civil War years Quakers played a major role in initiating penal reforms in the state, recommendations of both the Indiana Yearly Meeting and the Western Yearly Meeting of the Orthodox Society of Friends having led directly to the opening of the House of Refuge for Juvenile Offenders in Plainfield in 1868 and a separate prison and reformatory for women and girls in Indianapolis in 1873. In 1883 the House of Refuge was renamed the Reform School for Boys and twenty years later, in a movement to eliminate the reformatory stigma and to emphasize the educational rehabilitation of its youthful inmates, the Indiana Boys School. The school received boys from eight to sixteen years of age committed for the violation of criminal laws and from ten to seventeen years for incorrigibility, all remaining normally until attaining the age of twenty-one, though some were often released at eighteen. In 1899 the General Assembly passed legislation dividing the state's single prison-reformatory for female offenders, the Indiana Reformatory Institution for Women and Girls, into the Indiana Woman's Prison and the Indiana Industrial School for Girls. Although the legislature also authorized relocation of the girls' facility in 1903, both institutions occupied the same grounds until 1907, when the Indiana Girls' School, as it was renamed, was built outside the capital city in the rural suburb of Clermont. Girls from ten to eighteen years of age committed by the courts were confined at the school until they reached the age of twenty, unless released earlier by decision of the board of trustees. At the same time the quarters vacated by moving the Industrial School for Girls from the Woman's Prison in Indianapolis were converted into a Correctional Department for the confinement of women misdemeanants over tht age of eighteen, who were formerly sent to county jails.[25]

[25] Thornbrough, *Indiana in the Civil War Era,* pp. 591-596; *Laws of Indiana,* 1883, pp. 19-24; 1899, p. 22; 1903, pp. 524-528; 1907, pp. 139, 219-221; Butler, *Century of Progress,* pp. 26-27, 28, 31.

In the early twentieth century, moreover, Indiana played a significant role in the promotion of the juvenile court movement. In 1902 recently elected Judge George W. Stubbs of the Indianapolis Police Court began holding special weekly sessions for hearing charges against boys and girls under the age of sixteen. His efforts in their behalf attracted so much favorable attention that the next year the General Assembly passed a bill conferring jurisdiction over youthful offenders upon all the circuit courts of the state except in Marion County, where a separate juvenile court was established. This was the first separate court of its kind in the nation, though Illinois had provided for juvenile jurisdiction within the regular courts as early as 1899, and the legislature of Colorado enacted a similar measure just three days before passage of the Indiana law. Governor Durbin appointed Judge Stubbs to preside over the new Marion County Juvenile Court, which under his direction became a widely known and influential institution, especially for its system of employing volunteer probation officers as provided by the legislation of 1903.[26]

Measures were also taken to modify the often harsh and archaic treatment of adult convicts which prevailed during most of the nineteenth century, including the liberal application of the lash in the case of recalcitrant prisoners. In 1893, upon the recommendation of the committee on penal and reformatory institutions of the Board of State Charities, the General Assembly amended the penal code to halt the "indiscriminate" use of corporal punishment in the state prisons. According to the new regulations put into effect by this law, only the warden was permitted to order such punish-

[26] James A. Collins, "The Juvenile Court Movement in Indiana," *Indiana Magazine of History*, XXVIII (1932), 1-8; *Laws of Indiana*, 1903, pp. 516-522; George W. Stubbs, "The Mission of the Juvenile Courts," in National Conference of Charities and Correction, *Proceedings*, 1904, pp. 350-357; Helen W. Rogers, "The Probation System of the Juvenile Court of Indianapolis," in *ibid.*, pp. 369-379.

ment, which was to be administered only at specified hours of the day and in the presence of the prison physician and the chaplain. Although Quakers and others continued to protest strongly against capital punishment, bills calling for its abolition which were introduced into the legislature from time to time were repeatedly rejected. In this period crimes punishable by death in Indiana were limited to treason and first-degree murder, while the court could substitute life imprisonment at its discretion. Public hangings had long been outlawed, but until 1889 many executions still took place at the hands of sheriffs in the county jails. In that year the legislature fixed the two state prisons as the only locations where the death penalty could be legally carried out, and after 1897 it was restricted to the Michigan City prison. Finally, in 1913 legislation was enacted which replaced the old-fashioned gallows by the more efficient electric chair.[27]

The most far-reaching reforms of the penal system were initiated in 1897, when the General Assembly passed the indeterminate sentence and parole law, as recommended by a legislative commission established two years before. This act permitted the conditional release of male prisoners over sixteen years of age convicted of any felony except murder or treason who had served their minimum terms. Later, the so-called habitual criminals who were convicted of a felony for the third time, and those found guilty of rape upon a child under twelve years of age were excluded from the operation of the act. There was an immediate public outcry against the law in some quarters, which subsided after the Indiana Supreme Court upheld its constitutionality in 1898. In the following year the indeterminate sentence was also applied to women prisoners over the age of eighteen. Parole boards for each prison were constituted, first composed of the superintendent, physician, and chaplain as well as the board of trustees of the institution, but the former officers

27 Indiana Board of State Charities, *Annual Report,* 1893, pp. 35-36; *Laws of Indiana,* 1889, pp. 192-195; 1893, pp. 269-271; 1913, pp. 844-845; Butler, *Century of Progress,* p. 101.

were later excluded except in the case of women prisoners. Parolees remained under supervision for at least one year. As an integral part of the new system was the transformation of the Southern Prison at Jeffersonville into the Indiana Reformatory to house male convicts under the age of thirty who were not sentenced to death or life imprisonment. All others were committed to the Northern Prison in Michigan City.[28]

In 1907 the General Assembly took the further step of authorizing circuit and criminal court judges to suspend the sentences of persons convicted of certain felonies and misdemeanors and to place them under the supervision of probation officers. Finally, in 1915 the Indiana State Farm was opened at Putnamville for male misdemeanants above the age of sixteen, who were thus enabled to serve out their terms at work in healthful, unprisonlike surroundings rather than in the county jails. In general, the whole penal reform program was acclaimed a success. Between April 1, 1897, and September 30, 1915, a total of 9,338 prisoners were paroled from the various state prisons and reformatories in Indiana, 5,685 of whom served their year's parole and were given a final discharge, making the proportion of unsatisfactory cases 26.9 per cent. From April 1, 1907, to September 30, 1915, a total of 1,794 persons were given suspended sentences, only 604 or 33.7 per cent of whom were either delinquent or committed for violation during that time. In addition, within the first year of the operation of the Indiana State Farm, 73 counties had transferred 1,174 misdemeanants there.[29]

[28] *Laws of Indiana*, 1897, pp. 69-77, 219-222; 1899, p. 511; George Miller *v*. the State of Indiana, 149 Ind. 607 (1897); Amos W. Butler, "The Operation of the Indeterminate Sentence and Parole Law—a Study of the Record of Eighteen Years in Indiana," *Indiana Bulletin of Charities and Correction,* Special Number, January, 1916, pp. 2-6.

[29] *Laws of Indiana*, 1907, pp. 377-378; Helen Wilson, *The Treatment of the Misdemeanant in Indiana, 1816-1936* (University of Chicago, *Social Service Monographs*, 1938), pp. 45-50; Butler, *Century of Progress,* pp. 39-40, 99-100.

Besides the six state-operated penal institutions, Indiana had 202 city police stations and town lockups and 90 county jails in 1916. In that year the secretary of the Board of State Charities admitted that with few exceptions the last were "poorly planned, badly constructed, and often poorly administered." Many had no provision for the separation of inmates by age, sex, or other pertinent classification, and some were found absolutely unfit for the confinement of prisoners after state inspection was inaugurated in 1909. A law of 1901 required that the board of commissioners in any county of 50,000 or more population appoint a matron to take charge of women confined in jail, but only the largest cities had begun to employ female officers for similar duties in police stations.[30]

Contemporary currents of scientific interest in eugenics and the promulgation of theories of inherited criminal tendencies were apparently mainly responsible for the passage of Indiana's surgical sterilization law, one of the first of its kind anywhere in the world. As early as 1899 Dr. Harry C. Sharp, a physician employed by the Indiana Reformatory in Jeffersonville, had begun experimenting with the sterilization of prisoners on a voluntary basis. By 1907 he and others had gathered enough support for the legalization of this operation that the General Assembly in that year authorized the sterilization of "confirmed criminals, idiots, imbeciles and rapists" at the judgment of the administrators of the state penal institutions where such men were confined and on the advice of two consulting physicians. Although California, Connecticut, Iowa, and Washington passed similar acts within the next few years, strong opposition developed in Indiana, partly on constitutional grounds, for the 1907 law did not permit a court review of the prison officials' decision. Both Governors Marshall and Ralston halted enforcement of

[30] Butler, *Century of Progress*, pp. 96-97; *Laws of Indiana*, 1901, pp. 304-305; 1909, pp. 397-400. In 1895 the General Assembly authorized but did not require employment of police matrons in cities of 10,000 or more population. *Ibid.*, 1895, pp. 158-159.

the law during their respective terms of office, which stretched from 1909 to 1917, and in 1921 the Indiana Supreme Court ruled it invalid.[31]

One of the thorniest problems of prison policy in Indiana was the question of the employment of convict labor, which had long been handled on the contract system. Despite the opposition of both trade unions and manufacturing interests, the General Assembly in 1899 and 1903 authorized the Michigan City prison to continue to hire out to private employers the labor of about half of its total number of inmates, but all such contracts were to be permitted to expire by 1910. In 1909, however, the legislature passed an amendment which raised the ceiling on the number of prisoners so employed to 600, plus 50 per cent of the prison population above 800, and extending the time limit for the expiration of contracts to 1920. As a concession to critics of the system, it also provided that "such convict labor shall be employed at such trades and industries as shall least interfere and compete with outside labor and industries in the State of Indiana." In an attempt to work out an alternative method of employing labor, the state prison at Michigan City had begun to manufacture certain articles for its own use within the walls and after 1906 operated a binder-twine plant under the public account system. At the Indiana Reformatory, industries were carried on according to the trade-school law, under which most manufactured products were distributed to various state institutions, with the surplus being sold on the market. In 1917 the General Assembly finally abolished contract labor at the State Prison and placed its industrial enterprises and those of the State Farm on the same system as that of the Reformatory. Inmates of the Woman's Prison in Indianapolis were em-

[31] Rice, *The Hoosier Health Officer,* pp. 209-212; Alexander Johnson, "A State Aged 100: Glimpses of Social Progress in Indiana during One Hundred Years," *The Survey,* XXXVI (1916), 98; *Laws of Indiana,* 1907, pp. 377-378; Williams *et al. v.* Smith, 190 Ind. 526 (1920). In 1927, however, the Indiana General Assembly passed a new sterilization law which included provisions for a hearing and court appeal. *Laws of Indiana,* 1927, pp. 713-717.

ployed at such occupations as laundering and sewing, while those committed to the Indiana Boys' School or the Indiana Girls' School did not engage in any revenue-producing labor.[32]

§ § § §

The social reform movements of this era which provoked the most intense emotional response as well as political controversy in Indiana were those concerned with temperance and woman suffrage. Both were revived in the seventies and eighties after suffering virtual eclipse during the Civil War, and both went on to gain ultimate victories in the state and nation by 1920. Although the two were often closely linked in the minds of both advocates and opponents, temperance reform was generally considered to be somewhat less radical and received a broader hearing than the drive for equal suffrage. For example, many, if not most, Protestant congregations in the state wholeheartedly supported the temperance crusade, but few were willing even to provide a forum for discussion of voting rights for the disenfranchised sex.

Hoosier women, however, played an active role in the crusade against the use of intoxicating liquors, especially the members and leaders of the Indiana branch of the Woman's Christian Temperance Union, which was organized in 1874 under the presidency of Mrs. Zerelda G. Wallace of Indianapolis. In 1879, in preparation for a large-scale concerted effort to obtain state-wide prohibition legislation, a number of such organizations united in the Indiana Grand Council of Temperance. In the campaign which ensued, scores of petitions were submitted to the General Assembly, and Mrs. Wallace and others lobbied strenuously at the State House during the legislative session of 1881. The Republican-led legislature bowed to the unprecedented pressure to the extent of adopting in a bipartisan vote a constitutional amendment designed to prohibit the manufacture and sale of intox-

<hr>

[32] *Laws of Indiana,* 1899, pp. 27-30; 1903, p. 27; 1909, pp. 286-288; 1917, pp. 237-239; Butler, *Century of Progress,* pp. 97-98.

icating beverages within the state. In 1882 the Indiana Liquor League was formed to fight the amendment with funds supplied by brewing and whiskey interests. Once more the temperance forces girded for the struggle, but the fall elections produced a Democratic majority in the General Assembly which was opposed to the measure as a piece of sumptuary legislation, and the amendment was killed in the 1883 session, as discussed earlier.[33]

Defeat dampened the enthusiasm of the prohibitionists, and many temperance reformers turned their attention to other tactics and more modest objectives. For example, the Indiana W.C.T.U. initiated an educational and lobbying program which eventuated in 1895 in the passage of a state law requiring instruction in the public schools on the effect of alcohol and narcotics on the human system. In the same year the General Assembly also passed the Nicholson Law, which introduced a mild form of local option, whereby a majority of the voters in a township or city could file remonstrances to prevent the granting of licenses to individual saloon keepers. In 1905 the Moore Amendment widened the operation of the law by providing for blanket remonstrances halting the issuance of liquor licenses to all applicants in a given township or city ward. Since temperance sentiment tended to be more deeply rooted in most rural communities than in towns and cities, the next step of the reformers was to secure local option on a county-wide basis. In September, 1908, Republican Governor Hanly, an ardent prohibitionist himself, called a special session of the General Assembly, which proceeded to enact legislation authorizing the people of any county to ban the liquor traffic completely within its borders. These laws brought striking results. By November

---

[33] Thomas A. Goodwin, *Seventy-six Years' Tussle with the Traffic. Being a Condensation of the Laws Relating to the Liquor Traffic in Indiana from 1807 to 1883* . . . (Indianapolis, 1883), pp. 28-30; Charles E. Canup, "Temperance Movements and Legislation in Indiana," *Indiana Magazine of History,* XVI (1920), 120-121; Kettleborough, *Constitution Making in Indiana,* I, clx-clxi. For an account of the political struggle, see above, Chapter I, pp. 18-19.

1, 1909, 70 out of 92 counties, 922 out of 1,016 townships, 330 out of 360 towns, and 63 out of 89 cities, were dry by the operation of local-option remonstrances and elections, only a single county — Vanderburgh — remaining completely wet, without one or more dry townships. But in 1911 a Democratic-controlled legislature repealed the county-option measure and substituted a township-unit provision, which by the close of 1912 had reduced the number of dry counties to 26, dry townships to 825, dry towns to 300, and dry cities to 27.[34]

In the meantime, the movement for state-wide and national prohibition was reactivated in Indiana. In 1884, despite the opposition of many temperance advocates who preferred to work within the major political organizations, an Indianapolis attorney, Colonel Eli F. Ritter, and others organized a state branch of the National Prohibition party. Although this party regularly presented slates of candidates at election time, it was never able to mobilize more than a very small segment of the voters in highly politically conscious Indiana, and Ritter himself eventually became an advocate of local option and the chief author of the Nicholson Law of 1895. Popular appeal of the Prohibition party reached its peak in the state in 1904 when an Indianapolis banker, Felix T. McWhirter, received 22,690 votes for the governorship. Much more effective was the work of the Anti-Saloon League, organized in 1893 at Oberlin, Ohio, by the Reverend Howard H. Russell, who visited Indianapolis in 1898 in order to establish a state auxiliary under the leadership of a Presbyterian minister, the Reverend W. C. Helt. Shunning partisanship, the Anti-Saloon League rallied the churches and other temperance forces to help elect to office candidates who were committed to prohibitionist views, regardless of party affiliation.

---

[34] *Laws of Indiana,* 1895, pp. 248-252, 375; 1905, pp. 7-8; 1908 (special session), pp. 4-8; 1911, pp. 363-370; Dunn, *Indiana and Indianans,* II, 1064. Similar sentiment against the use of tobacco was expressed in a law passed in 1889 banning its sale to children under the age of sixteen. In 1905 the legislature enacted a law intended to prevent the manufacture or sale of cigarettes in Indiana, but four years later it was amended to prohibit only sales to minors. *Laws of Indiana,* 1889, p. 271; 1905, pp. 82-83; 1909, pp. 71-72.

Prominent leaders in Indiana were Timothy Nicholson, Quaker reformer of Richmond, Father John Kubacki, a Roman Catholic parish priest in South Bend, and the Reverend Edward S. Shumaker, a Methodist clergyman who became state superintendent of the League in 1907. In 1914 former Governor Hanly founded the Flying Squadron of America in Indianapolis to promote the cause of national prohibition by a program of lectures and publicity throughout the country. The next year he also established in the same city the *National Enquirer* as a leading temperance organ.[35]

The final drive of the prohibitionist crusade came during the war years, when moral and religious opposition to the use of intoxicating beverages was reinforced by a rising tide of anti-German sentiment. This was a particularly significant factor in Indiana, whose relatively large German population was often closely identified with hostility to the temperance movement. A contemporary Indiana historian has stated that "the race prejudice aroused by the war had a practical effect that could not have been attained by any amount of argument or persuasion; and prohibition was accepted by the great majority of the people with a satisfaction that would have been astonishing under other conditions." In December, 1916, all temperance organizations in the state except the Anti-Saloon League joined in the formation of the Indiana Dry Federation in order to present a united front against the politically powerful liquor interests. Both the Federation and the League launched strenuous campaigns for a state-wide prohibition law, which was finally enacted by a large majority in the General Assembly in February, 1917. Two years later, in January, 1919, Indiana became the twenty-fifth state to ratify the Eighteenth

[35] Ernest H. Cherrington (ed.), *Standard Encyclopedia of the Alcohol Problem* (6 volumes, Westerville, Ohio, 1924-30), III, 1308-1310; Robert J. Pitchell (ed.), *Indiana Votes* . . . (Bureau of Government Research, Indiana University, 1960), p. 33; Indianapolis *Journal,* October 10, 1898; Dunn, *Indiana and Indianans,* II, 1064-1066. For Hanly's extensive temperance activities, see Carson, The Life of J. Frank Hanly, Chapters XIII and XIV.

Amendment to the Constitution of the United States, which prohibited the manufacture, sale, and transportation of intoxicating liquors.[36]

§ § § § §

An often-heard argument for woman suffrage in temperance circles was that only female access to the ballot box would finally ensure the victory of the antiliquor crusade. In 1880, for example, ardent prohibitionists such as Zerelda G. Wallace and Helen M. Gougar had been converted to an equally strong advocacy of woman suffrage. After the rebirth of the Indiana branch of the American Woman Suffrage Association in 1869, Hoosier feminists set to work to try to persuade the state legislature to grant their sex the right to vote. As a result, several suffrage resolutions were introduced into the General Assembly in the seventies, though none received serious consideration. In 1878 a group of Indianapolis residents under the leadership of Mrs. Wallace and others formed the Equal Suffrage Society in order to press a more aggressive campaign. The secretary and active founder of the society, May Wright Sewall, later described the secretly summoned group as having "the air of a band of conspirators. Had we convened consciously to plot the ruin of our domestic life, which opponents predict as the result of women's enfranchisement, we could not have looked more guilty or have moved about with more unnatural stealth." Despite this clandestine beginning, the Equal Suffrage Society soon attracted a large, open membership of respectable and prominent citizens of Indianapolis, both men and women.[37]

In 1880 the leaders of both the Woman Suffrage Association and the Equal Suffrage Society served notice of their intention to make a serious fight for voting rights at the

36 Dunn, *Indiana and Indianans*, II, 1065; Canup, "Temperance Movements and Legislation in Indiana," *Indiana Magazine of History*, XVI, 138; *Laws of Indiana*, 1917, pp. 15-34; 1919, pp. 846-847.

37 Elizabeth Cady Stanton *et al.* (eds.), *History of Woman Suffrage* (6 volumes, New York and Rochester, 1881-1922), III, 535-536.

next session of the General Assembly. Like the campaign for a prohibition amendment, petitions in favor of woman suffrage were received from all over the state, and Mrs. Wallace and Mrs. Gougar led the lobbying efforts in the State House during the early months of 1881. Although a bill extending the ballot to women in choosing presidential electors was lost in the regular session, a resolution to amend the state constitution by deleting the word "male" in the section on the qualifications for voting passed both houses in a special session in April. Encouraged by this victory, suffragists launched a second campaign to secure adoption of the amendment by the succeeding legislature. In the spring of 1882 Mrs. Sewall presided over an enthusiastic mass meeting at the Grand Opera House in Indianapolis, which appointed delegates to attend the state political conventions to try to obtain pledges of support from the two leading parties. But the woman suffrage amendment went down to defeat with the prohibition amendment when the Democratic majority in the Fifty-third General Assembly cast aside both measures in 1883, largely because of the active opposition of the liquor industry.[38]

For several years after this climactic struggle Hoosier legislators showed little interest in woman suffrage. In 1887, during the discussion of a bill to permit women to vote in municipal elections, one member of the lower house announced that if he voted for it his constituents "would mob me after I went home; they don't believe in sickly sentimentality." One of the few who did stand uncompromisingly for the enfranchisement of women in the mid-eighties, however, was Senator William D. Foulke, the Quaker civil-service reformer of Richmond, who later served a term as president of the Indiana Woman Suffrage Association. Perhaps the most dramatic feminist gesture of the nineties was the attempt of Helen M. Gougar to cast her ballot in her home precinct in

[38] *Ibid.*, III, 540-544; Kettleborough, *Constitution Making in Indiana,* II, 193-195, 232-233.

the city of Lafayette in the fall of 1894. After being rebuffed by the startled officials she brought suit against the election board for restraint of her alleged constitutional right to vote. Having studied law with her attorney-husband, Mrs. Gougar gained admission to the bar in order to conduct her own case, carrying it all the way to the Indiana Supreme Court, which upheld the lower court's decision denying her unprecedented suit.[39]

Other Indiana feminists in this period turned their attention to broader fields. One of the most energetic was May Wright Sewall, who helped found and lead the International Council of Women in 1888 and the General Federation of Woman's Clubs in 1889, and who acted as the chief mover in the project of the Indianapolis Woman's Club to erect a headquarters building owned and operated entirely by women—the Propylaeum, which was completed in 1891. Moreover, two years later Mrs. Sewall took upon herself the task of organizing the Woman's Congress at the World's Columbian Exposition in Chicago.[40]

A sudden revival of interest in woman suffrage at the end of the century brought a flurry of petitions from twenty-four Indiana counties, which were presented to the Sixty-first General Assembly in 1899, but resolutions offered in both houses to widen the franchise by amending the state constitution failed to reach the floor of the legislature. Similar proposed amendments in 1901, 1911, and 1913 had no greater success, despite the heightened interest in constitutional revision manifested in the state during the progressive era. In the first two decades of the twentieth century a new generation of feminists attempted to reactivate the move-

[39] *Brevier Legislative Reports,* XXII (1885), 218, 256; *ibid.,* XXIV (1887), 451; Gougar *v.* Timberlake *et al.,* 148 Ind. 38 (1896). Mrs. Gougar published her brief in the losing suit as *The Constitutional Rights of the Women of Indiana: An Argument in the Superior Court of Tippecanoe County, Ind.* (n.p., 1895).

[40] Inez Haynes Irwin, *Angels and Amazons. A Hundred Years of American Women* (Garden City, N.Y., 1933), pp. 229-234.

ment for equal suffrage. In 1906 the Indiana Woman Suffrage Association held its first state conference in several years in the city of Kokomo, where a local society had precariously survived the long period of inactivity. Interest failed once more, however, until Anna Dunn Noland of Logansport called a second conference there in 1909 at her own expense. Two years later the association began publishing a monthly journal entitled *Woman Citizen* under the editorship of Antoinette D. Leach. Meanwhile, in 1909 Dr. Amelia R. Keller and Grace Julian Clarke of the Indianapolis Equal Suffrage Society took the lead in forming a Woman's School League with the object of seeking election of a woman to the municipal school board in the capital. Encouraged by their success in this campaign, in 1911 they enlarged their goal to work for universal suffrage under the new name of the Woman's Franchise League of Indiana. This organization soon became the leading feminist body in the state, with sixty branches and a total of three thousand members by May, 1916.[41]

In 1917, in order to mobilize broad support for suffrage measures in the General Assembly, a Legislative Council of Women was created under the presidency of Luella (Mrs. Felix T.) McWhirter of Indianapolis. For the first time in Indiana, moreover, suffragists encountered active opposition from women, especially a group headed by Mrs. Lucius B. Swift, wife of the former Mugwump and civil service reformer. But woman suffrage won impressive legislative victories in that year. The General Assembly not only adopted a resolution to amend the state constitution by deleting the word "male" from the section on voter qualifications, but also passed a partial suffrage bill granting women the right to vote immediately for presidential electors, municipal officials, and delegates to a proposed constitutional

[41] Kettleborough, *Constitution Making in Indiana,* II, 331-333, 353, 451, 569; Stanton *et al.* (eds.), *History of Woman Suffrage,* VI, 166-173. Membership in the Woman's Franchise League had risen to 16,000 by 1919. Its last convention was held in April, 1920, when it disbanded to be replaced by the Indiana State League of Women Voters. *Ibid.,* VI, 174.

convention. Yet the feminists' rejoicing over this apparent triumph proved to be premature. While the Franchise League hastened to get the women of the state registered as qualified voters in time for the fall municipal elections, suit was brought questioning the constitutionality of the partial suffrage act, and the Indiana Supreme Court invalidated it in October. Further action was deferred until 1919, when the legislature passed another presidential suffrage bill and also adopted a resolution calling for the passage of the Federal woman suffrage amendment then pending in the United States Senate, the House of Representatives having acted upon it in the previous year. On the other hand, modification of the state constitution was delayed by withdrawing the pending suffrage amendment in order to permit the legislature to initiate sixteen new amendments, including one granting voting rights to women. Moreover, when the Federal amendment finally won approval by the necessary two-thirds majority in the United States Senate in June, 1919, Indiana Governor James P. Goodrich refused to call a special session of the General Assembly to ratify it without assurances that the legislature would not take up any additional piece of business. After the Franchise League obtained pledges from a large majority of the legislators signifying their willingness to come together for this purpose only and to vote for ratification, the General Assembly was summoned in January, 1920, and brought to a conclusion the long-fought struggle for woman suffrage in Indiana by ratifying almost unanimously the Nineteenth Amendment to the United States Constitution.[42]

[42] *Ibid.,* VI, 175-180; Kettleborough, *Constitution Making in Indiana,* III, 22-23, 24-27, 40-42, 111; *Laws of Indiana,* 1917, pp. 73-74, 705; 1919, pp. 5, 845-846; 1920 (special session), pp. 5-6. The amendment to the state constitution which conferred the right to vote on women also restricted the suffrage to native-born persons and fully naturalized aliens. It was readopted by the legislature in 1921 and ratified by the voters at a special election held on September 6, 1921. Kettleborough, *Constitution Making in Indiana,* III, xiv, 193-194.

# CHAPTER XIII

# INDIANA WRITERS IN THE GOLDEN AGE

In a letter to Hoosier playwright George Ade in 1911, commenting on his native state's reputation for extraordinary literary fertility, Robert Underwood Johnson, the Earlham College-educated editor of *Century Magazine,* declared with humorous exaggeration that "it is difficult to fire off a shot-gun in Indiana without injuring a large section of the literary class of America." Extravagant claims of a more serious nature have been made concerning the quantity, if not the quality, of Hoosier literature, often by including the work of any person born or briefly resident in Indiana, no matter how slender in output or slight in literary significance or value. An anthology published in 1902, for example, contained a single page of poetry or prose from each of more than two hundred native Indiana authors, most of whom were exceedingly obscure. A single city boasted over half that number, as William Dudley Foulke of Richmond noted in an address before the Indiana Society of Chicago in 1908 by referring to a prospectus recently issued in celebration of his home city's centennial which listed the names of 112 Richmond authors. "If these great men are unknown to the rest of mankind," Foulke quipped, "why, that is the fault of the world, not ours."[1]

[1] Letter of Robert Underwood Johnson to George Ade, November 29, 1911, in the Indiana State Library; Edward J. Hamilton (comp.), *Indiana Writers of Poems and Prose* (Chicago, 1902); Foulke, *A Hoosier Autobiography,* p. 227. In his letter to Ade, Johnson himself added the warning: "At the same time I never without indignant denial allow the assertion to be made that a man becomes an Indiana author merely by passing through the State at night in a Pullman car." Roswell Smith, a lawyer in Lafayette, Indiana, for twenty years, was one of the founders of *Scribner's Monthly* in 1870 and became the chief proprietor of its successor in 1881, *Century Illustrated Monthly Magazine.* Under editors Richard Watson Gilder (1881-1909) and Robert U. Johnson (1909-1913) this journal especially welcomed the contributions of Hoosier writers. Robert U. Johnson, *Remembered Yesterdays* (Boston, 1923), pp. 81-84.

Along with the scores of little-known authors calculated in such fashion, however, Indiana produced an astonishingly large number of writers who earned national literary fame in the period extending from 1880 to 1920. Indeed, these were the years of the Golden Age of Indiana literature, during which appeared much of the best work of such popular Hoosier authors as Edward Eggleston, James Whitcomb Riley, Lew Wallace, Mary Hartwell Catherwood, Maurice Thompson, Meredith Nicholson, Charles Major, Gene Stratton Porter, and Booth Tarkington. While few of these received enduring critical acclaim, most reached an immense audience, and many achieved genuine national prominence. In the matter of book sales alone, Indiana literature fared extremely well, being represented by a disproportionate number of authors and titles on the best-seller lists compiled by various authorities.[2]

Many plausible reasons have been suggested by historians and others for the "prevalence of authorship" in the state at this time. In his pioneering study, *The Hoosiers,* published in 1900, Meredith Nicholson argued that from the beginning Indiana, far from being characterized by "uncouthness and ignorance of the inhabitants," as pictured in the Hoosier stereotype, was settled by men and women of hardy American stock who were "sustained and lifted by religion through all their formative years, and when aroused to the importance of education were quick to insure intelligence in their posterity." Thus, he added, "the artistic impulse appeared

[2] Arthur W. Shumaker describes the Golden Age of Indiana literature as falling in the fifty-year period between the publication of Edward Eggleston's *The Hoosier School-Master* in 1871 and Booth Tarkington's *Alice Adams* in 1921 in *A History of Indiana Literature* . . . (*Indiana Historical Collections,* Vol. XLII, Indianapolis, 1962), pp. 195-196. Twenty-one entries by Hoosier authors are included for the period 1895-1916 in the annual lists of the ten best-selling books of fiction compiled by Alice Payne Hackett, *Fifty Years of Best Sellers, 1895-1945* (New York, 1945), pp. 11-41. For the eighties Lew Wallace's *Ben-Hur* and Riley's *The Old Swimmin'-Hole and 'Leven More Poems* are considered to rank among the best sellers by Frank Luther Mott, *Golden Multitudes. The Story of Best Sellers in the United States* (New York, 1947), p. 310.

naturally in later generations." Others have stressed such factors as the mingling and rapid assimilation of many varied strains of population, the development of a distinctive Hoosier character and a considerable body of folklore concerning it, a popular tradition of pulpit, courthouse, and stump oratory, and a local pride which inspired writers of the region to emulate the literary accomplishments of the longer-settled East.[3]

The educational awakening of the seventies and eighties may have contributed to the flowering of literature, as the literary clubs which flourished throughout this period helped provide an appreciative environment for men of letters. One of the first and most influential of these latter institutions was the Indianapolis Literary Club, which was established in 1877 and comprised many of the leading writers as well as representatives of the capital city's professional, business, and political circles. The Indianapolis Literary Club was an all-male society, as was the Terre Haute Literary Club (1881) and the Ouiatenon Club of Crawfordsville (1883). Women's literary clubs also appeared, enough of them by 1890 to form a state federation, which was organized in that year on the initiative of the Indianapolis Woman's Club, founded in 1875. The literary columns of the daily and weekly press furnished an opportunity for yet-unknown authors like the young James Whitcomb Riley to publish their works of poetry or prose; many of the smallest county papers featured a "poet's corner" or similar department for literary contributions from readers. In Indianapolis such newspapers as the *Saturday Herald* and the *Sunday Journal* particularly promoted local writing. It was a group of contributors to the former paper who organized the Western Association of Writers at Plymouth Church in Indianapolis in the summer of 1886. Maurice Thompson served as its first president, and

---

[3] Julia Henderson Levering, *Historic Indiana* (New York, 1909), p. 350; Nicholson, *The Hoosiers*, pp. 1-28; Howard H. Peckham, "What Made Hoosiers Write?" *American Heritage*, I (1950), 25-27, 59-60; Shumaker, *A History of Indiana Literature*, pp. 8-13.

members of the standing of Riley, Mrs. Catherwood, and Meredith Nicholson lent the prestige of their names and often attended the annual meetings, which chiefly served as an occasion for mutual admiration and the outpouring of the literary effusions of amateur Hoosier bards. Originally created to encourage the development of a regional literature in the West distinct from that of the dominant East, the Western Association of Writers became largely an Indiana institution. While it failed to maintain high literary standards, it may have helped to keep alive for a time the ambitions of obscure but aspiring Hoosier authors but it finally faded out of existence by 1908.[4]

A signal factor in the promotion of a native literature was the appearance of a literary publishing house in Indiana. In 1883 an Indianapolis concern which published law books and judicial reports, Merrill, Meigs and Company, entered the field of belles lettres by the publication of James Whitcomb Riley's *"The Old Swimmin'-Hole," and 'Leven More Poems,* which the poet had originally issued privately. The commercial success of this book and subsequent volumes of Riley's verse as well as the works of other Hoosier authors quickly established this firm and its successors, as an important influence in the development of Indiana literature in the Golden Age.[5]

The literary talent of native Hoosiers often blossomed outside the state, as in the case of the well-known writers Ambrose Bierce, Theodore Dreiser, Edward Eggleston, William Vaughn Moody, George Jean Nathan, and David

[4] Shumaker, *A History of Indiana Literature,* pp. 13-14; Indiana Union of Literary Clubs, *Minutes,* 1890, pp. 3-4; George S. Cottman, "The Western Association of Writers: A Literary Reminiscence," *Indiana Magazine of History,* XXIX (1933), 187-197; James L. Weygand, *Winona Holiday. The Story of the Western Association of Writers* (Nappanee, Ind., 1948).

[5] W. J. Burke and Will D. Howe, *American Authors and Books, 1640 to the Present Day* (Revised edition, New York, 1962), p. 72; Shumaker, *A History of Indiana Literature,* pp. 14-15, 205-206. Merrill, Meigs and Company merged in 1885 with another book concern to form the Bowen-Merrill Company and in 1903 became the Bobbs-Merrill Company.

Graham Phillips, but a remarkably large body of reputable writers chose to live and work largely in Indiana in this period, despite the attraction of other American centers of literature and culture. Moreover, some of those who pursued careers in Chicago, New York, and elsewhere, such as Eggleston, Dreiser, and Phillips, often found in remembered scenes and personalities of Indiana literary inspiration and subject matter. On the other hand, the Hoosier novelists George Barr McCutcheon and Lew Wallace knew Indiana well but wrote instead mostly romances laid in Europe or the Orient.[6]

Hoosier men of letters were scattered throughout the state, though Indianapolis remained the literary, as it was the political, capital of Indiana. From the arrival of James Whitcomb Riley in that city in 1877 to the time of native-son Booth Tarkington's most productive writing, literary Indianapolis was composed of a close-knit circle of writers who knew each other intimately and were a dominant influence on the state's literature. Yet, Richmond, Shelbyville, Terre Haute, and even smaller cities in the state served as minor literary centers boasting the residence of one or more significant authors. A whole coterie of writers, for example, was associated with Crawfordsville, the "Hoosier Athens," as many of its inhabitants thought of it. This Montgomery County community contained the homes of three literary families in particular, Lew Wallace and his wife Susan Elston Wallace, Maurice and Will Thompson, and Mary Hannah and Caroline Virginia Krout. Crawfordsville was also the birthplace of Meredith Nicholson. However, when the author of *The Hoosiers* returned to Indiana after a few years' experience in business in Denver, Colorado, he took up residence in Indianapolis despite his advice to "Stay in Your Own Home Town."[7]

6 Richard A. Cordell, "Limestone, Corn, and Literature," *Saturday Review of Literature*, XIX, No. 8 (December 17, 1938), 3-4, 14-15.

7 Dorothy R. Russo and Thelma L. Sullivan, *Bibliographical Studies of Seven Authors of Crawfordsville, Indiana* (Indiana Historical Society, 1952),

Some general observations may be made about the content of Indiana literature in this period. The writers as a rule eschewed the bolder forms of literary realism though a few, as Tarkington in some of his best works, were willing to experiment with a milder version. Some of them had basic affinities with the school of local colorists, describing the native character in a generally favorable light and as part of a larger midwestern culture and sometimes, Riley and Eggleston, for instance, making effective use of local dialect. While living through a period of relatively rapid industrial-urban growth, moreover, many writers seemed to experience a nostalgia for the rural past, which they pictured as having greater virtue and a desirable simplicity. Humor was present in generous measure, but sentimentality and romanticism dominated the mood of most poets and novelists in Indiana, whether, like Lew Wallace and Charles Major, they wrote of far-off times and places or, like Riley and Maurice Thompson, of scenes close to home. Yet, despite similarities in approach and outlook, these writers did not constitute a distinct Hoosier school pursuing a common purpose with common methods. The Golden Age of Indiana literature in fact embraced a wide range of literary forms, techniques and subject matter.[8]

Poetry was a favorite type of imaginative expression in Indiana, especially among amateur literati, and nearly every aspiring Hoosier writer tried his hand at it at one time or another. One of the first successful poets in this period was Benjamin Stratton Parker, a New Castle newspaper editor who depicted the hardships of pioneer life and the beauty of unspoiled nature in such volumes as *The Cabin in the Clear-*

vii-viii; Nicholson, "Stay in Your Own Home Town," in *Old Familiar Faces,* pp. 147-148.

[8] In a personal letter to an Indiana historian in 1924 Booth Tarkington emphatically denied the existence of a Hoosier school of literature. "I do not see a school or group of writers working to a common end or with a common method, or from a common basis. The work of Riley, Wallace, Eggleston, Nicholson, and the others seems to me to bear no general resemblance and no particular resemblance." Tarkington to Robert LaFollette, March 24, 1924, quoted in LaFollette, "Interstate Migration and Indiana Culture," *Mississippi Valley Historical Review,* XVI (1929-30), 358.

*ing, and Other Poems* (1887) and *Rhymes of Our Neighbor-hood* (1895). He also compiled with Enos Boyd Heiney the first uncritical anthology of the state's native literature, *Poets and Poetry of Indiana* (1900), which listed 142 writers of verse in the state. Other versifiers of local fame were Civil War veterans Lee O. Harris and Ben D. House, the latter being known chiefly for his sonnet, "Appomattox," which was written upon the occasion of the death of Ulysses S. Grant in 1885. A much better-known poem on a somewhat similar theme was former Confederate soldier Will Thompson's often-anthologized salute to the defeated South, "High Tide at Gettysburg" (1888). Although this onetime Crawfordsville resident wrote very little poetry, he has also been remembered as the author of "Together against the Stream" (1892) and "The Bond of Blood" (1899), both published, as was his earlier poem, in *Century Magazine*. A Montgomery County farmer-poet who published many mediocre verses in both newspapers and in book form was James Buchanan Elmore, the "Bard of Alamo," author of such elocutionary classics as "The Monon Wreck" (1885). Also included among the ranks of minor poets were Albion Fellows Bacon, who with her sister Annie Fellows Johnston, author of the *Little Colonel* juvenile series, issued a collection of graceful poems entitled *Songs Ysame* (1897); the Roman Catholic devotional poets, Sister Mary Genevieve Todd of St. Mary-of-the-Woods and Father Charles Leo O'Donnell of Notre Dame; the highly literate William Dudley Foulke of Richmond and Max Ehrmann of Terre Haute, both of whom published volumes of rather conventional poetry along with many other kinds of writing; translators of Latin as well as modern European poetry, Charles R. Williams and John Augustine Wilstach; and homely, humorous versifiers, Silas B. McManus and Wilbur D. Nesbit.[9]

[9] Nicholson, *The Hoosiers,* 254-256, 265-266; Shumaker, *A History of Indiana Literature,* pp. 198-200, 221-223, 227-238, 251-254; De Forest O'Dell, "Unheralded Hoosier Poet," *American Mercury,* LI (September-December, 1940), 422-426.

Indiana offered, as Meredith Nicholson observed, a fair field for nature poets. "The prevailing note of the landscape," he wrote, "is tranquillity." This quiet beauty inspired the work of such poets as Maurice Thompson and Evaleen Stein, both of whom wrote verses about the Kankakee marsh and other romantic features of the Indiana landscape. Thompson's work was introduced to a wide audience in eastern magazines in the seventies and eighties and collected in volumes entitled *Songs of Fair Weather* (1883) and *Poems* (1892). Miss Stein, who was born and lived virtually her whole life in Lafayette, published two volumes of her verse in *One Way to the Woods* (1897) and *Among the Trees Again* (1902) which revealed, in Shumaker's words, "the advent of a fresh, new voice in Indiana letters." A traditionalist in the use of meter and rhyme as were most Hoosier poets, she occasionally could, as William Murray Hepburn has written, "stir the deeper emotions or take the mind on broad flights of fancy, but for the most part she preferred to portray the softer and less spectacular features of nature and of human life."[10]

Two major poets graced the Golden Age, though two men who differed as much in both manner and substance would be hard to imagine. Ranking higher in the view of the critical world was William Vaughn Moody, who spent his early youth in southern Indiana but experienced his most creative years outside the state, in Chicago and the East. His poetic achievements were of two kinds, a trilogy of verse dramas never presented on the stage but highly acclaimed by literary critics, and a relatively small number of shorter poems, many of great power, the best-known being "Gloucester Moors," "An Ode in Time of Hesitation," and "On a Soldier Fallen in the Philippines." He was an acute critic of his society, as these poems indicate, but he was not a radical innovator in American

[10] Nicholson, *The Hoosiers,* pp. 267-271; Russo and Sullivan, *Bibliographical Studies of Seven Authors of Crawfordsville,* pp. 185-193, 205-207; Shumaker, *A History of Indiana Literature,* pp. 224-226; Richard E. Banta (comp.), *Indiana Authors and Their Books* (Crawfordsville, Ind., 1949), pp. 301-303.

poetry, which at the beginning of the twentieth century was on the threshold of great changes. Yet Moody might have participated in the newer literary movements had he not died prematurely at the age of forty-one in 1910.[11]

James Whitcomb Riley, on the other hand, was a far more popular poet in his lifetime, though he was often criticized for excessive sentimentalism. A Greenfield sign painter who had begun to get his first verses published in newspapers, Riley accepted a position on the staff of the Indianapolis *Journal* in 1877 and moved to the capital city, where his composition and recitation of poetry evocative of rural childhood in an urbanizing age soon made him both a famous and beloved figure. His best-known poems, like "Little Orphant Annie," "When the Frost is on the Punkin," and "The Raggedy Man," were characterized by both sentimentality and humor and appealed to children and adults alike with their wholesome, cheerful, optimistic view of the world. A denizen of the state's largest city who was never tempted to live elsewhere, he gave voice to the antiurban bias of the rural Midwest:

> You kin boast about yer cities, and their stiddy growth and size,
> And brag about yer County-seats, and business enterprise,
> And railroads, and factories, and all sich foolery—
> But the little Town o'Tailholt is big enough for me!

So well did Riley capture the mood of his age, however, that he became the unofficial poet laureate of Indiana and of the children of America. In 1911 the Indiana Federation of Women's Clubs resolved that the poet's birthday be set aside annually for special celebrations and programs in schools and elsewhere, and the State Superintendent of Public Instruction decreed the first such "Riley Day" for October 7 of that year. By the time of Riley's death in 1916 his birthday was

---

11 David D. Henry, *William Vaughn Moody. A Study* (Boston, 1934), pp. 51-53, 55-56; Shumaker, *A History of Indiana Literature,* pp. 238-242, 248-251. Moody's literary reputation has declined considerably in the last few decades. See Martin Halpern, *William Vaughn Moody* (*Twayne's United States Authors Series,* New York, 1964), pp. 15-16.

being celebrated in communities throughout much of the nation. In those innocent years before the First World War, as a critical biographer has observed, James Whitcomb Riley became a hero of his age because he reflected in an uncomplicated way the popular nostalgia of his time and place; he was "the looking glass in which the Midwest saw its own archetypal reflection."[12]

Yet fiction—including the short story and the novel—was the most dominant product of Indiana's Golden Age of literature. Shumaker has counted thirty-four novelists in the period, of whom he considered eleven to have made significant contributions to American letters. Most wrote in the romantic tradition, their works about equally divided between historical tales set in foreign lands and stories of Indiana, past and present. An early movement in the direction of local-color realism, as represented by Edward Eggleston's series of western novels in the seventies and eighties and Maurice Thompson's collection of sketches of rural Indiana life published in 1875 as *Hoosier Mosaics,* quickly gave way to the popular taste for romances. Ohio-born Mary Hartwell Catherwood, who lived in Indianapolis from 1879 to 1882 and was briefly a friend and protégée of James Whitcomb Riley, wrote her first short stories about the drabness of small-town life and a rather harshly realistic novel, *Craque-O'-Doom,* a title taken from one of Riley's poems, before turning to the fictionalized historical accounts of New France which brought her fame beginning with the publication of *The Romance of Dollard* in 1889. Later novelists such as David Graham Phillips, who left Indiana for Cincinnati

12 Quotation from *The Biographical Edition of the Complete Works of James Whitcomb Riley,* p. 149, used by permission of the publishers, The Bobbs-Merrill Company, Inc., and of Lesley Payne and Elizabeth Eitel Miesse. Richard Crowder, *Those Innocent Years. The Legacy and Inheritance of a Hero of the Victorian Era, James Whitcomb Riley* (Indianapolis, 1957), pp. 13, 53-257. See also the essay by James T. Farrell, "The Frontier and James Whitcomb Riley," in Jeannette C. Nolan *et al., Poet of the People. An Evaluation of James Whitcomb Riley* (Bloomington, Ind., 1951), pp. 63-106.

and New York at an early point in his life but utilized his home state for many of his settings, and Booth Tarkington of Indianapolis brought about a revival of a mild literary realism. In general, however, the Indiana intellectual climate was inhospitable to writing of a severely realistic mode and rejected outright the naturalism of one of its greatest sons, Theodore Dreiser.[13]

Moreover, much local-color fiction in Indiana contained a strongly southern flavor. Maurice Thompson, who had lived in Georgia and Florida and served in the Confederate Army before settling in Crawfordsville, utilized a good deal of southern local color derived from his experiences below the Mason-Dixon Line. Its use is pronounced in his two early novels, *A Tallahassee Girl* (1882) and *His Second Campaign* (1883), both of which dealt with the problem of reconciliation of the postwar North and South through the vehicle of an intersectional love affair, as well as in the later *Stories of the Cherokee Hills* (1898). In his first historical novel, *The King of Honey Island* (1893), Thompson developed the Louisiana Creole character while telling the story of the Battle of New Orleans in the War of 1812, just as later he treated the French, the Indian, and the backwoods American character in recounting the conquest of Fort Sackville in *Alice of Old Vincennes* (1900), the book which brought him his greatest fame and financial reward near the end of his life. Similarly George Cary Eggleston, whose year as a teacher in a one-room schoolhouse near Madison, Indiana, inspired his brother Edward to write *The Hoosier School-Master,* drew upon his own experiences in the South and in the Confederate Army to produce *Southern Soldier Stories* (1898) and a long list of romantic novels of Virginia. Yet Eggleston, in collaboration

[13] John T. Flanagan's introduction to Maurice Thompson, *Hoosier Mosaics* (Facsimile reproduction, Gainesville, Fla., 1956), pp. v-vi; Robert Price, "Mrs. Catherwood's Early Experiments with Critical Realism," *American Literature,* XVII (1945), 140-151. It is interesting that Shumaker omits consideration of both Phillips and Dreiser as Indiana writers. Shumaker, *A History of Indiana Literature,* p. 18.

with Mary Schell Bacon, also published the partially realistic novel of Indiana, *Juggernaut,* in 1891. His other works dealing with the Indiana scene were *The First of the Hoosiers* (1903), an account of his more famous brother's early life and times, and three adventure books for boys entitled *The Last of the Flatboats* (1900), *Jack Shelby: A Story of the Indiana Backwoods* (1906), and *Long Knives: The Story of How They Won the West* (1907).[14]

Perhaps Maurice Thompson's best novel, however, was the semiautobiographical *A Banker of Bankersville* (1886), in which he came close to the moderately realistic canons of William Dean Howells, who visited the author in Crawfordsville in 1881 in order to obtain authentic local-color material on Indiana divorce courts which he used in writing *A Modern Instance.* But as both a novelist and a critic, Thompson, who as literary editor of the *Independent* after 1889 often attacked Howells and other realists and set forth in full his conservative critical views in a series of lectures at Hartford Theological Seminary in Connecticut published as *The Ethics of Literary Art* (1893), clearly preferred romanticism to realism. Like many, if not most Hoosier writers of this era, he subscribed to the midwestern version of the Genteel Tradition of letters. Despite his southern origins, Thompson took pride in his state and its literary culture. " 'As Indiana goes, so goes the Union,' " he wrote in 1900, "may yet be as true in literature as in politics."[15]

Another prominent exponent of Indiana and midwestern provincialism was Meredith Nicholson, the "Hoosier Cavalier," as one student of his work has dubbed him. Of his many successful novels published by the Bobbs-Merrill Com-

---

14 Otis B. Wheeler, *The Literary Career of Maurice Thompson* (*Louisiana State University Studies,* No. 14, Baton Rouge, La., 1965), pp. 119-121; Walter L. Fertig, "Maurice Thompson as a Spokesman for the New South," *Indiana Magazine of History,* LX (1964), 323-330; Shumaker, *A History of Indiana Literature,* pp. 273-285.

15 Wheeler, *Literary Career of Maurice Thompson,* pp. 27, 58-92, 138-141; Maurice Thompson, "Shall This Thing Be?" *Independent,* LII, No. 2699 (August 23, 1900), 2024.

pany in the early years of the twentieth century, several of them best sellers, Indiana settings were utilized in *Zelda Dameron* (1904), which was laid in Indianapolis, two romantic adventure stories, *The House of a Thousand Candles* (1905) and its sequel *Rosalind at Redgate* (1907), a light comedy inspired by his friendship with Governor-elect Thomas R. Marshall entitled *The Little Brown Jug at Kildare* (1908), and perhaps his best work, *A Hoosier Chronicle* (1912). The last, which dealt with Indiana politics and was set in Indianapolis, Crawfordsville, and the summer community at Lake Wawasee, contained many elements of literary realism. That Nicholson had not betrayed the prevailing sentimental optimism of Hoosier literature, however, was shown in the book's finale, when these words are placed in the mouth of the wealthy, down-to-earth Mrs. Sally Owen, the principal exemplar of native provincial wisdom in the story: "It's all pretty comfortable and cheerful and busy in Indiana, with lots of old-fashioned human kindness flowing around; and its getting better all the time. And I guess it's always got to be that way, out here in God's country." In his essays, which appeared intermittently while he was producing almost annual novels, Nicholson treated social and cultural aspects of Indiana and the Middle West in the same sympathetic, optimistic fashion. *The Hoosiers,* which he wrote in 1900 while in exile from Indiana in Denver and brought up to date in a second edition in 1915, has become a classic interpretation of the state and its literature. His remaining essays were published as magazine articles before being collected in *The Provincial American and Other Papers* (1912), *The Valley of Democracy* (1918), *The Man in the Street* (1921), and *Old Familiar Faces* (1929), all of which celebrated the homely, democratic virtues of his state and region.[16]

[16] Shumaker, *A History of Indiana Literature,* pp. 325-334; Jean Butler Sanders, Meredith Nicholson: Hoosier Cavalier (Unpublished Master's thesis in English, DePauw University, 1952), pp. 94-97, 129-144; Meredith Nicholson, *A Hoosier Chronicle* (Boston, 1912), p. 606. Nicholson continued to write novels, mostly of a picaresque or romantic type, until 1928, the date of publi-

The most successful novels of all in this period—and those for which Indiana was best known in the wider world—were historical romances, often dealing with far-off times and places. In 1880 General Lew Wallace of Crawfordsville, a veteran of both the Mexican War and the Civil War and author of two mediocre plays and a novel, *The Fair God* (1873), a story of the Spanish conquest of Mexico, put Indiana on the literary map of the United States by publishing *Ben-Hur. A Tale of the Christ.* The secret of the phenomenal popularity of this work, which eventually became one of the best-selling books of all time, was probably its artful combination of Oriental pageantry, personal heroics—as in the famed chariot race—and religious piety. While it had little real merit as literature, *Ben-Hur* inaugurated a whole genre of Biblical fiction, of which good examples were found in *The Yoke* (1904) and *Saul of Tarsus* (1906) by Elizabeth Miller Hack of Indianapolis, but none approached the success of the original until the publication of Indiana-born Lloyd Douglas' *The Robe* in 1942. Wallace's only other novel, *The Prince of India: or, Why Constantinople Fell* (1893) was inspired by his sojourn in Istanbul, Turkey, to which President James Garfield dispatched him as United States Minister in 1881 after having read and admired *Ben-Hur.* But *The Prince of India* never reached the heights of popularity of its predecessor, perhaps because it set forth a vague kind of universal religion less appealing to American readers than the muscular Christianity of *Ben-Hur,* which its author, who was not a member of any church, claimed to have written as an answer to Colonel Robert G. Ingersoll after having listened to the great agnostic's arguments during a chance encounter in a

cation of his historical romance about the life of Andrew Jackson, *The Cavalier of Tennessee.* From 1933 to 1941 he served in various diplomatic posts in South and Central American countries, returning in the latter year to private life in Indianapolis, where he died at the age of eighty-one in 1947. Shumaker, *A History of Indiana Literature,* pp. 335-336.

railway car en route to a Civil War veterans' reunion in Indianapolis in 1876.[17]

After returning from Turkey, the Hoosier soldier-author made his home once more in Indiana, alternating between Crawfordsville and Indianapolis, and leaving the state only briefly for lecture tours in other parts of the country. In the nineties, with his mounting book royalties, he erected an elegant modern apartment house in Indianapolis and named it "Blacherne" after the palace of Constantine in *The Prince of India,* and in Crawfordsville he built himself a palatial library-study in which to continue his writing. Yet little more came from the pen of the inveterate romanticist, who had always written of the colorful past of exotic lands rather than of his own state and nation which he had loved and served so long and so faithfully. In contrast to such fellow Hoosier novelists as Maurice Thompson or Meredith Nicholson, Wallace's output was small, and he contributed little or nothing in his writings to an understanding of the Indiana scene, which he was certainly as well qualified to do as any man of his age. Finally, in 1897 he put aside work on another historical romance and devoted his time to an autobiography, in which he traced his adventures from his early years in the state through the military experience in the Mexican War and the Civil War, devoting many thousands of words to a defense of the Second Indiana Regiment in the former and the Battle of Shiloh in the latter. This project, however, remained unfinished at Wallace's death in 1905, though his wife, Susan Elston Wallace, with the help of Mary

[17] Shumaker, *A History of Indiana Literature,* pp. 285-300, 413-414; Russo and Sullivan, *Bibliographical Studies of Seven Authors of Crawfordsville,* pp. 307-310; McKee, *"Ben-Hur" Wallace,* pp. 164-245. Wallace's most successful fictional character was not only transformed into a popular hero of the stage and, later, the motion pictures but also inspired the organization of a fraternal order, the Supreme Tribe of Ben-Hur, which was founded as a beneficial insurance association in Crawfordsville in 1894 by Dr. David W. Gerard with the author's blessing. The book's popularity contributed greatly to the rapid growth of the society, which by 1910 had enrolled over a quarter of a million men and women. Dunn, *Indiana and Indianans,* III, 1320-1322.

Hannah Krout contributed a short sketch of his later career in order to make possible publication in 1906 of two volumes of *Lew Wallace: An Autobiography*. In an Indianapolis newspaper poll taken shortly after his death, Wallace was chosen over ex-President Benjamin Harrison for inclusion among the state's heroes in Statuary Hall in Washington, D.C.[18]

Another Hoosier who met almost equal success as a historical novelist was Charles Major, a Shelbyville lawyer who drew upon his extensive study of English sixteenth-century history to write *When Knighthood Was in Flower,* a dramatic tale of the love of Mary Tudor for a commoner who was the favorite of her brother, King Henry VIII. Published in 1898 by the Indianapolis firm of Bowen-Merrill, it became an immediate best seller and established Major as a popular author overnight. Forsaking the courtroom, Major produced a number of similar romances with elaborately researched European historical settings including *Dorothy Vernon of Haddon Hall* (1902). Unlike Wallace, however, Charles Major utilized Indiana settings for three novels: the boys' adventure books, *The Bears of Blue River* (1901) and *Uncle Tom Andy Bill* (1908), and the less successful *A Forest Hearth: A Romance of Indiana in the Thirties* (1903). By the time of his death in 1913 the literary lawyer had become one of the best-known and wealthiest men of letters in the state.[19]

The tremendous success of *When Knighthood Was in Flower* induced its publisher, the Bowen-Merrill Company, to suggest to Meredith Nicholson the researching and writing of what became *Alice of Old Vincennes,* which the same firm issued in 1900. Other Hoosier residents who produced similar but much less successful historical romances were Charles Fleming Embree, Charles Test Dalton, Mary Elizabeth Jordan Lamb, and a professor of English at Indiana University, Henry Thew Stephenson, the scholarly

---

18 McKee, *"Ben-Hur" Wallace,* pp. 246-269.

19 Howard G. Baetzold, "Charles Major: Hoosier Romancer," *Indiana Magazine of History,* LI (1955), 31-42; Shumaker, *A History of Indiana Literature,* pp. 339-348.

author of *Patroon Van Volkenberg: A Tale of Old Manhat-*
*tan* (1900) and *The Fickle Wheel: A Tale of Elizabethan*
*London* (1901). George Barr McCutcheon, a Lafayette newspaperman who later lived in Chicago and New York, mined a
somewhat different vein in his *Graustark* (1901), a melodramatic adventure story of intrigue and love in a small,
mythical Balkan kingdom. The sudden, unexpected popularity
of this book launched McCutcheon on a long writing career,
during which he published five additional "Graustarkian" romances and several other novels, including a more serious
work partly laid in Indiana, *The Sherrods* (1903), and
*Viola Gwyn* (1922), a narrative of pioneer days in Lafayette.[20]

The number of Hoosier authors who made fictional use of
Indiana's historical background in this period was legion.
One of the best known was Caroline Virginia Krout of Crawfordsville, whose first book, *Knights in Fustian* (1900), was
based on the activities of the Knights of the Golden Circle
and a "Copperhead" insurrection in Montgomery County during the Civil War. Although her *On the We-a Trail* (1903)
treated the same events as the slightly earlier *Alice of Old*
*Vincennes* by her Crawfordsville neighbor, Maurice Thompson, it was well accepted, and in her last book she returned
to the same scenes to write about the founding of Post Vincennes in *Dionis of the White Veil* (1911). Among less-
known works of Indiana historical fiction, several dealing with
the Civil War period, were the following: Harriet Newell
Lodge, *A Bit of Finesse. A Story of Fifty Years Ago* (1894);
Anna Nicholas, *An Idyl of the Wabash, and Other Stories*
(1898); Millard F. Cox, *The Legionaires. A Story of the*

---

[20] Russo and Sullivan, *Bibliographical Studies of Seven Authors of Crawfordsville,* p. 225; Shumaker, *A History of Indiana Literature,* pp. 338-339,
390-393, 394-404. The novelist's brother, John T. McCutcheon, was also a successful Chicago newspaperman who was better known for his cartoons than his
writing, which included four mediocre novels, one of which dealt with a favorite Indiana theme, politics: *Congressman Pumphrey. The People's Friend*
(1907). *Ibid.,* pp. 417-419.

*Great Raid* (1899) ; Frank A. Myers, *Thad Perkins. A Story of Indiana* (1899) ; Grace C. Alexander, *Judith. A Story of the Candle-Lit Fifties* (1906) ; Harold M. Kramer, *Hearts and the Cross* (1906) ; Frederick Landis, *The Glory of His Country* (1910) ; Ulysses S. Lesh, *A Knight of the Golden Circle* (1911) ; Caroline Dale Snedeker, *Seth Way. A Romance of the New Harmony Community* (1917) ; and David W. Anderson, *The Blue Moon. A Tale of the Flatwoods* (1919). George W. Louttit, author of a historical romance laid in Indiana, *A Maid of the Wildwood* (1901), also produced an interesting political satire, *The Gentleman from Jay* (1903), of the same genre as the earlier work of a Lafayette newspaperman, Dwight LeRoy Armstrong, who wrote *An Indiana Man* (1890). There was even a novel about the Indianapolis Speedway, William Winter's *The Winner* (1915), as well as a clever piece of historical fiction in the guise of the travel diary of "John Parsons of Petersburg, Virginia," by Indianapolis *Star* columnist Kate Milner Rabb under the title of *A Tour Through Indiana in 1840* (1920).[21]

Quite a different sort of fiction came from the pen of Gene Stratton Porter, who extracted romance from nature rather than from history. While living with her husband and daughter in Geneva, Adams County, in an area still heavily forested and containing a huge marsh called the Limberlost Swamp, teeming with wild plant and bird life, she began her work in photography and natural history which led to the publication of *The Song of the Cardinal* in 1903. This was soon fol-

21 Shumaker, *A History of Indiana Literature,* pp. 348-349, 385-390, 393-394, 415-417, 419-424, 432-436. Despite the moderate success of her books, Caroline V. Krout ceased literary production during the last twenty years of her life following the publication of *Dionis of the White Veil* in 1911, apparently because of her shyness and sensitivity to criticism. Banta (comp.), *Indiana Authors and Their Books,* p. 184. Other little-known Hoosier authors who dealt with more or less indigenous material in their fiction were Margaret Holmes, Mary Jameson Judah, Martha Livingstone Moody, Angelin Teal, and James A. Wickersham. It is perhaps worth noting that so large a proportion of Indianans who wrote this type of fiction were women. Nicholson, *The Hoosiers,* pp. 221-223, 241.

lowed by the writing of her most popular books, *Freckles* (1904) and *A Girl of the Limberlost* (1909), which mingled romantic sentimentality and moralism in an idealized delineation of both man and nature. Three more best sellers, *At the Foot of the Rainbow* (1907), *The Harvester* (1911), and *Laddie* (1913), the last a fictionalized account of her own childhood experiences, had a similar saccharine quality, for their author made few concessions to realism. In 1913, after the draining of the marsh and the conversion of much of it to onion, celery, and sugar-beet beds virtually destroyed the Limberlost which had inspired her nature study and the books that had made her famous, Mrs. Porter moved to a wooded region on the shores of Sylvan Lake near Rome City. There she continued her writing until 1923, when she left the state permanently for California, but none of her later works proved nearly as successful as the Limberlost books.[22]

Of all the novelists Indiana produced in these years— many of whom celebrated the glories of rural and small-town Mid-America—only three dealt seriously and realistically with the problems of urban life. The most distinguished of these, Theodore Dreiser, was little appreciated in his home state and largely dissociated himself from Indiana to live and work mostly in the East, as also did the second member of this trio, David Graham Phillips. Both, however, made considerable use of their Hoosier background in their novels, Dreiser drawing upon his family and childhood experience in Terre Haute and elsewhere to portray the religious fanaticism and drab poverty found in the opening chapters of *Jennie Gerhardt* (1911) and the partly autobiographical *The "Genius"* (1915). Phillips, whose books had a realistic

[22] Jeannette Porter Meehan, *The Lady of the Limberlost. The Life and Letters of Gene Stratton-Porter* (Garden City, N.Y., 1928), pp. 111-239; Shumaker, *A History of Indiana Literature,* pp. 405-410. In 1924 Mrs. Porter was fatally injured in an automobile accident in Los Angeles and died at the age of sixty-one, one of America's most popular novelists. As a monument to her work the Indiana Department of Natural Resources has preserved her home in Geneva.

tone but lacked the searing quality of Dreiser's naturalistic writing, not only laid many of his scenes in Indiana but even modeled his hero in the political novels, *The Cost* (1904) and *The Plum Tree* (1905), on his good friend from college days at Indiana Asbury—later DePauw—University, Senator Albert J. Beveridge. In *The Conflict* (1911), he even created a Eugene V. Debs-type of socialist leader as the chief actor in a political and industrial conflict in "Remsen City, Indiana." In his most ambitious work, *Susan Lenox. Her Fall and Rise,* which was published posthumously in 1917, six years after the author's tragic murder in New York, Phillips writes of the heroine's birth and early life in an Ohio River town very much like Madison, Indiana, his own birth-place, before describing her spectacular career in Cincinnati and New York.[23]

The only one of the three novelists closely identified with Indiana, however, was Booth Tarkington of Indianapolis, who finally came to literary realism in his later novels after serving an apprenticeship with the more popular romantic mode of writing. His first book, *The Gentleman from Indiana* (1899), which immediately launched him upon a successful literary career, presented a somewhat sentimentalized version of midwestern small-town life, using such local-color touches as a vicious group of ruffians calling themselves White Caps, though they had no connection with the vigilante bands of the same name which terrorized parts of southern Indiana in the eighties and nineties. The publication of *Monsieur Beaucaire* (1900) and *The Two Vanrevels* (1902) took Tarkington into the field of historical romance, the first laid in eighteenth-century England and the second in Indiana during the Mexican War. His initial venture into realism was the writing of six short stories drawing upon his one-term experience in the state legislature, which were issued in 1905

23 Philip L. Gerber, *Theodore Dreiser* (*Twayne's United States Authors Series,* No. 52, New York, 1964), pp. 77-78, 147-148; Abe C. Ravitz, *David Graham Phillips* (*Twayne's United States Authors Series,* No. 96, New York, 1966), pp. 67-76, 126-128.

as *In the Arena. Stories of Political Life*. But not until 1913, after a bout with alcoholism and his divorce and remarriage, did Booth Tarkington begin to find himself as a serious novelist. In that year he published *The Flirt,* a domestic novel laid in Indianapolis, followed by *Penrod* (1914), the first in a popular series of relatively frank chronicles of boyhood. Tarkington reached the peak of his development, however, with four novels portraying Indianapolis middle-class family life in the midst of a deteriorating social order caused by urbanization and industrialization—*The Turmoil* (1915), *The Magnificent Ambersons* (1918), *Alice Adams* (1921), and *The Midlander* (1924), the second and third of which were awarded Pulitzer Prizes.[24]

Although Tarkington in his mature phase as represented by these four sociological novels appeared as both a social realist and a sincere critic of American materialism, he did not avoid completely the conservatism and sentimentalism which seemed to pervade so much of Indiana literature in the Golden Age. Not unlike his friend and fellow Hoosier, James Whitcomb Riley, he often tended to look back nostalgically at the simpler, happier times he envisaged as existing before the arrival of urban industrialism upon the Indiana scene. In *The Turmoil* Booth Tarkington expressed this attitude vividly in the description of Indianapolis found in the opening pages of the novel:[25]

Not quite so long ago as a generation, there was no panting giant here, no heaving, grimy city; there was but a pleasant big town of neighborly people who had understanding of one another, being, on the whole, much of the same type. It was a leisurely and kindly place—"homelike,"

[24] James Woodress, *Booth Tarkington, Gentleman from Indiana* (Philadelphia, 1955), pp. 59-203, 256-258; Shumaker, *A History of Indiana Literature,* pp. 350-373.

[25] Booth Tarkington, *The Turmoil* (New York, 1915), p. 2, quoted with the permission of Harper & Row, publishers. In 1927 three of the Indianapolis novels, *The Turmoil, The Magnificent Ambersons,* and *The Midlander,* were reissued as a trilogy entitled *Growth.* Until his death in 1946 Tarkington continued his prolific and versatile literary production, but nothing that he wrote subsequently attained the level he had reached in the trilogy and in *Alice Adams.* Shumaker, *A History of Indiana Literature,* pp. 373-385.

it was called—and when the visitor had been taken through the State Asylum for the Insane and made to appreciate the view of the cemetery from a little hill, his host's duty as Baedeker was done. The good burghers were given to jogging comfortably about in phaetons or in surreys for a family drive on Sunday. No one was very rich; few were very poor; the air was clean, and there was time to live.

The dramatic, not to say melodramatic, quality of many of the works of Indiana fiction writers in this period was manifested in their early and frequent transformation into theatrical productions. Of the novels thus dramatized, Wallace's *Ben-Hur,* Nicholson's *The House of a Thousand Candles,* and Major's *When Knighthood Was in Flower* were great popular successes on the stage. Booth Tarkington not only helped turn some of his own novels into plays, but he also wrote original farces and comedies, the most famous of which was his first, *The Man from Home,* written in collaboration with Harry Leon Wilson in 1907. Except for William Vaughn Moody, the expatriate Hoosier author of *The Great Divide* (1906) and *The Faith Healer* (1909), Indiana produced no outstanding dramatists. The first professional playwright in the state was probably Joseph Arthur, an Indianapolis actor who wrote *Blue Jeans* (1888) and other popular melodramas in the last quarter of the nineteenth century. William Oscar Bates, a newspaperman who began a career as a playwright in Indianapolis in 1900, wrote mostly one-act plays, many of them for the Little Theatre Society of Indiana which was organized in the capital city in 1915. One of them, *Polly of Pogue's Run* (1917), was a historical play having as its main character Civil War Governor Oliver P. Morton.[26]

One of the most popular playwrights in the whole country was George Ade, a native of Newton County, Indiana, who graduated from Purdue University and entered upon a ca-

[26] *Ibid.,* pp. 240-241, 294-295, 331, 343-344, 364-365n, 374-385, 498-502. Two Hoosiers who abandoned the state to carry on theatrical work in New York City were the Fort Wayne-born critic, George Jean Nathan, and Paul Wilstach of Lafayette, who was the author of several plays as well as the biography, *Richard Mansfield, the Man and the Actor* (1908). Banta, *Indiana Authors and Their Books,* pp. 234-235, 343-344.

reer as a journalist in Chicago, as did other Hoosiers such as John T. and George Barr McCutcheon and Theodore Dreiser. Becoming a well-known newspaper columnist with his "Stories of the Streets and of the Town," Ade achieved a literary reputation as a humorist and satirist with the publication in book form in 1900 of his *Fables in Slang,* which was quickly followed by a dozen more collections of similar "modern fables." In 1902 he wrote his first play, the libretto for a comic opera satirizing the American government's activities in the Philippine Islands, entitled *The Sultan of Sulu,* which with music by Alfred G. Wathall became an immediate popular success in the theater. The next year Ade followed it with another musical comedy, *Peggy from Paris,* and a drama based on small-town politics called *The County Chairman.* His best-known work was *The College Widow,* written in 1904 at his country estate, Hazelden, which he had recently built with part of his large literary earnings near his birthplace in Kentland, Newton County. This extraordinarily popular comedy was the first play in America about college life and football and had for its setting the Wabash College campus in Crawfordsville. Although George Ade's dramatic and other writings were more in the form of entertainment than permanent literature, his deft satirical wit and humor secured him an important place among Hoosier writers of the Golden Age.[27]

§ §

Journalism also flourished in the Golden Age of Indiana literature. Newspapers abounded, the vast majority of them country weeklies. Although the number of dailies increased

[27] Fred C. Kelly, *George Ade. Warmhearted Satirist* (Indianapolis, 1947), pp. 89-194; Shumaker, *A History of Indiana Literature,* pp. 444-470. Unlike most successful playwrights, George Ade did not become a New Yorker but retained his permanent residence in Indiana, making his country estate, Hazelden House, in Newton County, a gathering place for his literary friends and college and fraternity friends. After his death in 1944 his home was turned over to the county for the George Ade Memorial Hospital. Another monument to him is the Ross-Ade Stadium at Purdue University which was erected in large part through his efforts. Shumaker, *op. cit.,* pp. 472-473.

rapidly through most of this period, as late as 1918 thirty counties in Indiana had no daily press. In 1884 the Department of Statistics reported the existence of 336 weekly and 42 daily papers, five of the former and 18 of the latter printed in the German language. By 1909 the number of weeklies had risen to 517 and dailies to 172, plus 20 Sunday editions. But in 1919 mergers and failures had reduced the totals to 407, 138, and 18, respectively, including 13 foreign-language publications—seven in German, two in both German and English, one in English, Italian, and Slovak, one in Hungarian, and two in Polish. Five Negro newspapers were published in the state in this period, all in Indianapolis: the *Leader*, from 1879 to 1885; the *World*, from 1882 to 1924; the *Freeman*, from 1884 to 1926; the *Ledger*, from 1913 to 1927; and the only surviving paper, the *Recorder*, which was founded in 1897 by William H. Porter and George P. Stewart.[28]

Before the turn of the century most cities and even the smaller county seats in Indiana still maintained the tradition of competing party newspapers, whose editors took their politics seriously and often carried on colorful and vitriolic debates with each other. The main center of the political party press was Indianapolis, where the Democratic *Sentinel* under the editorship of Samuel E. Morse from 1888 to 1903 and the Republican *Journal*, published in this period by John C. and Harry S. New, served as outstanding examples of "partisan journalism of the slapstick variety," in the phrase of Louis Ludlow, the Washington correspondent of the *Sentinel* and later the Indianapolis *Star*. But it was the highly partisan leaders of the country press which inaugurated the movement for more active participation in party politics. In 1878 George J. Langsdale of the Greencastle *Banner* called a meeting of GOP editors in Indianapolis which resulted in the

[28] Indiana *Year Book*, 1918, pp. 983-1005; Indiana Department of Statistics, *Annual Report*, 1884, pp. 384-412; United States Bureau of the Census, *Fourteenth Census* (1920), IX, *Manufactures*, pp. 393-394; Thornbrough, *The Negro in Indiana*, pp. 384-388; Lyda, *The Negro in the History of Indiana*, p. 71.

organization of the Indiana Republican Editorial Association. Under the leadership of Langsdale, who was elected the first president, the association began a program of annual meetings, where resolutions were adopted and opinions on current party matters were aired. In 1896 President Charles B. Landis of the Delphi *Journal* organized the first Republican editorial banquet, and a state press bureau was established to work with the GOP state committee. Similarly, on November 19, 1880, eleven Democratic editors from northern Indiana met at Fort Wayne to discuss the recent election which had turned out so disastrously for their party. Out of that meeting came the organization on January 5, 1881, in Indianapolis of the Indiana Democratic Editorial Association, which elected John B. Stoll of the Ligonier *Banner* its first president. Stoll, who published the Elkhart *Monitor* from 1881 to 1883 and the South Bend *Times* from 1883 to 1912, was one of the most influential Democratic editors in the state; he later wrote a *History of the Indiana Democracy*.[29]

The leading newspaper chain in the state was the *Star* League, which was put together in 1903 by Muncie traction magnate George C. McCulloch, who founded the Indianapolis *Star* and the Terre Haute *Star* to add to his journal of the same name in Muncie, which had been begun in 1899. Within a year the Indianapolis *Star* had bought out the *Journal* and in 1906 the Sunday *Sentinel,* thus bringing an end to the old partisan press in the capital city. In the meantime, however, the *Star* papers came first into the hands of a company

29 Louis Ludlow, *From Cornfield to Press Gallery* . . . (Washington, D.C., 1924), pp. 95-106; Indiana Republican Editorial Association, *Souvenir of the 47th Annual Meeting 1878-1925* (Indianapolis, 1925), pp. 7-10; Luther Short, *Early History of the Democratic Editorial Association of Indiana* (Franklin, Ind., n.d.); Edna Miller, The Editorial Opinion of John B. Stoll (Unpublished Master's thesis in History, Butler University, 1946), pp. 24-25. Another Republican editor described George J. Langsdale as "extremely radical in his views, so radical, that upon the election of Grover Cleveland for President in 1884, he immediately resigned the postmastership of Greencastle, to take effect on March 4, 1885, he refusing to serve as postmaster under a Democratic administration." Marvin W. Pershing, *The Story of Our Association: The Indiana Republican Editorial Association* (Indianapolis, 1921).

headed by the former Richmond financier, Daniel G. Reid, and then by 1908 into receivership. Finally, in 1911 the Star League came under the control of Senator Beveridge's good friend, John C. Shaffer of Chicago, who also owned newspapers in that city as well as Denver and Louisville. Under Shaffer as publisher, the Indianapolis *Star* along with the Terre Haute and Muncie members of the chain became ardent exponents of the Progressive party. By 1906 the Scripps-McRae League was represented in the state by two newspapers of the J. C. Harper group, the Evansville *Press* and the Terre Haute *Post*. An extensive small-town newspaper chain was operated by William B. Harris of Ellettsville, Monroe County, who published weeklies for as many as 138 communities in southern Indiana and neighboring states in the eighties and nineties.[30]

Probably the best-written and best-edited newspaper in Indiana in this period was the Indianapolis *News,* an independent afternoon daily founded in 1869 by John H. Holliday. In 1892 Holliday sold his interest in the *News* to an Ohioan, William Henry Smith, former manager of the Associated Press, whose nephew, Charles W. Fairbanks, then a politically ambitious young Indianapolis attorney, was a silent partner in the venture. Under the leadership of the editor, Smith's son-in-law Charles R. Williams, and after Smith's death in 1896 his son, Delavan Smith, who acted as publisher, the Indianapolis *News* became the outstanding afternoon paper in the state, taking a vigorously independent line on most issues despite its generally Republican position. When the *News* boldly printed attacks upon the administration's han-

[30] Dunn, *Greater Indianapolis,* I, 412-413; John O. Carrington, The Foreign Policy of the Indianapolis Star, 1918-1939 (Unpublished Ph.D. thesis in History, University of Kentucky, 1958), pp. 1-10; Alfred M. Lee, *The Daily Newspaper in America. The Evolution of a Social Instrument,* (New York, 1937), p. 213; Robert D. Bickett, "William B. Harris and His Newspaper Chain," *Indiana Magazine of History,* XXXVI (1940), 117-122. In June, 1922, the Indianapolis *Times,* founded as the *Sun* in 1888, became a member of the Scripps-McRae chain of newspapers.

dling of the Panama Canal negotiations during the 1908 election campaign, President Theodore Roosevelt had a criminal libel indictment drawn up against the publisher, Delavan Smith, but Federal District Court Judge Albert B. Anderson in Indianapolis dismissed the charges, and the case entered the annals of the freedom of the press when the United States Supreme Court later handed down a decision in favor of the New York *World,* another target of Roosevelt's anger during the same incident.[31]

The secret of the success of the Indianapolis *News* lay chiefly in its excellent staff of editors and writers, which included such men as Hilton U. Brown, Louis Howland, Meredith Nicholson, and Morris Ross. Two of its most popular feature writers in this period were William Herschell, author of such Riley-like poems as "Ain't God Good to Indiana," which appeared in his newspaper column entitled "Songs of the Streets and Byways," and Juliet Virginia Strauss, wife of the publisher of the Rockville *Tribune* who began writing a weekly column for the *News* in 1903 over the signature "The Country Contributor." Edward Bok, editor of the *Ladies' Home Journal,* discovered Mrs. Strauss two years later and introduced her writings to the readers of his popular magazine as "The Ideas of a Plain Country Woman," the title under which a collection of her essays was published in 1906. Ohio-born Frank McKinney "Kin" Hubbard was a *News* political cartoonist who won a wide audience for "Hoosier humor" by his creation in 1904 of "Abe Martin of Brown County," a fictitious crackerbox philosopher, and his rustic southern Indiana friends and neighbors, who spoke a dialect not far from that found in some of James Whitcomb Riley's poetry. Through newspaper syndication as well as the publication of a series of books, Abe Martin's comments on the

31 Brown, *A Book of Memories,* pp. 184-195, 199-202; Clyde Pierce, "The Panama Libel Cases," *Indiana Magazine of History,* XXXIII (1937), 171-186; James E. Pollard, *The Presidents and the Press* (New York, 1947), pp. 585-589.

foibles of the human race earned Hubbard an enduring reputation as an Indiana humorist.[32]

A short-lived, unorthodox newspaper published in Indiana
was *The Coming Nation,* a socialist weekly established in 1893
in Greensburg by Julius A. Wayland, a Hoosier editor who
returned home in that year from Colorado, where he had
made his fortune in real estate dealings. Apparently because
he and his family were disliked in Greensburg for their unpopular social and economic views, Wayland moved to Rus-
kin, Tennessee, in 1894 to attempt to form a co-operative
colony. When this venture failed, he moved to Girard, Kansas, where he published for many years his *Appeal to Reason,*
a popular socialist successor to *The Coming Nation.*[33]

One of the first literary magazines in the state was *The
Telephone,* later named the *Midland Monthly,* published in
Indianapolis in 1882-1883 chiefly for a female audience. During the years 1889-1891 Charles B. Foster of the same city
edited *Hoosier,* a comic-illustrated weekly, and in 1895 Michael W. Carr, an Irish-born Roman Catholic publicist,
launched a short-lived illustrated literary journal under the
title, *The Pen.* Indianapolis was also briefly the home of a
"little magazine" modeled on Elbert Hubbard's *Philistine*
which was entitled *The Ishmaelite,* which Hewitt H. Howland edited from 1896 to 1899 with the help of contributors
including his brother, Louis Howland, and Meredith Nicholson, all staff members of the Indianapolis *News.* Of maga-

32 Brown, *A Book of Memories,* pp. 143-145, 210-212, 219-223, 229-230;
Edward Bok's introduction to Juliet V. Strauss, *The Ideas of a Plain Country
Woman* (New York, 1908), pp. v-vi; Fred C. Kelly, *The Life and Times of
Kin Hubbard, Creator of Abe Martin* (New York, 1952), pp. 81-111. Two
Hoosier newspapermen who achieved fame in their later careers outside of
Indiana were Roy W. Howard, who worked briefly for the Indianapolis *News,*
and Kent Cooper, who was once employed by that newspaper's short-lived
afternoon rival, the Indianapolis *Press,* as well as the more enduring Indianap-
olis *Sun. The Indiana Publisher* (Indianapolis), XXX, No. 1 (December, 1940),
12; Kent Cooper, *Kent Cooper and the Associated Press: An Autobiography*
(New York, 1959), pp. 21-25.

33 Howard H. Quint, "Julius A. Wayland, Pioneer Socialist Propagandist,"
*Mississippi Valley Historical Review,* XXXV (1948-49), 585-606.

zines of more general interest the most popular and enduring was E. E. Stafford's *The Indiana Woman. An Illustrated Indiana Weekly* (the first part of the title was dropped in 1899), which commented on social life, the arts, fashion, theater, and sports during its seven-year existence in Indianapolis from 1895 to 1902. In the year of its demise appeared *The Reader,* a literary and critical journal which was purchased by the Bobbs-Merrill Publishing Company in 1904 and under Hewitt H. Howland's editorial direction ranked "for a few years among the leading magazines of the country," according to the historian of the American magazine, Frank Luther Mott. Howland published articles on contemporary politics and public affairs including the widely read series of debates between William Jennings Bryan and Indiana's Senator Albert J. Beveridge in 1907. The Indiana capital could not long sustain such a journal, however, and in 1908 *The Reader* was merged with *Putnam's Monthly* in New York.[34]

§ § §

The Indiana literary renaissance was not confined to belles lettres and journalism but extended to many other types of writing as well. Politicians and other public men contributed a spate of autobiographies and volumes of reminiscences, including abolitionist George W. Julian's *Political Recollections* (1884); *Men and Measures of Half a Century* (1888) by Hugh McCulloch, Fort Wayne banker and Secretary of the Treasury under Presidents Andrew Johnson and Chester A. Arthur; *Recollections of Sixteen Presidents from Washington to Lincoln* (1894) by former Secretary of the Navy Richard W. Thompson of Terre Haute; United States Senator David Turpie's *Sketches of My Own Times* (1903); Julius A. Lemcke's whimsical *Reminiscences of an Indianian, from the Sassafras Log behind the Barn in Posey County to Broader Fields* (1905); former United States Secretary of State John Watson Foster's *Diplomatic Memoirs* (1909); university edu-

[34] *The Telephone. A Monthly Magazine Devoted to General Literature,* I (1882); *The Pen,* I (1895); *The Ishmaelite,* I (1896-1898), 1-4; Mott, *A History of American Magazines,* IV, 46, 96.

cator David Starr Jordan's *The Days of a Man* (1922); *Adventures in Social Work* (1923) by Alexander Johnson, first secretary of the Indiana State Board of Charities; and Governor and Vice-President Thomas R. Marshall's *Recollections* (1925). The Quaker reformer and writer, William Dudley Foulke, penned two accounts of his personal experiences in *Fighting the Spoilsmen* (1919) and *A Hoosier Autobiography* (1922).[35]

Indiana nonfiction writers were especially active in the fields of history and biography, the West and the Civil War frequently furnishing the settings. Two early studies of the western frontier were Indianapolis attorney Augustus Lynch Mason's *Romance and Tragedy of Pioneer Life* (1883) and *Massacre of the Mountains* (1886) by Jacob Piatt Dunn, a journalist and historian who became an earnest student of Indian language and lore as well as a prolific author of local history. Indiana can also claim James Mooney of Richmond, a self-taught anthropologist who spent his career in the United States Bureau of American Ethnology and produced such studies as *The Ghost-Dance Religion and the Sioux Outbreak of 1890* (1896) and *Myths of the Cherokee* (1900). In 1896 William H. English, a wealthy banker and politician who had been the Democratic vice-presidential candidate in 1880, published the two-volume *Conquest of the Country Northwest of the River Ohio, 1778-1783, and Life of Gen. George Rogers Clark,* a work which probably had an influence on the writing of both Maurice Thompson's *Alice of Old Vincennes* and Caroline V. Krout's *On the We-a Trail.*[36]

*Herndon's Life of Lincoln,* which was published in three slim volumes in 1889, was in no small part an Indiana prod-

35 Banta (comp.), *Indiana Authors and Their Books,* pp. 112-113, 168, 174-175, 190, 200, 324.

36 *Ibid.,* pp. 94, 105, 212, 227-228; Caroline Dunn, *Jacob Piatt Dunn: His Miami Language Studies and Indian Manuscript Collection* (Indiana Historical Society, *Prehistory Research Series,* Vol. I, No. 2, Indianapolis, 1937), pp. 31-42; Russo and Sullivan, *Bibliographical Studies of Seven Authors of Crawfordsville,* p. 216.

uct, for it was written by Lincoln's former law partner, William Herndon of Springfield, Illinois, in collaboration with Jesse W. Weik, a young Greencastle Federal pension agent who helped the old lawyer to prepare the biography. Weik, who did some independent field work in Kentucky and southern Indiana himself, finally inherited the Herndon-Lincoln papers and published *The Real Lincoln. A Portrait* in 1922. Other biographies dealing with the Civil War period were George W. Julian's *Life of Joshua R. Giddings* (1892), a eulogistic portrait of the Ohio abolitionist and Congressman who was also his father-in-law, and William D. Foulke's *Life of Oliver P. Morton* (1899), a well-researched account of the life and times of Indiana's wartime governor, which was written at the request of his son, Oliver T. Morton, who was himself the author of a collection of historical essays entitled *The Southern Empire* (1892). The most outstanding biographical work to come from a Hoosier pen, however, was the monumental four-volume *Life of John Marshall* (1916-1919), which Albert J. Beveridge wrote during his partial retirement from politics after the failure to bring Indiana into the camp of Theodore Roosevelt and the Progressive party in 1912. Concerned primarily with the constitutional issues over which the Civil War was in part fought, Beveridge intended to round off his studies with a definitive biography of Abraham Lincoln, a project which was cut off by the author's death in 1927, the four completed volumes dealing with Lincoln's early life and career being published in 1928.[37]

Among other Hoosier historians were Arthur Middleton Reeves, who pursued Scandinavian studies in Copenhagen and described the Viking explorations in America in *The*

[37] Benjamin P. Thomas, *Portrait for Posterity. Lincoln and His Biographers* (New Brunswick, N.J., 1947), pp. 132-164; David H. Donald, *Lincoln's Herndon* (New York, 1948), pp. 296-321; Foulke, *A Hoosier Autobiography*, p. 205; Bowers, *Beveridge and the Progressive Era,* pp. 545-589. Beveridge also used the Herndon-Lincoln papers which his friend Jesse W. Weik by then had possession of and placed fully at his disposal. Beveridge, *Abraham Lincoln* (4 volumes, Boston, 1928), I, vii.

*Finding of Wineland the Good* (1890) before his death in a
railroad accident on a visit to his home in Richmond, Indiana, in 1891, and Daniel Wait Howe, the former Marion
County Superior Court judge who turned to colonial Massachusetts for his subject in *The Puritan Republic* (1899) and
treated the coming of the Civil War in his *Political History of
Secession* (1914). Edward Eggleston published two volumes
of a projected history of American society and culture, *The
Beginners of a Nation* (1896) and *The Transit of Civilization
from England to America in the Seventeenth Century*
(1901), and was elected to the presidency of the American
Historical Association. His presidential address in 1900 was
an influential argument for the writing of social and cultural
history in place of the older type of political narrative. His
brother, George Cary Eggleston, contributed a sympathetic
*History of the Confederate War* (1910). The former editor
of the Indianapolis *News,* Charles R. Williams, was the author
of a two-volume *Life of Rutherford Birchard Hayes* (1914),
which he wrote after his retirement to Princeton, New Jersey, using the materials collected by his father-in-law, William Henry Smith, principal owner of the *News* who died in
1896. Significant works of academic historians in this period
included Paul L. Haworth's *The Hayes-Tilden Disputed
Presidential Election* (1906) and James A. Woodburn's *Life
of Thaddeus Stevens* (1913).[38]

Indiana's most prolific historian was John Clark Ridpath,
a native of Putnam County and professor of history and vice-
president of Indiana Asbury–DePauw University. His *Popular
History of the United States,* which was first issued in 1876
and was many times reprinted, became one of the most wide-

[38] Banta (comp.), *Indiana Authors and Their Books,* pp. 140, 158-159,
266, 347-348; James A. Rawley, "Edward Eggleston: Historian," *Indiana Magazine of History,* XL (1940), 341-352; Charles R. Williams, *Life of Rutherford
Birchard Hayes* (2 volumes, Boston, 1914), I, vii-viii. William H. Smith was
also the author of *A Political History of Slavery,* published posthumously by
the hand of his son, Delavan Smith, longtime publisher of the Indianapolis
*News.* See the introduction by Whitelaw Reid in Smith, *A Political History of
Slavery* (2 volumes, New York, 1903), pp. xii-xvi.

ly distributed volumes of its kind, and was made into an influential textbook. Retiring from his university post in 1885, Ridpath devoted most of the rest of his life to writing a popular series of multivolume works for the subscription trade including *Cyclopaedia of Universal History* (1885) and *Great Races of Mankind* (1893). Not works of original scholarship, his books were intended, he wrote, "for the practical man of the shop, the counter, and the plow." Indiana was also the birthplace of political scientist-historian Charles A. Beard, a DePauw University graduate who published his iconoclastic study, *An Economic Interpretation of the Constitution* (1913) while a professor at Columbia University. A classmate of Beard's at DePauw was Frederick A. Ogg who taught history for a few years at Manual Training High School in Indianapolis and at Indiana University before becoming the author of such works as *The Opening of the Mississippi—a Struggle for Supremacy in the American Interior* (1904) and *The Old Northwest. A Chronicle of the Ohio Valley and Beyond* (1919).[39]

Much historical writing was focused on Indiana itself in this period. In the eighties appeared the first flood of county and local histories, full of regional pride but often untrustworthy in detail. Two of the best of their kind were Judge David Demaree Banta's *Historical Sketch of Johnson County* (1881) and newspaper editor Berry Sulgrove's *History of Indianapolis and Marion County* (1884). A broader work of the same decade was William Wesley Woollen's *Biographical and Historical Sketches of Early Indiana,* which was published in Indianapolis in 1883. The awakening of interest in state and local history was also demonstrated by the reorganization in 1886 of the Indiana Historical Society, a private association founded in 1830 but long inactive. Jacob Piatt Dunn, who was chosen recording secretary, began the task

---

[39] Clifton J. Phillips, "John Clark Ridpath, DePauw Teacher and Historian," *DePauw Alumnus,* XXII (1957), 2-3; John Clark Ridpath, *A Popular History of the United States* (Cincinnati, 1876), p. iii; Banta (comp.), *Indiana Authors and Their Books,* pp. 21-22, 241.

of collecting and editing the society's historical papers, which were later published in 1897 under the terms of a bequest of William H. English. This series of *Publications* of the Indiana Historical Society included studies by Daniel W. Howe, George W. Julian, John H. Holliday, James A. Woodburn, and Dunn himself, who contributed such papers as his well-known disquisition on the word "Hoosier" and *The Mission to the Ouabache* (1902), which furnished the historical background for Caroline V. Krout's novel of the French occupation of Vincennes, *Dionis of the White Veil.*[40]

Jacob P. Dunn was also the author of *Indiana. A Redemption from Slavery* (1888), a volume in the *American Commonwealth Series* which gave most of its attention to the slavery question and did not carry the narrative beyond the Constitution of 1816. The first complete coverage of Indiana's history was essayed in *The History of the State of Indiana from the Earliest Explorations by the French to the Present Time* (1897), a two-volume work by William Henry Smith, a free-lance Indianapolis journalist who later wrote a campaign biography of vice-presidential candidate Charles W. Fairbanks as well as a *History of the Cabinet of the United States.* A useful specialized study was *A History of Education in Indiana* (1892) by Richard G. Boone, former superintendent of education in Frankfort and a professor of pedagogy at Indiana University. During the first two decades of the twentieth century a number of significant books on state history were published. Colonel William M. Cockrum's *Pioneer History of Indiana* (1907) and *History of the Underground Railroad* (1915) were based in large part on family reminiscences and documents. On the other hand,

---

[40] Banta (comp.), *Indiana Authors and Their Books,* pp. xii, 16, 309, 349; James A. Woodburn, "The Indiana Historical Society: A Hundred Years," in Christopher B. Coleman (ed.), *Centennial Handbook, Indiana Historical Society, 1830-1930* (Indiana Historical Society *Publications,* X, No. 1, Indianapolis, 1930), pp. 24-29; Dunn, *Indiana and Indianans,* V, 1924. A bibliography of county histories is found in Carolynne L. Wendel, *Aids for Genealogical Searching in Indiana* (Detroit Society for Genealogical Research, 1962).

George B. Lockwood, a young newspaperman made the first scholarly study of the Rappite and Owenite communities on the Wabash. Beginning his research into this subject while an undergraduate at DePauw University in the early nineties, Lockwood published the results of his scholarship in *The New Harmony Communities* in 1902.[41]

The best of a number of popular histories of the state was *Historic Indiana* (1909) by Julia Henderson Levering of Lafayette, whose "lifelong familiarity with the scenes, the characters, the movements, and the events mentioned," she declared in the preface, assured her readers a "sympathetic treatment of the subject." In the two historical volumes of his five-volume *Indiana and Indianans* (1919), Jacob P. Dunn presented a full, though often rambling, account containing a great deal of acute personal commentary along with occasional digressions into narrow subjects of special interest to the author. Two university studies by Hoosier social scientists dealing with specific aspects of the development of the state were William A. Rawles, *Centralizing Tendencies in the Administration of Indiana* (1903) and Newell Leroy Sims, *A Hoosier Village* (1912), a social history and sociological analysis of Angola in Steuben County. In the centennial year of 1916, an economist at DePauw University in Greencastle, Frank H. Streightoff, collaborated with his wife, Frances D. Streightoff, in preparing *Indiana. A Social and Economic Survey,* which gave attention to matters outside the usual political narratives found in histories of the state.[42]

In 1899 William Henry Smith, author of the *History of the State of Indiana,* assumed editorial control of *The Indianian,* a monthly journal begun two years earlier, which was devoted

---

[41] Banta (comp.), *Indiana Authors and Their Books,* pp. 38, 61-62, 194, 297-298; George B. Lockwood, *The New Harmony Communities* (Marion, Ind., 1902), pp. 279-280.

[42] Levering, *Historic Indiana,* p. vi; Banta (comp.), *Indiana Authors and Their Books,* pp. 291, 308; *Indiana Magazine of History,* I (1905), 39-40; VIII (1912), 98-99.

to the promotion of the study of Indiana history. It was discontinued in 1901 because of financial difficulties. Its successor was the *Indiana Magazine of History,* which George S. Cottman of Irvington, a job-printer with a consuming interest in local history, founded in 1905, printing the first issue on his own press. In 1907 the Indiana Historical Society made the magazine its official organ, with Christopher B. Coleman of Butler University as editor. Cottman resumed the editorship for two years from 1911 until 1913, when the Indiana University Department of History took over major responsibility for the magazine. The new editor was Logan Esarey, an instructor in history and secretary of the recently created Indiana Historical Survey, which had been organized to collect and publish documents and other materials on the history of the state. Although the survey project never received sufficient funds to become permanently established, Esarey was able to introduce courses and graduate seminars in Indiana and middle western history at the university and to make the *Indiana Magazine of History* one of the foremost journals of its kind in the Old Northwest. He also issued a *Guide to the Study of Indiana History* (1915) and edited with Leander J. Monks and Ernest V. Shockley the three volumes of *Courts and Lawyers of Indiana* (1916), but his major contribution was *A History of Indiana,* which was published in two volumes in 1915 and 1918.[43]

In the meantime, in 1907 the History Club at Indiana University proposed that the state plan a centennial celebration in 1916, the year of the hundredth anniversary of its admis-

[43] Dunn, *Greater Indianapolis,* I, 399; George S. Cottman, "The Indiana Magazine of History: A Retrospect," *Indiana Magazine of History,* XXV (1929), 281-287. In 1914 Cottman collaborated with Max R. Hyman to publish *Indiana, Past and Present: A Monthly Magazine of Hoosier Progress,* which lasted only eight months. Logan Esarey, who resigned as editor of the *Indiana Magazine of History* in 1927, continued to collect materials on the history of Indiana and the Middle West and left a few unpublished manuscripts when he died in 1942. In 1943 R. Carlyle Buley edited and published some of Esarey's essays as *The Indiana Home.* Buley, "Logan Esarey, Hoosier," *Indiana Magazine of History,* XXXVIII (1942), 348-381; Buley's foreword to Esarey, *The Indiana Home* (Crawfordsville, Ind., 1943).

sion to the Union. Professor James A. Woodburn, director of the Indiana Survey, and others promoted the idea, and in 1911 the General Assembly created a centennial commission which two years later recommended the construction of a $2,000,000 memorial building. The legislature refused to appropriate funds for this purpose, however, and instead submitted the proposition to a popular referendum, in which it was defeated along with a proposal to call a constitutional convention. Finally, in 1915 the General Assembly established the Indiana Historical Commission and appropriated $25,000, of which $20,000 was for the promotion of centennial celebrations in the state, and $5,000 for the collection and publication of historical documents. Not only were elaborate centennial pageants performed, notably at Bloomington, Corydon, and Indianapolis, but the state park system was begun with the acquisition of the McCormick's Creek and Turkey Run areas, and the Society of Indiana Pioneers was organized, all as part of the celebration of the state's hundredth anniversary.

Moreover, in 1916 the Indiana Historical Commission stretched the $5,000 appropriation, which Jacob P. Dunn disdainfully called a "beggarly amount," far enough to issue the first four volumes of the *Indiana Historical Collections*—two on *Constitution Making in Indiana* edited by Charles Kettleborough of the Indiana Bureau of Legislative Information, one a collection of travel writings edited by Harlow Lindley entitled *Indiana as Seen by Early Travelers,* and the last, Leah Jackson Wolford's book of Hoosier folksongs and games, *The Play-Party in Indiana.* More generous appropriations in the next few years made possible the publication of three volumes of the papers of the first governors of the Territory and State of Indiana edited by Logan Esarey of Indiana University.[44]

[44] Woodburn, "The Indiana Historical Society: A Hundred Years," in Coleman (ed.), *Centennial Handbook,* pp. 33-36; James A. Woodburn, "The Indiana Historical Commission and Plans for the Centennial," *Indiana Magazine of History,* XI (1915), 338-347; *Laws of Indiana,* 1915, pp. 455-457;

Hoosiers contributed to other kinds of literature as well, including general and topical essays, travel accounts, and scientific and nature studies. One of the most versatile writers of this period was William Dudley Foulke, whose earliest publication was a brief analysis of Russian autocracy entitled *Slav or Saxon* (1887). Albert J. Beveridge, who published a more sympathetic study on *The Russian Advance* (1903) based on his travels in Russia and Asia, was a prolific author of addresses and articles on a variety of topics, some of which were collected in book form as *The Young Man and the World* (1905), *The Bible as Good Reading* (1907), *The Meaning of the Times* (1907), and *Americans of To-day and To-morrow* (1908). Benjamin Harrison offered his thoughts on American government and other subjects in two collections of addresses and magazine articles, *This Country of Ours* (1897) and *Views of an Ex-President* (1901). Hoosier lawyers, who were responsible for the production of so many novels, also made significant contributions to general literature, including such works as William P. Fishback's *The Lawyer in Literature* (1892) and *Recollections of Lord Coleridge* (1895) and Colonel Eli F. Ritter's *Moral Law and Civil Law, Parts of the Same Thing* (1896). John H. Stotsenburg of New Albany, who was a member of the commission to revise the Indiana statutes in 1879-1881 and the author of a book on law, also published *An Impartial Study of the Shakespeare Title* in 1904.[45]

Women were also active in the field of nonfiction, as they had long been in fiction. Catharine Merrill, a popular professor of English literature at Butler University before her retirement in 1885, was the author of *The Man Shakespeare and*

Dunn, *Indiana and Indianans,* II, 781-783. The Society of Indiana Pioneers was organized on the initiative of Evaline R. Holliday of Indianapolis, wife of its first president, John H. Holliday. The Society inaugurated the annual state historical conferences in 1919 and sponsored pilgrimages to places of historical interest in Indiana, among other activities. A short-lived predecessor was the Indiana Pioneer Society (1878-1879). Society of Indiana Pioneers, *Year Book,* 1921, p. 4; 1937, pp. 3-22.

[45] Banta (comp.), *Indiana Authors and Their Books,* pp. 27, 110, 113, 137, 273, 306.

*Other Essays,* which was published posthumously in 1902. Several Indiana women wrote accounts of their far-flung travels, including Susan Elston Wallace's *The Storied Sea* (1883) and *Along the Bosphorus* (1898), Mary Hannah Krout's *Hawaii and a Revolution* (1898) and *A Looker-On in London* (1899), and Helen M. Gougar's *Forty Thousand Miles of World's Wandering* (1905). Ida Husted Harper, an active feminist who lived for several years in Terre Haute and Indianapolis, wrote *Associated Work of the Women of Indiana* for the Chicago World's Fair in 1893 as well as the three-volume *Life and Work of Susan B. Anthony* (1898-1909) and was the chief compiler of the last three volumes of the official *History of Woman Suffrage* (1903-1922). In 1917 Charity Dye, an Indianapolis schoolteacher who was the only woman member of the Indiana Historical Commission, issued a series of biographical sketches in honor of the state's centennial entitled *Some Torch Bearers in Indiana.*[46]

Indiana harbored many amateur naturalists who wrote articles and books describing their observations. One of the most popular writers of this kind was Maurice Thompson, novelist, civil engineer, and state geologist, who published two collections of nature stories, *By-Ways and Bird Notes* (1885) and *Sylvan Secrets* (1887). Moreover, he and his brother Will Thompson were both champion archers and helped to popularize that outdoor sport with their books, *The Witchery of Archery* (1878) and *How to Train in Archery* (1879), the first by Maurice alone and the second a joint production of the two Crawfordsville brothers. Two other amateur naturalists in this period were Gene Stratton Porter, who along with her novels wrote *What I have Done with Birds* (1907) and other accounts of bird life, and an Indianapolis attorney, William Watson Woollen, author of *Birds of Buzzard's Roost* (1907). The latter also founded the Nature Study Club of Indiana and presented a tract of land set aside as a bird sanctuary to the city of Indianapolis for the use of the public. Willis S. Blatchley, an entomologist who

46 *Ibid.,* pp. 94-95, 122, 184-186, 216.

served as state geologist from 1895 to 1911, expressed his lifelong passion for the world of nature in such books as *Gleanings from Nature* (1899) and *Woodland Idyls* (1912).[47]

In 1881 a young ornithologist, Amos W. Butler, and others organized the Brookville Society of Natural History in that Franklin County community. The society, which was the most active organization of its kind in the state, opened a natural history museum, and its members began publishing periodic scientific bulletins in 1885. Butler also took the lead in founding the Indiana Academy of Science, which came into existence at the annual meeting of the Brookville Society of Natural History in November, 1885, when President David Starr Jordan of Indiana University was chosen as the first presiding officer. Beginning in 1891 the Academy published a great variety of scientific papers in its annual *Proceedings* —the printing of which was financed by legislative appropriation after 1895—and became a major force in the promotion of natural science in the state. Its early membership rolls included such distinguished Indiana scientists as Joseph C. Arthur, plant rust authority at Purdue University; Amos W. Butler, who wrote *The Birds of Indiana* (1891); the China-born botanists, John Merle Coulter of Hanover and Wabash colleges and Stanley Coulter of Purdue, both of whom compiled catalogues of the flowering plants of Indiana, the former in 1881 and the latter in 1900; and Harvey W. Wiley, chief chemist of the United States Department of Agriculture and crusader for pure foods and drugs. David Starr Jordan, the author of many scientific studies on Indiana fish, was also a recognized writer of nature essays and stories.[48]

47 Russo and Sullivan, *Bibliographical Studies of Seven Authors of Crawfordsville,* viii-ix, 180-185, 289-292; Banta (comp.), *Indiana Authors and Their Books,* pp. 35, 258-259, 348-349.

48 Nadine K. Fichter, "The Brookville Society of Natural History," *Indiana Magazine of History,* XLII (1946), 305-310; *Laws of Indiana,* 1895, pp. 253-254; Indiana Academy of Science, *Proceedings,* 1891, p. 9; Will E. Edington, "There Were Giants in Those Days," *ibid.,* 1934, pp. 22-38; David H. Dickason, "David Starr Jordan as a Literary Man," *Indiana Magazine of History,* XXXVII (1941), 345-358.

# CHAPTER XIV

## THE FINE ARTS

THE FINAL PASSING OF THE PIONEER PERIOD in which the efforts of most citizens were directed chiefly to the management of practical affairs undoubtedly made it possible for Hoosiers to devote greater attention to the fine arts. In the last quarter of the nineteenth century the art of painting in particular began to flourish in the state in a manner and degree similar if not quite equal to the flowering of literature described in the preceding chapter. Although Indiana in earlier decades possessed a host of itinerant limners and other frontier artists, they were in large part self-trained semi-amateurs whose work belonged mostly to the category of "primitive" portraiture. Of the few pioneer painters who achieved higher standing, the most eminent according to Indiana art historian Wilbur D. Peat was the English-born George Winter, who studied art in New York before settling in 1837 in Logansport, where he produced workmanlike studies of the Miami Indians and painted scenes along the Wabash River. Moving to Lafayette in 1851 he continued to execute sensitive portraits and landscapes until his death in 1876.[1]

While many cities such as Evansville, Fort Wayne, Muncie, Richmond, Terre Haute, and Vincennes boasted small colonies of painters by the seventies, the largest contingent of resident artists in the state was to be found in Indianapolis. The greater size and wealth of the capital city afforded better op-

[1] Mary Q. Burnet, *Art and Artists of Indiana* (New York, 1921), pp. 38-50; Wilbur D. Peat, *Pioneer Painters of Indiana* (Indianapolis, 1954) pp. xi-xvii, 115-117, 123-124. For the definitive work on Winter's early activities, see *The Journals and Indian Paintings of George Winter, 1837-1839* (Indiana Historical Society, 1948).

portunities for the commissioning of portraits upon which the livelihood of most painters so largely depended, for there was still little demand for any other type of painting. In January, 1877, however, the Indianapolis Art Association was organized with the express design of familiarizing the citizenry with the wider scope of the work of local artists by public exhibitions of their canvases. Among its members were well-established older artists like Jacob Cox and Barton Stone Hays, both of whom had maintained studios in the city for many years, as well as such newcomers to Indianapolis as Dewey Bates and Theodore Clement Steele, who were elected to the offices of president and secretary, respectively, of the short-lived organization, which held only one exhibition before expiring. Besides the work of its members, however, the art association, which admitted only men to active membership, included in this showing some paintings by Charlotte Hillis "Lotta" Guffin, the city's leading woman artist and a student and colleague of Jacob Cox. At this time Indianapolis also enjoyed the services of Indiana's pioneer art critic, Alois Sinks, a native of Dayton, Ohio, who arrived in the capital city in the mid-seventies. A colorful Bohemian figure who had studied and worked in the art world of New York City, Sinks was a mediocre painter who turned to journalism and wrote many lively and often acerbic critiques of contemporary Hoosier art in the Indianapolis *Saturday Herald* before his death in 1881. Indeed, it may have been his harsh comments on an amateurish canvas of Lew Wallace which persuaded the versatile general to concentrate his talents upon literature rather than painting.[2]

Although Cox, Hays, and others had long offered private lessons in their studios, the first regular institution for the

2 Eva Draegert, "The Fine Arts in Indianapolis, 1875-1880," *Indiana Magazine of History,* L (1954), 105, 107-109, 193-194; Peat, *Pioneer Painters of Indiana,* pp. 131-133, 182-183, 190-192. Jacob Cox continued to work in Indianapolis until his death in 1892, but both Barton Hays and Mrs. Guffin departed from the city in the eighties, the latter dying in Chicago in 1896 and the former in Minneapolis in 1914. *Ibid.,* pp. 228, 232.

professional training of art students in the state was the Indiana School of Art, which opened its doors in Indianapolis in October, 1877, under the guidance of two talented European-trained painters, James Farrington Gookins, who acted as the school's director, and his assistant, John Washington Love. Gookins was a native of Terre Haute who had studied painting at the Bavarian Royal Academy in Munich, while Love, who was born in Ripley County but became a resident of Indianapolis at an early age, had been a student in the Ecole des Beaux-Arts in Paris. Although the school obtained the support of a relatively large number of patrons and sponsored an impressive exhibition of the work of its students and outstanding local artists, it survived for only two years. A major factor contributing to its demise was undoubtedly the severe economic depression of the time, but disagreement between the two directors may also have hampered its development. At the end of the first season Gookins resigned his place in the school in order to resume his painting and other interests in Terre Haute and later Chicago, returning only briefly to Indianapolis in 1887-1888 in the capacity of secretary of the Indiana Soldiers' and Sailors' Monument Commission. Moreover, John W. Love, who acted as the institution's sole director during the final year of its existence, died suddenly in 1880 before fulfilling his own promise as a painter.[3]

In spite of the brevity of its existence Gookins' and Love's Indiana School of Art had a significant impact upon the state by helping to launch a group of young artists in the city. Shortly after the school closed its doors several former students led by William Forsyth banded together as the Bohe—for Bohemian—Club and rented meeting rooms where they continued to sketch and paint for a number of years. Their ranks were thinned, however, by a veritable exodus

---

[3] Draegert, "The Fine Arts in Indianapolis, 1875-1880," *Indiana Magazine of History,* L, 109-111; Burnet, *Art and Artists of Indiana,* pp. 113-123; Peat, *Pioneer Painters of Indiana,* pp. 183-186; Dunn, *Greater Indianapolis,* I, 483-484.

of younger artists and art students which took place in the early eighties. One of the most promising of these was Charles Fiscus, who followed Gookins to Terre Haute and Chicago before returning to Indianapolis, where he died in 1884 at the age of twenty-three. Another departing Bohe Club member, Frank Edwin Scott, eventually became a permanent resident of Paris, where he attained a minor reputation as an expatriate American artist.[4]

With little or no opportunity at home for professional training and experience, many aspiring painters in Indiana looked abroad for artistic stimulation and opportunities for serious study. While the fashionable ateliers of Paris and Barbizon were attracting large numbers of American art students in these years, Hoosiers tended to prefer the more staid atmosphere of Munich and its Bavarian Royal Academy of Art. This institution had been the training ground not only for James F. Gookins but also for the better-known William Merritt Chase, an Indiana-born artist and pupil of Barton S. Hays, who after his return from Europe in the late seventies established his studio in New York City, where he became an influential still-life painter and teacher of painting. In the summer of 1880 a small band of artists and art students departed in a body to study and work in Munich. Included among the members of this Hoosier colony in Bavaria were John Ottis Adams, who had begun painting in Muncie after two years' study in London, and Theodore C. Steele, a native of Owen County who settled in the capital city in 1872, becoming a founding member and officer of the Indianapolis Art Association, as related above. Another talented young artist in the original band was Samuel G. Richards of Spencer, who had started to paint in Anderson, where he became a close acquaintance of James Whitcomb Riley, just then at the outset of his career as a journalist and poet. Both Richards and Steele, who were accompanied on the

---

[4] Burnet, *Art and Artists of Indiana*, pp. 124-131; William Forsyth, *Art in Indiana* (Indianapolis, 1916), pp. 10-12.

journey by their wives and children, had arranged to finance their European travel and study by obtaining prepayment for commissions to be executed after their return to America, Steele placing all arrangements in the capable hands of his friend and patron, Herman Lieber, an Indianapolis art dealer whose downtown gallery was a significant force in the promotion of the work of the city's artists in these years. In 1883 the Hoosier contingent in Munich was enlarged by the arrival of William Forsyth, an Ohio-born resident of Indianapolis who had been one of the first students enrolled in the short-lived Indiana School of Art and the chief founder of the Bohe Club. Moreover, in the next year Otto Stark, another Indianapolis painter who was closely associated with those of the Munich colony in later years, went to Paris to study at the Academie Julien.[5]

In Europe these expatriate Indiana artists acquired professional methods and techniques and came chiefly under the influence of a waning academic romanticism which left a lasting impression on their style. Despite their exposure to some of the unorthodox work of the French impressionists, they were little affected on the whole by any of the newer currents of European art which were eventually to have so great an impact upon most American painters. Nevertheless, the return of several of their number to Indiana in the middle and later eighties helped create a resurgence of interest and activity in painting which continued for many years and radically changed the Indiana art world. Unlike William M. Chase and some other European-trained Middle

[5] Burnet, *Art and Artists of Indiana,* pp. 132-148; Forsyth, *Art in Indiana,* pp. 12-14; Selma N. Steele *et al., The House of the Singing Winds: The Life and Work of T. C. Steele* (Indiana Historical Society, 1966), pp. 3-16. For an assessment of Chase see Katharine Metcalf Roof, *The Life and Art of William Merritt Chase* (New York, 1917). Samuel Richards, one of the most gifted of the Hoosier colony in Munich, became a victim of tuberculosis in Europe and upon his return to America in 1891 took up residence in Denver, Colorado, where he died in 1893. Marguerite Hall Albjerg, "A Nineteenth Century Artist, Samuel Richards, 1853-1893," *Indiana Magazine of History,* XLIV (1948), 143-160.

Westerners who preferred to work in the more favorable environment of established art centers in the United States or Europe, most of the members of the Hoosier colony decided to root themselves once more in the soil of Indiana and seek subject matter and inspiration on familiar home ground. In a series of newspaper articles prepared in honor of the state centennial in 1916, William Forsyth explained how he and his colleagues in Munich had been influenced by an ideal of national and regional expression which they had discovered in Europe, particularly in the work of certain Dutch and Scandinavian painters. "It dawned upon them," he wrote, "that if this kind of work could be developed in Holland and Norway, then why not in America; and, granted that it could be done in America, then why not in Indiana or any other part of the United States, if trained artists settled down at home and applied their knowledge to things they best knew?" Upon their actual return to Indiana, moreover, the repatriated Hoosier painters found to their great joy that "here was enough to engage their ambitions for the rest of their lives, and that here, perhaps, could be developed a school of painting distinctive and characteristic of the locality."[6]

T. C. Steele, who was the first to return home, arrived back in Indiana in 1885, followed by J. Ottis Adams two years later and William Forsyth in 1888. Otto Stark remained in the East for two years after leaving Paris before resettling in 1889 in Indianapolis, where he soon embarked upon a lengthy and influential career as supervisor of art in Manual Training High School. The three who had studied in Germany had become accustomed to leaving the studio and classroom for relatively long periods of painting outdoors in nearby villages and turned naturally to the Indiana landscape for material for their canvases. Singly or in pairs they began to

[6] Forsyth, *Art in Indiana,* pp. 15-16. After his return to Indiana, T. C. Steele, for example, occasionally defended the impressionists in papers and talks before various art groups. Steele, *The House of the Singing Winds,* pp. 43, 76.

explore the Hoosier countryside on sketching and painting expeditions, developing a strong interest in the seasonal variations of mood and color. Steele found subjects in the rural neighborhoods around Indianapolis itself and in Montgomery County and accompanied Forsyth on several outings to Vernon and the Muscatatuck River Valley. Both Steele and Forsyth separately visited Hanover on the spectacular bend of the Ohio River, and the latter also painted at Corydon and often took his pupils on tours in Morgan and Marion counties. In 1896 Steele and J. Ottis Adams began making annual expeditions to the picturesque old town of Brookville, where the two artists and their families joined in acquiring a summer home which they remodeled and named the Hermitage in 1898. Later Steele sold his share in the house to Adams, who with his artist-wife Winifred Brady Adams continued for several years to make it the center of a small colony of artists who spent summers in Brookville, the "Indiana Barbizon," as it was sometimes called.[7]

The most enduring art colony in the state devoted especially to rural landscape painting was established in and around Nashville, Brown County. In the nineties a few Hoosier artists made sketching trips on foot through parts of this isolated, hilly county southwest of Indianapolis, but it was a Chicago painter, Adolph Robert Shulz, who was chiefly responsible for discovering the unusual qualities of its landscape for his fellow artists. Paying his first visit to the region in the summer of 1900, Shulz returned again and again, finally settling permanently in Nashville in 1908 with his wife, Ada Walter Shulz, who was also a painter. Meanwhile, in 1907 T. C. Steele had built a summer studio-home

---

[7] Steele, *The House of the Singing Winds*, pp. 188-189; Burnet, *Art and Artists of Indiana*, pp. 165-167; Forsyth, *Art in Indiana*, pp. 15-16. Not restricting themselves to the Indiana landscape, Steele painted one or more summers in Vermont, Tennessee, Oregon, and California, and Adams spent several summers in Michigan and winters in Florida during the latter part of his painting career. Burnet, *Art and Artists of Indiana*, p. 169; Steele, *The House of the Singing Winds*, pp. 189-190.

—the "House of the Singing Winds"—near Nashville in the hamlet of Belmont, and soon more than a score of artists were located in the county, especially during the summer and fall seasons. Among them were John William "Will" Vawter of Greenfield, an illustrator of the poems of James Whitcomb Riley who later turned to landscape painting, and Gustave Baumann, a German commercial artist who established a successful wood-block printing and wood-engraving studio in Nashville in the second decade of the twentieth century. Others who frequently painted in Brown County in these years were Homer G. Davisson of Fort Wayne, Louis O. Griffith, a Greencastle native who lived in Chicago, and Frederick Polley of Indianapolis. By 1928 there were enough resident artists to make possible the establishment of the Brown County Art Gallery Association, which sponsored regular public exhibitions of the work done in the region.[8]

Indianapolis, however, continued to be the most important center of activity in the art world of Indiana. A main factor was the Art Association of Indianapolis, an active and prestigious organization called into existence largely through the efforts of May Wright Sewall, one of the city's most active feminists and educators, who had invited a Milwaukee woman, Nancy H. Adsit, to give a series of art lectures in her home in the winter of 1882-1883. These resulted in such an enthusiastic response that Mrs. Sewall called a special meeting of interested persons to form a permanent association for the promotion of art in the city. In November, 1883, the association sponsored its first annual exhibition of paintings and in January of the next year opened an art school

[8] Adolph Robert Shulz, "The Story of the Brown County Art Colony," *Indiana Magazine of History,* XXXI (1935), 283-285; Josephine A. Graf, "The Brown County Art Colony," *ibid.,* XXXV (1939), 365-367; Burnet, *Art and Artists in Indiana,* pp. 306-310; Steele, *The House of the Singing Winds,* pp. 57-167. After Steele's death in 1926, his widow preserved his Brown County studio-home and in 1945 presented it to the state of Indiana along with more than three hundred of his paintings and sketches as a permanent memorial to the painter. *Ibid.,* pp. 171-172.

under the direction of a Chicago artist, Charles F. McDonald, and Susan M. Ketcham of Indianapolis, who had been a student of Gookins and Love. Although classes were discontinued after two years for lack of patronage, a similar school was established in 1889 in the city by T. C. Steele, who was later joined by William Forsyth, both recently returned from Munich. In 1891 the Art Association of Indianapolis took over the management of this school, which continued in operation until the building in which it was located was razed in 1897. Meanwhile, in 1895 the association received a bequest from John Herron, an Englishman who had resided in Indianapolis for several years, for the establishment of a museum and art school. A long drawn-out contest of the Herron will was finally decided in favor of the association and an art school was opened in January, 1902, in a home formerly used as a studio by T. C. Steele. In the years 1906-1908 the Art Association of Indianapolis erected two handsome new buildings to house the varied activities —including exhibitions and public lectures as well as art classes—of the John Herron Art Institute, as the museum-school was named in honor of its benefactor. In 1908 the association began holding at the institute a series of annual exhibitions of the work of Indiana artists, including sculpture and applied arts as well as paintings, and later awarded special prizes for the best canvases by resident painters. Moreover, the John Herron Art Institute provided a permanent basis for the first time for the professional training of artists in Indianapolis.[9]

[9] May Wright Sewall, "The Art Association of Indianapolis: A Retrospect," in Art Association of Indianapolis, *A Record, 1883-1906* (n.p., 1906), pp. 5-6; Draegert, "The Fine Arts in Indianapolis, 1880-1890," *Indiana Magazine of History*, L, 325-327; Sister M. Dolorita Carper, A History of the John Herron Art Institute (Unpublished Master's thesis, Butler University, 1947). Susan M. Ketcham later studied in Europe and in New York City, where she made her home after 1889, painting on the Maine coast during the summers. She demonstrated her attachment to her home state by designing the official seal of the Daughters of Indiana in New York. Burnet, *Art and Artists of Indiana,* pp. 230-234.

The notion of an Indiana school of art consisting of a group of representative painters in the state whose work bore certain marks of similarity had its beginnings as early as 1885, when a number of canvases executed by William Forsyth and T. C. Steele while resident in Germany were shown in Plymouth Church, Indianapolis, with a catalogue illustrated by members of the Bohe Club entitled *Ye Hoosier Colony in München.* In 1894 the Art Association of Indianapolis organized a similar show at the Denison Hotel of the paintings, chiefly landscapes, of four local artists, including Richard Buckner Gruelle and Otto Stark as well as Forsyth and Steele. Gruelle, the only one of this quartet who had not studied abroad, was a self-taught painter from Kentucky and Illinois who became a resident of Indianapolis in 1882. Although not personally associated with the European-trained artists who had returned to Indiana, Gruelle produced landscapes and other canvases which were somewhat similar to and were often exhibited with their work. The well-known writer and critic, Hamlin Garland, who was passing through Indianapolis on a lecture tour, was so struck by the "Western" quality of the paintings of the four men that he persuaded the Central Art Association of Chicago to sponsor the same exhibition in that city later in the year. This Chicago showing, which included paintings by J. Ottis Adams as well, brought the struggling Indiana artists to the attention of a wider public as the "Hoosier Group" of landscapists. In a pamphlet published in connection with the exhibit by the Central Art Association, three Chicago critics—the famous sculptor, Lorado Taft, a painter, Charles Francis Brown, and Hamlin Garland himself— highly praised the canvases of the five Indiana artists as foreshadowing "ultimate victory" for "original Western art":[10]

[10] Burnet, *Art and Artists of Indiana,* pp. 159-161, 183-188, 221-222. Gruelle, who was something of an outsider in the Hoosier Group because of his lack of European training, moved to Norwalk, Connecticut, in 1910 but returned frequently to Indianapolis and died there in 1914. *Ibid.,* p. 194.

These men were isolated from their fellow-artists; they were surrounded by apparently the most unpromising material; yet they set themselves to their thankless task right manfully, and this exhibition demonstrates the power of the artist's eye to find floods of color, graceful forms, and interesting compositions everywhere.

These artists have helped the people of Indiana to see the beauty in their own landscape. They have not only found interesting things to paint near at hand—they have made these chosen scenes interesting to others. Therein lies their significance.

In subsequent years members of the Hoosier Group frequently had their work exhibited together in various parts of the country. In 1904 J. Ottis Adams, William Forsyth, and T. C. Steele won medals for their paintings shown at the Louisiana Purchase Exposition in St. Louis. Adams, Forsyth, Stark, and Steele all played prominent roles in the Society of Western Artists, an organization founded in 1896 which sponsored annual itinerant exhibitions until 1914 of the canvases of local painters in Indianapolis and five additional midwestern cities — Chicago, Cincinnati, Cleveland, Detroit, and St. Louis. A younger Indianapolis artist often associated with the Hoosier Group who later became a leading member of this society was Clifton A. Wheeler, noted especially for his winter scenes. After studying with William Forsyth in Indianapolis and with William M. Chase both in New York and Europe, Wheeler built a studio in the suburb of Irvington in 1911 and became an instructor in painting at the John Herron Art School.[11]

In the years 1914-1915 the erection of a new section of the Indianapolis City Hospital provided an opportunity for many of the resident artists of the capital to co-operate in an ambitious collective art project. Upon the advice of the city health officer, Dr. T. Victor Keene, who suggested the idea to the sponsoring agency, St. Margaret's Hospital Guild of St. Paul's Episcopal Church, the Board of Health as-

---

[11] Forsyth, *Art in Indiana*, p. 17; Burnet, *Art and Artists of Indiana*, pp. 227-229, 242-244; Society of Western Artists, *Third Annual Exhibition, 1899* (Indianapolis, 1899).

signed William Forsyth the task of recruiting a large corps of workmen and directing them in the painting of mural decorations for the children's ward and other units. Among the artists contributing to this major civic enterprise were J. Ottis Adams, Forsyth, Otto Stark, and T. C. Steele, as well as younger painters and art students in the city such as Wayman Adams, Martinus Andersen, Francis Brown, Simon P. Baus, Carl Graf, Walter Hixon Isnogle, Emma B. King, Dorothy Morlan, William E. Scott, and Clifton A. Wheeler. Scott, who studied under Otto Stark before going to France to work with the expatriate American Negro painter, H. O. Tanner, and John W. Hardrick, a pupil of Forsyth and Stark, were the outstanding Negro artists in the state, both of whom painted murals for some of the Indianapolis public schools. Other Indianapolis painters in the early years of the twentieth century, many of them products of the John Herron Art School, were E. Chase Cassady, Ada M. Comingore, Ruth Pratt Bobbs, Marie Chilton Gray, Anna Hasselman, Richard B. Hausdorfer, Julia Graydon Sharpe, Lucy Taggart, Sadie Weisenburger, and Lucy A. Wilson.[12]

Outside the capital city Richmond was the center of perhaps the most active and enthusiastic art movement in the state. In 1897 Ella Bond Johnston, William D. Foulke, and other civic leaders organized the Art Association of Richmond with the object of promoting a wider knowledge and more general appreciation of the fine arts, especially painting, among the citizens of that eastern Indiana community. The association's annual exhibition, which was sponsored in co-operation with the public school system, soon became a city-wide festival whose influence extended into the neighboring towns. In 1903 Daniel G. Reid, a wealthy financier and former resident of Richmond, donated an annual purchasing fund for the acquisition of a permanent col-

<hr/>

12 Forsyth, *Art in Indiana*, p. 23; Burnet, *Art and Artists of Indiana*, pp. 180-183, 237, 249.

lection of paintings and other works of art which grew gradually in both size and variety through other gifts and was
eventually housed in rooms specially designed for that purpose in a newly constructed high school building. The association also encouraged the work of Indiana and local artists
by annual awards for the best canvases submitted by residents of both the city and the state. Finally, in 1910 Mrs.
Johnston, who served as president of the association for
seventeen years, made Richmond the headquarters for an
extensive network of traveling exhibits of Indiana and other
American paintings which circulated annually under her
management among such cities as Anderson, Bloomington,
Evansville, Fort Wayne, Greensburg, Lafayette, Logansport,
Seymour, Terre Haute, and Vincennes.[13]

Richmond and its vicinity was also the site of a numerous and lively artists' colony, of which John Elwood Bundy
was the recognized leader. Bundy, a North Carolinian who
grew up on a farm in Morgan County, Indiana, and studied
painting briefly under Barton S. Hays in Indianapolis and
at the Metropolitan Museum in New York City, came to
Richmond in 1888 to take charge of the newly established
art department of Earlham College. Resigning from his
teaching position in 1896 in order to devote all his energies
to painting, he soon became one of the most admired inter-
preters of the Indiana landscape, specializing in beech-woods
scenes painted near his home on the outskirts of the city. A
long-time director of the Art Association of Richmond and
member of the Western Society of Artists, Bundy lent encouragement and assistance to many of the younger painters of the community. A talented contemporary Richmond
landscapist was Charles S. Conner, whose untimely death in
1905 cut short a promising career. Other painters who
worked in the same city, some of them pupils of John E.

[13] Burnet, *Art and Artists of Indiana,* pp. 268-278; Ella Bond Johnston,
"An Art Association for the People," *Outlook,* LXXXV (January-April,
1907), 943-951; Johnston, "Art in Indiana," *Outlook,* XCVIII (May-August,
1911), 433-440.

Bundy, were George Herbert Baker, Charles Howard Claw-son, Albert W. Gregg, Maude Kaufman Eggemeyer, Ed-gar Forkner, William T. Eyden, Jr., Frank J. Girardin, William A. Holly, Elwood Morris, Alden and Marcus Mote, Anna M. Newman and Micajah T. Nordyke.[14]

Muncie began to develop as an art center in 1887, when J. Ottis Adams returned there to open a studio and teach classes for a short time. One of his first pupils—and later his wife—was Winifred Brady Adams, who also studied in Philadelphia and New York and achieved recognition for her still-life paintings. In 1892 an Art Students' League was organized, and in 1906 an Art Association, which even-tually acquired a large collection of paintings which were hung in the Muncie Public Library. By 1910 the city could boast a small colony of resident artists, including Francis F. Brown, Harriet F. McCulloch, Susan R. Marsh, George An-drew Mock, and Margaret Ball Petty. Another flourishing art center was Fort Wayne, where J. Ottis Adams and William Forsyth had begun classes in painting as early as 1888. Partly as a result of their efforts an Art Association came into being under the patronage of the Hamilton family, sev-eral of whose female members became practicing artists in Fort Wayne or elsewhere—Agnes, Jessie, and Norah Ham-ilton along with Katherine H. Wagenhals. The most promi-nent painters in the city in the early decades of the twen-tieth century were Homer Gordon Davisson, the director of the Fort Wayne Art School, and Anna M. Newman, a pupil of John E. Bundy of Richmond, who taught in the Fort Wayne public schools.[15]

One of the best-known painters in the northern part of Indiana before his death in 1915 was L. Clarence Ball, who came to South Bend from Ohio as a young man in the early eighties. After beginning his artistic career as a sign painter

[14] Burnet, *Art and Artists of Indiana,* pp. 275-276, 278-288; Peat, *Pioneer Painters of Indiana,* pp. 77-79, 94-96.

[15] *Art Guide to Indiana* (Indiana University Extension Division, *Bulletin,* XVI, No. 8, 1931), pp. 99-100; Burnet, *Art and Artists of Indiana,* pp. 300-302.

decorating Studebaker wagons, Ball became a skilled interpreter of nature in both oil and water-color landscapes, most often painting scenes in the picturesque swamplands of the Kankakee and St. Joseph valleys. His protégé and portraitist, Leon A. Makielski, whom he discovered copying newspaper reproductions of famous paintings in the basement of the St. Joseph County Courthouse, left South Bend to study in the East and abroad before accepting a position in the Art Department of the University of Michigan. Robert W. Grafton, a Chicago painter long associated with Indiana who painted portraits of such Hoosier personages as Timothy Nicholson of Richmond and the humorist George Ade, eventually established his home and studio in Michigan City.[16]

In the eighties and nineties several painters worked in Logansport, including Charles E. Holbruner, James H. Newport, Joseph Mattes, and the two sisters, Mary MacDonald and Margaret MacDonald Pullman, but the chief figure remaining there after 1900 was Wils Berry, who had spent his earlier years as an itinerant artist in various parts of Canada and the United States. Crawfordsville was the home of painters George Vance and Fred Nelson Vance and Delphi of the impressionistic landscapist Roy Trobaugh. In the south, Paul A. Plaschke and Ferdinand Graham Walker lived in New Albany but maintained studios across the Ohio River in the city of Louisville, while Will Henry Stevens, a landscapist and pottery decorator, worked in his hometown of Vevay before moving to New Orleans in the twenties. Several women painters also pursued quiet careers in the smaller cities of the state—Helen M. Goodwin in New Castle, Emily Griffin Hyde in Spiceland, Lola Alberta St. John in Albany, Alice C. Winn in La Porte, Lillian Volland and Millie Roesgen Voris in Columbus, and Louise A. Zaring in Greencastle.[17]

[16] Burnet, *Art and Artists of Indiana*, pp. 289-299.

[17] Peat, *Pioneer Painters of Indiana*, pp. 122-123; Burnet, *Art and Artists of Indiana*, pp. 299-300, 303, 314-317, 357, 382, 388, 399-400.

While nearly every major Hoosier painter conducted art classes for a shorter or longer period, some artists made teaching their chief occupation. The company of art teachers active in the state in this period included Harold Haven Brown, the director of the Herron Art School after 1913, Margaret Overbeck and Emma Matern Weaver of DePauw University, Laura A. Fry of Purdue, and William T. Turman, who headed the art department at the State Normal School in Terre Haute after 1894. By the nineties the public schools in many cities were also employing trained artists as instructors, such as Margaret Beachey in Evansville, Lulu S. Boyd in Frankfort, Rosa B. Griffith in Terre Haute, and Florence Fitch, Estelle Peel Izor, Roda Selleck, Wilhelmina Seegmiller, Otto Stark, and Lillian Weyl in Indianapolis. Mary Y. Robinson taught art at the Girls' Classical School in Indianapolis for several years while Bessie Hendricks, Virginia Keep Clarke, Helen McKay Steele, and Temp Tice conducted children's classes at the Herron Institute.[18]

As in other fields of endeavor, moreover, many artists born and educated in Indiana pursued their professional careers outside the boundaries of the state. Daniel Garber worked in Philadelphia, Isaac Henry Caliga in Massachusetts, Daniel Kotz in New Jersey, and Herman H. Wessel in Cincinnati, while a whole colony of Hoosiers was located in New York, including Martinus Andersen, William Carey Brazington, Glen Cooper Henshaw, Henry R. MacGinnis, Frederick Webb Ross, and H. Vance Swope. One of the most extraordinarily successful Indiana-born artists of all was the miniaturist Amalia Kussner Coudert, who painted fashionable portraits on ivory of wealthy patrons in New York and members of the royalty and aristocracy of Europe. The East as a publishing center also attracted illustrators such as Fred-

---

18 Burnet, *Art and Artists of Indiana,* pp. 236-239, 257-266, 357-358, 359, 368, 369, 372, 386, 394, 399, 402. Estelle Peel Izor, who taught advanced life classes at the Manual Training High School in Indianapolis, was also a pioneer in the introduction of courses in clothing and home design and wrote a textbook entitled *Costume Designing and Home Planning* (New York, 1916).

erick Coffay Yohn of Indianapolis and three sets of brothers, George and Worth Brehm of Anderson, J. Franklin and Hanson Booth of Noblesville, and John B. and Justin C. Gruelle, sons of the Hoosier Group landscapist.[19]

By the turn of the century many of the larger newspapers in the state had begun to employ cartoonists and other illustrators, three of whom were Walter Galloway of the Indianapolis *News,* Bert J. Griswold of the Fort Wayne *Sentinel,* and Karl Kae Knecht of the Evansville *Courier.* Others found employment outside Indiana. John T. McCutcheon, a Tippecanoe County native and Purdue graduate who like his brother, the novelist George Barr McCutcheon, chose to make his career in Chicago, became a famous caricaturist on the staff of the *Tribune.* Another well-known Chicago *Tribune* cartoonist of a later period was Gaar Williams of Richmond, Indiana, who made his early reputation with the drawings which appeared in the Indianapolis *News* from 1909 to 1921. Two of the most successful newspaper artists in Indiana were Frank McKinney "Kin" Hubbard, creator of the "Abe Martin" cartoons, and Charles Bacon "Chic" Jackson of Muncie, who conceived and drew the popular comic strip, "The Bean Family," which made its initial appearance in the Indianapolis *Star* in 1913 and was later syndicated and widely distributed.[20]

Despite the growth of commercial photography and the nearly overwhelming interest in landscape on the part of the leading artists, portrait painting continued to flourish in

[19] Burnet, *Art and Artists of Indiana,* pp. 249-256, 312-314, 316: Forsyth, *Art in Indiana,* pp. 27-30; Walt Reed, *The Illustrator in America, 1900-1960's* (New York, 1967), pp. 46, 48, 74. For the work of one of the most noted of these Hoosier illustrators, see *Franklin Booth; Sixty Reproductions from Original Drawings* . . . (Robert Frank, publisher, New York, 1925). John B. "Johnny" Gruelle, who spent a few years drawing cartoons for the Indianapolis *Sentinel* and later the *Star,* was best known for his illustrations and retelling for children of some of James Whitcomb Riley's narrative verses, as in the *Orphant Annie Story Book* (Indianapolis, 1921), and other publications.

[20] Burnet, *Art and Artists of Indiana,* pp. 369, 372, 377, 378, 380, 382, 403; Indianapolis, *Star,* June 16, 1935; J. Harley Nichols, " 'Chic' Jackson's Bean Family," *Indiana Magazine of History,* XXXVI (1940), 208-216.

Indiana throughout this period, and most professional painters accepted commissions for this kind of work from time
to time. One of the most prolific portraitists was T. C.
Steele, who produced realistic likenesses of many of the
state's distinguished citizens, including Albert J. Beveridge,
Charles W. Fairbanks, Benjamin Harrison, David Starr Jordan, Herman Lieber, Colonel Eli Lilly, Catharine Merrill,
Harry S. New, James Whitcomb Riley, and May Wright
Sewall. He was also commissioned to execute the official portraits of Governors Albert J. Porter, Isaac P. Gray, Alvin P.
Hovey, Ira J. Chase, and Claude Matthews, which were done
from life, as well as a special centennial collection of portraits of four earlier chief executives, William Henry Harrison, Jonathan Jennings, Oliver P. Morton, and Thomas A.
Hendricks. Another member of the Hoosier Group, Otto
Stark, painted a full-length portrait of George Rogers Clark
for the Sons of the American Revolution in commemoration
of the state centennial, and several of the younger Indianapolis painters, such as Simon P. Baus, Ruth Pratt Bobbs,
Olive Rush, and Lucy B. Taggart, specialized in portraiture
and figure studies.[21]

Devoting himself wholly to portraiture was Wayman
Adams, the son of Nelson Perry Adams of Muncie, a stock
farmer-turned-painter who gave the young aspiring artist
his first lessons. Wayman Adams received his training at
the Herron Art School and with William M. Chase and Robert Henri in Europe before establishing studios in both Indianapolis and New York City early in the second decade of
the twentieth century. In Indiana he contributed the official
likeness of five governors of this period—Winfield T. Durbin, J. Frank Hanly, Thomas R. Marshall, Samuel M. Ralston, and James P. Goodrich—as well as those striking
character studies of Alexander Ernestinoff, director of the

21 Steele, *House of the Singing Winds,* pp. 149, 194-195; Wilbur D. Peat,
*Portraits and Painters of the Governors of Indiana, 1800-1943* (Indiana His-
torical Society *Publications,* XIV, No. 3, Indianapolis, 1944), pp. 416-420;
Burnet, *Art and Artists of Indiana,* pp. 206-207, 237, 247-248, 252-253.

Indianapolis Symphony, and the novelist Booth Tarkington, for which the painter was especially admired in the state. Most of Adams' work with its distinctly modern, cosmopolitan character, seemed to be little related to the main body of Hoosier painting. In 1921, however, he created a minor masterpiece in quite another vein with his humorous group portrait of J. Ottis Adams, William Forsyth, Otto Stark, and T. C. Steele entitled "The Jury," showing that quartet of senior Indiana artists characteristically engaged in the grave act of judging a canvas at an exhibition.[22]

Yet in the period 1880 to 1920 it was landscape painting upon which the reputation of Indiana artists chiefly rested. Given a strong impetus by the return of expatriate artists from abroad in the eighties, the outdoor landscape scene became the most characteristic expression of Hoosier sensibility in painting. Although these years were marked by a rapid rate of industrialization and urbanization in the state, the typical productions of its artists, like the poetry of their contemporary, James Whitcomb Riley, were evocative of the rural past. Hoosier landscapists for the most part also interpreted the Indiana countryside in their paintings in a generally nostalgic and sentimental fashion, though some of the younger artists, Wheeler, for instance, at times attained a more realistic quality in their canvases. Pastoral themes predominated, even among artists living and working in large cities, while the relatively small number of urban scenes painted by Indianapolis residents such as Otto Stark and T. C. Steele retained much of the romantic and poetic character of their rural landscapes. On the other hand, as Wilbur D. Peat has argued, the total output of Steele, who may be considered the central figure in Indiana painting in this era, showed a remarkable evolution of the artist's vision and technique away from the conservative "Mu-

22 Burnet, *Art and Artists of Indiana,* pp. 244-247; Peat, *Portraits and Painters of the Governors of Indiana,* pp. 422-426; Steele, *House of the Singing Winds,* p. 159. Wayman Adams also did the official portrait of Paul V. McNutt, governor, 1933-1937.

nich manner" in the direction of impressionist and even near-abstract art.[23]

Yet like much of the literature produced in Indiana in the same years, Hoosier painting as a whole might be summed up in the words of the anonymous authors of *Indiana. A Guide to the Hoosier State* as "conservative and provincial, pleasant in its mood, and reassuring in its optimistic point of view." Although such leading Hoosier artists of this time as J. Ottis Adams, John E. Bundy, William Forsyth, Otto Stark, T. C. Steele, and Clifton A. Wheeler pursued similar ideals and interests and had many students and imitators, they failed to found an influential school of painting or to carve out a very significant niche in the history of American art. In the centennial year of 1916 William Forsyth already perceived this failure but blamed it chiefly on a lack of public appreciation and patronage. "Artists can not work and produce their best for themselves alone," he stated. "To do that best there must be a response and encouragement from the people among whom they live sufficient to keep the springs of enthusiasm flowing." Under the circumstances, he thought that he and his fellow artists had accomplished as much as was humanly possible. "If the public has failed to encourage it [the Hoosier Group] adequately to full expression and accomplishment, perhaps it is a fault of our times, a lack of comprehension of what their work has meant."[24]

§ §

Outside of painting and closely related fields of artistic endeavor, there was comparatively little development of the

---

23 Steele, *House of the Singing Winds,* pp. 195-200. In 1922 T. C. Steele was named honorary professor by Indiana University, and he spent winters in Bloomington as a kind of painter in residence, but he died in 1926 before he was able to occupy the studio being built for him in the new wing of the university library. *Ibid.,* pp. 160-166.

24 *Indiana. A Guide to the Hoosier State,* p. 130; Forsyth, *Art in Indiana,* pp. 17-18. One art historian very briefly discusses Steele, Forsyth, Stark, J. Ottis Adams, Bundy, and Clifton Wheeler as members of a "Hoosier Group." Eugen Newhaus, *The History and Ideals of American Art* (Stanford, Calif., 1931), pp. 239-240.

creative arts in Indiana in this period. Despite the heroic efforts of three sisters, Elizabeth G., Hannah B., and Mary
F. Overbeck, who established a ceramic studio and school in
Cambridge City in 1911, the art of the potter failed to flourish in the state.[25]

Sculpture fared somewhat better. In the late seventies a
sculptor named Ferdinand Meersman taught briefly in the
Indiana School of Art, but apparently left no disciples and
little or no work of his own. Perhaps the first public statue
erected in Indianapolis was a full-size figure of Benjamin
Franklin which was placed over the main entrance of the
Franklin Insurance Building on the Circle in 1874, the work
of John H. Mahoney, a Welsh-born apprentice employed by
a stone-cutting firm in the capital city. Inspired by a display
of John Rogers statuary at the Indiana Exposition, the
self-taught Mahoney was emboldened to accept the Franklin
commission and later executed a marble likeness of General
Solomon Meredith on the Meredith estate near Cambridge
City. After studying abroad for over a year, he worked on
various monumental projects in the East before returning
in 1889 to Indianapolis, where he established a studio-
workshop. Another early Indianapolis sculptor was India
Underhill Kirkland, a student of the painter Jacob Cox, who
submitted a model for a statue of Oliver P. Morton in 1880,
but the commission was awarded instead to Franklin Simmons of Maine.[26]

[25] Burnet, *Art and Artists of Indiana*, pp. 302-303; *Art Guide to Indiana*,
p. 66.

[26] Indianpolis *Journal*, August 3, 1890; Forsyth, *Art in Indiana*, p. 22;
Burnet, *Art and Artists of Indiana*, pp. 91-92, 327-329; George S. Cottman,
"John Mahoney: An Indianapolis Sculptor," *Indiana Magazine of History*, XXV
(1929), 190-192. The Simmons statue of Morton, which was unveiled in 1884,
was not the last commission of that kind in Indianapolis to be awarded to
an out-of-state sculptor. In the next twenty-five years the following memorial
statues were similarly executed: Schuyler Colfax by Lorado Taft (1887);
Thomas A. Hendricks by Richard Henry Parks (1890); General Henry W.
Lawton by Andrew O'Connor under the supervision of Daniel C. French
(1907); Benjamin Harrison by Charles Henry Niehaus (1908). Dunn, *Greater
Indianapolis*, I. 489.

In the eighties and nineties the movement to build Civil War memorials around the state provided much work for sculptors. By far the most imposing of these was the Indiana Soldiers' and Sailors' Monument, which was erected in Circle Park in the center of Indianapolis. Authorized by the General Assembly in 1887 after several years of agitation by veterans' groups and others, the huge monument was completed only in 1902. After a worldwide competition the Monument Commission selected a design submitted by a German architect, Bruno Schmitz, who arrived in Indianapolis in 1889 to oversee the construction of the towering limestone shaft with its bronze and stone decorations. Of the three bronze astragals encircling the shaft, the lowest and largest was designed and cast in Germany while the remaining two were the work of George T. Brewster of Cleveland, Ohio, who also created the bronze female figure representing "Victory" which crowns the structure. In 1897, after the withdrawal of the American artist Frederick MacMonnies, who had been awarded a contract for the "War" and "Peace" groups which were to be cast in bronze relief on the east and west sides of the monument, Schmitz brought a young Austrian sculptor, Rudolph Schwarz, who had been trained at the Imperial Academy of Art in Vienna, to carve the designs in stone. Schwarz not only carried out the "Peace" and "War" designs successfully but later received the commission for the two smaller statuary groups placed over the fountains at the base of the monument entitled "The Return Home" and "The Dying Soldier," as well as the bronze sentries standing guard before the north and south entrances which were intended to represent the four branches of military service—Infantry, Cavalry, Artillery, and Navy.[27]

His reputation established by his work on the Soldiers' and Sailors' Monument, Rudolph Schwarz, who had become a permanent resident of Indianapolis, where he built

[27] Ernestine Bradford Rose, *The Circle: "The Center of our Universe"* (Indiana Historical Society *Publications*, XVIII, No. 4, Indianapolis, 1957), pp. 397-408; Burnet, *Art and Artists of Indiana*, pp. 321-323, 419-420.

the first bronze-casting foundry in the state, received numerous commissions for lesser Civil War memorials and similar monuments. Among his designs were the soldiers' monuments or memorial tablets which were erected in Crawfordsville, Franklin, Greencastle, Mount Vernon, Princeton, South Bend, Terre Haute, and Vincennes. He also executed the statue of Governor Oliver P. Morton which was placed in front of the east entrance to the State House and a bust of the Columbus industrialist, Joseph I. Irwin, as well as several large monuments outside the state. Yet the versatile Schwarz, who died in Indianapolis in 1912, achieved neither financial security nor lasting artistic fame from his work, which for the most part was done hastily and cheaply. "Had he not been obliged to compete for the miserable trade in monuments . . . ," Mary Q. Burnet has argued, "he might have developed into a sculptor of which Indiana would have been proud and have brought to light the great art qualities he possessed."[28]

In the meantime, John H. Mahoney, who was completely overlooked in the search for sculptors for the Soldiers' and Sailors' Monument, received the commission to execute the bronze statues of George Rogers Clark, William Henry Harrison, and James Whitcomb, which together with the Simmons statue of Governor Morton were placed in the Circle around the monument to represent four major epochs of Indiana history. In 1891 Mahoney also designed the bronze figure of William H. English which was cast in duplicate, one going to the banker-politician's home town of Scottsburg, Scott County, and the other being set up in the town named for him in Crawford County. On the whole, Mahoney's work displayed good design and vigorous execution if not exceptional artistic merit. His best work, according to Mrs. Burnet, was the George Rogers Clark statue, which portrayed the Gen-

[28] Burnet, *Art and Artists of Indiana*, pp. 323-327. Theodore Stempfel has described Schwarz's struggle to make a living as a sculptor in Indianapolis in his *Ghosts of the Past: Autobiographical Sketches* (Indianapolis, 1935), pp. 79-94.

eral not as "a statesman or a man trained in the schools, but as a leader of the frontier, bringing his men victoriously through the difficulties of the wilderness." Although Mahoney received two other commissions for monuments outside the state, he was virtually forced to abandon sculpture for lack of sufficient patronage long before his death in Indianapolis in 1919.[29]

Indiana was the birthplace of a large number of women artists whose talents and training directed them to a career as sculptors. One who turned from painting to sculpture in the midst of her art studies in Chicago was Frances M. Goodwin of New Castle, sister of the painter Helen M. Goodwin and creator of the bronze bust of Robert Dale Owen which was commissioned through the efforts of the Indiana Federation of Clubs and placed on the grounds of the state capitol in 1911. Miss Goodwin, who served as the first president of the Sculptors' Society of Indiana, also executed busts of such Hoosier notables as Vice-President Schuyler Colfax and the poet Benjamin S. Parker. Two younger contemporaries of hers, Helene C. Hibben and Myra Reynolds Richards of Indianapolis, were both former students of the Herron Art Institute who became known particularly for portrayals of Indiana personages. The former worked chiefly in miniatures and in bas-relief bronzes, while the latter executed larger busts and statues, including the Riley monument erected in the poet's native city of Greenfield in 1918. Indianapolis could also claim Rena Tucker Kohlmann, a competent painter as well as a sculptor of miniature figurines, and Clara Barth Leonard Sorenson, who executed a bronze bust of Judge Stephen Neal, drafter of the Fourteenth Amendment to the Federal constitution, for the State House and two memorial tablets for schools in the city before moving from the state. Other Indiana-born women sculptors who pursued careers elsewhere were Eleanor

29 Cottman, "John Mahoney: An Indianapolis Sculptor," *Indiana Magazine of History*, XXV, 191-192; Burnet, *Art and Artists of Indiana*, pp. 327-330.

Louise Guernsey, Katherine Stewart Lawson, Ida M. Stair, and Mary S. Washburn. Two who achieved a large measure of national recognition were Caroline Peddle Ball and Janet Scudder of Terre Haute, both of whom worked mostly in the East and in Europe. Miss Scudder designed many decorative fountains featuring statues of small boys, one of which was placed in the gallery of the Richmond Art Association. She was also the designer of the Indiana Centennial Medallion in 1916.[30]

Two Indianapolis sculptors born and trained abroad were the Russian, Alexander Sangernebo, an instructor at the Herron Art School, and an Englishman, Henry R. Saunders, who designed the portrait medallions of the English family on the English Hotel. Two younger sculptors, John G. Prasuhn and Walter R. Williams, maintained studios in Indianapolis for several years but were chiefly associated with Chicago art circles. Alfred N. Austin, of Terre Haute, was the designer of a bust of Richard W. Thompson placed in the Emeline Fairbanks Library in that city as well as the architect for the Indiana Building at the Columbian Exposition in Chicago in 1893. In the southern part of the state George H. Honig of Rockport executed the two statuary groups— the "Spirit of 1861" and the "Spirit of 1916"—flanking the front entrance of the Evansville Coliseum, and the Tell City sculptor, John C. Meyenberg, designed the Nancy Hanks Lincoln Monument in Lincoln City.[31]

§ § §

Most of the first professional architects in Indiana were born outside the state. John Elder, designer of the Central

[30] Burnet, *Art and Artists of Indiana*, pp. 331-343; Forsyth, *Art in Indiana*, pp. 22-23; Dye, *Some Torch Bearers in Indiana*, pp. 228-231; *Indiana Magazine of History*, IV (1908), 147. A bronze bust of Richard Owen, younger brother of Robert Dale Owen and commander of Camp Morton prison in 1862, was executed by Belle Kinney, daughter of a Confederate soldier, and presented to the State as a tribute from Confederate soldiers imprisoned at the camp during his command.

[31] Burnet, *Art and Artists in Indiana*, pp. 341-343, 377, 383; Forsyth, *Art in Indiana*, p. 22.

Hospital for the Insane and other Indianapolis buildings, came from Harrisburg, Pennsylvania, the Vevay architect George Kyle from Virginia, and Edwin May, builder of court-houses at Brookville, Fort Wayne, Greensburg, Shelbyville, Sullivan, and Vincennes in the fifties, from Boston. Francis Costigan, who designed the gracious Lanier home in Madison and several public buildings in Indianapolis, began his training as a carpenter's apprentice in Baltimore. Ireland was the birthplace of Isaac Hodgson, a prolific builder of county courthouses as well as the Rose Polytechnic Institute in Terre Haute, and William Tinsley, whose Gothic designs were used in Christ Church and Northwestern Christian University in Indianapolis, and Wabash College. Joseph Curzon, who built the Second Presbyterian Church and the first Union Railway Station in Indianapolis, was a native of Derbyshire, England. Dietrich A. Bohlen, who arrived in Indianapolis from Germany in the fifties, established one of the most enduring architectural firms in the city, which he headed until his death in 1890. Among his designs were St. John's Cathedral, Roberts Park Methodist Episcopal Church, and Tomlinson Hall, the last erected in 1885 as a convention center with its lower floor set aside for the Indianapolis municipal market. A native of Belgium, Josse Vrydagh, opened an architectural office in the sixties in Terre Haute, where he built the State Normal School and the Terre Haute House as well as courthouses at Bedford and Mount Vernon and one of the early college buildings at Indiana Asbury — later DePauw — University in Greencastle. Finally, it was a Swiss-born draftsman, Adolph Scherrer, who supervised the construction of the new state capitol in Indianapolis after the death in 1880 of Edwin May, who had drawn the original plans for the edifice.[32]

---

[32] Lee Burns, *Early Architects and Builders of Indiana* (Indiana Historical Society *Publications,* XI, No. 3, Indianapolis, 1935), pp. 193-201; Wilbur D. Peat, *Indiana Houses of the Nineteenth Century* (Indiana Historical Society, 1962), pp. 183-187.

The rapid growth of population and wealth in the last quarter of the nineteenth century was reflected in an outburst of architectural activity to meet the demand for large public buildings as well as more pretentious homes. Indianapolis alone gained a dozen or more new architects in this period, including such men as William H. Brown, George W. Bunting, Robert P. Daggett, B. V. Enos, and Herbert W. Foltz. The day of the self-taught carpenter-builder was coming to an end, as many of the younger designers had formal architectural training. Bernard Vonnegut, for example, studied at the Boston Institute of Technology and in Germany before forming a highly productive partnership with Arthur Bohn in 1888. Another Indianapolis graduate of the Massachusetts school was Louis H. Gibson, who with his partner, Edwin H. Ketcham, designed the State Hospitals for the Insane in Logansport, Richmond, and Evansville in the eighties.[33]

Fort Wayne had the largest contingent of architects outside the capital city, according to Wilbur D. Peat, who listed F. B. and Charles E. Kendrick, J. F. Wing and Marshall S. Mahurin, H. M. Matson and Brentwood S. Tolan, and Alfred Grindle among their number. Tolan's father, Thomas J. Tolan, who designed a few county courthouses in the late seventies and early eighties, should also be placed in the Fort Wayne group. Professional architects working in other Indiana cities before the turn of the century included William S. Kaufman and John A. Hasecoster in Richmond; Arthur LaBelle and Bert L. French, who practiced in Marion and Kokomo; A. D. Mohler at Huntington; John Link and H. L. Nichols at Bloomington; James F. Alexander, George S. Brown, and Alonzo Fleming at Lafayette. The

[33] Peat, *Indiana Houses of the Nineteenth Century,* pp. 188-189; Burnet, *Art and Artists of Indiana,* p. 400. Gibson, who died in 1907, was the author of a typescript document apparently prepared for the Columbian Exposition in Chicago in 1893 entitled Indiana Art, Artists and Architecture (Unpublished typescript, 1893, in the Indiana State Library). A brief sketch of his life is found in a letter from his brother, David Gibson, to Florence Venn, October 6, 1937, Indiana Biographical File, XVII, 9-14, Indiana State Library.

brothers James W. and Merritt Reid were residential build-
ers in Evansville and vicinity; W. H. Floyd, Charles N.
Gould, and Alfred N. Austin practiced at Terre Haute;
George H. Keeler and Edwin M. Cramer at Muncie; Joseph
E. Crain and J. H. Rhodes at Logansport; as well as S. R.
Berry at Peru, John W. Hammond at Frankfort, J. N. Jones
at Goshen, J. W. Gaddis at Vincennes, and George Pear-
son at Attica.[34]

Hoosier architects sought to organize themselves for the
purpose of advancing professional interests and standards as
early as 1884, when the first attempt to found a state chapter of the American Institute of Architects was made under
the leadership of Charles W. Wallingford of Indianapolis.
Two years later a chapter of the Western Association of
Architects came into existence briefly in the capital city, and
Oscar D. Bohlen, W. Scott Moore, Adolph Scherrer, and
others organized the Indianapolis Architects' Society, which
in 1889 received a charter from the A.I.A. None of these
associations long endured, however, and it was as late as
1910 before an Indiana chapter of the A.I.A. was permanently established, with Oscar D. Bohlen of the Indianapolis firm
founded by his father, Dietrich A. Bohlen, as first president. By 1912 this society, which sponsored annual exhibitions of architectural designs as well as a competition—won
by Adolph Scherrer—for the best design submitted for the
new buildings to be erected at Indianapolis City Hospital,
enrolled sixty members throughout the state.[35]

In 1918 the Hoosier historian Logan Esarey wrote rather
disparagingly that "Indiana cities contain few architectural

[34] Peat, *Indiana Houses of the Nineteenth Century,* pp. 188-189; David R.
Hermansen, *Indiana County Courthouses of the Nineteenth Century* (Muncie,
Ind., 1968), pp. 6-7, 22-23. Peat mentions neither Thomas J. Tolan nor Bert
L. French, whose names are found in the pamphlet by Hermansen.

[35] Draegert, "The Fine Arts in Indianapolis, 1880-1890," *Indiana Magazine
of History,* L, 344; Peat, *Indiana Houses of the Nineteenth Century,* p. 189;
"Historical Sketch of the Indiana Chapter of the American Institute of Architects," Indiana Chapter, American Institute of Architects, *Year Book and Catalogue of the Third Annual Exhibition,* 1912, no pagination.

features. The great majority of the buildings are only buildings and nothing more." Architectural styles in both public
buildings and private residences in Indiana, however, generally mirrored the American popular taste of the time.
In the decades following the Civil War domestic architecture
in particular reflected the influence of the French Second Empire, with its interest in the Renaissance and Baroque periods, and the so-called Queen Anne Revival in England. The
French mode was characterized by symmetry, simple classic
lines, and the mansard roof with ornamental dormer windows, as in the Stephen K. Fletcher home in Indianapolis
designed by John Stem in 1876. Midwestern adaptations of
Queen Anne, or what Wilbur D. Peat has rechristened "Neo-
Jacobean," followed a much freer and less formal design,
marked by projecting sections, an irregular floor plan, and a
wide variety of roof contours, with porches, balconies, and
towers usually adding to the complexity of its composition.
The latter style was most often represented by wood-frame
construction utilizing a great deal of lathe and jigsaw orna-
mentation, such as found in the Gilmore house (*ca* 1885) in
Greencastle, but Peat has noted some examples built of
brick and stone in a more restrained manner, like the John
W. Schmidt home (1890), now the Indianapolis Propylaeum.
The French Romanesque style popularized by Henry H.
Richardson was also applied to domestic architecture in this
period, usually employing massive stonework, as in the
Monroe Sieberling house (1889-1890) in Kokomo designed
by Arthur LaBelle and the imposing Studebaker mansion built
in South Bend in 1886 by a Chicago firm. Smaller, less pretentious homes were often constructed by carpenters according to designs combining convenience with beauty which
were found in house builders' manuals such as the two publications issued in 1889 and 1895 by Indianapolis architect
Louis H. Gibson.[36]

[36] Esarey, *History of Indiana,* II, 986; Peat, *Indiana Houses of the Nineteenth Century,* Plates 151, 165, 175, 186, 193; pp. 129-180. Louis H. Gibson's

In civic architecture the classical mode proved the most enduring of all modes throughout the late nineteenth and early twentieth century, abetted by the availability and growing popularity in this period of oolitic limestone, which possessed the monumental character and quality appropriate to this style of construction. One of the first buildings to utilize limestone in such a large structure and elaborate example of Greco-Roman architecture was the new state capitol which the General Assembly authorized in 1877 as a replacement for the much smaller Greek Revival edifice erected more than forty years before. Designed by Edwin May, one of the first professional architects to reside in Indianapolis, and brought to completion in 1888 by Adolph Scherrer, the finished State House was a massive structure with huge Corinthian columns on the exterior and a great copper dome over the central tower containing an imposing three-story rotunda. Inside, the first-floor columns were of the Doric order, those on the second floor, Ionic, and on the third, Corinthian.[37]

The French Renaissance-Baroque manner was seen in such public buildings as the rather ornate Marion County Courthouse (1877) in Indianapolis designed by Isaac Hodgson and the more conservative Vanderburgh County Courthouse (1891) in Evansville. But the Romanesque Revival of the eighties and nineties set in motion by the great American architect Henry H. Richardson posed an even greater challenge to the classical style in Indiana. Among Romanesque or modified Romanesque structures erected in these years were a remarkably large number of courthouses, including those in Bluffton, Wells County (1889) and Liberty, Union County (1890) designed by George W. Bunting; in Richmond, Wayne County (1892) by James W. McLaughlin and in Hartford City, Blackford County (1894) by Arthur

architectural handbooks were entitled *Convenient Houses* (New York, 1889) and *Beautiful Houses, a Study in Housebuilding* (New York, 1895).

[37] Draegert, "The Fine Arts in Indianapolis, 1880-1890," *Indiana Magazine of History*, L, 346-347.

LaBelle and Bert L. French; and in Greenfield, Hancock County (1896) and Knox, Starke County (1897) by the Fort Wayne architectural firm of Wing and Mahurin.[38]

One of the handsomest Romanesque buildings in Indianapolis before its demolition in 1924 to make room for the World War Memorial was the Propylaeum, which was designed by Adolph Scherrer and W. Scott Moore in 1889. Most such Richardson-inspired designs were carried out in massive stone masonry, but an outstanding exception was the cathedral-like Union Railway Passenger Station constructed of red brick and stone in Indianapolis in 1888. A unique example of authentic European Romanesque in Indiana was the large St. Meinrad's Abbey Church in Spencer County, which was built with locally quarried sandstone by the members of the Benedictine monastic community themselves over the span of years from 1899 to 1907, after the original structure had been destroyed by fire.[39]

Yet the early years of the twentieth century witnessed a strong resurgence of classical influences in architecture, as revealed in the design of most of the scores of Carnegie libraries which were scattered over the state during this period as well as the Federal buildings erected in some of the larger cities. The most successful of the latter type of edifice was the imposing United States Courthouse and Post Office which was finished in downtown Indianapolis in 1904. A smaller but more graceful version of this style of architecture was the Indianapolis City Hall, which was completed in 1910 and now serves as the Indiana State Museum. An Evansville architect, Clifford Shopbell, created several classically inspired structures in the southern section of the state, including Carnegie libraries in Shelbyville, Greens-

---

[38] Burns, *Early Architects and Builders of Indiana,* p. 201; Howard E. Wooden, *Architectural Heritage of Evansville: An Interpretive Review of the Nineteenth Century* (Evansville Museum of Arts and Science, 1962), pp. 54-56; Hermansen, *Indiana County Courthouses,* pp. 4-7, 20-22.

[39] Draegert, "The Fine Arts in Indianapolis, 1880-1890," *Indiana Magazine of History,* L, 345; *Indiana. A Guide to the Hoosier State,* pp. 212, 397-398; Kleber, *History of St. Meinrad Archabbey,* pp. 429-432.

burg, Franklin, Seymour, Salem, Princeton, Mount Vernon, and Poseyville, as well as the Evansville Soldiers' and Sailors' Memorial Coliseum, which the city erected in honor of its Civil War veterans in 1916.[40]

The completion of the magnificent new Indianapolis Public Library in 1917 was in itself a solid refutation of Esarey's complaint that Indiana urban architecture lacked distinction. Designed by the French-born Paul Philippe Cret of the University of Pennsylvania, who also drew the plans for the main building of the John Herron Art Institute, the library exterior was a model of pure Doric form which excited the admiration of many of the nation's critics. One architectural historian called it "the best Greek building in the United States." The initial appearance of the modern functional type of architecture took place in 1914, when the Louis Sullivan-designed Purdue State Bank was constructed in West Lafayette. This building, while one of the smallest and simplest ever designed by the outstanding Chicago architect, was a fair representative of his mature style, but it had little immediate impact upon the generally conservative architectural tradition in Indiana.[41]

§ § § §

The musical culture of Indiana in the last decades of the nineteenth century owed a great deal to the members of the German communities which existed in such cities as Evansville, Fort Wayne, Indianapolis, and South Bend, where various German-American instrumental and vocal groups flourished. In South Bend one family alone supplied a major part of the city's musical leadership, forming the Elbel Band and other musical organizations under the baton of Lorenz and Louis Elbel, while Indianapolis from an early

40 Cottman, *Centennial History and Handbook of Indiana*, pp. 324-325; Wooden, *Architectural Heritage of Evansville*, pp. 74-75; Morlock, *The Evansville Story*, p. 167; *Memoirs of the Lower Ohio Valley* . . . (2 volumes, Madison, Wis., 1905), I, 329-330.

41 *Indiana. A Guide to the Hoosier State*, p. 157; Suzanne LaFollette, *Art in America*, quoted in *ibid.*, p. 220; Hugh Morrison, *Louis Sullivan: Prophet of Modern Architecture* (New York, 1935), p. 220.

period enjoyed the orchestral activities of a number of German-born musicians such as Max Leckner, Reinhold A. Miller, Adolph Schellschmidt, and Bernhardt Vogt.[42]

By the eighties and nineties the German singing societies were in their heyday. The oldest such society in the state was the Indianapolis Maennerchor, a large choral group which celebrated its twenty-fifth anniversary in June, 1880, with the most impressive music festival ever held in the capital city up to that time. The Maennerchor had its headquarters in the old City Hall, which it renovated extensively in 1897, but ten years later was able to erect its own hall. Rival organizations in the Indianapolis German community were the Lyra, a mixed chorus and orchestra founded in 1870, and Musikverein, an association sponsoring a sixty-piece orchestra and both a male and a mixed chorus which was created in 1898 in connection with the building of Das Deutsche Haus. Although these groups were composed chiefly of amateur performers, they were led by professional musicians like Alexander Ernestinoff, who was born in St. Petersburg, Russia, and came to Indianapolis in 1880 to direct first the Maennerchor and then the Lyra, before accepting leadership of the Musikverein upon its founding in 1898, and Carl Barus, a German-born musician active in Cincinnati since the fifties who conducted the Maennerchor from 1882 until his retirement in 1896. Evansville, another important center of German culture, also had a singing society called the Germania Maennerchor.[43]

Several English-language singing groups also appeared in this period. One of the most enduring of these was the Terre Haute Oratorio Society, which was founded in 1877 and continued to flourish for many years. Among the earliest musical organizations of this kind were the Indianapolis Choral

42 Elizabeth E. Gunn Seebirt, *Music in Indiana* (n.p., n.d.), pp. 12-14, 125; Martha F. Bellinger, "Music in Indianapolis, 1821-1900," *Indiana Magazine of History,* XLI (1945), 360-361; South Bend *Tribune,* October 30, 1927.

43 Bellinger, "Music in Indianapolis, 1821-1900," *loc. cit.,* XLI, 352-355; Seebirt, *Music in Indiana,* p. 72.

Union, which was established in 1869, and the Harmonic Society, formed by a division within the former group in 1875.
Directed by James S. Black and William H. Clarke, respectively, these two societies performed oratorios and other
music of a religious character for several seasons but were
dissolved by the eighties, when three new groups, the Indianapolis Choral Society, the Indianapolis Chorus, and the Men-
delssohn Society, enjoyed a brief existence. During the decade
of 1880 to 1890, which one historian of Indianapolis has
called the "Golden Decade" of musical culture in that city,
amateur groups were frequently formed to produce the works
of Gilbert and Sullivan and other popular composers of light
opera. In 1882 a local music teacher, Ora Pearson, organized
the Indianapolis Opera Company for the production of such
performances, while both Barus and Ernestinoff conducted
similar groups at the height of the popularity of light opera
in the late eighties.[44]

The chief musical event of the decade was the ambitious
music festival held in June, 1886, in newly completed Tomlinson Hall in Indianapolis. Planned as a benefit for the Soldiers' and Sailors' Monument under the auspices of the
Grand Army of the Republic, the program included only
one paid, imported performer—the operatic singer, Miss
Lilli Lehman—in addition to a 650-voice chorus and 60-
piece orchestra made up of local talent and conducted by Carl
Barus of the Maennerchor. Although the festival was enthusiastically received and financially successful, raising approximately five thousand dollars for the monument fund,
it was not repeated the next summer because the General
Assembly had in the meantime voted an official appropriation for the memorial structure. In 1889, however, Carl Barus
and others organized a May Music Festival Association in
order to sponsor similar annual concerts which brought well-
known musical artists to the city. The festivals held that

[44] Seebirt, *Music in Indiana,* pp. 55-56; Eva Draegert, "Cultural History of
Indianapolis: Music, 1875-1890," *Indiana Magazine of History,* LIII (1957), 275-
278, 288-291.

spring and each succeeding year but one for nearly a decade were brilliant successes, but the complete financial fiasco of the 1898 season brought the series to an abrupt close. Although various Indianapolis organizations sponsored performances of visiting musicians in later years, especially the People's Concert Association founded in 1905 by Edward B. Birge and others, the only musical event comparable to the May Festivals was the National Saengerfest held in Indianapolis in 1908 by the German singing societies. In 1911, however, Birge, who was the director of music in the Indianapolis public schools, organized a People's Chorus, which presented annual concerts under his direction until his departure from the city in 1921.[45]

Moreover, the struggle to establish a modern professional orchestra in the capital city made only sporadic progress in this period. In 1895 Karl Schneider, an Indianapolis musician, began organizing a symphony orchestra which he conducted in a notable series of public concerts in 1904-1905. Schneider departed from the city shortly afterwards, leaving the orchestra to his German-born colleague, Ferdinand Schaefer, who was soon forced to disband the organization for lack of financial support. Finally, in 1911 a group of Indianapolis citizens led by Herman Lieber and Leo Rappaport founded the Indianapolis Orchestra as a co-operative society under a board of directors composed entirely of women. This orchestra under the experienced hand of its conductor, Alexander Ernestinoff, survived for seven seasons and closed its career without a deficit after presenting its last concert on November 11, 1917. This wartime interruption halted the movement to create a permanent orchestra until 1930, when Ferdinand Schaefer organized a group of musicians in Indianapolis for the performance of a series of concerts which

[45] Dunn, *Greater Indianapolis,* I, 533-534; Bellinger, "Music in Indianapolis, 1821-1900," *Indiana Magazine of History,* XLI, 350; Bellinger, "Music in Indianapolis, 1900-1944," *loc. cit.,* XLII (1946), 47-49.

led to the formation of the Indiana State Symphony Society the next year.[46]

Although the Fort Wayne Conservatory of Music had been in existence since 1871, the development of professional musical education in the state as a whole was relatively slow. A major step forward in the training of musicians was taken in 1889, when pianist-composer Clarence Forsythe opened the Indianapolis School of Music. In 1895 the Metropolitan School of Music was established in the same city and in 1907 the College of Musical Art, which eleven years later was merged with the Indianapolis College of Music and Fine Arts, a successor to Forsythe's institution. Finally, in 1928 all the existing music schools in Indianapolis were absorbed into the newly founded Arthur Jordan Conservatory of Music, which later became an affiliate of Butler University. Schools of music were also organized at DePauw University in 1884 and at Indiana University in 1921.[47]

Indiana produced few notable musical composers in this period. Two who achieved a local reputation were Charles F. Hansen, a native of Lafayette, who during a long career as a church organist in Indianapolis, though blind, composed many hymns and other pieces of religious music, and Frederic Krull, an Indianapolis singer trained in Berlin who set thirty or more of James Whitcomb Riley's poems to music. The best-known Hoosier composer of popular songs was Theodore Dreiser's brother, Paul Dresser, who wrote the music for "On the Banks of the Wabash" at Dreiser's suggestion in 1895. A composer of more serious music was Charles Diven Campbell, a professor at Indiana University from 1906 until his death in 1919, whose sonorous "Hymn to In-

[46] Dunn, *Greater Indianapolis,* I, 536; Bellinger, "Music in Indianapolis, 1900-1944," *Indiana Magazine of History,* XLII, 61-63.

[47] Bellinger, "Music in Indianapolis, 1821-1900," *Indiana Magazine of History,* XLI, 360; Bellinger, "Music in Indianapolis, 1900-1944," *loc. cit.* XLII, 56; Manhart, *DePauw through the Years,* I, 194-197; Woodburn and Myers, *History of Indiana University,* II, 238.

diana" was written in honor of the state's centennial in 1916.[48]

Another field of art which flowered in Indiana during the period 1880 to 1920 was the theater. Buildings with facilities for stage performances began to be erected in the late 1860's and early 1870's and before long every progressive town wanted one. Many were called opera houses though this was a misnomer in the early days; it was apparently used, as one historian has suggested, because the word theater was in bad repute. Buildings were financed in various ways—by wealthy and influential citizens, by the local government, or by subscriptions of local citizens.[49]

The 1880 Census listed the opera houses or theaters in the principal cities, with their capacity. Evansville had an opera house built in 1866 by a stock company with a capacity of 1,266, and a Turners Hall built by the German Turnverein for theatrical performances and other activities. Fort Wayne had an Academy of Music with a seating capacity of 1,200. For Indianapolis, four theaters were listed: the Grand Opera House, opened in 1875 with a capacity of 1,600; Park Theatre (originally called the Metropolitan), 1,200; and the Germania and Maennerchor with a capacity of 600 and 500, respectively. The last two were used for amateur theatricals as well as for musical productions. In Lafayette an opera house had been built in 1872 with a capacity of 2,500. New Albany had a theater that could take care of 1,200, and in addition a Turners Hall where concerts and lectures were held. Richmond had two theaters, each with a capacity of 1,200. Probably the most elaborate of the early buildings was Naylor's Opera House in Terre Haute, built in 1870 at a cost of $178,000. More than 250 theatrical companies were

---

[48] Indiana Federation of Music Clubs, *Indiana Composers, Native and Adopted* (Bloomington, Ind., 1936), pp. 12, 21, 24; *The Songs of Paul Dresser with an Introduction by . . . Theodore Dreiser* (New York, 1927), pp. v-x; Lindley (ed.), *The Indiana Centennial 1916*, p. 211.

[49] Louis Atherton, *Main Street on the Middle Border* (Indiana University Press, 1954), pp. 135-142.

traveling throughout the United States in 1880, playing one-night stands in smaller cities while in the larger ones they often gave three evening performances plus a matinee. The programs were varied to suit the tastes of the audiences.[50]

Indianapolis with four theaters in 1880 to serve a population of 75,056, would seem to have been well supplied, and the announcement by William H. English, banker and Democratic politician, early in 1880 that he planned to erect a theater on the Circle caused considerable comment. The *Saturday Herald,* an Indianapolis newspaper, tried to discourage him, arguing that the city could not very well support another theater, but Mr. English went ahead with his plans to erect a building modeled after one in New York City which would be larger and more elaborate than any yet erected in the state. The opening night on September 27, 1880, was a notable occasion with Lawrence Barrett playing the leading role in *Hamlet.* To meet their new competition, Dickson's Grand Opera House and the Park Theatre, both of which were under the same management, had been renovated and offered that same day the attractions of James A. Herne's *Hearts of Oak* and W. D. Eaton's *All the Rage.*[51]

The opening of English's Opera House gave a new impetus to the cultural life of Indianapolis and the surrounding area, and in time its influence reached out to include the entire state. Some of the outstanding artists who appeared season after season were Henry Irving, Joseph Jefferson, Sarah Bernhardt, Richard Mansfield, Edwin Booth, Edwin Forrest, John Drew, Julia Marlowe, Minnie Maddern Fiske, Nat Goodwin, Clara Morris, Maggie Mitchell, Madame Januschek, Lillian and Annie Russell, Marie Dressler, Eugenia Blair, James

[50] United States Bureau of the Census, *Tenth Census* (1880), *Report on Social Statistics of Cities,* Pt. 2, pp. 441, 446, 452, 459, 462, 467; William Winter, *The Wallet of Time. Containing Personal, Biographical, and Critical Reminiscence of the American Theatre* (2 volumes, New York, 1913), I, 23.

[51] Sullivan, *English's Opera House,* pp. 337-340, 345-350; Indianapolis *News,* September 27 and 28, 1880.

O'Neill, Otis Skinner, Maude Adams, Anna Held, Ethel Barrymore, and Walker Whiteside.[52]

New theaters were being built in other cities of the state, also. Bucklen Opera House was opened in Elkhart in the 1880's; a new opera house was built in Evansville, and the Alcazar in New Castle in 1893. At Terre Haute a new Grand Opera House was completed in 1897 to replace Naylor's which had burned the year before. Although the seating capacity of the New Castle Alcazar was only one thousand, it had a stage as large as the one at English's and was able to book the same attractions as those showing in Indianapolis. It reached the peak of its popularity from 1906 to 1909. Crump's Opera House in Columbus was advertising in 1902 Robert B. Mantell in *Monbars*, Porter J. White in *David Caruth*, and a return engagement of W. E. Nankeville's play *Human Hearts*. South Bend, with its Oliver Opera House and The Auditorium, both with excellent facilities, had such top attractions in the decade 1900 to 1910 as John Drew in *Richard Carvel*, Joseph Jefferson in *The Rivals*, Anna Held in *Mam'selle Napoleon*, and Ethel Barrymore in *Cousin Kate*. The premier performance of George Ade's *Artie* was presented in 1907.[53]

Another theater was built in Indianapolis in 1909-1910, the Murat, with a capacity of two thousand. Its bookings were handled by Sam and Lee Shubert, a New York syndicate, while English's Opera House booked through Klaw and Erlanger, another New York syndicate. The Murat was advertising for the 1910 season such performances as *The Lottery Man*, with the original cast headed by Cyril Scott; Henry E. Dixey in *The Naked Truth* ("the laughter rage of London"), Lew Field's musical play *The Midnight Sons,* and

[52] Chronological list of attractions at English's, 1880-1948, in Raymond J. Feld Papers, Indiana State Library.

[53] George W. Butler, *The Manual of Elkhart* . . . (Elkhart, Ind., n. d.), no pagination; Morlock, *The Evansville Story,* 145-150; New Castle *Courier-Times,* August 6, 1941; *Crump's Theatre Herald,* December 5 and 10, 1902; J. J. Detzler, *South Bend, 1900-1910. The Awakening of a Small Town* (South Bend, Ind., 1959), p. 60.

Eddie Foy in the musical revue, *Up and Down Broadway*.[54]
By this time transportation facilities between Indianapolis
and the surrounding towns had greatly improved, making it
possible for persons outside the city to attend performances
in the capital city.

Another important event in the history of the theater in
Indianapolis was the coming of Stuart Walker, playwright
and producer, to that city in 1916 to launch his stock company
at the Murat; he returned the next four years for the summer months. Walker's ability to discover new talent and in
directing made the Murat a workshop in theatrical production.[55]

Another form of traveling theatricals was the showboats
that went up and down the Ohio River in the summer months,
stopping at the towns along the way for one-night performances. Two of the best-known were "Price's Sensation," built
in 1883 by Captain J. D. Price, and "The Golden Rod" built
in 1904 by Ralph Emerson. The latter had a capacity of
1,200 in the theater part. Melodrama and vaudeville were the
principal fare of the showboat troupes. The boat's approach
to a town was heralded by the playing of the calliope. After
the boat docked, the townspeople were invited to come aboard
and meet the members of the troupe; with this introduction
and the spreading of leaflets through the town, the evening
performance was advertised.[56]

Having the opportunity of seeing theatrical performances
in their home town or in a neghboring city, it would be expected that a number of Indiana's young men and women
would be drawn to the theater world. Among those who
achieved distinction in the period 1880 to 1920 were: Laura
Arnold, Indianapolis; Richard Bennett, of Cass County;
Ed Blondell, Columbus; Frederick Burton, Gosport; Charles
W. Dingle, Wabash; Alice Fischer, Terre Haute; Edna

[54] Dunn, *Greater Indianapolis*, I, 472; *Indianapolis Dramatic Review*, November 19, 1910.

[55] Indianapolis *News*, July 3, 1920.

[56] *Ibid.*, June 23, 1923.

Goodrich, Logansport; Louise Closser Hale, Indianapolis; Louise Josephine Kerlin (Louise Dresser), Evansville and Indianapolis; Warren Kerrigan, New Albany; Charles Murray, Laurel; Mignon McGibeny, Indianapolis; John Sigvard Olsen (Ole Olson), Peru and Wabash; and Walker Whiteside, Logansport.[57]

Not all the theater productions were by professionals. In Indiana as elsewhere there were people who liked to act for the fun of it. Austin H. Brown was the moving spirit in the Indianapolis Dramatic Society which was active in the 1870's and continued this interest into the next decade in his work with the Dramatic, Literary, and Musical Association of the Scottish Rite. The Dramatic Society was reorganized in 1890 as the Dramatic Club. The Propyleum was used for its performances.[58]

Then in 1915 a group of Indiana citizens met at the John Herron Art Institute to organize the Little Theatre Society of Indiana. George Ade was elected president; Samuel A. Eliot, Jr., grandson of the former president of Harvard, was named the first director, and George Sommes later served in that capacity. The Sculpture Court of the Herron Institute was used for its performances in the beginning, and later the Masonic Temple. Plays presented by the Little Theatre Society during its first four years included *Polly of Pogue's Run*, by W. O. Bates; *Laughing Gas*, by Theodore Dreiser; *The Drawing of the Sword*, by Thomas Wood Stevens; *Lithuania*, by Rupert Brooke; *Three Pills in a Bottle*, by Rachel Field; *Bernice*, by Susan Glaspell; and *Deidre of the Sorrows*, by John M. Synge. Players included Mrs. Carl Lieber, Arthur J. Beriault, George C. Calvert, Carl Goe, Carl Graf, Mary H. Flanner, Miss Jeanette Orlopp, Mrs. Elizabeth

[57] Actors and Actresses, in clipping file, Indiana Division, Indiana State Library.

[58] Dunn, *Greater Indianapolis*, I, 471-472; Eva Draegert, "The Theatre in Indianapolis, 1880-1890," *Indiana Magazine of History*, LII (1956), 45-46.

Schofield, H. L. Earnest, Miss Caroline B. Hendricks, Lulu Kanagy, Charles Williams, and Edward LaShelle.[59]

After 1900 students in most of the colleges as well as those in the larger high schools were presenting plays and musical productions. Upon returning to their home towns, many of the college students with acting experience organized local dramatic groups, thus spreading the interest in this form of recreation and entertainment.

The origin and rise of the motion picture industry during the first two decades of the twentieth century brought an end to the "golden age" of the theater. Although Thomas Edison is given credit for inventing motion pictures, the kinetoscope or viewing machine which he produced in 1889 was the culmination of research by a number of individuals working in the same field. Edison saw no commercial value in the invention and it was not until four years later that he obtained a patent for it and placed it on exhibition. It was only a peep-show device in which one dropped a coin in a slot and looked through an aperture to see a bit of slapstick comedy lasting about thirteen seconds. The projection of pictures on a screen followed shortly and the length of the films was increased to one thousand feet, occupying about fifteen minutes.[60]

The first story with a plot was produced in 1903 when an Edison cameraman filmed *The Great Train Robbery*. With this as its entire program a movie theater was opened in

[59] *Booth Tarkington Civic Theatre, Golden Anniversary Yearbook, 1914-1964* (n. p., n. d.), no pagination; programs of the Little Theatre Society of Indiana, 1916-1920, in Indiana State Library.

[60] *Dictionary of American History,* IV, 31-32; A. R. Fulton, *Motion Pictures. The Development of an Art from Silent Films to the Age of Television* (University of Oklahoma Press, 1960), pp. vii, 7-9, 15. Charles Francis Jenkins, a government clerk from Washington, D. C., is supposed to have made one of the first successful demonstrations of projecting pictures on a screen on June 6, 1894, while visiting in his hometown of Richmond, Indiana. Apparently he was not successful in capitalizing on his discovery for Thomas Armat is credited with building in 1895 the first machine (called the "Vitascope") for projecting pictures on a screen. Indianapolis *News,* May 7, 1921; Fulton, *Motion Pictures,* p. 15.

Pittsburgh in 1905. The entrance fee was a nickel and thus it was called a nickelodeon. James West who reportedly opened a movie theater in Evansville the same year found the public fearful of entering the building because of the dark interior. The first movie house in Indianapolis, called the Bijou, was started by C. L. Sutherland in July, 1906. One reel of film was shown over and over for an entire week. The possibilities of the new amusement soon became apparent and within the next decade the production of films and the operation of movie houses grew by leaps and bounds. In 1914 David W. Griffith, director of the Biograph Company, filmed *The Birth of a Nation* in twelve reels, a picture that is still regarded as a masterpiece.[61] Actors and actresses of the stage at first spurned the idea of working for the motion picture companies, but in time some were lured into making films. It is well to remember that these first films were silent films and the adaptation from stage to screen would not have been easy.

The legitimate theater was not long in feeling the effect of the new industry by decreased attendance at its productions. The opera houses, not being suited to the showing of films, were converted to other uses and less elaborate structures, with seating on one floor, appeared on the main streets of Hoosier towns. By 1919 Evansville had twelve movie houses while Indianapolis had a total of fifty-five the following year. In spite of the attraction of the movies, the Murat and English's Opera House continued to play host to the patrons of the theater, bringing to them the outstanding artists and productions of the stage.

61 Fulton, *Motion Pictures,* pp. 45, 59-61; Indianapolis *News,* June 26 and October 16, 1915.

# CHAPTER XV

# INDIANA IN THE FIRST WORLD WAR

THE OUTBREAK OF WAR IN EUROPE in the summer of 1914 awakened Indianans to a heightened awareness of world affairs. While the immediate reaction was one of shock and amazement at the unexpected turn of events, most of the newspaper press in the state concurred in placing the chief blame for the conflict squarely at the door of the Central Powers, which were generally considered unpopular, autocratic states. On August 5 the normally rather cautious Indianapolis *News* summed up the case editorially: "No amount of special pleading can alter the judgment of mankind. Germany and Austria could have prevented this war by refusing to take the first foolish step." Yet within a few weeks, as the war became a familiar feature of the news, a more balanced and even neutral point of view predominated in the secular press as many Indiana newspapers softened their previously anti-German attitudes, as Cedric C. Cummins has shown.[1]

By the end of August, 1914, however, the flood of news stories depicting the German invasion and occupation of neutral Belgium in a largely unfavorable light brought an end to this relatively fluid state of public opinion. Although most Hoosier editors gave little space to the more flagrant examples of "atrocity" propaganda, the general tenor of news reportage as well as the editorial comment was damning of Germany for its apparently unduly harsh treatment of the

---

[1] Indianapolis *News*, August 5, 1914; Cummins, *Indiana Public Opinion, 1914-1917*, pp. 3-21. Cummins points out that about this time several newspapers shifted from a pro-Ally to a largely pro-German point of view, including the New Albany *Ledger* and the Richmond *Palladium*, as well as three Chicago papers circulating in Indiana, the *American*, the *Examiner*, and the *Tribune*.

Belgian people. Sympathy for the victims of war in that unhappy country generated a newspaper-supported relief campaign which elicited contributions in money and commodities totaling more than $80,000. According to the estimate of Cummins in his study of Indiana public opinion toward the war, between two thirds and three fourths of the population of the state may have favored the Allies by the close of the year.[2]

Two additional factors reinforced the pro-Ally position in 1915—German submarine warfare, particularly the torpedoing of the British luxury liner "Lusitania" with the loss of some 1,500 lives, including 124 Americans, and the reports of sabotage in American factories filling war orders for the Allies. Yet, despite editorial condemnation of Germany, there was little inclination to call for American intervention in what was still considered a purely European affair. In fact, by the spring of 1916, when Francisco Villa and his band of raiders crossed the Mexican border into United States territory, most Indianans would probably have preferred war with Mexico to one with Germany. In an election year, moreover, Hoosier politicians were reluctant to offend the extensive German-American community in the state, which was eagerly wooed by both major parties in the presidential campaign of 1916.[3]

A strong current of positive pro-German sentiment also existed in Indiana, where persons of German birth or descent

2 Cummins, *Indiana Public Opinion, 1914-1917*, pp. 21-41. According to Cummins, the drive for Belgian relief in Indiana reached its climax in December, 1914, though the Indiana committee of the Commission for Relief in Belgium was not officially organized until April of the following year under the chairmanship of Charles W. Fairbanks. *Ibid.*, pp. 32-33n. A young teacher of history at Indiana University, James G. McDonald, attempted to defend Germany's actions in Belgium in a pamphlet published by the Germanistic Society of Chicago entitled *German "Atrocities" and International Law* (Chicago, 1914).

3 Cummins, *Indiana Public Opinion, 1914-1917*, pp. 83-141, 201-205, 208-234. The German-born Congressman from Evansville, Charles Lieb, however, lost his German-American constituency's support by his loyalty to President Wilson and did not run for re-election in 1916. *Ibid.*, pp. 192-193.

constituted the largest and most closely knit ethnic minority. Throughout the first years of the war German-language newspapers in Evansville, Fort Wayne, Indianapolis, and Terre Haute rallied their readers to the cause of the Fatherland, attacking war loans to the Allies and urging on the nation an embargo on the shipment of munitions to Germany's enemies. Active in the same movement were the German cultural, religious, and other societies in the state, many of which were represented in the Indiana German-American Alliance, a branch of the national body of the same name which was organized in 1905. Led from the outset by Joseph H. Keller, an Indianapolis businessman and one-time president of the city's board of school commissioners, the Alliance by 1915 comprised 123 local societies. Its annual state convention in August, 1914, was held in the heavily German city of Hammond, which gave a warm welcome to the delegates, who sang both "Die Wacht am Rhein" and the "Star Spangled Banner" at a picnic attended by about five thousand persons. Two years later the members of the German-American Alliance meeting in state convention in Indianapolis passed resolutions affirming their loyalty to the United States while maintaining their belief in the justice of the German cause.[4]

Irish-Americans, less numerous in Indiana though very influential, especially in Roman Catholic ecclesiastical circles, seconded the pro-German efforts, chiefly out of antagonism to Great Britain. Perhaps the most important pro-German journal in the state was Joseph Patrick O'Mahony's *Indiana Catholic*—by 1916 the *Indiana Catholic and Record*—which seldom missed an opportunity to strike an anti-British note. During the year 1915 joint German-Irish rallies were held

---

[4] *Ibid.*, pp. 46-54; William A. Fritsch, *German Settlers and German Settlements in Indiana* (Evansville, Ind., 1915), p. 61; Moore, *The Calumet Region,* p. 159; Indianapolis *News,* September 5, 1916. Fritsch gave the number of members of the Indiana German-American Alliance as 10,000, but its president, Joseph H. Keller, claimed 25,000 members in his testimony before the Senate Judiciary Committee in 1918. Indianapolis *News,* March 7, 1918.

in several Hoosier cities to protest American partiality toward the Allies. Among other minority ethnic groups in Indiana the Hungarians of South Bend and the Calumet Region gave ardent support to the Central Powers, while the Belgians, Serbians, Croatians, Czechs, Slovaks, Romanians, and Poles were pro-Ally. Italians were caught in the middle between supporters of both sides and took little part in the controversy prior to Italy's adherence to the Allies in May, 1915.[5]

The war in Europe was a stimulus to the organized peace movement in America, though pacifism as such found little lodgment in Indiana except among certain religious groups. In March, 1915, the Indiana Peace Society, which had been founded a year before under the chairmanship of President William Lowe Bryan of Indiana University, held a meeting in Indianapolis to plan concerted efforts with other organizations such as the recently formed Woman's Peace Party. In May the Indiana branch of the World Peace Foundation was organized, with Charles W. Fairbanks as chairman and Amos W. Butler secretary. During 1915 David Starr Jordan, formerly a professor at Butler College and president of Indiana University before becoming head of Stanford University in California, returned to the state to lecture under the auspices of the World Peace Foundation. Both the Indiana Federation of Women's Clubs and the Woman's Franchise League of Indiana adopted the peace issue, and the indefatigable Hoosier feminist May Wright Sewall became a member of Henry Ford's ill-conceived peace expedition to Europe in December, 1915.[6]

[5] *Indiana Catholic and Record* (Indianapolis), December 15, 1916, and following issues; *Lake County Times* (Hammond), February 3, 1915; Fort Wayne *Sentinel,* August 17, 1915; Indianapolis *Star,* February 9, 1915; Cummins, *Indiana Public Opinion, 1914-1917,* pp. 56-64.

[6] Indianapolis *Star,* March 14, 1914, March 30, 1915; Cummins, *Indiana Public Opinion, 1914-1917,* pp. 157-164. Mrs. Sewall wrote an open letter to "My Friends in Hoosierland," dated December 16, 1915, concerning the Ford peace expedition which is found in the Sewall Collection in the Indiana State Library and is quoted in Cummins, *op. cit.,* p. 163.

Although pro-German advocates were occasionally found in these peace organizations, most of their leaders leaned to the side of the Allies, and some later became active interventionists. Many peace societies also seemed less interested in ending the current war than in preventing a future one. The leading example of this type of organization was the League to Enforce Peace, founded in Philadelphia in June, 1915, under the leadership of ex-President William Howard Taft. William D. Foulke, a former Mugwump and civil service reformer who was one of the original members of the League, helped organize an Indiana branch in April, 1916, under largely Republican auspices. The first president of the Indiana League to Enforce Peace, Henry Lane Wilson, a Republican and former United States minister to Mexico, actually resigned from the society in January, 1917, after Democratic President Woodrow Wilson endorsed the idea of such a league.[7]

The war split the churches, at least partly, along ethnic lines. German and Irish Catholics, German Lutherans, German Methodists, and Evangelicals usually favored the Central Powers, while Episcopalians and Christian Scientists were pro-British. Most other churches tended to show less interest in the war during the period of American neutrality, though they eventually became pro-Ally. One of the strongest statements by a religious body came from the committee on social service of the Indiana Baptist Convention in October, 1914. Describing the war's cause as "predatory capitalism, intrenched behind hoary despotisms," the committee flatly declared: "This is not a Christian war. It is pagan and brutal. It shows how far the nations engaged in it are from being Christian." Most consistent in their opposition to war were the historic pacifist sects in Indiana—the Brethren or Dunkards, the Mennonites and Amish, and the Society of Friends. The two former groups,

[7] Foulke, *A Hoosier Autobiography,* pp. 182-186; Cummins, *Indiana Public Opinion, 1914-1917,* pp. 164-169, 238-239.

largely German in origin, took virtually no part in public peace agitation, but the Quakers of Indiana held mass meetings opposing war and sent resolutions to the President and Congress. In July, 1915, a well-attended national Friends Peace Conference was convened at Winona Lake, and throughout the war period the *American Friend,* organ of the Five Years Meeting published in Richmond, Indiana, maintained a firm antiwar attitude. Other smaller churches which denounced the war, often in Biblical terms, were the Seventh-Day Adventist, Free Methodist, Nazarene, and the Church of God, while from a different point of view Unitarians remained aloof from it.[8]

More powerful an expression than pacifism in Indiana in these years was an isolationist attitude common to most of the Middle West and much of the rest of the nation. Long after the outbreak of the war in Europe Hoosiers evinced little concern over any possible threat to American security and took little or no interest in military affairs. Despite Indiana's record of patriotic readiness in both the Civil War and the Spanish-American War, by 1914 the state militia had suffered a severe decline in enrollment, morale, and public support. In 1915 United States Army inspectors found some units so inefficient and under strength that they were ultimately dismissed. Under the new Congressional legislation of the next year providing for Federal assistance to state elements of the National Guard, funds were denied several Indiana companies for failing to meet established standards, and the annual brigade encampment was abandoned. Nevertheless, in June, 1916, the two remaining infantry regiments of the Guard were mustered into Federal service and a third regiment organized, all of which were dispatched, with three artillery batteries, to the Mexican border in July under the command of a regular Army officer, Lieutenant Colonel

[8] Cummins, *Indiana Public Opinion, 1914-1917,* pp. 64-71; Indiana Baptist Convention, *Proceedings,* 1914, p. 67; Woodward, *Timothy Nicholson,* pp. 157-160; Indiana Yearly Meeting, *Minutes,* 1914, pp. 72-75; 1915, pp. 82-83; 1916, pp. 87-100; *American Friend,* N.S. III (1915), 497 and passim.

Edward M. Lewis. Although they proved not to be needed, the Indiana troops were not demobilized until the end of the year.[9]

In general Indiana and the Middle West moved much more slowly than the East toward the notion of military preparedness, which was rejected outright at this time by such national Hoosier political leaders as Vice-President Marshall and Senator Kern. The leading advocates of preparedness in the state were more often Republicans or Progressives than Democrats, and were usually ardent backers of the Allies, while of course the Socialists were utterly opposed to the whole system of militarism. In the forefront of the preparedness drive in Indiana was the novelist Booth Tarkington, whose advocacy of a bigger Navy in the summer of 1915 drew criticism from even the generally pro-Ally Indianapolis *News*. Tarkington, whose travels abroad had made him a strong Francophile, also attacked the pro-German attitudes of the German-American "hyphenates." Other Hoosier men of letters in the pro-Ally preparedness camp were James Whitcomb Riley, George Ade, William D. Foulke, and Meredith Nicholson. On the other hand, former Senator Albert J. Beveridge, who traveled to the European war zone in the winter of 1914-1915 and published his observations in *Collier's Weekly* and the *Saturday Evening Post,* took a fairly neutral stand at first which offended many of his pro-Ally friends.[10]

One of the chief proponents of military preparedness in Indiana was Lucius B. Swift, former Mugwump and Pro-

[9] Indianapolis *News,* June 3, 5, December 20, 1915; Indianapolis *Star,* May 19, June 4, 1916; Esarey, *History of Indiana,* II, 1085-1090. The Indiana National Guard at the time of the Mexican border affair was ranked only fortieth in the nation in percentage of war strength. Indianapolis *Star,* December 27, 28, 1916.

[10] Cummins, *Indiana Public Opinion, 1914-1917,* pp. 72-77; Indianapolis *News,* June 26, July 2, 1916; Woodress, *Booth Tarkington,* pp. 198-203; Bowers, *Beveridge and the Progressive Era,* pp. 457-485. Foulke, a birthright Quaker, resigned from the Society of Friends after the outbreak of the war because of his opposition to its nonresistance tenets. Foulke, *A Hoosier Autobiography,* p. 219.

gressive party leader who opened a one-man campaign for a larger army in an address before the Economic Club of Indianapolis on May 25, 1915, which was later issued as a pamphlet under the title *The Military Situation in the United States* (1915). Noting the effect of the European war in undermining American security, he discussed the need for immediate defense preparations. "We are no longer immune from attack by reason of isolation," he stated, "and we have not only our own country but the Monroe Doctrine and the Panama Canal to take care of." Swift's chief contribution to the pro-Ally cause, however, was an anti-German polemic first presented at the prestigious Indianapolis Literary Club on October 4, 1915, and widely distributed in pamphlet form as *Germans in America* by such organizations as the American Rights Committee, a pro-Ally organization of which Tarkington, Swift, and Professor James A. Woodburn of Indiana University were officers. A third propaganda pamphlet by Swift entitled *America's Debt to England: The Failure to Teach the Foundations of Liberty* (1917) originated in an address before the American Historical Association in Cincinnati in December, 1916, which was frequently repeated before Indiana audiences.[11]

During the year 1916 an ever-widening group of Hoosiers came over publicly to the Allied cause. Among the sixteen Indiana signers of the "Address to the People of the Allied Nations" which was issued in April, 1916, to advertise American sympathy for the Allies were the names of elev-

11 Lucius B. Swift, *The Military Situation in the United States* (Indianapolis, 1915), p. 8; Lucius B. Swift, *Germans in America* (Indianapolis, 1916); Lucius B. Swift, *America's Debt to England: The Failure to Teach the Foundations of Liberty* (Indianapolis, 1917), p. 31; Foulke, *Lucius B. Swift,* pp. 99-115; Cummins, *Indiana Public Opinion, 1914-1917,* pp. 148-151. Swift's *Germans in America* was translated into French and published in the French propaganda series, *Voix Americains sur la Guerre de 1914-1916* (Paris, 1916), IV, 46-68. Another anti-German propagandist in Indianapolis was William N. Cochran, who in a privately published pamphlet in September, 1915, described the war as a "great world contest between Christian civilization and paganism." William N. Cochran, *The Soul of the German Empire* [Indianapolis, 1915], p. 78.

en Indiana University professors as well as Rollo Walter Brown of Wabash College, Indianapolis attorney William H. H. Miller, and Episcopal Bishop John Hazen White. In December, four hundred prominent Indiana citizens joined Swift and Tarkington in a statement to President Wilson approving his protest against the deportation of Belgian workers to Germany, including Demarchus C. Brown, Evans Woollen, William Fortune, Christopher B. Coleman, John H. Holliday, Dr. John N. Hurty, William P. Hapgood, Barton W. Cole, Hugh McK. Landon, Dr. John Courtland Van Camp, and George J. Marott. Since economic prosperity was related to America's trade with the Allies, farmers and others rejected any embargo on the shipment of American food to them, as a resolution of the Indiana State Grange in 1916 and statements in various farm journals made clear.[12]

The German decision on the last day of January, 1917, to resume unrestricted submarine warfare stirred Indianans, and President Wilson's announcement on February 3 breaking off relations with the German Empire won immediate approval in most quarters. Both houses of the General Assembly unanimously voted resolutions of support, while Governor Goodrich wrote the President that Hoosiers were behind him. The disclosure of the Zimmerman Note with its plans for an alliance of Germany with Mexico and Japan against the United States, together with the reports of attacks by German submarines on American merchantmen in March, brought most Indianans to an acceptance of United States' entry into the war. Many felt like Louis Howland, an editor of the Indianapolis *News*, who wrote in a letter to Swift on March 22: ". . . the war is one between civilization and barbarism, and we should stand for civilization. We should also stand for the great English race, to which we owe our religion, our language, our literature, our law, and

12 Cummins, *Indiana Public Opinion, 1914-1917,* pp. 206-207, 235n; Indiana State Grange, *Journal of Proceedings,* 1916, p. 59, *Farmer's Guide,* December 9, 1916, and *Indiana Farmer,* December 16, 1916, cited in Cummins, *op. cit.,* p. 236.

our liberty." In some cities mass meetings were held urging Congress to declare war on the Central Powers, such as the one convened in Indianapolis on March 31 under the chairmanship of Episcopal Bishop Joseph M. Francis. The unanimity of Indiana's two Senators, James E. Watson and Harry S. New, and thirteen Congressmen in voting for war on April 4 and 5, 1917, reflected the general consensus reached among most of the state's population concerning the necessity for finally entering the conflict. Yet, as Cummins has pointed out, unlike the wildly enthusiastic response to the Spanish-American War in Indiana, Hoosiers joined with the Allied Powers in the First World War with sobriety and a sense of the great seriousness of the moment.[13]

The great majority of Indianans quickly closed ranks after the declaration of war. On April 6, 1917, the *Indiana Catholic and Record,* one of the bitterest critics of the Allies, announced that all Americans must be loyal supporters of what was now their country's cause. Almost all of the German-Americans who had hitherto clung to the side of the Fatherland accepted the inevitable and prepared to support the war effort. One of the chief movers in this matter was Richard Lieber, the German-born conservationist and Indianapolis businessman whom Governor Goodrich appointed to his staff as military secretary with the rank of Colonel on April 13, 1917. During 1917-1918 Lieber gave a series of speeches in Indianapolis and other cities in an attempt to rally German-American opinion to the American cause. In these addresses, which were later published and distributed by the "Friends of German Democracy," he explained how his fellow countrymen's natural love for the Fatherland had blinded them to the "diabolical plotting and depth of depravity of official Germany," and expressed the hope that with the German-American change of heart after

---

[13] Indiana *House Journal,* 1917, pp. 257-258; Indiana *Senate Journal,* 1917, pp. 1206, 1213-1214; Indianapolis *Star,* February 5, April 6, 1917; Louis Howland to Swift, March 22, 1917, Swift Papers; Cummins, *Indiana Public Opinion, 1914-1917,* pp. 239-252.

United States' entry into the war the "old American will straighten his path."[14]

§ §

Governor Goodrich anticipated the Congressional declaration of war by calling a conference of farmers, grain dealers, bankers, and others on April 5 at the State House to discuss measures concerning the production and conservation of food in wartime. Out of this meeting came plans for organizing the efforts of farmers and other food producers which were first co-ordinated by Professor George I. Christie, superintendent of the agricultural extension division at Purdue University. Under his leadership Indiana increased its corn acreage by about 600,000 and its wheat acreage by 524,000 during 1917, while planting more than 500,000 individual war gardens. Christie's work was so well regarded in Washington that he was brought to the Department of Agriculture to supervise the national farm effort and became Assistant Secretary of Agriculture in October, 1918.[15]

Not long after American entry into the conflict Indiana businessmen went to Washington to see about procuring war contracts for the state's industries, and a plan was drawn up for a central clearinghouse to provide information concerning government contracts. In Indianapolis the Chamber of Commerce established a war contract bureau for that purpose. Indiana's industrial plants furnished munitions and other war materials on a large scale, their total value approximating $300,000,000.[16]

[14] *Indiana Catholic and Record* (Indianapolis) April 6, 1917; Richard Lieber, *A Plea to German Americans for Unity of Purpose* (New York, 1918), p. 4; Richard Lieber, *Democracy: The Heritage of All* (New York, 1918), p. 10; Frederick, Colonel Richard Lieber, pp. 173-177. In his testimony before the Senate Judiciary Committee in 1918, Joseph H. Keller, president of the Indiana German-American Alliance, insisted that his organization had been inactive since 1916 and that he himself was a loyal, patriotic American with two sons in the United States Army. Indianapolis *News,* March 7, 12, 1918.

[15] Indianapolis *Star,* April 6, 1917; Roll, *Indiana,* II, 453; Dunn, *Indiana and Indianans,* III, 1255.

[16] Walter Greenough, *The War Purse of Indiana (Indiana Historical Collections,* VIII, Indianapolis, 1922), pp. 26n, 43n.

On May 19, 1917, at the request of the national government Governor Goodrich named a State Council of Defense to co-ordinate Indiana's total war effort. The original seventeen men and one woman on the council included Will H. Hays, chairman of the Republican state committee, ex-Vice-President Fairbanks, Thomas Taggart, a former mayor of Indianapolis and national Democratic chairman, Charles Fox, president of the Indiana State Federation of Labor, and George Ade, the well-known playwright-humorist. One of its first tasks was to organize county councils of defense consisting of seven persons to be nominated by the judges of the circuit courts, including one woman and a representative of organized labor. With no legislative appropriation available, the Indiana Council of Defense had to be financed by a loan of $100,000 from ninety-eight banks and trust companies in the state. Its first chairman was Hays, who resigned in April, 1918, in order to become head of the Republican national committee and was replaced by Michael E. Foley, an Indianapolis lawyer. Committees or sections were formed on education, scientific research, highway transportation, communications, labor and employers' co-operation, medical work, coal production, public morals, and similar matters, and the council co-operated with the national government in organizing such agencies as the Indiana branches of the Boys' Working Reserve under Isaac D. Strauss, the Federal Food Administration under Dr. Harry E. Barnard of the State Board of Health, and the Federal Fuel Administration under Indianapolis banker Evans Woollen.[17]

A woman's section headed by Anne Studebaker Carlisle of South Bend organized the efforts of thousands of Indiana women in food production, child welfare, sale of Liberty Bonds, soldiers' entertainment and recreation, education and propaganda, motor corps work, Americanization, and the problems pertaining to women in industry. Included among

17 Indianapolis *Star*, May 18, 1917; Indiana State Council of Defense, *A Report, 1917;* Indiana *Year Book,* 1918, pp. 581-591; Hays, *Memoirs,* pp. 114-123.

the active leaders of this section were Indianapolis educator
Julia E. Landers, Hortense Tapp Moore of Rockville, Mary
L. Matthews of Purdue University, Katharine Merrill Gray-
don of Butler College, Albion Fellows Bacon of Evansville,
Alice Foster McCulloch of Fort Wayne, Vida Newsom of
Columbus, and Marie Chomel, Julia C. Henderson, and Dr.
Amelia R. Keller of Indianapolis. A total of 626,292 women
were registered for war work in Indiana, a figure second only
to that of Michigan in proportion to population.[18]

George Ade was the chairman of the publicity committee
of the State Council of Defense, which consisted of five representatives from both the Republican and the Democratic
Editorial associations and five members at large, three of
whom were from Indianapolis newspapers. Ade threw himself into the task, "determined," he was alleged to have
said, "to keep the Germans out of Indiana." He wrote a series
of pamphlets for various age groups, one of which, entitled
"Helping to Win the War," was distributed nationally by
George Creel's Committee on Public Information in Washington. An *Indiana War Service Text-Book* (1918) was
prepared for use in high school classes which contained
statements by President Wilson, Governor Goodrich, and
former Governor Ralston, war poems, a description of the
work of the Councils of Defense by George Ade, and an
essay on the meaning of the war by Louis Howland.[19]

One of the most prolific propagandists for the American
war effort was Booth Tarkington, who according to his biographer published twice as many articles on the war after

[18] Indiana *Year Book,* 1918, pp. 591-593; Indianapolis *Star,* March 20, 1919.
An organization founded in Indiana in 1917 on the initiative of the State
Council of Defense was the American War Mothers composed of women with
sons in military service. The president of the Indiana chapter, Alice M. French,
was chosen the first National War Mother at the state convention in Indianapolis on August 15, 1918, when with the assistance of a few delegates from Pennsylvania the national organization was launched. *Indianian,* I, No. 1 (August,
1920), 67-71.

[19] Indiana State Council of Defense, *A Report, 1917,* pp. 7-8; Kelly, *George
Ade,* p. 235; *Indiana War Service Text-Book for Indiana High Schools* (Indianapolis, 1918).

American entry than in the nearly three preceding years of pro-Ally agitation. Tarkington, moreover, infused his fiction writing with the war spirit, publishing during 1918 a story, "Captain Schlotterwerz," about the patriotic awakening of a German-American family in the Middle West and the novel *Ramsay Milholland,* whose hero left college to join the Army while counteracting the arguments of a college girl who held pacifist views. College professors lectured on the causes of the war. At Indiana University Samuel B. Harding, Albert L. Kohlmeier, James G. McDonald, and James A. Woodburn of the History Department, as well as Alfred M. Brooks in fine arts and William B. Elkins in philosophy, were among those most active in war writing.[20]

Reams of war poetry were produced in Indiana, most of it ephemeral. The best-known versifier was Indianapolis *News* columnist William Herschell, whose comic opening lines in the refrain of the war song "Long Boy" achieved a kind of immortality: "Good-by, Ma! Good-by, Pa! Good-by mule, with yer old hee-haw!" Two other sets of war verses written by Herschell in 1917 and also set to music were the extremely sentimental "The Kid Has Gone to the Colors" and the martial "We Are Coming, Little Peoples."[21]

The chief note struck in Hoosier war propaganda was simple patriotism; there was little said about a "war for democracy." In his widely circulated address before the GOP state convention in May, 1918, Governor Goodrich pled for unity: "There can be no middle course in this war. There are just two kinds of people in America—patriots and traitors. Every man must take his place on one side or the other. He who does not wholeheartedly and unreservedly stand by his government in this war must be counted against it." The Republican governor, moreover, specifically repudiated

20 Woodress, *Booth Tarkington,* pp. 199-201; *Indiana University Alumni Quarterly,* IV (1917), 362-370, 489-524; V (1918), pp. 4-34, 131-150, 308-328.

21 Indianapolis *News,* April 14, May 5, July 10, 1917; William Herschell, *The Kid Has Gone to the Colors. And Other Verse* (Indianapolis, 1917), pp. 1-2, 56-57, 104-107.

the Wilsonian concept of a war to "make the world safe for democracy." Americans were fighting, he said, "in defense of American rights, within the sanctity of international law, the rights of all nations to govern themselves as they see fit and according to their own light, without interference from more powerful and insolent neighbors. . . ." In addition, the Governor defended the loyalty of the German-Americans and warned his fellow citizens against taking private action against persons thought to be disloyal.[22]

The intense drive toward conformity in wartime Indiana, however, took its toll of civil liberties. In some cities and counties schoolteachers were required to take an oath of allegiance before receiving their contracts, and a few lost their positions on suspicion of disloyalty. A young instructor at Indiana University, W. E. Zeuch, was forced to resign over a letter he had written to an Iowa newspaper in November, 1917, protesting the propagandistic nature of the German atrocity stories. "The University has no place for such a man," declared President William Lowe Bryan in announcing the recommendation brought in by an investigating committee of the faculty that Zeuch resign. A similar incident took place at the State Normal School in Terre Haute, where Professor John J. Schlicher, head of the Latin Department, gave a chapel talk in the spring of 1917 which contained a mild warning that America might lose its democratic freedoms in fighting a war for democracy. Although Schlicher was attacked by patriotic groups in Terre Haute, the board of trustees at first refused to dismiss him, but by January, 1918, the board reversed itself and asked him to resign, which he did the following June.[23]

22 Indianapolis *Star,* May 30, 1918; James P. Goodrich, *Speech of Hon. James P. Goodrich Governor of Indiana as Temporary Chairman of the Republican State Convention . . . 1918* [Indianapolis, 1918], pp. 2-5, 9, 14.

23 H.S.K. Bartholomew and Carrie Nusbaum, History of Elkhart County, Indiana, in the World War (Typed MS [1925], in Indiana State Library), no pagination; Howard K. Beale, *Are American Teachers Free?* . . . (Commission on the Social Studies, *Report,* Part XII, New York, 1936), pp. 27, 64; Cynthia L. Baxter, Indiana University 1917-1929 (Unpublished Master's thesis in

Cases were reported of attacks on German individuals, of homes and shops being broken into to remove the Kaiser's picture, and of severe community pressure being exerted on persons who showed too little zeal for the American war effort. The County Councils of Defense often investigated cases of suspected disloyalty in their jurisdiction, sometimes with the aid of the so-called Liberty Guards, a paramilitary group organized by order of the Governor in December, 1917, to help keep order and eliminate subversion in the state. Under the leadership of George S. Harney of the military department of the State Council of Defense, the Liberty Guards grew to more than 30,000 men organized into 15 regiments and over 200 companies and located in almost every county of the state. Besides their activities in uncovering "slackers" and other suspicious persons, they served as a preliminary training cadre for Hoosier young men drafted into the United States military service.[24]

Various patriotic societies and similar groups were also active in the hunt for disloyal elements in many parts of Indiana. Most secretive of all were the local branches of the American Protective League, which co-operated closely with the United States Department of Justice. Even the American Rights Committee, originally organized as a pro-Ally interventionist body before America's entry into the war, became involved in searching out suspicious behavior on the part of fellow Hoosiers. A letter of April 12, 1917, from the secretary of the Indianapolis branch of the American Rights Committee to Lucius B. Swift, indicates some of the methods used:[25]

History, 1953), pp. 19-20; Lynch, *A History of Indiana State Teachers College,* pp. 253-255.

[24] Gary *Post,* March 26, 1918; Terre Haute *Star,* July 3, 1918; Ginger, *The Bending Cross,* pp. 351-352; Liberty Guards (Typed MS, undated, in Archives Division, Indiana State Library); Indiana *Year Book,* 1918, pp. 191, 589; 1919, p. 745; Indianapolis *News,* December 2, 1918.

[25] C. V. Haworth, *History of Howard County in the World War* (Indianapolis, 1920), p. 332; Garvin M. Brown to Swift, April 12, 1917, Swift Papers; Howland to Swift, January 7, 1918, in *ibid.* William D. Foulke, another early

Instruct your Section to obtain accurate data that can be substantiated. Get name and address of suspected persons—what was said—or done—when and where—and names of persons present at the time.

Tell them to investigate all possible rumors, as while they often lead to nothing—they sometimes point the way to activities of the utmost importance.

Hoosiers displayed perhaps their greatest degree of unity of effort and purpose in the four great Liberty Loan campaigns of 1917 and 1918 and the final Victory Loan campaign of 1919, all of which was described as a "financial awakening" for the state. Indiana was divided into two regions for the campaigns, sixty-eight northern and central counties coming under the direction of the Seventh Federal Reserve District centered in Chicago, and the remaining twenty-four counties to the south in the jurisdiction of the Eighth District headquarters in St. Louis. The total amount of money raised in these strenuous war-financing efforts, including the sale of war savings stamps, came to approximately $500,000,000. In many instances, tremendous pressure was brought to bear upon recalcitrant residents who tried to avoid purchasing bonds. In one noteworthy case in Carroll County a banker and other local citizens were eventually indicted for forcing Dunkard farmers to buy bonds during the last two campaigns by dragging them out of their homes at night and painting their houses red and yellow.[26]

Some municipalities enacted legislation against disloyal utterances, such as Indianapolis City Ordinance No. 35 of 1917, which made it unlawful not only to speak or write against the government of the United States but also to "incite, urge or advise strikes or disturbances" in war-re-

pro-Ally interventionist, was distressed to find himself and his wife classified as pro-German by the Wayne County Council of Defense. Foulke to James P. Goodrich, February 15, 1918, in Governors' Papers, Archives Division, Indiana State Library.

26 Greenough, *The War Purse of Indiana*, pp. 13-17, 20-22; Indianapolis *News*, June 24, 1919. The directors of the Liberty Bond campaigns met with representatives of the Mennonites and Amish at South Bend in September, 1918, to devise a system for the indirect purchase of bonds through certificates of deposit. Greenough, *The War Purse of Indiana*, pp. 118-119.

lated industrial plants.[27] One of the main casualties of the war spirit in Indiana was the German language. Efforts were made to halt the use of German in church services and especially in schools. In November, 1917, the Indiana State Teachers Association passed a resolution requesting a ban upon the instruction in German in both public and private schools, and in January of the next year the Indianapolis Board of School Commissioners voted to end German-language teaching in all of the city elementary schools. Enrollment in German classes in Indianapolis high schools dropped significantly in 1917 and 1918, though the General Assembly did not act to prohibit all teaching of German until after the war's end in 1919. The unpopularity of the German name led to its abrupt removal from churches, banks, and other institutions in these years, and in February, 1918, Das Deutsche Haus in Indianapolis was rechristened the Athenaeum.[28]

Opposition to the war after American entry in April, 1917, was limited largely to a few religious organizations with historic nonresistance traditions. In general most ecclesiastical leaders shouldered arms willingly, as in the state meeting called by Governor Goodrich at Indianapolis in May, 1917, when all the clergymen present pledged support to the war effort. On April 22, 1917, however, Indiana Quakers sponsored a conference at Richmond to discuss ways of meeting the war crisis, including support for relief measures in war-ravaged countries and the establishment of a program of noncombatant national service. Hoosier Friends were well represented in the first unit of the newly organ-

27 Indianapolis Common Council, *Journal*, 1917, pp. 231-232, 241-242, 283.

28 Indianapolis *Star*, November 4, 1917; Ellis, "German Instruction in the Public Schools of Indianapolis, 1869-1919," *Indiana Magazine of History*, L (1954), 373-378; *Laws of Indiana*, 1919, pp. 50-51, 822-823; United States Comptroller of the Currency, *Annual Report*, 1918, I, 67-68; Indianapolis *Star*, February 23, 1918. The innocuous poem, "Kaiserblumen," was cut out of *Third Readers* in the hands of Hoosier school children by school boards. Ellis, "German Instruction in the Public Schools of Indianapolis, 1869-1919," *Indiana Magazine of History*, L, 375.

ized American Friends Service Committee sent to France in 1917, with seventeen young men among the original contingent of one hundred. Other Indiana Quakers were drafted and sent to Camp Zachary Taylor in Kentucky, where for the most part they were segregated from ordinary soldiers and assigned to noncombatant work.[29]

The war was the main topic at the Mennonite biennial conference held at Yellow Creek Church near Goshen, Indiana, from August 29 to September 1, 1917, which sent a delegation to confer with Secretary of War Newton D. Baker concerning exemption of its members from military service. Indiana Mennonite leaders subscribed to the statement drawn up at the conference which recommended refusal of both combatant and noncombatant service in the uniform of the United States Army. Although many Mennonite and Amish youth accepted military service, most of them as noncombatants, some experienced severe penalties for radical adherence to their nonresistance principles. An extreme example of this was illustrated by the case of John H. Smeltzer, who was inducted into the Army at South Bend in July, 1918, and sent to Camp Taylor, where upon refusal to wear the uniform or obey military orders, he was subjected to harsh and inhumane treatment by both commissioned and noncommissioned officers. He was eventually tried by court-martial and sentenced to serve five years at hard labor. At a special conference of the Church of the Brethren held at Goshen in January, 1918, a paper prepared by a committee of seven ministers and laymen was addressed to the President and Secretary of War setting forth the church's position of nonresistance; a second paper urged members to con-

[29] Indianapolis *News,* May 16, 1917; *American Friend,* N.S. V (1917), 350-351, 534, 550-551; Woodward, *Timothy Nicholson,* pp. 159-160. Foulke, who was a member of the Wayne County Conscription Board, claimed that no more than "a score or two" of Friends in the Richmond area sought exemption from the Army on conscientious grounds, and these accepted noncombatant duty without difficulty. Foulke, *A Hoosier Autobiography,* p. 202.

tribute to war relief. Young Brethren were also among those accepting noncombatant service in the United States uniform.[30]

Thirty to forty men and women were present at a meeting of conscientious objectors held at Indianapolis on May 31, 1917. Although a second meeting of the same group a week later resulted in the formation of the Indianapolis Union for Democracy under the leadership of C. G. Maurer and A. J. Hornung, nothing more was heard of this organization during the remaining months of the war.[31] Indiana's most prominent opponent of the war was the Socialist leader Eugene V. Debs of Terre Haute. After remaining relatively quiet during the first fourteen months of American participation in the conflict, in June, 1918, Debs finally began to speak out publicly against the war. The press, however, paid little attention to the former Socialist presidential candidate as he addressed small groups of sympathizers in Indiana, Illinois, and Ohio. Even his arrest and indictment under the Federal Espionage Act for an antiwar speech in Canton, Ohio, on June 16 did not stimulate much editorial response, though the Socialist party of Indiana nominated him to run for Congress in his home district a second time—an honor he declined. The Terre Haute *Tribune* sent a special correspondent to Cleveland to cover Debs's trial in September, 1918, and published a front-page drawing of the old Socialist addressing the court on his own behalf, but heartily endorsed his conviction in these words: "any success for Debs here meant the highest German triumph, and America, as long as she is America, cannot tolerate that."[32]

30 Bartholomew and Nusbaum, History of Elkhart County, Indiana, in the World War; Wenger, *The Mennonites in Indiana and Michigan*, pp. 38-41.

31 Indianapolis *Star*, June 1, 8, 1917.

32 Ginger, *The Bending Cross*, pp. 353-376; Terre Haute *Tribune*, June 30, September 13, 1918. A later editorial in the *Tribune* pointed out that the trial showed that Debs was more dangerous than was thought by many of his fellow citizens in Terre Haute, who had grown accustomed to his presence among them. A quick survey of public opinion in Terre Haute after the trial indicated that local sentiment was strongly against Debs. Terre Haute *Tribune*, September 14, 16, 1918.

§ § §

By the latter half of 1916 there was a flurry of interest
in military training in Indiana. In June of that year the
trustees of Indiana University approved the establishment of
a Reserve Officers Training Corps on the campus. Delays
in organizing such a unit, because of a shortage of Army
officers to act as instructors, moreover, led to student demonstrations in favor of some kind of military program in
March, 1917. As a result, the university administration permitted the formation of five companies of students under
the temporary command of Kenneth P. Williams, a young
mathematics teacher with some military experience.[33]

A poll of newspaper editors in the state, conducted by the
Indianapolis *Star* in late April, 1917, revealed a near-consen-
sus on the need for universal military conscription in order
to prosecute the war successfully. Out of 162 editors who
answered the questionnaires, 135 favored a draft and 15 a
system of volunteers; only six voiced strong opposition to conscription, while another six seemed undecided or noncommit-
tal.[34] On April 28, while Congress was still debating the
Selective Service bill, Governor Goodrich named the members of local conscription boards, which met the following day
in Indianapolis to receive their instructions. County boards
were composed of the sheriff, the county clerk, and a private citizen. Additional three-man boards were also established in the state's larger cities. On May 7 the Governor appointed as state conscription director the former speaker
of the Indiana house, Jesse E. Eschbach, who established his

[33] Baxter, Indiana University, 1917-1929, pp. 1-4. After the ROTC was
finally established at Indiana University, it was replaced by the Student Army
Training Corps program in October, 1918, and then re-established after the
latter's demise near the end of the year. *Ibid.*, pp. 6-8. Kenneth P. Williams
became the commanding officer of an artillery battery composed mostly of Indiana University students and Bloomington citizens which was mustered into
the Indiana National Guard and fought in France with the 150th Field Artillery in the Rainbow Division. *Battery F, 150th F.A., Under the Rainbow. A History of Its Service in the War against Germany* (Indianapolis, 1919), p. 1.

[34] Indianapolis *Star*, April 25, 1917.

office in the State House on May 24, after the final passage of the Selective Service Act, and was chiefly responsible for the initial organization of the draft machinery in Indiana, though his place was soon taken by an Army officer, Major Robert C. Baltzell. In accordance with instructions from the Federal government the third member of the county board was replaced by a physician; and on July 4 four district appeal boards were appointed. The first registration on June 5, 1917, produced the names of 257,311 draft-eligible men between the ages of 21 and 31; the second on July 5 and August 24 added 24,015 who had reached the age of 21 since the first registration; and the third on September 12, 1918, another 354,812, including all men between the ages of 18 and 45 not previously registered.[35]

On July 13, 1917, the Secretary of War allotted Indiana a draft quota of 17,510 men, who were mobilized on August 21 at Camp Zachary Taylor near Louisville, Kentucky. There they were trained and organized into the Eighty-fourth Division with other draftees from Kentucky, as well as later contingents of Hoosiers called to the colors by their conscription boards. For the most part, however, they did not remain together as a unit but were separated and scattered among other military organizations both in the United States and abroad, largely as replacements. As part of the national military policy, Negro soldiers were drafted separately, a group of 1,258 men from the Indianapolis area leaving for camp in August, 1918, after a parade and mass meeting in the capital city.[36]

The War Department's plans to utilize existing educational facilities for military training purposes was finally put into effect in the fall of 1918, when nineteen Student Army Training Corps units were established at Indiana and Purdue universities, the State Normal Schools at Terre Haute and Muncie, and the following private institutions: Butler College,

35 *Ibid.*, April 29, May 8, 1917; Indiana *Year Book*, 1918, pp. 599-602.

36 Indiana *Year Book*, 1919, p. 750; Esarey, *History of Indiana*, II, 1092, 1094; Indianapolis *Star*, August 21, 1918.

Central Normal College, DePauw University, Franklin College, Hanover College, Huntington College, Indiana Dental College, Indiana Veterinary College, University of Notre Dame, Oakland City College, Rose Polytechnic Institute, Taylor University, Tri-State University, Valparaiso University, and Wabash College. In addition to these collegiate units, eleven vocational units were also established at Interlaken School for Boys, Indiana, Purdue, and Valparaiso universities, and under the auspices of the Chambers of Commerce in Indianapolis, Richmond, and Warsaw. Late in getting organized, the SATC lasted only a few months and was deactivated not long after the Armistice in November.[37]

The Indiana National Guard, with an enlisted strength of only 3,100 on March 1, 1917, was authorized to increase its size to 10,419 officers and men and on August 5 was mustered into Federal service. The First Regiment, Indiana Field Artillery, was sent to Camp Mills, Long Island, where it became part of the 42d or Rainbow Division as the 150th Field Artillery. In October the regiment sailed for France, becoming an element in the first 60,000 American troops to reach that country. After several weeks of training behind the lines it saw action at the front from February through the first part of November, 1918, and later served in the Army of Occupation in Germany until April 7, 1919, when it received orders to return to the United States. The regiment was finally mustered out at Camp Taylor, Kentucky, on May 24, 1919.[38]

All the remaining units of the Indiana National Guard, including four regiments of infantry, a battalion of engineers, four troops of cavalry, two field hospitals, three ambu-

[37] United States Department of War, Committee on Education and Special Training, *A Review of Its Work during 1918* (Washington, D.C., 1919), pp. 88, 92.

[38] Indiana *Year Book,* 1917, p. 531; 1919, pp. 745-746. Two accounts of Hoosiers who served in the 150th Artillery Regiment of the 42d Division are Elmer F. Straub, *A Sergeant's Diary in the World War* . . . (*Indiana Historical Collections,* X, Indianapolis, 1923) and Elmer W. Sherwood, *The Diary of a Rainbow Veteran Written at the Front* (Terre Haute, 1929).

lance companies, and a signal corps battalion, were sent to Camp Shelby at Hattiesburg, Mississippi. The Guard spent fifty-one weeks there in the "heart of a cut-over pine district," the chief products of which, according to the report of the Indiana adjutant general, were "goats, sand and pine stumps." Together with guardsmen from West Virginia and Kentucky, the Indiana troops at Camp Shelby were organized into the 38th Division, which did not go overseas until late September, 1918. A number of enlisted men, however, had been transferred from the division and sent overseas as replacement troops in June, 1918, and their places taken by draftees from other states. In general, the War Department followed a policy of breaking up state units in order to create a truly national army. As a result, even after arrival in France the Indiana elements of the 38th Division were largely separated and assigned to various other organizations, making it virtually impossible to identify Hoosier military units in the war, with the exception of the 150th Artillery Regiment serving with the Rainbow Division as described above.[39]

A smaller Indiana unit of a highly specialized type was the Eli Lilly Base Hospital, or Base Hospital No. 32, which was organized through the efforts of a group of Indianapolis physicians. In February, 1917, the Eli Lilly Company through its president, Josiah K. Lilly, offered to donate $25,000 to the Indianapolis chapter of the American Red Cross to furnish a military hospital staffed by local physicians and nurses. With this money and additional funds raised in the city a 500-bed hospital was equipped and staffed. The personnel were inducted into military service and trained briefly at

[39] Indiana *Year Book*, 1919, pp. 746-749. The failure to keep Indiana regiments of the National Guard intact caused unhappiness in some quarters in the state. Adjutant General Harry B. Smith complained in his official report in 1919: "Why it was necessary to completely disrupt Indiana regiments has never been explained, and no explanation has ever been offered as to why a splendid division of troops, thoroughly trained, was kept in camp in the United States when there were repeated calls for troops to resist and check the forward movement of the German Army." *Ibid.*, p. 749.

Fort Benjamin Harrison outside of Indianapolis before sailing in December to France, where they established Base Hospital 32 at Contrexeville, returning to the United States in April, 1919.[40]

A second regiment of artillery was also organized as part of the Indiana National Guard in October, 1917, but for some reason it was never called into Federal service and was eventually dissolved. With the federalization of the Guard, Indiana was left without any troops for domestic peacekeeping purposes; therefore, in November, 1917, Governor Goodrich authorized the formation of a new state militia, which was largely composed of men beyond the age limits of selective service. Organized into three regiments of infantry, the militia was called out several times during 1918 and 1919 for guard and riot duty in industrial disturbances. Adjutant General Harry B. Smith described its work in the following exaggerated, if not indeed inflammatory, fashion:[41]

> There were enemies at home as well as in France and the Militia was ready for them. They were seditionists, traitors, and breeders of disorder. The Militia was ready to deal with any trouble they started. It was the only guard we had for the rear and its existence and the spirit it showed put a stop to attacks from within.

Altogether, Indiana furnished 130,670 troops during the war. Most of these were drafted into service by the state's conscription boards, but a large number—39,586 by April 1, 1918—served as volunteers in the Army, Navy, and Marines. After the end of the war a great homecoming celebration for Hoosier troops was held in Indianapolis on May 7, 1919, a date chosen to take advantage of the return to the state at that time of its two identifiable overseas units, Base Hospital

---

[40] Benjamin D. Hitz (comp.), *A History of Base Hospital 32* (Indianapolis, 1922), pp. 1-57; Marie and Anselm Chomel, *A Red Cross Chapter at Work* (Indianapolis, 1920), pp. 234-256. The Indianapolis Red Cross chapter was organized in 1916 under the presidency of William Fortune at the request of Ernest P. Bicknell, director of the American National Red Cross and a former secretary of the Indiana Board of State Charities and Correction. *Ibid.,* pp. 6-15.

[41] Indiana *Year Book,* 1919, pp. 734-740, 750; 1920, pp. 226-231.

32 and the 150th Field Artillery. Indiana later honored its more than three thousand war dead, the majority dying as a result of diseases — chiefly influenza and pneumonia — contracted at home or abroad during the conflict, by publishing their names and brief biographical sketches in a volume issued by the Indiana Historical Commission in 1921 entitled the *Gold Star Honor Roll*.[42]

§ § § §

In an attempt to exploit the unity achieved in wartime for postwar reconstruction, Governor Goodrich called a conference of business, labor, educational, and other leaders at Indianapolis on November 26, 1918. Although the conference attracted national attention for its discussion of the reconversion of industry to a peacetime basis and the special problems of the Negro and working women, no concrete program emerged, and the Governor failed to name the nine-man commission on reconstruction suggested by the delegates.[43] On the other hand, Governor Goodrich himself presented to the next session of the General Assembly in 1919 a whole set of recommendations for the centralization and greater efficiency of the state government based in part, at least, upon lessons learned in wartime administration. These included strengthening of the State Board of Tax Commissioners, establishment of a State Highway Commission, Conservation Commission, and a separate Department of Banking and Insurance, and the consequent elimination of the

[42] Roll, *Indiana*, II, 452-453, 460-463; Indianapolis *Star*, May 8, 1919. Letters from the War and Navy departments to the Indiana Adjutant General in 1933 give the figure for the Army as 118,098 and for the Navy as 12,253, making a total of 130,351 men and women who served in the war from Indiana. Supplementary Index, Indiana Division, Indiana State Library—Military Statistics. The first American soldier to lose his life on the battlefield in France was Corporal James B. Gresham of Evansville, Indiana. A member of the Regular Army since 1914, he was killed in a German air raid near Artois on November 3, 1917. *Gold Star Honor Roll, 1914-1918 (Indiana Historical Collections,* VII, Indianapolis, 1921), pp. 10, 638.

[43] Indianapolis *Star*, November 27, 1918; *The Survey*, XLI (October, 1918-March, 1919), 326-327; Charles Kettleborough, Reconstruction and Readjustment in Indiana (Typed MS, 1920, in Indiana State Library).

office of state statistician and the elective office of state geologist. Other similar recommendations which, however, failed to find favor among the legislators were elimination of the elective offices of state superintendent of public instruction, clerk of the supreme court, and attorney general, and their replacement by appointed officials. The Governor was also unsuccesful in obtaining legislation to permit counties to have full-time health officials and to establish a commission to investigate a social insurance program for the state.[44]

The General Assembly, moreover, showed a greater interest than the Governor in attempting to combat the influence of Bolshevism in postwar Indiana, as displayed in its passing of one of the several state sedition laws of the era. This statute, after a preamble which recognized the civil rights of American citizens, argued that the "claim to those rights should never be allowed to cover treasonable acts or utterances, the advocacy of anarchy, the overthrow of government, or the abrogation of constitutional means for the maintenance of law and order and the protection of the lives and rights of persons, or the advocacy of or the practice of sabotage." After noting also that "recent occurrences in Russia and elsewhere warn us that the toleration of such unbridled license of speech and of such practices involves great danger to civilization and to organized society, and threatens a possible lapse into barbarism," the law made it unlawful to display certain flags or other symbols of any movement to overthrow by force or violence the government of Indiana or the United States, or the advocacy in writing of such a movement.[45]

May Day celebrations in a few Indiana cities in 1919 were an occasion for some radical agitation and considerable concern among conservative elements in the state. A peaceful demonstration in Terre Haute in which thousands of persons marched to the courthouse to listen to speeches in honor of

[44] Indiana *Senate Journal,* 1919, pp. 10-24.
[45] *Laws of Indiana,* 1919, pp. 588-589.

Eugene V. Debs, then in prison in Moundsville, West Virginia, for defying the Federal Espionage Act, was organized by the Central Labor Union of that city. More violent incidents took place in South Bend and Gary, where agitators stirred up the large foreign-born working population. In the latter city a crowd of three hundred people, including representatives from East Chicago and Indiana Harbor, attempted to hold a street parade after being refused permission by the mayor. After the parade was halted by police and a group of war veterans, a meeting was held in Roumanian Hall in which speakers allegedly denounced the "government of the United States, the government of Indiana, and the city government of Gary." In an editorial on May 6 the Indianapolis *Star* blamed the demonstrations on foreigners and stated baldly that "the logical course to pursue with aliens who make trouble or sympathize with trouble-makers is to deport them. . . . Those who are citizens and can not be deported should be dealt with as unsparingly as the laws will permit."[46]

The immediate thrust of the war was to stimulate an interest in internationalism in some quarters, as manifested in the continuing movement for a League of Nations among many churchmen, clubwomen and others, including such prominent public figures as William D. Foulke, Louis Howland, and Booth Tarkington. Both the Indianapolis *News* and the Indianapolis *Star* gave at least moderate support to the idea of American co-operation with the Allies in preserving the peace, the latter going so far as to endorse a statement made by the Secretary of War that "the day of isolation for the United States has passed. For good or ill this republic must concern itself with every problem that touches the

[46] Terre Haute *Tribune,* May 5, 1919; Indianapolis *Star,* May 5, 6, 1919. Veterans' and other patriotic groups, especially the recently organized American Legion, which chose Indianapolis for its national headquarters in November, 1919, took the lead in opposing Socialist "agitators" in Indiana, such as the radical sociologist Scott Nearing, who lectured at Lafayette Labor Temple in 1919 on the question of amnesty for such political prisoners as Eugene V. Debs. Indianapolis *News,* November 11, 26, 1919.

people of every portion of the world." On the other hand, former Progressives Albert J. Beveridge and Lucius B. Swift, fearful of the possible loss of national sovereignty, wrote and spoke actively against the League. Moreover, Indiana Senators New and Watson, conservative Republicans both, adamantly opposed President Wilson's proposed system of international organization. In February, 1919, while the covenant of the League of Nations was being debated at Versailles, Senator New urgently implored the Indiana Governor to use all his influence to prevent an endorsement of the League by the General Assembly then in session. Although resolutions endorsing the League were introduced in both houses, the GOP-controlled legislature refused to even consider them.[47]

Indiana entered the postwar era in a cautious, conservative frame of mind. While apparently willing to accept a greater degree of centralized state government, including its extension to some new areas of the public interest, Hoosiers balked at widening the scope of individual nonconformity after a period of intense wartime unity. Although participation in a European war tended to make all Indianans more aware of their stake in world affairs, it failed to eradicate the latent isolationist attitudes and sentiments common to much of the Middle West. As a result of the First World War, Indiana became both more unified and more integrated into the total political, economic, and social fabric of the nation, but not yet deeply involved in the world beyond the United States.

[47] Foulke, A Hoosier Autobiography, pp. 185-189; Louis Howland to Swift, January 5, 1920, Swift Papers; Indianapolis News, June 21, 1918; Bowers, Beveridge and the Progressive Era, pp. 496-513; Indianapolis Star, December 17, 1918; New to Goodrich, February 24, 1919, Governors' Correspondence, Archives, Indiana State Library. John C. Shaffer, editor and publisher of the Indianapolis Star, broke sharply with his good friend Beveridge in order to plump for the League of Nations. Desite his support for the League, which never wavered, Shaffer bitterly denounced Wilson and supported the GOP in the election of 1920. John O. Carrington, The Foreign Policy of the Indianapolis Star, 1918-1939 (Unpublished Ph.D. thesis in History, University of Kentucky, 1958), pp. 55-98.

BIBLIOGRAPHY

# BIBLIOGRAPHY

This bibliography does not purport to be all inclusive. Instead, the author has attempted to list the most significant materials, published and unpublished, for the study of the history of Indiana for the period from 1880 to 1920. All items cited in the footnotes are not included, while some material not cited has been included in the belief that it will be useful to persons seeking to do more intensive research on some subjects than was possible within the limits of the present volume.

The bibliography is organized partly on the basis of type of material, partly on the basis of subject matter.

## UNPUBLISHED MATERIALS

### MANUSCRIPTS

The most extensive collections of manuscripts on the history of Indiana are to be found in the Indiana Division of the Indiana State Library, the Indiana Historical Society Library, and the Lilly Library of Indiana University.

*Indiana Division, Indiana State Library*

There is a card index of the manuscripts organized according to subject and also a useful chronological catalogue. Many of the larger collections are important principally for political history, but there are numerous smaller collections of letters, diaries, and account books which throw light on various aspects of the history of the period. As a part of the celebration of the state's sesquicentennial in 1966, a concerted effort was made to collect manuscript material in its original form or, where this was not possible, to make microfilm or Xerox copies. Since 1966 the Indiana Division has continued to add original and copied material as well as beginning a new venture, the recording of interviews with prominent individuals or with individuals who were participants in some historic event or movement. A list of the material collected by Thomas Krasean, field agent, during the sesquicentennial and following year was published in the June and September, 1968, issues of the *Indiana Magazine of History*.

Some of the more important collections in the Indiana Division which contain materials on the period from 1880 to 1920 are listed below.

Albert J. Beveridge Papers. There are additional Beveridge letters in the Shaffer and Taylor Papers.

Amos W. Butler Papers. State charities and prison reform; Western Association of Writers; Indiana Academy of Science.

Ira J. Chase Diary, 1882-1894.

Church history. Numerous records of individual churches. See card index under name of denomination.

Grace Julian Clarke Papers (Mrs. Clarke was the daughter of George W. Julian). Suffrage movement, housing, and child welfare; activities of Indiana Federation of Women's Clubs, Woman's Franchise League, and various peace organizations; records of Equal Suffrage Society of Indianapolis, 1878-1880.

John Coburn Papers (Coburn was an Indianapolis lawyer and Congressman). Political and economic material; natural gas boom.

Schuyler Colfax Papers. Political, personal, and business papers. Mostly for period before 1880.

County superintendents of public instruction, Association Proceedings, 1895-1929. Earlier records, 1887-1894, in Archives Division.

Eugene V. Debs Papers. Correspondence, clippings, and printed and typed articles and speeches; scrapbooks, 1887-1924 (microfilm).

Deutscher pioneer verein (Indianapolis ?), minutes of meetings, 1880-1909. In German script.

Lucius C. Embree Papers (Embree was a Princeton, Indiana, lawyer and active in the Republican party). Politics; railroads; World War I.

John W. Foster Papers (Foster was a lawyer, diplomat, and secretary of state, 1892-1893). Microfilm.

William Dudley Foulke Papers. Civil service reform, progressive movement, woman suffrage, and League to Enforce Peace.

Agnes McCulloch Hanna Collection (Mrs. Hanna was the daughter of Oscar McCulloch). Papers of Hugh Hanna; papers and diaries of Oscar McCulloch; Indianapolis Monetary Convention, 1897-1898.

Benjamin Harrison Papers. Business, politics.

Will H. Hays Papers (Hays was chairman of the state and national Republican committees). Extensive collection, not yet catalogued.

David W. Henry Collection. Politics, appointments under civil service, letters of Fairbanks, Hanly, Durbin, etc.

Jere Hershey Diary, 1873-1922 (Hershey was a civil engineer at Vincennes). Diary covers economic conditions, prices, weather, and accounts of elections and use of Australian ballot.

William S. Holman Papers. Letters received from constituents while Holman was a member of Congress.

Indiana Civil Service Reform Asociation, Minutes, 1885-1890.

Indiana State Grange, account book, 1877-1889; record book, 1869-1896.

Indianapolis German Literary Society, minutes and club programs, 1893-1918.

Indianapolis Literary Club, constitution, minutes, miscellaneous papers, 1907-1910.

George W. Julian Papers. Journal, 1869-1899.

John Worth Kern Papers (partly Xerox copies). Politics.

Thomas R. Marshall Papers. Speeches, articles, scrapbooks; some letters on social, economic, and political questions.

Claude Matthews Papers. Correspondence relating to strikes. Additional papers in Archives Division.

Louis T. Michener Papers (Michener was Indiana attorney general and Benjamin Harrison's political manager). (Microfilm). Politics.

William H. H. Miller Papers (Miller was attorney general in Harrison's cabinet). Business papers, letterbooks, speeches.

Harry S. New Papers (partly on microfilm). Politics.

Benjamin S. Parker Papers. Politics, Indiana authors, Western Association of Writers.

May Wright Sewall Papers. Scrapbooks.

John C. Shaffer Papers. Mainly letters from Albert J. Beveridge.

Spanish-America War. Some letters and diaries of servicemen.

Lucius B. Swift Papers. Civil service reform, politics, World War I.

Thomas Taggart Papers (Taggart was a Democratic political leader). Scrapbooks relating to politics; French Lick Springs Hotel.

Robert S. Taylor Papers (Taylor was a Fort Wayne attorney). Business papers, politics, Indianapolis Monetary Convention, 1897-1898.

World War I. Liberty loan drives, selective service, state council of defense, letters of servicemen.

## Indiana Historical Society Library

The greater part of the manuscripts in the the Society library relates to the period before 1880, but in recent years later materials have been added as they have become available. Some of the more important collections which contain material on the period from 1880 to 1920 are listed below.

John C. Chaney Papers, 1883-1942 (Chaney was a Congressman from Sullivan County). Politics, family papers.

Orange V. Darby Papers, 1901-1909 (Darby was the owner of a dry-goods store in Kokomo). Business, electric railroads.

William H. English Collection. Politics. Mostly for earlier period.

Goodwin Family Papers, 1827-1924 (microfilm). Diaries, scrapbooks, miscellany, relating to a Brookville family.

Merton W. Grills Collection, 1827-1956. Diaries, account books, etc., principally relating to Wayne and Henry counties.

Benjamin Harrison Letters, 1889-1909.

Mrs. Otto H. Hasselman Papers, 1879-1905 (Mrs. Hasselman was a resident of Indianapolis). Diaries, correspondence.

Alexander Heron Papers. Include the period 1872-1900 when Heron was secretary of the State Board of Agriculture.

Judah-Brandon Papers, 1820-1950. Personal letters relating to social events. Mostly for period after 1880.

New Albany United Charities. Minutes, 1895-1942 (microfilm).

Patrons of Husbandry, Olive Grange No. 189, Randolph County. Proceedings, 1883-1892.

Schramm Diaries, 1851-1903. In German. Diary entries pertain primarily to agricultural matters of a Hancock County family, but also record daily happenings.

Lorenz G. Schumm Collection. Includes Beveridge material.

Delavan and William Henry Smith Papers (William Henry Smith was co-owner of the Indianapolis *News;* his son Delavan Smith was later co-owner and publisher of the *News*).

Spanish-American War. Letters of Capt. C. E. Reese, active in Philippine campaign.

James A. Stuart Papers, 1907-1965 (Stuart was editor of the Indianapolis *Star*). Politics, literary material, and letters from prominent Hoosiers.

Lew Wallace Papers. Family papers, Spanish-American War, miscellany.

*Lilly Library, Indiana University*

The manuscript collections are described in some detail in a card catalogue. Most of the material deals with politics and business for the period from 1880 to 1920 though some is of a more general nature. Listed below are the more important collections for the period.

Willis S. Blatchley Papers (Blatchley was a naturalist and state geologist).

George W. Camp Papers. Business papers of the Dublin Agricultural Company, manufacturers of farm implements, 1880-1905.

Columbia Conserve Company. Business records of Indianapolis canning company, 1903-1953, an experiment in ownership and management by employees.

William Cumback Papers (Cumback, of Greensburg, was a Congressman). A few letters and other papers on Republican politics.

Charles Warren Fairbanks Papers. Extensive collection of letters dealing chiefly with Fairbanks' career as United States Senator and Vice-President.

Nicholas Filbeck Papers, 1843-1915 (Filbeck was a Republican political leader and hotel operator in Terre Haute).

James A. Hemenway Papers, 1904-1921 (Hemenway was a Congressman and United States Senator from Warrick County).

Hoffman Brothers Company. Business records of a band sawmill company, 1867-1949.

Alvin P. Hovey Papers. A few letters for period of his governorship, 1889-1891.

Indiana Forestry Association. Records of the association founded by Charles W. Fairbanks, 1910-1917.

Joseph I. Irwin Papers. Correspondence and other papers of prominent Columbus businessman.

Mary Hannah Krout Papers (Crawfordsville journalist-author, 1851-1927).

Richard Lieber Papers. Large collection of materials relating to Lieber's career as a music and art critic for Indianapolis newspapers, conservationist, and leader of movement for state parks.

Louis Leon Ludlow Papers (Ludlow was a Washington correspondent for Indianapolis newspapers and later Congressman).

Joseph Ewing McDonald Papers. Scrapbooks of newspaper clippings dealing with Senator McDonald's political career.

Samuel M. Ralston Papers. Extensive collection.

James Whitcomb Riley Papers. Large collection of letters and other materials.

Lew Wallace Papers. Relate to Wallace's career as an author.

William Albert Wirt Papers. Prominent Gary educator.

James Albert Woodburn Papers (Woodburn was professor of history at Indiana University).

## ARCHIVES

A variety of records relating to the period covered by the present volume are preserved in the Archives Division of the Indiana State Library. A summary guide to the collection, prepared by Margaret Pierson in 1962, will give the researcher some idea of what is available. Only a very small part of the collection has been catalogued.

*Governor*

For this most important of state offices, an inventory of the correspondence, documents, and reports of each successive administration has been prepared by the Archives staff. Though very limited in extent for the governors who served in the 1880's, the material becomes more voluminous with each administration until at the end of the period under consideration one finds seven file drawers of material for the Ralston administration and four drawers for his successor, Governor Goodrich.

*Adjutant General*

The papers from this office are extensive and have been catalogued. For the period 1880-1920 they include the following: correspondence of the adjutant general and quartermaster general; state militia and National Guard records; records of the Spanish-American War, Mexican border conflict, and World War I; records and correspondence of the Liberty Guards, 1917-1919; State Council of Defense, 1917-1918; records of the various G.A.R. posts in the state.

*Agriculture, State Board of*

General correspondence, 1860-1933.

*Attorney General*

Letterbooks dating from 1880 are available and files of correspondence, briefs, and opinions in civil and criminal cases.

*Auditor of State*

Here are materials on banking including correspondence, papers of incorporation, stocks and notes, and an index of state banks, 1873-1893; list of building and loan associations, 1894-1909, and a record of the examination of these associations, 1911-1924.

*Conservation, Department of*
Records begin with the creation of the department in 1919.

*Health, State Board of*
General correspondence, 1902-1932; letterbooks, 1907-1909.

*Insurance Department*
Annual statements of insurance companies doing business in Indiana, correspondence, 1900-1937, and reports of various companies.

*Public Service Commission*
Tariff regulations of railroads.

*Public Welfare, Department of*
Here are correspondence and institutional reports of the State Board of Charities, predecessor of the Department of Welfare, 1889-1935. There is related material in Governors' files.

*Secretary of State*
Correspondence; incorporation papers of companies and corporations that have been dissolved or charters revoked; record of pardons and paroles.

*Soldiers' and Sailors' Monument Commission*
Material relating to building of monument on the Circle in Indianapolis. Related material is in the Governors' files.

*State Soldiers' Home*
Records of the home at Lafayette.

*State Board of Tax Commissioners*
These papers have been catalogued and include proceedings, 1891-1934; correspondence relating to corporation assessments, 1883-1915; petitions by civil corporations for permission to issue bonds, 1919-1921; tax returns of banks, 1919-1920, of foreign corporations, 1919-1921, of electric and steam railroads, telegraph companies, pipelines, etc., 1896-1934; and of telephone companies, 1902-1934; and beginning in 1872, annual returns of public utilities to the State Tax Board, predecessor of the Board of Tax Commissioners.

*Superintendent of Public Instruction*
This material has been catalogued and includes records of the various agencies connected with the office. The following will give some idea of its extent: correspondence, 1865-1921; circulars to school officials, 1855-1890; material on school financing; enumeration of children, 1859-1907 (scattered); consolidated reports of private, commercial, and business schools, and training schools for nurses for year ending June, 1920; records of State Board of Education, Division of School Inspection, School Book Commission, School Survey Commission, State Board of Attendance, and Division of Teacher Training and Licensing; minutes of State Teachers Association, 1854-1915; minutes and proceedings of County Superintendents' Association, 1887-1894.

*Treasurer of State*
Journal, ledger, and letterbooks; register of taxes of fire insurance companies, 1913-1931, and life insurance companies, 1906-1921; and reports of condition of state banks, 1900-1909.

### UNPUBLISHED THESES
Much important research is contained in unpublished doctoral and masters' theses in history and related subjects. The titles of individual theses are cited under the appropriate subject headings below.

## PUBLISHED MATERIALS

### DOCUMENTS—UNITED STATES
Interstate Commerce Commission, *Statistics of Railways,* 1916, 1921, 1927.
United States Bureau of the Census. All of the decennial censuses for the period covered by this volume were useful, especially those dealing with agriculture, manufacturing, and population. Other special volumes that were helpful are:
*Tenth Census* (1880). Volumes on Social Statistics of Cities and on Statistics of Wages.
*Compendium of the Tenth Census* (1880). 2 volumes.
*Eleventh Census* (1890). Volume on Churches.
*Compendium of Eleventh Census* (1890). 3 volumes
*Twelfth Census* (1900). Special report on Occupations.
*Thirteenth Census* (1910). Volume on Mines and Quarries.
*Thirteenth Census* (1910), *Abstract, with Supplement for Indiana.*
*Fourteenth Census* (1920). Volume on Irrigation and Drainage.
The following special reports of the Bureau of the Census have been useful:
*Electric Industries, 1915, Telephones.*
*Fisheries of the United States, 1908.*
*Census of Manufactures, 1905* (4 vols.) ; *1914* (2 vols.).
*Mines and Quarries, 1902.*
*Negro Population, 1790-1915* (1918) ; *Negroes in the United States, 1920-32* (1935).
*Religious Bodies, 1906* (2 vols.), *1916* (2 vols.), *1926* (2 vols.).
*Telephones and Telegraphs, 1902.*
*Transportation by Water, 1906* and *1916.*
United States Congress, *Congressional Record,* 46th to 66th Congress.
————, *House Miscellaneous Documents,* 47 Congress, 2 session, No. 6. Report of Tariff Commission.
————, *Senate Reports,* 60 Congress, 1 session, No. 325. Report of Inland Waterways Commission.
————, *Senate Reports,* 61 Congress, 2 session, No. 645. Report on Condition of Women and Child Wage-Earners in the United States.
United States Department of Agriculture. *Bulletins, Circulars, Reports, Yearbooks.*

United States Department of Commerce, *Statistical Abstract,* 1920, 1922.
United States Department of Labor. *Bulletins, Reports.*
United States Geological Survey, *Mineral Resources of the United States,* 1882-1920.

## GOVERNMENT DOCUMENTS—INDIANA

Adjutant General, *Reports,* 1880-1914.
Agriculture, State Board of, *Reports,* 1880-1907.
Attorney General, *Reports,* 1880-1916; *Opinions,* 1917-1920.
Charities, Board of State, *Bulletin,* 1890-1920; *Reports,* 1891-1920.
Fisheries and Game, Commissioner of, *Reports,* 1881-1916.
Forestry, State Board of, *Reports,* 1901-1907.
General Assembly, *Brevier Legislative Reports,* 1881-1887.
————, *Documentary Journal,* 1880-1912. Usually two volumes a year. Includes messages of governors; reprieves and pardons granted by governors; reports of state offices and commissions; reports of state schools, state institutions, state prisons.
Geology and Natural History, Department of, *Reports,* 1881-1888.
Geology and Natural Resources, Department of, *Reports,* 1891-1916.
Health, State Board of, *Bulletins,* 1899-1920; *Reports,* 1882-1916.
Inspection, Department of, *Reports,* 1909-1916.
Labor Commission, *Reports,* 1899-1910.
Medical Registration and Examination, Board of, *Reports,* 1897-1916.
Mine Inspector, *Reports,* 1879-1890. Continued in *Reports* of Department of Geology and Natural Resources and then of Bureau of Inspection.
Pharmacy, Board of, *Reports,* 1899-1914 (1900-1906 in MS form).
Public Instruction, State Superintendent of, *Reports,* 1880-1916.
Public Library Commission, *Reports,* 1900-1920.
Public Service Commission, *Reports,* 1914-1915.
Railroad Commission, *Reports,* 1906-1912. Continued in *Reports* of Public Service Commission.
Secretary of State, *Reports,* 1880-1916.
Statistics, Department of, *Reports,* 1881-1916.
Statistics and Geology, Department of, *Reports,* 1879-1880.
Supreme Court, *Reports,* 1880-1920.
*Year Book,* 1917-1920. Contains reports of bureaus, departments, and offices formerly issued separately as well as reports of new departments such as Conservation and Highway.

## NEWSPAPERS

The largest collections of Indiana newspapers are found in the Indiana State Library and the Indiana University Library. The leading newspaper covering the entire period from 1880 to 1920 was the Indianapolis *News,* while the Republican *Journal* and the Democratic *Sentinel* of the same city were most useful for political events as seen from their respective partisan viewpoints. The Indianapolis *Star,* which purchased the *Journal* in 1904 and the *Sentinel* in 1906, was first Republican and then Progressive before returning to the allegiance of the GOP in 1916. The capital city had no newspaper fully committed to the Democratic party after 1906, though the *Sun,* later the *Times,* leaned in the direction of the Democracy.

Outside the capital the state's leading newspapers in this period included the Evansville *Courier,* Fort Wayne *Sentinel* and *Gazette,* Gary *Post,* Hammond *Lake County Times,* Muncie *Star,* New Albany *Ledger* and *Tribune,* South Bend *Tribune,* and the Terre Haute *Express, Star,* and *Tribune.* Newspapers of some of the smaller cities and towns include the Columbus *Republican,* Crown Point *Lake County Star,* Greencastle *Banner,* Greensburg *Weekly Review,* Rockport *Democrat,* Shoals *Referendum,* Versailles *Republican,* Vevay *Reveille,* and the Vincennes *Commercial* and *Western Sun.*

## GENERAL WORKS

Barnhart, John D., and Carmony, Donald F., *Indiana: From Frontier to Industrial Commonwealth* (4 vols. [vols. 3-4 biographical], New York, 1954).

Bowman, Heath, *Hoosier* (Indianapolis, 1941).

Carmony, Donald F. (ed.), *Indiana: A Self-Appraisal* (Indiana University Press, Bloomington, 1966).

Cottman, George S., *Centennial History and Handbook of Indiana* (Indianapolis, 1915).

Dunn, Jacob Piatt, *Indiana and Indianans: A History of Aboriginal and Territorial Indiana and the Century of Statehood* (5 vols. [vols. 3-5 biographical], Chicago and New York, 1919).

Esarey, Logan, *History of Indiana from Its Exploration to 1922* (Third edition, 2 vols., Fort Wayne, Ind., 1924).

*Indiana: A Guide to the Hoosier State (American Guide Series,* New York, 1941).

Levering, Julia, *Historic Indiana* . . . (New York, 1910).

Martin, John Bartlow, *Indiana: An Interpretation* (New York, 1947).

Roll, Charles, *Indiana: One Hundred and Fifty Years of American Development* (5 vols. [vols. 3-5 biographical], Chicago, 1931).

Smith, William Henry, *The History of the State of Indiana from the Earliest Explorations by the French to the Present Time* (2 vols., Indianapolis, 1903).

Thornbrough, Emma Lou, *Indiana in the Civil War Era, 1850-1880 (The History of Indiana,* Vol. III, Indianapolis, 1965).

Wilson, William E., *Indiana: A History* (Indiana University Press, Bloomington, 1966).

The *Indiana Historical Collections,* published by the Indiana Historical Bureau, and the Indiana Historical Society *Publications* include a number of scholarly works on aspects of the period from 1880 to 1920. The *Indiana History Bulletin,* published by the Bureau, is useful for the material on automobiles manufactured in Indiana.

The *Proceedings* of the Indiana Academy of Science, beginning in 1891, are valuable for biographical material, as well as for articles on the various sciences.

The *Indiana Magazine of History,* a quarterly published by the Department of History of Indiana University in co-operation with the Indiana Historical Society, is the most important journal for the publication of scholarly articles on Indiana history. Research embodied in articles has been most helpful in the writing of this volume, and numerous articles published in the *Magazine* are cited. There are composite indexes covering Volumes 1-25 and 26-50, and indexes by volume beginning with Volume 51.

### City, County, and Regional Histories

The most recent compilation of Indiana county histories is that contained in *Aids for Genealogical Searching in Indiana,* by Carolynne L. Wendel (Detroit Society for Genealogical Research, 1962). Many of these histories were published in the 1880's, but a number of county and city histories appeared in the early years of the twentieth century. Though sometimes uncritical and overly laudatory, they contain biographical information and material on social, economic, and cultural developments not found elsewhere. There is a complete collection of these histories in the Indiana Division of the Indiana State Library. The Division also has a complete collection of Indianapolis city directories beginning in 1869 as well as directories from the other principal cities of the state.

The most noteworthy of the city histories are those by Jacob P. Dunn, *Greater Indianapolis* . . . (2 vols., Chicago, 1910); Max Hyman, *Hyman's Hand Book of Indianapolis* (Indianapolis, 1897); Frederick D. Kershner, A Social and Cultural History of Indianapolis, 1860-1914 (Unpublished Ph.D. thesis in History, University of Wisconsin, 1950); Jeannette C. Nolan, *Hoosier City: The Story of Indianapolis* (New York, 1943); Kate Milner Rabb and William Herschell, *An Account of Indianapolis and Marion County* (Vols. III and IV of Logan Esarey, *History of Indiana* . . . [Dayton, Ohio, 1924]); Robert R. Drummond, Terre Haute, A City of Non-Growth (Unpublished Ph.D. thesis, Northwestern University, 1953); Bert J. Griswold, *The Pictorial History of Fort Wayne Indiana* (2 vols., Chicago, 1917); James E. Morlock, *The Evansville Story: A Cultural Interpretation,* Evansville, Ind. 1956).

The principal regional histories are those concerned with the Calumet area: Timothy H. Ball, *Northwestern Indiana from 1800 to 1900* (1900); *The Calumet Region Historical Guide* (1939); and Powell Moore, *The Calumet Region* (1959).

### Biographical Materials

GENERAL. *Encyclopedia of Biography of Indiana* (2 vols., Chicago, 1895, 1899); Charity Dye, *Some Torch Bearers in Indiana* (Indianapolis, 1917);

Francis M. Trissal, *Public Men of Indiana* (2 vols., Hammond, Ind., 1923). In the Indiana Division of the Indiana State Library are the Indiana Biographical Series, a compilation of newspaper clippings, and the George S. Cottman Collection of newspaper clippings. Indexes to both of these collections as well as other biographical material are included in the card file of Indiana Biography in the Indiana Division.

POLITICAL. Claude Bowers has written a classic biography of an outstanding Hoosier politician in *Beveridge and the Progressive Era* (Cambridge, Mass., 1932). It should be supplemented, however, by John Braeman's scholarly Albert Beveridge: From Imperialism to Progressivism (Unpublished Ph.D. thesis in History, Johns Hopkins University, 1960) and the same author's articles in the *Indiana Magazine of History*, LIII (1957), 355-382, and LX (1964), 1-36. Bowers, who also wrote *The Life of John Worth Kern* (Indianapolis, 1918), described his own early political career in Indiana in his autobiography, *My Life. The Memoirs of Claude Bowers* (New York, 1962). McAlister Coleman, *Eugene V. Debs. A Man Unafraid* (New York, 1930) and Floy R. Painter, *That Man Debs and His Life Work* (Bloomington, Ind., 1929) are early biographies of the Socialist leader, but a later work by Ray Ginger, *The Bending Cross. A Biography of Eugene V. Debs* (Rutgers University Press, 1949) is more authoritative. David A. Shannon, Anti-war Thought and Activities of Eugene V. Debs, 1914-1921 (Unpublished Master's thesis in History, University of Wisconsin, 1947), covers well that specific topic and period. There is no definitive published work on Charles W. Fairbanks. William Henry Smith wrote the uncritical campaign biography, *The Life and Speeches of Hon. Charles Warren Fairbanks* (Indianapolis, 1904), while Herbert Rissler is the author of a penetrating study, Charles Warren Fairbanks: Conservative Hoosier (Unpublished Ph.D. thesis in History, Indiana University, 1961).

William Dudley Foulke published two accounts of his own career, *Fighting the Spoilsmen. Reminiscences of the Civil Service Reform Movement* (New York, 1919) and *A Hoosier Autobiography* (New York, 1922), as well as a eulogistic life of his close friend and fellow reformer, *Lucius B. Swift. A Biography* (Indianapolis, 1930). Martha Alice Tyner, The Political Career of Walter Quintin Gresham (Unpublished Master's thesis in History, Indiana University, 1933) and her article in *Indiana Magazine of History*, XXIX, 297-338, add little to Matilda Gresham's *Life of Walter Quintin Gresham, 1832-1895* (2 vols., Chicago, 1919). There is no definitive biography of Governor Hanly, though Leslie Ward Carson's The Life of J. Frank Hanly: Log Cabin Boy to Governor (Unpublished Master's thesis in History, University of Illinois, 1928) is a useful though somewhat uncritical study. Harry J. Sievers, S. J., has completed the last two volumes of his detailed, heavily documented biography of Indiana's only President of the United States, *Benjamin Harrison, Hoosier Statesman, From the Civil War to the White House, 1865-1888* (New York, 1959) and *Benjamin Harrison, Hoosier President, The White House Years and After, 1889-1901* (Indianapolis, 1968). Will H. Hays tells something of his political career in Indiana in the first part of *The Memoirs of Will H. Hays* (New York, 1955), which is also partly the subject of Garland C. Routt, Will

Hays: A Study in Political Leadership and Management (Unpublished Master's thesis in Political Science, University of Chicago, 1937).

The only extended account of the Indiana governor who was twice the Democratic vice-presidential candidate is the uncritical John W. Holcombe and Hubert M. Skinner, *Life and Public Services of Thomas A. Hendricks* (Indianapolis, 1886). A less-known Hoosier politician, Republican Congressman William S. Holman, is the subject of the last part of Israel George Blake, *The Holmans of Veraestau* (Oxford, Ohio, 1943). The biography of Julian by his daughter, Grace Julian Clarke, *George W. Julian* (Indianapolis, 1923) has been largely superseded by Patrick W. Riddleberger, *George Washington Julian. Radical Republican* (Indianapolis, 1966). The witty but disorganized *Recollections of Thomas R. Marshall, Vice-President and Hoosier Philosopher. A Hoosier Salad* (Indianapolis, 1925) needs to be supplemented at almost every point by the scholarly Charles M. Thomas, *Thomas Riley Marshall, Hoosier Statesman* (Oxford, Ohio, 1939). Treating a critical point in Governor Marshall's career are Lawrence M. Bowman, Stepping Stone to the Vice Presidency: A Story of Thomas Riley Marshall's 1908 Gubernatorial Victory (Unpublished Master's thesis in History, University of Kansas, 1967) and Keith S. Montgomery, "Thomas R. Marshall's Victory in the Election of 1908," *Indiana Magazine of History,* LIII (1957), 147-166.

H. S. K. Bartholomew is the author of brief sketches of two minor political figures: "Governor Claude Matthews," *Indiana Magazine of History,* XXVI (1930), 271-278, and "The Political Career of Benjamin F. Shively," *ibid.,* XXVIII (1932), 251-268. The only attempt at a full-scale biography of Thomas Taggart is the interesting but one-sided account by his private secretary, Alva C. Sallee, T. T. The Master Mind that Wrought Brilliant and Bewildering Achievements in Political Legerdemain (Typed MS, undated, in Indiana State Library), though his business career is partly treated in Richard W. Haupt, History of the French Lick Springs Hotel (Unpublished Master's thesis in History, Indiana University, 1953). Two autobiographical accounts by United States Senators are David Turpie's *Sketches of My Own Times* (Indianapolis, 1903) and James E. Watson's *As I Knew Them* (Indianapolis, 1936). Besides Leonard S. Kenworthy, *The Tall Sycamore of the Wabash: Daniel Wolsey Voorhees* (Boston, 1936), another study of Senator Voorhees is Forrest L. Seal, The Oratory of Senator Daniel W. Voorhees of Indiana (Unpublished Ph.D. thesis in Speech, Purdue University, 1954). An Indiana-born politician-diplomat is the subject of Frances Marie Phillips, John Watson Foster, 1836-1917 (Unpublished Ph.D. thesis in History, University of New Mexico, 1956).

MISCELLANEOUS. Several autobiographies shed some light on this period, including Jay Allen, *Autobiography* (Philadelphia, 1910); Frank Clayton Ball, *Memoirs* (Muncie, Ind., 1937); Maurice Francis Egan, *Recollections of a Happy Life* (New York, 1924); Daniel Fisher, *A Human Life: An Autobiography with Excursuses* (New York, 1909), Alexander Johnson, *Adventures in Social Work* (Fort Wayne, 1923); David Starr Jordan, *The Days of a Man* . . . (2 vols., New York, 1922); Millard F. Kennedy, *Schoolmaster of Yesterday: A Three-Generation Story* (New York, 1940); J. A. Lemcke, *Reminiscences of an Indianian* . . . (Indianapolis, 1905); Elbert Russell, *Elbert Russell, Quaker. An*

*Autobiography* (Jackson, Tenn., 1956); Theodore Stempfel, Sr., *Ghosts of the Past: Autobiographical Sketches* (Indianapolis, 1935); and Harvey W. Wiley, *An Autobiography* (Indianapolis, 1930).

Useful secondary accounts of the lives of businessmen are Jane Fisher's biography of her husband Carl G. Fisher, *Fabulous Hoosier. A Story of American Achievement* (New York, 1947); Gavin Dalglish's eulogy of a Batesville furniture manufacturer, *Of This Heritage. The Biography of John A. Hillenbrand* (n. p., 1954); Emma Lieber, *Richard Lieber* ([Indianapolis], 1947); Milton Rubincam, "David M. Parry," *Indiana Magazine of History,* XXXIV (1938), 165-174; and Edwin Corle, *John Studebaker: An American Dream* (New York, 1948). Two scholarly manuscripts dealing with important industrial leaders are Richard H. Gemmecke, W. G. Irwin and Hugh Thomas Miller. A Study in Free Enterprise in Indiana (Unpublished Ph.D. thesis in History, Indiana University, 1955); Douglas L. Meikle, James Oliver and the Oliver Chilled Plow Works (Unpublished Ph.D. thesis in History, Indiana University, 1958). Studies of educators include Emma Lou Thornbrough, *Eliza A. Blaker. Her Life and Work* (Indianapolis, 1956); John G. Coulter's biography of his brother, Stanley Coulter, *The Dean. An Account of His Career and His Contributions* (Lafayette, Ind., 1940); Edward McNall Burns, *David Starr Jordan: Prophet of Freedom* (Stanford, Calif., 1953); H. S. K. Bartholomew, "Virginia C. Meredith," *Indiana Magazine of History,* XXXV (1939), 49-57; Vernon F. Schwalm, *Otho Winger 1877-1946* (Elgin, Ill., 1952); and Ralph E. Weber, *Notre Dame's John Zahm. American Catholic Apologist and Educator* (Notre Dame, Ind., 1961).

## POLITICAL HISTORY

The general history of the two major parties for part of the period 1880-1920 is covered from a partisan point of view in Russell M. Seeds, *History of the Republican Party of Indiana* (Indianapolis, 1899), and John B. Stoll, *History of the Indiana Democracy, 1816-1916* (Indianapolis, 1917). There is also a small pamphlet, *Greenback Party History in Brief 1875-1952* (Indianapolis, 1952). More critical are William G. Carleton, "Why Was the Democratic Party in Indiana a Radical Party, 1865-1890?" *Indiana Magazine of History,* XLII (1946), 207-228; Ora Ellen Cox, "Socialist Party in Indiana since 1896," *ibid.,* XII (1916), 95-130; Carl Painter, "The Progressive Party in Indiana," *ibid.,* XVI (1920), 173-283; Ernest C. Stewart, "The Populist Party in Indiana," *ibid.,* XIV (1918), 332-367, XV (1919), 53-74; and Arthur J. Rhoads, The Populist Movement in Indiana (Unpublished Master's thesis in History, Indiana University, 1955).

William E. Henry (comp.), *State Platforms of the Two Dominant Political Parties in Indiana, 1850-1900* (Indianapolis, 1902), is useful for the period covered, while party platforms for later years are found in the Indianapolis newspapers and in the Indiana *Year Book,* 1917-1920. Other works are Charles Kettleborough (ed.), *Constitution Making in Indiana . . .* (3 vols., Indianapolis, 1916, 1930); Robert J. Pitchell (ed.), *Indiana Votes: Election Returns for Governor, 1852-1956, and Senator, 1914-1958* (Bureau of Government Research, Indiana University, 1960); and William A. Rawles, *Centralizing Tendencies in the Administration of Indiana* (New York, 1903). General interpretations of Indiana politics include John H. Fenton, *Midwest Politics* (New York, 1966), Frank Munger, Two-Party Politics in the State of Indiana (Unpublished Ph.D. thesis in Government, Harvard University, 1955), and V. O. Key, Jr., and Frank Munger, "Social Determinism and Electoral Decision," in Eugene Burdick and Arthur J. Brodbeck (eds.), *American Voting Behavior* (Glencoe, Ill., 1959). Also useful for specific aspects are Robert D. Seltzer, Rotten Boroughism in Indiana (Unpublished Ph.D. thesis in Government, Indiana University, 1952) and articles in the *Indiana Magazine of History* by A. Dale Beeler, R. C. Buley, William G. Carleton, Albert V. House, Robert LaFollette, H. Wayne Morgan, Charles F. Remy, and Paul T. Smith.

A large number of pamphlets were published on political controversies of the times. Some of the more significant were Charles H. Bliss (ed.), *The Populist Compendium: References for Reformers* (Auburn, Ind., 1894); William D. Bynum, *A Revenue vs. A Protective Tariff* (Indianapolis, 1884); Simeon Coy, *The Great Conspiracy. A Complete History of the Famous Talley-Sheet Cases* (Indianapolis, 1889); Jacob P. Dunn, *The World's Silver Question* (Indianapolis, 1894); William P. Fishback, *A Plea for Honest Elections* (Indianapolis, 1886); Charles H. McCarer, *The Gerrymander* . . . (Indianapolis, 1886); R. S. Robertson, *The Indiana Rebellion of 1887: The Case of the Lieutenant-Governor* (n. p., 1887); Newell H. Motsinger, *The Way Out. A Mathematical Solution of Labor, Capital, Money and Trusts* (Shoals, Ind., 1899). Besides the official *Report of the Monetary Commission of the Indianapolis Convention* (University of Chicago Press, 1898), there are arguments for and against the Commission's work in Russel M. Seeds, The Story of a Great Movement (Unpublished MS, 1900, in Indiana State Library) and Flavius J. Van Vorhis, *The Currency Trust Conspiracy* (Indianapolis, 1910).

Collected political addresses include Albert J. Beveridge, *The Meaning of the Times* (Indianapolis, 1907); George B. Lockwood (comp.), *Public Addresses and State Papers of Governor J. Frank Hanly of Indiana* (Marion, Ind., 1906); George W. Julian, *Later Speeches on Political Questions with Select Controversial Papers,* edited by Grace Julian Clarke (Indianapolis, 1889); Harriet C. Voorhees (ed.), *Forty Years of Oratory. Daniel Wolsey Voorhees: Lectures, Addresses and Speeches* (2 vols., Indianapolis, 1897).

On the temperance issue in politics there are two valuable compilations, Harold C. Feightner, Wet and Dry Legislation in Indiana (1790-1957) (2 vols., mimeographed [Indianapolis, 1957]) and Frank A. Horner, *Horner's Treatise on the Liquor Laws of Indiana* (Indianapolis, 1900), as well as the narrative by Charles E. Canup, "Temperance Movements and Legislation in Indiana," *Indiana Magazine of History,* XVI (1920), 3-37, 112-151. Also useful are the *Minutes* and *Annual Reports* of the Indiana Women's Christian Temperance Union, 1874-1920, and such pamphlets as Michael W. Carr, *A Criticism of Fanatical Temperance* (Indianapolis, 1895) and Eli F. Ritter, *Prohibition Party in Indiana: The Necessity for Separate Political Organization* (Indianapolis, 1884).

## Economic History

Brief accounts of general economic developments are contained in Frances Doan Streightoff and Frank H. Streightoff, *Indiana. A Social and Economic Survey* (Indianapolis, 1916), and Stephen S. Visher, *Economic Geography of Indiana* (New York, 1923).

## Transportation

An indispensable source of information on railroads is Henry V. Poor (comp.), *Manual of the Railroads of the United States* (New York), 1880-1920. The *Annual Reports* of the major railroad systems are also useful.

The following are secondary accounts of steam railroads: John W. Barriger, *A Hoosier Centenarian "The Monon"* (New York, 1947); George H. Burgess and Miles C. Kennedy, *Centennial History of the Pennsylvania Railroad Company, 1846-1946* (Philadelphia, 1949); Carlton J. Corliss, *Main Line of Mid-America. The Story of the Illinois Central* (New York, 1950); Taylor Hampton, *The Nickel Plate Road* (Cleveland, 1947); Frank P. Hargrave, *A Pioneer Indiana Railroad. The Origin and Development of the Monon* (Indianapolis, 1932); Alvin F. Harlow, *The Road of the Century. The Story of the New York Central* (New York, 1947); W. T. Hicks, Indianapolis Southern Railroad (Unpublished MS, 1911, in Indiana University Library); Edward Hungerford, *Men of Erie. A Story of Human Effort* (New York, 1946); Edward Hungerford, *The Story of the Baltimore & Ohio Railroad, 1827-1927* (2 vols., New York, 1928); Ared Maurice Murphy, "The Big Four Railroad in Indiana," *Indiana Magazine of History,* XXI (1925), 109-273; John A. Rehor, *The Nickel Plate Story* (Milwaukee, Wis., 1965); Howard W. Schotter, *The Growth and Development of the Pennsylvania Railroad Company* (Philadelphia, 1927); Robert F. Smith, *From the Ohio to the Mississippi* (Cincinnati, Ohio, 1965); Earle Steele, *The Chicago & Atlantic Railway Company. Forty-third Anniversary, 1883-1926* (Huntington, Ind., 1926); and Charles W. Turner, *Chessie's Road* (Richmond, Va., 1956).

Street and electric railways are treated in Glen A. Blackburn, "Interurban Railroads of Indiana," *Indiana Magazine of History,* XX (1924), 400-464; George K. Bradley, *Fort Wayne's Trolleys, 1870-1963* (Chicago, 1963); George K. Bradley, *The Northern Indiana Railways* (Electric Railway Historical Society, *Bulletin 6,* Chicago, 1953); David W. Chambers, *The Lafayette Street Railway* (Electric Railway Historical Society, *Bulletin 32,* Chicago, 1958); Robert M. Haley, The American Electric Railway Interurban (Unpublished Ph.D. thesis in Economics, Northwestern University, 1936); Fred B. Hiatt, "Development of Interurbans in Indiana," *Indiana Magazine of History,* V (1909), 122-130; and Jerry Marlette, *Electric Railroads of Indiana* (Indianapolis, 1959).

*A Short History of the Indiana State Highway Commission,* by J. M. Henry (Indianapolis, 1926), traces the early history of that agency.

## Natural Resources

The best single guide to Indiana's natural resources in this period is William N. Logan *et al., Handbook of Indiana Geology* (Indiana Department of Conservation, *Publication No. 21,* 1922). Other useful publications are William N. Logan, *Petroleum and Natural Gas in Indiana: A Preliminary Survey* (Indiana Department of Conservation, *Publication No. 8,* 1920) and Charles H. Parrish, *Natural Resources of Indiana: A Survey* (Department of Conservation, *Publication No. 16,* 1921).

Special subjects are covered in Joseph A. Batchelor, *An Economic History of the Indiana Oolitic Limestone Industry* (Indiana University *Studies in Business, No. 27,* Bloomington, 1944); William Edward Bean, The Soft Coal Industry of Southern Indiana (Unpublished A.B. thesis in Economics, Indiana University, 1922); Osmond LaVar Harline, Economics of the Indiana Coal Mining Industry (Unpublished Ph.D. thesis in Economics, Indiana University, 1958); C. C. Lydick, Natural Gas in Indiana (MS, 1946, in Indiana State Library); Oliver C. Lockhart, *The Oolitic Limestone Industry of Indiana* (Indiana University *Studies, No. 9,* Bloomington, 1910); Katherine D. Schakel, Some Aspects of Coal Mining in Indiana (Unpublished Master's thesis in History, Butler University, 1934).

Extremely valuable for the conservation movement is Robert A. Frederick, Colonel Richard Lieber, Conservationist and Park Builder: The Indiana Years (Unpublished Ph.D. thesis in History, Indiana University, 1960).

### AGRICULTURE

In addition to the publications of the United States Bureau of the Census and the Department of Agriculture, the *Annual Reports* of the Indiana State Board of Agriculture, the Indiana Corn Growers Association, and similar societies, the *Proceedings* of the Indiana State Grange, the *Transactions* of the Indiana Horticultural Society, and the various *Bulletins* and other publications of the Agricultural Experiment Station and the Extension Division of Purdue University are particularly useful.

The only general survey is William Latta, *Outline History of Indiana Agriculture* (Lafayette, Ind., 1938), which contains much valuable information organized in a rather unsystematic fashion. An extremely valuable work is Stephen S. Visher, *The Climate of Indiana* (Indiana University Publications, Science Series No. 13, Bloomington, 1944). Two pamphlets prepared for the Columbian Exposition of 1893 are John B. Conner, *Agricultural Resources and Development of the State* (Indianapolis, 1893) and Virginia C. Meredith, *A Monograph on the Live Stock of the State of Indiana* (Indianapolis, 1893). Studies of specific aspects of farm organization or technology are Robert H. Bahmer, "The American Society of Equity," *Agricultural History,* XIV (1940), 33-63; Dudley D. Davis, The History of the Indiana Farm Bureau Cooperative Association (Unpublished Master's thesis, Butler University, 1941); Donald P. Greene, Prairie Agricultural Technology 1860-1900 (Unpublished Ph.D. thesis in History, Indiana University, 1957); James A. Everitt, *The Third Power: Farmers to the Front* (Indianapolis, 1903); Dave O. Thompson, *A History: Fifty Years of Cooperative Extension Service in Indiana* (Lafayette, Ind., 1962); Paul Turner, *They Did It in Indiana: The Story of the Indiana Farm Bureau Co-operatives* (New York, 1947).

MANUFACTURING

George W. Starr, *Industrial Development of Indiana* (Indiana University *Studies in Business, No. 14,* Bloomington, 1937), is a general study of manufacturing which needs to be supplemented by George D. King, The Industrialization of Indiana, 1860-1920 (Unpublished Ph.D. thesis in History, Indiana University, 1963).

Aspects of the glass industry are treated in William E. Aiken, *The Roots Grow Deep* (Cleveland, Ohio, 1957) and Ruth Herrick, *Greentown Glass. The Indiana Tumbler and Goblet Company and Allied Manufacturers* (Grand Rapids, Mich., 1959). The iron and steel industry is the subject of John B. Appleton, *The Iron and Steel Industry of the Calumet District. A Study in Economic Geography* (University of Illinois *Studies in the Social Sciences,* XIII, No. 2, Urbana, 1927); Alden Cutshall, "Terre Haute Iron and Steel: A Declining Industry," *Indiana Magazine of History,* XXXVII (1941), 237-244; and Howard A. Knox, "Development of the American Tin Plate Industry," *The Iron Age,* October-December, 1943. Significant studies of the automobile industry include Howard R. DeLancy, The History of the Cole Motor Car Company (Unpublished D.B.A. thesis in Business, Indiana University, 1954) and the same author's "The Cole Motor Car Company," *Business History Review* (Boston), XXX (1956), 260-273; Wallace S. Huffman's three articles in the *Indiana History Bulletin,* XXXVIII (1961), 143-168; XLI (1964), 195-202; XLIV (1967), 9-44; William C. Oursler, *From Ox-Carts to Jets. Roy Ingersoll and the Borg-Warner Story: A Biography* (Englewood Cliffs, N. J., 1959); Joseph S. Powell, History of Elwood Haynes and the Automobile Industry (Unpublished Master's thesis in History, Indiana University, 1948); as well as a trio of books on the Studebaker Corporation: Albert R. Erskine, *History of the Studebaker Corporation* (South Bend, Ind., 1924); Stephen Longstreet, *A Century on Wheels. The Story of Studebaker, 1852-1952* (New York, 1952); and Kathleen Ann Smallzreid and Dorothy J. Roberts, *More Than You Promise. A Business At Work in Society* (New York, 1942).

Paul H. Giddens, *Standard Oil Company (Indiana). Oil Pioneer of the Middle West* (New York, 1955) is a definitive account. Studies of individual companies are Roscoe C. Clark, *Threescore Years and Ten. A Narrative of the First Seventy Years of Eli Lilly and Company, 1876-1946* (n. p., 1946) and Fred C. Kelly's story of the Commercial Solvents Company of Terre Haute, *One Thing Leads to Another: The Growth of an Industry* (New York, 1936). Brief accounts of other manufacturing companies are found in the pamphlets, *Berghoff Brewing Corporation* (Fort Wayne, 1940), *Fort Wayne Corrugated Paper Company. Forty Years of Container Making* (Chicago, 1949), *Nordyke & Marmon Company: An Institution. A History of the Development of a Leading Indianapolis Industry* (n. p., 1920), and Douglas A. Fisher, *Steel Serves the Nation, 1901-1951. The Fifty Year Story of United States Steel* (n. p., 1951).

LABOR

Important documents of the labor movements are the *Proceedings* and other publications of the Knights of Labor, the Central Labor Union of Indianapolis, and the Indiana Federation of Labor. Two articles on the formation of the last-named organization are Hugh Gormley, "Indiana: A Union State," *American Federationist,* LV, No. 6 (June, 1948), and Ralph W. Van Valer, "The Indiana State Federation of Labor," *Indiana Magazine of History,* XI (1915), 40-58. Useful accounts of individual labor unions include Chris Evans, *History of the United Mine Workers of America* . . . (2 vols., n. p., n. d.) ; Ellsworth Steele, "The Flint Glass Workers' Union in the Indiana Gas Belt and the Ohio Valley in the 1890's," *Indiana Magazine of History,* L (1954), 227-250; and George A. Tracy (comp.), *History of the Typographical Union* (Indianapolis, 1913). Dealing with labor disturbances are Louis Adamic, *Dynamite. The Story of Class Violence in America* (New York, 1931) ; William J. Burns, *The Masked War* (New York, 1913) ; William Z. Foster, *The Great Steel Strike and Its Lessons* (New York, 1920) ; Ortie E. McManigal, *The National Dynamite Plot* (Los Angeles, 1913).

The following are studies on labor legislation: Jay B. Kennedy, Protective Labor Legislation in Indiana (Unpublished Ph.D. thesis, Indiana University, 1961) ; Carl H. Mote, *Industrial Arbitration* . . . (Indianapolis, 1916) ; Charles Emery Reed, Factory Inspection (Unpublished A.B. thesis, Indiana University, 1912) ; S. W. Schaefer, Protective Labor Legislation in Indiana (Unpublished A.B. thesis, Indiana University, 1911) ; Ben F. Small, *Workmen's Compensation Law of Indiana* (Indianapolis, 1950) ; and Fred Witney, *Indiana Labor Relations Law* (*Indiana Business Report No. 30,* Bloomington, 1960).

## POPULATION

The only general study of immigration in this period is Robert R. LaFollette, "Foreigners and Their Influence on Indiana," *Indiana Magazine of History,* XXV (1929), 14-27. There are a few significant works on the German element, including Vonneda Dunn Bailey, The Germans in Indiana, with Economic Emphasis (Unpublished Master's thesis in Economics, Indiana University, 1946) ; Fred J. Bartel, *The Institutional Influence of the German Element of the Population in Richmond, Indiana* (Wayne County Historical Society *Papers,* I, No. 2, Richmond, 1905) ; William A. Fritsch, *German Settlers and German Settlements in Indiana* (Evansville, 1915) ; and Theodore G. Probst, The Germans in Indianapolis, 1850-1914 (Unpublished Master's thesis in History, Indiana University, 1951). Also useful is Myra Auerbach, A Study of the Jewish Settlement in Indianapolis (Unpublished Master's thesis in Economics and Sociology, Indiana University, 1937).

On the Negro John W. Lyda has written the brief sketch, *The Negro in the History of Indiana* (Terre Haute, 1953), which has been superseded for the period up to 1900 by Emma Lou Thornbrough, *The Negro in Indiana. A Study of a Minority* (Indianapolis, 1957). The latter author has also brought the story down to 1963 in *Since Emancipation. A Short History of Indiana Negroes, 1863-1963* (Indiana Division, American Negro Emancipation Centennial Authority [1963]). Two studies deal with the movement of white population: James V. Chittick, The Greater Indiana: A Study of the Movement of Hoosiers to Other States (Unpublished Master's thesis in History, Indiana University, 1940), and Robert R. LaFollette, "Interstate Migration and Indiana Culture," *Mississippi Valley Historical Review,* XVI (1929-30), 347-358.

## EDUCATION

The best study of education for the period up to its date of publication is Richard G. Boone, *A History of Education in Indiana* (New York, 1892, reprinted by Indiana Historical Bureau, Indianapolis, 1941). It is supplemented by Fassett A. Cotton's pamphlet prepared for the Louisiana Purchase Exposition entitled *Education in Indiana: An Outline of the Growth of the Common School System* (Indianapolis, 1904) and his expanded version, *Education in Indiana (1793 to 1934)* (Bluffton, Ind., 1934).

PUBLIC SCHOOLS. The published *Reports* of the State Superintendent of Public Instruction and of the Indianapolis and other municipal school boards contain useful information. Accounts of various aspects of public education are found in the following: C. Ross Dean, The Development of State Control of Secondary Education in Indiana (Unpublished Ph.D. thesis in Education, Indiana University, 1947); Frances H. Ellis, "German Instruction in the Public Schools of Indianapolis, 1869-1919," *Indiana Magazine of History*, L (1954), 119-138, 251-276, 357-380; Oscar Findley, *Development of the High School in Indiana* (n. p., 1925); Roy R. Roudebush, School Consolidation in Indiana (Unpublished Master's thesis in Education, Indiana University, 1927); William O. Lynch, "The Great Awakening: A Chapter in the Educational History of Indiana," *Indiana Magazine of History*, XLI (1945), 107-130. A critical summary of the public school system at the end of this period is found in Indiana Education Survey Commission, *Public Education in Indiana* (New York, 1923).

The Gary school system is the subject of a large number of books, including William P. Burris, *The Public School System of Gary, Ind.* (United States Bureau of Education, *Bulletin No. 18,* 1914); A. H. Bell, *The Work-Study-Play Program* (Columbus, Ohio, 1932); Randolph S. Bourne, *The Gary Schools* (Boston, 1916); Roscoe D. Case, *The Platoon School in America* (Stanford, Calif., 1931); John and Evelyn Dewey, *Schools for Tomorrow* (New York, 1915); Charles R. Richards, *The Gary Public Schools, Industrial Work* (New York, 1918).

PRIVATE SCHOOLS. Besides the catalogues and bulletins of various individual schools, a good collection of which is found in the Indiana State Library, the following secondary accounts are useful: Elizabeth Denehie, "Catholic Education in Indiana: Past and Present," *Indiana Magazine of History*, XII (1916), 337-350; Raymond W. Elliott, The History of Fairmount Academy (Unpublished Master's thesis, Indiana University, n. d.); Sister M. Salesia Godecker, *History of Catholic Education in Indiana: A Survey of the Schools, 1702-1925* (St. Meinrad, Ind., 1926); Sadie Bacon Hatcher, *A History of Spiceland Academy, 1826-1921* (Indianapolis, 1934); Ethel Hittle McDaniel, *The Contribution of the Society of Friends to Education in Indiana* (Indianapolis, 1939); Albert Mock, The Academy Movement in Indiana from 1850 to 1900 (MS, 1933, in Indiana State Library); James C. Standiford, A History of Borden Institute (Unpublished Master's thesis, Butler University, 1933); John H. Thomas, "The Academies of Indiana," *Indiana Magazine of History*, X (1914), 331-358; XI (1915), 8-39.

HIGHER EDUCATION. The only general study is James A. Woodburn, *Higher Education in Indiana* (United States Bureau of Education, *Circular of*

*Information No. 1,* 1891). Catalogues, bulletins, and other publications of the colleges and universities contain useful information, many of which are in the Indiana State Library collection. Individual institutions represented by full-scale histories are as follows:

BUTLER COLLEGE. By Thomas Benton Fields (Unpublished Master's thesis in Education, Indiana University, 1928).

DEPAUW UNIVERSITY. By William W. Sweet (New York, 1937) and by George B. Manhart (2 vols., Greencastle, Ind., 1962).

EARLHAM COLLEGE. By Opal Thornburg (Richmond, Ind., 1963).

FRANKLIN COLLEGE. By John F. Cady (Franklin, Ind., 1934).

GOSHEN COLLEGE. By John Sylvanus Umble (Scottdale, Pa., 1955).

HANOVER COLLEGE. By William A. Millis (Hanover, Ind., 1927).

INDIANA CENTRAL COLLEGE. By Russell E. Vance, Jr. (n. p., 1955).

INDIANA DENTAL COLLEGE. By Jack D. Carr (Unpublished Master's thesis in Education, Butler University, 1957).

INDIANA STATE NORMAL SCHOOL. By William O. Lynch (Terre Haute, Ind., 1946).

INDIANA UNIVERSITY. By Theophilus A. Wylie (Indianapolis, 1890) ; by James A. Woodburn and Burton D. Myers (2 vols., Bloomington, Ind., 1940, 1952) ; by Cynthia Baxter (Unpublished Master's thesis in History, Indiana University, 1953).

MANCHESTER COLLEGE. By Ira H. Frantz (ed.) (Elgin, Ill., 1964).

MOORES HILL COLLEGE (Evansville College). By John W. Winkley (Evansville, Ind., 1954).

PURDUE UNIVERSITY. By William M. Hepburn and Louis M. Sears (Indianapolis, 1925) ; by H. B. Knoll (West Lafayette, Ind., 1963).

NOTRE DAME UNIVERSITY. By Arthur J. Hope, C.S.J. (Notre Dame, Ind., 1943).

SAINT MARY'S COLLEGE. By Marion McCandless (Notre Dame, Ind., 1952).

TRI-STATE COLLEGE. By Alice A. Parrott (Angola, Ind. 1959).

UNION CHRISTIAN COLLEGE. By James W. Conlin (Unpublished Master's thesis in Education, Indiana University, 1931).

VALPARAISO UNIVERSITY, By John Streitelmeier (Valparaiso, Ind. 1959).

WABASH COLLEGE. By James I. Osborne and Theodore G. Gronert (Crawfordsville, Ind., 1932).

LIBRARIES. Jacob P. Dunn prepared a short monograph for the Columbian Exposition, *The Libraries of Indiana* (Indianapolis, 1893). A somewhat more extensive work is William E. Henry, *Municipal and Institutional Libraries of Indiana* . . . (n. p., 1904), written for the Louisiana Purchase Exposition. Two useful theses are Thomas Hunt, Origins and Development of the Indianapolis Public Library, 1873-1899 (Unpublished Master's thesis, University of Kentucky, 1956) and LaVern Walther, Legal and Governmental Aspects of Public Library Development in Indiana, 1816-1953 (Unpublished Ph.D. thesis in Education, Indiana University, 1957).

## RELIGION

Church records for various denominations are found in the Indiana State Library and in the archives of several educational institutions,

# BIBLIOGRAPHY

including Christian Theological Seminary (Disciples), DePauw University (Methodist), Earlham College (Society of Friends), Franklin College (Baptist), Goshen College (Mennonite), and the University of Notre Dame (Roman Catholic). Denominational journals also contain useful information.

Secondary accounts of religious institutions are available for many denominations represented in the state, as indicated below:

ROMAN CATHOLIC. The basic work though old is Charles Blanchard (ed.), *History of the Catholic Church in Indiana* (2 vols., Logansport, Ind., 1898). Herman J. Alerding is the author of both *A History of the Catholic Church in the Diocese of Vincennes* (1885) and *The Diocese of Fort Wayne 1856—September 22, 1907* . . . (Fort Wayne, 1907). A later pamphlet is Humbert P. Pagani, *200 Years of Catholicism in Indiana: An Authentic History of the Diocese of Indianapolis, formerly the Diocese of Vincennes* (Indianapolis, 1934). The life of a distinguished journalist-prelate is related in Richard Ginder, *With Ink and Crozier. A Biography of John Francis Noll, Fifth Bishop of Fort Wayne and Founder of Our Sunday Visitor* (Huntington, 1952). The following are accounts of individual institutions and orders: Sister Mary Borromeo Brown, *The History of the Sisters of Providence of Saint Mary of the Woods* (New York, 1949); Mother M. Clarissa and Sister Mary Olivia, *With the Poverello: History of the Sisters of Saint Francis, Oldenburg, Indiana* (New York, 1948); Sister M. Eleanore, *On the King's Highway: A History of the Sisters of the Holy Cross of St. Mary of the Immaculate Conception, Notre Dame, Indiana* (New York, 1931); and Albert Kleber, *History of St. Meinrad Archabbey, 1854-1954* (St. Meinrad, Ind., 1954).

DISCIPLES OF CHRIST. Commodore Wesley Cauble's *Disciples of Christ in Indiana: Achievement of a Century* (Indianapolis, 1930) has been superseded by Henry K. Shaw, *Hoosier Disciples: A Comprehensive History of the Christian Churches (Disciples of Christ) in Indiana* (St. Louis, Mo., 1966). There is also Alfred T. DeGroot, *The Church of Christ in Owen County, Indiana* (Spencer, Ind., n. d.).

BAPTIST. One of the most critical and scholarly denominational histories is John F. Cady, *The Origin and Development of the Missionary Baptist Church in Indiana* (Franklin, Ind., 1942), which replaces William T. Stott, *Indiana Baptist History* (Franklin, Ind., 1908). Accounts of a small Baptist sect are found in D. B. Montgomery (ed.), *General Baptist History* (Evansville, 1882), and Theophilus A. H. Laslie, *Laslie's History of the General Baptists* (Revised edition, Poplar Bluff, Mo., 1938).

METHODIST. The various conferences are covered in the following: Jack J. Detzler, *The History of the Northwest Indiana Conference of the Methodist Church 1852-1951* (Nashville, Tenn., 1953); Herbert L. Heller, *Indiana Conference of the Methodist Church 1836-1956* (Greencastle, Ind., 1956); Horace N. Herrick and William W. Sweet, *A History of the North Indiana Conference of the Methodist Episcopal Church from Its Organization in 1844 to the Present* (Indianapolis, 1917); Frederick A. Norwood, *History of the North Indiana Conference 1917-1956: North Indiana Methodism in the Twentieth Century*

(Winona Lake, Ind., 1957). There is also an account of a dissenting group, John C. Coons, *A Brief History of the Methodist Protestant Church in Indiana* (n. p., 1939).

SOCIETY OF FRIENDS. Fragments of Quaker history are found in the *Reminiscences* of Nathan T. and Esther G. Frame (Cleveland, Ohio, 1907); Willard Heiss, *A Brief History of Western Yearly Meeting of Conservative Friends and the Separation of 1877* (Indianapolis, 1963); Opal Thornburg, *Whitewater: Indiana's First Monthly Meeting of Friends, 1809-1959* (Richmond, Ind., 1959).

UNITED BRETHREN. There are accounts of two different conferences: Adam B. Condo, *History of the Indiana Conference of the Church of the United Brethren in Christ* (n. p., 1926), and Augustus C. Wilmore, *History of the White River Conference of the Church of the United Brethren in Christ . . .* (Dayton, Ohio, 1925).

CHURCH OF GOD. The best accounts are Charles Ewing Brown, *When the Trumpet Sounded. A History of the Church of God Reformation Movement* (Anderson, Ind., 1951); Enoch E. Byrum, *Life Experiences* (Anderson, Ind., 1928); Frederick G. Smith, *Brief Sketch of the Origin, Growth and Distinctive Doctrine of the Church of God Reformation Movement* (Anderson, Ind., 1926).

Other denominations are represented by the following: W. T. Allen (comp.), *The Presbytery of Indianapolis* (n. p., 1951); C. R. Defenderfer, *Lutheranism at the Crossroads of America: A Study of the Indiana Synod of the U. L. C. A.* (n. p., n. d.); John A. Hostetler, *Amish Life* (Scottdale, Pa., 1952); Sarah S. Pratt, *Episcopal Bishops in Indiana. A Church Woman's Retrospect* (Indianapolis, 1934); Anna Stockinger, "The History of Spiritualism in Indiana," *Indiana Magazine of History,* XX (1924), 280-287; John C. Wenger, *The Mennonites in Indiana and Michigan* (Scottdale, Pa., 1961); Herbert L. Whitehead, *History of Indiana Congregationalism* (n. p., 1919); and Otho Winger, *History of the Church of the Brethren in Indiana* (Elgin, Ill., 1917).

There are also a number of historical accounts of individual congregations, one of the best of which is Eli Lilly, *History of the Little Church on the Circle. Christ Church Parish Indianapolis 1837-1955* (Indianapolis, 1957). Judge Kelly has written the *First History of Allen Chapel A. M. E. Church, Indianapolis, Indiana* (Indianapolis, 1916). Useful information is also found in Vincent H. Gaddis and John A. Huffman, *The Story of Winona Lake. A Memory and a Vision* (Revised edition, Winona Lake, 1960); Edith Iredale, *A Promise Fulfilled* (Elgin, Ill., 1962); and Genevieve C. Weeks, "Oscar C. McCulloch Transforms Plymouth Church, Indianapolis, into an 'Institutional' Church," *Indiana Magazine of History,* LXIV (1968), 87-108. Collections of sermons include William Henry Book (ed.), *The Indiana Pulpit* (Cincinnati, 1912), and volumes by such Protestant ministers as Frederick E. Dewhurst, Oscar C. McCulloch, William H. Nelson, Arthur T. Pierson, and Myron W. Reed.

## Benevolent and Penal Institutions

A brief general treatment is found in Amos W. Butler, *A Century of Progress. A Study of the Development of Public Charities and Correction, 1790-1915* (n. p., 1916). Also useful are Walter C. Woodward's biography of a long-time member of the State Board of Charities and Correction, *Timothy Nicholson, Master Quaker* (Richmond, Ind., 1927), and two articles by Genevieve C. Weeks on the work of Oscar C. McCulloch in *The Social Service Review*, XXXIX (1965), 38-52, 209-221. Albion Fellows Bacon's autobiography, *Beauty for Ashes* (New York, 1914), is a beautifully told story of her activities in housing reform. Other significant writings on social welfare are Evelyn C. Adams, "The Growing Concept of Social Responsibility Illustrated by a Study of the State's Care of the Insane in Indiana," *Indiana Magazine of History*, XXXII (1936), 1-22; Hazel Irene Hansford, *A Social Study of Mental Defectives in County H, Indiana, in 1918* (Bloomington, 1923); Alice Shaffer *et al.*, *The Indiana Poor Law. Its Development and Administration with Special Reference to the Provision of State Care for the Sick Poor* (Chicago, 1936). The following writings deal with penal conditions and reforms: James A. Collins, "The Juvenile Court Movement in Indiana," *Indiana Magazine of History*, XXVIII (1932), 1-8; Lucian V. Rule, *The City of Dead Souls and How It Was Made Alive Again; A Hundred Years within the Walls* (Louisville, Ky., 1920); and Helen Wilson, *The Treatment of the Misdemeanant in Indiana, 1816-1936* (Chicago, 1938).

## PUBLIC HEALTH

Thurman B. Rice, *The Hoosier Health Officer. A Biography of John N. Hurty* (Indianapolis, 1946), a collection of articles originally published in the *Monthly Bulletin* of the State Board of Public Health, is virtually a history of the public health movement in Indiana in this period. G. W. H. Kemper's pioneer study, *A Medical History of the State of Indiana* (Chicago, 1911), has been superseded by the encyclopedic volume, Dorothy R. Russo (ed.), *One Hundred Years of Indiana Medicine 1849-1949* (Indianapolis, 1949). Burton D. Myers, *The History of Medical Education in Indiana* (Bloomington, Ind., 1956), traces the history of the various medical schools. On the nursing profession, information is found in Charlotte Akins, History of the Visiting Nurse Association of Indianapolis, 1913-1959 (Unpublished Master's thesis in Education, Butler University, 1960), and Dotaline E. Allen, *History of Nursing in Indiana* (Indianapolis, 1950).

## CULTURAL AND INTELLECTUAL HISTORY

SOCIETIES. The development of literary clubs is treated in Loring C. Halberstadt, "Terre Haute Literary Club, 1881-1931," *Indiana Magazine of History*, XXVII (1931), 316-325, 350-351; Martha Nicholson McKay, *Literary Clubs of Indiana* (Indianapolis, 1894); Stephen C. Noland (comp.), *Indianapolis Literary Club. Summarized Record 1877-1934* (Indianapolis, 1934). Useful for the woman's club movement are Grace Gates Courtney (comp.), *History of Indiana Federation of Clubs* (Fort Wayne, 1939); Caroline Dunn, *Indianapolis Propylaeum, 1883-1938* (Indianapolis, 1938); Indiana Union of Literary Clubs, *Minutes and Constitution*, 1890-1906, succeeded by the *Proceedings* and *Year Books* of the Indiana Federation of Clubs, 1907-1920; and *Indianapolis Woman's Club, 1875-1940* (Indianapolis, 1940). On the Chautauqua movement there is James M. Conlin, A History of Merom Bluff Chautauqua 1905-1935 (Merom Bluff, n. d.). German societies are the subject of *Indianapolis Turn-*

*verein. Seventy-fifth Anniversary, 1851-1926* (n. p., 1926) and Theodore Stempfel, *Festschrift zur der Vollendung des Deutschen Hauses in Indianapolis* (Indianapolis, 1898).

LITERATURE. The best single, comprehensive work is Arthur W. Shumaker, *A History of Indiana Literature (Indiana Historical Collections,* XLII, Indianapolis, 1962). Briefer interpretations are Richard A. Cordell, "Limestone, Corn, and Literature," *Saturday Review of Literature,* December 17, 1938; Meredith Nicholson, *The Hoosiers* (Revised edition, New York, 1915); and Howard H. Peckham, "What Made Hoosiers Write?" *American Heritage,* I (1950), 25-27, 59-60. Richard E. Banta (comp.), *Indiana Authors and Their Books* (Crawfordsville, Ind., 1949) and Dorothy Russo and Thelma L. Sullivan, *Bibliographical Studies of Seven Authors of Crawfordsville, Indiana* (Indianapolis, 1952), are useful reference works. Important individual authors are treated in the following: Howard G. Baetzold, "Charles Major: Hoosier Romancer," *Indiana Magazine of History,* LI (1955), 31-42; Richard Crowder, *Those Innocent Years. The Legacy and Inheritance of a Hero of the Victorian Era, James Whitcomb Riley* (Indianapolis, 1957); Philip L. Gerber, *Theodore Dreiser* (New York, 1964); Fred C. Kelly, *George Ade. Warmhearted Satirist* (Indianapolis, 1947); Irving McKee, *"Ben-Hur" Wallace. The Life of General Lew Wallace* (Berkeley, Calif., 1947); Jeannette Porter Meehan, *The Lady of the Limberlost. The Life and Letters of Gene Stratton-Porter* (Garden City, N. Y., 1928); Robert Price, "Mrs. Catherwood's Early Experiments with Critical Realism," *American Literature,* XVII (1945), 140-151; Abe C. Ravitz, *David Graham Phillips* (New York, 1966); Jean Butler Sanders, Meredith Nicholson: Hoosier Cavalier (Unpublished Master's thesis in English, DePauw University, 1952); Otis B. Wheeler, *The Literary Career of Maurice Thompson* (Baton Rouge, La., 1965); and James Woodress, *Booth Tarkington, Gentleman from Indiana* (Philadelphia, 1955).

JOURNALISM. Two newspapermen have left valuable reminiscences: Hilton U. Brown, *A Book of Memories* (Indianapolis, 1951) and Louis L. Ludlow, *From Cornfield to Press Gallery . . .* (Washington, D. C., 1924). A briefer recollection is H. S. K. Bartholomew, "Newspaper Work at the Turn of the Century," *Indiana Magazine of History,* XXXV (1939), 303-306. The same author has written "Editor John B. Stoll," *ibid.,* XXVIII (1932), 73-83, which is supplemented by Edna Miller, The Editorial Opinion of John B. Stoll (Unpublished Master's thesis, Butler University, 1946). The only other study of editorial policy is John O. Carrington, The Foreign Policy of the Indianapolis Star, 1918-1939 (Unpublished Ph.D. thesis in History, University of Kentucky, 1958). Charles C. Clayton is the author of a history of a journalistic fraternity founded at DePauw University, *Fifty Years of Freedom: The Story of Sigma Delta Chi's Service to American Journalism 1909-1959* (Carbondale, Ill., 1959). Other useful accounts are Marvin W. Pershing, *The Story of Our Association: The Indiana Republican Editorial Association* (Indianapolis, 1921); Clyde Pierce, "The Panama Libel Cases," *Indiana Magazine of History,* XXXIII (1937), 171-186; and Luther Short, *Early History of the Democratic Editorial Association of Indiana* (Franklin, Ind., n. d.).

ART AND ARCHITECTURE. An over-all view is presented in Mary Q. Burnet, *Art and Artists of Indiana* (New York, 1921). The painter William Forsyth's newspaper articles reprinted as *Art in Indiana* (Indianapolis, 1916) and the *Art Guide to Indiana* published as Indiana University Extension *Bulletin*, XVI, No. 8 (1931) are useful supplements. Eva Draegert's survey of fine arts in Indianapolis is found in the *Indiana Magazine of History*, L (1954), 105-118, 321-348. Wilbur D. Peat has contributed two scholarly works on painting, *Pioneer Painters of Indiana* (Indianapolis, 1954) and *Portraits and Painters of the Governors of Indiana, 1800-1943* (Indianapolis, 1944), as well as a perceptive essay in Selma Steele *et al., The House of the Singing Winds: The Life and Work of T. C. Steele* (Indiana Historical Society, 1966). Information on art associations and schools is found in *Art Association of Indianapolis, A Record, 1883-1906* (n. p., 1906); Sister M. Dolorita Carper, A History of John Herron Art Institute (Unpublished Master's thesis, Butler University, 1947); Albert F. Diserens, "The Fort Wayne Art School and Museum . . .," *Old Fort News*, XV, Nos. 1 and 2 (March-June, 1952); and Ella Bond Johnston, "An Art Association for the People," *The Outlook*, LXXXV (January-April, 1907), 943-951.

Architect Louis H. Gibson is the author of Indiana Art, Artists and Architecture (MS, 1893, in Indiana State Library). For the period up to 1900, Wilbur D. Peat's *Indiana Houses of the Nineteenth Century* (Indiana Historical Society, 1962) is an indispensable and beautiful book on domestic architecture. One aspect of civic architecture is covered in David R. Hermansen, *Indiana County Courthouses of the Nineteenth Century* (Muncie, Ind., 1968). Both private and public structures are represented in Howard E. Wooden, *Architectural Heritage of Evansville. An Interpretive Review of the Nineteenth Century* (Evansville, Ind., 1962).

MUSIC AND THE THEATRE. Indianapolis' leading theater in this period is the subject of William G. Sullivan, *English's Opera House* (Indiana Historical Society *Publications,* XX, No. 3, Indianapolis, 1960). Information on music is found in Martha F. Bellinger's two articles on music in Indianapolis in the *Indiana Magazine of History*, XLI (1945), 345-362 and XLII (1946), 47-65; Eva Draegert, "Cultural History of Indianapolis: Music, 1875-1890," *ibid.*, LIII (1957), 265-304; Indiana Federation of Music Clubs, *Indiana Composers, Native and Adopted* (Bloomington, 1936); Indianapolis Saengerbund, *Golden Jubilee Concert, 1885-1935* (Indianapolis, 1935); Joseph Keller (ed.), *Festschrift zur Feier des Goldenen Jubilaums des Indianapolis Maennerchor* (Indianapolis, 1904); Elizabeth E. Gunn Seebirt, *Music in Indiana* (n.p., n.d.); and *The Songs of Paul Dresser* (New York, 1927).

## World War I

An excellent survey of attitudes toward the war is found in Cedric Cummins, *Indiana Public Opinion and the World War, 1914-1917* (*Indiana Historical Collections,* XXVIII, Indianapolis, 1945). Personal accounts and unit histories include *Battery F, 150th F. A., Under the Rainbow. A History of Its Service in the War against Germany* (Indianapolis, 1919); Benjamin D. Hitz (comp.),

*A History of Base Hospital 32* (Indianapolis, 1922); Elmer W. Sherwood, *Rainbow Hoosier* (Indianapolis, n. d.) and by the same author, *Diary of a Rainbow Veteran Written at the Front* (Terre Haute, 1929). Another personal account is *A Sergeant's Diary in the World War,* by Elmer F. Straub (*Indiana Historical Collections,* X, Indianapolis, 1923).

Indianans who gave their lives in the service of their country are commemorated in *Gold Star Honor Roll, 1915-1918* (*Indiana Historical Collections,* VI, Indianapolis, 1921), while the *Indiana Book of Merit* (*Indiana Historical Collections,* XVIII, Indianapolis, 1932) records the names and service of those who were decorated.

Other useful accounts are Marie Cecile and Anselm Chomel, *A Red Cross Chapter at Work* (Indianapolis, 1920); Walter Greenough, *The War Purse of Indiana* (*Indiana Historical Collections* VIII, Indianapolis, 1922); Indiana State Council of Defense, *A Report, 1917* (n. p., 1918); *Indiana War Service Text-Book for Indiana High Schools* (Indianapolis, 1918).

The Indiana State Library compiled 44 volumes of clippings from Indianapolis newspapers giving a chronological account of the war and its aftermath, 1917-1923.

## County War History Records

At the close of the war, Governor Goodrich delegated to the Indiana Historical Commission the task of collecting and preserving the record of Indiana's participation in the war. Special committees were appointed in each county to work with the Commission in collecting all types of material, including service records; civilian war records; letters and diaries of servicemen; war pictures, posters, and photographs; reports of war organizations including county councils of defense, selective service boards, liberty loan committees, Red Cross, fuel and food administrators; and newspapers, complete files or clippings. Nearly all the ninety-two counties participated in the program and sent the material collected to Indianapolis for preservation in the Indiana State Library; it has been kept together as a unit and constitutes a valuable source for Indiana's part in the war. About a dozen counties published their war histories. The following list describes the material collected in each county and the name of the principal compiler.

Allen. Mrs. Samuel R. Taylor, History (1 vol.); service records (9 vols.).

Bartholomew. County Historical Society, History (1 vol.). Newspaper clippings (1 vol.).

Benton. Mrs. John Lee Dinwiddie, History (1 vol.).

Blackford. Lula Haddon, History (1 vol.); Mrs. Charles Ritter and Mrs. James D. Sturgis, service records (2 vols.).

Boone. O. H. Carmichael and Mrs. George M. Conley, History (2 vols.). Newspaper clippings (1 vol.).

Brown. Mamie Moser, service records, pictures, clippings (1 vol.).

Carroll. Lou Bonnell, History (1 vol.).

CASS. Ora E. Cox, History (1 vol., printed).

CLARK. Mrs. Fannie Sparks, History (1 vol.).

CLAY. American Legion, History (1 vol., printed).

CLINTON. Mrs. Nora Kramer *et al.,* History (1 vol.) ; service records (1 vol.).

CRAWFORD. Newspaper clippings (1 vol.).

DAVIESS. Newspaper clippings (1 vol.).

DECATUR. Mrs. George Deiwert, History (1 vol., printed). Service records and clippings (1 vol.).

DEKALB. J. Y. McClellan, History and service records (1 vol.).

DELAWARE. Lannes McPhetridge, History (1 vol., printed) ; W. H. H. Kemper, newspaper clippings (2 vols.) ; service records (1 vol.).

DUBOIS. Margaret A. Wilson, History (1 vol.) ; service records (3 vols.).

ELKHART, H. S. K. Bartholomew, History (1 vol.). Newspaper clippings (2 vols.).

FLOYD. Julia I. Penn, History and service records (2 vols.).

FOUNTAIN. Verna Glascock, History and service records (1 vol.).

FRANKLIN. John L. Stewart and Fred E. Bartlett, History (1 vol.).

FULTON. William H. Deniston, History and service records (3 vols.) ; Harold Van Trump, History (1 vol., printed).

GIBSON. A. A. Rhodes, History (1 vol.).

GRANT. Mrs. Frances W. Davis, History (1 vol.) ; service records (1 vol.).

GREENE. Newspaper clippings (1 vol.).

HAMILTON. Meade Vestal, service records (3 vols.).

HANCOCK. Defense council, History (1 vol.) ; George Richman, service records (2 vols.).

HARRISON. Robert Kirkham, History and service records (2 vols.).

HENRY. John J. Powell, clippings and miscellany (1 vol.).

HOWARD. Clarence V. Haworth, History (1 vol., printed).

HUNTINGTON. Mrs. Frank Felter, History (1 vol.) ; service records (1 vol.).

JASPER. Mrs. Charles W. Hanley, History and service records (4 vols.).

JAY. Milton T. Jay, History and service records (1 vol.).

JEFFERSON. George S. Cottman, History and Sociological Study (1 vol., printed). Service records and photographs (1 vol.).

KOSCIUSKO. Newspaper clippings (1 vol.).

LA GRANGE. Frank Dunten, History (1 vol.). Newspaper clippings (1 vol.).

LAKE. Mrs. Emma Leary, History (1 vol.) ; service records (3 vols.) ; Mrs. Frank J. Sheehan, Gary in the War (2 vols.).

MADISON. J. J. Netterville, War History included in his county history; Benjamin F. Alvord, service records (1 vol.).

MARION. Ellis Searles, History and photographs (2 vols.) ; E. W. Diggs, Negroes in the War (1 vol.) ; War Mothers, service records (4 vols.).

MARSHALL. Mrs. J. H. Willey, History and service records (1 vol.).

MARTIN. Della Taylor, History (1 vol.).

MIAMI. Eleanor Kartholl and Zelma O. Wilson, History and service records (2 vols.).

MONROE. John F. Shuman, Brief history.

MONTGOMERY. Harriet H. Cranston, History and service records (2 vols.).

NOBLE. Newspaper clippings (1 vol.).

OHIO. Lucian Harris and William D. Ricketts, History and service records (1 vol.). Newspaper clippings (1 vol.).

OWEN. David E. Beem, History (1 vol.).

PARKE. History and service records (1 vol., printed).

PIKE. Arthur H. Taylor, Brief history and roster of soldiers.

PULASKI. Newspaper clippings (1 vol.).

PUTNAM. Arthur Deen, History and photographs (1 vol.).

RANDOLPH. Newspaper clippings (2 vols.).

RIPLEY. Minnie E. Wycoff, History (1 vol., printed); miscellaneous papers, clippings, photographs (1 vol.); service records (4 vols.).

RUSH. Newspaper clippings (6 vols.).

SCOTT. Permelia Boyd, History (1 vol.).

SHELBY. Hortense H. Montgomery, History (1 vol.); Mrs. Harry Morrison, service records (3 vols.).

SPENCER. Charles Lieb *et al.,* History (1 vol.); service records (1 vol.); scrapbooks (6 vols.).

STARKE. Sylva R. Jonas, History (1 vol., printed). Newspaper clippings (1 vol.).

SULLIVAN. James B. Maple, History and service records (1 vol.).

SWITZERLAND. Earl S. Brown, History (1 vol., printed).

TIPPECANOE. Newspaper clippings (1 vol.); Haywood Publishing Company, Honor Roll, including photographs and biographical notes (1 vol., printed).

TIPTON. Ebert Allison, History (1 vol., printed); service records (2 vols.).

UNION. Mrs. Albert Bertch, History and service records (1 vol.).

VANDERBURGH. Heiman Blatt, History (1 vol., printed); Ethel F. McCullough, service records (9 vols.).

VERMILLION. Mrs. Nelle Wait, service records (1 vol.).

VIGO. Mrs. May Dodson and Mrs. Sallie C. Hughes, History and service records (1 vol.). Newspaper clippings (2 vols.).

WARRICK. American Legion, History (1 vol.).

WASHINGTON. Mrs. Harvey Morris and Mrs. Elizabeth Cauble, service records (1 vol.).

WAYNE. Edgar M. Haas, service records (3 vols.).

WELLS. Charles E. Sturgis, History (1 vol.); Mrs. Harry Heath, service records (2 vols.); Monon *News, Monon Township in the War* (1 vol., printed).

WHITLEY. Newspaper clippings (2 vols.).

INDEX

# INDEX

(647)

**4546**